Dimensions of HUMAN BEHAVIOR

Second Edition

In memory of Robert E. Hutchison, Gertrude Hutchison,
and James M. Doran Sr., who added so much to my life journey

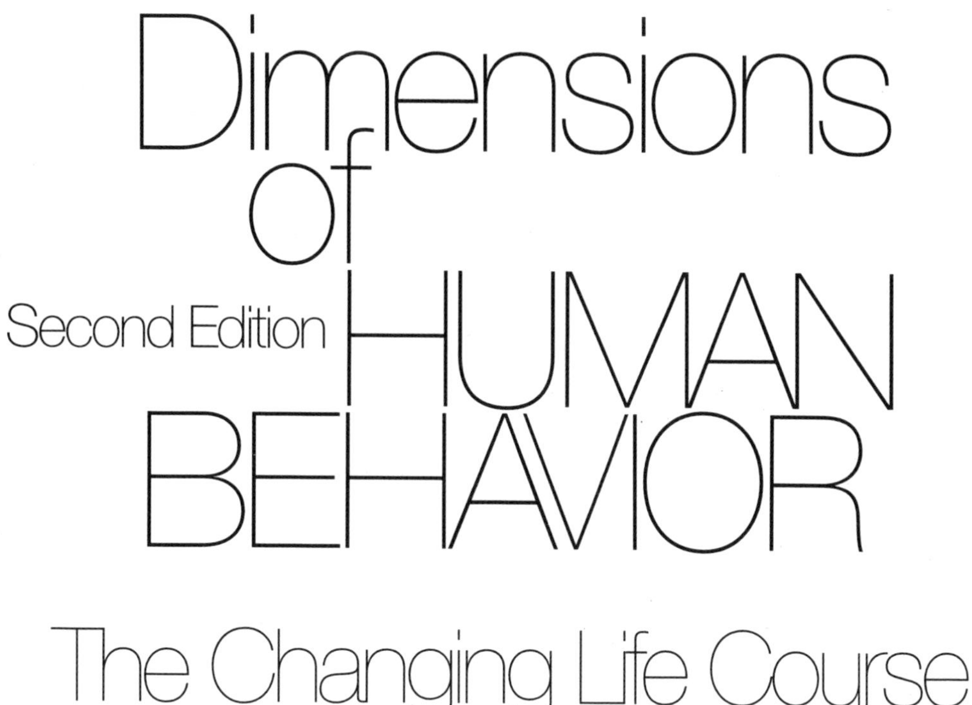

Dimensions of Human Behavior

Second Edition

The Changing Life Course

Elizabeth D. Hutchison
Virginia Commonwealth University

SAGE Publications
International Educational and Professional Publisher
Thousand Oaks ▪ London ▪ New Delhi

For information:

Sage
2455 Teller Road
Thousand Oaks, California 91320
E-mail: order@sagepub.com

Sage Publications Ltd.
6 Bonhill Street
London EC2A 4PU
United Kingdom

Sage Publications India Pvt. Ltd.
B-42, Panchsheel Enclave
Post Box 4109
New Delhi 110 017

Printed in the United States of America

Library of Congress Cataloging-in-Publication Data

Dimensions of human behavior. The changing life course /
edited by Elizabeth D. Hutchison.- 2nd ed.
p. cm.
Includes bibliographical references and index.
ISBN 0-7619-8764-9 (pbk.)
1. Social psychology. 2. Human behavior. 3. Social structure. 4. Social service.
I. Title: Changing life course. II. Hutchison, Elizabeth.
HM1033 .D553 2003
302—dc21

2002151763

03 04 05 10 9 8 7 6 5 4 3 2

Acquiring Editor:	Alison Muddritt
Editorial Assistant:	Mishelle Gold
Developmental Editor:	Rebecca Smith
Production Editor:	Claudia A. Hoffman
Typesetter:	C&M Digitals (P) Ltd.
Copy Editor:	Barbara Coster
Indexer:	Molly Hall
Cover Designer:	Michelle Lee

About the Author

Elizabeth D. Hutchison, M.S.W., Ph.D., is Associate Professor in the School of Social Work at Virginia Commonwealth University. She has practiced in health, mental health, and child and family welfare. Her major areas of interest are child and family welfare, social work practice with nonvoluntary clients, and the human behavior curriculum. She has taught human behavior courses at the B.S.W., M.S.W., and doctoral levels, and currently teaches human behavior, social justice, and child and family policy courses.

Brief Contents

Contents

PREFACE

Like many people, my life has been full of change since the first edition of this book was published in 1999. After a merger/acquisition, my husband took a new position in Washington, D.C., and we moved to the nation's capitol from Richmond, Virginia, where we had lived for 13 years. I changed my teaching affiliation from the Richmond campus of the Virginia Commonwealth University School of Social Work to the satellite program in northern Virginia. Just as I began to think about revisions of this book, my mother-in-law, for whom my husband and I had served as primary caregivers, began a fast decline and died rather quickly. A year later, my mother had a stroke and my father died a month after that. In the past month, my daughter started graduate school and my son relocated from Pennsylvania to North Carolina. These events have all had an impact on my life course.

But, change has not been confined to change in my multigenerational family. Since the first edition of the book was published, we have had a presidential election for which the outcome stayed in limbo for weeks. The economy has peaked and declined. And, most notably, on September 11, 2001, terrorists hijacked airplanes and forced them to be flown into the twin towers of the World Trade Center in New York City and into the Pentagon near my school. The latter event will become an important life course marker for people of all generations in the United States.

Since I was a child listening to my grandmother's stories about the challenges, joys, and dramatic as well as mundane events in her life, I have been captivated by people's stories. I have learned that a specific event can be understood only in the context of an ongoing life story. Social work has historically used the idea of person-in-environment to develop a holistic understanding of human behavior. This idea has become popular as well with most social and behavioral science disciplines. Recently, we have recognized the need to add the aspect of time to the person-environment construct, to capture the dynamic, changing nature of person-in-environment.

Organized around time, this book tries to help you understand the relationship between time and human behavior. The companion volume to this book, *Person and Environment*, analyzes relevant dimensions of person and environment and presents up-to-date reports on theory and research about each of these dimensions. The purpose of this volume is to show how these multiple dimensions of person and environment work together with dimensions of time to produce patterns in unique life course journeys.

Life Course Perspective

As in the first edition, my colleagues and I have chosen a life course perspective to capture the dynamic, changing nature of person-environment transactions. In the life course perspective, human behavior is not a linear march through time, nor is it simply played out in recurring cycles. Rather, the life course journey is a moving spiral, with both continuity and change, marked by both predictable and unpredictable twists and turns. It is influenced by changes in the physical and social environment as well as by changes in the personal biological, psychological, and spiritual dimensions.

The life course perspective recognizes *patterns* in human behavior related to biological age, psychological age, and social age norms. In the first edition, we discussed theory and research about six age-graded periods of the life course, presenting both the continuity and the change in these patterns. Because mass longevity is leading to finer distinctions among life phases, nine age-graded periods are discussed in this edition. The life course perspective also recognizes *diversity* in the life course related to historical time, gender, race, ethnicity, social class, and so forth, and we emphasize group-based diversity in our discussion of age-graded periods. Finally, the life course perspective recognizes the *unique life stories* of individuals, the unique configuration of specific life events and person-environment transactions over time.

General Knowledge and Unique Situations

The purpose of the social and behavioral sciences is to help us to understand *general patterns* in person-environment transactions over time. The purpose of social work assessment is to understand *unique configurations* of person and environment dimensions at a given time. Those who practice social work must weave what they know about unique situations with general knowledge. To assist you in this process, as we did in the first edition, we begin each chapter with stories, which we then intertwine with contemporary theory and research. Most of the stories are composite cases and do not correspond to actual people known to the authors. We also call attention to the successes and failures of theory and research to accommodate human diversity related to gender, race, ethnicity, culture, sexual orientation, and disability.

The bulk of this second edition will be familiar to instructors who used the first edition of *Dimensions of Human Behavior: The Changing Life Course.* Many of the changes that do occur came at the suggestion of instructors who have been using the first edition. To respond to the rapidity of changes in complex societies, all chapters have been updated. As in the first edition, key terms are presented in bold type in the chapters and defined in the Glossary.

Also New in This Edition

The more substantial revisions for this edition include the following:

- More content has been added on the effects of gender, race, ethnicity, social class, sexual orientation, and disability on life course trajectories.
- Greater attention has been given to how the individual life course intersects with the family life course.
- New exhibits have been added and others updated.
- Some new case studies have been added to reflect events of the past few years.
- Web resources have been updated.
- Orienting questions have been added to the beginning of each chapter to help the student to begin to think about why the content of the chapter is important for social workers.
- Key ideas have been summarized at the beginning of each chapter to give students an overview of what is to come.
- Active Learning exercises have been added at the end of each chapter.
- An introductory chapter has been added to lay out the major themes of the life course perspective and connect those themes to the person-environment-time framework presented in the companion volume to this book, *Dimensions of Human Behavior: Person and Environment.*
- The chapter on infancy and early childhood has been divided into two chapters: Chapter 3, "Infancy and Toddlerhood," and Chapter 4, "Early Childhood."
- The chapter on adulthood has been divided into two chapters: Chapter 7, "Young Adulthood," and Chapter 8, "Middle Adulthood." Chapter 7 captures recent theorizing and research on "emerging adulthood." Chapter 8 includes the very recent theorizing and research about midlife adulthood.
- The chapter on late adulthood has been divided into two chapters: Chapter 9, "Late Adulthood," and Chapter 10, "Very Late Adulthood." Chapter 10 captures the new territory being charted by the growing group living well into their 80s and beyond, and presents material on the dying and bereavement processes.

One Last Word

I hope that reading this book helps you to understand how people change from conception to death, and why different people react to the same stressful situations in different ways. I also hope that you will gain a greater appreciation for the ongoing life stories in which specific events are embedded. In addition, when you finish reading this book, I hope that you will have new ideas about how to reduce risk and increase protective factors during different age-graded periods and how to help clients find meaning and purpose in their own life stories.

You can help me in my learning process by letting me know what you liked or didn't like about the book.

—*Elizabeth D. Hutchison*
School of Social Work
Northern Virginia Program
Virginia Commonwealth University
6295 Edsall Road
Alexandria, VA 22314
ehutch@atlas.vcu.edu

Acknowledgments

A project like this book is never completed without the support and assistance of many people. A second edition stands on the back of the first edition, and by now I have accumulated a large number of people to whom I am grateful.

Steve Rutter, former publisher and president of Pine Forge Press, shepherded every step of the first edition and provided ideas for many of the best features of the book. Along with Paul O'Connell, Becky Smith, and Maria Zuniga, he helped to refine the outline for the second edition.

The contributing authors and I are grateful for the assistance of Dr. Maria E. Zuniga, of San Diego State University School of Social Work, who served as cultural competency consultant for the second edition. She contributed the David Sanchez case study in Chapter 1 and provided many valuable suggestions of how to improve the coverage of cultural diversity in each chapter. Her suggestions have improved the book immensely.

I am grateful once again to work with a fine group of contributing authors. They were gracious about tight timelines and requests for new features. Most important, they were committed to providing a state-of-the-art knowledge base for understanding human behavior across the life course.

I was so fortunate to have the developmental editorial services of Becky Smith for both the first and second editions. She is such a joy to work with! She took our drafts and returned them to us in a much more coherent and polished form. The contributing authors and I appreciated her mastery of both language and ideas. We also appreciated her ability to give feedback in a kind and gentle manner. In addition, Becky served as editor for the visual essays.

In the later stages of this project, a whole host of people connected to Sage Publications became part of my life and helped me with the many processes and procedures that turn ideas and words into a coherent printed product. Mishelle Gold, Alison Mudditt, and Claudia Hoffman provided valuable editorial assistance. Barbara Coster provided further editorial refinement.

I am also grateful to Dr. Shirley Bryant, Program Director, and my colleagues at the VCU School of Social Work Program in Northern Virginia. They have provided me with much care and support through a difficult year and tolerated my preoccupation without complaint. My conversations about the human behavior curriculum with colleagues Holly Matto and Connie Laurent-Roy have produced new ideas that ended up in this book. I am lucky to have such colleagues.

My students also deserve a special note of gratitude. They teach me all the time, and many things that I have learned interacting with them show up in the pages of this book. They also provide a great deal of joy to my life journey. Those moments when I encounter former students doing informed, creative, and humane social work are special moments indeed.

My deepest gratitude goes to my husband, Hutch. Since the first edition of this book was published, we have weathered several challenging years. Without his support, and his patience about forgoing vacations, this book could not have been completed in this year of loss.

Elizabeth D. Hutchison
September 2002

Contributing Authors

Marian A. Aguilar, M.S.W., Ph.D., is Associate Professor and Chair of the Department of Sociology, Psychology, and Social Work at Texas A & M International University. Her research and publications have focused on issues of diversity, welfare, education, and health delivery as they affect women, persons with disabilities, older adults, and people of color. She has taught courses in social policy, program evaluation, administration and planning, and psychosocial aspects of health and illness.

Suzanne M. Baldwin, B.S.N., R.N., M.S.W., L.C.S.W., is a doctoral candidate in the School of Social Work at Virginia Commonwealth University. She works as a clinical social worker in private practice with families and as a clinical nurse specialist in newborn intensive care. Her major areas of interest are health social work and family systems. She has taught human behavior, practice, communications, and research courses at Old Dominion University and at the School of Social Work at Virginia Commonwealth University.

Leanne Wood Charlesworth, M.S.W., Ph.D., is a senior associate with Caliber Associates, a research and consulting firm. She has held various child welfare and research positions. Her areas of interest include social welfare policy and child and family issues. She has taught human behavior and research courses.

Marcia P. Harrigan, M.S.W., Ph.D., is Associate Professor and Director of the M.S.W. Program in the School of Social Work at Virginia Commonwealth University. She has practiced in child welfare and juvenile justice. Her major areas of interest are family systems, family assessment, multigenerational households, and long distance family caregiving. She has taught human behavior and practice courses.

Pamela J. Kovacs, M.S.W., Ph.D., is Associate Professor in the School of Social Work at Virginia Commonwealth University. Her practice experience includes work with individuals, families, and groups in oncology, hospice, and mental health settings. Her major areas of interest are HIV/AIDS, hospice and palliative care, volunteerism, caregiving, and preparing social workers for health care social work. She teaches social work practice, health care and social work, qualitative research, and serves as a field liaison.

Susan Ainsley McCarter, M.S., M.S.W., Ph.D., lives in Charlotte, North Carolina. She has worked as a juvenile probation officer, mental health counselor for children, adolescents, and families, AmeriCorps coordinator, mentor trainer, and mother. Her current research interest is minority overrepresentation in the juvenile justice system. She has taught human behavior, social policy, and sociology courses at both the undergraduate and graduate levels.

Peter Maramaldi, C.S.W., M.P.H., Ph.D., is Assistant Professor at the University of Utah College of Social Work, the Associate Director of the WD Goodwill Social Work Initiatives on Aging, and a Hartford Social Work Faculty Scholar. His current research focuses on behavioral oncology and aging. He worked in a broad range of practice settings for more than 25 years in New York City before moving to Utah. He has taught courses in various areas of social work practice, health policy, and research methodology on the graduate level.

Holly C. Matto, M.S.W., Ph.D., L.C.S.W.-C., is Assistant Professor in the School of Social Work at Virginia Commonwealth University. Her research focuses on substance abuse assessment and treatment. She has taught courses in human behavior, social work practice, art therapy in social work practice, and research methodology.

Matthias J. Naleppa, M.S.W., Ph.D., is Associate Professor in the School of Social Work at Virginia Commonwealth University and a Hartford Geriatric Social Work Scholar. His research focuses on social work with elderly clients, specifically on applying the task-centered model to case management and gerontological practice. He has taught courses in human behavior, social work practice, and research methodology at the University at Albany, Marywood University, and Virginia Commonwealth University.

Pamela Viggiani, M.S.W., Ph.D., is Assistant Professor in the Social Work Department at Nazareth College. Her clinical and research interest is in school-based dropout prevention programs for at-risk elementary and middle school students. She teaches social policy, human behavior, and practice courses.

Jim Wood, Ed.D., is the Coordinator of Curriculum and Instruction for the Sodus Central School District, a small school district in Upstate New York. His areas of interest include achievement gap issues and school culture. In his 32 years of teaching, he has taught students from kindergarten through the graduate level.

Debra J. Woody, Ph.D., L.M.S.W.-A.C.P., is Assistant Professor in the School of Social Work at the University of Texas at Arlington. Her most recent practice experience is in child and family practice. Her major areas of interest are child and family issues, particularly as they are influenced by race. She currently teaches both undergraduate and graduate practice courses and graduate research courses. She taught B.S.W. courses for several years at Baylor University.

Maria E. Zuniga, M.S.W., Ph.D., is Professor in the School of Social Work at San Diego State University. She previously taught at Sacramento State University. Her areas of focus are direct practice, gerontological practice, and practice with multicultural populations, in particular, practice with Latinos. She has taught human behavior courses. She was a member of the board of directors of the Council on Social Work Education (CSWE) and helped to develop a CSWE-sponsored conference on Cultural Competence held at the University of Michigan in 1999. She is a consultant on cultural competence for local, state, and national agencies and publishing houses.

VISUAL ESSAY

Tracking Time

The expression "the march of time" conjures an image of a simple progression through the years. But time is not just linear. It is also cyclical. Consider the way the four seasons return, one after another, year after year.

Lives, too, are both linear and cyclical.

As time passes, we progressively age, and we move from one life situation to another.

VISUAL ESSAY

Consider the dual nature of time in this couple's anniversary photographs, which span 30 years. We see the linear progression of time in the environmental and biological changes affecting the couple. But we also see the cyclical nature of the life course in the fact that this couple took time every year to celebrate their marriage.

Cyclical celebrations like wedding anniversaries and birthdays are cultural markers drawing attention to significant relationships and important features of life.

Some cultural markers are not cyclical, however. They mark special events that might occur only once (or a limited number of times) in a person's life. Consider occasions like the first day of school, the loss of the last baby tooth, the first romantic kiss, the birth of a child, the first gray hair, and the retirement party after a long career. Events like these mark our place along the life course.

A wedding is one such event. To a certain extent, it marks the transition from carefree youth to responsible adulthood. It also marks a change in family affiliations. Instead of "belonging" to their family of birth, the newlyweds simultaneously form their own family and extend their family circle to include their in-laws.

VISUAL ESSAY

Most of us participate in such life events, but the particular form they take is specific to our era, culture, and social setting and uniquely shaped by who we are. Notice the similarities and differences in these wedding pictures, all from the United States.

© Dennis Degnan/CORBIS.

© Ariel Skelley/CORBIS.

© Walter Hodges/CORBIS.

Just as life events take shape from our lives, our lives take shape with each new life event. Life events give us roles—such as spouse or parent—and those roles change over time.

A woman becomes a mother, taking on new responsibilities and new relationships with the people in her world.

One day the woman's child becomes a mother herself.

In the process, the woman gains a new role: grandmother.

Eventually the grandson grows up and shifts into the role of father. But the way he plays that role reflects his own era, personality, and life situation, not those of his grandmother.

VISUAL ESSAY

As social workers, our job is to pay attention to a client's place in the life course and the way that life events may be affecting the client. But we must not forget that each person experiences the life course in a unique manner.

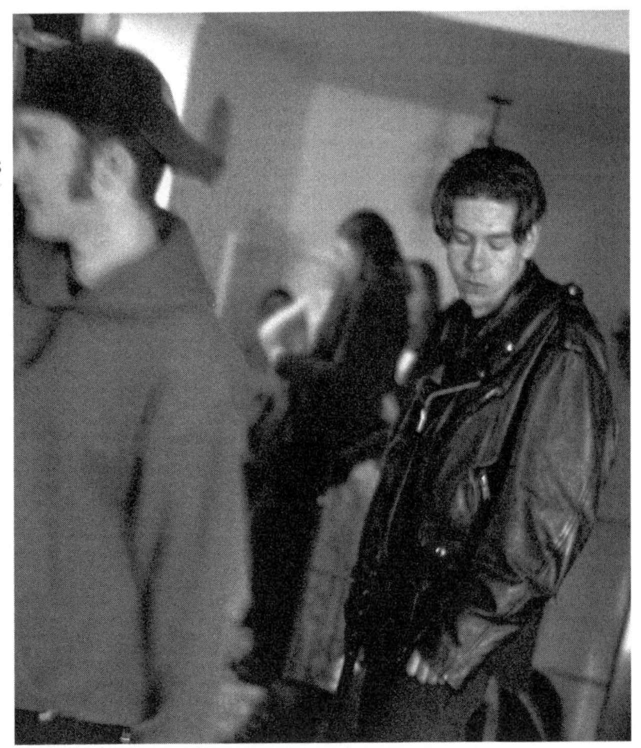

© Cheryl Maeder/CORBIS.

For instance, a person's chronological age—the age indicated by the calendar—may give us a general idea of the issues and events shaping the person. But by thinking about variations in biological age, psychological age, social age, and spiritual age as well, we have an even clearer picture of how the timing of life events is likely to affect the individual.

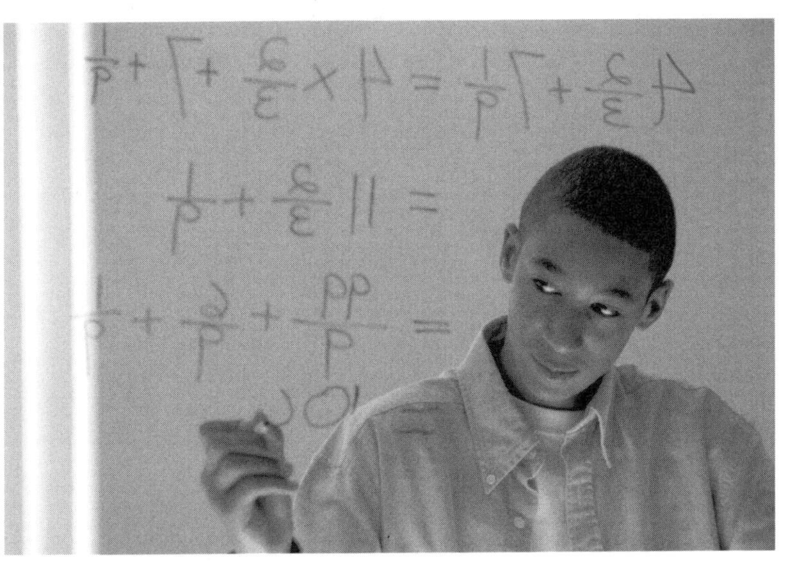

© George Disario/CORBIS.

Keep in mind, too, that things don't always happen to people. Human beings also have the capacity to chart their own course in life.

For example, physical disability places a person at risk for many disappointments in life—poor self-esteem, problems in forming relationships with other people, poor job prospects, and lifelong economic disadvantage. But many individuals have the personal and social resources to overcome the risk and create a satisfying life.

The social worker's job is to work toward eliminating environmental barriers to such participation and at the same time to help individuals facing developmental risk to find the resources within their own lives that will enable them to participate fully in the world they inhabit.

© Tim Pannell/CORBIS.

CHAPTER 1

A Life Course Perspective

Elizabeth D. Hutchison

Key Terms

Active Learning

Web Resources

CHAPTER 1

A Life Course Perspective

Elizabeth D. Hutchison
Virginia Commonwealth University

Why do social workers need to understand how people change from birth to death?

What do social workers need to know about biological, psychological, social, and spiritual changes over the life course?

Why do different people react to the same type of stressful life event in different ways?

Key Ideas

As you read this chapter, take note of these central ideas:

1. The life course perspective attempts to understand the continuities as well as the twists and turns in the paths of individual lives.
2. The life course perspective recognizes the influence of historical changes on human behavior.
3. The life course perspective recognizes the importance of timing of lives not just in terms of chronological age but also in terms of biological age, psychological age, social age, and spiritual age.
4. The life course perspective emphasizes the ways in which humans are interdependent and gives special attention to the family as the primary arena for experiencing and interpreting the wider social world.
5. The life course perspective sees humans as capable of making choices and constructing their own life journeys, within systems of opportunities and constraints.
6. The life course perspective emphasizes diversity in life journeys and the many sources of that diversity.
7. The life course perspective recognizes the linkages between childhood and adolescent experiences and later experiences in adulthood.

Case Study 1.1

David Sanchez's Search for Connections

David Sanchez has a Hispanic name, but he explains to you, as you ready him for discharge from the hospital, that he is a member of the Navajo tribe. He has spent most of his life in New Mexico but came to Los Angeles to visit his son Marco, age 29, and his grandchildren. While he was visiting them, he was brought to the emergency room and then hospitalized for what has turned out to be a diabetic coma. He had been aware of losing weight during the past year, and felt ill at times, but thought these symptoms were just signs of getting older or, perhaps, the vestiges of his alcoholism from the ages of 20 to 43. Now in his 50s, although he has been sober for 7 years, he is not surprised when his body reminds him how he abused it.

You suggest to Mr. Sanchez that he will need to follow up in the outpatient clinic, but he indicates that he needs to return to New Mexico. There he is eligible, as a Vietnam veteran, for health services at the local VA hospital outpatient clinic. He also receives a disability check for a partial disability from the war. He has not been to the VA since his rehabilitation from alcohol abuse, but he is committed to seeing someone there as soon as he gets home.

During recent visits with Marco and his family, David started to recognize how much his years of alcohol abuse hurt his son. After Mrs. Sanchez divorced David, he could never be relied on to visit Marco or to provide child support. Now that Marco has his own family, David hopes that by teaching his grandchildren the ways of the Navajo, he will pay Marco back a little for neglecting him. During the frequent visits of this past year, Marco has asked David to teach him and his son how to speak Navajo. This gesture has broken down some of the bad feelings between them.

David has talked about his own childhood during recent visits, and Marco now realizes how much his father suffered as a child. David was raised by his maternal grandmother after his father was killed in a car accident when David was 7. His mother had been very ill since his birth and was too overwhelmed by her husband's death to take care of David.

Just as David became attached to his grandmother, the Bureau of Indian Affairs (BIA) moved him to a boarding school. His hair was cut short with a tuft left at his forehead, which gave the teachers something to pull when he was being reprimanded. Like most Indian children, David suffered this harshness in silence. Now he feels that it is important to break this silence. He has told his grandchildren about having his mouth washed out with soap for speaking Navajo. He jokes that he has been baptized in four different

CASE STUDY 1.1

religions—Mormon, Catholic, Lutheran, and Episcopalian—because these were the religious groups running the boarding schools he attended. He also remembers the harsh beatings for not studying, or for committing other small infractions, before the BIA changed its policies for boarding homes and the harsh beatings diminished.

David often spent holidays at the school, because his grandmother had no money for transportation. He remembers feeling so alone. When David did visit his grandmother, he realized he was forgetting his Navajo and saw that she was aging quickly.

He joined the Marines when he was 18, like many high school graduates of that era, and his grandmother could not understand why he wanted to join the "white man's war." David now recognizes why his grandmother questioned his decision to go to war. During his alcohol treatments, especially during the use of the Native sweatlodge, he often relived the horrible memories of the bombings and killings in Vietnam; these were the memories he spent his adult life trying to silence with his alcohol abuse. Like many veterans, he ended up on the streets, homeless, seeking only the numbness his alcoholism provided. But the memories were always there. Sometimes his memories of the children in the Vietnam villages reminded him of the children from the boarding schools who had been so scared; some of the Vietnamese children even looked like his Indian friends.

It was through the Indian medicine retreats during David's rehabilitation that he began to touch a softer reality. He began to believe in a higher order again. Although his father's funeral had been painful, David experienced his grandmother's funeral in a more spiritual way. It was as if she was there guiding him to enter his new role. David now realizes this was a turning point in his life.

At his grandmother's funeral, David's great-uncle, a medicine man, asked him to come and live with him because he was getting too old to cut or carry wood. He also wanted to teach David age-old cures that would enable him to help others struggling with alcohol dependency, from Navajo as well as other tribes. Although David is still learning, his work with other alcoholics has been inspirational, and he finds he can make special connections to Vietnam veterans.

Recently, David attended a conference where one of the First Nations speakers talked about the transgenerational trauma that families experienced because of the horrible beatings children encountered at the boarding schools. David is thankful that his son has broken the cycle of alcoholism

CASE STUDY 1.1

and did not face the physical abuse to which he was subjected. But he is sad that his son was depressed for many years as a teen and young man. Now, both he and Marco are working to heal their relationship. They draw on the meaning and strength of their cultural and spiritual rituals. David's new role as spiritual and cultural teacher in his family has provided him with respect he never anticipated. Finally he is able to use his grandmother's wise teachings and his healing apprenticeship with his great-uncle to help his immediate family and his tribe.

As the social worker helping Mr. Sanchez with his discharge plans, you are aware that discharge planning involves one life transition that is a part of a larger life trajectory.

By Maria E. Zuniga

Case Study 1.2

Mahdi Mahdi's Shared Journey

In your refugee resettlement work, you are eager to learn all you can about the refugee experience. You are learning from your clients, but you also find it helpful to talk with other resettlement workers who have made a successful adjustment after entering the United States as a refugee. You have been particularly grateful for what you have learned from conversations with Mahdi Mahdi. Mahdi works as an immigration specialist at Catholic Social Services in Phoenix, providing the kind of services that he could have used when he came to Phoenix as a refugee 10 years ago.

Mahdi was born in Baghdad, Iraq, in 1957. His father was a teacher, and his mother stayed at home to raise Mahdi and his four brothers and two sisters. Mahdi remembers the Baghdad of his childhood as a mix of old and new architecture and traditional and modern ways of life. Life in Baghdad was "very good" for him until about 1974, when political unrest and military control changed the quality of life.

Mahdi and his wife were married after they graduated from Baghdad University with degrees in fine arts in 1982. Mahdi started teaching art in high school when he graduated from college, but he was immediately

CASE STUDY 1.2

drafted as an officer in the military to fight in the Iran-Iraq War. He was supposed to serve for only 2 years, but the war went on for 8 years, and he was not able to leave the military until 1989. Mahdi recalls that many of his friends were killed in the war.

By the end of the war, Mahdi and his wife had two daughters, and after the war Mahdi went back to teaching. He began to think, however, of moving to the United States, where two of his brothers had already immigrated. He began saving money and was hoping to immigrate in November 1990.

But on August 2, 1990, Iraq invaded Kuwait, and the second Persian Gulf War began. Mahdi was drafted again to fight in this war, but he refused to serve. According to the law in Iraq, anyone refusing the draft would be shot in front of his house. Mahdi had to go into hiding, and he remembers this as a very frightening time.

After a few months, Mahdi took his wife, two children, and brother in a car and escaped from Baghdad. He approached the American army on the border of Iraq and Kuwait. The Americans took Mahdi and his family to a camp at Rafha in northern Saudi Arabia and left them there with the Saudi Arabian soldiers. Mahdi's wife and children were very unhappy in the camp. The sun was hot, there was nothing green to be seen, and the wind storms were frightening. Mahdi also reports that the Saudi soldiers treated the Iraqi refugees like animals, beating them with sticks.

Mahdi and his family were in the refugee camp for about a year and a half. He was very frightened because he had heard that some members of the Saudi Arabian army had an unofficial agreement with the Iraqi army to drop any refugees that they wanted at the Iraq border. One day he asked a man who came into the camp to help him get a letter to one of his brothers. Mahdi also wrote to the U.S. embassy. Mahdi's brother petitioned to have him removed from the camp, and Mahdi and his family were taken to the U.S. Embassy in Riyadh. Mahdi worked as a volunteer at the embassy for almost a month, and then he and his family flew to Switzerland, on to New York, and finally to Arizona. It was now September of 1992.

Mahdi and his family lived with one of his brothers for about a month and a half, and then they moved into their own apartment. Mahdi worked as a cashier in a convenience store and took English classes at night. He wanted to be able to help his daughters with their schoolwork. Mahdi reports that although the culture was very different from what he and his family were accustomed to, it did not all come as a surprise. Iraq was the first Middle

CASE STUDY 1.2

Eastern country to get television, and Mahdi knew a lot about the United States from the programs he saw.

After a year and a half at the convenience store, Mahdi decided to open his own moving company, USA Moving Company. He also went to school half time to study physics and math. He kept the moving company for 2 years, but it was hard. Some customers didn't like his accent, and some of the people he hired didn't like to work for an Iraqi.

After he gave up the moving company, Mahdi taught seventh grade fine arts in a public school for a couple of years. He did not enjoy this job, because the students were not respectful to him.

For the past 6 years, Mahdi has worked as an immigration specialist for Catholic Social Services. He enjoys this work very much, and has assisted refugees and immigrants from many countries, including Somalia, Vietnam, and the Kosovo region of Yugoslavia. Mahdi has finished 20 credits toward a master's degree in art education, and he thinks he might go back to teaching someday.

Mahdi's father died in 1982 from a heart attack; Mahdi thinks that worries about his sons' safety killed his father. Mahdi's mother immigrated to Arizona in 1996 and lives about a mile from Mahdi and his family, next door to one of Mahdi's brothers. (Three of Mahdi's brothers are in Phoenix and one is in Canada. One sister is in Norway and the other is in Ukraine.) Mahdi's mother loves being near the grandchildren, but she does not speak English and thus has a hard time meeting new people. In 1994, Mahdi and his wife had a third daughter. About 11 months ago, Mahdi's mother- and father-in-law immigrated to the United States and came to live with Mahdi and his family. His wife now stays home to take care of them. Mahdi is sensitive to how hard it is for them to move to a new culture at their age.

Mahdi and his family live in a neighborhood of white Americans. His daughters' friends are mostly white Americans and Hispanic Americans. Although Mahdi and his family are Sahih Muslim, Mahdi says that he is not a very religious person. They do not go to mosque, and his wife does not wear a veil—although his mother does. Mahdi says that his faith is a personal matter, and he does not like to draw attention to it. It is much better, he says, to keep it personal.

This part of the conversation brings Mahdi to mention the aftermath of September 11, 2001, and what it is like living in the United States as an Iraqi American since the terrorist attack. He says that, overall, people have been very good to him, although he has had some bad experiences on the

CASE STUDY 1.2

street a few times, when people have stopped him and pointed their fingers angrily in his face. His neighbors and colleagues at work have offered their support.

Mahdi suggests that you might want to talk with his daughter, Rusel, to get another view of the family's immigration experience. Rusel recently graduated from high school and is preparing to enroll at the University of Arizona to study civil engineering.

When Rusel thinks of Baghdad, it is mostly the war that she remembers. She remembers the trip in the car that took her family away from Baghdad, and she remembers being confused about what was happening. Her memories of the refugee camp in Rafha are not pleasant. The physical environment was strange and frightening to her: no trees, hot sand, flies everywhere, no water for a shower, no way to get cool, living in a tent with the sound of sandstorms.

When the Mahdi family left the camp, Rusel did not know where they were going, but she was glad to be leaving. Her memories of coming to the United States are very positive. She was happy to be living in a house instead of a tent and to be surrounded by uncles, aunts, and cousins. At first, it was very hard to communicate at school, but her teacher assigned another student, Nikki, to help Rusel adjust. Rusel is still grateful for the way that Nikki made her feel comfortable in her new surroundings. Rusel is also quick to add that she was in an English as a second language (ESL) program for 3 years, and she wants everybody to know how important ESL is for immigrant children. Certainly, she now speaks with remarkable English fluency. Rusel also is grateful that she had "Aunt Sue," an American woman married to one of her uncles, who helped her whole family adjust. She knows that many immigrant families come to the United States without that kind of built-in assistance, and she is proud of the work her father does at the Catholic Social Services.

Rusel is an exuberant young woman, full of excitement about her future. She turned somber, however, at the end of the conversation when she brought up the subject of September 11, 2001. She was very frightened then, and continues to be frightened, about how people in the United States view her and other Arabic people. She says, "I would not hurt a fly," but she fears that people will make other assumptions about her.

As a social worker who will assist many refugee families, you appreciate learning about Mahdi Mahdi's preimmigration experience, migration journey, and resettlement adjustments. You know, however, that each immigration journey is unique.

Case Study 1.3

The Suarez Family After September 11, 2001

Maria is a busy, active 3-year-old whose life was changed by the events of September 11, 2001. Her mother, Emma Suarez, worked at the World Trade Center and is still listed as missing.

Emma was born in Puerto Rico and came to the mainland to live in the South Bronx when she was 5, along with her parents, a younger brother, two sisters, and an older brother. Emma's father, Carlos, worked hard to make a living for his family, sometimes working as many as three jobs at once. After the children were all in school, Emma's mother, Rosa, began to work as a domestic worker in the homes of a few wealthy families in Manhattan.

Emma was a strong student from her first days in public school, and was often at the top of her class. Her younger brother, Juan, and the sister closest to her in age, Carmen, also were good students, but they were never the star pupils that Emma was. The elder brother, Jesus, and sister, Aida, struggled in school from the time they came to the South Bronx, and both dropped out before they finished high school. Jesus has returned to Puerto Rico to live on the farm with his grandparents.

During her summer vacations from high school, Emma often cared for the children of some of the families for whom her mother worked. One employer was particularly impressed with Emma's quickness and pleasant temperament and took a special interest in her. She encouraged Emma to apply to colleges in her senior year in high school. Emma was accepted at City College and was planning to begin as a full-time student after high school graduation.

A month before Emma was to start school, however, her father had a stroke and was unable to return to work. Rosa and Aida rearranged their work schedules so that they could share the care of Carlos. Carmen had a husband and two young children of her own. Emma realized that she was now needed as an income earner. She took a position doing data entry in an office in the World Trade Center and took evening courses on a part-time basis. She was studying to be a teacher, because she loved learning and wanted to pass on that love to other students.

And then Emma found herself pregnant. She knew that Alejandro Padilla, a young man in one of her classes at school, was the father. Alejandro said that he was not ready to marry, however. Emma returned to work a month after Maria was born, but she did not return to school. At first, Rosa and Aida were not happy that Emma was pregnant with no plans to marry, but once Maria

CASE STUDY 1.3

was born, they fell hopelessly in love with her. They were happy to share the care of Maria, along with Carlos, while Emma worked. Emma cared for Maria and Carlos in the evenings so that Rosa and Aida could work.

Maria was, indeed, an engaging baby, and she was thriving with the adoration of Rosa, Carlos, Aida, Juan, and Emma. Emma missed school, but she held on to her dreams to be a teacher someday.

On the morning of September 11, 2001, Emma left early for work at her job on the 84th floor of the south tower of the World Trade Center, because she was nearing a deadline on a big project. Aida was bathing Carlos when Carmen called about a plane hitting the World Trade Center. Aida called Emma's number, but did not get through to her.

The next few days, even weeks, are a blur to the Suarez family. Juan, Carmen, and Aida took turns going to the Family Assistance Center, but there was no news about Emma. At one point, Juan brought Rosa to the Red Cross Disaster Counseling Center where you were working because he was worried about her. She seemed to be near collapse.

Juan, Rosa, and Aida all missed a lot of work for a number of weeks, and the cash flow sometimes became problematic. They have been blessed with the generosity of their Catholic parish, employers, neighbors, and a large extended family, however, and financial worries are not their greatest concerns at the moment. They are relieved that Maria will have access to money for a college education. But they miss Emma terribly and struggle to understand the horrific thing that happened to her. They all still have nightmares about planes hitting tall buildings.

Maria is lucky to have such a close loving family, and she has gradually quit asking for her mother. She seems keenly aware, however, that there is enormous sadness in her home, and her hugs don't seem to take away the pain.

As a social worker doing disaster relief, you are aware of the large impact that disasters have on the multigenerational family, both in the present and for years to come.

A Definition of the Life Course Perspective

One of the things that the stories of David Sanchez, Mahdi Mahdi, and the Suarez family have in common is that they unfolded over time, across multiple generations. We all have stories that unfold as we progress through life. A useful way to understand this

EXHIBIT 1.1
The Relationship of Person, Environment, and Time

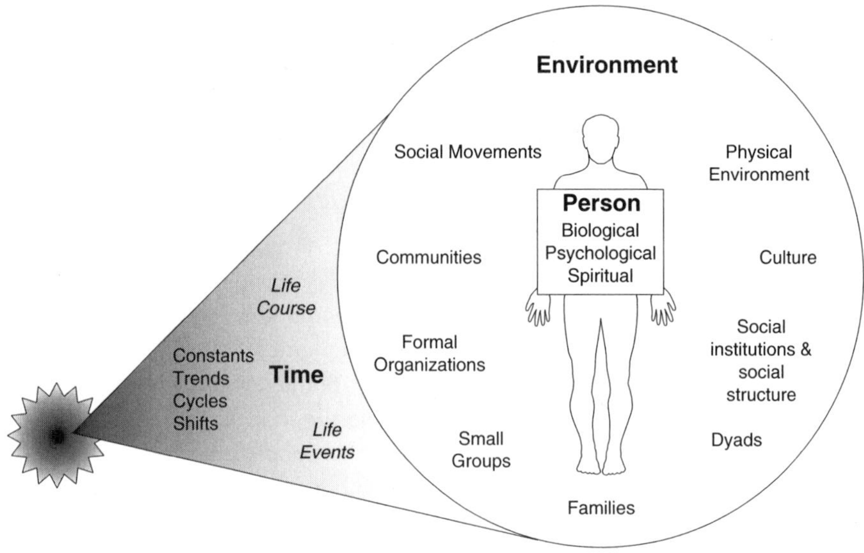

relationship between time and human behavior is the **life course perspective,** which looks at how chronological age, common life transitions, and social change shape people's lives from birth to death. Of course, time is only one dimension of human behavior; characteristics of the person and the environment in which the person lives also play a part (see Exhibit 1.1). But it is common and sensible to try to understand a person by looking at the way that person has developed throughout different periods of life.

You could think of the life course as a path. But note that it is not a straight path; it is a path with both continuities and twists and turns. Certainly, we see twists and turns in the life stories of David Sanchez, Mahdi Mahdi, and Emma Suarez. Think of your own life path. How straight has it been to date?

If you want to understand a person's life, you might begin with an **event history,** or the sequence of significant events, experiences, and transitions in a person's life from birth to death. An event history for David Sanchez might include suffering his father's death as a child, moving to live with his grandmother, being removed to a boarding school, fighting in the Vietnam War, getting married, becoming a father, divorcing, being treated for substance abuse, participating in Indian medicine retreats, attending his grandmother's funeral, moving to live with his great-uncle, and reconnecting with Marco. Mahdi Mahdi's event history would most likely include the date he was drafted, the end of the Iran-Iraq War, escape from Baghdad, and resettlement in the United States. For little Maria Suarez, the events of September 11, 2001 will become a permanent part of her life story.

You might also try to understand a person in terms of how that person's life has been synchronized with family members' lives across time. David Sanchez has begun to have a clearer understanding of his linkages to his great-uncle, father, son, and grandchildren. Mahdi Mahdi tells his story in terms of family connections, and Maria's story is thoroughly entwined with that of her multigenerational family.

Finally, you might view the life course in terms of how culture and social institutions shape the pattern of individual lives. David Sanchez's life course was shaped by cultural and institutional preferences for placing Indian children in boarding schools during middle childhood and adolescence and for recommending the military for youth and young adults. Mahdi Mahdi's life course was also heavily influenced by cultural expectations about soldiering. The economic system is shaping Maria Suarez's life, through its influence on work opportunities for her family members.

Theoretical Roots of the Life Course Perspective

The life course perspective is a theoretical model that has been emerging over the last 40 years, across several disciplines. Sociologists, anthropologists, social historians, demographers, and psychologists—working independently and, more recently, collaboratively—have all helped to give it shape.

Glen Elder Jr., a sociologist, was one of the early authors of a life course perspective, and continues to be one of the driving forces behind its development. In the early 1960s, he began to analyze data from three pioneering longitudinal studies of children that had been undertaken by the University of California, Berkeley. As he examined several decades of data, he was struck with the enormous impact of the Great Depression of the 1930s on individual and family pathways (Elder, 1974). He began to call for developmental theory and research that looked at the influence of historical forces on family, education, and work roles.

At about the same time, social history emerged as a serious field. Social historians were particularly interested in retrieving the experiences of ordinary people, from their own vantage point, rather than telling the historical story from the vantage point of the wealthy and powerful. Tamara Hareven (1978, 1982b, 1996, 2000) has played a key role in developing the subdiscipline of the history of the family. She is particularly interested in how families change and adapt under changing historical conditions and how individuals and families synchronize their lives to accommodate to changing social conditions.

As will become clearer later in the chapter, the life course perspective also draws on traditional theories of developmental psychology, which look at the events that typically occur in people's lives during different stages. The life course perspective differs from these psychological theories in one very important way, however. Developmental

EXHIBIT 1.2
Basic Concepts of the Life Course Perspective

Cohort: Group of persons who were born at the same historical time and who experience particular social changes within a given culture in the same sequence and at the same age.

Transition: Change in roles and statuses that represents a distinct departure from prior roles and statuses.

Trajectory: Long-term pattern of stability and change, which usually involves multiple transitions.

Life Event: Significant occurrence involving a relatively abrupt change that may produce serious and long-lasting effects.

Turning Point: Life event that produces a lasting shift in the life course trajectory.

psychology looks for universal, predictable events and pathways, but the life course perspective calls attention to how historical time and the person's culture affect the individual experience of each life stage.

Basic Concepts of the Life Course Perspective

Scholars who write from a life course perspective and social workers who apply the life course perspective in their work rely on a handful of staple concepts: cohorts, transitions, trajectories, life events, and turning points (see Exhibit 1.2 for concise definitions). As you read about each concept, imagine how it applies to the lives of David Sanchez, Mahdi Mahdi, and Maria Suarez, as well as to your own life.

Cohorts

With their attention to the historical context of developmental pathways, life course scholars have found the concept of cohort to be very useful. In the life course perspective, a **cohort** is a group of persons who were born at the same historical time and experience particular social changes within a given culture in the same sequence and at the same age (Rosow, 1978; Ryder, 1965; Settersten & Mayer, 1997).

Cohorts differ in size, and these differences affect opportunities for education, work, and family life. For example, the baby boom that followed World War II produced a large cohort. When this large cohort entered the labor force, surplus labor drove wages down and unemployment up (Pearlin & Skaff, 1996; Uhlenberg, 1996). Similarly, the large "baby boom echo" cohort is now competing for slots in prestigious universities (Argetsinger, 2001).

EXHIBIT 1.3
Population Pyramids: Kenya, United States, and Italy, 1995

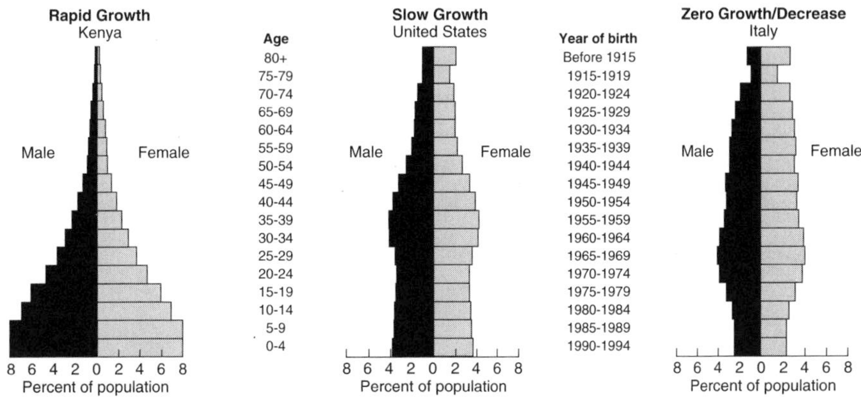

Source: McFalls, J. (1998). Population composition. *Population Bulletin, 53*(3), 26-34. Used by permission.

Some observers suggest that cohorts develop strategies for the special circumstances they face (Easterlin, Schaeffer, & Macunovich, 1993). They suggest that "boomers" responded to the economic challenges of their demographic bubble by delaying or avoiding marriage, postponing childbearing, having fewer children, and increasing the presence of mothers in the labor force.

One way to visualize the configuration of cohorts in a given society is through the use of a **population pyramid,** a chart that depicts the proportion of the population in each age group. As Exhibit 1.3 demonstrates, different countries have significantly different population pyramids. In rapid-growth countries, like Kenya, fertility rates are high and the majority of people are young (McFalls, 1998). Slow-growth countries, like the United States, have a high number of older adults and are becoming increasingly dependent on immigration (typically more attractive to young adults) for a work force to support the aging population. Migration of legal and illegal immigrants accounted for more than one fourth of the U.S.'s population growth in the 1980s and for about one third of the growth in the 1990s. In zero-growth or decreasing countries, like Italy, fertility is at or below replacement level. If it goes and stays below replacement level, the population will begin to decline.

Exhibit 1.3 also shows the ratio of males to females in each population. A cohort's **sex ratio** is the number of males per 100 females. Sex ratios affect a cohort's marriage rates, childbearing practices, crime rates, and family stability (McFalls, 1998). For some time, sex ratios at birth have been lower for blacks than for whites in the United States, meaning that fewer black boy babies are born per 100 girl babies than is the case in the white population (see Ulizzi & Zonta, 1994). This disparity holds up across the life course, with a sex ratio of 81 men to 100 women among black adults over 18 compared to 94 men to 100 women among white adults. When this difference in sex ratios is juxtaposed with a growing disadvantage of black men in the labor market and their increasing rates of incarceration, it is not surprising that a greater percentage of black adults (39%) than white adults (21%) had never been married in 1999 (U.S. Census Bureau, 2000). As shown in Exhibit 1. 3, the ratio of men to women declines across adulthood in all three countries. In the United States, the sex ratio drops to 40 men for every 100 women in the 85 and older population (McFalls, 1998).

Transitions

A life course perspective is stage-like because it proposes that each person experiences a number of **transitions,** or changes in roles and statuses that represent a distinct departure from prior roles and statuses (George, 1993). Life is full of such transitions: starting school, entering puberty, leaving school, getting a first job, leaving home, retiring, and so on. Leaving his grandmother's home for boarding school and enrolling in the military were important transitions for David Sanchez. Rusel Mahdi is excited about the transition from high school to college.

Many transitions relate to family life: marriages, births, divorces, remarriages, deaths (Carter & McGoldrick, 1999b). Each transition changes family statuses and roles and generally is accompanied by family members' exits and entrances. We can see the dramatic effects of birth and death on the Suarez family as Maria entered and Emma exited the family circle.

Transitions in collectivities other than the family, such as small groups, communities, and formal organizations, also involve exits and entrances of members, as well as changes in statuses and roles. In college, for example, students pass through in a steady stream. Some of them make the transition from undergraduate to graduate student, and in that new status they may take on the new role of teaching or research assistant.

Trajectories

The changes involved in transitions are discrete and bounded; when they happen, an old phase of life ends and a new phase begins. In contrast, **trajectories** involve long-term patterns of stability and change in a person's life, and usually involve multiple transitions. We do not necessarily expect trajectories to be a straight line, but we do expect them to have some continuity of direction. For example, we assume that once David Sanchez became addicted to alcohol, he set forth on a path of increased use of alcohol and deteriorating ability to uphold his responsibilities, with multiple transitions involving family disruption and job instability.

Because individuals and families live their lives in multiple spheres, their lives are made up of multiple, intersecting trajectories—for example, educational trajectories,

EXHIBIT 1.4
My Lifeline
(Interlocking
Trajectories)

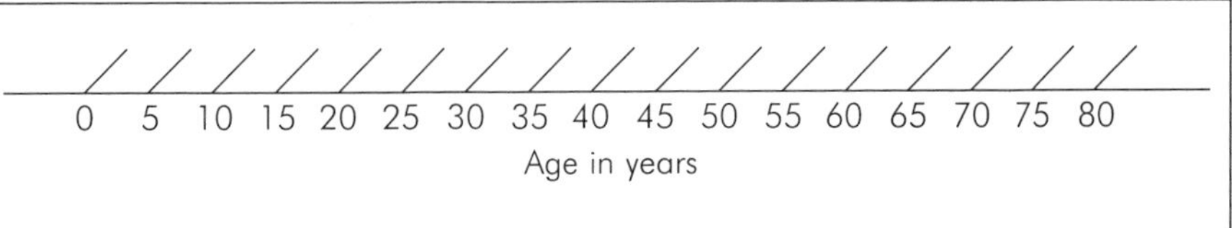

Assuming that you will live until at least 80 years of age, chart how you think your life course trajectory will look. Write in major events and transitions at the appropriate ages. To get a picture of the interlocking trajectories of your lifeline, you may want to write family events and transitions in one color, educational events and transitions in another, occupational events and transitions in another, and health events and transitions in another.

family life trajectories, health trajectories, and work trajectories (Cooksey, Menaghan, & Jekielek, 1997; Settersten & Mayer, 1997; Shanahan, Miech, & Elder, 1998). These interlocking trajectories can be presented visually on separate lifeline charts or as a single lifeline. See Exhibit 1.4 for instructions on completing a lifeline of interlocking trajectories.

Life Events

Specific events predominate in the stories of David Sanchez, Mahdi Mahdi, and Maria Suarez: death of a parent, escape from the homeland, terrorist attack. A **life event** is a significant occurrence involving a relatively abrupt change that may produce serious and long-lasting effects (Settersten & Mayer, 1997). "Life event" refers to the happening itself and not to the transitions that will occur because of the happening.

One common method for evaluating the effect of such stressful events is Thomas Holmes & Richard Rahe's Schedule of Recent Events, also called the Social Readjustment Rating Scale (Holmes, 1978; Holmes & Rahe, 1967). The Schedule of Recent Events, along with the rating of the stress associated with each event, appears in Exhibit 1.5. Holmes and Rahe constructed their schedule of events by asking respondents to rate the relative degree of adjustment required for different life events.

Inventories like the Schedule of Recent Events can remind us of some of the life events that affect human behavior and life course trajectories, but they also have limitations:

> Life events inventories are not finely tuned. One suggestion is to classify life events along several dimensions: "major versus minor, anticipated versus unanticipated, controllable versus uncontrollable, typical versus atypical, desirable versus undesirable, acute versus chronic." (Settersten & Mayer, 1997, p. 246)

EXHIBIT 1.5
Life Change Events from the Holmes and Rahe Schedule of Recent Events

Life Event	Stress Rating
Death of a spouse	100
Divorce	73
Marital separation from mate	65
Detention in jail or other institutions	63
Death of a close family member	63
Major personal injury or illness	53
Marriage	50
Being fired at work	47
Marital reconciliation with mate	45
Retirement from work	45
Major change in the health or behavior of a family member	44
Pregnancy	40
Sexual difficulties	39
Gaining a new family member (e.g., through birth, adoption, elder moving in)	39
Major business readjustment (e.g., merger, reorganization, bankruptcy)	39
Major change in financial state (a lot worse off or a lot better off than usual)	38
Death of a close friend	37
Changing to a different line of work	36
Major change in the number of arguments with spouse (more or less)	35
Taking out a mortgage or loan for a major purchase	31
Foreclosure on a mortgage or loan	30
Major change in responsibilities at work (e.g., promotion, demotion, lateral transfer)	29
Son or daughter leaving home	29
Trouble with in-laws	29
Outstanding personal achievement	28
Wife beginning or ceasing work outside the home	26
Beginning or ceasing formal schooling	26
Major change in living conditions (e.g., building a new home, remodeling, deterioration of home or neighborhood)	25
Revision of personal habits (e.g., dress, manners, associations)	24
Trouble with the boss	23
Major change in working hours or conditions	20
Change in residence	20
Change to a new school	20
Major change in usual type and/or amount of recreation	19
Major change in church activities (e.g., a lot more or a lot less than usual)	19
Major change in social activities (e.g., clubs, dancing, movies, visiting)	18
Taking out a mortgage or loan for a lesser purchase (e.g., for a car, TV, freezer)	17

(continued)

Exhibit 1.5

Life Change Events from the Holmes and Rahe Schedule of Recent Events *(continued)*

Life Event	Stress Rating
Major change in sleeping habits (a lot more or a lot less sleep, or change in part of day when asleep)	16
Major change in number of family get-togethers (e.g., a lot more or a lot less than usual)	15
Major change in eating habits (a lot less food intake or very different meal hours or surroundings	15
Vacation	13
Christmas	12
Minor violations of the law (e.g., traffic tickets, jaywalking, disturbing the peace)	11

Source: Holmes, T. (1978). Life situations, emotions, and disease. *Psychosomatic Medicine, 19, 747.*

Existing inventories are biased toward undesirable, rather than desirable, events. Not all life events prompt harmful life changes (Pearlin & Skaff, 1996).

Specific life events have different meanings to various individuals and to various collectivities. Those distinctive meanings have not been measured in most research on life events (George, 1996; Hareven, 2000). One example of a study that has taken different meanings into account found that women report more vivid memories of life events in relationships than men report (Ross & Holmberg, 1992).

Life events inventories are biased toward events more commonly experienced by certain groups of people: young adults, men, whites, and the middle class (Settersten & Mayer, 1997, p. 246). In one small exploratory study that used a lifeline rather than an inventory of events in an attempt to correct for this bias, women reported a greater number of life events than men did (de Vries & Watt, 1996).

Turning Points

David Sanchez describes becoming an apprentice medicine man as a turning point in his life. For Mahdi Mahdi, the decision to refuse the draft was a turning point. Even though Maria Suarez was too young to think of September 11, 2001, as a turning point in her life, there is no doubt that the events of that day changed the course of her life. A **turning point** is a special life event that produces a lasting shift in the life course trajectory. It must lead to more than a temporary detour. As significant as they are to individuals' lives, turning points usually become obvious only as time passes (Wheaton & Gotlib, 1997). Yet in one survey, more than 85% of the respondents reported that there had been turning points in their lives (Clausen, 1990, cited in Wheaton & Gotlib, 1997). According to traditional developmental theory, the developmental trajectory is more or less continuous, proceeding steadily from one phase to another. But life course trajectories are seldom so smooth and predictable. They involve many discontinuities, or sudden breaks, and some special life events become turning points that produce a lasting shift in the life course trajectory. Inertia tends to keep us on a particular trajectory, but turning points add twists and turns or even reversals to the life course (Wheaton & Gotlib, 1997). For example, we expect someone who is addicted to alcohol to continue to organize his or her life around that substance unless some event becomes a turning point for recovery.

Three types of life events can serve as turning points (Rutter, 1996):

1. Life events that either close or open opportunities
2. Life events that make a lasting change on the person's environment
3. Life events that change a person's self-concept, beliefs, or expectations

Some events, such as migration to a new country, are momentous because they qualify as all three types of events. Migration, whether voluntary or involuntary, certainly makes a lasting change on the environment in which the person lives; it may also close and open opportunities and cause a change in self-concept and beliefs. Certainly, that seems to be the case with Mahdi Mahdi. Keep in mind, however, that individuals make subjective assessments of life events (George, 1996). The same type of life event may be a turning point for one individual, family, or other collectivity, but not for another. Less dramatic transitions may also become turning points, depending on the individual's assessment of its importance. A transition can become a turning point under five conditions (Hareven, 2000):

1. When the transition occurs simultaneously with a crisis or is followed by a crisis
2. When the transition involves family conflict over the needs and wants of individuals and the greater good of the family unit
3. When the transition is "off-time," meaning that it does not occur at the typical stage in life
4. When the transition is followed by unforeseen negative consequences
5. When the transition requires exceptional social adjustments

Loss of a parent is not always a turning point, but when such a loss occurs off-time, as it did with David Sanchez and Maria Suarez, it is often a turning point. Emma Suarez may not have thought of her decision to take a job in the World Trade Center as a turning point, because she could not foresee the events of September 11, 2001.

Most life course pathways include multiple turning points, some that get life trajectories off track and others that get life trajectories back on track (Wheaton & Gotlib, 1997). David Sanchez's Vietnam experience seems to have gotten him off track, and his grandmother's death seems to have gotten him back on track. In fact, we could say that the intent of many social work interventions is to get life course trajectories back on track. We do this when we work with a family that has gotten off track and on a path to divorce. We also do this when we plan interventions to precipitate a turning point toward recovery for a client with an addiction. Or we may plan an intervention to help a deteriorating community reclaim its lost sense of community and spirit of pride. It is interesting to note that many social service organizations have taken "Turning Point" for their name.

Major Themes of the Life Course Perspective

Almost a decade ago, Glen Elder (1994) identified four dominant, and interrelated, themes in the life course approach: interplay of human lives and historical time, timing of lives, linked or interdependent lives, and human agency in making choices. The meaning of these themes is discussed below, along with the meaning of two other related themes that Elder (1998) and Michael Shanahan (2000) have recently identified as important: diversity in life course trajectories and developmental risk and protection. The meaning of these themes is summarized in Exhibit 1.6.

Interplay of Human Lives and Historical Time

As sociologists and social historians began to study individual and family life trajectories, they noted that persons born in different years face different historical worlds, with different options and constraints—especially in rapidly changing societies, such as the United States at the beginning of the 21st century. They suggested that historical time may produce **cohort effects**, which occur when social change affects one cohort differently than it affects subsequent cohorts. For example, Elder's (1974) research on children and the Great Depression found that the life course trajectories of the cohort that were young children at the time of the economic downturn were more seriously affected by family hardship than the cohort that were in middle childhood and late adolescence at the time.

Analysis of large data sets by a number of researchers provides forceful evidence that changes in other social institutions impinge on family and individual life course trajectories (e.g., Cooksey, Menaghan, & Jekielek, 1997; Elder, 1986; Rindfuss,

Exhibit 1.6
Major Themes of the Life Course Perspective

Interplay of human lives and historical time: Individual and family development must be understood in historical context.

Timing of lives: Particular roles and behaviors are associated with particular age groups, based on biological age, psychological age, social age, and spiritual age.

Linked or interdependent lives: Human lives are interdependent, and the family is the primary arena for experiencing and interpreting wider historical, cultural, and social phenomena.

Human agency in making choices: The individual life course is constructed by the choices and actions individuals take within the opportunities and constraints of history and social circumstances.

Diversity in life course trajectories: There is much diversity in life course pathways, due to cohort variations, social class, culture, gender, and individual agency.

Developmental risk and protection: Experiences with one life transition have an impact on subsequent transitions and events, and may either protect the life course trajectory or put it at risk.

Swicegood, & Rosenfeld, 1987; Shanahan et al., 1998). Tamara Hareven's historical analysis of family life (2000) documents the lag between social change and the development of public policy to respond to the new circumstances and the needs that arise with social change (see also Riley, 1996). One such lag today is the lag between trends in employment among mothers and public policy regarding child care during infancy and early childhood. Social work planners and administrators confront the results of such a lag in their work. Thus, they have some responsibility to keep the public informed about the impact of changing social conditions on individuals, families, communities, and formal organizations.

Timing of Lives

"How old are you?" You have probably been asked that question many times, and no doubt you find yourself curious about the age of new acquaintances. Every society appears to use age as an important variable, and many social institutions in advanced industrial societies are organized, in part, around age—the age for starting school, the age of majority, retirement age, and so on (Settersten & Mayer, 1997). In the United States, our speech abounds with expressions related to age: "terrible 2s," "sweet 16," "20-something," "life begins at 40," "senior discounts."

Age is also a prominent attribute in efforts by social scientists to bring order and predictability to our understanding of human behavior. Life course scholars are interested in the age at which specific life events and transitions occur, which they refer to as the timing of lives. They may classify entrances and exits from particular statuses and roles as "off-time" or "on-time," based on social norms or shared expectations about the timing of such transitions (George, 1993). For example, childbearing in adolescence is considered off-time in modern industrial countries, although it is seen as on-time in many preindustrial societies. Likewise, death in early or middle adulthood, as happened in large numbers during the early stages of the AIDS epidemic, is considered off-time in modern industrial societies. Survivors' grief is probably deeper in cases of "premature loss" (Pearlin & Skaff, 1996), which is perhaps why Emma Suarez's family keeps saying, "She was so young; she had so much life left." Certainly, David Sanchez reacted differently to his father's and his grandmother's deaths.

Dimensions of Age. Chronological age itself is not the only factor involved in timing of lives. Age-graded differences in roles and behaviors are the result of biological, psychological, social, and spiritual processes. Thus, age is often considered from each of the perspectives that make up the biopsychosocial framework (e.g., Cavanaugh, 1996; Kimmel, 1990; Settersten & Mayer, 1997). Although life course scholars have not directly addressed the issue of spiritual age, it is an important perspective as well.

Biological age indicates a person's level of biological development and physical health, as measured by the functioning of the various organ systems. It is the present position of the biological person in relation to the potential life cycle. There is no simple, straightforward way to measure biological age. Any method for calculating it has been altered by changes in life expectancy (Shanahan, 2000) and by changes in the main causes of death (Bartley, Blane, & Montgomery, 1997). With the development of modern medicine, the causes of death have shifted from infectious diseases to chronic diseases (National Center for Health Statistics, 2001b). Life course researchers need to collaborate with geneticists to understand the effect on biological age of late-emerging genetic factors and with endocrinologists to understand how social processes are related to biological aging (Shanahan, 2000).

Psychological age has both behavioral and perceptual components. Behaviorally, psychological age refers to the capacities that people have and the skills they use to adapt to changing biological and environmental demands. Skills in memory, learning, intelligence, motivation, emotions, and so forth are all involved (Settersten & Mayer, 1997). Perceptually, psychological age is based on how old people perceive themselves to be. Life course researchers have explored the perceptual aspect of psychological age since the 1960s, sometimes with questions such as, "Do you feel that you are young, middle aged, old, or very old?" (e.g., Barak & Stern, 1986; Markides & Boldt, 1983). More recently, researchers have used a more multifaceted way of exploring perceived age. Some have distinguished between "feel-age, look-age, do-age, and interests-age" (Henderson, Goldsmith, & Flynn, 1995). Anthropological examination of life transitions suggests that men and women attach different social meanings to age and use different guidelines for measuring how old they are (Hagestad, 1991), but empirical research on the role gender plays in self-perceived age is mixed. Culture is another factor in perceptions of age. In one study, the researchers found less discrepancy between chronological age and self-perceived age among a Finnish sample than among a U.S. sample, with the U.S. sample demonstrating a definite tendency to say they considered themselves more youthful than their chronological age (Uotinen, 1998).

Social age refers to the age-graded roles and behaviors expected by society—in other words, the socially constructed meaning of various ages. The concept of **age norm** is used to indicate the behaviors that are expected of people of a specific age in a given society at a particular point in time. Age norms may be informal expectations, or they may be encoded as formal rules and laws. For example, cultures have an informal age norm about the appropriate age to begin romantic dating, if at all. On the other hand, we have developed formal rules about the appropriate age for driving, drinking alcohol, and voting. Life course scholars suggest that age norms vary not only across historical time and across societies but also by gender, race, ethnicity, and social class within a given time and society (Chudacolff, 1989; Kertzer, 1989; Settersten & Mayer, 1997). Although biological age and psychological age are recognized in the life course perspective, social age receives special emphasis. For instance, life course scholars use life phases such as early childhood and middle adulthood, which are based in large part on social age, to conceptualize human lives from birth to death. In this book, we talk about nine phases, from conception to very late adulthood. Keep in mind, however, that the number and nature of these life phases are socially constructed and have changed over time, with modernization and mass longevity leading to finer gradations in life phases and consequently a greater number of them (Settersten & Mayer, 1997).

Spiritual age indicates the current position of a person in the ongoing search for "meaning and morally fulfilling relationships" (Canda, 1997, p. 302). David Sanchez is certainly at a different position in his search for life's meaning than he was when he came home from Vietnam. Although life course scholars have not paid much attention to spiritual age, it has been the subject of study by some developmental psychologists and other social scientists. In an exploration of the meaning of adulthood edited by Erik Erikson in 1978, several authors explored the markers of adulthood from the viewpoint of a number of spiritual and religious traditions, including Christianity, Hinduism, Islam, Buddhism, and Confucianism. Several themes emerged across the various traditions: balance between contemplation and moral action, reason, self-discipline, character improvement, loving actions, and close community with others. All the authors noted that spirituality is typically seen as a process of growth, a process with no end. James Fowler (1981) has presented a theory of faith development, based on 359 in-depth interviews, that strongly links it with chronological age. Ken Wilber's (1977, 1995) Full-Spectrum Model of Consciousness also proposes an association between age and spiritual development, but Wilbur does not suggest that spiritual development is strictly linear. He notes, as do the contributors to the Erikson book, that there can be regressions, temporary leaps, and turning points in a person's spiritual development.

Standardization in the Timing of Lives. Life course scholars debate whether the trend is toward greater standardization in age-graded social roles and statuses or toward greater diversification (Settersten & Lovegreen, 1998; Shanahan, 2000). Ironically, life patterns seem to be becoming, at the same time, more standardized and more diversified. The implication for social workers is that we must pay attention to the uniqueness of each person's life course trajectory, but we can use research about regularities in the timing of lives to develop prevention programs. The "Knowledge Into Practice" story at the end of this book is a good example of a prevention program based on such research.

Some societies engage in **age structuring,** or standardizing of the ages at which social role transitions occur, by developing policies and laws that regulate the timing of these transitions. For example, the United States has laws and regulations about the ages for compulsory education, working (child labor), driving, drinking, being tried as an adult, marrying, holding public office, and receiving pensions and social insurance. However, countries vary considerably in the degree to which age norms are formalized (Settersten & Mayer, 1997; Shanahan, 2000). Some scholars suggest that formal age-structuring becomes more prevalent as societies modernize (Buchmann, 1989; Meyer, 1986). Also, formal age structuring, as we know it, may not have been possible until we could predict that large numbers of people would survive to late adulthood (Kohli, 1986). This is one clear way in which social age is interrelated with biological age.

Formalized age structuring has created a couple of difficulties that affect social workers. One is that cultural lags often lead to a mismatch between changing circumstances and the age structuring in society (Foner, 1996). Consider the trend for corporations to offer early retirement, before the age of 65, in a time when people are living longer and with better health. This mismatch has implications both for public budgets and for individual lives. Another problem with the institutionalization of age norms is increasing age segregation; people are spending more of their time in groups consisting entirely of people their own age. Social work services are increasingly organized around the settings of these age-segregated groups: schools, the workplace, senior centers, and so forth.

Some life course scholars argue, however, that modernization has allowed the life course to become more flexibly structured (Guillemard & van Gunsteren, 1991;

Neugarten & Hagestad, 1976). Indeed, there is much diversity in the sequencing and timing of adult life course markers, such as completing an education, beginning work, leaving home, marrying, and becoming a parent (George & Gold, 1991). Trajectories in the family domain may be more flexible than work and educational trajectories (Elder, 1998; Settersten & Lovegreen, 1998). Life course trajectories also vary in significant ways by gender, race, ethnicity, and social class (Elder, 1998; Settersten & Lovegreen, 1998; Shanahan, 2000). This issue will be discussed further later in the chapter.

To gain a better understanding of regularities and irregularities in life course trajectories, researchers have studied the order in which life events and transitions occur (George, 1993). Most of the research has been on the entrance into adulthood, focusing specifically on the completion of school, first full-time job, and first marriage (Hogan, 1978, 1981; Modell, Furstenberg, & Hershberg, 1976; Settersten, 1998; Shanahan, Miech, & Elder, 1998). Life course scholars also are interested in the length of time that an individual, family, or other collectivity spends in a particular state, without changes in status or roles. In general, the longer we experience specific environments and conditions, the more likely it is that our behavior will be affected by them (George, 1996). The duration of Mahdi Mahdi's stays in various settings and statuses—soldier, refugee, convenience store clerk, immigration specialist—was important. Finally, life course scholars are studying the pace of transitions. Transitions into adult roles in young adulthood (such as completing school, leaving home, getting the first job, getting married, having the first child) appear to be more rapidly timed than transitions in middle and late adulthood (such as launching children, retiring, losing parents) (Hareven, 1978, 2000).

Linked or Interdependent Lives

The life course perspective emphasizes the interdependence of human lives and the ways in which relationships both support and control an individual's behavior. **Social support**, which is defined as help rendered by others that benefits an individual (Thoits, 1985), is an obvious element of interdependent lives. Relationships also control behavior through expectations, rewards, and punishments.

Particular attention has been paid to the family as a source of support and control. In addition, the lives of family members are linked across generations, with both opportunity and misfortune having an intergenerational impact. The cases of David Sanchez, Mahdi Mahdi, and Maria Suarez are rich examples of lives linked across generations. But they are also rich examples of how people's lives are linked with those of people outside the family.

Links Between Family Members. Certainly, parents' and children's lives are linked. Elder's longitudinal research of children raised during the Great Depression found that as parents experienced greater economic pressures, they faced a greater risk of depressed feelings and marital discord. Consequently, their ability to nurture their children was compromised, and their children were more likely to exhibit emotional distress, academic trouble, and problem behavior (Elder, 1974). The connection between family hardship, family nurturance, and child behaviors is now well established (e.g., Conger, Elder, Lorenz, Simons, & Whitbeck, 1992; Conger et al., 1993). These findings might help to explain recent reports that adolescents in the United States and Canada exhibited more academic and behavioral problems when their mothers moved from welfare to work if the family's economic situation became less stable in the process (Stepp, 2001). In addition to the economic connection between parents and children, parents provide social capital for their children, in terms of role models and networks of social support (Cooksey, Menaghan, & Jekielek, 1997).

It should also be noted that parents' lives are influenced by the trajectories of their children's lives. For example, parents may need to alter their work trajectories to respond to the needs of a terminally ill child. Or parents may forgo early retirement to assist their young adult children with education expenses. Mahdi Mahdi says that his father died from worrying about his sons.

Older adults and their adult children are also interdependent. The pattern of mutual support between older adults and their adult children is formed by life events and transitions across the life course (Hareven, 1996). It is also fundamentally changed when families go through historical disruptions such as wars or major economic downturns. For example, the traditional pattern of intergenerational support—parents supporting children—is often disrupted when one generation migrates and another generation stays behind. It is also disrupted in immigrant families when the children pick up the new language and cultural norms faster than the adults in the family and take on the role of interpreter for their parents and grandparents (Hernandez & McGoldrick, 1999).

What complicates matters is that family roles must often be synchronized across three or more generations at once. Sometimes this synchronization does not go smoothly. Divorce, remarriage, and discontinuities in parents' work and educational trajectories may conflict with the needs of children (see, e.g., Ahrons, 1999; Cooksey, Menaghan, & Jekielek, 1997). Similarly, the timing of adult children's educational, family, and work transitions often conflicts with the needs of aging parents (Hareven, 1996). The "generation in the middle" may have to make uncomfortable choices when allocating scarce economic and emotional resources. When a significant life event in one generation (such as death of a grandparent) is juxtaposed with a significant life event in another generation (such as birth of a child), families and individual family members are especially vulnerable (Carter & McGoldrick, 1999b).

Links With the Wider World. We know a lot more at this point about the ways that individuals and their multigenerational families are interdependent than about the interdependence between individuals and families and other groups and collectivities. However, we may at least note that work has a major effect on family transitions (George, 1993). In this vein, using data for 6- and 7-year-old children from the National Longitudinal Survey of Youth, researchers found that the children's depression and aggressive behavior were not associated with whether their mothers were employed but rather with the type of work those mothers did (Cooksey et al., 1997). Children whose mothers are in occupations requiring complex skills are less likely to be depressed and behave aggressively than children whose mothers are in less skilled work environments. Perhaps performing complex tasks at work enhances parenting skills. Or perhaps the mothers in more skilled occupations benefit emotionally from having greater control over their work environments. This finding would, of course, have meaning only in an advanced industrial society and would offer no insight about parenting skills in traditional societies.

The family seems to have much more influence on child and adolescent behaviors than the neighborhood does (Elder, 1998; Furstenberg, Cook, Eccles, Elder, & Sameroff, 1999; Klebanov, Brooks-Gunn, Gordon, & Chase-Lansdale, 1997). More differences in the behavior of children and adolescents have been found among families within a given neighborhood than have been found when comparing the families in one neighborhood with families in other neighborhoods. There is evidence, however, that the neighborhood effects may be greater for children living in high-poverty areas, which are often marked by violence and environmental health hazards, than for children living in low-poverty neighborhoods (Katz, Kling, & Liebman, 1999, cited in Shonkoff & Phillips, 2000; Rosenbaum, 1991).

It is important for social workers to remember that lives are also linked in systems of institutionalized privilege and oppression. The life trajectories of members of minority groups in the United States are marked by discrimination and lack of opportunity, which are experienced pervasively as daily insults and pressures. However, various cultural groups have devised unique systems of social support to cope with the "mundane extreme environments" in which they live (McAdoo, 1986). Examples include the extensive and intensive natural support systems of Hispanic families like the Suarez family (Falicov, 1999) and the special role of the church for African Americans (Billingsley, 1999).

Human Agency in Making Choices

Mahdi Mahdi made a decision to refuse the draft, and this decision had a momentous impact on his own life course as well as the trajectory of members of his extended family. Like all of us, he made choices that fundamentally changed his life (Elder, 1998). In other words, he participated in constructing his life course through the exercise of **human agency,** or the use of personal power to achieve one's goals. The emphasis on human agency may be one of the most positive contributions of the life course perspective (Hareven, 2000).

A look at the discipline of social history might help to explain why considering human agency is so important to social workers. Social historians have attempted to correct the traditional focus on lives of elites by studying the lives of common people (Hareven, 2000). By doing so, they discovered that many groups once considered passive victims—for example, working-class people and slaves—actually took independent action to cope with the difficulties imposed by the rich and powerful. Historical research now shows that couples tried to limit the size of their families even in preindustrial societies (Wrigley, 1966), that slaves were often ingenious in their struggles to hold their families together (Gutman, 1976), and that factory workers used informal networks and kinship ties to manage, and sometimes resist, pressures for efficiency (Hareven, 1982a). These findings are consistent with social work approaches that focus on individual, family, and community strengths (Saleeby, 1996).

Clearly, however, human agency has limits. Individuals' choices are constrained by the structural and cultural arrangements of a given historical era. For example, Mahdi Mahdi's choices did not seem limitless to him; he faced the unfortunate choices of becoming a soldier again or refusing the draft. Unequal opportunities also give some members of society more options than others have. Elder (1998) notes that the emphasis on human agency in the life course perspective has been aided by Albert Bandura's (1986) work on the two concepts of *self-efficacy*, or sense of personal competence, and *efficacy expectation*, or expectation that one can personally accomplish a goal. It is important to remember, however, that Bandura (1986) makes specific note about how social inequalities can result in low self-efficacy and low efficacy expectations among members of oppressed groups.

Diversity in Life Course Trajectories

Life course researchers have long had strong evidence of diversity in individuals' life patterns. Early research emphasized differences between cohorts, but increasing attention is being paid to variability within cohort groups. Elder's four themes of the life course perspective are linked to the sources of both kinds of variability:

1. *Interplay of human lives and historical time.* Cohorts tend to have different life trajectories because of the unique historical events each cohort encounters. Mahdi Mahdi wanted his daughter to tell her story because he knew that he and she had experienced the war, escape, and resettlement very differently.

2. *Timing of lives.* Age norms change with time and place and culture; they also vary by social location, or place in the social structure, most notably by gender, race,

ethnicity, and social class (Settersten & Mayer, 1997). These variables create differences from one cohort to another as well as differences among the individuals within a cohort.

3. *Linked or independent lives.* The differing patterns of social networks in which persons are embedded produce differences in life course experiences. The intersection of multiple trajectories—for example, the family lifeline, the educational lifeline, and the work lifeline—introduces new possibilities for diversity in life course patterns. Like many midlife adults, Mahdi Mahdi must find a way to balance his family lifeline, educational lifeline, and work lifeline.

4. *Human agency in making choices.* Human agency allows for extensive individual differences in life course trajectories, as individuals plan and make choices between options. It is not surprising, given these possibilities for unique experience, that the stories of individuals vary so much.

A good indication of the diversity of life course trajectories is found in an often cited study by Ronald Rindfuss and colleagues (Rindfuss et al., 1987). They examined the sequencing of five roles—work, education, homemaking, military, and other—among 6,700 men and 7,000 women for the 8 years following their high school graduation in 1972. The researchers found 1,100 different sequences of these five roles among the men and 1,800 different sequences among the women. This and other research on sequencing of life course transitions has called increasing attention to the heterogeneity of life course trajectories (Settersten, 1998; Settersten & Lovegreen, 1998; Shanahan et al., 1998).

As these research results indicate, men's life course trajectories are more rigidly structured, with fewer discontinuities, than women's. One explanation for this gender difference is that women's lives have been more strongly interwoven with the family domain than men's, and the family domain operates on nonlinear time, with many irregularities (Settersten & Lovegreen, 1998). Men's lives are still more firmly rooted in domains outside the family, such as the paid work world, and these domains operate in linear time. Men's and women's life trajectories have started to become more similar, but this convergence is primarily because women's schooling and employment patterns are moving closer to men's, and not because men have become more involved in the family domain (Settersten & Lovegreen, 1998).

Life course trajectories also vary by social class. In neighborhoods characterized by concentrated poverty, large numbers of youth drop out of school by the ninth grade (Kliman & Madsen, 1999). This was the case for Jesus and Aida Suarez. In contrast, youth in upper middle-class and upper-class families expect an extended period of education with parental subsidies. These social class differences in educational trajectories are associated with differences in family and work trajectories. Affluent youth go to school and postpone their entry into adult roles of work and family. Less affluent youth, however, often enter earlier into marriage, parenting, and employment.

Research suggests that the family life trajectories in minority groups in the United States are different from the family life trajectories of whites. Minority youth tend to leave home to live independently later than white youth do, at least in part because of the high value put on "kinkeeping" in many minority cultures (Stack, 1974). However, in a random sample from a major urban U.S. city, minority respondents gave earlier deadlines for leaving home than white respondents when questioned about the appropriate age for leaving home—even though the minority respondents actually left home at a later age than the white respondents (Settersten, 1998). This finding may reflect the bicultural conflict that complicates the lives of young adults in ethnic minority groups. It also reflects differences in financial resources for leaving home.

Another source of diversity in a country with considerable immigration is the individual experience leading to the decision to immigrate, the journey itself, and the resettlement period (Devore & Schlesinger, 1999; Hernandez & McGoldrick, 1999). The individual's decision to immigrate may involve social, religious, or political persecution. Or, as in Mahdi Mahdi's case, it may involve war and a dangerous political environment. The transit experience is sometimes traumatic, and Mahdi Mahdi does not like to recall his escape in the middle of the night. The resettlement experience requires establishment of new social networks, may involve changes in socioeconomic status, and presents serious demands for acculturating to a new physical and social environment. Mahdi Mahdi speaks of the struggles in being a convenience store clerk with a college education. Gender, race, social class, and age all add layers of complexity to the migration experience. Family roles often have to be renegotiated as children outstrip older family members in learning the new language. Tensions can develop over conflicting approaches to the acculturation process (Fabelo-Alcover, 2001). Just as they should investigate their clients' educational trajectories, work trajectories, and family trajectories, social workers should be interested in the migration trajectories of their immigrant clients.

Developmental Risk and Protection

As the life course perspective has continued to evolve, it has more clearly emphasized the links between the life events and transitions of childhood, adolescence, and adulthood (Shanahan, 2000). Studies indicate that childhood events sometimes shape people's lives 40 or 50 years later (George, 1996).

In fact, the long-term impact of developmental experiences was the subject of the earliest life course research, Glen Elder's (1974) examination of longitudinal data for children from the Great Depression. He compared a group of children (referred to as the

Oakland children) who were born in 1920 and 1921 with a group of children (referred to as the Berkeley children) who were born in 1928 and 1929. The Oakland children experienced a relatively stable and secure childhood before they encountered the economic deprivations of the Great Depression during their adolescence. They also made the transition to adulthood after the worst of the economic downturn. The Berkeley children, on the other hand, experienced early childhood during the worst years of the Depression. When they reached adolescence, their parents were involved in World War II, with many fathers away in military roles and many mothers working long hours in "essential industry." Although both groups experienced economic hardship and later difficulties in life transitions, the Berkeley children were more negatively affected than the Oakland children.

Elder has recently more clearly enunciated the idea of developmental risk and protection as a major theme of the life course perspective: "[T]he developmental impact of a succession of life transitions or events is contingent on when they occur in a person's life" (1998, p. 3). Other life course scholars have suggested that it is not simply the timing and sequencing of hardships but also their duration and spacing that provide risk for youth as they make the transition into adulthood. For instance, poverty alone is much less of a risk than extended poverty (Shanahan, 2000). Families are more vulnerable to getting off track when confronted simultaneously by multiple events and transitions (Carter & McGoldrick, 1999b). Life course scholars have borrowed the concepts of **cumulative advantage** and **cumulative disadvantage** from sociologist Robert Merton to explain inequality within cohorts across the life course (Bartley et al., 1997; O'Rand, 1996). Merton (1968) found that in scientific careers, large inequalities in productivity and recognition had accumulated. Scholarly productivity brings recognition, and recognition brings resources for further productivity, which of course brings further recognition and so on. Merton proposed that, in this way, scientists who are productive early in their careers accumulate advantage over time, whereas other scientists accumulate disadvantage. Sociologists propose that cumulative advantage and cumulative disadvantage are socially constructed; social institutions and societal structures develop mechanisms that ensure increasing advantage for those who succeed early in life and increasing disadvantage for those who struggle (Settersten & Lovegreen, 1998).

Consider the effect of advantages in schooling. Young children with affluent parents attend well-equipped primary and secondary schools, which position them for successful college careers, which position them for occupations that pay well, which provide opportunities for good health maintenance, which position them for healthy, secure old age. This trajectory of unearned advantage is sometimes referred to as **privilege** (McIntosh, 1988). Children who do not come from affluent families are more likely to attend underequipped schools, experience school failure or dropout, begin work in low-paying sectors of the labor market, experience unemployment, and arrive at old age with compromised health and limited economic resources.

Early deprivations and traumas do not inevitably lead to a trajectory of failure, but without intervention that reverses the trajectory, these early experiences are likely to lead to accumulation of disadvantage. Individual trajectories may be moderated not only by human agency but also by historical events and environmental supports. As one example of the positive impact of historical events, many children of the Great Depression were able to reverse disadvantages in their life trajectories through their military service in World War II (Elder, 1986). On the other hand, military service in wartime may involve traumatic stress, as we see with David Sanchez and Mahdi Mahdi. In terms of environmental support, governmental safety nets to support vulnerable families at key life transitions have been found to reduce the effects of deprivation and trauma on health (Bartley et al., 1997). Researchers have found that home nurse visitation during the first 2 years of a child's life can reduce the risk of child abuse and criminal behavior among low-income mothers (Olds et al., 1997).

The life course perspective and the concept of cumulative disadvantage is beginning to influence community epidemiology, or the study of the prevalence of disease across communities (e.g., Brunner, 1997; Kellam & Van Horn, 1997; Kuh & Ben-Shlomo, 1997). Researchers in this tradition are interested in social and geographical inequalities in the distribution of chronic disease. They suggest that risk for chronic disease gradually accumulates over a life course through episodes of illness, exposure to unfavorable environments, and unsafe behaviors. They are also interested in how some experiences in the life course can break the chain of risk.

This approach to public health mirrors efforts in developmental psychology and other disciplines to understand developmental risk and protective factors (Fraser, 1997; Rutter, 1996; Werner, 2000). The study of risk and protection has led to an interest in the concept of **resilience**, which refers to the ability of some people to fare well in the face of risk factors. Researchers studying resilient children are examining the interplay of risk factors and protective factors in their lives. Although the study of protective factors lags behind the study of risk factors, researchers speculate that a cumulative effect will also be found for protective factors (Fraser, 1997).

Many scholars now recommend that we think of risk and protection as processes over time, which is very much like the way that life course scholars write about life trajectories. Exhibit 1.7 shows how phases of life are interwoven with various risks and protective factors.

Strengths and Limitations of the Life Course Perspective

As a framework for thinking about the aspect of time in human behavior, the life course perspective has several advantages over traditional theories of human development. It

EXHIBIT 1.7
Risk and Protective Factors for Specific Life Course Phases

Life Course Phase	Risk Factors	Protective Factors
Infancy	Poverty Child abuse/neglect Parental mental illness Teenage motherhood	Active, alert, high vigor Sociability Small family size
Infancy-Childhood	Poverty Child abuse/neglect Divorce Parental substance abuse	"Easy," engaging temperament
Infancy-Adolescence	Poverty Child abuse/neglect Parental mental illness Parental substance abuse Teenage motherhood Divorce	Maternal competence Close bond with primary caregiver (not necessarily biological parent) Supportive grandparents
Infancy-Adulthood	Poverty Child abuse/neglect Teenage motherhood	Low distress/low emotionality Mother's education
Early Childhood	Poverty	Advanced self-help skills
Preschool-Adulthood	Poverty Parental mental illness Parental substance abuse Divorce	Supportive teachers Successful school experiences
Childhood-Adolescence	Poverty Child abuse/neglect Parental mental illness Parental substance abuse Divorce	Internal locus of control Strong achievement motivation Special talents, hobbies Positive self-concept For girls: emphasis on autonomy with emotional support from primary caregiver For boys: structure and rules in household For both boys and girls: assigned chores Close, competent peer friends who are confidants

(continued)

EXHIBIT 1.7
Risk and Protective Factors for Specific Life Course Phases *(continued)*

Life Course Phase	Risk Factors	Protective Factors
Childhood-Adulthood	Poverty Child abuse/neglect Parental mental illness Parental substance abuse Divorce	Average/above-average intelligence Ability to distance oneself Impulse control Strong religious faith Supportive siblings Mentors
Adolescence-Adulthood	Teenage parenthood Poverty	Planning, foresight

Source: Based on Werner, 2000, pp. 118-119.

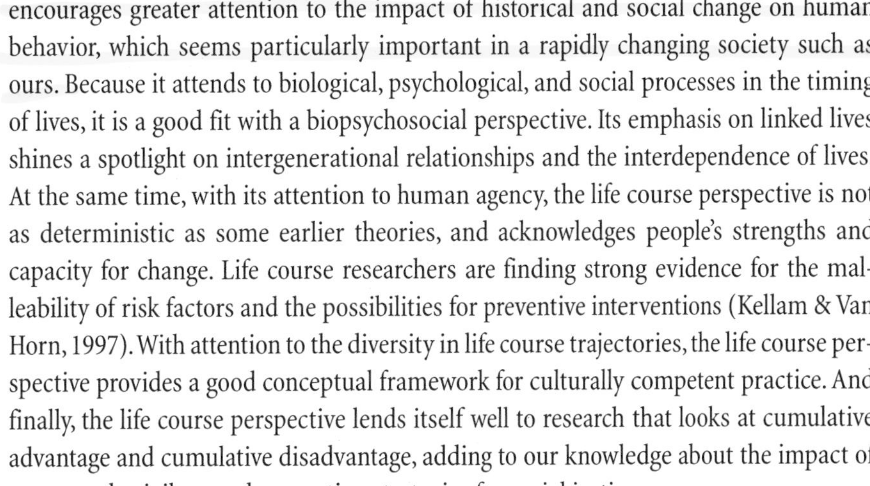

encourages greater attention to the impact of historical and social change on human behavior, which seems particularly important in a rapidly changing society such as ours. Because it attends to biological, psychological, and social processes in the timing of lives, it is a good fit with a biopsychosocial perspective. Its emphasis on linked lives shines a spotlight on intergenerational relationships and the interdependence of lives. At the same time, with its attention to human agency, the life course perspective is not as deterministic as some earlier theories, and acknowledges people's strengths and capacity for change. Life course researchers are finding strong evidence for the malleability of risk factors and the possibilities for preventive interventions (Kellam & Van Horn, 1997). With attention to the diversity in life course trajectories, the life course perspective provides a good conceptual framework for culturally competent practice. And finally, the life course perspective lends itself well to research that looks at cumulative advantage and cumulative disadvantage, adding to our knowledge about the impact of power and privilege and suggesting strategies for social justice.

To answer questions about how people change and how they stay the same across a life course is no simple task, however. Take, for example, the question of whether there is an increased sense of generativity, or concern for others, in middle adulthood. Should the researcher study different groups of people at different ages (perhaps a group of 20-year-olds, a group of 30-year-olds, a group of 40-year-olds, a group of 50-year-olds, and a group of 60-year-olds) and compare their responses, in what is known as a cross-sectional design? Or should the researcher study the same people over time (perhaps at 10-year intervals from age 20 to age 60) and observe whether their responses stay the same or change over time, in what is known as a longitudinal design? I hope you are already raising the question, What happens to the cohort effect in a cross-sectional study? That is, indeed, always a problem with studying change over time with a cross-sectional design. Suppose we find that 50-year-olds report a greater sense of generativity than those in younger age groups. Can we then say that generativity does, indeed, increase in middle adulthood? Or do we have to wonder if there was something in the social and historical contexts of this particular cohort of 50-year-olds that encouraged a greater sense of generativity? Because of the possibility of cohort effects, it is important to know whether research was based on a cross-sectional or longitudinal design.

Although attention to diversity and heterogeneity may be the greatest strength of the life course perspective, heterogeneity may also be its biggest challenge. The life course perspective, like other behavioral science perspectives, searches for patterns of human behavior. But the current level of heterogeneity in countries such as the United States may well make discerning patterns impossible (George, 1993).

Another possible limitation of the life course perspective is a failure to adequately link the micro world of individual and family lives to the macro world of social institutions and formal organizations (George, 1993). Social and behavioral sciences have, historically, divided the social world up into micro and macro and studied them in isolation. The life course perspective was developed by scholars like Glen Elder Jr. and Tamara Hareven, who were trying to bring those worlds together. Sometimes, however, this effort is more successful than at other times.

Integration With a Multidimensional, Multitheoretical Approach

A companion volume to this book, *Dimensions of Human Behavior: Person and Environment*, recommends a multidimensional, multitheoretical approach for understanding human behavior. This recommendation is completely compatible with the life course perspective. The life course perspective clearly recognizes the biological and psychological dimensions of the person and can accommodate the spiritual dimension. The life course emphasis on linked or interdependent lives is consistent with the idea of the unity of person and environment presented in Volume I of this book. It can also easily accommodate the multidimensional environment (physical environment, culture, social institutions and social structure, families, small groups, formal organizations, communities, and social movements) discussed in the companion volume.

Likewise, the life course perspective is consistent with the multitheoretical approach presented in Volume I. The life course perspective has been developed by scholars across several disciplines, and they have increasingly engaged in cross-fertilization of ideas from a variety of theoretical perspectives (see, e.g., George, 1993, 1996; Kellam & Van Horn, 1997; O'Rand, 1996; Pearlin & Skaff, 1996). Because the life course can be approached from the perspective of the individual, from the perspective

EXHIBIT 1.8

Overlap of the Life Course Perspective and Eight Theoretical Perspectives on Human Behavior

Theoretical Perspective	Life Course Themes and Concepts
Systems Perspective: Human behavior is the outcome of reciprocal interactions of persons operating within organized and integrated social systems.	Theme: Timing of Lives; Linked or Interdependent Lives Concepts: Biological Age, Psychological Age, Social Age, Spiritual Age
Conflict Perspective: Human behavior is driven by conflict, dominance, and oppression in social life.	Theme: Developmental Risk and Protection Concepts: Cumulative Advantage; Cumulative Disadvantage
Rational Choice Perspective: Human behavior is based on self-interest and rational choices about effective ways to accomplish goals.	Theme: Human Agency in Making Choices Concepts: Choices; Opportunities; Constraints
Social Constructionist Perspective: Social reality is created when actors, in social interaction, develop a common understanding of their world.	Themes: Timing of Lives; Diversity in Life Course Trajectories; Developmental Risk and Protection Concepts: Making Meaning of Life Events; Social Age; Age Norms; Age Structuring; Acculturation; Cumulative Advantage and Disadvantage
Psychodynamic Perspective: Internal processes such as needs, drives, and emotions motivate human behavior; early childhood experiences are central to problems of living throughout life.	Themes: Timing of Lives; Developmental Risk and Protection Concepts: Psychological Age; Capacities; Skills
Developmental Perspective: Human behavior both changes and stays the same across the life cycle.	Themes: Interplay of Human Lives and Historical Times; Timing of Lives; Developmental Risk and Protection Concepts: Life Transitions; Biological Age, Psychological Age, Social Age, Spiritual Age; Sequencing
Social Behavioral Perspective: Human behavior is learned when individuals interact with the environment; human behavior is influenced by personal expectations and meanings.	Themes: Interplay of Human Lives and Historical Time; Human Agency in Making Choices; Diversity in Life Course Trajectories; Developmental Risk and Protection Concepts: Life Events; Human Agency
Humanistic Perspective: Human behavior can be understood only from the internal frame of reference of the individual; human behavior is driven by a desire for growth and competence.	Themes: Timing of Lives; Human Agency in Making Choices Concepts: Spiritual Age; Meaning of Life Events and Turning Points; Individual, Family, and Community Strengths

of the family or other collectivities, or seen as a property of cultures and social institutions that shape the pattern of individual lives, it builds on both psychological and sociological theories. Exhibit 1.8 demonstrates the overlap between the life course perspective and the eight theoretical perspectives presented in Chapter 2, Volume I, of *Dimensions of Human Behavior: Person and Environment.*

IMPLICATIONS FOR SOCIAL WORK PRACTICE

The life course perspective has many implications for social work practice, including the following:

- Help clients make sense of their unique life's journeys and to use that understanding to improve their current situations. Where appropriate, help them to construct a lifeline of interlocking trajectories.
- Try to understand the historical contexts of clients' lives and the ways that important historical events have influenced their behavior.
- Where appropriate, use life event inventories to get a sense of the level of stress in a client's life.
- Be aware of the potential to develop social work interventions that can serve as turning points that help individuals, families, communities, and organizations to get back on track.
- Work with the media to keep the public informed about the impact of changing social conditions on individuals, families, communities, and formal organizations.
- Recognize the ways that the lives of family members are linked across generations and the impact of circumstances in one generation on other generations.
- Use existing research on risk, protection, and resilience to develop prevention programs.
- When working with recent immigrant and refugee families, be aware of the age norms in their countries of origin.
- Be aware of the unique systems of support developed by members of various cultural groups, and encourage the use of those supports in times of crisis.
- Support and help to develop clients' sense of personal competence for making life choices.

Key Terms

age norm
age structuring
biological age
cohort
cohort effects
cumulative advantage
cumulative disadvantage
event history
human agency
life course perspective
life event
population pyramid
privilege
psychological age
resilience
sex ratio
social age
social support
spiritual age
trajectories
transitions
turning point

Active Learning

1. Prepare your own lifeline of interlocking trajectories (see Exhibit 1.4 for instructions). What patterns do you see? What shifts? How important are the different sectors of your life—for example, family, education, work, health?

2. One researcher found that 85% of respondents to a survey on turning points reported that there had been turning points in their lives. Interview five adults and ask whether there have been turning points in their lives. If they answer no, ask about whether they see their life as a straight path or a path with twists and turns. If they answer yes, ask about the nature of the turning point(s). Compare the events of your interviewees as well as the events in the lives of David Sanchez, Mahdi Mahdi, and Emma Suarez, with Rutter's three types of life events that can serve as turning points and Hareven's five conditions under which a transition can become a turning point.

3. Think of someone whom you think of as resilient, someone who has been successful against the odds. This may be you, a friend, coworker, family member, or a character from a book or movie. If the person is someone you know and to whom you have access, ask them to what they owe their success. If it is you or someone to whom you do not have access, speculate about the reasons for the success. How do their life journeys compare to the common risk and protective factors summarized in Exhibit 1.7?

Web Resources

Each chapter of this textbook contains a list of Internet resources and Web sites that may be useful to readers in their search for further information. Each site listing includes the address and a brief description of the contents of the site. Readers should be aware that the information contained in Web sites may not be truthful or reliable and should be confirmed before being used as a reference. Readers should also be aware that Internet addresses, or URLs, are constantly changing; therefore, the addresses listed may no longer be active or accurate. Many of the Internet sites listed in each chapter contain links to other Internet sites containing more information on the topic. Readers may use these links for further investigation.

Information not included in the Web Resources sections of each chapter can be found by using one of the many Internet search engines provided free of charge on the Internet. These search engines enable you to search using keywords or phrases, or you can use the search engines' topical listings. You should use several search engines when researching a topic, as each will retrieve different Internet sites.

GOOGLE
www.google.com
ASK JEEVES
www.askjeeves.com
YAHOO
www.yahoo.com
EXCITE
www.excite.com
LYCOS
www.lycos.com

A number of Internet sites provide information on theory and research on the life course:

Bronfenbrenner Life Course Center

www.lifecourse.cornell.edu

Site presented by the Bronfenbrenner Life Course Center at Cornell University contains information on the Center, current research, working papers, and links to work/family Web sites, demography Web sites, and gerontology Web sites.

The Finnish Twin Cohort Study

kate.pc.helsinki.fi/twin/twinhome.html

Site presented by the Department of Public Health at the University of Helsinki contains information on an ongoing project begun in 1974 to study environmental and genetic factors in selected chronic diseases with links to other related resources.

Michigan Study of Adolescent and Adult Life Transitions (MSALT)

www.rcgd.isr.umich.edu/msalt/home.htm

Site presented by the Michigan Study of Adolescent and Adult Life Transitions project contains information about the longitudinal study begun in 1983, publications on the project, and family-oriented Web resources.

Sociology and the Study of the Life Course

www.mpib-berlin.mpg.de/en/forschung/bag

Site presented by the Max Planck Institute for Human Development in Berlin, Germany, contains information on comprehensive research on social structure and the institutional contexts of the life course.

Life Course Project

lifecourse.anu.edu.au/lcp_info.html

Site presented by the Life Course Project of the Australian National University contains information on a longitudinal study of gender roles.

Project Resilience

www.projectresilience.com

Site presented by Project Resilience, a private organization based in Washington, D.C., contains information on teaching materials, products, and training for professionals working in education, treatment, and prevention.

Chapter 2

Conception, Pregnancy, and Childbirth

Marcia P. Harrigan

Suzanne M. Baldwin

CHAPTER 2

Conception, Pregnancy, and Childbirth

Marcia P. Harrigan and Suzanne M. Baldwin
Virginia Commonwealth University

What biological, psychological, social, or spiritual factors influence the beginning of the life course?

What recent technological advances related to conception, pregnancy, and childbirth are important to social work intervention?

What unique knowledge do social workers bring to multidisciplinary teams working with issues of conception, pregnancy, and childbirth?

Key Ideas

As you read this chapter, take note of these central ideas:

1. Conception, pregnancy, and childbirth should be viewed as normative life transitions that require family or family-like supportive relationships to maximize favorable outcomes.
2. Conception, pregnancy, and childbirth are influenced by changing family structures and gender roles.
3. Variations in human behavior at this life stage relate to social class, race and ethnicity, and religion, and their interplay must be considered in assessment and intervention.
4. Women who are poor or lack social support—and therefore experience greater stress than other women—are most at risk for poor pregnancy outcomes.
5. Prenatal care, including childbirth education, ensures the most positive pregnancy outcome possible. Universal access to prenatal care should be a social work priority.

6. Although we are increasingly learning about the role of genetics in human development, 80 to 90% of fertilized ova with a genetic anomaly will abort spontaneously, resulting in 94 to 96% of all births occurring without genetic anomaly.
7. The incidence of low birth weight infants continues to be high, particularly for neonates born to poor and minority women and those exposed to teratogens such as nicotine, illegal drugs, and alcohol.

Case Study 2.1

A Change of Plans for Tahesha Gibbon

For as long as 15-year-old Tahesha Gibbon can remember, her mother has told her that she would be the first in the family to go to college. Tahesha's mother had once planned to live out this dream herself, but the dream began to fade when Tahesha was born. Her mother was 13 years old at the time. Over and over, Tahesha's mother has told her about the reality that displaced the dream: years of poverty and struggle, multiple pregnancies, spontaneous abortion, and four children ages 15, 14, 9, and 6, the last born with sickle-cell anemia. Diagnosed with acquired immune deficiency syndrome (AIDS) 4 years ago, Tahesha's mom now increasingly focuses on Tahesha's future—as a college-educated woman and the family caretaker. "Don't play the fool, Tahesha. Get you an education, a steady pay job, one that makes the rent and the doctor . . . then have your babies."

Tonight Tahesha lies in her own bed, listening to the sounds of her brothers who share the room next to hers. Outside, tires screech. She holds her breath and then quickly lets it out when she does not hear metal crashing. Then she hears the familiar "pop"—perhaps a gunshot. Tahesha feels relieved that everyone is in bed and out of the line of any stray bullet.

Tahesha closes her eyes, trying to recapture how she felt that night over a month ago. She wanted to say, "No, I don't do that," but it did not seem to fit the occasion. She had already declined the heroin that many of her friends used as a buffer against the strain of living in a violence-infested neighborhood. But Tahesha remembers saying yes to some wine, thinking a little would not hurt; maybe it would even offer some relief from her constant feelings of dread and anxious anticipation of more "bad news." But the wine only led to other things: "Come on, Tahesha, you'll like it. Ain't nothing you ever felt. Don't deny me my manhood, girl. Heck, there's nothin' to worry for . . . this is God's gift." God. Comfort. Hope. But in the end what she felt was not the promise she had felt a few years ago, singing in the choir,

CASE STUDY 2.1

listening to the preacher talk about the promised land and better times. "Is there any more wine?" Tahesha remembers asking, while thinking it was not really her voice giving in to the moment. She had made a request. Or was it a choice? Are they the same? What "choice" did she have? Why did she think she was so different from her friends, who laughed and seemed to enjoy the moment?

Now, 6 weeks later, Tahesha feels nauseous for the second morning in a row. A missed period: pregnant. What will her mother say? Tahesha cringes to think that her life goals may have been sacrificed for an hour spent pursuing peace and pleasure—a high price for any 15-year-old girl. Yet, maybe her mother would be proud. Tahesha recalls how her mother had responded to her aunt's first pregnancy: "You're no woman until you have that first one."

A few days later, Tahesha drops by the community center—where, until 2 years ago, she was an active member of your after-school program—and shares her confusion with you.

Case Study 2.2

The Randolphs' Premature Birth

The movement of her growing infant drew Karen into an entrancing world of hope and fantasy. For 8 weeks her husband, Bob, had been watching Karen's abdomen rise and fall to the rhythm of their son's gymnastics. Although they were only 6 months into the pregnancy, the colors for the nursery had been selected and a baby shower was being planned. Already her changing figure was eliciting comments from her coworkers in the office where she worked part time as a secretary. With weeks of nausea and fatigue behind her, a general sense of well-being pervaded Karen's mind and body.

Then, with dawn hours away, Karen woke to cramping and blood. With 14 more weeks before her delivery date, Karen was seized with fear. Wishing that Bob was not 1,500 miles away, Karen fervently prayed for herself and her baby. The ambulance ride to the hospital became a blur of pain mixed with feelings of unreality. When she arrived in the labor and delivery suite, masked individuals in scrubs took control of her body while demanding

CASE STUDY 2.2

answers to a seemingly endless number of questions. Karen knew everything would be fine if only she could feel her son kick. Why didn't he kick?

As the pediatrician spoke of the risks of early delivery, the torrent of words and images threatened to engulf her. Suddenly, the doctors were telling her to push her son into the world—her fragile son who was too small and vulnerable to come out of his cocoon so soon. Then the pain stopped. Oblivious to the relief, Karen listened for her baby's cry. It didn't come. Just a few hours earlier, she had fallen asleep while her baby danced inside her. Now there was only emptiness. Her arms ached for the weight of her infant, and her heart broke with her failure as a parent.

In the newborn intensive care unit (NICU), a flurry of activity revolved around baby boy Randolph. Born weighing only 1 pound 3 ounces, this tiny red baby's immature systems were unprepared for the demands of the extrauterine world. Rapidly he was connected to a ventilator, intravenous lines were placed in his umbilicus and arm, and monitor leads were placed on all available surfaces. Nameless to his caregivers, the baby his parents had already named Joseph was now the recipient of some of the most advanced technological interventions available in modern medicine.

About an hour after giving birth, Karen saw Joseph for the first time. Lying on a stretcher, she counted 10 miniature toes and fingers. Through a film of tears, trying to find resemblance to Bob, who is of Anglo heritage, or herself, a light-skinned Latina, in this tiny form, Karen's breathing synchronized to Joseph's as she willed him to keep fighting.

Alone in her room, she was flooded with fear, grief, and guilt. What had she done wrong? Could Joseph's premature birth have been caused by paint fumes from decorating his room?

Karen greeted Bob's arrival the next day with mixed feelings. Although she told herself she was being unreasonable, she was angry that he had not been available during the past day. Simultaneously, she was grateful to see him. She was not left to face her feelings alone.

Thirteen days after his arrival, Joseph took his first breath by himself. His hoarse, faint cry provoked both ecstasy and terror in his parents. Off the ventilator, he would periodically miss a breath, which would lead to a decreased heart rate, then monitors flashing and beeping. Throughout the next 10 weeks, Joseph's struggle to survive led Karen and Bob on the most exhilarating yet terrifying roller-coaster ride of their lives. Shattered hopes were mended, only to be reshattered with the next telephone call. Each visit to Joseph was followed by the long trip home to the empty nursery.

CASE STUDY 2.2

The close relationship that Karen and Bob had previously experienced began to fray. Karen was remote during their times alone. They had unaccustomed arguments and little time or energy for intimacy. Bob's attempt to concentrate on his job had limited success, although his job was more important than ever as the medical bills continued to accumulate.

As the weeks passed and Joseph's survival seemed assured, the medical staff continued to equivocate about possible long-term problems. Attempting to focus on the present, slowly Bob and Karen learned to recognize Joseph's preference for gentle stroking during waking periods and to anticipate his angry crying when procedures were performed.

Great joy and equally intense anxiety pervaded Joseph's homecoming day. After spending 53 days in the NICU and still weighing only 4 pounds 13 ounces, Joseph was handed to his parents. With more questions than answers about their son's future and their abilities to take care of him, Bob and Karen took their baby to his new home.

As the NICU social worker, your major goal is to support these individuals as a family unit facing this challenging transition to parenthood. In the past 53 days, you have helped Bob and Karen get their questions answered, understand the unfamiliar medical language of the health care providers, and understand and cope with the strong emotions they are experiencing.

CASE STUDY 2.3

THE GEREKES' LATE-LIFE PREGNANCY

Thirty-one years ago, at age 44, Hazel Gereke gave birth to her fifth child, Terry. At the time of his birth, Terry's siblings ranged in age from 2 to 25, and his father was 48. The following interview tells the story of this German American family:

Q: It's been 31 years, but what do you remember about your pregnancy with Terry?

A: Well, I menstruated regularly and had long, heavy bleeding. It lasted 2 to 3 weeks every month, so I went to the doctor. He said I was

CASE STUDY 2.3

4-1/2 months pregnant! I cried . . . I was too far along to do anything. You see, back then you had to have three doctors go before the hospital board to say the pregnancy jeopardized the mother's health. Well, my doctor was Catholic, so I knew that would not happen.

Q: Do you remember how Mr. Gereke reacted to this pregnancy?

A: I can remember exactly what he said like it was yesterday: "Hazel, we'll love it!"

Q: What was the rest of the pregnancy like?

A: Horrible! Right after I found out, in October, Grandma and Grandpa moved in to live with us, and in November, Ann, our oldest child, got married! I wasn't feeling the best in the world. I would wake up at 3:00 A.M. with pains in my hand, elbows, and arm . . . I walked the floor. I had carpel tunnel, but at the time I thought it was the pregnancy. In December, I had false labor and was due in January. Terry was born on February 7, 1966.

Q: What was Terry's pregnancy like compared to the other four?

A: Ann's was normal; she was born in 1941 at home, with a doctor and a nurse who came with gas, oxygen, and a birthing table. John was more difficult; I had a prolapsed uterus and difficult delivery. He was premature and blue at birth. Gail, I carried breech, but she was turned in labor. You could tell by her black-and-blue nose, mouth, chin, and forehead! But everything was OK. Mike was normal. I had no morning sickness but a long delivery. Terry I don't remember because I was put under when I went into the delivery room. They said the delivery was hard due to my age.

Q: What do you remember right after Terry's birth?

A: I bottle-fed him but had difficulty, so the nurse taught me how. The doctor said, "He might be a little slow."

Q: When and how did you find out that Terry had Down's syndrome?

A: I first heard "Down's" when I enrolled him in school and saw on the record "Down's child"! I went right away to the doctor, who said the test would cost $75. Well, I said, "there's no need for a test—it won't change what he is." He wasn't that bad. After his first birthday, he sat, began to walk, and said "Mama," "Daddy," "bye-bye," and

CASE STUDY 2.3

"eat"—about 7 to 10 words. He was beginning to dress and potty train. At birth the nurses said, "You won't have any problem training this one; when he's wet, he screams!" But when he was 15 to 18 months old he had terrible seizures . . . all summer. He left the table, walked into the living room, and we heard a terrible sound. He had fallen backwards and hit his head on the table. He was limp. They put him on dilantin and phenobarbital and kept increasing it. He became a vegetable. I gradually withdrew him from his medication . . . boy, was the doctor upset when he found that out, but Terry was doing better!

Q: What impact do you remember Terry's difficulties having on the rest of the family?

A: Gail and Mike were still at home. Gail said, "He doesn't look good—he looks funny." I took Terry to the mirror to teach him his eyes, ears, and mouth like I had the others. "Look at the pretty baby!" I said. He hung his head . . . he never looked in the mirror again. He was down about himself; he knew he was different. I worried that Mike was teased by the other kids when the bus came for Terry—they called it "the dummy bus." I always knew who had compassion, because if they did, Terry stayed around. Otherwise, he went to his room.

Five years ago, the Gerekes followed advice they had received and arranged for Terry to go to a group home, but no one in the family felt comfortable about this plan. The day he was to move into the group home, Hazel Gereke learned that Terry would be sharing a room with five other adult males, and she refused to let him live there. After 2 more years at home, at age 29, Terry moved to a different group home. Now, he visits his parents every Saturday and helps his father mow the grass, but he is always eager to return to the group home.

When asked if she thinks anything should have happened differently over the years, Hazel reluctantly but honestly replies that "the pregnancy should have been stopped." When asked "What has Terry contributed to your family?" she replies, "He has kept the family together and taught us not to take things for granted."

Although the Gerekes did not have contact with a social worker when they first encountered their late-life pregnancy, Hazel Gereke has reminded us about the ambivalences and ambiguities that social workers need to keep in mind when working with issues of problem pregnancies.

Sociocultural Organization of Childbearing

These three stories tell us that conception, pregnancy, and childbirth are experienced in different ways by different people. But they do not tell us about all the possible variations, which reflect the complex interplay of person, environment, and time. The biological processes vary little for the vast majority of women and their families, but researchers continue to study the psychological, social, and spiritual dimensions of childbearing. This chapter presents a multidimensional overview of current knowledge about conception, pregnancy, and childbirth gleaned from the literatures of anthropology, genetics, medicine, nursing, psychology, social work, and sociology.

In what other ways might culture affect the childbearing experience?

As you read, keep in mind that all elements of childbearing have deep meaning for a society. Procreation allows a culture to persist, as children are raised to follow the ways of their predecessors. Procreation may also allow a culture to expand if the birthrate exceeds the rate at which the society loses members. Thus, as Valsiner (1989a) reminds us, "Human procreation is socially organized in all its aspects. In any cultural group around the world, society regulates the conditions under which a woman is to become pregnant, how she and her husband should conduct themselves during the pregnancy, how labor and delivery take place, and how the newborn child is introduced into society" (p. 117).

In the United States, the social meaning of childbearing has changed rather dramatically over the past 20 years, in several ways (Carter & McGoldrick, 1989; Chadiha & Danziger, 1995; Danziger & Danziger, 1993; Ellman & Taggart, 1993; Furstenberg, 1994; Moss, 1987; Skolnick & Skolnick, 1996):

- Marriage and childbirth are more commonly delayed.
- People want smaller families.
- Various options for controlling reproduction are more available and accessible.
- Sexual freedom has increased.
- More single women of all ages get pregnant and keep the baby.
- Family values and sexual mores vary more.
- Parents are less subject to gender role stereotyping—Mom takes care of the baby while Dad earns a paycheck, and so on.
- Fathers are considered more important, beyond their genetic contributions.

Despite continued emphasis on childbearing, elected childlessness is more common and more acceptable.

These trends have prompted considerable debate over how our society should define *family.* The family operates at the intersection of society and the individual. For most people it serves as a safe haven and a cradle of emotional relationships. It is both the stage and partial script for the unfolding of the individual life course.

Family Diversity

Less than 50% of family households today comprise married couples and their children. Some people have voiced dismay, decrying the demise of the nuclear family structure and "family values." Others have noted that we are simply witnessing what family historians call **family pluralism,** or recognition of the many viable types of family structures. Such pluralism is nothing new, but our tolerance for all types of families has grown over the past few decades. The definition of *family* must reflect this pluralism. Yet, unresolved moral, political, and economic issues abound (Stacey, 1996). These debates influence which family research proposals are funded (Udry, 1993); how abortion and family policy is constructed (Figueira-McDonough, 1990), particularly at the national level; and who gets access to such family resources as birth control pills and prenatal care.

We know that increasingly fewer children are born into a family comprising a married couple and their offspring all living together. We are well aware that some children are born to single women with and without significant others, some are relinquished at birth, some lose their parents to war and other disasters, and some are removed by society from the birth parent(s) due to neglect, abuse, and abandonment. Yet, all these children live, formally or informally, for better or for worse, with a family of some type: foster, adoptive, extended, fictive kin, blended, and reunited are examples. Rarely does a child live without some type of family configuration, even those who live in arrangements such as group homes; thus, almost all children still experience the life course through a family lens.

In addition, longevity coupled with a continuing high divorce rate, increasing types of new family structures, and more racial/ethnic diversity results in a more complex tapestry of families in the United States than in the past. Over the life course, a child born today may experience a biological parent, a foster parent, a stepparent, siblings, half siblings, step siblings, or foster siblings accompanied by all the related "others" implicit in a complex family web.

The multigenerational family—with perhaps four or five generations living simultaneously—is becoming especially common. In 1900, in contrast, 76% of all 15-year-olds already had experienced the death of at least one parent (Brody, 1985). By 2020, one fourth of the U.S. population will be age 80 or older (Walsh, 1998), so the chances of having a living great-grandparent will be excellent. In poor African American families, where grandparenthood may occur for persons in their 30s, the chances of having five generations of family members alive at the same time are good too (Hines, 1999). These extended families have the potential to provide greater support for parents in general, and many of these older family members may become the caretakers of newborns. In fact, an increasing number of grandparents are raising grandchildren on their own because of parental inability or absence, typically related to substance abuse or incarceration (Beeman, Kim, & Bullerdick, 2000; Flint & Perez-Porter, 1997; Goodman, 2001; Grant, 2000; Scannapieco & Jackson, 1996; Walsh, 1999).

The physical presence of "family" members is not the only factor influencing the experience of conception, pregnancy, and childbirth. When a child is born, a new role emerges for people other than the mother: grandma, uncle, second cousin, half sibling, and foster brother, to name a few. This new family role influences expectations both for the parents and the other caretakers. Furthermore, all families have a life cycle that includes a past, present, and hopes for the future (Carter & McGoldrick, 1999b). This family life cycle influences individual development in complex ways. For example, the timing and other circumstances of pregnancy are influenced by the family constellation. Consider your own family beliefs about favorable and unfavorable circumstances of conception, pregnancy, and childbirth. Perhaps these views vary across the generations, but the views of past generations can still create an expectation for certain circumstances and behaviors. Consider the story of Tahesha Gibbon, who uses the words that her mother spoke to her aunt to help wrestle with the awareness of being pregnant: "You're no woman until you have that first one." Although Tahesha's unplanned pregnancy may well alter her life course, this family belief buffers the negative impact.

In the absence of a biological family "history," individuals tend to seek a substitute history. The literature is replete with accounts of the quest to find one's birth family in order to discover the past and predict the future. Yet, other children who were separated from their birth parents decide to accept their surrogate parents and the accompanying family network as sufficient for support of the necessary tasks of parenthood and other family roles over the life course.

For families separated by major cultural differences and great geographical distances, as is the situation for most immigrant families, the response to multigenerational family expectations, rituals, and themes related to conception, pregnancy, and childbirth may be difficult or problematic. Such experiences pressure families to adapt and change. Still, responses to conception, pregnancy, and childbirth continue to resonate with the themes, myths, legacies, and secrets that bind families across many generations.

Conception and Pregnancy in Context

The three case studies at the beginning of the chapter remind us that the emotional reaction to conception may vary widely. The Randolphs' conception brought joy, in contrast to Tahesha Gibbon's initial dismay followed by rising hopefulness; Mr. Gereke voiced confidence in contrast to his wife's apprehension. The conception experience is influenced by expectations the parents learned growing up in their own families of birth, as well as by many other factors: the mother's age, health, marital status, social status, cultural expectations, peer expectations, school or employment circumstances, and prior experiences with conception and childbearing, as well as the interplay of these factors with those of other people significant to the mother.

The conception experience may also be influenced by organized religion. Church policies reflect different views about the purpose of human sexual expression: pleasure, procreation, or perhaps both. Many mainstream religions, in their denominational policy statements, specify acceptable sexual behaviors (Bullis & Harrigan, 1992). Unwanted conception may be seen as an act of carelessness, promiscuity, or merely God's will—perhaps even punishment for wrongdoing. These beliefs are usually strongly held and have become powerful fodder for numerous social, political, and religious debates related to conception.

Even the mechanisms of conception are socially constructed. Some traditional cultures, such as the Telefomin of New Guinea, believe that repeated intercourse is necessary to conceive, but they forbid intercourse after conception so that multiple births will not occur. In contrast, the Dusan of Borneo believe that conception occurs when the body heat created between males and females causes the woman's blood to boil, forming the child drop by drop; consequently, intercourse must occur throughout pregnancy for the child to develop fully (Valsiner, 1989a). In the United States, conception is believed to be a complex biological event.

Just as the experience of conception has varied over time and across cultures, so has the experience of pregnancy. It too is influenced by religious orientations, social customs, changing values, economics, and even political ideologies. For example, societal expectations of pregnant women in the United States have changed, from simply waiting for birth to actively seeking to maintain the mother's—and hence the baby's—health, preparing for the birth process, and sometimes even trying to influence the baby's cognitive and emotional development while the baby is in the womb.

Childbirth in Context

Throughout history, families and particularly women have passed on to young girls the traditions of childbirth practices. These traditions have been shaped by cultural and institutional changes. At the same time, the social function of childbirth has been institutionalized, changing the historical dynamics of pregnancy and childbirth dramatically.

Place of Childbirth. Until the early 20th century, 95% of births occurred at home with a midwife (a trained birthing specialist). Most U.S. presidents were born at home; Jimmy Carter (the 39th president) was the first to be born in a hospital (Rothman, 1991). The family was intimately involved. During the "lying-in month" following birth, the mother was sheltered from outside influences, often lying in a darkened room while being taught by family members how to care for her newborn (Devitt, 1977). Yet, home births faced some danger: in 1900, 8 of every 1,000 women who labored at home died (Achievements in Public Health, 1999). Hospital births presented great risk at this time also: one in six who delivered in a hospital also died, primarily from sepsis (Vellery-Rodot, 1926). As formalized medical training developed, so did the medicalization of childbirth. By 1940, over 50% of deliveries occurred in hospitals (Campbell & MacFarlane, 1986), structuring the birthing process and ending the traditional lying-in month. To further the trend away from home births, the American College of Obstetricians and Gynecologists issued a policy statement in 1975, affirmed in 1999, that protested out-of-hospital births and asserted that acceptable levels of safety were only available in the hospital. In fact, the former president of the organization labeled home births as child abuse (Hosmer, 2001). By 1998, a study of 26,000 births in the United States found that only 1% occurred at home (Ventura et al., 1998), despite approximately a 75% cost savings for home births over hospital births (Anderson & Anderson, 1999). Reflecting this trend, Hazel Gereke's first child was born at home, but her later children were born in a hospital.

The role of fathers in childbirth has also changed over time. During the 16th century, men were excluded by law and custom from observing deliveries, because labor was viewed as "something to be endured by women under the control of other experienced and knowledgeable women" (Johnson, 2002, p. 165). During the 1960s, even though childbirth had moved out of the home, hospitals still excluded fathers from participating in the labor process (Kayne, Greulich, & Albers, 2001). This became accepted practice but began to change in the 1970s. As more women were subjected to episiotomies (incisions to enlarge the opening for the baby during birth), enemas, and anesthesia in a male-dominated arena, often without their full knowledge or consent (Ashford, LeCroy, & Lortie, 2001), fathers were first invited in by physicians to serve as witnesses to avoid litigation (Odent, 1998, 1999). A 1995 survey found that in the United Kingdom, fathers were present at 80% of all births, often serving as a "coach" (Woollett et al., 1995).

Whatever the original reason for encouraging the father's presence in the delivery room, father-supported childbirth appears to increase the mother's satisfaction in the birth process and decrease the amount of pain medication needed (Smith et al., 1991). However, one study found that men felt some coercion to attend the birth to avoid the label of a "bad father," and perceived themselves excluded psychologically, with little direction or elucidation of what was expected of them (Odent, 1998, 1999). Nevertheless, father involvement as active "witness" and advocate improves the experience of both partners. In the Randolphs' story, the birth was traumatic, with Karen surrounded by strangers and unsupported by her husband.

The feminist movement contributed to the return to natural birthing practices, as women advocated for less invasive deliveries in more friendly environments (Johanson,

Newburn, & Macfarlane, 2002). Today, some mothers continue to give birth at home. Most mothers who have reported participating in planned home births were over 30, were married, lived in less populated areas, and either had less than 8 years of education or had college or graduate degrees; they also had lower mortality rates than hospital deliveries (Scott, Berkowitz, & Klaus, 1999). This later finding, of lower mortality rates, must be interpreted carefully, because women with high-risk pregnancies are less likely to deliver at home. Three other major changes have occurred in the past 30 years: the reemergence of midwives with advanced education and training (Bain, Gau, & Reed, 1995), the use of doulas (laywomen who are employed to stay with the woman through the entire labor, encouraging her and providing comfort measures), and the recent growth of **birthing centers** located close to a major hospital or within the hospital itself (Klaus, Kennel, & Klaus, 1993). The birthing centers feature comfortably decorated rooms and increase the ability of extended family members, including siblings, to participate in the birth.

How does childbirth education support human agency in making choices?

Childbirth Education. Childbirth education was not formalized until the early 1900s, when the Red Cross set up hygiene and health care classes for women as a public health initiative. In 1912, the U.S. Children's Bureau (created as a new federal agency to inform women about personal hygiene and birth) published a handbook titled *Prenatal Care*, emphasizing the need for medical supervision during pregnancy (Barker, 1998). Thus, when Dr. Grantley Dick-Read published *Childbirth Without Fear* in 1944, the medical establishment reacted negatively. The idea that women who were educated about childbirth would have less fear and therefore less need for pain medication was summarily rejected.

Not until the 1950s did the idea of childbirth education gain credibility. A French obstetrician, Dr. Fernand Lamaze, learned of Russian attempts to use hypnosis to reduce childbirth pain. His book *Painless Childbirth* (1958) has become the foundation for contemporary childbirth education. It instructs women, and more recently fathers and significant others, about female anatomy, the physiology of pregnancy, and relaxation techniques based on hypnosis (DeHart, Sroufe, & Cooper, 2000; Novak & Broom, 1995).

Childbirth education became a governmental priority during the 1980s as the gap widened between African Americans and other ethnic groups regarding the incidence of low birth weights and infant mortality (Armstrong, 2000). The need for childbirth classes cuts across demographic lines in theory but, in many cases, not in practice. Studies show that better-educated women of higher socioeconomic status are more likely to participate in childbirth classes (Grossman, Fitzsimmons, Larsen-Alexander, Sachs, & Harter, 1990; Riedmann, 1996a). The Maternity Care Access Act of 1989 created a means-tested program called First Steps to provide parenting and childbirth classes to women who previously could not afford them (Rabkin, Balassone, & Bell, 1995). Healthy People 2000, the federal government's national health goals, supported prenatal education as a way to alter individual women's behavior, thereby improving pregnancy outcomes (Armstrong, 2000). Childbirth classes are seen by some as a method to reduce the gap between the organizational structure of the hospital and the individual preferences of the pregnant family. Some claim that classes acculturate the family to the hospital's protocols and expectations and thus facilitate medical management of labor and delivery (Armstrong, 2000). But childbirth classes do seem to help. Outcome studies have shown that childbirth classes result in decreased pain and anxiety (Dickason, Schult, & Silverman, 1990), shorter labor, decreased use of forceps, improved infant outcome, and an overall positive experience (Riedmann, 1996b). However, classes must address the needs of all involved in this major life event. In one study, the researchers found that fathers who tended to avoid information were more dissatisfied with the childbirth experience after attending childbirth classes than fathers who had not attended. There was no relationship between fathers' attendance at childbirth classes and attachment to the infant 6 weeks after birth (Tiedje, 2001). Clearly, more information is needed to understand how prenatal education can meet the father's needs as well as the mother's needs—and not just the obstetrician's needs.

Hospital Stay. Pregnancy is one of the most common reasons for hospital admission. Each year there are approximately four million deliveries, 22% of which are cesarean, 14% assisted vaginal, and the remaining 64% spontaneous vaginal deliveries (Lydon-Rochelle, Holt, Martin, & Easterling, 2000).

What historical trends are related to these changes in the view of pregnancy?

Despite the frequent use of hospital delivery, we are in the midst of a changing philosophy. The view of pregnancy as an "illness" is giving way to the view that giving birth is a normal life transition. We are also living in an era that values cost-effective, innovative, comprehensive health services. Thus, policies regarding the length of the new mother's stay in the hospital are also changing.

Forty years ago, women remained hospitalized for 7 to 10 days following birth. By the early 1990s, the norm was 2 to 3 days. During the mid-1990s, however, controversial managed-care policies pushed for women with uncomplicated deliveries to be discharged within 24 hours, a savings of 2 hospital days. However, both mother and infant undergo rapid transitions during the period following delivery. The infant must adjust to a new environment, learn to nurse, and begin the process of **bonding**—development of a close emotional attachment—with parents. Life-threatening problems, such as heart problems, jaundice, or infections, may not be detected until the second or 3rd day of life. As compensation for early discharge, some birthing facilities sent a nurse to visit the home for the first few days after discharge to assess the mother and the infant for any problems. These home visitors also provided education and emotional support.

However, the early discharge protocols were based on inadequate studies and created difficulties for many new mothers and infants. The outcry from patients and physicians led to congressional hearings about "drive-through deliveries" and the subsequent enactment of the Newborns' and Mothers' Health Protection Act of 1996. This federal legislation compelled insurers to provide a minimum stay of 2 days for mother and newborn following a vaginal delivery and 4 days following a cesarean section (Sitzer, 1998). It also has spurred studies focusing on the risks of premature discharge, with early results showing increased readmission rates of the newborn for jaundice, dehydration, and infection (Sacchetti, Gerardi, Sawchuck, & Bihl, 1997). Women over 32, African American women who have a cesarean delivery, and women who are giving birth for the first time have been at greatest risk for readmission (Lydon-Rochelle et al., 2000).

Breastfeeding. Throughout history, most infants have been breastfed. However, alternatives to breastfeeding by the mother have always existed. Archeological records from 2000 B.C. show that at least some infants had a wet nurse (a woman employed to breastfeed someone else's infant) or were fed animal milks (Coates, 1993). Following World War II, breastfeeding ceased to be the primary nutritional source for infants because of the promotion of manufactured formula in industrialized and nonindustrialized countries. Since the 1980s, cultural attitudes have shifted again in favor of breastfeeding. The *Healthy People 2010* report states that 75% of new mothers breastfeed during the early postpartum period and 50% continue for 6 months (*Healthy People 2010*, 2000).

In the United States in the early 1980s, nursing mothers were typically older than average, white, more affluent, better-educated nonsmokers and had more social support (Coates, 1993, p. 18). It is still true that older mothers are more likely to breastfeed, but recent statistics indicate that Hispanic and foreign-born mothers have a higher rate of breastfeeding than native-born mothers (Humphreys, Thompson, & Miner, 1998; Ryan, 1997). Karen Randolph had planned to breastfeed, but that plan has been disrupted in Joseph's struggle to survive. First-born and healthy children are more likely to be breastfed as well as those born by vaginal delivery (Hirschman & Butler, 1981; Starbird, 1991). Negative indicators for breastfeeding include Protestantism, maternal employment, single parenthood, and a poor maternal self-image (American Dietetic Association, 2001; Cahill & Wagner, 2002; Hirschman & Butler, 1981; Humphreys, Thompson, & Miner, 1998; Pesa & Shelton, 1999; Wright et al., 1988). The greatest decline in breastfeeding has been among young, unmarried, African American women of lower income, with a rate 60% less than a nonblack woman (Forste, Weiss, & Lippincott, 2001). They are less likely to have education regarding the benefits of breastfeeding and the flexibility in the workplace to pump and store milk (Fletcher, 1994; Forste et al., 2001; Grossman et al., 1990).

In an attempt to address these racial and economic differences, the federally subsidized **Women, Infants, and Children (WIC) program,** which was initiated in 1972, expanded food benefits from 6 to 12 months for breastfeeding mothers in the late 1980s (Coates, 1993). Providing supplemental food, nutrition education, health referrals, and breastfeeding support for low-income women during and after pregnancy, as well as for children up to the age of 5, WIC served approximately 47% of infants born in 1998. Yet, another 11% who were eligible did not participate (American Academy of Pediatrics, 2001b). Establishing hospital policies to promote breastfeeding (Philipp et al., 2001) and employer support for nursing mothers (such as on-site day care most likely to be available in large corporations but seldom available to lower-income working women) would assist in reaching the Healthy People 2010 goal (Pascoe, Pletta, Beasley, & Schellpfeffer, 2002).

Cultural norms also influence breastfeeding. In European American and Mexican American families, the mother seeks the opinion of the baby's father and maternal and paternal grandparents, whereas in African American families, the maternal grandmother and peers are most influential in the decision to breastfeed (Baranowski, 1983). Korean mothers-in-law care for the new mother and are a powerful influence in choices about breastfeeding. In Saudi Arabia, a woman may breastfeed her infant openly and receive no notice, although otherwise she is fully veiled. In France, topless swimming is culturally acceptable, but breastfeeding in public is not (Riordan, 1993a).

Studies have demonstrated that the breastfeeding decision is typically made in the first trimester of pregnancy, pointing to the need for breastfeeding information early in the pregnancy (Aberman & Kirchoff, 1985; Kaufman & Hall, 1989; Meyers, 2001). The length of time a child is nursed is proportional to the number of persons supporting the decision (Cronenwett & Reinhardt, 1987; Walker, 1992). One study found that a corporate-sponsored lactation program established to educate men in the workplace about breastfeeding (including supplying each man with free breast pump rental, double breast pump kit, and instruction from a lactation consultant) increased the mother's breastfeeding at 6 months to 21.7% above the national average (Ascribe Higher Education News Services, 2002). Women decide to nurse primarily for infant health benefits. One benefit is increased immunity—which begins in the third trimester—to viruses such as mumps, chicken pox, and influenza (Riordan, 1993b). A study of children in the United Arab Emirates found that infants breastfed less than 6 months were more than twice as likely to develop acute lymphocytic leukemia (ALL) and four times more vulnerable to non-Hodgkin's lymphomas (NHL), two serious childhood cancers ("Breastfeeding protects," 2001). The mother's sterile milk is always at the correct temperature, has lower but higher-quality protein content than cow's milk, has well-absorbed fat content (Fletcher, 1994), has more efficient vitamin and mineral balance, and results in a 50% decrease in the rate of infant hospitalizations and illness such as gastrointestinal illness and ear infections (Chen, Yu, & Li, 1988; Howie, Forsyth, Ogston, Clark, & Florey, 1990). Early research into the links between breastfeeding and childhood and adolescent obesity have shown a lower risk of obesity for infants breastfed at least 6 months.

Postpartum maternal benefits of breastfeeding include increased calorie consumption without weight gain; the release of the hormone oxytocin, causing uterine contractions; reduced uterine bleeding; and lower cost. Mothers also choose to bottle-feed for a variety of reasons, including convenience and flexibility of scheduling

(Aberman & Kirchoff, 1985)—particularly important to women who work outside the home (Frederick & Auerbach, 1985).

Contraindications to breastfeeding are few, but they include maternal medical conditions such as untreated tuberculosis, leukemia, breast cancer diagnosed during lactation, drug abuse, and sexually transmitted diseases (STDs) (Dickason, Silverman, & Kaplan, 1998). Mothers who are positive for the human immunodeficiency virus (HIV) are often advised to avoid breastfeeding because they could pass the virus on to the infant. However, in poor countries the contaminated water supply may pose a more serious health risk. One unreplicated study showed that HIV-positive mothers trebled the risk of dying within 2 years of giving birth if they breastfed their newborns (Africa News Services, 2001; Guay & Ruff, 2001). The challenge for the social worker as a member of the health delivery team is tremendous when working with this at-risk population in making decisions around pregnancy and childbirth.

Finally, the threat of bioterrorism extends to pregnant women and children. The U.S. government recommends that infants and pregnant women use amoxicillin when exposure to anthrax is suspected or known. If the mother is unable to take amoxicillin, the safety of the long-term use of the other standard medications is unknown, and it is suggested that breastfeeding resume after completion of treatment ("Update: Interim recommendations," 2001).

Reproductive Genetics

Recognition of the need for genetics knowledge is not new to social work. In fact, Mary Richmond (1917) advocated that a social worker "get the facts of heredity" in the face of marriage between close relatives, miscarriage, tuberculosis, alcoholism, mental disorder, nervousness, epilepsy, cancer, deformities or abnormalities, or an exceptional ability.

What are the implications of this knowledge explosion for social work practice?

Almost 50 years later, James Watson and Francis Crick first described the mechanisms of genetic inheritance. But it was not until 1970 that our knowledge of genetics began to explode. In 1990 the Human Genome Project was funded by the U.S. Department of Energy and the National Institutes of Health as an international effort to map all the human genes by 2003. The goal was to treat, cure, and prevent disease. By June 2000, the first working draft of the human genome was completed. This knowledge has altered social work practice in many areas, primarily in working with persons of reproductive age.

Genetic Mechanisms

Chromosomes and genes are the essential components of the hereditary process. Genetic instructions are coded in **chromosomes** found in each cell; each chromosome carries **genes,** segments of deoxyribonucleic acid (DNA), that contain the codes producing particular traits and dispositions. Each mature **germ cell**—ovum or sperm—contains 23 chromosomes, half of the set of 46 present in each parent's cells. As you can see in Exhibit 2.1, when the sperm penetrates the ovum (**fertilization**), the parents' chromosomes combine to make a total of 46 chromosomes arrayed in 23 pairs.

As recently as June 2000, genetic researchers estimated that *each chromosome* may have as many as 20,000 genes, with an average of 3,000 to 5,000 genes per chromosome. However, the working genome draft now estimates that humans have just over 30,000 total genes, slightly more than the number mice have (Human Genome Project, 2002).

The genes constitute a "map" that guides the protein and enzyme reactions for every subsequent cell in the developing person and across the life span. Thus, every physical trait and many behavioral traits are influenced by the combined genes from the ovum and sperm.

Every person has a unique **genotype,** or array of genes, unless the person is an identical twin. Yet, the environment may influence how each gene pilots the growth of cells. The result is a **phenotype** (observable trait) that differs somewhat from the genotype. Thus, even a person who is an identical twin has some unique characteristics. On initial observation, you may not be able to distinguish between identical twins, but if you look closely enough, you will probably find some variation, such as differences in the size of an ear, hair thickness, or temperament.

A chromosome and its pair have the same types of genes at the same location. The exception is the last pair of chromosomes, the **sex chromosomes**, which, among other things, determine sex. The ovum can contribute only an X chromosome to the 23rd pair, but the sperm can contribute either an X or a Y and therefore determines the sex of the developing person. A person with XX sex chromosomes is female; a person with XY sex chromosomes is male (refer to Exhibit 2.1).

Genes on one sex chromosome that do not have a counterpart on the other sex chromosome create **sex-linked traits.** A gene for red/green color blindness, for example, is carried only on the X chromosome. When an X chromosome that carries this gene is paired with a Y chromosome, which could not carry the gene, red/green color blindness is manifested. So, almost all red/green color blindness is found in males. This gene for color blindness does not manifest if paired with an X chromosome unless the gene is inherited from both parents, which is rare. However, if a woman inherits the gene from either parent, she can unknowingly pass it on to her sons.

Whether genes express certain traits depends on their being either dominant or recessive. Traits governed by **recessive genes** (e.g., hemophilia, baldness, thin lips) will only be expressed if the responsible gene is present on each chromosome of the relevant pair. In contrast, traits governed by **dominant genes** (normal blood clotting, curly hair, thick lips) will be expressed if one or both paired chromosomes have the gene. When the genes on a chromosome pair give competing, yet controlling, messages, they are

EXHIBIT 2.1
Germ Cell Division, Fertilization, and Chromosome Pairs

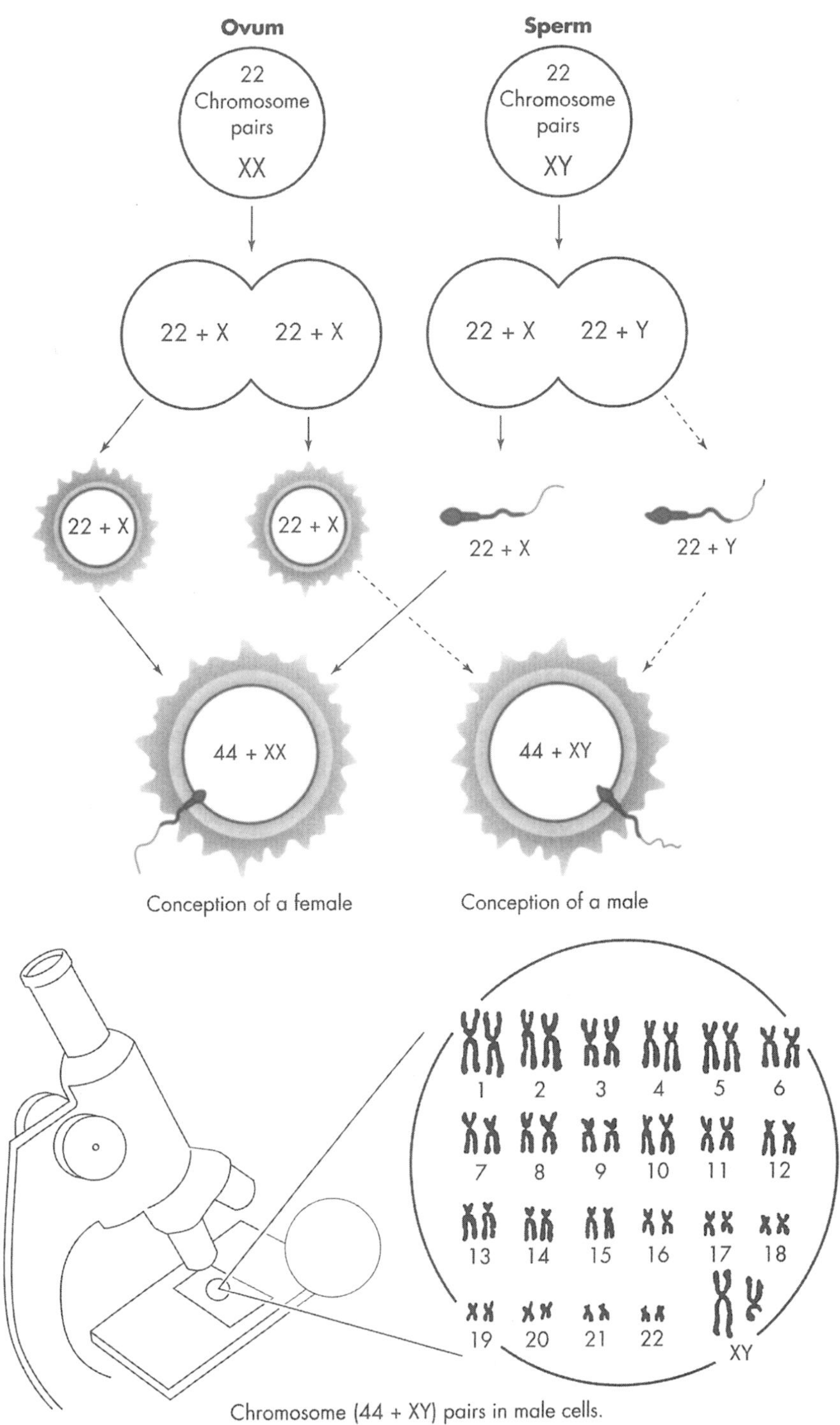

Chromosome (44 + XY) pairs in male cells.

called **interactive genes**, meaning that both messages may be followed to varying degrees. Hair, eye, and skin color often depend on such interactivity. For example, a light-skinned person with red hair and hazel eyes may mate with a person having dark skin, brown hair, and blue eyes and produce a child with a dark complexion, red hair, and blue eyes.

Genetic Counseling

Although Mary Richmond in 1917 noted that many physical traits, medical problems, and mental health problems have a genetic basis, only recently has technology allowed us to identify the specific genes governing many of these traits. Now that the initial mapping of the human genome is complete, the next step is to further identify the complex interactions between the genes. The goal is to develop genetic interventions to prevent or cure various diseases or disorders as well as affect conception, pregnancy, and childbirth in other ways. At present, research is underway to genetically alter sperm, leading to male contraception ("Good news," 2002). Our understanding of physical and psychological traits heretofore attributed to factors other than genetics, such as the environment, is therefore advancing rapidly (Takahashi & Turnbull, 1994).

Our rapidly increasing ability to read a person's genetic code and understand the impact it could have on the person's life has led to the relatively new discipline of **genetic counseling**, which provides information and advice to guide decisions of persons concerned about hereditary abnormalities. Social workers, with their biopsychosocial perspective, are well positioned to assess the need and in some circumstances provide such services (Bishop, 1993; Schild & Black, 1984; Takahashi & Turnbull, 1994). The interdisciplinary field of genetics acknowledges social work as one of its essential disciplines, thereby making at least a rudimentary understanding of genetics and related biothethical issues essential for social work practice (Garver, 1995; Human Genome Project, 2002; Rauch, 1988; Reed, 1996).

Social workers need to understand the rising bioethical concerns that genetic research fosters and use such knowledge to help clients faced with genetically related reproductive decisions. The U.S. government has the largest bioethics program in the world to address questions such as, Who should have access to genetic information? Do adoptive parents have the right to know the genetic background of an adoptee? Will genetic maps be used to make decisions about a pregnancy? Which genes should be selected for reproduction? Will persons who are poor be economically disadvantaged in the use of genetic information?

A major concern of genetic counseling is whether all genetic information should be shared with a client. Some information may only cause distress, because the technology for altering genes is in its infancy and applicable to only a few situations. But recent advances allow for earlier diagnosis and give some clients more decision options. Today, for example, a late-life pregnancy such as Hazel Gereke's could be evaluated genetically using amniocentesis or chorion villi testing. Such evaluation could lead to decisions ranging from abortion to preparation for parenting a child with a disability. However, these options typically are laced with economic, political, legal, ethical, moral, and religious considerations (Andrews, 1994; Chadwick, Levitt, & Shickle, 1997).

Ethical issues related to genetic engineering have an impact not only at the individual and family levels but also at the societal level. For example, when we are able to manipulate genes at will, we will need to be on guard against genetic elitism. It is one thing to use genetic engineering to eliminate such inherited diseases as sickle-cell anemia, but quite another to use it to select the sex, body type, or coloring of a child. We are living in a time of tremendous ethical complexity, involving the interplay of new reproductive technologies; changing family structures, values, and mores; political and religious debate; and economic considerations. This ethical complexity extends to issues of social justice: as increasing numbers of persons gain the ability to control conception, plan pregnancy, and control pregnancy outcomes, social workers need to protect the interests of those who lack the knowledge and other resources to do so.

Control Over Conception and Pregnancy

How are decisions about timing of childbearing related to biological age, psychological age, social age, and spiritual age?

The desire to plan the timing of childbearing is an ancient one, as is the desire to stimulate pregnancy in the event of infertility. Contraception and induced abortion have probably always existed in every culture. Effective solutions for infertility are more recent. But it is important to remember that not all methods of controlling conception and pregnancy are equally acceptable to all people. Cultural and religious beliefs, as well as personal circumstances, make some people more accepting of some methods than others.

Contraception

The range of birth control options available today provides women and men the ability to plan pregnancy and childbirth more than ever before. Women in the United States are having more children than at any other time in almost 30 years; at the same time, remarkable new methods of contraception have become available (Martin, Hamilton, Ventura, Menacker, & Park, 2002).

Each birth control option needs to be considered in light of its cost, failure rate, potential health risks, and probability of use, given the user's sociocultural circumstances. The National Survey of Family Growth, completed in 1995, is the largest statistically accurate study that highlights such considerations.

In 2000, the World Health Organization increased medical restrictions on contraception, decreasing the number of women who are eligible for oral contraceptives and intrauterine device (IUD) insertion, citing health concerns. However, the risk of pregnancy is generally higher than the risk of adverse reactions to contraceptives (Best, 2002). With the world population doubling every 30 to 40 years and uneven overpopulation distribution, there is an urgent need to provide inexpensive, safe, convenient, and appropriate contraceptive devices to women worldwide (Goldenberg & Jobe, 2001).

Complete sexual abstinence is the only certain form of contraception. Without any contraception, an estimated 85% of heterosexual couples who engage in regular intercourse will conceive within 1 year. Contraceptive failure rate data vary across studies. Data from Fu and colleagues provide an estimate of possible failure rates for several types of contraception (Fu, Darroch, Haas, & Ranjit, 1999). Sexually active women have these options:

- *Breastfeeding.* Women who are breastfeeding are less likely to conceive than other women are. It is estimated that if breastfeeding were stopped and not replaced with other contraceptives, the fertility rate would increase by 12% a year (Thapa, Short, & Potts, 1988). Breastfeeding is not recommended as a reliable contraceptive method, however.

- *Coitus interruptus.* Premature withdrawal of the penis from the vagina, before ejaculation, is probably the oldest form of birth control. However, the failure rate is approximately 27.1% a year, and coitus interruptus offers no protection from STDs and HIV (Fu et al., 1999; Hatecher et al., 1994).

- *Periodic abstinence.* Natural family planning or the rhythm method involves daily tracking of changes in the woman's body associated with the menstrual cycle and an avoidance of intercourse during fertile periods. The failure rate is 25.3% per year (Fu et al., 1999).

- *Barrier methods.* The male condom (failure rate 14.7% over a 12-month period), the diaphragm (6% failure rate), and the cervical cap (20-36% failure rate) provide increased protection against STDs. But except for the condom, protection against HIV is uncertain (Fu et al., 1999). The female condom has met with resistance although it increases women's contraceptive choices. It costs between $2 and $3 per use, is visible after insertion (some women are requesting colored condoms), and may be noisy. Originally thought to provide protection for low-income women internationally, it has not been well accepted (Severy & Spieler, 2000). Male condom usage among adolescents dramatically increased from 21% in 1979 to 58% in 1988. However, recent data show that only 45% of adolescent males use condoms each time they have intercourse, and the rate decreases with age (American Academy of Pediatrics, 2001a). Spermicides, acting as chemical barriers, have a high failure rate (25%) and provide minimal protection against STDs and HIV (Fu et al., 1999).

- *Oral contraceptives.* The introduction of birth control pills in the United States in 1960 precipitated major changes in reproduction. With a failure rate of only about 1 to 3%, they revolutionized family planning. The results of recent studies have raised concerns about long-term problems associated with "the pill," especially among women who smoke, but this continues to be one of the most popular forms of birth control.

- *Intermuscular injections.* In 1992, the introduction in the United States of Depo-Medroxyprogestrone acetate (Depo-Provera), a drug used for many years in Europe, allowed women protection against pregnancy for 3 months. There are concerns that Depo-Provera may reduce absorption of calcium, leading to decreased bone density at the same time (during adolescence) that almost half of adult bone mass is being formed ("Providers examine," 2001). There is a 2.6% failure rate over 12 months (Fu et al., 1999).

- *Intrauterine devices.* The use of IUDs has been marked by controversy and legal disputes for a number of years. They were introduced in the early 1900s, but high rates of infection and tissue damage discouraged their use until the 1960s. Most manufacturers discontinued production in the 1980s following expensive legal settlements. However, newer IUDs are widely used and considered safe and reliable. Approximately 15% of women discontinue use of the IUD within 1 year because of complications, but they have a contraceptive failure rate over 1 year of only 0.1 to 0.6% (Fu et al., 1999).

- *Voluntary surgical sterilization.* Sterilization is considered effective but permanent. However, recent advances in microsurgery have increased the success rates for reversal procedures. Fertility can be restored in up to 50% of men and 70% of women with reversal surgery. Informed consent is required prior to surgical sterilization. Tubal ligations reduce the risk of pelvic inflammatory disease and ovarian cancer (Fu et al., 1999).

- *Emergency contraception (EC).* Postcoital administration of hormones (estrogen and progesterone) given twice within 72 hours of unprotected intercourse, 12 hours apart, is estimated to reduce the risk of pregnancy by 75%. The U.S. Agency for International Development (USAID) has recommended EC for women who have been raped, women whose partner's condoms break, women who run out of other forms of contraceptives, women who have forgotten to take several consecutive oral contraceptives doses, and women who did not expect to have sexual relations (Severy & Spieler, 2000). However, concerns have been expressed that women may rely upon EC as a routine method of contraception rather than as an emergency form (leading to increased risk behaviors), and it offers no protection from STDs (Harvey, Beckman, Sherman & Petitti, 1999). The cost is low but there may be side effects, including nausea, vomiting, and bleeding (American Medical Association, 2002).

- *New contraceptive methods.* A rash of new choices became available early in 2002. The *vaginal ring* remains in place for 3 weeks and then is removed for 1 week. It provides protection by releasing hormones similar to oral contraceptives but with steadier levels in the blood. A *contraceptive patch* is applied to the lower abdomen, buttocks, or upper body for 3 weeks and then discontinued for 1 week. Early efficacy studies found failure rates to be 0.65%, and approximately 15% of users discontinued use due to side effects (Mechcatie, 2002). Women over 198 pounds experienced a higher failure rate (Chatfield, 2002). Several European countries allow a *single-rod contraceptive implant* that can remain for 3 years and may replace the six-rod Norplant implant. *Oral contraceptives* that only need to be taken four times per year are also being tested ("What to expect," 2001). The recent introduction of a *monthly injectable contraceptive*, Lunelle, provides an alternative to quarterly Depo-Provera shots ("Providers examine," 2001). Finally, early studies are being conducted on a *new contraceptive gel*, GufferGel. It changes the vaginal acidity, thereby potentially killing both sperm and the bacteria that cause STDs ("New gel tested," 2002).

Consider the circumstances of both Tahesha Gibbon and Hazel Gereke. What contraception options might they have today that they did not have at the time they got pregnant? What personal, familial, and cultural factors would possibly influence their use, or nonuse, of contraceptive options that are now available?

Medical Abortion

Abortion may be the most politicized, hotly debated social issue related to pregnancy today. But it was not always so controversial. Prior to the mid-1800s, abortion was practiced in the United States but was not considered a crime if performed before the fetus quickened (or showed signs of life). After 1860, however, physicians advocated banning abortion because of maternal harm caused by the use of dangerous poisons and practices (Figueira-McDonough, 1990). Legislators also wanted to see growth in the U.S. population. By 1900, all states had legislation prohibiting abortion except in extreme circumstances, typically medically related. Over the years, moral issues increasingly became the basis for debate.

Despite laws controlling abortion, it has remained an option for those with the economic means. Poor women have been the ones whose access to abortion services is limited. Hazel Gereke recounted that as late as 1966, legal abortion had to be "medically related," which did not cover the difficulty of another child for older parents or the difficulty of raising a child with Down's syndrome, a condition that at that time could not be ascertained prenatally. Hazel's situation was also influenced by the moral or religious stance of the physician and perhaps the hospital.

In 1973, in ***Roe v. Wade,*** the U.S. Supreme Court legalized abortion in the first trimester and left it to the discretion of the woman and her physician. However, the Supreme Court ruled in 1989, in ***Webster v. Reproductive Health Services,*** that Medicaid could no longer fund abortions and that much of the decision making related to abortion should return to the states. Today, states vary considerably in who has access to abortion, when, how, and at what cost. In some states, new rules are effectively decreasing access, particularly for poor and minority populations. Some poor African American women have no greater access to abortion now than they did more than 100 years ago (Ross, 1992). It is unlikely that Tahesha would have access to a legal and safe abortion if she were interested in that option.

Today, approximately half of all unintended pregnancies in the United States end in abortion. During the first trimester and until **fetal viability** (the point at which the baby could survive outside the womb) in the second trimester, a pregnant woman can legally choose an abortion. Approximately 88% of abortions are performed during the first 12 weeks of pregnancy (Centers for Disease Control & Prevention [CDC], 2000). Later-term or partial birth abortions continue to be hotly debated by state legislators from moral, medical, and religious perspectives. Recent controversy regarding procedures for terminating a pregnancy after fetal viability have raised ethical and legal dilemmas that are being addressed in the legal system, by most religions, and in other parts of the culture. Opinion polls continually reveal, however, that like Hazel Gereke, the majority of Americans favor abortion as an option under specified conditions (Cook, Jelen, & Wilcox, 1992; Figueria-McDonough, 1990). Still, the rate of induced abortion declined by 16% between 1990 and 1996 (Centers for Disease Control & Prevention, 2000). Abortion procedures fall into three categories:

1. *Menstrual regulation.* The hormone prostaglandin is given to the woman within 6 to 7 weeks after the last period to stimulate shedding of the uterine lining and, with it, the embryo. It accounts for only 0.5% of abortions and is associated with such complications as threatened spontaneous ("natural") abortions and **ectopic pregnancy** (implantation of the embryo outside the uterus).
2. *Instrumental evacuation.* One of two types of instruments is used in 98.9% of all abortions. The standard first-trimester **vacuum curettage** is the one most frequently performed in an outpatient clinic. A suction device is threaded through the cervix to remove the contents of the uterus. It is fairly safe, but because it is invasive, it introduces greater risks than the use of prostaglandin. The second-trimester **curettage abortion** requires even greater dilatation of the cervix to allow passage of a surgical instrument used to scrape the walls of the uterus. If cutterage abortion is performed on an outpatient basis, a second visit is required. With both types of instrumental evacuation, the woman faces risks of bleeding, infection, and subsequent infertility.

3. *Amnioinfusion.* In the second trimester, a saline solution can be infused into the uterus to end the pregnancy. **Amnioinfusion** is used in only 0.4% of abortions and requires the greatest medical expertise and follow-up care.

Regardless of the timing or type of abortion, all women should be carefully counseled before and after the procedure. Unplanned pregnancies typically create considerable psychological stress, and social workers can help pregnant women consider all alternatives to an unwanted pregnancy—including abortion—consistent with the client's personal values and beliefs. Following an abortion, most women experience only mild feelings of guilt, sadness, or regret that abate fairly soon, followed by relief that the crisis is resolved (David, 1996). Nevertheless, some women have a more severe response and may require ongoing counseling (Erikson, 1993; Speckland, 1993). Counseling is also particularly important from a prevention perspective, because women receiving counseling following a first abortion have been found to practice contraception with greater frequency and success (David, 1996). Social workers need to be mindful of their personal views about abortion in order to help a client make an informed decision that reflects the client's values, religious beliefs, and available options.

Infertility Treatment

How does infertility affect the multigenerational family?

Children in most segments of today's society are taught that one of their major goals in life should be to become a parent. Thus, **infertility,** the inability to create a viable embryo, is often a life crisis. In one study, 50% of women and 15% of men experiencing infertility reported that it was the most upsetting experience in their lives (Collins, Freeman, Boxer, & Tureck, 1992). It combines threats to sexuality, self-esteem, and the marital relationship with perceived failure to meet societal expectations and with social isolation from family and friends (Keye, 1995). Couples struggling to conceive report higher rates of marital dissatisfaction because of the need to have sex on schedule, the specific details of techniques meant to increase fertility, and the pain that may accompany sexual intercourse (Keye, 1995).

The causes of infertility are many. New studies demonstrate a possible link between fertility and the reaction to stress created by infertility itself. Conditions that affect male erectile function or ejaculation impair both male fertility and female receptivity. An alarming increase in STDs has contributed to rising infertility rates. Pelvic adhesions and endometriosis (abnormal growth of the uterine lining) in the female reproductive system also decrease conception rates.

Many other factors have been implicated in infertility recently. Research has shown that men who drive more than 2 consecutive hours per day have an increased rate of infertility due to increased scrotal temperatures ("Is driving a risk factor?" 2000). In addition, exposure to indoor insecticides (such as products that control ticks,

Exhibit 2.2
Causes and Cures for Infertility

Male Infertility		Female Infertility	
Problem	**Treatment**	**Problem**	**Treatment**
Low sperm count	Change of environment; antibiotics; surgery; hormonal therapy; artificial insemination	Vaginal structural problem Abnormal cervical mucus Abnormal absence of ovulation	Surgery Hormonal therapy Antibiotics for infection: hormonal therapy
Physical defect affecting transport of sperm	Microsurgery	Blocked or scarred fallopian tubes	Surgery; in vitro fertilization
Genetic disorder	Artificial insemination	Uterine lining unfavorable to implantation	Hormone therapy; antibiotics; surgery

Source: Based on Cahill & Wardle, 2002, and Sadovsky, 2002.

mosquitoes, lice) may disrupt reproductive hormones and possibly contribute to cancer in women ("Household pesticides," 2000), and women whose mothers took diethylstilbestrol (DES) during pregnancy have higher infertility rates and a 30% higher chance of spontaneous abortion during the first trimester (Hollander, 2001). Clearly, there is a need to continue to explore contributors to infertility.

In the past, infertile couples could keep trying and hope for the best, but medical technology has given today's couples a variety of options, summarized in Exhibit 2.2.

The use of **replacement hormonal therapy (RHT),** which restores key hormones to normal levels, often mitigates infertility problems that are due to hormonal deficiency. The resultant pregnancy rate is variable, ranging from 20 to 90% (Dickason, Silverman, & Kaplan, 1998). The risk of multiple births with RHT can be as high as 30%, however, depending on the medication regimen selected (Dickason, Schult, & Silverman, 1990). Many physicians recommend in vitro fertilization over RHT due to increased ability to regulate multiple births (Gottlieb, 2000).

If the problem is male infertility (diagnosed by a sperm analysis), the preferred method is artificial insemination, using fresh or frozen donor sperm. The success rate is typically 15 to 20% and costs approximately $250 per cycle (Fertility Plus, n.d.). Ethical and legal questions have been raised, however, regarding the legal status of the sperm donor (what parental rights does he have?) and the psychosocial impact on the mother. Sperm donors are routinely screened for genetic defects and physical suitability, but psychological screening remains controversial—in large part because it is nonstandardized and thus easily misinterpreted.

The birth of the first "test tube baby" in 1978, demonstrating the first of many **assisted reproductive technologies (ART)**, initiated a new era in infertility management and research. The first test tube baby was conceived in the United States in 1983, and the number of such births has increased each year since that time. Half of ART pregnancies result in multiple births ("Infant mortality," 2002). In 1998, 370 clinics nationwide performed over 81,899 ART cycles, with more than 30,000 babies (20,143 deliveries) born that year (approximately 25% success rate) ("Use of assisted reproductive technology," 2002). Women under the age of 35 have a 32% success rate, and those over 42 only conceive 5 to 8% of the time (Vastag, 2001; "CDC: 30,000 babies," 2002).

By the time a couple considers the use of ART, they have often struggled for a long time, emotionally and physically, with infertility and may be desperate. But the high cost and limited success rates deter some prospective candidates. Some ART centers require a psychological evaluation of the couple to assess competency to parent, although studies have demonstrated that those couples seeking ART are generally psychologically healthy and that in any case they tend to minimize problems when applying for ART (Keye, 1995).

The most common types of ART are the following:

- **In vitro fertilization (IVF)** has a success rate of only 15 to 20% and costs approximately $10,000 per attempt. In this procedure, ova are surgically removed during ovulation, mixed with donor sperm, then inserted into the uterus after fertilization and the beginning of cell division. This form of ART accounted for 97% of all ART procedures in 1999 (CDC, 1999).

- **Gamete intrafallopian tube transfer (GIFT)** has a success rate of 35 to 40%. GIFT uses the same procedure as IVF, except that the fertilized ova are surgically returned to the woman's fallopian tubes. Like IVF, this technique requires daily participation. It also entails an increased risk for ectopic pregnancy, multiple births, and surgical complications, and represents 1% of ART procedures (CDC, 1999).

- **Intrauterine insemination (IUI)** is a very costly procedure that may take several attempts over a 6- to 9-month period before pregnancy occurs (Dickason, Silverman, & Kaplan, 1998). IUI involves bypassing the cervix (usually altered by antibodies or infection) and surgically implanting the ovum and spermatozoa into the uterus. The highest success rate for a healthy woman with no known fertility problems is 25%. It usually takes at least three cycles, with costs ranging widely between $750 to $7,000, depending on the treatment center and medications (San Francisco Fertility Centers, 2002).

- **Preservation and gestational surrogacy** is the harvesting of embryos to preserve for future use. This procedure is often used when women face surgery due to cancer and will not be able to conceive in the future (Plante, 2000). In cases of cervical cancer, it occurs 10 to 15% of the time during childbearing years. For example, 10 to 15% of women of childbearing age are faced with cervical cancer, and some of them may desire a future pregnancy that is threatened or precluded by the cancer.

All of these procedures except preservation and gestational surrogacy may use donated ova, but that practice has raised further legal and ethical questions, especially regarding parental rights and responsibilities. Psychological and emotional issues may also arise, related to the introduction of third-party genetic material, secrecy, and confidentiality.

Although ART was originally limited to married couples, unattached females in increasing numbers are using this method of conception. Their reasons include unsuccessful relationships with men in the past, prior abuse, or a lesbian lifestyle. Women well beyond traditional childbearing age have also begun to use ART. This trend has raised additional moral and ethical questions in some segments of society, such as, How well can a single mother, a lesbian mother, or an older mother raise a child? These questions have led not only to hot debate but also to research to provide evidence of successful parenting outcomes.

Adoption is one last alternative for the infertile couple. It is not much less daunting than infertility treatment, however. A time-consuming multiphase evaluation, which includes a home study, is required before finalization of custody. The idea of parenting an infant with an unknown genetic heritage may also be a challenge for some people, particularly because an increasing number of problems previously thought to be environmentally induced are being linked—at least in part—to genetics. On the positive side, however, some individuals and couples prefer adoption to the demands and uncertainties of ART. Some adoptive parents are also committed to giving a home to children in need of care.

Normal Fetal Development

The 40 weeks of **gestation,** during which the fertilized ovum becomes a fully developed infant, are a remarkable time. **Gestational age** is calculated from the date of the beginning of the woman's last menstrual period, a fairly easy time for the woman to identify. In contrast, **fertilization age** is measured from the time of fertilization, approximately 14 days after the beginning of the last menstrual period. The average pregnancy lasts 280 days when calculated from gestational age and 266 from the time of fertilization. Conventionally, the gestation period is organized by trimesters of about 3 months each.

This is a convenient system, but note that these divisions are not supported by clearly demarcated events.

First Trimester

In some ways, the first 12 weeks of pregnancy are the most remarkable. In an amazingly short time, sperm and ovum unite and are transformed into a being with identifiable body parts. The mother's body also undergoes dramatic changes.

Fertilization and the Embryonic Period. Sexual intercourse results in the release of an average of 200 million to 300 million sperm. Their life span is relatively short, and their journey through the female reproductive tract is fraught with hazards. Thus, only about 1 or 2 in 1,000 of the original sperm reach the fallopian tubes, which lead from the ovaries to the uterus. Typically, only one sperm penetrates the ripened ovum, triggering a biochemical reaction that prevents entry of any other sperm. The **zygote** (fertilized egg) continues to divide and begins about a 7-day journey to the uterus.

Following implantation in the uterine wall, the zygote matures into an **embryo**. The placenta, which acts like a filter between the mother and the growing embryo, also forms. The umbilical cord connects the fetus to the placenta. Oxygen, water, and glucose, as well as many drugs, viruses, bacteria, vitamins, and hormones, pass through the placenta to the embryo. Amniotic fluid in the uterus protects the embryo throughout the pregnancy.

By the 3rd week, tissue begins differentiating into organs. During this period, the embryo is vulnerable to **teratogens**—substances that may harm the developing organism—but most women do not know they are pregnant. Exhibit 2.3 shows how some relatively common drugs may have a teratogenic effect in the earliest stage of fetal development.

The Fetal Period. By the 8th week, the embryo is mature enough to be called a **fetus** (meaning "young one") (Novak & Broom, 1995), and as we see in Tahesha's story, the mother is experiencing signs of her pregnancy. Usually the mother has now missed one menstrual period, but if her cycle was irregular, this may not be a reliable sign. Approximately 50% of women experience nausea and vomiting (morning sickness) during the first trimester. A few experience vomiting so severe that it causes dehydration and metabolic changes requiring hospitalization. **Multigravidas**, women who have had a previous pregnancy, often recognize the signs of excessive fatigue and soreness in their breasts as a sign of pregnancy.

Between the 8th and 12th week, the fetal heart rate can be heard using a Doppler device. At 12 weeks, the gender of the fetus can be detected, and the face is fully formed. The fetus is moving within the mother, but it is still too early for her to feel the movement.

Newly pregnant women often feel ambivalence. Because of hormonal changes, they may experience mood swings and become less outgoing. Concerns about the changes

EXHIBIT 2.3
Potential Teratogens During the First Trimester

Substance	Effects on Fetal Development
Acetaminophen (Tylenol)	None
Amphetamines	Cardiac defects, cleft palate
Antacids	Increase in anomalies
Antianxiety medications	Increase in anomalies
Antihistamines	None
Barbiturates	Increase in anomalies
Gentamycin (antibiotic)	Eight cranial nerve damage
Glucocorticoids (steroids)	Cleft palate, cardiac defects
Haloperidol	Limb malformations
Insulin	Skeletal malformations
Lithium	Goiter, eye anomalies, cleft palate
LSD	Chromosomal abnormalities
Penicillin	None
Phenobarbital	Multiple anomalies
Podophyllin (in laxatives)	Multiple anomalies
Tetracycline (antibiotic)	Inhibition of bone growth, discoloration of teeth
Tricyclic antidepressants	Central nervous system and limb malformations

in their bodies, finances, the impact on their life goals, lifestyle adjustments, and other interpersonal interactions may cause anxiety. Often the father experiences similar ambivalence, and he may be distressed by his partner's mood swings. Parents who have previously miscarried may have a heightened concern for the well-being of this fetus.

Second Trimester

By the 16th week, the fetus is approximately 19 centimeters (7.5 inches) long and weighs 100 grams (3.3 ounces). The second trimester is generally a period of contentment and planning for most women, as it seems to have been for Karen Randolph. For problem pregnancies, or in troubled environments, quite the opposite may occur. However, the fatigue, nausea and vomiting, and mood swings that often accompany the first few weeks usually disappear in the second trimester.

Hearing the heartbeat and seeing the fetus via ultrasound often bring the reality of the pregnancy home. As seen in the story of the Randolphs, **quickening**—the experience of feeling fetal movement—usually occurs around this time, further validating the personhood of the fetus. **Fetal differentiation,** whereby the mother separates the individuality of the fetus from her own personhood, is usually completed by the end of this trimester. Many fathers too begin to relate to the fetus as a developing offspring.

Some fathers enjoy the changing shape of the woman's body, but others may struggle with the changes. Unless there are specific contraindications, sexual relations may continue throughout the pregnancy, and some men find the second trimester a period of great sexual satisfaction. Often during the second trimester the pregnant woman also experiences a return of her prepregnancy level of sexual desire.

Third Trimester

By 24 weeks, the fetus is considered viable in many hospitals. However, the parents may be less confident. Karen Randolph, for instance, was not prepared for the birth of her son, Joseph, who at 26 weeks' gestation, struggled to survive. Clearly, mothers are usually not psychologically prepared for delivery so early in the third trimester, and the risks to newborns are very great if birth occurs prior to the 26th week of pregnancy.

The tasks of the fetus during the third trimester are to gain weight and mature in preparation for delivery. As delivery nears, the increased weight of the fetus can cause discomfort for the mother, and often she looks forward to delivery with increasing anticipation. Completion of preparations for the new arrival consume much of her attention.

Labor and Delivery of the Neonate

Predicting when labor will begin is impossible. However, one indication of imminent labor is **lightening** (the descent of the fetus into the mother's pelvis). For a **primipara**—a first-time mother—lightening occurs approximately 2 weeks before delivery. For a multipara—a mother who has previously given birth—lightening typically occurs at the beginning of labor. Often the mother experiences **Braxton-Hicks contractions**, brief contractions that prepare the mother and fetus for labor—what Hazel Gereke referred to as "false labor." Usually, true labor begins with a show or release of the mucous plug that covered the cervical opening.

Labor is divided into three stages:

1. In the first stage, the cervix thins and dilates. The amniotic fluid is usually released during this stage ("water breaking"), and the mother feels regular contractions that intensify in frequency and strength as labor progresses. Many factors determine the length of this stage, including the number of pregnancies this mother has experienced, the weight of the fetus, the anatomy of the mother, the strength of the contractions, and the relaxation of the mother in the process. Despite the stories that abound, most mothers have plenty of time to prepare for the upcoming birth. Near the end of this phase, "transition" occurs, marked by a significant increase in the intensity and frequency of the contractions and heightened emotionalism. The head crowns (is visible at the vulva) at the end of this stage.

2. The second stage is delivery, when the **neonate** (newborn) is expelled from the mother. If the newborn is born breech (feet or buttocks first) or is transverse (positioned horizontally in the birth canal) and cannot be turned prior to birth, the mother may require a cesarean section.

3. Typically, within 1 hour after delivery, the placenta, the remaining amniotic fluid, and the membrane that separated the fetus from the uterine wall are delivered with a few contractions. If the newborn breastfeeds immediately, the hormone oxytocin is released to stimulate these contractions.

Following birth, the neonate undergoes rapid physiological changes, particularly in its respiratory and cardiac systems. Prior to birth, oxygen is delivered to the fetus through the umbilical vein, and carbon dioxide is eliminated by the two umbilical arteries. Although the fetus begins to breathe prior to birth, breathing serves no purpose until after delivery. The neonate's first breath, typically in the form of a cry, creates tremendous pressure within the lungs, which clears amniotic fluid and triggers the opening and closing of several shunts and vessels in the heart. The blood flow is rerouted to the lungs.

Many factors, such as maternal exposure to narcotics during pregnancy or labor, can adversely affect the neonate's attempts to breathe—as can prematurity, congenital anomalies, and neonatal infections. Drugs and other interventions may be administered to maintain adequate respiration. To measure the neonate's adjustment to extrauterine life, **Apgar scores**—rather simple measurements of physiological health—are assessed at 1, 5, and 10 minutes after birth. Apgar scores determine the need for resuscitation and indicate the effectiveness of resuscitation efforts and long-term problems that might arise. The other immediate challenge to the newborn is to establish a stable temperature. Inadequately maintained body temperature creates neonatal stress and thus increased respiratory and cardiac effort, which can result in respiratory failure. Close monitoring of the neonate during the first 4 hours after birth is critical to detect any such problems in adapting to extrauterine life.

Pregnancy and the Life Course

As the three case studies at the beginning of the chapter indicate, pregnancy is a period of transition. Each family member faces changes in role identification and prescribed tasks.

Regardless of her age or number of previous births, the pregnant woman must complete four different developmental tasks:

1. Provide safety for herself and the infant throughout pregnancy, labor, and delivery
2. Help people in her social support system to accept this event
3. Bond with her unborn infant
4. Come to terms with the inequality inherent in a mother/neonate relationship (Rubin, 1995)

Under what conditions might the transition to parenthood become a turning point?

Although the tasks were the same for Tahesha Gibbons, Karen Randolph, and Hazel Gereke, each had very different resources for negotiating the tasks. To some extent, those resources were specific to their position in the life course. Remember, however, that the tasks are the same regardless of maternal age.

Teen Pregnancy

Tahesha Gibbon represents a well-known situation in the United States. Fifty percent of adolescents are sexually active, resulting in over 880,000 pregnancies per year in women aged 15 to 19. Approximately half of these pregnancies result in a live birth, 35% end in abortion, and 14% in miscarriage or stillbirth.

The good news is that despite an 8% increase in birthrates between 1991 and 2000, teen birthrates decreased by 22%, with the most marked decline among black teenagers (down 31%) and teens between 15 and 17 (down 29%). Hispanic births show the slowest decline rates (12%) (Kaplan et al., 2001; Koshar, 2001). Although the birthrate to unmarried mothers rose by 3% between 1994 and 2000, the number of births to unmarried teens declined 2 years in a row (U.S. Department of Health and Human Services, 2001a).

Nevertheless, adolescent pregnancy in the United States is among the highest in the industrialized world, with teen pregnancies accounting for 13% of babies born (Tomal, 1999). The social costs are high: an estimated $7 billion is spent each year on adolescent pregnancy, only one third of the teens are able to earn a high school diploma, and 3 million teens contract an STD each year (Kaplan et al., 2001; Koshar, 2001).

One study showed that twice as many teens coerced into sex or raped experienced teenage pregnancy compared to their nonabused peers (Kenney, Reinholtz, & Angelini, 1997). A boyfriend was identified as the perpetrator in almost 30% of these rapes. Approximately 5% of all rapes result in pregnancy regardless of age (Holmes, Resnick, Kilpatrick, & Best, 1996). In addition, a study found that 29% of pregnant teens between the ages of 12 and 19 were victims of violence during their pregnancy. The victims of violence (physical and sexual) were more likely to use cigarettes, alcohol, and illicit drugs than nonvictims (Martin, Clark, Lynch, Kupper, & Cilenti, 1999). Social workers are often on the front line helping these teens as they struggle with emotional and physical suffering.

Pregnant adolescents are at risk medically also. They have higher incidences of toxemia (pregnancy-induced high blood pressure) and anemia than adult women, and their neonates are at greater risk for low birth weight, prematurity, and infant mortality than neonates born to adult women. The rate of prematurity and low birth weight among African American adolescents is twice as high as the rate for Hispanic and European American adolescents. Although pregnancy-related complications are not limited to teen mothers, it is important for social workers to note that black women are three times as likely to die from such complications as Caucasian women are (a rate that has risen 33% in the past 100 years) (Population Council, Inc., 1999).

Limited financial resources, the inadequate and fragmented facilities often found in poverty-stricken communities, and the normal adolescent avoidance of problems frequently contribute to a delayed diagnosis of pregnancy for disadvantaged young women. Of course, delayed diagnosis hampers timely prenatal care (Osofsky, Osofsky, & Diamond, 1988) and limits pregnancy options, increasing the risks of both mortality and morbidity (sickness) for fetus, newborn, and mother.

The experience of pregnancy varies somewhat with stage of adolescence:

- *Young adolescents, ages 12 to 14.* Following years of increases, pregnancy rates for this group are dropping. Nine percent of 14-year-old sexually active women become pregnant each year, but they account for only 3% of all teen births and abortions (Kaplan, 2001; Tomal, 1999). The bulk of teen pregnancies are still occurring at later ages. One study found that the rate of pregnancy for this age group was significantly affected by the parents' marital status, indicating that family stability may be a more powerful influence in pregnancy prevention than socioeconomic status (Tomal, 1999). Some of the pregnancies in this age group can be attributed to increased rates of child sexual abuse (National Center for Child Abuse and Neglect, 1995). Long-standing incest can result in pregnancy as the teen becomes fertile. As the average age of first menstruation decreases, it is not uncommon for girls as young as 10 years old to ovulate. At the same time, the interval between the onset of menstruation and the completion of the educational process has lengthened, increasing the possibility of disrupting pregnant teens' education and thus condemning them to a lifetime of poverty. Long-term commitment and financial support from the father of the pregnant teen's child are unusual, further contributing to the isolation and impoverishment of the young adolescent mother. Premature birth is 3.4 times more common for young adolescents than for non-adolescent women, possibly because of the difficulty of meeting the nutritional demands of both the growing fetus and the growing adolescent (DuPlessis, Bell, & Richards, 1997).

- *Middle adolescents, ages 15 to 17.* Young women at this age have completed most of their physical growth but are still emotionally immature. They may engage in sexual activity to demonstrate independence, maintain status in their peer group (which appears to be part of the story for Tahesha), explore self-identity, or experiment with new behaviors. The sense of invulnerability that permeates adolescence often provides a false sense of security.

- *Late adolescents, ages 18 to 20.* The relatively recent phenomenon of "adolescence" has redefined pregnancy for this age group. Until the 20th century, marriage and childbearing were normative during this life stage. Late adolescents who become pregnant tend to be more mature than younger teens and often have a positive relationship with the infant's father. They are more focused on the future and may have more social supports. However, if the teen's education is disrupted, the pregnancy may be viewed as a major impediment to achieving career goals.

How important is the multigenerational family in social work practice with pregnant teens?

One significant feature of teen pregnancy is the extent to which the adolescent mother connects with other family members. From a family systems perspective, the pregnant teen may be repeating her mother's behaviors, as seen in Tahesha's story. Research also suggests that younger sisters of pregnant teens, compared to younger sisters without a pregnant older sister, show more acceptance of at-risk behaviors for pregnancy, engage in more problem behaviors, and have more interaction with the older sibling's social network (East, 1996; East & Shi, 1997). The family's response to the pregnancy and the teen mother's emotional stability will significantly influence her parenting behaviors. Positive role modeling of family dynamics and social support are especially important.

Many initiatives have focused on pregnancy prevention, important because 60 to 80% of adolescent pregnancies are unintended (Cowley & Farley, 2001). A metaanalysis of studies found that pregnancy prevention programs had no effect on reducing teen sexual activity but did lead to the increased use of condoms and a reduction in pregnancy rates (Franklin & Corcoran, 2000). Communities are increasingly allocating resources to facilitate education programs, at times funded by local businesses (Koshar, 2001; National Campaign to Prevent Teen Pregnancy, 2002). Effective prevention programs must be developed and implemented with attention to issues of violence and substance abuse.

The role and needs of the adolescent father have been woefully neglected in the research on adolescent pregnancy. Teen fathers who remain involved with the mother and infant provide a significant source of support for both (Osofsky, Hann, & Peebles, 1993). One study showed that the best predictor of an adolescent girl's attitude toward her pregnancy was her boyfriend's desire for a baby (Cowley & Farley, 2001). Pregnant adolescents who maintain a relationship with the baby's father seek prenatal care earlier than teens who terminate the relationship (Moss, 1987). For these reasons, many programs targeting teen mothers also provide services to engage teen fathers.

Early Adulthood Pregnancy

Physiologically, the young woman in her 20s and 30s is at the optimal age for pregnancy. Psychologically, young adults are involved in establishing life goals, and these often involve parenthood. Thus, pregnancy during this period of the life course is a normative event in most cultures.

Research suggests that even during the prime childbearing years, women who have appropriate social support are healthier psychologically and physically during their pregnancies. Their infants are six times less likely to experience problems, and they have more positive developmental outcomes, compared to women who lack social support (Hogoel, Van-Raalte, Kalekin-Fishman, & Shlfroni, 1995; Oakley, Hickey, Rojan, & Rigby, 1996). Social support is an important protective factor for mother and child.

Delayed Pregnancy

What cohort effects can you recognize in attitudes toward delayed pregnancy?

An increasing number of women are delaying childbirth until their late 30s and 40s, even into their 50s and 60s. Many have been struggling with infertility for several years; others deliberately have chosen to wait until their careers are established. Other women are choosing to have children with a new partner. Some single women, driven by the ticking of the so-called biological clock, finally choose to go ahead and have a child on their own, often using artificial insemination.

Waiting until later in the life cycle to reproduce raises significant problems. The fertility rate for women aged 40 to 47 is only between 5 and 7% (Berryman & Wendridge, 1991; Fleming, 2000). The rate of miscarriage for women over 45 is 75% (Fleming, 2000). The trend to delay childbearing has also led to increased maternal mortality rates for women over 35, especially those delivering their first child (Waterstone, Bewley, Wolfe, & Murphy, 2001). Most fertility clinics discourage women over 40 from using their own eggs for in vitro fertilization because the woman's eggs age as she does, with an increased risk of chromosomal abnormalities. Some infertility clinics are using the DNA from the older woman's egg and transferring it into the cytoplasm of a younger woman's donated egg. Research is being conducted into the efficacy of freezing a slice of ovarian tissue (containing thousands of immature eggs) for later implantation (Klotter, 2002).

Unlike Hazel Gereke, who 31 years ago unexpectedly became pregnant in later life, many women are purposely choosing to face the risks of delayed pregnancy and childbirth. They are often less traditional than their peers, have a more autonomous personality, and are more likely to have younger partners (Berryman & Wendridge, 1991). Ethical and sociological questions are being raised as to the appropriateness of older women bearing children when they may not live long enough to raise their offspring. Historically, infants were killed if the community and the family felt that there were inadequate resources to provide for their care. Social workers are faced with the challenge of working with families when infants are born to mothers of advanced maternal age (AMA) as well as providing guidance to older persons considering pregnancy.

Women who conceive after 35 may have more difficulty adjusting to the pregnancy during the first trimester than do their younger cohorts, but by the third trimester there is no difference in acceptance (Berryman & Wendridge, 1996). Preexisting medical conditions, such as diabetes or hypertension, may increase the risks of pregnancy, and older women, like Hazel Gereke, face the increased risk of giving birth to an infant with Down's syndrome. Older women have higher incidences of complications during labor and delivery and an increased rate of cesarean births. With appropriate physical care, however, most women can successfully negotiate most of the hazards of later-life pregnancy (Waterstone, Bewley, Wolfe, & Murphy, 2001).

In some cases, *elderly gravidas*—the medical term for pregnant women over 35—may be embarrassed by their pregnancy and resent the disruption of their established routine. They may be concerned about care for the child as they age, leading to increased stress. Older children may also have difficulty accepting the mother's pregnancy and the arrival of a new sibling. However, older women may be more financially stable and feel more self-confident in their mothering role (Pridham & Chang, 1992), and increasing numbers of women are choosing to have a child after age 35, despite the greater risks.

Risk and Protective Factors in Conception, Pregnancy, and Childbirth

Despite significant advances in the medical management of pregnancy and childbirth, the United States ranks 25th in the world in infant mortality and 21st in maternal mortality, worse than most industrialized nations (Homer, 2001). Thus, the understanding and prevention of **risk factors,** the characteristics that increase the likelihood of a problem, are of particular concern. Risk factors include biological, psychological, social, familial, environmental, and societal dimensions. Like risk factors, **protective factors,** which help reduce or protect against risk, also range from biological to societal dimensions. Exhibit 2.4 presents selected risk and protective factors for conception, pregnancy, and childbirth.

What do social workers need to know about the effects of aspects of fetal development on subsequent development?

Social workers must be knowledgeable about the risk and protective factors that are associated with the most commonly occurring problems they address with individuals and families. It is also critical that social workers remember that the presence of a risk or protective factor cannot totally predict any one outcome. Even when a risk factor is present, it may not be sufficient to result in the related outcome, or the effect may have a rather broad range of impact. For example, pregnant women's prenatal

EXHIBIT 2.4
Selected Risk and Protective Factors for Conception, Pregnancy, and Birth

	Risk Factors	Protective Factors
Conception	Low sperm count	Father drug abstinence (marijuana)
	Fallopian tubal factors	Gynecological care
	Genetic abnormality	Genetic counseling
	Adolescent promiscuity	Family life education; contraception; abstinence
	Endometriosis	Hormone therapy; surgery
	Inadequate nutrition for sexually active women of childbearing age	Folic acid supplement
Pregnancy	Female age (<18 or >35)	Family life education; birth control
	Delivery before 38 weeks	Prenatal care; WIC Program
	Gestation, toxemia, diabetes	Prenatal care
	Stress due to inadequate resources	Social and economic support
	Trauma	Accident prevention (falls, fire, car)
	Smoking	Prenatal care; smoking cessation programs
Birth	Venereal diseases such as gonorrhea and positive GBS	Prenatal care; antibiotic eye drops for neonate; maternal testing
	Meconium aspiration; anoxia	C-section delivery; drug during pregnancy; well-managed labor and delivery
	Prolonged and painful labor	Birthing classes; social support; father presence at birth; adequate pain control

heroin use is known as a risk factor for their children's intelligence, but children exposed to heroin in the womb have had IQ scores ranging from 50 to 124 (Wachs, 2000).

Another consideration is timing. One child with a defective gene may experience the onset of a genetic illness much earlier or later than another child with the same gene.

And finally, most outcomes are determined by several factors. Seldom is an environmental, social, or biological risk solely responsible for an outcome (Epps & Jackson, 2000). We are unlikely to ever be able to predict all the developmental patterns that might result from a given set of risks (Vallacher & Nowak, 1998; Wachs, 2000).

One explanation for the great variability in individual outcomes when risk factors are present is the concept of resiliency, or the ability to cope and adapt (Garmezy, 1993; Werner, 2000). Both individuals and families are faced with stressful situations, chronic or crisis, over the life course (Walsh, 1998). And both the individual and family may possess characteristics that have been identified as the ability to bounce back, respond, adapt, or successfully cope with these life events. Certain family characteristics related to resiliency—such as good communication and problem-solving processes—can serve as protective factors for individual development (Hawley & DeHaan, 1996). Family risk factors with individual impact may include marital discord and inadequate parenting skills.

The Gereke family demonstrated characteristics of resiliency in how it responded to Terry's birth. The parents' life courses were dramatically altered, from anticipating the arrival of adulthood for their youngest child (empty nest) to becoming the parents of a newborn with a major disability. In fact, however, the lives of all family members were altered by this one event. Ultimately, they said that Terry's birth changed their family for the better, bringing them all emotionally closer and making them more responsive to others' needs. For each person, Terry's birth also set into motion multiple transitions, and in a like manner Terry's life course was affected by these family and individual transitions.

Social Work and Problems of Childbearing

The events related to childbearing are affected by economic, political, and social forces. Social workers, with their understanding of changing configurations of person and environment, are well equipped to address the needs of all persons of reproductive age that derive from these forces. Although most pregnancies result in favorable outcomes, for those that do not, social workers can play an important role. Moreover, many negative outcomes can be prevented through social work interventions: prenatal care, childbirth education, introduction to new medical technologies, and genetic counseling. The social worker who participates in these interventions requires knowledge of, and collaboration with, a range of other professionals.

Problem Pregnancies

In some sense, each of the pregnancies described at the beginning of this chapter is a problem pregnancy. Pregnancy can become problematic for a variety of reasons, but only three types of problem pregnancies are discussed here: undesired pregnancy, ectopic pregnancy, and miscarriage and stillbirth.

Undesired Pregnancy. Pregnancies that are unplanned are a problem because they are associated with increased stress. They carry a higher risk for inadequate prenatal care, health problems late in the pregnancy and right after birth, and significant postnatal problems. Some data indicate that women who are unhappy about their pregnancy during the first trimester may experience up to two times greater neonatal mortality than women who are accepting of their pregnancy (Bustan, 1994).

Women who experience unplanned pregnancies are more likely to have been influenced by their partner's choice of birth control and more likely to have used unreliable methods of birth control compared to women who do not become pregnant (Rosenfeld & Everett, 1996). Social workers can use this knowledge to target at-risk teens, provide essential information, link teens to reproductive resources, and assist in problem solving about other reproductive concerns.

Ectopic Pregnancy. An ectopic pregnancy occurs if the zygote implants outside the uterus, usually in the fallopian tubes. The rate of ectopic pregnancy rose sixfold in the United States between 1970 and 1992 and continues to increase. Each year over 100,000 pregnancies are terminated due to ectopic implantation, and it accounts for over 9% of the maternal deaths in the first trimester (Walling, 2001). Women who have had previous ectopic pregnancies, tubal damage from surgeries or infection (especially Chlamydia trachomatis—the major cause of pelvic inflammatory disease), a history of infertility, in vitro fertilization, or a maternal age over 35 are at greater risk for an ectopic pregnancy (Ankum, 2000).

The initial clinical symptoms, abdominal pain and vaginal bleeding, are nonspecific, but if tubal rupture occurs, the situation is life threatening and requires a visit to the emergency clinic. Early diagnosis is critical to the outcome. New techniques such as imaging studies and measurement of pregnancy hormonal levels may help decrease maternal mortality (Splete, 2002). However, because the diagnosis of ectopic pregnancy cannot be made without sophisticated medical equipment, all sexually active women with lower abdominal pain and vaginal bleeding should be evaluated (Tay, Moore, & Walker, 2000).

When found within the first 6 weeks of pregnancy, ectopic pregnancy is typically treated with medication (methotrexate); otherwise, abdominal surgery is necessary (Cooper, 2000). Approximately one half of women who are treated for an ectopic pregnancy will spontaneously conceive again within a year (Ego, 2001).

Miscarriage and Stillbirth. **Miscarriage** is the naturally occurring loss of a fetus prior to 20 weeks' gestation—a **spontaneous abortion**. Approximately 10 to 15% of all pregnancies end in spontaneous abortion, without a discernible cause and often unrecognized by the mother. An estimated 50% of threatened spontaneous abortions become complete abortions. If the abortion is incomplete, any placenta or fetus that is not expelled must be surgically removed (Novak & Broom, 1995) or the mother risks hemorrhage and infection.

In late pregnancy, if the fetus does not breathe or exhibit a heartbeat, or if the umbilical cord stops pulsating, the birth is considered a **stillbirth** or **intrauterine fetal death (IUFD).** Stillbirths account for up to 50% of deaths of the baby just before, during, or just after birth (perinatal mortality) (Dickason, Schult, & Silverman, 1990). Stillbirths are caused by numerous maternal problems and fetal conditions. In cases of stillbirth, labor generally proceeds immediately and is allowed to occur naturally. But the pregnancy may continue for several days following cessation of movement, and in extreme cases surgery may be needed to end the pregnancy. Stillbirth frequently occurs without explanation, typically resulting in great stress and anguish for parents, who blame themselves and struggle with unresolved guilt. Social workers can help parents to understand and cope with the strong emotions they are experiencing.

At-Risk Newborns

Not all pregnancies proceed smoothly and end in routine deliveries. The newborn may face a variety of risks related to genetics, pregnancy complications, and birth complications.

Prematurity and Low Birth Weight. A radical shift has occurred in our culture over the past 20 years: the desire for a positive pregnancy outcome has been replaced by the assumption that the pregnancy will be flawless and the baby will be perfect (Forrest, 1993; McCarton, 1986). But alarming statistics debunk this myth. Over 400,000 **premature births** (births after less than 37 weeks' gestation) occur in the United States each year (Van Riper, 2001). In the United States, 1 in 14 babies born each year is preterm, and the rate of preterm births continues to rise, despite increased availability of prenatal care, nutrition programs for pregnant women, and labor-stopping medications (Guyer et al., 1999; Stevens, 2002).

The overall rate of **low birth weight (LBW)** infants—infants weighing less than 2,500 grams (5 pounds 8 ounces) at birth—has changed little over the past 30 years. Although the rate for black women dropped by 10% over the last decade and rose 11% for white women, the rate for LBW infants born to African American women remains almost twice as high as Caucasian women ("Infant mortality," 2002).

Very low birth weight (VLBW) infants—infants weighing less than 1,500 grams (3 pounds 3 ounces)—occur 1.42% of the time but have a mortality rate 96% greater than larger newborns (Hoybert, Friedman, Strobino, & Guyer, 2001). There are significant racial differences in the number of VLBW infants born, with Caucasians accounting for 59.1%, African Americans 12.9%, Puerto Ricans 9.3%, Filipinos 8.3%, Mexicans 5.2%, and Chinese 5.2%. These statistics have remained relatively stable through the past decade despite advances in obstetrical and neonatal care (Hoybert, Friedman, Strobino, & Guyer, 2001).

The United States ranks the highest in infant mortality and LBW deliveries among all developed countries. The apparent failure of prevention programs is relevant to the social worker's intervention (Heck, Schoendorf, & Chavez, 2002). There are 34.6 infant deaths per 1,000 births for women who received no prenatal care compared to 6.2 infant deaths per 1,000 for women who saw a medical professional in the first trimester. Unmarried mothers had an infant death rate of 10.2 per 1,000 versus 5.5 per 1,000 for married mothers (National Vital Statistics Report, 2002). Clearly, there is a need for social workers to help impoverished, poorly educated, young, and unmarried mothers access and use the appropriate services. Otherwise babies die.

What impact will these changes in health care for premature infants have on families and schools?

The survival rates of premature infants have improved, largely because of explosive growth in the field of neonatal medicine and the establishment of regional NICUs. Less than 5% of infants of normal birth weight are affected by cerebral palsy, hydrocephalus and microcephaly (disorders of the cranium), blindness, deafness, and seizures. However, neonates weighing less than 1,000 grams (2.2 pounds) have a 49% chance for abnormal neurodevelopment and sensory assessments, 17% have cerebral palsy, 23% have long-term disabilities, and 33% require frequent hospitalizations during their first years of life (Jones, Guildea, Stewart, & Cartlidge, 2002; Koeske & Koeske, 1992; Vohr et al., 2000).

Studying the long-term effects of prematurity is difficult because today's 5-year-old who was LBW received significantly less sophisticated care than the current patients in the NICU. However, we know that on the average, LBW children score significantly lower than children of normal birth weight on intelligence tests; have decreased fine and gross motor coordination; have impaired perceptual-motor skills; and demonstrate greater difficulties in language, nonverbal reasoning, and problem solving (Hack, Breslau, & Aram, 1992; Hack, Taylor, Klein, & Eiben, 1994; McDermott, Cokert, & McKeown, 1993; Peterson, Greisen, & Kovacs, 1994; Teplin, Burchinal, Johnson-Martin, Humphrey, & Kraybill, 1991). VLBW infants who escape cerebral palsy are exhibiting subnormal academic achievement 30 to 50% of the time, 30% have a diagnosis of attention deficit hyperactivity disorder, and, interestingly, 25 to 30% are affected by psychiatric disorders in adolescence. It is proposed that the vulnerability of the premature brain during this critical period of fetal development is negatively affected by the stressful neonatal environmental conditions (Elley, 2001; Perlman, 2001). Therefore, neonatal environmental conditions may be as much of a risk factor for negative pregnancy outcomes as simple prematurity. Thus, the Randolphs have reason to wonder what the future holds for their baby.

Until recently, it had been assumed that the major risk factors for prematurity included maternal age, race or ethnicity, health, and risk-taking behaviors. However, pregnant African Americans, who have a three- to fourfold disadvantage in delivering extremely low birth weight (ELBW) neonates, are more likely than European Americans to be unmarried, have less education, and be younger. African Americans also have higher rates of hypertension, anemia, and low-level lead exposure, indicating that their general health status may be a factor (National Center for Health Statistics [NCHS], 1993a). In addition, 30% of LBW births can be attributed to natal environmental factors, such as maternal illness (e.g., stress and genital infections), some maternal working conditions, smoking, poor maternal weight gain during pregnancy along with being underweight before the pregnancy, intrauterine infections, and maternal short stature (Goldenberg, Hauth, & Andrews, 2000; Heck, Schoendorf, & Chavez, 2002; Spencer & Logan, 2002).

One of the greatest risk factors for the infant's LBW and mortality is the mother's smoking (NCHS, 1997b). Smoking during pregnancy has declined steadily since 1989, but in 1999, 12.6% of women still smoked during their pregnancy. Pregnant teens have the highest smoking rate (18%), with the rate of African American teens' smoking rising the fastest (Hoybert et al., 2001). The death rate for mothers who smoked is 10.5 per 1,000 births, versus 6.6 deaths per 1,000 for the nonsmokers (National Vital Statistics Report, 2002). Thirty percent of pregnant adolescents who had experienced violence also smoked, demonstrating the effects of cumulative risks. Because smoking reduces the amount of oxygen and the flow of nutrients to the fetus, smoking during the third trimester, a period of rapid fetal weight gain, is especially harmful. Cessation of smoking at any time during the pregnancy will have a positive effect, although if the pregnant woman is smoking by the 32nd week of pregnancy, there are no negative effects on birth weight. However, continued smoking is associated with higher rates of miscarriage, LBW, sudden infant death syndrome (SIDS), and cleft palates (Higgins, 2002).

Other risk factors for prematurity and LBW include alcohol use and other drug use. The mother's adequate nutrition prior to conception, as well as during pregnancy, is another important factor in fetal health. It is normal to gain between 20 and 35 pounds with a singleton pregnancy. Overweight mothers may have larger babies and are at a higher risk for diabetes, whereas women who are 10% below average weight run the risk of premature delivery, preeclampsia, and bleeding (Cooper, 2000). VLBW neonates such as Joseph Randolph run an even greater risk of problems associated with prematurity.

Newborn Intensive Care. As the Randolphs know all too well, parents' expectations for a healthy newborn are shattered when their child is admitted to an NICU. Their fear and anxiety often make it hard for them to form a strong emotional bond with their newborn. About 90% of mothers and 80% of fathers report that they develop an attachment to the infant during the third trimester of pregnancy. But when an infant is premature, the parents have not had the same opportunity. In addition, the fear that a sickly newborn may die inhibits some parents from risking attachment. Others are consumed with guilt at their baby's condition and believe that they will only harm the newborn by their presence. Karen and Bob Randolph had to work hard to contain their anxiety about Joseph's frailties.

Early disruption in bonding may have a more significant long-term impact on the child than the infant's actual medical condition (Wittenberg, 1990). The response has been a movement toward family-centered NICU environments, which are structured to promote interaction between the infant and the parents, siblings, and others in the family's support system. Ample opportunity to interact with Joseph facilitated Karen and Bob Randolph's attempts to bond with him.

Understanding the psychological stresses confronting the family with a baby in the NICU is the basis for social work interventions. As the Randolphs' story suggests, deciding whether to invest in the newborn and risk great loss or to withdraw in an effort to protect oneself against pain causes continuing tension. Witnessing the suffering and death of other neonates is traumatizing as well (Yu, Jamieson, & Asbury, 1981). Social workers can help parents understand and cope with this stress.

Neonatology, the care of critically ill newborns, has only recently been recognized as a medical specialty. It is a much-needed specialty, however. Preemies in the NICU are estimated to account for 5 million hospital days per year, costing approximately $5 billion annually (Joffe, Symonds, Alverson, & Chilton, 1995). In 1998, 65% of all infant deaths occurred to the 7.6% of infants born with LBW, and 51% of all infant deaths occurred to the 1.5% of infants born with VLBW. Almost 9 out of 10 infants weighing less than 500 grams (1 pound 1 ounce) die within the 1st year of life, many dying within the 1st week (Hoybert et al., 2001). Since the advent of the NICU in the 1970s, the survival rate of critically ill neonates has continued to increase. It is highly unlikely that Joseph Randolph would have survived in 1970, when an infant weighing 1,500 grams (3.3 pounds) had a 50% chance of survival. By 2000, however, an infant weighing between 1,250 and 1,500 grams had a 98% chance of survival (Glass, 1994; Hoybert et al., 2001).

Social workers in an NICU must negotiate a complex technological environment requiring specialized skill and knowledge while attempting to respond with compassion, understanding, and appropriate advocacy. It helps to remember that the effort could affect a neonate's life course.

Major Congenital Anomalies. Overall, only 2 to 4% of all surviving newborns have a birth defect. However, the number of neonates born with anomalies due to genetics and exposure to teratogens, or nonhereditary factors that affect development of the fetus, during their development does not reflect the number of abnormal embryos. Fewer than half of all fertilized ova result in a live birth; the rest are spontaneously aborted. The probability that a fertilized ovum with a genetic anomaly will abort spontaneously ranges from 80 to 90% (Opitz, 1996). Social workers need to be mindful of the low probability that a child will be born with a genetic disorder or congenital anomaly when responding to parental fears.

Preventing, diagnosing, and predicting the outcome of genetic disorders is very difficult because of the complexities of genetic processes:

- **Variable expressivity**. Genes manifest differently in different people. For example, persons with cystic fibrosis, caused by a recessive gene, display wide variability in the severity of symptoms. The expression of the disorder appears to be influenced by the interplay of psychological, social, political, economic, and other environmental factors. The effects can be exacerbated by maternal substance abuse, inadequate maternal nutrition, and birth trauma. Children with cystic fibrosis born into poverty may not have benefited from early diagnosis, may live in an inner city that exposes them to increased levels of pollution, or may lack adequate home medical care because the primary caregiver is also responsible for meeting the family's economic needs.

- **Genetic heterogeneity.** The same characteristic may be a consequence of one of a number of genetic anomalies. For example, neural tube defects may result either from gene mutations or from exposure to specific teratogens.
- **Pleiotropy principle**. The same gene may influence seemingly unrelated systems (Rauch, 1988). Hair color, for example, is typically linked to a particular skin color (such as blonde hair with light complexion, black hair with olive complexion).

Genetic disorders fall into four categories, summarized in Exhibit 2.5 (Opitz, 1996; Rauch, 1988; Reed, 1996; Vekemans, 1996):

1. *Inheritance of a single abnormal gene.* An inherited anomaly in a single gene may lead to a serious disorder. The gene may be recessive, meaning that both parents must pass it along, or it may be dominant, in which case only one parent needs to have the gene in order for it to be expressed in the child. A third possibility is that the disorder is sex-linked, meaning that it is passed along by either the father or the mother.

2. *Multifactorial inheritance.* Some genetic traits, such as height and intelligence, are influenced by environmental factors such as nutrition. Their expression varies because of **multifactorial inheritance,** meaning that they are controlled by multiple genes. Multifactorial inheritance is implicated in traits that predispose a person to mental illnesses, such as depression. However, these traits are merely predisposing factors, creating what is called **genetic liability**. Siblings born with the same genetic traits may thus vary in the likelihood of developing a specific genetically based disorder, such as alcoholism or mental illness (Rauch, 1988; Takahashi & Turnbull, 1994).

3. *Chromosomal aberration.* Some genetic abnormalities are not hereditary but rather are caused by a genetic mishap during development of the ovum or sperm cells. Sometimes the cells end up missing chromosomes or having too many. When the ovum or sperm cell has fewer than 23 chromosomes, the probability of conception and survival is minimal. But in the presence of too many chromosomes in the ovum or the sperm, various anomalies occur. Down's syndrome, or trisomy 21, the most common chromosomal aberration, is the presence of 47 chromosomes—specifically, an extra chromosome in the 21st pair. Its prevalence is 1 in 600 to 1,000 live births overall, but as seen in the Hazel Gereke's story, it increases to 1 in 350 for women over age 35 (Vekemans, 1996). Other chromosome anomalies include Turner's syndrome (a single sex chromosome, X) and Klinefelter's syndrome (an extra sex chromosome, XXY).

EXHIBIT 2.5

Four Categories of Genetic Anomalies

Inheritance of Single Abnormal Gene		
Recessive	**Dominant**	**Sex-Linked**
Sickle-cell anemia Tay-Sachs disease Cystic fibrosis	Neurofibromatosis Huntington's disease	Hemophilia Duchenne's muscular dystrophy
Multifactorial Inheritance		
Possible mental illness	Alcoholism	
Chromosomal Aberration		
Down's syndrome (additional 21st chromosome)	Turner's syndrome (X)	Klinefelter's syndrome (XXY)

Exposure to Teratogens			
Radiation	**Infections**	**Maternal Metabolic Imbalance**	**Drugs and Environmental Chemicals**
Neural tube defects	Rubella: deafness, glaucoma Syphilis: neurological, ocular, and skeletal defects	Diabetes: neural tube defects Folic acid deficiency: brain and neural tube defects Hyperthermia (at 14-28 days): neural tube defects	Alcohol: mental retardation Heroin: attention deficit disorder Amphetamines: urogenital defects

4. *Exposure to teratogens.* Teratogens can be divided into four categories: radiation, infections, maternal metabolic imbalance, and drugs and environmental chemicals. In the Randolph story, Karen wondered if Joseph's premature birth was a result of prenatal exposure to paint fumes. It may have been, depending on what specific chemicals were involved, when exposure occurred, and to what degree. Parents who, like the Randolphs, are experiencing considerable guilt over their possible responsibility for their baby's problems may take comfort from the knowledge that the impact of exposure to teratogens can vary greatly. Much depends on the

Exhibit 2.6
Sensitive Periods in Prenatal Development

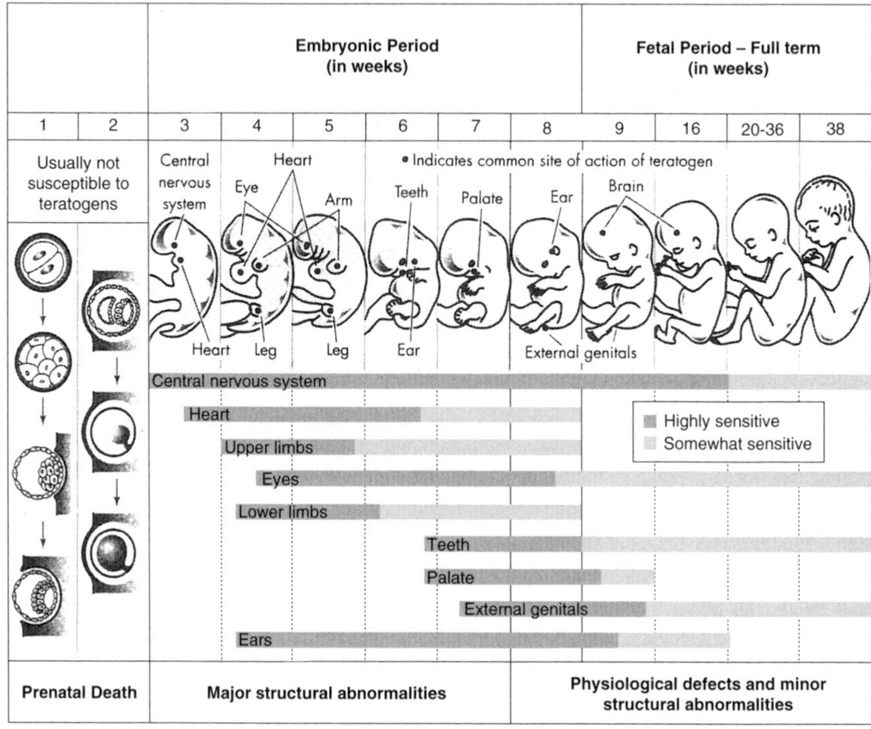

Source: Moore and Persand, 1993.

timing of exposure. The various organ systems have different critical or **sensitive periods,** summarized in Exhibit 2.6.

Parents who have reason to fear these congenital anomalies often opt for diagnosis during pregnancy. **Amniocentesis** is the extraction of amniotic fluid for chromosomal analysis; it involves inserting a hollow needle through the abdominal wall during the second trimester. **Chorion villi testing (CVT)** involves the insertion of a catheter through the cervix into the uterus to obtain a sample of the developing placenta; it can be done as early as 8 weeks but carries a slightly higher risk of causing spontaneous abortion (miscarriage). A more frequent procedure is **ultrasonography** (ultrasound), which produces a visual image of the developing fetus.

How might culture, social class, and religious orientation affect these decisions?

If an anomaly is detected, the decisions that need to be made are not easy ones. The possibility of false readings on these tests makes the decisions even more complicated. Should the fetus be aborted? Should fetal surgery—a surgical specialty still in the early stages of development—be undertaken? Could **gene replacement therapy**, implantation of genetic material to alter the genotype—still a costly experimental procedure—prevent an anomaly or limit its manifestation? Do the parents have the financial and psychological means to care for a neonate with a disability? This was a question that the Gerekes asked of themselves. What is the potential impact on the marriage and extended family system? Nonurgent decisions should be postponed until parents have an opportunity to adjust to the crisis and acquire the necessary information (Fost, 1981). The multidimensional perspective of social workers can contribute to a more holistic understanding of a client's situation, leading to appropriate and effective interventions when genetic anomalies are likely to, or do, occur.

Special Parent Populations

Social workers should recognize the risks involved in the configurations of person and environment for some special parent populations. Six of these special populations are discussed here.

Pregnant Substance Abusers. Our knowledge of the developmental impact of maternal use of illegal and legal substances is rapidly increasing. The good news is that health care professionals are increasingly able to avoid prescribing legal drugs that might harm the developing fetus, once pregnancy is confirmed. The bad news is that too many pregnant women are still harming their babies through use of illegal drugs or abuse of legal substances. And, unfortunately, many women do not know they are pregnant during the first trimester, a period when the fetus is very vulnerable to teratogens.

Although it is difficult to obtain reliable statistics, an estimated 22% of females of childbearing age abuse substances. Moreover, approximately 25% of pregnant women use two or more teratogenic substances. Among pregnant substance abusers, 91% use heroin, methadone, or other opiates, 35% use stimulants, 25% cannabis, 22% benzodiazepines, and 7% hallucinogens—with 38% injecting their main drug (McElhatton, 2000).

Possible effects of commonly abused legal and illegal substances are presented in Exhibit 2.7. Cocaine and crack use is connected with increased chances of the placenta separating from the uterine wall, which can lead to maternal and fetal death, intracranial hemorrhage for both mother and newborn, urinary and genital defects in the neonate, and increased risk of SIDS as well as neonatal withdrawal that can last for several weeks. Amphetamines are associated with increased rates of spontaneous abortions and possible heart defects. Ecstasy seems to increase the likelihood of cardiovascular and musculoskeletal anomalies in the fetus (McElhatton, 2000). **Fetal alcohol syndrome (FAS),** a complex of anomalies, is the leading cause of mental retardation worldwide (Abel & Sokol, 1987; Beckman & Brent, 1994; LaDue, 2001; Light, Irvine, & Kjerulf, 1996). Pregnant substance abusers in general have a higher incidence of miscarriages, prematurity, and LBW, as well as STDs, tuberculosis, and AIDS, than other pregnant women. Furthermore, the neonate who was exposed prenatally to substances like alcohol, tobacco, and illegal drugs is 46 times more likely than normal to die in the

Exhibit 2.7
Commonly Abused Drugs and Fetal Effects

	Alcohol	Cocaine	Amphetamines	Cigarettes	Heroin
Abortion	X	X	X		X
Stillbirth	X	X	X		X
Prematurity	X	X	X	X	X
Intrauterine growth retardation	X	X	X	X	X
Respiratory distress	X	X			X
Withdrawal	X	X	X		X
Fine motor problems	X				X
Malformations	X	X	X		X
Developmental delays	X	X	X		X

1st month of life (Larson, 1995). Possible effects of commonly abused legal and illegal substances are presented in Exhibit 2.7.

Interestingly, some individuals appear to be "resistant" to teratogens like alcohol, and no teratogen causes defects all the time (Opitz, 1996). In fact, about 60% of babies born to alcoholic mothers show no signs of being affected by their mother's drinking (Opitz, 1996).

Still, teratogenic substances should be avoided during pregnancy to increase the chances of a healthy outcome. Social workers are collaborating with other professionals to provide public education to women in the childbearing years about the teratogenic effects of alcohol, tobacco, and other drugs.

Mothers With Eating Disorders. During the past 15 years, there has been a striking increase in eating disorders, primarily anorexia nervosa (self-imposed starvation) and bulimia (binging and purging), among U.S. teenagers and women (Pirke, Dogs, Fichter, & Tuschil, 1988). Because eating disorders frequently result in menstrual disorders, reduced sex drive, and infertility, pregnancy is frequently overlooked in this population (Bonne, Rubinoff, & Berry, 1996). Apparently, however, some women first develop eating disorders during pregnancy, perhaps in response to their weight gain and change in shape (Fahy, 1991).

An eating disorder is likely to result in poor pregnancy outcomes, such as fetuses **small for gestational age (SGA)**, LBW infants, and increased neonatal mortality (Bakan, Birmingham, & Goldner, 1991; Pomeroy & Mitchell, 1989). Premature delivery occurs at twice the expected rate, and perinatal mortality is six times the expected rate. The length of time the mother is able to breastfeed her infant has not been found to be affected by eating disorders, however (Brinch, Isager, & Tolstrup, 1988). Social workers who work regularly with women with eating disorders or with pregnant women need to be knowledgeable about the possibilities for poor pregnancy outcomes in pregnant women with eating disorders.

Lesbian Mothers. In recent years, the number of lesbians who are or who desire to be mothers has increased, but these women continue to face many obstacles and dilemmas (Gartrell et al., 1996). More than one third of lesbians are estimated to be mothers, and it is reasonable to assume that more would choose motherhood if the larger society offered greater support.

Perhaps one of the major risk factors for lesbian mothers is the potential for rejection or disapproval by the members of a society with negative views of homosexuality (King, 2001; Laird & Green, 1996). Conception, pregnancy, and childbirth demand role realignments for heterosexual couples and create stress. These same dynamics occur in lesbian couples, but they often face a greater challenge due to society's reluctance to recognize lesbian relationships.

Lesbian mothers face other challenges. Despite increased availability of alternative fertilization methods, many health care providers remain insensitive to issues that lesbian women may face when using them. Lesbian women who become pregnant may lack the support of family and friends, and birthing facilities may not allow female partners to be involved with the birth process. In addition, employers may limit access to, or reluctantly provide, resources such as medical benefits for pregnancy and childbirth (Laird & Green, 1996).

Yet, lesbian mothers have advantages that some other special parent populations do not have. A study of 27 lesbian mothers indicated that these family households are strong, individual functioning is good, and a variety of parenting skills are common (Dundas & Kaufman, 2000). Other studies of lesbian mothers report that all respondents sought prenatal care and that 89 to 100% attended childbirth education classes (Gartrell et al., 1996; Harvey, Carr, & Bernheime, 1989). Social workers can help health care providers recognize both the strengths of and the special challenges facing lesbian mothers.

Mothers and Fathers With Disabilities. One in five persons reports a physical or mental disability, and over half of these people are female (Jans & Stoddard, 1999). People with physical or mental disabilities tend to be perceived as "asexual," and thus conception, pregnancy, and childbirth frequently are not considered relevant issues for them (Cole & Cole, 1993; Sawin, 1998). This is not the case. For one thing, not all disabilities negatively affect reproduction. For example, 75% of women with rheumatoid arthritis experience remission of disease during pregnancy (Connie, 1988; Corbin, 1987). Other interesting data come from a 4-year national study funded by the National Institutes of Health (NIH), which compared 506 women with physical disabilities to 444 women without a disability. Women with disabilities reported a 32% marriage rate, compared to 36% of nondisabled women. For women living with partners, 71% of those with disabilities were sexually active at the time of the study, compared to 96% of nondisabled women. Birthrates were 38% for women with disabilities and 51% for nondisabled women (Nosek, 1995).

The NIH study found a remarkable difference between the two populations in the use of contraception, however, because women with disabilities have more limited options. For example, the use of barrier methods may be compromised by limited use of hands. Overall, women with disabilities were less likely to use oral contraception, possibly because their access to it was limited. Disabled and nondisabled women did not differ in their rates of tubal ligation and partner vasectomy, but women with disabilities were much more likely to have had a hysterectomy (22% versus 12%), the most invasive and risky surgical sterilization option (Nosek, 1995).

Perhaps one of the most striking findings of the NIH study was that 10% of women with disabilities reported abuse—such as coerced sterilization—by health care providers, compared to only 3% of nondisabled women. In addition, for the women who had access to medical care, 37% of women with disabilities perceived their physician as uninformed about the effect of their disability on reproductive health (Nosek, 1995).

Women with disabilities who do decide to become pregnant must be monitored more closely than nondisabled women to offset the increased risks associated with the disability. Although women with disabilities have higher rates of complications during pregnancy (Nosek, Howland, Rintal, Young, & Chanpong, 1997), with careful planning they can make the adaptations needed to care for newborns. For a summary of the effects of selected disabilities on conception, pregnancy, and childbirth, see Sawin (1998).

Despite public distaste for the practice, some persons with disabilities continue to be targets of involuntary sterilization (Rock, 1996; Smith & Polloway, 1993; Waxman, 1994). Professionals do not agree about how to handle the reproductive rights of individuals with severe inheritable disorders or with limited capacity to care for a child (Brantlinger, 1992). Many do agree, however, that physical, environmental, interpersonal, informational, and policy barriers leave people with disabilities disenfranchised from both the reproductive health system and other reproductive options.

Not surprisingly, a 1997 study identified reproductive health as one of the four top research priorities for disabled persons (Berkeley Planning Associates, 1997). As society slowly begins to recognize persons with disabilities as full members of society, some of the negative implications of conception, pregnancy, and childbirth with this population may be dispelled. Meanwhile, however, social workers, who have traditionally been a voice for this population, must not let that voice be lost at this stage of the life course.

Incarcerated Pregnant Women. An estimated one out of four women inmates are pregnant when they are incarcerated or have delivered a baby within the preceding year (Wooldredge & Masters, 1993). These women and their babies are at particular risk because most of the mothers are poor, many abuse drugs both prior to and after incarceration, many have severe physical and mental health problems, and most lack education and skills related to pregnancy, childbirth, and prenatal care (Kaplan & Sasser, 1996). The children of these women face high rates of perinatal mortality and illness, intrauterine growth retardation, and other problems associated with drug abuse (Cordero, Hines, Shibley, & Landon, 1992; Egley, Miller, Granados, & Ingram-Fogel, 1992).

With the rise in the proportion of women who are incarcerated, services for pregnant inmates have increased some, considerably improving the odds of good pregnancy outcomes (U.S. Federal Bureau of Prisons, 1998). In fact, one study found that the birth weights of children of incarcerated mothers were no different from those of nonincarcerated women; rather, longer incarceration was related to higher birth weights (Martin, Kim, Kupper, Meyer, & Hays, 1997). However, good prenatal care is typically found only in larger prisons associated with academic medical centers (Cordero et al., 1992; Gabel & Johnston, 1995). Pregnant women in other types of facilities are at greater risk.

Regardless of the type of facility, prison life in general is stressful, and thus pregnant inmates cannot count their environment as a protective factor (Young, 1996). Alternative living environments that provide adequate services are a possible means of improving pregnancy outcomes (Blinn, 1997; Bloom & Steinhart, 1993; Siefert & Pimlott, 2001; Stevens & Patton, 1998).

HIV-Infected Mothers. The United Nations program on HIV and AIDS (UNAIDS) estimates that over 600,000 mother-to-newborn HIV transmissions occur each year, with the numbers increasing rapidly, especially in Southeast Asia. In the United States, however, there are fewer newborns infected in 1 year than in 1 morning in the rest of the world; approximately 200 infants in the United States were born with HIV in 2000 (Medical Letter, 2002).

Elective cesarean sections reduce the risk of mother-to-infant transmission by 50%, and the use of Antiretroviral (AZT) has reduced the rate of transmission to less than 5% (McIntyre & Gray, 2002). However, the cost of either treatment is prohibitive to women in third world countries. What is typically used to prevent transmission—cleansing of the birth canal during labor—has not proved effective.

Breastfeeding is an area of special concern. HIV can be transmitted through breast milk and is significant in the high rates of this disease in Africa, but accurate data regarding the rate of transmission are difficult to obtain. To further complicate the issue, infant mortality rates have increased in poor countries where formula feeding has been implemented—partially due to contaminated water supplies used to make the formula. The United Nations suggests that in poorer countries, breastfeeding is a better option because it does help prevent infectious disease and malnutrition (Guay & Ruff, 2001; Kent, 2002). However, it also recommends that women be informed about their choices for infant feeding.

The standard protocol for neonates born to HIV-positive mothers is to treat them with AZT for 6 weeks, whether or not they test positive. However, this medication is not widely available in poorer countries, increasing the number of children who will die from AIDS. Perhaps the lack of AZT is not all bad: recent studies are suggesting that AZT is a teratogen, causing mutations of the DNA. Fortunately, an explosion in research in this area is leading to newer, less dangerous medications (Klotter, 2002; McIntyre & Gray, 2002).

The news is encouraging in other ways too. In 1994, the American Society for Reproductive Medicine discouraged women who were HIV-positive from having children because transmission of the virus could not be prevented. In 2002, the same group said that the recent advances in therapies greatly reduce the rate of transmission, and withdrew their recommendations to avoid childbearing. The Society (2002) suggested cesarean sections, bottle feeding, special sperm washing and testing if the father is HIV-positive, and counseling if both mother and father are HIV-positive, due to the possibility of orphaning the baby (Medical Letter, 2002).

The social worker must be aware of the complexities of this issue as well as societal prejudices against women with HIV infections. Working to increase HIV awareness and promote clear notification of HIV status will continue to be important social work roles in the next decade.

IMPLICATIONS FOR SOCIAL WORK PRACTICE

Social workers practicing with persons at the stage of life concerned with conception, pregnancy, and childbirth should follow these principles:

- Respond to the complex interplay of biopsychosocial and spiritual factors related to conception, pregnancy, and childbirth.
- When working with any client of childbearing age, always consider the possibility of conception, pregnancy, and childbirth, their potential outcomes, and their impact on the changing person/environment configuration.
- Identify the needs of vulnerable or at-risk groups, and work to provide services for them. For example, structure birth education classes to include not only family but family-like persons, and provide interpreters for the hearing impaired.
- Actively pursue information about particular disabilities and their impact on conception, pregnancy, and childbirth.
- Acquire and apply skills in advocacy, education about reproductive options, consumer guidance in accessing services, and case management.

- Assume a proactive stance when working with at-risk populations to limit undesirable reproductive outcomes and to help meet their reproductive needs. At-risk groups include adolescents, low-income women, women involved with substance abuse, women with eating disorders, and women with disabilities who lack access to financial, physical, psychological, and social services.
- Assist parents faced with a potential genetic anomaly to gain access to genetic screenings, prenatal diagnosis, postnatal diagnosis, treatment, and genetic counseling.
- Involve parents in decision making to the greatest extent possible by delaying nonurgent decisions until parents have had a chance to adjust to any crisis and acquire the necessary information to make an informed decision.
- Establish collaborative relationships with other professionals to enhance and guide assessment and intervention.
- Identify and use existing programs that provide education and prenatal services to women, such as the WIC program, particularly for those most at risk of undesirable outcomes.

Key Terms

amniocentesis
amnioinfusion
Apgar score
assisted reproductive technologies (ART)
birthing center
bonding
Braxton-Hicks contractions
chorion villi testing (CVT)
chromosomes
curettage abortion
dominant genes
ectopic pregnancy
embryo
family pluralism
fertilization
fertilization age
fetal alcohol syndrome (FAS)
fetal differentiation
fetal viability
fetus
gamete intrafallopian tube transfer (GIFT)
genes
gene replacement therapy
genetic counseling
genetic heterogeneity
genetic liability
genotype
germ cell

gestation
gestational age
infertility
interactive genes
intrauterine fetal death (IUFD)
intrauterine insemination (IUI)
in vitro fertilization (IVF)
lightening
low birth weight (LBW)
miscarriage
multifactorial inheritance
multigravida
neonate
neonatology
phenotype
pleiotropy principle
premature birth
preservation and gestational surrogacy
primipara
protective factors
quickening
recessive genes
risk factors
replacement hormonal therapy (RHT)
Roe v. Wade
sensitive period
sex chromosome
sex-linked trait
small for gestational age (SGA)
spontaneous abortion
stillbirth
teratogen
ultrasonography (ultrasound)
vacuum curettage
variable expressivity
very low birth weight (VLBW)
Webster v. Reproductive Health Services
Women, Infants, and Children (WIC) program
zygote

Active Learning

1. Select one topic from the chapter outline. Identify a community service setting that addresses the chosen topic. Interview a professional from that setting, preferably a social worker, to solicit the following information:

- Services provided
- The role of the social worker
- The roles of the other disciplines
- The mechanisms used to acquire new knowledge on the topic
- The challenges and rewards of social work practice in that setting

2. Locate the National Association of Social Workers Code of Ethics on the organization's Web site at www.naswdc.org. Choose an ethical issue from the list below.

Using the Code of Ethics as a guide, what values and principles can you identify to guide decision making related to the issue you have chosen?

- Should all women, regardless of marital status or income, be provided with the most current technologies to conceive when they are unable to do so?
- What are the potential issues of preservation and gestational surrogacy in terms of social justice and diversity?
- Should pregnant women who abuse substances be incarcerated to protect the developing fetus?
- Do adoptive parents have the right to know the genetic background of an adoptee?
- Which genes should be selected for reproduction?
- Will persons who are poor be economically disadvantaged in the use of genetic information?

3. Select one of the three life journeys that introduced this chapter: Tahesha Gibbons, the Randolphs, or the Gerekes. Identify the risk and protective factors related to their conception, pregnancy, and childbirth experience. Then change one factor in the story; for example, assume Tahesha was age 20 when she became pregnant. How might that alter her life course and that of her child? Then try changing another factor; for example, assume Tahesha had completed 3 years of college. How does that change the trajectory of her story? Try again; for example, assume Tahesha was being treated for depression when she became pregnant. Again, how does that factor alter her life course and that of her child?

Web Resources

Information About Pregnancy

www.thebabiesplanet.com/bbpregna.htm

Site presented by The Last Planet Internet Services contains links to various sites concerning pregnancy and childbirth.

Childbirth.org

www.childbirth.org

Award-winning site maintained by Robin Elise Weiss contains information on birth plans, cesareans, complications, episiotomies, feeding, fertility, health, and labor, and a FAQ section.

Family and Social Demographic Data

www.census.gov

Site presented by the U.S. Census Bureau provides current census data related to the family and social context of conception, pregnancy, and childbirth.

Infertility Center

www.womens-health.com/InfertilityCenter

Site presented by Women's Health Interactive and the National Council on Women's Health contains information on human reproduction, assessment of pregnancy factors, infertility evaluations and treatments, emotional aspects of infertility, and a FAQ section.

Planned Parenthood

www.plannedparenthood.org

Official site of the Planned Parenthood Federation of America Inc. contains information about Planned Parenthood, health and pregnancy, birth control, abortion, STDs, pro-choice advocacy, and a guide for parents.

Human Genome Project

www.ornl.gov/hgmis

Site of the Human Genome Program of the U.S. Department of Energy that has sequenced the genes present in human DNA.

Center for Research on Women with Disabilities (CROWD)

www.bcm.tmc.edu/crowd

Site presented by the Center for Research on Women with Disabilities contains reports on women with disabilities, educational materials, and links to other research on women with disabilities.

CHAPTER 3

Infancy and Toddlerhood

Debra J. Woody

CHAPTER 3

Infancy and Toddlerhood

Debra J. Woody
University of Texas at Arlington

Why is it important for social workers to know about brain development?

Why is it important for social workers to understand attachment issues between infants and parents?

How do day care provisions in the United States compare to those in other countries?

Key Ideas

As you read this chapter, take note of these central ideas:

1. Although growth and development in young children have some predictability and logic, the timing and expression of many developmental skills vary from child to child and depend in part on the environment and culture in which the child is raised.
2. Physical growth, brain development, and the development of sensory abilities and motor skills are all important aspects of physical development in infants and toddlers.
3. According to Piaget, infants and toddlers are in the sensorimotor stage of cognitive development, responding to what they hear, see, taste, touch, smell, and feel.
4. Erikson describes two stages of psychosocial development relevant to infants and toddlers, each with its own central task: trust versus mistrust (birth to age 1½) and autonomy versus shame and doubt (1½ to 3 years).
5. The attachment relationship between infants and toddlers and their caregivers serves as the model for future relationships.

6. Researchers have found that children who live in poor economic conditions are at high risk for delays in physical, cognitive, and emotional development.

7. Prenatal care, diet, education, and social support are thought to influence infant mortality rates in the United States.

CASE STUDY 3.1

HOLLY'S EARLY ARRIVAL

Although Marilyn Hicks had been very careful with her diet, exercise, and prenatal care during pregnancy, Holly arrived at 23 weeks' gestation, around 6 months into the pregnancy. Initially she weighed 3 pounds 11 ounces, but she quickly lost the 11 ounces. Immediately after birth, Holly was whisked away to the neonatal unit in the hospital, and her parents had just a quick peek at her. Your first contact with Marilyn and Martin Hicks, an Anglo couple, was in the neonatal unit. Although Marilyn Hicks began to cry when you spoke with her, overall both parents seemed to be coping well and had all their basic needs met at that time. You left your business card with them and instructed them to call you if they needed anything.

Despite her early arrival, Holly did not show any signs of medical problems, and after 6 weeks in the neonatal unit, her parents were able to take her home. You allowed the newly formed Hicks family time to adjust, and in keeping with the policy of the neonatal program, you scheduled a follow-up home visit within a few weeks.

When you arrive at the house, Marilyn Hicks meets you at the door in tears. She states that taking care of Holly is much more than she imagined. Holly cries "constantly" and does not seem to respond to Mrs. Hicks's attempts to comfort her. In fact, Mrs. Hicks thinks that Holly cries even louder when her mother picks her up or tries to cuddle with her. Mrs. Hicks is very disappointed, because she considers herself to be a nurturing person. She is unsure how to respond to Holly's "rejection of her." The only time Holly seems to respond positively is when Mrs. Hicks breastfeeds her.

Mrs. Hicks has taken Holly to the pediatrician on several occasions and has discussed her concerns. The doctor told her that nothing is physically wrong with Holly and that Mrs. Hicks has to be more patient.

Mrs. Hicks confides in you that she read some horrifying material on the Internet about premature infants. According to the information she read, premature infants often have difficulty bonding with their caretaker, which in some children may ultimately result in mental health and emotional problems. Mrs. Hicks is concerned that this is the case with Holly.

CASE STUDY 3.1

You note that in addition to her fears, Mrs. Hicks must be exhausted. Her husband returned to work shortly after the baby came home, and Mrs. Hicks has not left the house since then. She tried taking a break once when her aunt came for a visit, but Holly cried so intensely during this time that her aunt refused to be left alone with Holly again. As the social worker, you will help Mrs. Hicks cope with the powerful feelings that have been aroused by Holly's premature birth, get any needed clarification on Holly's medical condition, and find ways to get Mrs. Hicks a break from caregiving. You will also want to help her to begin to feel more confident about her ability to parent Holly.

CASE STUDY 3.2

MYON'S ISOLATION

During the first few weeks of your Human Behavior and Social Environment class, all your students are asked to tell "their story." Eventually you call on Myon, a student who identifies herself as Korean. You immediately notice that her English is okay but you must listen attentively to understand.

Myon explains that this is her 2nd year in the United States. She moved here with her husband, who is an engineer and works for a major company. She recently gave birth to a daughter who is 8 months old. Myon was a full-time student last year but is only taking one class this semester because she must care for her daughter. Myon states that although the birth of her daughter is a great event for her, she feels all alone. If she were still in Korea, her mother and aunts would help her raise her daughter. She is hoping that eventually her mother can come for an extended stay, but the immigration department is still considering her application.

One of your students asks Myon how much her husband helps with caregiving. Myon blushes (even more than she already was) and states that she did not mean to imply that he was not helpful, but, she confesses, she views caregiving as mainly her responsibility. Other students eager to help ask her about day care or other possible child care arrangements. Myon has a friend, also from Korea, who baby-sits while Myon takes this one class, but again Myon articulates that caring for her daughter is her own responsibility. Myon smiles and looks relieved when you indicate that she can be seated.

Case Study 3.3

Demarcus's Violent Neighborhood

Ynecka Green is a 17-year-old African American single parent who needs help overcoming depression and anxiety. She has told you that she still cries each night about the death of both of her brothers in unrelated shootings. She always felt that her older brother, Marcus, would probably die at a young age because he had long been involved in "questionable" activities. He had skipped school since fifth grade and "hung out" with several convicted felons. At the time of his death, he was awaiting trial for a burglary in which a store attendant was killed. Even so, Ynecka and her parents were shocked when he was killed outside his parents' home in what appeared to be a drive-by shooting.

In contrast, Robert, Ynecka's younger brother, had been a good student. He was on the honor roll and was very excited about beginning junior high in the fall. He looked forward to all the additional activities junior high would offer—band, art classes, and the science fair. But his good grades and good behavior had not saved him either. The Green family had teased Robert about his "nosiness" and had warned him on several occasions that his curiosity would one day get him in trouble. And then he too was gunned down in front of his parents' home after happening upon an unrelated shooting. "If only he had not looked up and been able to identify the shooter, maybe then his life would have been spared," Ynecka thought to herself many times.

Robert seemed to be on his way to escaping from their drug-infested, high-crime neighborhood. Ynecka had been secretly hoping that once he made his way out, he would help her, and she too would have a better life. But she also loved her younger brother very much. Robert made her feel special because he spent many hours telling her great stories about African kings and queens, and once saved his allowance to buy her a plastic tiara.

Ynecka's heart has literally ached since Robert's death a year ago. The only thing that has kept her going is the birth of her child, Demarcus, 2 years ago. Ynecka has admitted to you, though, that she felt panic when she found out the baby was a boy. How would she be able to save him from the perils that had taken the lives of her brothers? Her fears have become barely controllable over the past month because she has noted the same "nosy" personality in her son that she saw in her brother Robert. Ynecka reports that Demarcus, now age 2, is curious about everything. He explores every corner of their home, and when out in public, he seems interested in everyone they meet. She fears that he too will eventually be a witness to the "wrong" event.

Healthy Development in Infants and Toddlers

We were all infants and toddlers once, but sometimes, in our work as social workers, we may find it hard to understand the experience of someone 2 years old or younger. (Young children are typically referred to as **infants** in the 1st year, but as they enter the 2nd year of life and become more mobile, they are usually called **toddlers,** from about 12 to 36 months of age.) As adults, we have become accustomed to communicating with words, and we are not always sure how to read the behaviors of the very young child. And we are not always sure how we are to behave with them. The best way to overcome these limitations, of course, is to learn what we can about the lives of infants and toddlers.

What must social workers know about biological age, psychological age, and social age to understand whether an infant or toddler's behavior is healthy or problematic?

In all three of the case studies at the beginning of this chapter, factors can be identified that may adversely affect the children's development. However, we must begin by understanding what is traditionally referred to as "normal" development. But because *normal* is a relative term with some judgmental overtones, we will use the term *healthy* instead.

Social workers employed in schools, hospitals, community mental health centers, and other public health settings are often approached by parents and teachers with questions about development in young children. To assess whether any of the children they bring to your attention require intervention, you must be able to distinguish between healthy and problematic development in three areas: physical, cognitive, and socioemotional development. As you will see, young children go through a multitude of changes in all three areas simultaneously. Inadequate development in any one of them—or in multiple areas—may have long-lasting consequences for the individual.

Keep in mind, however, that what is considered to be healthy is relative to environment and culture. Every newborn enters a world with distinctive features structured by the social setting that he or she encounters (Valsiner, 1989b). Therefore, all aspects of development must be considered in a cultural context.

To make the presentation of ideas about early childhood manageable, this chapter follows a traditional method of organizing the discussion by type of development: physical development, cognitive development, emotional development, and social development. In this chapter, emotional development and social development are combined under the heading Socioemotional Development. Of course, all these types of development and behavior are interdependent, and often the distinctions blur.

Physical Development

Newborns depend on others for basic physical needs. They must be fed, cleaned, and kept safe and comfortable until they develop the ability to do these things for themselves. At the same time, however, newborns have an amazing set of physical abilities and potentials right from the beginning.

With adequate nourishment and care, the physical growth of the infant is quite predictable. Most newborns weigh between 5 and 10 pounds at birth and are between 15 and 25 inches long. Infants grow very rapidly throughout the first 2 years of life, but the pace of growth slows a bit in toddlerhood. For example, infants double in weight by age 4 months, and by age 2 most infants are quadruple their original weight and double their original height (inches long). Thus, the average 2-year-old weighs between 20 and 40 pounds and is between 30 and 50 inches long.

As you can see, the size of individual infants and toddlers can vary quite a bit. Some of the difference is due to nutrition, exposure to disease, and other environmental factors; much of it is due to genetics. Some ethnic differences in physical development have also been observed. For example, Asian American children tend to be smaller than average, and African American children tend to be larger than average (Tanner, 1990).

Self-Regulation. Before birth, the bodily functions of the fetus were regulated by the mother's body. After birth, the infant must develop the capacity to engage in self-regulation (Shonkoff & Phillips, 2000). At first, the challenge is to regulate bodily functions, such as temperature control, sleeping, eating, and eliminating. That challenge is heightened for the premature or medically fragile infant, as Holly's mother is finding.

As any new parent will tell you, infants are not born with regular patterns of sleeping, eating, and eliminating. With maturation of the central nervous system in the first 3 months, and with lots of help from parents or other caregivers, the infant's rhythms of sleeping, eating, and eliminating become much more regular (Davies, 1999). A newborn usually sleeps about 16 hours a day, dividing that time evenly between day and night. Of course, this is not a good fit with the way adults organize their sleep lives. At the end of 3 months, most infants are sleeping 14 to 15 hours per day, primarily at night, with some well-defined nap times during the day. Parents also gradually shape infants' eating schedules so that they are eating mainly during the day.

What have you observed about how culture influences the parenting of infants and toddlers?

There are cultural variations in, and controversies about, the way caregivers shape the sleeping and eating behaviors of infants. In some cultures, infants sleep with parents, and in other cultures, infants are put to sleep in their own beds and often in their own rooms. In some cultures, putting an infant to sleep alone in a room is considered to be neglectful (Korbin, 1981). Chapter 2 outlined some of the cultural variations and controversies about breastfeeding versus bottle feeding. It is interesting to note that both breastfeeding and sleeping with parents induce shorter bouts of sleep and less sound sleep than the alternatives (Shonkoff & Phillips, 2000). Some researchers have speculated that the infant's lighter and shorter sleep pattern may protect against sudden infant death syndrome (SIDS). Of course, parents sleeping with infants must be aware of the hazard of rolling over and suffocating the infant. Luckily, parents have also been found to sleep less soundly when they sleep with infants (Shonkoff & Phillips, 2000).

Parents become less anxious as the infant's rhythms become more regular and predictable. At the same time, if the caregiver is responsive and dependable, the infant becomes less anxious and begins to develop the ability to wait to have needs met.

There are cultural variations in beliefs about how to respond when infants cry and fuss, whether to soothe them or leave them to learn to soothe themselves. When parents do attempt to soothe infants, however, they seem to use the same methods across cultures: "They say something, touch, pick up, search for sources of discomfort, and then feed" (Shonkoff & Phillips, 2000, p. 100). Infants who have been consistently soothed usually begin to develop the ability to soothe themselves after 3 or 4 months. This ability is the precursor to struggles for self-control and mastery over powerful emotions that occur in toddlerhood.

Sensory Abilities. Full-term infants are born with a functioning **sensory system**—the senses of hearing, sight, taste, smell, touch, and sensitivity to pain—and these abilities continue to develop rapidly in the first few months. Indeed, in the early months the sensory system seems to function at a higher level than the motor system, which allows movement. The sensory system allows infants, from the time of birth, to participate in and adapt to their environments. A lot of their learning happens through listening and watching (Bornstein, 1995). The sensory system is an interconnected system, with various sensory abilities working together to give the infant multiple sources of information about the world.

Hearing is the earliest link to the environment; in the uterus the fetus is sensitive to auditory stimulation. Newborns show a preference for their mother's voice over other female voices (De Casper & Fifer, 1980). Young infants can distinguish changes in loudness, pitch, and location of sounds (Kuhl, 1987), and they appear to be particularly sensitive to language sounds.

The newborn's vision improves rapidly during the first 4 months. By about the age of 4 months, the infant sees objects the same way that an adult would. Of course, infants do not have the same cognitive associations with objects that adults have. Infants respond to a number of visual dimensions, including depth, brightness, movement, color, and distance. Human faces have particular appeal for newborns. One to 2 days after birth, infants are able to discriminate among, and even imitate, happy, sad, and surprised expressions, but this ability wanes after a few weeks (Field, Woodson, Greenberg, & Cohen, 1982). By 3 months, most infants are able to distinguish a parent's face from the face of a stranger (Zucker, 1985). Some researchers have found that infants are distressed by a lack of facial movement in the people they look at (Stack & Muir, 1992).

Taste and smell begin to function in the uterus, and newborns can differentiate sweet, bitter, sour, and salty tastes. Sweet tastes seem to have a calming effect on newborns (Blass & Ciaramitaro, 1994). Breastfed babies are particularly sensitive to their mother's body odors.

Both animal and human research tells us that touch plays a very important role in infant development. In many cultures, swaddling, or wrapping a baby snugly in a blanket, is used to soothe a fussy newborn. We also know that gentle handling, rocking, stroking, and cuddling are all soothing to an infant. Regular gentle rocking and stroking have been very effective in soothing low birth weight (LBW) babies, who may have underdeveloped central nervous systems. Infants also use touch to learn about their world and their own bodies. Young infants use their mouths for exploring their worlds, but by 6 months of age, infants can make controlled use of their hands to explore objects in their environment (Blass & Ciaramitaro, 1994).

There is clear evidence that from the first days of life, babies feel pain. Recently, pediatric researchers have been studying newborn reactions to medical procedures such as heel sticks. One researcher found that newborns who undergo repeated heel sticks learn to anticipate pain and develop a stronger reaction to pain than other infants (Taddio, Shah, Gilbert-Macleod, & Katz, 2002). These findings are leading pediatricians to reconsider their stance on the use of pain medications with newborns.

Reflexes. Although dependent on others, newborns are equipped from the start with tools for survival that are involuntary responses to simple stimuli, called **reflexes**. Reflexes aid the infant in adapting to the environment outside the womb.

Newborns have two critical reflexes:

1. *Rooting reflex.* When you gently stroke infants' cheeks or the corners of their mouth with a finger, they will turn their head in the direction of the touch and open their mouth in an attempt to suck the finger. This reflex aids in feeding, because it guides the infants to the nipple.

2. *Sucking reflex.* When a nipple or some other suckable object is presented to the infant, the infant sucks it. This reflex is another important tool for feeding.

Many infants would probably perish without the rooting and sucking reflexes. Imagine the time and effort it would require for one feeding if they did not have them. Instead, infants are born with the ability to take in nutriment.

Reflexes disappear at identified times during infancy (see Exhibit 3.1). Both the rooting reflex and sucking reflex disappear between 2 and 4 months (Sroufe, Cooper, & DeHart, 1996). By this time, the infant has mastered the voluntary act of sucking and is therefore no longer in need of the reflexive response. Several other infant reflexes appear to have little use now, but probably had some specific survival purposes in earlier times.

Reflexes are important in the evaluation of neurological functioning. The absence of reflexes can indicate a serious developmental disorder. Given Holly's early arrival, her reflex responses were thoroughly evaluated.

EXHIBIT 3.1
Infant Reflexes

Reflex	Description	Visible
Sucking	The infant instinctively sucks any object of appropriate size that is presented to it.	First 2 to 4 months
Rooting	The head turns in the direction of a stimulus when the cheek is touched. The infant's mouth opens in an attempt to suck.	First 3 months
Moro/Startle	The arms thrust outward when the infant is released in midair, as if attempting to regain support.	First 5 months
Swimming	When placed face down in water, the infant makes paddling, swimlike motions.	First 3 months
Stepping	When the infant is held in an upright position with the feet placed on a firm surface, the infant moves the feet in a walking motion.	First 3 months
Blinking	The eyes blink in response to light, air, and other stimuli.	Lifetime
Grasping	The infant grasps objects placed in its hand.	First 4 months
Babinski	The toes spread when the soles of the feet are stroked.	First year

How do these motor skills help to promote a sense of human agency in making choices?

Motor Skills. The infant gradually advances from reflex functioning to motor functioning. The development of **motor skills**—the ability to move and manipulate—occurs in a more or less orderly, logical sequence. It begins with simple actions such as lifting the chin and progresses to more complex acts such as walking, running, and throwing. Infants usually crawl before they walk.

Motor development is somewhat predictable, in that children tend to reach milestones at about the same age. Typical ages for some significant developmental milestones are listed in Exhibit 3.2. Remember, however, that development of motor skills varies from child to child. Many parents, for example, become concerned if their child has not attempted to walk unassisted by age 1. However, some children walk alone at age 9 months; others do not even attempt to walk until age 15 months.

The development of motor skills (and most other types of skills, for that matter) is a continuous process. Children progress from broad capacities to more specific refined abilities. For example, toddlers progress from eating cereal with their fingers to eating with a spoon.

EXHIBIT 3.2 Selected Developmental Milestones

Milestone	Age of Onset
Sits unassisted	8 to 12 months
Pulls to a standing position	8 to 12 months
Feeds self with fingers	8 to 10 months
Waves "bye-bye"	8 to 10 months
Crawls	10 to 12 months
Drinks from a cup	10 to 12 months
Uses spoon proficiently	12 to 18 months
Scribbles with crayon	12 to 18 months
Walks independently	18 months
Walks and runs well	2 to 3 years

Parents are usually quite patient with their child's motor development. However, toilet training (potty training) is often a source of stress and uncertainty for new parents. Until recently, many child development experts recommended that babies be potty trained during the 1st year of life. Consequently, many parents exercised strong measures, including scolding and punishment, to ensure timely toilet training. Even now, many grandparents proudly report that they tied their infants to the potty chair at times of predicted elimination (after eating, for example) until the child was able to master the skill. T. Berry Brazelton (1983), one of the best known pediatricians in the United States, has endeavored to change this negative perspective. He advocates that parents begin potty training during the 2nd year of life, during the lull time after standing and walking have been accomplished. Only then, he says, is the infant physiologically and psychologically ready to master this skill. By age 3, most children have mastered toilet training, but even 5-year-olds are still prone to soiling accidents.

Culture and ethnicity appear to influence motor development in infants and toddlers. For example, African American and Hispanic children may develop motor skills at a faster rate than do European American children of the same age. One extensive series of studies compared African American, Hispanic, and white families of similar socioeconomic status (Bartz & Levine,1978). The researchers attributed ethnic differences in motor ability to different parental expectations. African American and Hispanic parents expected their children to become more independent earlier. They therefore encouraged skills that lead to independence, such as walking, self-feeding, and potty training. Parents in violent neighborhoods like the one in which Demarcus lives may worry that advanced motor skills can get a toddler into trouble.

The Growing Brain. In recent years, we have been bombarded with media reports about new brain research that indicates the importance of the first 2 to 3 years of life for healthy brain development. These reports have gone so far as to suggest that the first

2 to 3 years are a sensitive period for brain development and have emphasized how important a nurturing environment is for stimulating brain development. The implication in these reports is that future brain growth will be seriously jeopardized if brain development is not adequately nurtured in the first 2 years.

However, behavioral scientists have criticized these media reports for exaggerating what is actually known about the developing brain (see, e.g., Bruer, 1999; Thompson & Nelson, 2001). They suggest that brain development is lifelong, and caution against overemphasizing the first 2 years. In fact, the brain maintains a great deal of **plasticity**, or susceptibility to influence, after early childhood (Thompson & Nelson, 2001). In addition, the prenatal period may be a more important period of brain development than the first 2 years after birth, because the basic architecture of the brain is laid down during that time, a time when the developing brain is very susceptible to environmental toxins.

What is known about brain development is that the human brain, like the brains of other primates, overproduces **synapses,** or neural connections, on a massive scale during early development (Huttenlocher & Kabholkar, 1997). The human newborn has more synapses than the human adult. The period of overproduction of synapses, or **blooming,** is followed by a period of **pruning,** or reduction, of the synapses to improve the efficiency of brain functioning. The blooming and pruning of synapses operate on different timetables in different regions of the brain. For example, overproduction of synapses in the visual cortex of the brain peaks in the 4th month after birth, and pruning in that region continues until sometime toward the end of the early childhood period (Huttenlocher and Kabholkar, 1997). By contrast, in the medial prefrontal cortex part of the brain, where higher-level cognition and self-regulation take place, synaptic blooming peaks at about 1 year of age, and pruning continues until middle to late adolescence.

The available evidence suggests that both genetic processes and early experiences with the environment influence the timing of brain development, but little is really known about the processes involved in humans (Thompson & Nelson, 2001). What is known is that exposure to speech in the 1st year expedites the discrimination of speech sounds. In addition, exposure to patterned visual information in the first few years of life is necessary for normal development of some aspects of vision. It is not as clear, however, whether emotional and cognitive development have similar sensitive periods.

How could these aspects of contemporary popular culture contribute to a cohort effect in parenting styles?

Parents are often advised in the media to talk to, sing to, play with, and otherwise provide stimulation to their infant in order to develop the brain. Such parenting efforts are beneficial because they are likely to promote secure attachments and an overall sense of well-being in the infant; they also enhance learning. But, contrary to media hype about listening to classical music and other such methods of infant stimulation, no magic bullets have been found for brain stimulation (Shonkoff & Phillips, 2000). What is clearer from the research is that good nutrition is essential for brain development, and exposure to environmental toxins is hazardous. There is also growing evidence from animal research that early emotional trauma and deprivation are detrimental to brain development (Shonkoff & Phillips, 2000; Teicher, 2002).

The best approach to enhancing brain development thus may be public health policies that ensure the physical and mental health of pregnant women and parents, minimize environmental toxins, and ensure adequate nutrition during early childhood (Thompson & Nelson, 2001; Zuckerman & Kahn, 2000). Barry Zuckerman and Robert Kahn (2000) emphasize that the "breadth and depth of the influence of women's physical and mental health on child health" (p. 101) get lost in the discussion of child welfare policy. Early vision and hearing screening is also important, because of the consequences of early sensory experience for brain development (Thompson and Nelson, 2001).

Childhood Immunizations. **Immunization,** also called vaccination or inoculation, is a method of administering microorganisms, bacteria, or viruses that have been modified or killed to protect humans from disease. Most vaccinations are administered by injection. The purpose of immunization is to stimulate the body's immune system to build a defense against a specific disease.

Important breakthroughs in vaccine development have led to eradication or near eradication of such life-threatening diseases as smallpox, poliomyelitis, diphtheria, and tetanus, and this has been a boon to health during infancy, toddlerhood, and early childhood (Betts, 2002). Since the early 1980s, the development of vaccines has proliferated, and vaccines have now been developed for much less serious childhood illnesses such as mumps, measles, rubella, and chickenpox. The development of these new vaccines has resulted in an increase in the total number of vaccinations administered to young children. The National Vaccine Information Center (NVIC) reports that currently 34 doses of 10 different vaccines are administered before the child's fifth birthday.

Since the 1980s, some child advocates have challenged both the quality and quantity of vaccinations being administered. They suggest that the increased use of immunization has become harmful to many children, both because of the quantity of vaccines being taken and because of inadequate vaccine safety research. Congressman Dan Burton, from Indiana, joined with these advocacy groups to argue for vaccine reform by the federal government. His interest in the issue of vaccines developed when a granddaughter became seriously ill after receiving a hepatitis B shot and a grandson became autistic at age 14 months after receiving nine vaccines on one day (Betts, 2002).

Three vaccines have been targeted by child advocates as most questionable: the hepatitis B vaccine; the measles, mumps, rubella (MMR) vaccine; and the pertussis (whooping cough) portion of the diphtheria, pertussis, tetanus (DPT) vaccine. The hepatitis B vaccine has been linked to a number of serious health problems, and in 1998, France became the first country to discontinue requirement of hepatitis B vaccination for school-age children. Some researchers have linked the pertussis portion of the DPT to SIDS. The MMR vaccine is suspected as playing a role in the rapid increase of autism since the 1980s, an increase from 1 in 2,500 children before 1980 to 1 in 150 children currently (NVIC, n.d.). The practice of adding thimerosol as a preservative in multidose vaccines has been a particular concern of the child advocacy groups. Thimerosol is 49% mercury, and mercury is known to cause neurological damage. Mercury in vaccines was banned in the United Kingdom, Finland, and Sweden by 1995 and in the United States in 1999.

Most parents are unaware of the immunization controversy, but the debate over immunization safety creates hard decisions for those parents who are aware. They want to protect their children from the harmful effects of disease, but they do not welcome potential harms from vaccines. Some researchers argue that the benefits of immunizations outweigh the hazards, and many health care workers fear the public health consequences if parents begin to avoid immunizing their young children (Trifiletti, 2001). Many public school systems do not allow children to be admitted without up-to-date vaccinations. Luckily, both scientists and government reformers are currently investigating the issue of vaccine safety as this book is being written. On the basis of the above discussion about early brain development, vaccine safety is an important issue in infancy and toddlerhood. Some infants and toddlers will be more vulnerable than others to multiple doses of multiple vaccines.

Cognitive Development

How do the drives to learn and be in interaction with the environment promote interdependence?

As the brain develops, so does its ability to process and store information and to solve problems. These abilities are known as **cognition**. When we talk about how fast a child is learning, we are talking about cognitive development. Researchers now describe the infant as "wired to learn," and agree that infants have an intrinsic drive to learn and to be in interaction with their environment (Shonkoff & Phillips, 2000). A central element of cognition is language, which facilitates both thinking and communicating. Exhibit 3.3 lists some milestones in cognitive development.

Piaget's Stages of Cognitive Development. To assess children's cognitive progress, many people use the concepts developed by the best-known cognitive development theorist, Jean Piaget (1952). Piaget believed that cognitive development occurs in successive stages, determined by the age of the child. His overall contention was that as a child grows and develops, cognition changes not only in quantity but also in quality.

Piaget used the metaphor of a slow-motion movie to explain his theory, which is summarized in Exhibit 3.4 as follows:

1. **Sensorimotor stage** (ages birth to 2 years). Infants at this stage of development can look at only one frame of the movie at a time. When the next picture appears on the screen, infants focus on it and cannot go back to the previous frame.

EXHIBIT 3.3
Selected Milestones in Cognitive Development

Milestone	Age of Onset
Coos responsively	Birth to 3 months
Smiles responsively	3 to 4 months
Smiles at self in mirror	3 to 4 months
Laughs out loud	3 to 4 months
Plays peek-a-boo	3 to 4 months
Shows displeasure	5 to 6 months
Babbles	6 to 8 months
Understands simple commands	12 months
Follows directions	2 years
Puts two to three words together	2 years
Uses sentences	2 to 3 years

2. **Preoperational stage** (ages 2 to 7). Preschool children and children in early grades can remember (recall) the sequence of the pictures in the movie. They also develop **symbolic functioning**—the ability to use symbols to represent what is not present. However, they do not necessarily understand what has happened in the movie or how the pictures fit together.

3. **Concrete operations stage** (ages 7 to 11). Not until this stage can children run the pictures in the movie backward and forward to better understand how they blend to form a specific meaning.

4. **Formal operations stage** (ages 11 and beyond). Children gain the capacity to apply logic to various situations and to use symbols to solve problems. Adding to Piaget's metaphor, one cognitive scientist describes formal operations as the ability of the adolescent not only to understand the observed movie but also to add or change characters and create an additional plot or staging plan (Edwards, 1992).

The first of Piaget's stages applies to infants and toddlers. During the sensorimotor period, they respond to immediate stimuli—what they see, hear, taste, touch, and smell—and learning takes place through the senses and motor activities. Piaget suggests that infant and toddler cognitive development occurs in six substages during the sensorimotor period.

Substage 1: Reflex Activity (birth to 1 month). Because reflexes are what the infant can "do," they become the foundation to future learning. Reflexes are what infants build on.

EXHIBIT 3.4
Piaget's Stages of Cognitive Development

Stage	*Characteristics*
Sensorimotor (birth to 2 years)	Infant is egocentric; he or she gradually learns to coordinate sensory and motor activities and develops a beginning sense of objects existing apart from the self.
Preoperational (2 to 7 years)	The child remains primarily egocentric but discover rules (regularities) that can be applied to new incoming information. The child tends to overgeneralize rules, however, and thus makes many cognitive errors.
Concrete operations (7 to 11 years)	The child can solve concrete problems through the application of logical problem-solving strategies.
Formal operations (11 years and beyond)	The person becomes able to solve real and hypothetical problems using abstract concepts.

Substage 2: Primary Circular Reactions (1 to 4 months). During this stage, infants repeat (thus the term *circular*) behaviors that bring them a positive response and pleasure. The infant's body is the focus of the response; thus the term *primary*. If, for example, infants by chance hold their head erect or lift their chest, they will continue to repeat these acts because they are pleasurable. Infants also have limited anticipation abilities.

Substage 3: Secondary Circular Reactions (4 to 8 months). As in the second substage, the focus is on performing acts and behaviors that bring about a response. In this stage, however, the infant reacts to responses from the environment. If, for example, 5-month-old infants cause the rattle to sound inadvertently as their arms move, they will continue attempts to repeat this occurrence.

Substage 4: Coordination of Secondary Circular Reactions (8 to 12 months). The mastery of **object permanence** is a significant task during this stage. Piaget contended that around 9 months of age, toddlers develop the ability to understand that an object or a person exists even when they don't see it. Piaget demonstrated this ability by hiding a favored toy under a blanket. Infants are able to move the blanket and retrieve the toy. Object permanence is related to the rapid development of memory abilities during this period (Rovee-Collier, 1999). Two other phenomena are related to this advance in memory. **Stranger anxiety**, in which the infant reacts with fear and withdrawal to unfamiliar persons, has been found to occur at about

9 months across cultures. Many first-time parents comment, "I don't know what has gotten into her; she has always been so outgoing." **Separation anxiety** also becomes prominent in this period. The infant is able to remember previous separations and becomes anxious at the signs of an impending separation from parents. With time, the infant also learns that the parent always returns.

Substage 5: Tertiary Circular Reactions (12 to 18 months). During this stage, toddlers become more creative in eliciting responses and are better problem solvers. For example, if the first button on the talking telephone does not make it talk, they will continue to press other buttons on the phone until they find the correct one.

Substage 6: Mental Representation (18 months to 2 years). Piaget described toddlers in this stage as actually able to use thinking skills in that they retain mental images of what is not immediately in front of them. For example, the toddler will look in a toy box for a desired toy and move other toys aside that prohibit recovery of the desired toy. Toddlers can also remember and imitate observed behavior. For example, toddlers roll their toy lawn mower over the lawn, imitating their parents' lawn mowing.

As much as Piaget's work has been praised, it has also been questioned and criticized. Piaget constructed his theory based on his observations of his own three children. Thus, one question has been how objective he was and whether the concepts can really be generalized to all children. Also, Piaget suggested that his developmental model describes the "average" child, but he did not define or describe what he meant by average. Finally, Piaget also did not address the influence of environmental factors—such as culture, family, and significant relationships and friendships—on cognitive development.

Findings from more recent research have also called into question some aspects of Piaget's theory. For example, Piaget described young children as being incapable of object permanence until at least 9 months of age. However, infants as young as 3½ and 4½ months of age have been observed who are already proficient at object permanence (Baillargeon, 1987). Other researchers (Munakata, McClelland, Johnson, & Siegler, 1997) have found that although infants seem aware of hidden objects at 3½ months, they fail to retrieve those objects until about 8 months of age. These researchers suggest that cognitive skills such as object permanence may be multifaceted and gradually developed. Findings like these suggest using Piaget's model with caution. It remains, however, our most useful view of how cognition develops.

Prelanguage Skills. Some of the developmental milestones for language development are listed in Exhibit 3.3. Although infants communicate with their caretaker from the beginning (primarily by crying), language development truly begins around 2 months of age. These first sounds, cooing, are pleasing to most parents. By age

4 months, infants babble. Initially, these babbles are unrecognizable. Eventually, between 8 and 12 months, infants make gestures to indicate their desires. The babble sounds and gestures together, along with caretakers' growing familiarity with the infant's "vocabulary," make it easier for infants to communicate their desires. For example, 12-month-old infants may point to their bottle located on the kitchen cabinet and babble "baba." The caretaker soon learns that "baba" means "bottle."

By the age of 18 to 24 months, the toddler can speak between 50 and 200 words. Piaget asserts that children develop language in direct correlation to their cognitive skills. Thus, most of the words spoken at this age relate to people and significant objects in the toddler's environment. These include words such as "mama," "dada," "cat," and "sissy" (sister), for example. Toddlers' first words also include situational words such as "hot," "no," and "bye." Between 20 and 26 months, toddlers begin to combine two words together, also in tandem with growing cognitive abilities. For example, children can say "all gone" as they develop an understanding of object permanence (Berk, 2002).

Even with these skills, toddlers may be difficult to understand on occasion. Cindy, the mom of 24-month-old Steven, describes collecting her son from day care. During the trip home, Steven initiated conversation with Cindy by calling out "Mama." He began to "tell" her about something that Cindy assumes must have occurred during the day. Steven continued to babble to his mother with animation and laughs and giggles during the story. Although Cindy laughed at the appropriate moments, she was unable to understand most of what Steven was sharing with her.

The most important thing that adults can do to assist with language development is to provide opportunity for interactions. Adults can answer questions, provide information, explain plans and actions, and offer feedback about behavior. Adults can also read to infants and toddlers and play language games. The opportunity for interaction is important for deaf children as well as hearing children, but deaf children need interaction that involves hand and eye, as with sign language (Shonkoff & Phillips, 2000).

Children who are bilingual, or multilingual, from birth seem to develop language ability at the same pace as children who are monolingual (Shonkoff & Phillips, 2000). Of course, language ability in any language is not retained unless the environment provides an opportunity for using the language.

Socioemotional Development

Infants and toddlers face vital developmental tasks in the emotional arena (some of which are listed in Exhibit 3.5), as well as in the social arena. Development during these early ages may set the stage for socioemotional development during all other developmental ages. This section addresses these tasks.

Erikson's Theory of Psychosocial Development. Erik Erikson's (1950) theory explains socioemotional development in terms of eight consecutive, age-defined stages

EXHIBIT 3.5 Selected Milestones in Emotional Development

Milestone	Age
Emotional life centered on physical states. Exhibits distress, fear, and rage.	Newborn
Emotional life begins to be centered on relationships. Exhibits pleasure and delight.	3 months
Emotional life continues to be relational, but distinctions are made between those relationships, as in stranger anxiety and separation anxiety. Exhibits joy, fear, anxiety, and anger.	9 months
Emotional life becomes sensitive to emotional cues from other people. Exhibits a range of emotion from joy to rage.	End of first year
Emotional life becomes centered on regulation of emotional states.	Second and third year

Source: Based on Davies, 1999, and Shonkoff & Phillips, 2000.

of emotional development. Each stage requires the mastery of a developmental task. Mastery at each stage depends on mastery in the previous stages. If the "task facilitating factors" for a stage are absent, the individual will become stuck in that stage of development.

Each of Erikson's stages is overviewed in Exhibit 3.6 and discussed in the chapter about the part of the life course to which it applies. The following two stages are relevant to infants and toddlers:

How does the development of trust during infancy affect future relationships?

1. *Trust versus mistrust* (ages birth to 1½). The overall task of this stage is for infants to develop a sense that their needs will be met by the outside world and that the outside world is an okay place to be. In addition, the infant develops an emotional bond with an adult, which Erikson believes becomes the foundation for being able to form intimate, loving relationships in the future. Erikson argues the need for one consistent mother figure. The most important factor facilitating growth in this stage is consistency in having physical and emotional needs met: being fed when hungry, being kept warm and dry, and being allowed undisturbed sleep. In addition, the infant has to be protected from injury, disease, and so on, and receive adequate stimulation. Infants who develop mistrust at this stage become suspicious of the world and withdraw, react with rage, and have deep-seated feelings of dependency. These infants lack drive, hope, and motivation for continued growth. They cannot trust their environment and are unable

to form intimate relationships with others. Given Ynecka Green's view that the outside world is not a safe place, described at the beginning of the chapter, her young son, Demarcus, is at risk of developing feelings of mistrust.

How does the toddler's experience with autonomy contribute to the capacity for human agency?

2. *Autonomy versus shame and doubt* (ages 1½ to 3). A child with autonomy has a growing sense of self-awareness and begins to strive for independence and self-control. These children feel proud that they can perform tasks and exercise control over bodily functions. They relate well with close people in the environment and begin to exercise self-control in response to parental limits. To develop autonomy, children need firm limits for controlling impulses and managing anxieties, but at the same time still need the freedom to explore their environment. Exhibit 3.7 summarizes possible sources of anxiety for toddlers (Davies, 1999). Toddlers also need an environment rich with stimulating and interesting objects and with opportunities for freedom of choice. Adults must accept the child's bodily functions as normal and good and offer praise and encouragement to enhance the child's mastery of self-control. At the other end of the spectrum are children who doubt themselves. They fear a loss of love and are overly concerned about their parents' approval. These children are ashamed of their abilities and develop an unhealthy kind of self-consciousness.

Erikson does not address whether tasks that should be mastered in one stage can be mastered later if the facilitating factors—such as a dependable, nurturing caregiver—are introduced. At what point is it too late to undo psychosocial damage? Critics also question Erikson's emphasis on the process of individualization, through which children develop a strong identity separate from that of their family. Many believe this to be a North American, Western value and therefore not applicable to collectivistic societies such as many African and Asian societies or to collectivistic subcultures within society in the United States.

Emotional Control. Researchers have paid a lot of attention to the strategies infants develop to cope with intense emotions, both positive and negative ones. They have found that by the middle of the 2nd year, toddlers have built a repertoire of ways to manage strong emotions. They make active efforts to avoid or disregard situations that arouse strong emotions. They engage in reassuring self-talk. And they develop substitute goals if they become thwarted in goal-directed behavior (Shonkoff & Phillips, 2000).

You may not be surprised to learn that researchers have found that one of the most important elements in how an infant learns to manage strong emotions is the assistance provided by the caregiver for emotion management (Kopp, 1989). The child's temperament also makes a difference, as you will see in the next section.

Finally, there are cultural differences in expectations for management of emotions in infants. For example, Japanese parents try to shield their infants from the frustrations that would invite anger. In other words, some emotions are regulated by protecting the

Exhibit 3.6
Erikson's Stages of Psychosocial Development

Life Stage	Psychosocial Challenge	Characteristic
Infancy (birth to about 1 year)	Basic trust versus basic mistrust	Infants must form trusting relationships with caregivers or they will learn to distrust the world.
Toddlerhood (about 1 to 3 years)	Autonomy versus shame and doubt	Toddlers must develop self-confidence and a sense of mastery over themselves and their worlds and they use newly developed motor skills or they will develop shame and doubt about their inability to develop control.
Early childhood (3 to 5 years)	Initiative versus guilt	Young children must develop a growing capacity to plan and initiate actions or they may feel guilt about their taking initiative.
Middle childhood (6 to 11 years)	Industry versus inferiority	School-aged children must develop a sense of competence to master and complete tasks or they learn to feel inferior or incompetent.
Adolescence (11 to 20 years)	Identity versus role diffusion	Adolescents must develop a sense of who they are and where they are going in life or they become confused about their identity.
Young adulthood (21 to 40 years)	Intimacy versus isolation	Young adults must develop the capacity to commit to deep associations with others or they feel a sense of isolation.
Middle adulthood (40 to 65 years)	Generativity versus stagnation	Midlife adults must develop the capacity to transcend self-interest to guide the next generation or they feel stagnated.
Late adulthood (over 65 years)	Ego integrity versus despair	Older adults must find integrity and contentment in their final years by accepting their life as it has been or they feel a sense of despair.

Source: Based on Erikson, 1950, 1978.

child from situations that would arouse them (Miyake, Campos, Kagan, & Bradshaw, 1986). There are also cultural differences in how much independence infants and toddlers are expected to exercise in managing emotions. In one study comparing

EXHIBIT 3.7
Some Possible Sources of Anxiety for Toddlers

Difficulty understanding what is happening.

Difficulty communicating.

Frustration over not being able to do what others can do or what they imagine others can do.

Conflicts between wanting to be independent and wanting their parents' help.

Separation or threat of separation from caregivers.

Fears of losing parental approval and love.

Reactions to losing self-control.

Anxieties about the body.

Source: Adapted from Davies, 1999.

Anglo and Puerto Rican mothers, Harwood (1992) found that Anglo mothers expected their infants to manage their stranger anxiety and separation anxiety without clinging to the mother. The Puerto Rican mothers, on the other hand, expected their infants to rely on the mother for solace.

Temperament. Another way to look at emotional development is by evaluating **temperament**—the individual's innate disposition. The best-known study of temperament in infants and young children was conducted by Alexander Thomas, Stella Chess, and Herbert Birch (1968, 1970). They studied nine components of temperament: activity level, regularity of biological functions, initial reaction to any new stimulus, adaptability, intensity of reaction, level of stimulation needed to evoke a discernible response, quality of mood, distractibility, and attention span or persistence. From their observations, the researchers identified three types of temperament: easy, difficult, and slow to warm up.

For an idea of the differences in infant temperament, consider the range of reactions you might see at a baptism service. One infant might scream when passed from one person to the other and when water is placed on his or her forehead. The mother might have difficulty calming the infant for the remainder of the baptism service. At the other extreme, one infant might make cooing noises throughout the entire service and seem unbothered by the rituals. The slow-to-warm-up infant might cautiously check out the clergy administering the baptism and begin to relax by the time the ritual is completed.

Thomas and his colleagues believed that a child's temperament appears shortly after birth and is set, or remains unchanged, throughout life. Recent research indicates, however, that a stable pattern of temperament is not evident until about 4 months, when the central nervous system is further developed (Shonkoff & Phillips, 2000). Whether temperament is permanent or not is still unresolved.

Thomas, Chess, and Birch cautioned that a difficult temperament does not necessarily indicate future childhood behavior problems, as one might logically assume. More significant than an infant's temperament type is the "goodness of fit" between the infant and the expectations, temperament, and needs of those in the child's environment (Thomas & Chess, 1986). In other words, how well the infant's temperament matches with that of parents, caregivers, and siblings is crucial to the infant's emotional development. For example, there appears to be a "problematic fit" between Holly and her mother. Although Mrs. Hicks is able to meet Holly's basic needs, she feels rejected and overwhelmed by Holly's "difficult" temperament. Holly seems to get irritated with Mrs. Hicks's nurturing style. Thomas and Chess suggest that regardless of a child's temperament, caregivers and others in the child's environment can learn to work with a child's temperament. Thus, helping Mrs. Hicks develop a better fit between herself and Holly will help Holly develop toward healthy functioning.

Research investigating temperament as a predictor of preschool behavior problems yielded a surprising result (Oberklaid, Sanson, Pedlow, & Prior, 1993). Investigators found that the parent's perception of the preschool child's temperament had more influence on the development of behavior problems than did the child's actual temperament. Children who were perceived by their caregivers as having a "difficult" temperament were twice as likely to develop a behavior problem during the preschool years, regardless of their empirically measured temperament type. You may see Demarcus's curiosity as a healthy trait, but if Ynecka perceives it as difficult, behavior problems may develop.

Studies like these call into question whether temperament is genetically determined or environmentally induced. In a study of temperament among twins and among adopted siblings, investigators found that genetics contributed more than environment to temperament development (Braungart, Plomin, DeFries, & Fulker, 1992). The twins' temperaments were more alike than were those of the adopted siblings. The researchers concluded that environment contributes very little to temperament. However, another team of researchers (deVries & Sameroff, 1984) studied temperament among infants from three distinct East African societies and concluded that factors in the infants' environment—such as child-rearing practices, level of social change or modernization, maternal attitudes, ecological setting, and specific early life events—have more influence on temperament development than genetics. We could infer from this study that temperament is "neutral" and then molded and shaped by parental characteristics and expectations (Oberklaid et al., 1993). As with other aspects of personality, however, perhaps children are born with a genetic predisposition to a temperament type that is then significantly influenced by environmental factors.

How important is the early attachment relationship for the quality of future relationships?

Bowlby's Theory of Attachment. Another key component of emotional development is **attachment**—the ability to form emotional bonds with other people. Many child development scholars have suggested that attachment is one of the most important issues in infant development, mainly because attachment is the foundation for emotional development and a predictor of later functioning. Note that this view of attachment is similar to Erikson's first stage of psychosocial development. This perspective is similar to the one Mrs. Hicks found on the Internet, which raised issues of concern for her.

The two most popular theories of attachment were developed by John Bowlby (1969) and Mary Ainsworth and colleagues (Ainsworth, Blehar, Waters, & Wall, 1978). Bowlby, who initially studied attachment in animals, concluded that attachment is natural, a result of the infant's instinct for survival and consequent need to be protected. Attachment between infant and mother ensures that the infant will be adequately nurtured and protected from attack or, in the case of human infants, from a harsh environment. The infant is innately programmed to emit stimuli (smiling, clinging, etc.) to which the mother responds. This exchange between infant and mother creates a bond of attachment. The infant initiates the attachment process, but later the mother's behavior is what strengthens the bond.

Bowlby hypothesized that attachment advances through four stages: preattachment, attachment in the making, clear-cut attachment, and goal-corrected attachment. This process begins in the 1st month of life, with the infant's ability to discriminate the mother's voice. Attachment becomes fully developed during the 2nd year of life, when the mother and toddler develop a partnership. During this later phase of attachment, the child is able to manipulate the mother into desired outcomes, but the child also has the capacity to understand the mother's point of view. The mother and the child reach a mutually acceptable compromise.

Bowlby contends that infants can demonstrate attachment behavior to others; however, attachment to the mother occurs earlier than attachment to others and is stronger and more consistent. It is thought that the earliest attachment becomes the child's working model for subsequent relationships (Bowlby, 1982). Myon seems to understand the importance of her relationship with her infant.

Attachment explains the child's anxiety when the parents leave. However, children eventually learn to cope with separation. Toddlers often make use of **transitional objects**, or comfort objects, to help them cope with separations from parents and to handle other stressful situations. During such times, they may cuddle with a blanket, teddy bear, or other stuffed animal. The transitional object is seen as a symbol of the relationship with the caregiver, but toddlers also see it as having magic powers to soothe and protect them (Davies, 1999).

Ainsworth's Theory of Attachment. One of the most widely used methods to investigate infant attachment, known as the strange situation procedure, was developed by Ainsworth and colleagues (Ainsworth et al., 1978). The Ainsworth group believed that you could assess the level of infant attachment to the mother through the infant's response to a series of "strange" episodes. Basically, the child is exposed over a period of 25 minutes to eight constructed episodes involving separation and reunion with the mother. The amount of child attachment to the mother is measured by how the child responds to the mother following the "distressing" separation.

Ainsworth and her colleagues identified three types of attachment:

1. *Secure attachment.* The child uses the mother as a home base and feels comfortable leaving this base to explore the playroom. The child returns to the mother every so often to ensure that she is still present. When the mother leaves the room (act of separation), the securely attached child will cry and seek comfort from the mother when she returns. But this child is easily reassured and soothed by the mother's return.

2. *Anxious attachment.* The child is reluctant to explore the playroom and clings to the mother. When the mother leaves the room, the child cries for a long time. When the mother returns, this child seeks solace from the mother but continues to cry and may swat at or pull away from the mother. Ainsworth and colleagues described these infants as somewhat insecure and doubted that their mothers would ever be able to provide the security and safety they need.

3. *Avoidant attachment.* Some infants seem indifferent to the presence of their mother. Whether the mother is present or absent from the room, these children's responses are the same.

Recent scholars have added a fourth possible response, known as the insecure disorganized/disoriented response (Main & Hesse, 1990). These children display contradictory behavior: they attempt physical closeness, but retreat with acts of avoidance. These infants typically have mothers who either have a history of abusive behavior or continue to struggle with a traumatic experience in their own lives. As a result, these infants become confused in the "strange" situation. They fear the unknown figure and seek solace from the mother, but retreat because they are also fearful of the mother. Some authors have suggested that the behavior associated with the disorganized style is actually an adaptive response to harsh caregiving (Stovall & Dozier, 1998).

According to Ainsworth's attachment theory, children whose mothers are consistently present and responsive to their needs and whose mothers exhibit a warm, caring relationship develop an appropriate attachment. The implication is that infants and toddlers need their mother as the sole caregiver for healthy development. This assumption probably seemed unquestionable when these theories were constructed. However, over the past 20 to 30 years, more women have entered the workforce. Thus, many more children experience alternative forms of child care, including day care.

The effect day care has on the development of attachment in young children continues to be a hotly debated topic. Some argue that day care has a negative effect on infant attachment and increases the risk of the infant's developing insecure and avoidant forms of attachment (see, e.g., Belsky, 1987; Belsky & Braungart, 1991). The risks are especially high if the infant attends day care during the 1st year of life. Others argue that day care does not have a negative effect on infant and early childhood attachment (Griffith, 1996; Shonkoff & Phillips, 2000).

The question of how day care attendance affects attachment is probably not as simplistic as either side contends. Many factors appear to be associated with the development of attachment for children in day care. The overriding factor is the quality of the relationship between the infant and parents, regardless of the child's care arrangements. For example, mothers who have a positive attitude toward their infant, are emotionally available to their infant, and encourage age-appropriate levels of independence produce infants with secure attachment (Clarke-Stewart, 1988; Shonkoff & Phillips, 2000).

Other investigations suggest that the amount of involvement by the father and the quality of the marital relationship between the mother and father are also relevant to the development of secure infant attachment. Infants whose parents have a stable and loving marriage and whose father is significantly involved in their nurturing and care tend to develop secure attachment, even if they spend a significant portion of the day in child care (Schachere, 1990).

Recently, researchers have begun to study attachment among children in foster care. Over a half million children are in foster care in the United States (Children's Defense Fund, 2001a). Most of these children come into foster care without secure attachments. Once in foster care, many children are subjected to frequent changes in their foster homes (Smith, Stormshak, Chamberlain, & Whaley, 2001). Problems with attachment may contribute to foster home disruptions, but foster home disruptions also contribute to attachment problems. The child welfare system has paid too little attention to issues of attachment.

One final note on the issue of attachment. The manner in which infant attachment is measured raises some concerns. Most studies of attachment have used the Ainsworth group's strange situation method. However, this measure may not yield valid results with some groups or under certain conditions. For example, the avoidant pattern of attachment some investigators have noted among children in day care may not indicate lack of attachment, as some have concluded (Clarke-Stewart, 1989). These children may be securely attached but seem indifferent to the exit and return of the mother simply because they have become accustomed to routine separations and reunions with their mother.

In what other ways does culture affect infant and toddler development?

The appropriateness of using the strange situation method with certain ethnic groups has also been questioned. Researchers evaluating attachment in Puerto Rican and Dominican infants (Fracasso, Busch-Rossnagel, & Fisher, 1994) have concluded that the pattern of attachment in these ethnic groups is different from that identified in studies of European American infants and is thus often mislabeled. More specifically, multiple caregiving is traditional in the African American community (Jackson, 1993). Many extended-family members (both blood and nonblood relations) participate in the rearing of children—for a number of reasons, including accommodation of parents' unconventional work schedules. This multiple caregiving arrangement encourages African American infants to befriend "strangers" introduced to them by their mothers. As a result, African American children often are more independent and do not experience the same level of anxiety that European American children experience when left by their mother. The "apathy" of African American children toward the mother may not be apathy at all, but rather an indication that they have adapted to the multiple caregiver arrangement. Interestingly, this tradition of shared child rearing echoes the African proverb "It takes a village to raise a child," which has become a popular adage in the United States. Also, it should be noted that the extended kinship network has been found to be a strength of African American families (Hill, 1972; Logan, Freeman, & McRoy, 1990).

At the other end of the continuum, Asian mothers like Myon have traditionally rarely left their infants in the care of others. One researcher found that Japanese mothers leave their babies in the care of others an average of 2.2 times in a given month, and only in the care of an immediate family relative such as the father or grandmother. They also keep their infants in close proximity; they often sleep in the same room and infants are carried on the mother's back (Takahashi, 1990). As a result, Japanese infants tend to be highly anxious when their mothers leave the room. The response to the mother leaving is so intense that these infants are not easily comforted when the mother returns. Some might label the response by these infants as a sign of insecure attachment, although the response is consistent with the environment they have experienced. Quite likely, the infants in fact have a secure and appropriate attachment to their mother (Takahashi, 1990).

The Role of Play

Historically, play was thought to be insignificant to development, especially for infants and toddlers. However, we now know that play allows infants and toddlers to enhance motor, cognitive, emotional, and social development.

Because of their differences in development in all areas, infants and toddlers play in different ways. Exhibit 3.8 describes four types of infant play and three types of play observed in very young children. These later types of play begin in toddlerhood.

EXHIBIT 3.8 Types of Play in Infancy and Toddlerhood

Types of Infant Play	
Vocal play	Playful vocalizing with grunts, squeals, trills, vowels, etc. to experiment with sound and have fun with it.
Interactive play	Initiating interactions with caregivers (at about 4-5 months), by smiling and vocalizing, to communicate and make connection.
Exploratory play with objects	Exploring objects with eyes, mouth, and hands to learn about their shape, color, texture, movement, and sounds and to experience pleasure.
Baby games	Participating in parent-initiated ritualized, repetitive games, such as peek-a-boo, that contain humor, suspense, and excitement and build an emotional bond.
Types of Toddler Play	
Functional play	Engaging in simple, repetitive motor movements.
Constructive play	Creating and constructing objects.
Make-believe play	Acting out everyday functions and tasks and playing with an imaginary friend.

Source: Types of Infant Play based on Davies, 1999; Types of Toddler Play based on Rubin, Fein, & Vandenberg, 1983.

Play develops in union with cognitive and motor development. For example, young toddlers will play with a mound of clay by hitting and perhaps squishing it. More developed toddlers will mold the clay into a ball, and older toddlers will try to roll or throw the molded ball.

One zealous mother describes joining the Toy of the Month Club in which she received developmental toys through the mail each month for the first 2 years of her child's life. This mother wanted to be sure that her child had every opportunity to advance in terms of motor and cognitive skills. Although this mother's efforts are to be applauded, she admits that these toys were very costly and that perhaps she could have achieved the same outcome with other less costly objects. For example, there is no evidence that a store-bought infant mobile is any more effective than a homemade paper one hung on a clothes hanger. The objective is to provide stimulation and opportunities for play.

Another important aspect of play is parent/child interaction. Parent/infant play may increase the likelihood of secure attachment between the parent and child (Call, 1995). The act of play at least provides the opportunity for infants and parents to feel good about themselves by enjoying each other and by being enjoyed (Call, 1995; McCluskey & Duerden, 1993). Even before infants can speak or understand language spoken to them, play provides a mechanism of communication between the parent and infants. Infants receive messages about themselves through play, which promotes their sense of self (McCluskey & Duerden, 1993).

Play also is a vehicle for developing peer relations. A few decades ago, it was thought that babies really aren't interested in each other and cannot form relationships with each other. Recent research challenges this view (Shonkoff and Phillips, 2000). The peer group becomes more important at earlier ages as family size decreases and siblings are no longer available for daily social interaction. Researchers have found that very young infants get excited by the sight of other infants; by 6 to 9 months, infants appear to try to get the attention of other infants; and by 9 to 12 months infants imitate each other. Although toddlers are capable of establishing relationships, their social play is a struggle, and a toddler play session is quite a fragile experience. Toddlers need help in structuring their play with each other. And yet, researchers have found that groups of toddlers in preschool settings develop play routines that they return to again and again over periods of months (Corsaro, 1997). These toddler play routines are primarily nonverbal, with a set of ritualized actions. For example, Corsaro notes a play routine in one Italian preschool in which a group of toddlers would rearrange the chairs in the room and work together to move them around in patterns. They returned to this routine fairly regularly over the course of a year, modifying it slightly over time. Peer relations are being built by "doing things together."

Developmental Disruptions

Providing interventions to infants and toddlers with disabilities is mandated by the Developmental Disabilities Assistance and Bill of Rights Act. However, accurately assessing **developmental delays** in young children is difficult (Zipper & Simeonsson, 1997). One reason is that although we have loose guidelines for healthy development in infants and toddlers, development varies by individual child. Young children walk, master potty training, and develop language skills on different time tables. It is therefore difficult to assess whether a particular child has a case of delayed development—and if so, which faculties are delayed. Premature infants like Holly, for example, often need time to catch up in terms of physical, cognitive, and emotional development. At what point do you decide Holly is not developing fast enough and label her developmentally delayed?

The other reason that accurate assessment of developmental difficulties in infants and toddlers is hard is that although many physical and cognitive disabilities have been found to be genetic and others to be associated with environmental factors, the cause of most disabilities is unknown. For example, mental retardation has 350 known causes, yet the cause of most identified cases of mental retardation is unknown (Zipper & Simeonsson, 1997). Anticipating what the risk factors might be for a particular child and how they might influence developmental delays is therefore difficult.

Regardless, early intervention services for infants and toddlers who truly are delayed appear to be effective, especially in enhancing cognitive development (Shonkoff, Hauser-Cram, Krauss, & Upshur, 1992). The earlier the intervention begins, the better. Parent involvement is also crucial to the child's progress.

Child Care Arrangements in Infancy and Toddlerhood

Human infants start life in a remarkably dependent state, in need of constant care and protection. On their own, they would die. Toddlers are full of life and are making great strides in development in all areas, but they are also "not ready to set out for life alone in the big city" (Newman & Newman, 1997, p. 344). Societal health is dependent on finding good solutions to the question, Who will care for infants and toddlers?

With large numbers of mothers of infants and toddlers in the paid work force, and not at home, this question becomes a challenging one. The United States seems to be responding to this challenge more reluctantly than other highly industrialized countries are. This difference becomes clear in comparative analysis of two solutions for early child care: family leave and paid child care.

Family Leave

What impact might this trend have over time on the current cohort of infants and toddlers?

Because of changes in the economic institution in the United States between 1975 and 1999, the proportion of infants with mothers in paid employment increased from 24% to 54% (Shonkoff & Phillips, 2000). A similar trend is occurring in all highly industrialized countries.

In response, most industrialized countries have instituted social policies that provide for job-protected leaves for parents to allow them to take off from work to care for their young children. Sweden was the first country to develop such a policy in 1974. The Swedish policy guaranteed paid leave.

By the early 1990s, the United States was the only industrialized country without a family leave policy (Kamerman, 1996). But in 1993, the U.S. Congress passed the Family and Medical Leave Act (FMLA) of 1993 (P.L. 103-3). FMLA requires businesses with 50 or more employees to provide up to 12 weeks of unpaid, job-protected leave during a 12-month period for workers to manage childbirth, adoption, or personal or family illness. Eligible workers are entitled to continued health insurance coverage during the leave period.

Exhibit 3.9 highlights the family leave policies in selected countries. As you can see, the United States is one of a few industrialized countries to provide no paid leave and falls at the bottom of the range in terms of duration of leave. This is an area for social work advocacy.

Paid Child Care

Historically in the United States, mothers were expected to provide full-time care for infants and toddlers at home. If mothers were not available, it was expected that children would be cared for by domestic help or a close relative but still in their home setting (Kamerman & Kahn, 1995). Even in the 1960s, with the development of Head Start programs, the focus was on preschool age children; infants and toddlers were still expected to be cared for at home (Kamerman & Kahn, 1995). Thus, historically there was very little provision of alternative child care for most children below school age.

This phenomenon has changed dramatically, however, over the last 20 years. In 1999, about 61% of women in the United States with children age 6 and under worked outside the home, and 54% of women with children age 1 year and younger worked outside the home (Shonkoff & Phillips, 2000). Therefore, alternative child care has become a necessity in the United States.

Many advocates for day care refer to the European model as an ideal for the United States. Countries in Europe provide "universal" child care for all children, regardless of the parents' income, employment status, race, age, and so forth. These programs are supported through national policy and funded through public funds. If they pay at all, parents pay no more than a quarter of the monies needed. Parents in Europe thus pay far less than parents in the United States typically pay.

Currently, there are some innovative programs in Europe in which the focus is on providing alternative group care for toddlers in group settings outside the home (Kamerman & Kahn, 1995). The thought is that the cognitive and social skills of children age 2 and older can be enhanced in a group setting. This care is also funded and regulated through public funds. Workers who provide this care are well trained in child development and are paid well (by United States' standards) for their services. Most important, this care is available to all families and children.

Research results indicate that day care in general is not harmful to infants and toddlers (Shonkoff & Phillips, 2000). The primary concern is the quality of the day care provided. Researchers conclude that quality day care can even enhance cognitive development among 9-month-old infants (Schuetze, Lewis, & DiMartino, 1999). The National Research Council (1990) has identified three factors essential to quality day care,

Exhibit 3.9

Family Leave Policies in Selected Countries, 1998-2002

Country	Duration of Leave	Percentage of Wage Replaced
Australia	1 year parental	Unpaid
Belgium	15 weeks maternity 3 months parental for each parent 3 days paternity	75 to 80% Low Flat Rate Benefit
Canada	17 weeks maternity 35 weeks parental, either parent or shared Unpaid family leave	55% 55%
Denmark	18 weeks maternity, including 4 weeks prebirth 10 weeks parental 2 weeks paternity Child care leave up to 52 weeks for either parent up to child's 8th birthday.	90% 60% 100% 60%
Greece	17 weeks maternity 3.5 months parental leave for each parent	50% Unpaid
Italy	5 months maternity, including 1 month prebirth Additional 10 months parental leave, 20 months for multiple births Family (sick) leave: 5 days/year for children 3–8 years old	80% 30% Paid
Mexico	12 weeks maternity (6 weeks prebirth)	100%
Norway	52 weeks parental leave (or 42 weeks at 100%) Childrearing leave up to age 2	80% Flat rate
Sweden	Full parental leave until child is 13 months; includes adoption Next 3 months Last 3 months	80% Flat rate Unpaid
United States	12 weeks family leave, includes maternity	Unpaid

Source: Based on Clearinghouse on International Developments in Child, Youth and Family Policies at Columbia University (2002).

described in Exhibit 3.10. Others propose that quality day care must include a well-defined curriculum and be based on child development theory (Bredekamp, 1992; Dodge, 1995).

EXHIBIT 3.10
Identified Factors of Quality Day Care

Staff/child ratio	1:3 for infants, 1:4 for toddlers, and 1:8 for preschoolers
Group/age ratio	no larger than 6 for infant, 8 for toddlers, and 16 for preschoolers
Staff training	on child development and age-appropriate child care.

Source: National Research Council, 1990.

Infants and Toddlers in the Multigenerational Family

What have you observed about how family relationships change when a baby is born?

Maria, a new mom, describes the first visit her mother and father made to her home after the birth of Maria's new infant. "Mom and Dad walked right past me as if I was not there, even though we had not seen each other for 6 months. I quickly realized that my status as their 'princess' was now replaced with a new little princess. During their visit, my husband and I had to fight to see our own child. When she cried, they immediately ran to her. And my mother criticized everything I did—she didn't like the brand of diapers I used, she thought the color of the room was too dreary for an infant—and she even scolded my husband at one point for waking the baby when he went to check on her. I appreciated their visit, but I must admit that I was glad when it was time for them to leave." Maria's description is not unique. The involvement of grandparents and other extended family members in the care of infants and toddlers may be experienced either as a great source of support or as interference and intrusion (and sometimes as a little of each).

Yet, the specific roles of grandparents and other extended family members is rarely discussed within the family, which is why conflicts often occur (Hines, Preto, McGoldrick, Almeida, & Weltman, 1999). When these roles are clearly articulated and agreed upon, extended family members can provide support that enhances infant and toddler development (Hines et al., 1999). Family involvement as a form of social support is further discussed as a "protective factor" later in this chapter.

The birth of a child, especially of a first child, brings about a major transition not only for parents but also for the entire kin network. Partners become parents; sons and daughters become fathers and mothers; fathers and mothers become grandfathers and grandmothers; and brothers and sisters become aunts and uncles. The social status of the extended family serves as the basis of the social status of the child, and the values and beliefs of the extended family will shape the way they care for and socialize the child (Carter & McGoldrick, 1999b; Newman & Newman, 1997). In addition, many children's names and child-rearing rituals, decisions, and behaviors are passed from past generations to the next.

To illustrate this point, there is an old joke about a mother who prepared a roast beef for most Sunday family dinners. She would always cut the roast in half and place it in two pans before cooking it in the oven. Observing this behavior, her young daughter asked her why she cut the roast in half. After some thought she told her daughter that she did not know for sure; she remembered that her mother had always cut her roast in half. Later the mother asked her mother why she had cut her roast in half before cooking it. The senior mother explained that she did not have a pan large enough for the size roast she needed to feed her family. Thus, she would cut the roast in half in order to fit it into the two pans that she did own.

Similar behavior affects decisions regarding infants and toddlers. One mother reports giving her infant daughter herb tea in addition to an ointment provided by her physician for a skin rash. It seems that this skin rash was common among infant girls in each generation in this family. A specific herb tea was traditionally used to treat the rash. This mother confesses that she did not tell her mother or grandmother that she used the ointment prescribed by her doctor. It is interesting for us to note that although the mother did not have complete faith in the tea, she also did not have complete faith in the ointment. The mother states that she is not sure which one actually cured the rash. Violation of family and cultural rituals and norms can be a source of conflict between new parents and other family members (Hines et al., 1999). For example, differences of opinion about baptism, male circumcision, and even child care arrangements can create family disharmony.

Risks to Healthy Infant and Toddler Development

You have probably already surmised what some of the environmental factors are that inhibit healthy growth and development in infants and toddlers. This section addresses a few of those factors that social workers are especially likely to encounter: poverty, inadequate caregiving, and child abuse.

Poverty

In what ways does social class affect the development of infants and toddlers?

In recent years, the greatest increase in poverty in the United States has been among families with young children (Schmitz & Hilton, 1996). Although the poverty rate for children under 3 dropped from 27% in 1993 to 18% in 2000, the poverty rate for children under 3 was about 80% higher than the rate for adults in 2000. The situation looks even more grim when young children living with "near poor" families are included: nearly 40% of children under 3 lived either in poverty or in near poor low-income families (families with incomes below 200% of the poverty line) in 2000 (Song & Lu, 2002). The upsurge of female-headed households is a major factor in the high poverty rate among young children (Canino & Spurlock, 1994; Song & Lu, 2002; McWhirter, McWhirter, McWhirter, & McWhirter, 1993). Other contributors have been a significant decrease in the real incomes of families, growing inequality in income distribution, stagnant wages for young workers, high unemployment among minority men, and a decrease in cash benefits available to young families (Children's Defense Fund, 2001b). Finally, African American children and Hispanic children are three times more likely than European American children to live in poverty (Song & Lu, 2002).

Although some young children who live in poverty flourish, poverty presents considerable risks to children's growth and development. (That risk continues into preschool and middle childhood, as Chapters 4 and 5 explain.) Children living in poverty often suffer the consequences of poor nutrition and inadequate health care. Many of these children do not receive proper immunizations, and many minor illnesses go untreated, increasing the potential for serious health problems. This phenomenon is particularly disturbing because many of these minor illnesses are easily treated. Most childhood ear infections, for example, are easily treated with antibiotics; left untreated, they can result in hearing loss.

In addition to inadequate health care and nutrition, children living in poverty often experience overcrowded living conditions. Overcrowding restricts opportunities for play, and thus, because most learning and development in young children takes place in the context of play, restricts healthy development. A study of development among 12-month-old Haitian American children found that the poorer children experienced more overcrowded conditions than those not living in poverty and consequently had less play time, fewer toys, a smaller number of safe areas to play, and less private time with parents (Widmayer, Peterson, & Larner, 1990). The living conditions of the children who were poor were associated with delayed motor development and lower cognitive functioning.

Children are affected not only by the direct consequences of poverty but also by indirect factors such as family stress, parental depression, and inadequate or nonsupportive parenting (Kirby & Fraser, 1997; McLoyd & Wilson, 1991). Ynecka Green's depression and anxiety will affect her relationship with Demarcus. Poor children are more likely to be exposed to environmental toxins (Song & Lu, 2002).

Most disturbing is the link between poverty and **infant mortality**—the death of a child before his or her first birthday. Infant mortality rates in the United States are high compared to other industrialized nations (National Center for Health Statistics [NCHS], 2000). Within the United States, mortality rates for infants are higher among the poor, and the rate among African Americans is twice that of European Americans (U.S. Census Bureau, 2000). As discussed in Chapter 2, low birth weight (LBW) as a result of inadequate prenatal care is the primary factor that contributes to the high infant mortality rate (Frank, Strobino, Salkever, & Jackson, 1992; Halpern, 1992; Klerman, 1991).

Interestingly, the infant mortality rate for Hispanic women is lower than that of European American women (NCHS, 1990), even though inadequate prenatal care is prominent among Hispanic women. This fact suggests that differences in prenatal care explain only part of the disparity in infant mortality rates. The mother's diet and social support network have been suggested as other factors that may affect infant mortality rates (NCHS, 1990). One comparative study found lower rates of alcohol and tobacco use among Hispanic women than among women of other racial/ethnic groups and the presence of stronger family, cultural, and social ties (Rogers, 1989). These findings suggest that social support may offset the consequences of inadequate prenatal care.

Inadequate Caregiving

The most pervasive response to inadequate caregiving is nonorganic failure to thrive (NOFTT). This diagnosis is used to describe infants, usually between ages 3 to 12 months, who show poor development, primarily in terms of weight gain. These infants weigh less than 80% of the ideal weight for their age. The "nonorganic" feature refers to the lack of medical causes for the poor development, and is thought to be a consequence of environmental neglect (lack of food) and stimulus deprivation (Bassali & Benjamin, 2002). Overall, NOFTT is a consequence of the infant's basic needs going unmet, primarily the needs for feeding and nurturing.

A review of the literature identified several parental factors that appear to increase the likelihood of the development of NOFTT (Bassali & Benjamin, 2002; Marino, Weinman, & Soudelier, 2001). These include maternal depression, maternal malnutrition during pregnancy, marital problems between parents, and mental illness and/or substance abuse in the primary caretaker.

Parental mental illness and depression are associated with other problems among infants and toddlers as well. For example, infants of depressed mothers demonstrate less positive expressions of mood and personality and are less attentive in play (Gomez, 2001). Overall, they demonstrate less joy, even when they were securely attached to the mother. One analysis of the literature on parental mental illness and infant development concluded the following (Seifer & Dickstein, 2000):

- Parental mental illness increases the likelihood of mental health problems among their children.
- Mothers who are depressed are more negative in interaction with their infants.
- Similarly, infants with depressed mothers are more negative in their exchange with their mothers.

- There is an association between parental mental illness and insecure attachment between parents and infants.
- Depressed mothers view their infant's behavior as more negative than non-depressed mothers.

Child Abuse

How might child abuse or neglect experienced as an infant or toddler affect later development?

Almost all parents in the United States use some type of physical punishment, and hitting children usually begins in infancy (McGoldrick, Broken Nose, & Potenza, 1999). Apparently, many parents are simply not aware of how dangerous it can be to use physical punishment with such young children. Infants and toddlers who are abused demonstrate delayed cognitive and language development (Veltman & Browne, 2001). As abuse and neglect continue, the infant's cognitive skills continue to decline and reach levels of "intellectual disability" (Strathearn, Gary, & O'Callaghan, 2001). Interestingly, these infants also have smaller than average head sizes. Also, according to reports from the U.S. Department of Health and Human Services (1995), most children who die from child abuse or neglect are under age 5, and the majority of these children are less than 1 year of age.

Several factors are thought to contribute to the abuse of infants and toddlers. Consistently, poverty is reported as a factor that contributes to abuse and neglect (Lee & George, 1999). Factors that interact with poverty and increase the likelihood of abuse are young motherhood and single parenthood.

An association also has been found between infant temperament and abuse (Brayden, Altemeier, Tucker, Dietrich, & Veitze, 1992). Infants who have "difficult" temperament are more likely to be abused and neglected. Others suggest that the combination of difficult temperament and environmental stress interact (Roberts, 1979). Similarly, infants and toddlers with mental, physical, or behavioral abnormalities are also at a higher risk for abuse (Frodi, 1981).

Parental characteristics such as lack of education, poor self-esteem, lack of family support, and parental depression also contribute to child abuse and neglect (Coohey, 1998; Levine & Sallee, 1999). Of course, parents who abuse their children were often abused themselves as children (Zuravin & Di Blasio, 1996).

The number of infants removed from their home due to parental substance abuse has increased (Chasnoff, 1998), and thus the relationship between substance abuse and child abuse has become a focus of research. The abuse of alcohol and other substances is reported to contribute to child abuse (Sun, Shillington, Hohman, & Jones, 2001). Some suggest that parental substance abuse is present in at least half of all families in Child Protective Service caseloads (Murphy, Jellinek, Quinn, Smith, Poitrast, & Goshko, 1991); others predict that this number may be as high as 80% (Barth, 1994). Many advocate for substance abuse treatment programs that include mothers and their infants and toddlers (Clark, 2001).

Regardless of cause, contrary to what most of us believe, most abusive parents feel terrible afterward and express feelings of guilt and remorse (Kempe & Kempe, 1976).

Protective Factors in Infancy and Toddlerhood

Many young children experience healthy growth and development despite the presence of risk factors. They are said to have **resilience**. Several factors have been identified as mediating between the risks children experience and their growth and development (Kirby & Fraser, 1997; Werner, 2000). These factors are "protective" in the sense that they shield the child from the consequences of potential hazards (Kirby & Fraser, 1997). Following are some protective factors that help diminish the potential risks to infants and toddlers.

Education. Research indicates that the education of the mother directly affects the outcome for infants and toddlers. This effect was found even in the devastating poverty that exists in Nicaragua (Pena & Wall, 2000). The infant mortality rate is predictably high in this country. However, investigators found that the higher the mother's level of formal education, the lower the infant mortality rate. Investigators hypothesize that mothers with higher levels of formal education provide better quality of care to their infants by feeding them more conscientiously, using available health care, keeping the household cleaner, and generally satisfying the overall needs of the infant. These mothers simply possessed better coping skills.

Similar results were found in a study of mothers and infants with two strikes against them—they are living in poverty and the infants were born premature (Bradley et al., 1994). Infants whose mothers had higher intellectual abilities demonstrated higher levels of cognitive and social development and were more likely to be in the normal range of physical development.

Social Support. Social support is often found in informal networks, such as friends and extended family members, or in formal support systems, such as the church, community agencies, day care centers, social workers, and other professions. The availability of social support seems to buffer many risk factors, such as stress experienced by parents (Koeske & Koeske, 1990). For example, Mrs. Hicks could truly benefit from having the opportunity to take a break from the stresses of caring for Holly. Both formal and informal social support can fill this gap for her. Even child abuse is reduced in the presence of positive social support networks (Coohey, 1996).

Extended family members often serve as alternative caregivers when parents cannot provide care because of physical or mental illness or job demands. Reliance on an extended family is particularly important in some cultural and socioeconomic groups. Myon, for example, feels isolated in raising her daughter due to the absence of social support in her new country. In fact, lacking help from extended family members, Myon's pursuit of further education has been interrupted.

Easy Temperament. Infants with a positive temperament are less likely to be affected by risk factors (Kirby & Fraser, 1997). The association between easy temperament and "protection" is both direct and indirect. Infants with a positive temperament may simply perceive their world more positively. Infants with a positive temperament may also induce more constructive and affirming responses from those in their environment.

Social Work Interventions: Promoting Resilience in Infants and Toddlers

Social workers can draw on the growing literature on risk factors, protection factors, and resilience to develop interventions that promote resilience in infants and toddlers. Our efforts should attempt to reduce risk factors and to enhance protective factors.

Advocacy for Social Equity. Poverty is one of the main conditions that obstructs healthy growth and development among infants and toddlers. Because of poverty, infants and toddlers may not receive the nutrition and health care that is crucial to their development. Other factors related to poverty include their parents' lack of education, substandard housing, poor sewerage, and faulty child-rearing practices (Brosco, 1999). So obvious is the link between poverty and poor outcomes for infants that one traditional mission for the social work profession has been the elimination of poverty. That mission has been pursued through direct services to poor families, political and social action, and the promotion of social and economic justice.

An example of the type of program advocated by social workers is the effort to increase breastfeeding among low-income mothers. Mothers living in poverty are less likely than other mothers to breastfeed, although the many benefits of breastfeeding are well documented (Kramer, 1991). In addition, for parents with few financial resources, breastfeeding is a low-cost way to meet the initial nutritional needs of their infants. The Women, Infants and Children (WIC) supplemental food program is a major factor in promoting breastfeeding. Education and information about breastfeeding is offered when pregnant women receive WIC vouchers. For those mothers who choose to breastfeed, WIC clinics offer counseling regarding problems the mothers encounter while nursing. Also, mothers can call a breastfeeding hot line.

Many programs offering support to parents of infants and toddlers have been threatened as welfare reform continues. Thus, the need is all the greater for social workers to address the availability, affordability, and quality of services for poor families. Some needed services include health insurance, adequate food and housing for women and children, and ways of securing sufficient income from fathers (Brosco, 1999). Social workers can also help by creating neighborhood-based programs that reduce class conflict, counter feelings of alienation, localize control of social institutions, create jobs and reverse neighborhood economic decline, and improve human services (Halpern, 1993).

Preventing Risk Through Education. Logically, if risk factors could be prevented, children would have a greater opportunity for healthy development. Some suggest that next to elimination of poverty, education geared toward prevention of risk factors is the best ammunition available to increase the resilience of infants and toddlers (Brosco, 1999). Relevant topics include home hygiene, including information on how to protect infants from flies that carry diseases, why hand washing is important, and why and how to keep milk fresh.

Other useful educational efforts are community-based prenatal outreach programs, federally funded family planning programs, and groups focused on parenting skills for expectant parents. One innovative program was a parent education group for parents of young children in a housing project (Dubrow & Garbarino, 1989). The group focused on helping the parents understand the effects of neighborhood violence on young children. Parents were advised about how to recognize signs of distress and when to seek services for their children. A group like this one could be beneficial to Ynecka Green, Demarcus's mother. This type of experience would provide a place for her to express her grief and to gain survival skills. She would then have more freedom to encourage and support Demarcus's development.

Building Community Support. Social workers can facilitate informal helping and mutual aid at the community level. The challenge is to create more comprehensive programs and to develop better collaboration among existing services. One suggestion has been "one-stop shopping" (National Commission to Prevent Infant Mortality, 1992), which involves creating one application form for multiple services, shortening application forms, expediting the determination of eligibility, maintaining the case manager model, and creating interagency partnerships.

One attempt at providing more comprehensive services was a day care program set up for children, ages newborn to 5, of migrant workers (Achata, 1993). In addition to regular day care services, the program provided extended meal service and immunizations, thus increasing the number of children with up-to-date vaccinations.

Advocating for Better Day Care. A large percentage of women with infants and toddlers work full time outside the home. High-quality day care is essential. In particular, child care providers must be trained. One analysis of the social work literature suggests that social work as a profession is not involved enough in child care systems on either a local or national level (Frankel, 1991). Social workers could provide more services at day care sites and advocate for more affordable, higher-quality day care services.

Promoting Adequate Caregiving. Given that infants and toddlers are greatly dependent on adults to meet their needs, social workers can often help a great deal at the individual level by promoting sufficient and effective caregiving. Social workers must continue to provide services to parents that enable them to manage or eliminate problems that interfere with their ability to meet the needs of their children. In addition, helping parents work toward fulfillment of their own needs, by connecting or reconnecting them to formal and informal social support networks, will help them be more effective parents. Myon, for example, may not have her extended family available to help with child care, but perhaps she can explore other acceptable sources of support.

Promoting adequate caregiving may also involve providing innovative programs and interventions to meet the needs of parents. For example, infants with several identifiable risk factors—namely, poverty, maternal depression, and inadequate caretaking—received weekly intervention services through home visits (Lyons-Ruth, Connell, Grunebaum, & Botein, 1990). Infants who received these services increased in cognitive and emotional development and were better off than a group of infants with similar risk factors who served as a comparison group and did not receive the services. Infants who received the services were also twice as likely to be assessed as securely attached. In another program, families were screened for abuse before they left the hospital with their newborn infant (Duggan & Windham, 2000). Families who were determined to be at risk for abuse were provided with in-home services to improve family functioning and prevent child maltreatment. This type of early detection and immediate intervention proved to be effective.

IMPLICATIONS FOR SOCIAL WORK PRACTICE

In summary, knowledge about infants and toddlers has several implications for social work practice:

- Become well acquainted with theories and empirical research about growth and development among infants and toddlers.
- Assess infants and toddlers in the context of their environment, culture included.
- Promote continued use of formal and informal social support networks for parents with infants and toddlers.
- Continue to promote the elimination of poverty and the advancement of social justice.
- Advocate for compulsory health insurance and quality health care.

- Advocate for more affordable, quality child care.
- Collaborate with news media and other organizations to educate the public about the impact of poverty and inequality on early child development.
- Learn intervention methods to prevent and reduce substance abuse.
- Help parents understand the potential effects of inadequate caregiving on their infants.
- Provide support and appropriate intervention to parents to facilitate effective caregiving for infants and toddlers.

Key Terms

attachment
blooming
cognition
concrete operations stage
developmental delay
formal operations stage
immunization
infant
infant mortality
motor skills
object permanence
plasticity (brain)
preoperational stage
pruning
reflex
resilience
sensorimotor stage
sensory system
separation anxiety
stranger anxiety
symbolic functioning
synapses
temperament
toddler
transitional object

Active Learning

1. Spend some time at a mall or other public place where parents and infants frequent. List behaviors that you observe that indicate attachment between the infant and caretaker. Note any evidence you observe that may indicate a lack of attachment.

2. Ask to tour a day care facility. Describe the things you observe that may have a positive influence on cognitive development for the infants and toddlers who are placed there. List those things that you think are missing from that setting that are needed to create a more stimulating environment.

3. Social support is considered to be a protective factor for individuals throughout the life course. List the forms of social support that are available to Marilyn Hicks, Myon, and Ynecka Green. How do they help them with their parenting? In what ways could they be more helpful? How do they add to the level of stress?

Web Resources

The Jean Piaget Society

www.piaget.org/main.html

Site presented by The Jean Piaget Society, an international interdisciplinary society of scholars, teachers, and researchers, contains information on the society, a student page, a brief biography of Piaget, and Internet links.

Erikson Tutorial Home Page

snycorva.cortland.edu/~ANDERSMD/ERIK/welcome.HTML

Site maintained by the State University of New York-Cortland contains a summary chart of Erik Erikson's eight stages of psychosocial development, a brief biography of Erikson, critiques and controversies, references, and links to other pertinent Internet sites.

National Center for Children in Poverty (NCCP)

cpmcnet.columbia.edu/dept/nccp

Site presented by the NCC of the Mailman School of Public Health of Columbia University contains media resources, child poverty facts, as well as information on child care and early education, family support, and welfare reform.

Zero to Three

www.zerotothree.org

Site presented by Zero to Three: National Center for Infants, Toddlers & Families, a national nonprofit charitable organization with the aim to strengthen and support families, contains Parents' Tip of the Week, Parenting A-Z, BrainWonders, a glossary, and links to the Erikson Institute and other Internet sites.

National Network for Child Care

www.nncc.org/homepage.html

Site presented by the Cooperative Extension System's National Network for Child Care contains a list of over 1,000 publications and resources related to child care, an e-mail listserve, and a newsletter.

CHAPTER 4

Early Childhood

Debra J. Woody

CHAPTER 4

Early Childhood

Debra J. Woody
University of Texas at Arlington

Why do social workers need to know about the ability of preschool-age children to express emotions and feelings?

What is the process of gender and ethnic recognition and development among young children?

What do social workers need to know about play among young children?

Key Ideas

As you read this chapter, take note of these central ideas:

1. Healthy development is in many ways defined by the environment and culture in which the child is raised. In addition, although growth and development in young children have some predictability and logic, the timing and expression of many developmental skills vary from child to child.

2. According to Piaget, preschoolers are in the preoperational stage of cognitive development and become capable of cognitive recall and symbolic functioning.

3. Erikson describes preschoolers' task as being the development of initiative versus guilt (ages 3 to 6).

4. As young children struggle to discover stability and regularity in the environment, they are often rigid in their use of rules and stereotypes.

5. Regardless of country of residence or culture, all preschool children engage in spontaneous play.

6. Three types of parenting styles have been described: authoritarian, authoritative, and permissive. Parenting styles are prescribed to some extent by the community

and culture in which the parent resides. However, authoritarian and permissive styles often lead to emotional and behavioral problems.

7. Poverty, ineffective discipline, divorce, and exposure to violence all pose special challenges for early childhood development.

Case Study 4.1

Terri's Terrible Temper

Terri's mother and father, Mr. and Mrs. Smith, really seem at a loss about what to do. They adopted Terri, age 3, when she was an infant. They describe to you how happy they were to finally have a child. They had tried for many years, spent a lot of money on fertility procedures, and had almost given up on the adoption process when Terri seemed to be "sent from heaven." Their lives were going well until a year ago, when Terri turned 2. Mrs. Smith describes an overnight change in Terri's behavior. Terri has become a total terror at home and at preschool. In fact, the preschool has threatened to dismiss Terri if her behavior does not improve soon. Terri hits and takes toys from other children, she refuses to cooperate with the teacher, and does "what she wants to do."

Mr. and Mrs. Smith admit that Terri runs their household. They spend most evenings after work coaxing Terri into eating her dinner, taking a bath, and going to bed. Any attempt at a routine is nonexistent. When the Smiths try to discipline Terri, she screams, hits them, and throws things. They have not been able to use time-outs to discipline her because Terri refuses to stay in the bathroom, the designated time-out place. She runs out of the bathroom and hides. When they attempt to hold her in the bathroom, she screams until Mr. Smith gets too tired to continue to hold her or until she falls asleep. Mr. and Mrs. Smith admit that they frequently let Terri have her way because it is easier than saying no or trying to discipline her.

The "straw that broke the camel's back" came during a family vacation. Mrs. Smith's sister and family joined the Smiths at the beach. Mr. Smith describes the vacation as a total disaster. Terri refused to cooperate the "entire" vacation. They were unable to eat at restaurants because of her tantrums, and they were unable to participate in family activities because Terri would not let them get her ready to go. They tried allowing her to choose the activities for the day, which worked until other family members tired of doing only the things that Terri wanted to do. Terri would scream and

CASE STUDY 4.1

throw objects if the family refused to eat when and where she wanted or go to the park or the beach when she wanted. Terri's sister became so frustrated with the situation that she vowed never to vacation with them again. In fact, it was the sister who insisted that they get professional help for Terri.

CASE STUDY 4.2

JACK'S NAME CHANGE

Until last month, Jack, age 4, lived with his mother, Joyce, and father, Charles, in what Joyce describes as a happy home. She was shocked when she discovered that her husband was having an affair with a woman at work. She immediately asked him to leave and has filed for divorce. Charles moved in with his girlfriend and has not contacted Joyce or Jack at this point. Joyce just can't believe that this is happening to her. Her mother had the same experience with Joyce's father but had kept the marriage going for the sake of Joyce and her siblings. Joyce, on the other hand, is determined to live a different life from the life her mother chose. She saw how depressed her mother was until her death at age 54. Joyce states that her mother died of a broken heart.

Although Joyce is determined to live without Charles, she is concerned about how she and Jack will live on her income alone. They had a comfortable life before the separation, but it took both incomes. Although she plans to seek child support, she knows she will need to move, because she cannot afford the mortgage on her own.

Joyce would prefer for Jack not to have contact with his father. In fact, she is seriously considering changing Jack's name because he was named after his father. Joyce has tried to explain the situation to Jack as best she can. However, in your presence, she told Jack that she hopes he does not grow up to be like his father. She also told Jack that his father is the devil and is now living with a witch.

Joyce tells you that Jack has had difficulty sleeping and continues to ask when his father is coming home. Joyce simply responds to Jack by telling him that they probably will never see Charles again.

Case Study 4.3

A New Role for Ron and Rosiland's Grandmother

Ron, age 3, and Rosiland, age 5, have lived with Ms. Johnson, their grandmother, for the last year. Their mother, Shirley, was sent to prison a year ago after conviction of drug trafficking. Shirley's boyfriend is a known drug dealer and had asked Shirley to make a "delivery" for him. Shirley was arrested as she stepped off the bus in another state where she had taken the drugs for delivery. Ron and Rosiland were with her when she was arrested, because she had taken them with her. Her boyfriend thought that a woman traveling with two younger children would never be suspected of delivering drugs.

Ron and Rosiland were put into foster care by Child Protective Services until Ms. Johnson arrived to pick them up. It had taken her 2 weeks to save enough money to get to the children and fly them all home. Ms. Johnson shared with you how angry she was that Shirley's boyfriend refused to help her get the children home. Shirley calls the children when she can, but because her crime was a federal offense, she has been sent to a prison far away from home. The children ask about her often and miss her terribly. Ms. Johnson has told the children that their mom is away but has not told them that she will be away for some time. She is also unsure how much they understand about what happened, even though they were present when their mom was arrested.

Ms. Johnson shares with you that she has no choice but to care for the children, although this is definitely not the life she has planned. She was looking forward to living alone; her husband died several years ago. With her small savings, she was planning to visit her sister in another state for an extended visit. But that money is gone now, because these funds were used to get the children home. She seems to love both of the children but confides that the children "drive her crazy." She is not accustomed to all the noise, and they seem to need so much attention from her. Getting into the habit of having a scheduled day is also difficult for Ms. Johnson. Both children attend preschool, an arrangement Shirley made before her incarceration. Ms. Johnson describes the fact that the children attend preschool as a blessing, because it gives her some relief. You suspect that preschool is a blessing for the children as well.

Healthy Development in Early Childhood

As children like Terri, Jack, Ron, and Rosiland emerge from toddlerhood, they turn their attention more and more to the external environment. Just as in infancy and toddlerhood they worked at developing some regularity in their body rhythms, attachment relationships, and emotional states, they now work to discover some stability and regularity in the external world. That is not always an easy task, given their limitations in cognitive and language development. Much happens in all interrelated dimensions of development between 3 and 6, however, and children emerge from early childhood with a much more sophisticated ability to understand the world and their relationships to it. They work out this understanding in an increasingly wider world, with major influences coming from family, school, peer groups, neighborhood, and the media.

What historical trends are influencing our understanding of social age in early childhood?

Some child development scholars still refer to the period between ages 3 and 6 as the preschool age, but others have recently begun to refer to this period as early school age, reflecting the fact that most children are enrolled in some form of group-based experience during this period. We will simply refer to this period between 3 and 6 years of age as early childhood. Remember as you read that the various types of development discussed in this chapter under separate headings actually are interdependent, and sometimes the distinctions between the dimensions blur.

Physical Development in Early Childhood

As Chapter 3 explained, infants and toddlers grow rapidly. From ages 3 to 6, physical growth slows significantly. On average, height during this stage increases about 2 to 3 inches per year, and the young child adds about 5 pounds of weight per year. As a result, young children look leaner and better proportioned than they did as toddlers. Logically, there is great variation in the height and weight of young children. Also, cultural differences in height and weight are still evident in the early childhood years. For example, African American children in early childhood on average are taller and heavier than white children of the same age (Lowery, 1986).

One of the main arenas for physical development at this age is the brain. By age 5, the child's brain is 90% of its adult size. Motor and cognitive abilities increase by leaps and bounds because of increased interconnections between brain cells, which allow for more complex cognitive and motor capability. In addition, through a process called **lateralization,** the two hemispheres of the brain begin to operate slightly differently, allowing for a wider range of activity. Simply stated, brain functioning becomes more specialized. The left hemisphere is activated during tasks that require analytical skills, including speaking and reading. Tasks that involve emotional expression and spatial skills, such as visual imagery, require response from the right hemisphere.

Children also obtain and refine some advanced motor skills during this time, such as running, jumping, and hopping. A 3-year-old can pedal a tricycle, a 4-year-old can gallop, and a 5-year-old can jump rope and walk on a balance beam. In addition to these gross motor skills—skills that require use of the large muscle groups—young children develop fine motor skills, including the ability to scribble and draw, cut with scissors, and by age 5, print their name.

Increases in fine motor skills also allow young children to become more self-sufficient. At age 3, children can manage toilet needs without supervision; by age 4, they can dress and undress themselves and pour water into a glass. Most young children enjoy the independence that performing these skills allows. However, allowing the extra time needed for young children to perform these tasks can be frustrating to adults. Ms. Johnson, for example, has lived alone for some time now and may need to readjust to allowing extra time for the children to "do it themselves." Spills and messes, which are a part of this developmental process, are also often difficult for adults to tolerate.

Cognitive and Language Development

Recently I was at a doctor's office when a mother walked into the waiting area with her son, about age 3. The waiting area was very quiet, and the young child's voice seemed loud in the silence. The mother immediately began to "shh" her son. He responded by saying, "I don't want to shh, I want to talk." Of course, we all laughed, which made the child talk even louder. The mother moved immediately to some chairs in the corner and attempted to get her son to sit. He refused, stating that he wanted to stand on one foot. The mother at once attempted to engage him with the toys she had with her. They played with an electronic game in which the child selects pieces to add to a face to make a complete face. This game kept the child's attention for awhile until he became bored. The mother told him to "make the game stop." The child responded by yelling at the game, demanding that it stop making the face. The mother, understanding that her son had taken a literal interpretation of her comments, rephrased her directions and showed her son how to push the stop button on the game.

Next, the two decided to read a book about the Lion King. The child became very confused, because in the book, different from his memory of the movie, the main character, Simba, was already an adult at the beginning of the book. The child, looking at the pictures, argued that the adult lion was not Simba but instead was Simba's father. The mother attempted to explain that this book begins with Simba as an adult. She stated that just as her son will grow, Simba grew from a cub to an adult lion. The son looked at his mother bewildered, responding with, "I am not a cub, I am a little boy." The mother then tried to make the connection that just like the son's daddy was once a boy, Simba grew up to be a lion. The boy responded by saying that men and lions are not the same. Needless to say, the mother seemed relieved when her name was called to see the doctor.

This scene encapsulated many of the themes of cognitive and moral development in early childhood. As memory improves, and the store of information expands, young children begin to think much more in terms of categories, as the little boy in the doctor's office was doing. He was now thinking in terms of cubs, boys, lions, and men. They also begin to recognize some surprising connections between things. No doubt, in a short time, the little boy will recognize a connection between boys and cubs, men and lions, boys and men, as well as cubs and lions. Young children are full of big questions such as where do babies come from, what happens to people when they die, where does the night come from. They make great strides in language development and the ability to communicate. And they make gradual progress in the ability to judge right and wrong and to regulate behavior in relation to that reasoning.

Piaget's Stages of Cognitive Development. In early childhood, children fit into the second stage of cognitive development described by Piaget, the preoperational stage. This stage is in turn divided into two substages:

> *Substage 1: Preconceptual stage* (ages 2 to 4). The most important aspect of the preoperational stage is the development of symbolic representation, which occurs in the preconceptual stage. Through play, children learn to use symbols and actively engage in what Piaget labeled deferred imitation. Deferred imitation refers to the child's ability to view an image and then, significantly later, recall and imitate the image. For example, 3-year-old Ella, who watches the *Dora the Explorer* cartoon on TV, fills her backpack with a pretend map and other items she might need, such as a blanket and a flashlight, puts it on, creates a pretend monkey companion named Boots, and sets off on an adventure, using the kitchen as a barn, the space under the dining table as the woods, and keeping her eyes open all the while for the "mean" Swiper the Fox. Ella's cousin, Zachery, who is enthralled with the *Bob the Builder* cartoon, often pretends that he is Bob the Builder when he is playing with his toy trucks and tractors. Whenever Zachery encounters a problem, he will sing Bob's theme song, which is "Bob the Builder, can we fix it, yes we can!!"

> *Substage 2: Intuitive stage* (ages 4 to 7). During the second part of the preoperational stage, children use language to represent objects. During the preconceptual stage, any object with long ears may be called "bunny." However, during the intuitive stage, children begin to understand that the term *bunny* represents the entire animal, not just a property of it. However, although young children are able to classify objects, their classifications are based on only one attribute at a time. For example, given a set of stuffed animals of various sizes and colors, the young child will group the animals either by color or by size. In contrast, an older child who has reached the intuitive stage may sort them by both size and color.

In early childhood, children also engage in what Piaget termed **transductive reasoning**, or a way of thinking about two or more experiences without using abstract logic. This can be explained best with an illustration. Imagine that 5-year-old Sam immediately smells chicken when he enters his grandmother's home. He comments that she must be having a party and asks who is coming over for dinner. When the grandmother replies that no one is coming over and that a party is not planned, Sam shakes his head in disbelief and states that he will just wait to see when the guests arrive. Sam recalls that the last time his grandmother cooked chicken was for a party. Because grandmother is cooking chicken again, Sam thinks another party is going to occur. This type of reasoning is also evident in the example of the mother and child in the doctor's office. Because the child saw Simba as a cub in the movie version of the *Lion King*, he reasons that the adult lion in the picture at the beginning of the book cannot possibly be Simba.

One last related preoperational concept described by Piaget is **egocentrism**. According to Piaget, in early childhood, children perceive reality only from their own experience and believe themselves to be at the center of existence. They are unable to recognize the possibility of other perspectives on a situation. For example, a 3-year-old girl who stands between you and the television to watch a program believes that you can see the television because she can. This aspect of cognitive reasoning could be problematic for most of the children described in the case examples. Jack may believe that it is his fault that his father left the family. Likewise, Ron and Rosiland may attribute their mother's absence to their behavior, especially given that they were present when she was arrested.

Language Skills. Language development is included under cognitive development because it is the mechanism by which cognitive interpretations are communicated to others. Note that for language to exist, children must be able to "organize" their experiences (Hopper & Naremore, 1978).

At the end of toddlerhood, young children have a vocabulary of about 1,000 words, and they are increasing that store by about 50 words per month (Davies, 1999). They can speak in two-word sentences, and they have learned the question form of language. They are asking "why" questions, persistently and often assertively, to learn about the world. Three-year-old speech is generally clear and easy to understand.

How does language development in early childhood promote human agency in making choices?

By the fourth year of life, language development is remarkably sophisticated. The vocabulary is becoming more and more adequate for communicating ideas, and 4-year-olds are usually speaking in sentences of 8 to 10 words. They have mastered language well enough to tell a story mostly in words, rather than relying heavily on gestures, as toddlers must do. But perhaps the most remarkable aspect of language development in early childhood is the understanding of grammar rules. By age 4, young children in all cultures understand the basic grammar rules of their language. They accomplish this mostly by a figuring out process. As they figure out new grammar rules, as with other aspects of their learning, they are overly regular in using those rules, because they have not yet learned the exceptions. So we often hear young children make statements such as "she goed to the store," or perhaps "she wented to the store."

There has been a long-standing debate about how language is acquired. How much of language ability is a result of genetic processes, and how much of it is learned? B. F. Skinner (1957) argued that children learn language by imitating what they hear in the environment and then being reinforced. When children utter sounds heard in their environment, he contended, parents respond in a manner (smiling, laughing, clapping) that encourages young children to repeat the sounds. As children grow older, they are often corrected by caregivers and preschool teachers in the misuse of words or phrases. At the other end of the spectrum, Noam Chomsky (1968) contended that language ability is primarily a function of genetics. Although somewhat influenced by the environment, children develop language skills as long as the appropriate genetic material is in place.

Some scholars assert that both perspectives have merit and that language development is best thought of as "innate-learned" (Hopper & Naremore, 1978). They propose that the ability to develop language skills is genetic, but this ability must be activated and cultivated by forces in the environment. Research seems to support this premise. In studies of healthy young children, researchers have found that language development is influenced more by biological factors during the first 2 years of life and more by environmental factors during the third year (Molfese, Holcomb, & Helwig, 1994). Studies involving research on young children who were preterm infants also support the idea that language skill is due to an interaction of biological and environmental factors (Beckwith, 1984). Neonatal medical problems were found to have some influence on cognitive development, including language development; however, the development of cognitive skills was more influenced by the amount of maternal attention the children received.

How do social class, culture, and gender affect the "developmental niche" during early childhood?

Developmental niche is another environmental factor considered important in the development of language skills (Harkness, 1990). From observation of their environment—physical and social surroundings, child-rearing customs, and caregiver personality—children learn a set of regulations or rules for communication that shape their developing language skills. Children have an innate capacity for language, but the structuring of the environment through culture is what allows language development to occur.

Moral Development

During early childhood, children move from a moral sense that is based on outside approval to a more internalized moral sense, with a rudimentary moral code. They engage in a process of taking society's values and standards as their own. They begin to integrate these values and standards into both their worldview and their self-concept. There are three components of moral development during early childhood (Newman & Newman, 1997):

1. *Knowledge* of the moral code of the community and how to use that knowledge to make moral judgments
2. *Emotions* that produce both the capacity to care about others and the capacity to feel guilt and remorse
3. *Actions* to inhibit negative impulses as well as to behave in a **prosocial**, or helpful and empathic manner

Understanding Moral Development. Moral development has been explored from several different theoretical perspectives that have been found to have merit. Three of these approaches to moral development are explored here:

1. *Psychodynamic approach.* Sigmund Freud's psychoanalytic theory proposed that there are three distinct structures of the personality: id, ego, and superego. According to Freud, the superego is the personality structure that guides moral development. There are two aspects to the superego: the *conscience*, which is the basis of a moral code, and the *ego ideal*, which is a set of ideals expected in a moral person. Freud (1927) thought that the superego is formed between the ages of 4 and 7, but more recent psychodynamic formulations suggest that infancy is the critical time for the beginning of moral development (Kohut, 1971). Freud thought that children would have more highly developed superegos when their parents used strict methods to inhibit the children's impulses. Contemporary research indicates the opposite, however, finding that moral behavior is associated with parental warmth, democratic decision making, and modeling of temptation resistance (Maccoby, 1992). New psychodynamic models emphasize a close, affectionate bond with the caregiver as the cornerstone of moral development (Emde, Biringen, Clyman, & Oppenheim, 1991). Freud also believed that males would develop stronger superegos than females, but research has not supported this idea.

2. *Social learning approach.* From the perspective of social learning theory, moral behavior is shaped by environmental reinforcements and punishments. Children are likely to repeat behaviors that are rewarded, and they are also likely to feel tension when they think about doing something that they have been punished for in the past. From this perspective, parental consistency in response to their children's behavior is important. Social learning theory also suggests that children learn moral conduct by observing models. Albert Bandura (1977) found that children are likely to

EXHIBIT 4.1
Kohlberg's Stages of Moral Development

Level I:	**Preconventional** Stage 1: Moral reasoning is based on whether behavior is rewarded or punished. Stage 2: Moral reasoning is based on what will benefit the self or loved others.
Level II:	**Conventional** Stage 3: Moral reasoning is based on the approval of authorities. Stage 4: Moral reasoning is based on upholding societal standards.
Level III:	**Postconventional** Stage 5: Moral reasoning is based on social contracts and cooperation. Stage 6: Moral reasoning is based on universal ethical principles.

Source: Based on Kohlberg, 1969, 1976.

engage in behaviors for which they see a model rewarded and to avoid behaviors that they see punished.

3. *Cognitive developmental approach.* Piaget's theory of cognitive development has been the basis for stage models of moral reasoning, which assume that children's moral judgments change as their cognitive development allows them to examine the logical and abstract aspects of moral dilemmas. Moral development is assisted by opportunities to encounter new situations and different perspectives. The most frequently researched stage model is the one presented by Lawrence Kohlberg (1969, 1976) and summarized in Exhibit 4.1. Kohlberg described three levels of moral reasoning, with two stages in each level. It was expected that in early childhood, children will operate at the **preconventional level**, with their reasoning about moral issues based, first, on what gets them rewarded or punished. This type of moral reasoning is thought to be common among toddlers. In the second stage, moral reasoning is based on what benefits either the child or someone the child cares about. This is consistent with the child's growing capacity for attachments. There is some empirical evidence that children between the ages of 3 and 6 do, indeed, begin to use the type of moral reasoning described in Stage 2 (Walker, 1989).

Why is the development of empathy important for future capacity for relationships?

All of the above approaches to moral development in early childhood have been criticized for leaving out two key ingredients of moral development: **empathy**, or the ability to understand another person's emotional condition, and **perspective taking**, or the ability to see a situation from another person's point of view (Eisenberg & Strayer, 1987; Iannotti, 1985). There is growing agreement that empathy begins in infancy and grows throughout early childhood. By age 3 or 4, children across cultures have been found to be able to recognize the type of emotional reaction that other children might have to different situations (Borke, 1973). Perspective taking has been found to grow gradually, beginning at about the age of 4 or 5 (Iannotti, 1985).

Helping Young Children to Develop Morally. There is growing evidence that some methods work better than others for helping children develop moral reasoning and conduct. Activities that are particularly helpful are those that help children control their own behavior, help them understand how their behavior affects others, show them models of positive behavior, and get them to discuss moral issues (Walker & Taylor, 1991).

Although religious beliefs play a central role in most societies in clarifying moral behavior, little research has been done to explore the role of religion in moral development in young children. Recent research (Roof, 1999) has indicated that adults often become affiliated with a religious organization when their children are in early childhood, even if the parents become "religious dropouts" after the children are out of the home. Religious rituals link young children to specific actions and images of the world as well as to a community that can support and facilitate their moral development. The major world religions also teach parents about how to be parents. Young children, with their comfortable embrace of magic, easily absorb religious stories on topics that may be difficult for adults to explain. Religion that emphasizes love, concern, and social justice can enrich the young child's moral development. On the other hand, religion that is harsh and judgmental may produce guilt and a sense of worthlessness, which do not facilitate higher levels of moral reasoning.

Personality and Emotional Development

The key concern for Jack and for Ms. Johnson's grandchildren—Ron and Rosiland—is their emotional development. Specifically, will they grow into happy, loving, well-adjusted people despite the disruptions in their lives? Young children do face important developmental tasks in the emotional arena. This section addresses these tasks, drawing on Erikson's theory of psychosocial development.

Erikson's Theory of Psychosocial Development. Erikson labeled the stage of emotional development that takes place during the early childhood years as *initiative versus guilt* (ages 3 to 6). (Refer back to Exhibit 3.6 for the complete list of Erikson's stages.) Children who pass successfully through this stage learn to get satisfaction from completing tasks. They develop imagination and fantasies and learn to handle guilt about their fantasies.

At the beginning of this stage, children's focus is on family relationships. They learn what roles are appropriate for various family members, and they learn to accept parental limits. In addition, they develop gender identity through identification with the parent of the same sex. Age and sex boundaries must be appropriately defined at this stage, and parents must be secure enough to set limits and resist the child's possessiveness.

By the end of this stage, the child's focus turns to friendships outside the family. Children engage in cooperative play and enjoy both sharing and competing with peers. Children must also have the opportunity to establish peer relationships outside the family. This is one of the functions the preschool program serves for Ms. Johnson's grandchildren.

Children who become stuck in this stage are plagued with guilt about their goals and fantasies. They become confused about their gender identity and about family roles. These children are overly anxious and self-centered.

What are our societal expectations for regulation of emotions during early childhood?

Emotions. Growing cognitive and language skills give young children the ability to understand and express their feelings and emotions. They are able to label their own emotions—"I feel sad; I feel happy." However, they attribute most of their feelings to external causes—"I am sad because Mommy took my toy; I feel happy because Daddy is home from work" (Fabes, Eisenberg, Nyman, & Michealieu, 1991).

Children in early childhood can also identify feelings expressed by others and use creative ways to comfort others when they are upset. A friend describes the response of her 5-year-old son Marcus when he saw her crying about the sudden death of her brother in a car accident. Marcus hugged his mom and told her not to cry, because, although she was sad about Uncle Johnny, she still had Marcus. Marcus promised his mother to never drive a car so she would not have to worry about the same thing happening to him. This attempt to reduce his mother's sadness is a typical response from a child of this age (Fabes et al., 1991).

The ability to understand emotion continues to develop as young children have more opportunity to practice these skills. Children reared in homes in which emotions and feelings are openly discussed are better able to understand and express feelings (Denham, Zoller, & Couchoud, 1994).

Aggression. One behavior that increases during the early childhood years is aggression. Two types of aggression are observed in young children: **instrumental aggression,** which occurs while fighting over toys and space, and **hostile aggression,** which is an attack meant to hurt another individual.

Although some children continue high levels of aggression into middle childhood, usually aggression peaks early in the early childhood years (Cummings, Iannotti, & Zahn-Waxler, 1989). By the end of the early childhood years, children learn better negotiation skills and become better at asking for what they want and using words to express feelings. Terri, in the first case study in this chapter, obviously has not developed these moderating skills.

Attachment. In early childhood, children still depend on their attachment relationships for feelings of security. In particularly stressful times, the attachment behavior of the young child may look very much like the clinging behavior of the 2-year-old. For the most part, however, securely attached children will handle their anxieties by verbalizing their needs. For example, at bedtime, the 4-year-old child may say, "I would like you to read one more story before you go." This increased ability to verbalize wants is a source of security. In addition, many young children continue to use transitional objects, such as blankets or a favorite teddy bear, to soothe themselves when they are anxious.

Social Development

In early childhood, children become more socially adept than they were as toddlers, but they are still learning how to be social and how to understand the perspectives of other people. The many young children who enter group care face increasing demands for social competence.

Peer Relations. In early childhood, children form friendships with other children of the same age and gender; boys gravitate toward male playmates and girls choose girls. When asked about the definition of a friend, most children in this age group think of a friend as someone with whom you play (Youniss, 1980). My neighbor children, for example, made their initial approach to my young son by saying, "Let's be friends; let's play" and "I'll be your friend if you will be mine." They do not view friendship as a trusting, lasting relationship. Even this limited view of friendship is important for this age group, however. For example, children who enter kindergarten with identified friends adjust better to school (Johnson, Ironsmith, Snow, & Poteat, 2000).

Research indicates that young children are at a higher risk of being rejected by their peers if they are aggressive and comparatively more active, demonstrate a difficult temperament, are easily distracted, and demonstrate lower perseverance (Johnson et al., 2000; Walker, Berthelsen, & Irving, 2001). One would wonder, then, how young peers respond to Terri. The rejection of some children is long lasting. Even when they change their behavior and fit better with the norm, often they continue to be rejected (Walker et al., 2001).

Self-Concept. In early childhood, the child seems to vacillate between grandiose and realistic views of the self (Davies, 1999). On the one hand, children are aware of their growing competence, but at the same time, they have normal doubts about the self, based on realistic comparisons of their competence with the competence of adults.

Some investigators have suggested that during early childhood, the child's ever increasing understanding of the self in relation to the world begins to become organized into a **self-theory** (Epstein, 1973, 1991; Epstein, Lipson, Holstein, & Huh, 1993). As children develop the cognitive ability to categorize, they use categorization to think about the self. By age 2 or 3, children can identify their gender and race (discussed in greater detail shortly) as a factor in understanding who they are. Between the ages of 4 and 6, young children become more aware that different people have different perspectives on situations. This helps them to begin to understand cultural expectations and sensitizes them to the expectations that others have for them.

This growing capacity to understand the self in relation to others leads to self-evaluation, or **self-esteem**. Very early interpersonal experiences provide information that becomes incorporated into self-esteem. Messages of love, admiration, and approval lead to a positive view of the self. Messages of rejection or scorn lead to a negative view of the self. In addition to these interpersonal messages, young children observe their own competencies and attributes, and compare them with the competencies of other children as well as adults. And they are very aware of being evaluated by others, their peers as well as important adults.

Of course, a young child may develop a positive view of the self in one dimension, such as cognitive abilities, and a negative view of the self in another dimension, such as physical abilities. Children also learn that some abilities are more valued than others in the various environments in which they operate.

How does gender influence early childhood development?

Gender Identity and Sexual Interests. During early childhood, gender becomes an important dimension of how children understand themselves and others. There are four components to gender identity during early childhood (Newman & Newman, 1997):

1. *Making correct use of the gender label.* By age 2, children can usually accurately identify others as either male or female, based on appearance.
2. *Understanding gender as stable.* Later, children understand that gender is stable, that boys grow up to be men and girls to be women.
3. *Understanding gender constancy.* Even with this understanding of gender stability, young children, with their imaginative thinking, continue to think that girls can turn into boys and boys into girls by changing appearance. For example, a 3-year-old given a picture of a girl is able to identify the person as a girl. But if the same girl is shown in another picture dressing as a boy, the 3-year-old will label the girl a boy. It is not until sometime between age 4 and 7 that children understand *gender constancy*, the understanding that one's gender does not change, that the girl dressing as a boy is still a girl.
4. *Understanding the genital basis of gender.* Gender constancy has been found to be associated with an understanding of the relationship between gender and genitals (Bem, 1989).

Human societies use gender as an important category for organizing social life. There are some rather large cultural and subcultural variations in gender role definitions, however. Existing cultural standards about gender are pervasively built into adult interactions with young children and into the reward systems that are developed for shaping child behavior. There is much research evidence that parents begin to use gender stereotypes to respond to their children from the time of birth (O'Brien, 1992). They cuddle more with infant girls and play more actively with infant boys. Later, they talk more with young girls and expect young boys to be more independent.

Once toddlers understand their gender, they begin to imitate and identify with the same-sex parent, if he or she is available. Once young children begin to understand gender role standards, they become quite rigid in their playing out of gender roles—only girls cook, only men drive trucks, only girls wear pink flowers, only boys wear shirts with footballs. This gender understanding also accounts for the preference of same-sex playmates and sex-typed toys (Davies, 1999). Remember, though, that the exaggeration of gender stereotypes in early childhood is in keeping with the struggle during this period to discover stability and regularity in the environment.

A few researchers have found, with longitudinal research, that young boys who engage in unusual amounts of play with girls and female-identified activities are more likely than boys who engage in gender stereotypical play to have a bisexual or homosexual orientation in adolescence and young adulthood. This finding is usually interpreted to indicate an early biological factor in sexual orientation (Bailey & Zucker, 1995).

During early childhood, children become increasingly interested in their genitals. They are interested, in general, in how their bodies work, but the genitals seem to hold a special interest as the young child learns through experimentation that the genitals can be a source of pleasure. Between 3 and 5, children may have some worries and questions about genital difference; little girls may think they once had a penis and wonder what happened to it. Little boys may fear that their penises will disappear, like their sister's did. During early childhood, masturbation is used both as a method of self-soothing and for pleasure. Young children also "play doctor" with each other, and often want to see and touch their parents' genitals. Many parents and other caregivers are confused about how to handle this behavior, particularly in our era of heightened awareness of childhood sexual abuse. In general, parents should not worry about genital curiosity or about children experimenting with touching their own genitals. They should remember, however, that at this age children may be overstimulated by seeing their parents' genitals. And we should always be concerned when children want to engage in more explicit adult-like sexual play that involves stimulation of each other's genitals.

How important is racial and ethnic identity in early childhood?

Racial and Ethnic Identity. Findings from research suggest that children first learn their own racial identity before they are able to identify the race of others (Kowalski, 1996). However, identification of others by race is limited to skin color. Young children may label a Hispanic individual, for example, as either African American or white, depending on the individual's skin color. Young children also show a preference for members of their own race over another (Katz, 1976). Perhaps this choice is similar to the preference for same-sex playmates, a result of young children attempting to learn their own identity.

Social scientists concerned about the development of self-esteem in children of color have investigated racial bias and preference using children in early childhood as subjects. The most famous of these studies was conducted by Kenneth Clark and Mamie Clark in 1939. They presented African American children with black dolls and white dolls and concluded that African American children responded more favorably to the white dolls and had more negative reactions to the black dolls. A similar study 40 years later, observing young African American children in New York and Trinidad, reported similar results (Gopaul-McNicol, 1988). The young children from both New York and Trinidad preferred and identified with the white dolls. Interestingly, the same results have been reported more recently in studies of Taiwanese young children (Chang, 2001). Most of the Taiwanese children in the study indicated a preference for the white dolls and demonstrated a "pro-white attitude."

It is questionable, however, whether these preferences and biases are equated with self-concept and low self-esteem for children of color. Most argue that they are not. For example, racial bias and self-concept were not related among the young Taiwanese children (Chang, 2001). Likewise, findings from studies about young African American children indicate high levels of self-concept despite the children's bias in favor of the white culture and values (Spencer, 1985). Spencer concludes, "Racial stereotyping in black children should be viewed as objectively held information about the environment and not as a manifestation of personal identity" (p. 220).

The Role of Play

The young child loves to play, and play is essential to all aspects of early child development. We think of the play of young children as fun-filled and lively. And yet it serves a serious purpose. Through play, children develop the motor skills essential for physical development, learn the problem-solving skills and communication skills fundamental to cognitive development, and express the feelings and gain the self-confidence needed for emotional growth. Essentially, play is what young children are all about; it is their work.

Play may be one of the few elements in the development of young children that is universal, regardless of culture. Comparing children from six different countries with significantly different cultures, one study found that all children in early childhood constructed spontaneous play activities (Whiting & Whiting, 1975). Even children in cultures that require young children to work or complete chores included play in their work activities. Some suggest that the act of play is almost automatic, driven by physiological functions (Gandelman, 1992; Panksepp, 1986).

The predominant type of play in early childhood, beginning around the age of 2, is **symbolic play**, otherwise known as fantasy play, pretend play, or imaginary play (Pelligrini & Galda, 2000). Children continue to use vivid imaginations in their play, as they did as toddlers, but they also begin to put more structure into their play. Thus, their play is intermediate between the fantasy play of toddlers and the structured, rules-oriented play of middle childhood. Although toddler play is primarily nonverbal, the play of young children often involves highly sophisticated verbal productions. There is some indication that this preference for symbolic play during early childhood exists across cultures, but the themes of the play reflect the culture in which it is enacted (Roopnarine, Shin, Donovan, & Suppal, 2000).

Symbolic play during early childhood has four primary functions: providing an opportunity to explore reality, contributing to cognitive development, allowing young children to gain control over their lives, and serving as a shared experience and opportunity for development of peer culture. These functions are explained in more detail below.

Play as an Opportunity to Explore Reality. Young children imitate adult behavior and try out social roles in their play (Davies, 1999). They play house, school, doctor, police, firefighter, and so on. As they "dress up" in various guises of adult roles, or even as spiders and rabbits, they are using fantasy to explore what they might become. Their riding toys allow them to play with the experience of having greater mobility in the world.

Play's Contribution to Cognitive Development. The young child uses play to think about the world, to understand cause and effect (Roskos & Christie, 2000). Throughout early childhood, young children show increasing sophistication in using words in their dramatic play.

Some researchers have asked the question, Does symbolic play facilitate cognitive development, or does symbolic play require mature cognitive abilities? The question is unresolved; the available evidence indicates only that cognitive development is connected with play in early childhood (Roopnarine et al., 2000). Childhood sociologists have found that children create sophisticated language games for group play that facilitate the development of language and logical thinking (Corsaro, 1997). A number of researchers have studied how young children build literacy skills through play, particularly play with books (Roskos & Christie, 2000). Play that is focused on language and thinking skills has been described as **learning play** (Meek, 2000).

How does play develop skills for human agency in making choices?

Play as an Opportunity to Gain Control. In his cross-cultural study of play, William Corsaro (1997), a childhood sociologist, demonstrates that young children typically use dramatic play to cope with fears. They incorporate their fears into their group play and thus develop some mastery over stress and anxiety. This perspective on young children's play is the cornerstone of play therapy (Winnicott, 1971). Anyone who has spent much time in a child care center has probably seen a group of 4-year-olds engaged in superhero play, their flowing capes improvised with towels pinned on their shirts. Such play is "an attempt to master anxiety connected with the young child's growing perception that he's a small person in a big world who is incompetent compared to adults" (Davies, 1999, p. 240). Corsaro (1997) suggests that the love for climbing toys that bring small children high over the heads of others serves the same purpose.

Children in preschool settings have also been observed trying to get control over their lives by subverting some of the control of adults. Corsaro (1997) describes a preschool where the children had been told that they could not bring any play items from home. The preschool teachers were trying to avoid the kinds of conflicts that can occur over toys brought from home. The children in this preschool found a way to subvert this rule, however: they began to bring in very small toys, such as matchbox cars, that would fit in their pockets out of sight when teachers were nearby. Corsaro provides a number of other examples from his cross-cultural research of ways that young children use play to take some control of their lives away from adults.

Play as a Shared Experience. There is increasing emphasis on the way that play in early childhood contributes to the development of peer culture. Many researchers who study the play of young children suggest that **sociodramatic play**, or group fantasy play in which children coordinate their fantasy, is the most important form of play during this time. Indeed, one researcher has reported that two thirds of the play among North American young children is sociodramatic play (Rubin, 1986). Young children are able to develop more elaborate fantasy play and sustain it by forming friendship groups, which in turn gives them experience with group conflict and group problem solving that carries over into the adult world (Corsaro, 1997).

As young children play in groups, they attempt to protect the opportunity to keep the play going by restricting who may enter the play field (Corsaro, 1997). Young children can often be heard making such comments as, "We're friends; we're playing, right?" Or perhaps, "You're not our friend, you can't play with us." The other side of the coin is that young children must learn how to gain access to play in progress (Garvey, 1984). An important social skill is being able to demonstrate that they can play without messing the game up. Young children learn a set of do's and don'ts to accomplish that goal (see Exhibit 4.2) and develop complex strategies for gaining access to play.

Conflict often occurs in young children's play groups, and researchers have found gender and cultural variations in how these conflicts get resolved. Young girls have been found to prefer dyadic (two-person) play interactions, and young boys enjoy larger groups (Benenson, 1993). These preferences may not hold across cultures, however. For example, white middle-class young girls in the United States are less direct and assertive in challenging each other in play situations than either African American girls in the United States or young girls in an Italian preschool (Corsaro, 1997). Greater assertiveness may allow for more comfortable play in larger groups.

EXHIBIT 4.2
Do's and Don'ts of Getting Access to Play in Progress

Do's

Watch what's going on.
Figure out the play theme.
Enter the area.
Plug into the action.
Hold off making suggestions about how to change the action.

Don'ts

Don't ask questions for information (if you can't tell what's going on, you'll mess it up).
Don't mention yourself or your reactions to what is going on.
Don't disagree or criticize what is happening.

Source: Based on Garvey, 1984.

Developmental Disruptions

Most developmental problems in infants and young children are more accurately described as **developmental delays**, offering the hope that early intervention, or even natural processes, will mitigate the long-term effects. In contrast, developmental problems in school-age children are typically labeled disabilities and classified into groups, such as mental retardation, learning disabilities, and motor impairment (Zipper & Simeonsson, 1997).

Many young children with developmental difficulties, including emotional and behavioral concerns, are inaccurately assessed and misdiagnosed—often because young children are assessed independently of their environment (Freeman & Dyer, 1993). After interviewing professionals who work with children age 6 and under, one research team compiled a list of traits observed in young children that indicate emotional and behavioral problems: extreme aggressive behavior, difficulty with change, invasion of others' personal space, compulsive or impulsive behavior, low ability to trust others, lack of empathy or remorse, and cruelty to animals (Schmitz & Hilton, 1996). Parents and teachers often handle these behaviors with firmer limits and more discipline. However, environmental risk factors, such as emotional abuse or neglect and domestic violence, may be the actual cause.

Given the difficulty of accurate assessment, assessment in young children should include many disciplines, to gain as broad an understanding as possible (Zipper & Simeonsson, 1997). Assessment and service delivery should also be culturally relevant (Parette, 1995). In other words, culture and other related issues—such as family interaction patterns and stress, the social environment, ethnicity, acculturation, social influences, and developmental expectations—should all be considered when evaluating a child's developmental abilities.

For those children who have been labeled developmentally delayed, the main remedy has been social skill development. In one such program, two types of preschool classrooms were evaluated (Roberts, Burchinal, & Bailey, 1994). In one classroom, young developmentally delayed children were matched with nondelayed children of the same age; in another classroom, some of the "normal" children were the same age as the developmentally delayed children and some were older. Social exchange between the children with disabilities and those without disabilities was greater in the mixed-aged classroom. Another study evaluated the usefulness of providing social skills training to children with mild developmental disabilities (Lewis, 1994). In a preschool setting, developmentally delayed children were put in situations requiring social interaction and were praised for successful interaction. This method increased social interaction between the young children.

Early Childhood in the Multigenerational Family

Curiosity and experimentation are the hallmarks of early childhood. Young children are sponges, soaking up information about themselves, their worlds, and their relationships. They use their families as primary sources of information and as models for relationships. Where there are older siblings, they serve as important figures of identification and imitation. Aunts, uncles, cousins, and grandparents may also serve this role, but parents are, in most families, the most important sources of information, support, and modeling for young children.

Parents play two very important roles for their age 3 to 6 child: educator and advocate (Newman & Newman, 1997). As educators, they answer children's big and little questions, ask questions to stimulate thinking and growth in communication skills, provide explanations, and help children figure things out. They teach children about morality and human connectedness by modeling honest, kind, thoughtful behavior, and by reading to their children about moral dilemmas and moral action. They help children develop emotional intelligence by modeling how to handle strong feelings, and by talking with children about the children's strong feelings. They take young children on excursions in their real physical worlds as well as in the fantasy worlds found in books. They give children opportunities to perform tasks that develop a sense of mastery.

Not all parents have the same resources for the educator role or the same beliefs about how children learn. And some parents take their role as educators too seriously, pushing their young children into more and more structured time with higher and higher expectations of performance (Elkind, 1981). Many of these parents are pushing their own frustrated dreams onto their young children. The concern is that these children are deprived of time for exploration, experimentation, and fantasy.

In the contemporary era, children are moving into organized child care settings at earlier ages. As they do so, parents become more important as advocates who understand their children's needs. The advocate role is particularly important for parents of young children with disabilities. These parents may need to advocate to ensure that all aspects of early childhood education programs are accessible to their children.

For some children, like Ron and Rosiland, it is the grandparent and not the parent who serves as the central figure. Estimates are that 5.4 million children live in homes headed by a grandparent or other relative (Children's Defense Fund, 2001a). In about 50% of these families, no biological parent is present in the home. Substance abuse, divorce, teen pregnancy, the AIDS epidemic, and imprisoned mothers like Shirley account for the large number of children living in grandparent-headed homes (Jendrek, 1993). Some custodial grandparents describe an increased purpose for living (Roe & Minkler, 1998/99), but others describe increased isolation, worry, physical and emotional exhaustion, and financial concerns (Roe & Minkler, 1998/99). These are some of the same concerns expressed by Ms. Johnson. In addition, grandparents caring for children with psychological and physical problems experience high levels of stress (Sands & Goldberg, 2000).

The literature indicates that young children often do better under the care of grandparents than in other types of homes (Jendrek, 1993). However, children parented by their grandparents must often overcome many difficult emotions (Smith, Dannison, & Vach-Hasse, 1998). These children struggle with issues of grief and loss related to loss of their parent(s) and feelings of guilt, fear, embarrassment, and anger. These feelings may be especially strong for young children who feel they are somehow responsible for the loss of their parent(s).

Although children in this age group are capable of labeling their feelings, their ability to discuss these feelings with any amount of depth is very limited. In addition, grandparents may feel unsure about how to talk about the situation with their young grandchildren.

Professional intervention for the children is often recommended (Smith et al., 1998). Some mental health practitioners have had success providing group sessions that help grandparents gain control over their grandchildren's behavior, resolve clashes in values between themselves and their grandchildren, and help grandparents avoid overindulgence and set firm limits (Stokes & Greenstone, 1981).

Risks to Healthy Development in Early Childhood

Why is it important to recognize risk factors and protective factors in early childhood?

This section addresses a few risk factors that social workers are likely to encounter in work with young children and their families: poverty, ineffective discipline, divorce, and violence (including child abuse). In addition, the section outlines the protective factors and social work interventions that ameliorate the risks.

Poverty

Over 11 million children live in poverty in the United States—including 17% of children age 6 and younger. About 40% of U.S. children 6 years and younger live in low-income families, with incomes below 200% of the poverty level (National Center for Children in Poverty, 2002). Poverty, in the form of poor nutrition, inadequate health care, and overcrowded living conditions, presents considerable risks to children's growth and development. Estimates are that thousands of young children, especially those from poor African American communities, are not being immunized, threatening their long-term health (Copeland, 1996). Overcrowding is particularly problematic to young children in that it restricts opportunities for play, the means through which most development occurs. Research indicates that young children reared in poverty are significantly delayed in language and other cognitive skills (Locke, Ginsborg, & Peers, 2002). The effects of poverty on children in early childhood appear to be long lasting. Children who experience poverty during their early years are less likely to complete school than children whose initial exposure to poverty occurred in the middle childhood years or during adolescence (Brooks-Gunn & Duncan, 1997). Researchers have also found that children who live in poverty are at high risk for low self-esteem, peer conflict, depression, and childhood psychological disorders (McLoyd & Wilson, 1991; McWhirter et al., 1993). These problems are primarily the outcome of living in a violent setting or in deteriorated housing and of the instability that results from frequent changes in residence and schools (McLoyd & Wilson, 1991). Overall, children who live in poverty, regardless of other adversities, suffer the worst consequences (Brooks-Gunn & Duncan, 1997).

Ineffective Discipline

A popular guidebook for parents declares, "Under no circumstances should you ever punish your child!!" (Moyer, 1974, p. 40). Punishment implies an attempt to get even with the child, whereas **discipline** involves helping the child overcome a problem.

Parents often struggle with how forceful to be in response to undesired behavior. The Smiths are a good example of this struggle. Because parents are not formally trained in parenting skills in the United States, the type of discipline they use, and the circumstances in which they use it, is often molded by how they were disciplined as children and by cultural and societal norms. However, parenting styles are not permanent (Hemenway, Solnick, & Carter, 1994). Even adults who experienced the most punitive type of correction as children are able to escape the "transgenerational cycle" of punitive child-rearing practices.

How can social workers help parents with parenting young children? Following extensive research, Diana Baumrind (1971) described three parenting styles: authoritarian,

Exhibit 4.3
Three Parenting Styles

Parenting Style	Description	Type of Discipline
Authoritarian	Parents who use this type of parenting are rigid and controlling. Rules are narrow and specific, with little room for negotiation, and children are expected to follow the rules without explanation.	Cold and harsh. Physical force. No explanation of rules provided.
Authoritative	These parents are more flexible than authoritarian parents. Their rules are more reasonable, and they leave opportunities for compromises and negotiation.	Warm and nurturing. Positive reinforcement. Set firm limits and provide rationale behind rules and decisions.
Permissive	The parents' rules are unclear, and children are left to make their own decisions.	Warm and friendly toward their children. No direction given.

Source: Adapted from Baumrind, 1971.

authoritative, and permissive (see Exhibit 4.3). The **authoritative parenting** style is considered the most desirable approach to discipline and behavior management. Baumrind suggests that children reared from the authoritative perspective are energetic, competent, and more socially adept than others. Children reared from the **permissive parenting** orientation are said to be cheerful but demonstrate little if any impulse control. In addition, these children are overly dependent and have low levels of self-reliance. The Smiths' style of parenting probably fits here. Certainly, Terri's behavior mirrors behavior exhibited by children reared with the permissive style. Children reared under an **authoritarian parenting** style become hostile and moody and have difficulty managing stress. Discipline that is punitive, especially spanking, is associated with increased levels of aggression in children (Carey, 1994; Welsh, 1985).

Parenting styles are prescribed in part by the community and the culture. For example, West Indian and Puerto Rican communities typically use physical punishment as a discipline technique (Canino & Spurlock, 1994).

Also, some differences in parenting styles are a product of the socioeconomic environment in which they occur. Low-income parents are often more authoritarian than other parents, exercising rigid, controlling techniques (Maccoby, 1980). This practice, however, may seem more legitimate in context. Parents usually respond with discipline to three types of situations: physical danger, their children's expression of psychobiological drives such as sex and aggression, and their children's socializing inside and outside of the family (Epstein, Bishop, Ruan, Miller, & Keitner, 1993). Logically, dangerous situations require more rigid and uncompromising forms of discipline. A middle-income mother who professes to be radically opposed to physical punishment may admit that she spanked her child once for running out of a store into a busy parking lot. Low-income parents are likely to be confronted with many dangerous situations involving their children. In neighborhoods where violence is a part of everyday life, rules become a matter of protection, and adherence to the rules is a survival tactic. Physical punishment for disobeying the rules is not necessarily the best or only solution. But for many low-income parents, harsh punishment may be less an issue of control or "bad parenting" than an effort to cope with a desperate situation.

Divorce

How are young children affected by this historical trend toward high rates of divorce?

The divorce rate has quadrupled over the past 20 years, and in 1997, over one third of all U.S. families were families where children were being raised by one parent, usually the mother (Children's Defense Fund, 1997). It is estimated that over half of the children born in the 1990s spent some of their childhood in a single-parent household (Anderson, 1999). These single-parent families often live in poverty, and as I have already mentioned, poverty can have a negative effect on children's development.

Regardless of family income level, many children suffer when their parents divorce. It has been suggested, however, that the negative effects children experience may actually be the result of parents' responses to divorce rather than of the divorce itself (Brown, Eichenberger, Portes, & Christensen, 1991). In fact, parental coping and adjustment may be solely responsible for the negative adjustment of children after a divorce (Kurtz, 1995).

One significant parental issue is the relationship that the parents maintain during and after the divorce. With minimal conflict between the parents about custody, visitation, and child-rearing issues, and with parents' positive attitude toward each other, children experience fewer negative consequences (Wallerstein & Kelly, 1980). Unfortunately, many children, like Jack in the case study, end up as noncombatants in the middle of a war, trying to avoid or defuse raging anger and disagreement between the two parents.

Many divorced parents have difficulty maintaining effective levels of parenting. Consequently, children often experience inconsistent discipline and a decrease in attention and nurturing. For example, divorced mothers of young children provide less stimulation and support to their children, a consequence of the mothers' dissatisfaction with and concern about their own lives (Poehlmann & Fiese, 1994). This lack of stimulation and support has a negative effect on the children's cognitive development.

How does psychological age affect children's responses to domestic violence?

In early childhood, children are more vulnerable than older children to the emotional and psychological consequences of separation and divorce (Wallerstein & Blakeslee, 1989; Wallerstein & Corbin, 1991; Wallerstein, Corbin, & Lewis, 1988). One reason may be that young children have difficulty understanding divorce and often believe that the absent parent is no longer a member of the family and will never be seen again. In addition, because of young children's egocentrism, they often feel that the divorce is a result of their behavior and experience the absent parent's leaving as a rejection of them. One wonders if Jack thinks he not only caused his father to leave but also caused him to become the devil.

The good news/bad news is that children's adaptation to divorce is not necessarily permanent. One study found that many children who initially were negatively affected by their parents' divorce were well adjusted when evaluated 10 years later (Wallerstein & Blakeslee, 1989). Conversely, however, many children who initially seemed to adjust well to their parents' divorce were not as well adjusted 10 years later.

To successfully adjust to their parents' divorce, children must accomplish six tasks (Wallerstein, 1983):

1. Come to accept that their parents are divorced and that their access to at least one parent will change
2. Disengage from their parents' conflict and get on with their own "work" (school, play, friends, etc.)
3. Cope with such losses as moving, losing income, and losing a parent
4. Acknowledge and resolve their feelings of anger at themselves or at one or both parents
5. Accept that the divorce is permanent
6. Realize that just because their parents' marriage failed does not mean they are incapable of healthy relationships with others—in other words, that their parents' divorce does not preclude a successful marriage for them

Task 6 is the most important, and the child's ability to accomplish it depends on successful resolution of the other five tasks. Most young children are not capable of resolving all these tasks, but they can begin working toward resolution during the early childhood years.

Violence

Many parents complain that keeping violence away from children requires tremendous work even in the best of circumstances. Children witness violence on television and through video and computer games and hear about it through many other sources. In the worst of circumstances, young children not only are exposed to violence but become victims of it as well. This section discusses three types of violence experienced by many young children: community violence, domestic violence, and child abuse.

Community Violence. In some neighborhoods, acts of violence are so common that the communities are labeled "war zones." However, most residents prefer not to be combatants. When surveyed, mothers in a Chicago housing project ranked neighborhood violence as their number one concern and as the condition that most negatively affects the quality of their life and the lives of their children (Dubrow & Garbarino, 1989). Unfortunately, neighborhood violence has become a major health issue for children (Pennekamp, 1995).

A few years ago, I had the opportunity to observe the effects of community violence up close when I took my daughter to get her hair braided by someone who lived in a housing project, an acquaintance of a friend. Because the hair-braiding procedure takes several hours, my daughter and I were in the home for an extended period. While we were there, the news was released that Tupac Shakur (a popular rap singer) had died from gunshot injuries received earlier. An impromptu gathering of friends and relatives of the woman who was doing the braiding ensued. Ten men and women in their early 20s, along with their young children, gathered to discuss the shooting and to pay tribute to Tupac, who had been one of their favorite artists. As Tupac's music played in the background, I was struck by several themes:

- Many in the room told of a close relative who had died as a result of neighborhood violence. I noticed on the wall of the apartment three framed programs from funerals of young men. I later learned that these dead men were a brother and two cousins of the woman who lived in the apartment. All three had been killed in separate violent incidents in their neighborhood.
- A sense of hopelessness permeated the conversation. The men especially had little hope of a future, and most thought they would be dead by age 40. Clinicians who work with young children living in neighborhoods in which violence is prevalent relate similar comments from children (National Center for Clinical Infant Programs, 1992). When asked if he had decided what he wanted to be when he grew up, one child is quoted as saying, "Why should I? I might not grow up" (p. 25).
- Perhaps related to the sense of hopelessness was an embracing of violence. I observed that during lighter moments in the conversation, the guests would chuckle about physical confrontations between common acquaintances.

Ironically, as my daughter and I were about to leave, gunshots sounded and the evening get-together was temporarily interrupted. Everyone, including the children, ran out of the apartment to see what had happened. For me, the significance of the evening was summarized in one of the last comments I heard before leaving. One of the men stated, "If all that money didn't save Tupac, what chance do we have?" It is interesting to note that Tupac's music and poetry continue to be idolized. Many still identify with his descriptions of hopelessness.

These sorts of conditions are not favorable for adequate child development (Dubrow & Garbarino, 1989). Investigations into the effects of living in violent neighborhoods support this claim. Children who grow up in a violent environment are reported to demonstrate low self-esteem, deficient social skills, and difficulty coping with and managing conflict (MacLennan, 1994). When my daughter and I visited the housing project, for example, we witnessed a 3-year-old telling her mother to "shut up." The mother and child then began hitting each other. Yes, some of this behavior is a result of parenting style, but one cannot help wondering about the influence of living in a violent community.

For many children living in violent neighborhoods, the death of a close friend or family member is commonplace. My husband, who is also a social worker, was employed at a community child guidance center. He reported that appointments were often canceled so the parents could attend funerals.

Living so intimately with death has grave effects on young children. In one study of young children whose older siblings had been victims of homicide, the surviving siblings showed symptoms of depression, anxiety, psychosocial impairment, and post-traumatic stress disorder (Freeman, Shaffer, & Smith, 1996). These symptoms are similar to those observed in young children in situations of political and military violence—for example, in Palestinian children in the occupied West Bank (Baker, 1990) and in children in South African townships during apartheid (Magwaza, Kilian, Peterson, & Pillay, 1993). Perhaps the label "war zone" is an appropriate one for violent communities.

Domestic Violence. Domestic violence may take the form of verbal, psychological, or physical abuse, although physical abuse is the form most often implied. An estimated 3 million to 10 million children per year witness their mothers being assaulted by their fathers (Silvern & Kaersvang, 1989; Vissing, Straus, Gelles, & Harrop, 1991). The number of children who witness domestic violence is even higher when instances of abuse by stepfathers, boyfriends, and other male liaisons—as well as abuses perpetrated by women—are included.

In early childhood, children respond in a number of ways during violent episodes (Smith, O'Connor, & Berthelsen, 1996). Some children display fright—that is, they cry and scream. Others attempt to stop the violence by ordering the abuser to stop, by physically placing themselves between the mother and the abuser, or by hitting the abuser. Many children attempt to flee by retreating to a different room, turning up the volume on the TV, or trying to ignore the violence.

The effects of domestic violence on children's development are well documented. Distress, problems with adjustment, characteristics of trauma, and increased behavior problems have all been observed in children exposed to domestic violence (Hughes, 1988; Perloff & Buckner, 1996; Shepard, 1992; Silvern & Kaersvang, 1989). In addition, these children develop either aggressive behaviors or passive responses, both of which make them potential targets for abuse as teens and adults (Suh & Abel, 1990; Tutty & Wagar, 1994).

In early childhood, children are more vulnerable than older children to the effects of living with domestic violence (O'Keefe, 1994; Smith et al., 1996). Younger children simply have fewer internal resources to help them cope with the experience. In addition, older children have friendships outside the family for support, whereas younger children rely primarily on the family. Many parents who are victims of domestic violence become emotionally unavailable to their young children. Battered mothers, for example, often become depressed and preoccupied with the abuse and their personal safety, leaving little time and energy for the attention and nurturing needed by young children. Another reason that young children are more vulnerable to the effects of domestic violence is that children between the ages of 3 and 6 lack the skills to verbalize their feelings and thoughts. As a result, thoughts and feelings about the violence get trapped inside and continually infringe upon the child's thoughts and emotions. Finally, as in the case of divorce, because of their egocentrism, young children often blame themselves for the domestic abuse.

Domestic violence does not always affect children's long-term development, however. In one study, one third of the children seemed unaffected by the domestic violence they witnessed at home; these children were well adjusted and showed no signs of distress, anxiety, or behavior problems (Smith et al., 1996). Two factors may buffer the effect domestic violence has on children (O'Keefe, 1994):

1. *Amount of domestic violence witnessed by the child.* The more violent episodes children witness, the more likely they are to develop problematic behavior.

2. *Relationship between the child and the mother, assuming the mother is the victim.* If the mother/child relationship remains stable and secure, the probability of the child developing behavioral difficulties decreases significantly—even when the amount of violence witnessed by the child is relatively high.

Interestingly, the father/child relationship in cases of domestic abuse was not found to be related to the child's emotional or psychological development (O'Keefe, 1994). Perhaps either the father figure in many of these cases is not the biological father or the mother/child attachment is more significant for younger children.

Child Abuse. Every day in the United States, 7,942 children are reported abused or neglected (Children's Defense Fund, 2001a). Child abuse may take the form of verbal, emotional, physical, or sexual abuse or child neglect. Child abuse creates risks to all aspects of growth and development, as shown in Exhibit 4.4. Young children who have been abused or neglected are often withdrawn, fatigued, immobile, and lacking in age-appropriate curiosity (Veltkamp & Miller, 1994). They are often overly dependent on others and excessively concerned about parental needs, at the expense of their own needs. These young children are also leery of physical contact and are excessively self-controlled.

Although child abuse and neglect occur across gender, ethnic, and socioeconomic divisions, some of these factors present a higher risk than others. Poverty and the lack of economic resources are correlated with abuse, especially physical abuse and neglect. In addition, family isolation and lack of a support system, parental drug and alcohol abuse, lack of knowledge regarding child rearing, and parental difficulty in expressing feelings are all related to child abuse (Gelles, 1989; Veltkamp & Miller, 1994; Wolfner & Gelles, 1993). An association has also been noted between abuse of young children and the overload of responsibilities that women often encounter. Mothers who work outside the home and are also responsible for most or all of the domestic responsibilities, and mothers with unemployed husbands, are more prone to abuse their young children than other groups of mothers are (Gelles & Hargreaves, 1981).

There is also a high correlation between domestic violence and child abuse. Results from one study indicated that men who physically abuse their spouses are also more likely to abuse their children (Ross, 1996).

Protective Factors in Early Childhood

Many of the factors listed in Chapter 3 that promote resiliency during the infant and toddler years are equally relevant during the early childhood years. Other protective factors also come into play (Kirby and Fraser, 1997):

- *Social support.* Social support mediates many potential risks to the development of young children. The presence of social support increases the likelihood of a positive outcome for children whose parents divorce (Garvin, Kalter, & Hansell, 1993), moderates the effects for children who experience violence (Nettles, Mucherah, & Jones, 2000), facilitates better outcomes for children of mothers with mental illness (Oyserman, Bybee, Mowbray, & MacFarlane, 2002), and is even thought to reduce the continuation of abuse for 2- and 3-year-olds who have experienced parental abuse during the first year of life (Kotch et al., 1997). Social support aids young children in several ways (Kirby & Fraser, 1997). Having a consistent and supportive

EXHIBIT 4.4

Some Potential Effects of Child Abuse on Growth and Development

Physical Impairments	Cognitive Impairments	Emotional Impairments
Physical Abuse and Neglect		
Burns, scars, fractures, broken bones, damage to vital organs and limbs Malnourishment Physical exposure Poor skin hygiene Poor (if any) medical care Poor (if any) dental care Serious medical problems Serious dental problems Death	Delayed cognitive skills Delayed language skills Mental retardation Failure-to-thrive syndrome Delayed reality testing Overall disruption of thought processes	Negative self-concept Increased aggressiveness Poor peer relations Poor impulse control
Sexual Abuse		
Trauma to mouth, anus, vaginal area Genital and rectal pain Genital and rectal bleeding Genital and rectal tearing Sexually transmitted disease	Hyperactivity Bizarre sexual behavior	Overly adaptive behavior Overly compliant behavior Habit disorders (nail biting) Sleep disturbances Night terrors Self-mutilation
Psychological/Emotional Abuse		
	Pessimistic view of life Anxiety and fear Distorted perception of world Deficits in moral development	Alienation Intimacy problems Low self-esteem Depression

Source: Adapted from Drisko, 1992. See also Veltkamp & Miller, 1994.

aunt or uncle or preschool teacher who can set firm but loving limits, for example, may buffer the effects of a parent with ineffective skills. At the community level, preschools, church programs, and the like may help to enhance physical and cognitive skills, self-esteem, and social development. Through social support from family and nonfamily relationships, young children can receive care and support, another identified protective factor.

- *Positive parent-child relationship.* A positive relationship with at least one parent helps children to feel secure and nurtured (Kirby & Fraser, 1997). Remember from

Chapter 3 that a sense of security is the foundation on which young children build initiative during the early childhood years. Even if Jack never has contact with his father, Charles, a positive relationship with Joyce, his mother, can mediate this loss.

- *Effective parenting.* In early childhood, children need the opportunity to take initiative but also need firm limits, whether they are established by parents or grandparents or someone else who adopts the parent role. Terri, for example, has not been able to establish self-control because her boundaries are not well defined. Effective parenting promotes self-efficacy and self-esteem and provides young children with a model of how they can take initiative within boundaries (Kirby & Fraser, 1997).
- *Self-esteem.* A high level of self-worth may allow young children to persist in mastery of skills despite adverse conditions. Perhaps a high level of self-esteem can enhance Ron's, Rosiland's, and Jack's development despite the disruptions in their lives. In addition, research indicates that self-esteem is a protective factor against the effects of child abuse (Kirby & Fraser, 1997).
- *Intelligence.* Even in young children, a high IQ serves as a protective factor. For example, young children with high IQs were less likely to be affected by maternal psychopathology (Tiet et al., 2001). Others suggest that intelligence results in success, which leads to higher levels of self-esteem (Kirby & Fraser, 1997). For young children, then, intelligence may contribute to mastery of skills and independence, which may enhance self-esteem. Intelligence may also protect children through increased problem-solving skills, which allow for more effective responses to adverse situations.

Social Work Interventions: Promoting Resilience in Early Childhood

Young children need the opportunity for growth, health, and achievement. But a large percentage of young children today face substantial risks to healthy development. As social workers, we must be prepared to help them develop the resilience they need to overcome those risks.

Advocating for Services for Poor Children

Poor children in their early childhood years continue to need adequate nutrition and health care. Improving access to existing programs, facilitating community organization, assisting families to take self-help measures, and supporting national efforts to improve immunization among poor children are all methods to help mediate the effects of poverty on young children (Copeland, 1996).

Alleviating Emotional and Behavioral Problems

The risks to healthy development have increased for children of all socioeconomic levels over the past decade, and the needs of younger children have grown and have become more complex (Schmitz & Hilton, 1996). The result has been an increase in the number of emotional and behavioral problems observed in children age 6 and younger. Research indicates that older children and adolescents with behavior disorders first exhibited problems at a very young age (Schmitz & Hilton, 1996).

Children under 6, however, are often excluded from therapeutic services because of their age. Many assume these children are too young to benefit from therapeutic intervention because they lack the verbal skills to participate and because the "real" problem is with the parents. Parents have described their futile attempts to solicit therapeutic services for their young children who exhibit emotional and behavioral problems. They are usually turned away with the recommendation that they consider a parenting class. Even when a traumatic event occurs, such as the murder of an older sibling, younger children are unlikely to receive any type of mental health services (Freeman et al., 1996). In fact, younger children of battered women are often referred to as "the forgotten victims" (Grusznski, Brink, & Edleson, 1988).

Given these findings and the fact that younger children respond more quickly than older ones to treatment, it seems therapeutically and financially wise to target this age group for therapeutic services. The idea of offering services at an earlier age is supported by an evaluation of a child abuse prevention program providing the same type of intervention to children of various ages (Dhooper & Schneider, 1995). The researchers found that the younger the child, the more the child gained from the intervention experience. Some have also suggested that services must begin with younger children to break the transgenerational cycle of disruptive behavior often associated with such risk factors as poverty and violence (Frey, 1989).

Innovative programs also enhance parents' ability to assess their child's functioning and provide techniques that parents can use to promote healthy development. In one such program, parents were provided with assessment materials and educated on how to use these materials to assess their child's functioning in the home (Bloch & Seitz, 1989). In other programs, parents were instructed on how to teach cognitive skills to their children and how to use play to enhance parent/child relationships (Coleman & Ganong, 1983; McLaren, 1988).

Preschools offer a natural setting for mental health services to this age group. For example, mental health professionals provided intervention services to day care centers in Jerusalem (Frank, Bell, Nowik, & Faber, 1989). Alternative forms of intervention—such as play, drawings, and storybooks, which give children an opportunity to act out feelings and problems—have been successful in alleviating symptomatic behavior in younger children (Magwaza et al., 1993; Tutty & Wagar, 1994).

Promoting Effective Parenting

At one level, promoting effective parenting means helping to eliminate such risk factors to healthy development as poverty and domestic abuse. But social workers can also help a great deal at the individual level by promoting positive parent/child relationships. This approach fits well with the social work concept of the person in the environment: the parent is the most important component of a young child's environment. Social workers must continue to provide services to parents from this perspective, which often means helping parents diminish their own level of stress in order to meet the needs of their children. In addition, helping parents work toward fulfillment of their own needs will help them be more effective. Research indicates that parents' response to stress, especially mothers' response, is a better predictor of the young child's adjustment than is the stressful situations experienced by the child (Hodges, Tierney, & Buchsbaum, 1984).

Promoting Self-Efficacy and Self-Esteem

Social workers can promote the healthy development of young children by helping to create opportunities for them to increase self-efficacy and self-esteem. For example, groups in which young children learn and demonstrate problem-solving and safety skills have been effective in helping them anticipate potential violence and practice potential responses (Grusznski et al., 1988; Tutty & Wagar, 1994). Such groups help children gain more feelings of control.

IMPLICATIONS FOR SOCIAL WORK PRACTICE

In summary, knowledge about early childhood has several implications for social work practice with young children:

- Become well acquainted with theories and empirical research about growth and development among young children.
- Continue to promote the elimination of poverty and the advancement of social justice.
- Collaborate with other professionals in the creation of laws, interventions, and programs that assist in the elimination of violence.
- Create and support easy access to services for young children and their parents.

- Assess younger children in the context of their environment.
- Become familiar with the physical and emotional signs of child abuse.
- Directly engage younger children in an age-appropriate intervention process.
- Provide support to parents and help facilitate positive parent/child relationships.
- Encourage and engage both mothers and fathers in the intervention process.
- Provide opportunities for children to increase self-efficacy and self-esteem.
- Help parents understand the potential effects of negative environmental factors on their children.

Key Terms

authoritarian parenting
authoritative parenting
developmental delay
discipline
egocentrism
empathy
hostile aggression
instrumental aggression
lateralization
learning play
permissive parenting
perspective taking
preconventional level of moral reasoning
self-esteem
self-theory
sociodramatic play
symbolic play
transductive reasoning

Active Learning

1. Watch any child-oriented cartoon on television. Describe the apparent and implied messages (both positive and negative) available in the cartoon about race and ethnicity, and gender differences. Consider how these messages might affect gender and ethnic development in young children.

2. Observe preschool-age children at play. Record the types of play that you observe. How well do your observations fit with what is described about play in this chapter?
3. The case studies at the beginning of this chapter (Terri, Jack, and Ron and Rosiland) do not specify race or ethnicity of the families. How important an omission did that appear to you? What assumptions did you make about the racial and/or ethnic background of the families? On what basis did you make those assumptions?

Web Resources

Children of Separation and Divorce

www.divorceabc.com/./default.htm

Site presented by the Children of Separation and Divorce Center Inc. (COSD) contains information about support groups, resources for professionals, library of articles, news and events, KIDS Newsletter, and Frequently Asked Questions.

Facts for Families

www.aacap.org/publications/factsfam/index.htm

Site presented by American Academy of Child & Adolescent Psychiatry contains concise and up-to-date information on a variety of issues facing children and their families, including day care, discipline, children and divorce, child abuse, children and TV violence, and children and grief.

The Office for Studies in Moral Development and Education

tigger.uic.edu/~1nucci/MoralEd/office.html

Site presented by the Office for Studies in Moral Development and Education at the College of Education at the University of Illinois at Chicago contains an overview of Piaget's, Kohlberg's, and Gilligan's theories of moral development and the domain theory of moral development.

Play Therapy Central

playtherapycentral.com/center.html

Site presented by Kid Power, a play therapy training center in Red Bluff, California, contains information on home study courses, workshops, therapist resources, and parent resources.

Children's Defense Fund

www.childrensdefense.org/

Site presented by the Children's Defense Fund, a private nonprofit child advocacy organization, contains information on issues, the Black Community Crusade for Children, the Child Watch Visitation Program, and a parent resource network.

U.S. Department of Health & Human Services

www.dhhs.gov

Site maintained by the U.S. Department of Health & Human Services contains information on child care, child support enforcement, and children's health insurance.

CHAPTER 5

Middle Childhood

Leanne Wood Charlesworth

Pamela Viggiani

Jim Wood

CHAPTER 5

Middle Childhood

Leanne Wood Charlesworth
Caliber Associates

Pamela Viggiani
Nazareth College

Jim Wood
Sodus Central School District

What types of school, family, and community environments are most conducive to positive development during middle childhood?

How does the socioeconomic system, both within the United States and globally, affect child development during the middle childhood years?

How does resilience develop in children?

Key Ideas

As you read this chapter, take note of these central ideas:

1. In general, during middle childhood, reasoning becomes more logical, an internally based system of morality develops, the child becomes able to understand the perspectives of others, and the child acquires an enhanced sense of mastery.
2. Schools are the primary context for development in middle childhood and have many positive effects, but they have traditionally presented a number of challenges to development for children belonging to nondominant groups.
3. As children progress through middle childhood, peers have an increasingly important impact on behavior, emotions, and activities; peer acceptance becomes very important for psychological adjustment.

4. Socially competent children begin to develop close friends and fairly stable friendship networks—although family remains an extremely important influence.

5. Poverty, biculturalism, attention deficits, family disruption, physical disabilities, and family and community violence pose significant challenges for many children in middle childhood.

Case Study 5.1

Malik's High Spirits

Malik is a 6-year-old boy living in an impoverished area of a large city. Malik's mother, Traci, and father, Jean, married when Traci was just 17 and divorced after 2 years of marriage, when Malik was 3. Although Traci has custody of Malik, Jean is still quite involved in his life and typically cares for him on weekends. Jean came to the United States as a teenager. His family performed migrant farmwork and he rarely attended school, but he is an outgoing person with many friends. He takes Malik everywhere with him on weekends, including to social events such as pick-up basketball games and card games with the group of men that he works with at a local factory. Jean speaks Creole and English and is proud of the fact that Malik is also bilingual. Jean dreams of someday returning to Haiti with Malik to visit relatives he has not seen in years.

Malik is in first grade at a private Catholic school (St. Joseph's Academy). He is a very energetic, enthusiastic child. Although his teachers view him as very bright, he is at times disruptive in the classroom and is frequently aggressive with peers when disputes occur. Most of these incidents have been minor, but on a few occasions Traci has had to visit the school. Traci is not concerned, however, about Malik's school behavior. His Head Start teachers described him as extremely smart, though easily frustrated, particularly with his peers when things did not go his way. Traci feels Malik is brighter than most children his age and has a great deal of potential. She decided to enroll him at St. Joseph's because she felt he was learning very little in the public school where he attended kindergarten and Malik hated going there, complaining that his teachers yelled at him constantly. The extra cost of the private school has been a significant burden, particularly since Traci lost her job. However, Traci is proud of her Italian Catholic upbringing and thinks the school is the best choice for Malik.

Traci and her new boyfriend, James, recently became engaged and moved in together. James seems resentful of Malik and complains that

CASE STUDY 5.1

he receives too much attention. James has two children of his own who reside with their mother. He says that in his opinion, Malik is spoiled and needs discipline. Traci admits that her relationship with Malik is changing and he is becoming harder to handle. She says he is always on the go, increasingly involved in school activities, and always wanting to go outside or to friends' homes to play. Although he is often sullen and angry when he comes home from visits with his father, he often complains that he has more fun when he is with Jean, asserting that Jean lets him do whatever he wants. Lately, he has begun to ignore Traci's requests and attempts at discipline, telling her that he does not like to be told what to do.

CASE STUDY 5.2

RHODA'S DISLIKE OF SCHOOL

Rhoda, a 9-year-old fourth grade student, attends a rural elementary school in an all-white community. Rhoda lives with her grandmother in a small house on a country road half a mile away from the small town where her school is located. Rhoda doesn't know her mother or father. Her father died in a car accident when she was an infant and her mother's whereabouts are unknown.

Rhoda, who is about 5 feet tall and weighs approximately 160 pounds, is very sensitive about her weight and tries to hide her body under baggy sweaters and her winter coat. Rhoda's grandmother, Elaine, has difficulty getting Rhoda to shower on a regular basis. Rather than arguing, Elaine allows Rhoda to skip showering most nights. As a result, Rhoda's hair is rather greasy, her fingernails often have dirt under them, and she has strong body odor. Elaine insists that Rhoda shower when she notices that Rhoda smells bad, but Rhoda recently commented that she'd prefer not to shower at all.

Elaine is a loving caregiver, but she readily admits that she has a hard time asserting authority over Rhoda. She and Rhoda struggle over school attendance. Often when Elaine wakes her in the morning, Rhoda complains

CASE STUDY 5.2

of a headache; Elaine usually lets her stay home. On a few recent occasions, Rhoda has left home for school on time but never actually made it to school. She walked around the small town for a while; by the time she noticed how much time had passed, it seemed too late to go to school, so she didn't go at all. When Rhoda does make it to school, she frequently calls her grandmother and asks to come home because she doesn't feel well. On these occasions, Elaine often feels sympathetic and picks Rhoda up from school.

Rhoda is open about her dislike of school, telling you bluntly that she hates her teacher because the teacher picks on her when she tries to answer questions and can't get them right. Rhoda also says that she hates all of her classmates. She says they are mean, they call her names, and they refuse to sit by her in class. Things are especially bad in gym class. Rhoda despises Ms. Jones, the gym teacher. Rhoda has been placed on detention for the past several weeks because she refuses to change for gym. Recently, Ms. Jones sent a note home to Elaine explaining that Rhoda will fail gym for the year if she continues to refuse to change for class. Rhoda is also performing poorly in most of her other subjects.

When you ask Rhoda about any positive feelings toward school, she shrugs her shoulders at first. Finally, after a long pause, she reports "loving" the school nurse, Ms. Joy. Ms. Joy always greets Rhoda with a smile when she comes to the nurse's office and listens to Rhoda when she talks about her various ailments. Rhoda visits the nurse almost every day she is at school. Rhoda also eventually mentions that she likes another fourth grader, Jane, who is often in the nurse's office when Rhoda comes to visit. Jane is a very shy, timid fourth grader. She likes to talk with Rhoda about video games and favorite television shows when they are both in the nurse's office.

In general, Rhoda seems to be a very isolated, often unhappy fourth grader with few friends. She is not doing well academically and does not like the way she looks. She doesn't have many hobbies, but she does like watching television, playing video games, and eating ice cream. When you talk with her, she tells you that she is not treated fairly at school, and she insists that everyone at school hates her. Rhoda adds that she "hates them back." But once Rhoda admitted to you that she sometimes wishes she could make a few more friends and that she would like to do a little better in school.

CASE STUDY 5.3

JUAN'S UNSETTLED LIFE

Juan's life has been full of change. A slightly built 12-year-old, Juan is in an English as a second language (ESL) class at Charlotte Middle School. He speaks very little English. He emigrated from El Salvador 5 months ago with his mother, Silvia, and his 16-year-old brother, Jaime. Until Juan was 3, he lived in a rural village on the Pacific coast of El Salvador with his parents and three siblings. Just before his first birthday, Juan's family witnessed the abduction of his father by a "death squad" (the name used in El Salvador for a military group supported by the government). His father never returned. At the age of 4, Juan and his family moved to his aunt and uncle's home in Las Colinas, a neighborhood within the small city of Santa Tecla. Last year, most of Las Colinas was destroyed in a devastating earthquake. Juan's uncle, two sisters, and cousin were killed in the earthquake.

After the earthquake, Silvia contacted her cousin, Arturo, in the United States. Arturo made arrangements for a "coyote" (the Spanish nickname for a person who smuggles people across the border) to bring Silvia, Jaime, and Juan to the United States. The trip was exhausting; the family was harassed at each border they crossed. After traveling by bus to Mexico City, Juan and his family finally met the coyote in the border town of Agua Prieta. With eight other people, they crossed the border on foot through the desert outside Douglas, Arizona. They went 2 days without water and the temperatures in the desert at night dipped below freezing, but they eventually made it to Arturo's home. Arturo paid the coyote all the money he and his family had managed to save since arriving in the United States 3 years earlier. Now Silvia must pay back the $8,000 to Arturo and his wife.

An immigration lawyer is trying to help the family obtain legal residency documents, but right now it is difficult for Silvia and Jaime to find jobs. Without papers, Silvia is worried about getting caught in the United States. Also, without papers, the family is afraid to apply for public assistance or Medicaid.

Silvia recently obtained a job as a housekeeper and nanny for a wealthy family with three young children. She leaves her home very early each morning to catch the bus to the family's house. The family, however, is not paying her each week as they promised, and when they do pay her, they sometimes pay less than the agreed on amount. Silvia is afraid to complain because she fears the family may then turn her in to the

CASE STUDY 5.3

immigration authorities. She is searching for other work but has yet to find anything.

Jaime works as often as possible—on busy nights, at a local restaurant busing tables and washing dishes. More often, he goes to a nearby parking lot where employers come looking for day laborers to do short-term landscaping or construction work. When he is lucky, he gets picked from the group of immigrant men waiting there. It is hard work and the pay is low, because there are more men waiting for work than are hired each day, but it pays more than his restaurant job. Lately, Jaime has had a very short temper and does not appear to be sleeping. He seems to want to do nothing but work, and he complains constantly that the family will never be able to pay off their huge debt to Arturo. On several recent occasions, he has come home extremely late and very intoxicated. Although Jaime and Juan used to be close, Jaime now seems constantly angry with Juan.

You have begun working with Juan in the school setting because his ESL teacher is concerned about him. His teacher reports that he shows no interest in classroom activities or his peers and always seems exhausted. She also states that he often appears to be daydreaming, and when she tries to talk to him, he seems to withdraw further. To date, no educational or psychological assessments have taken place. When you ask Juan about El Salvador and his background, he avoids eye contact with you and will not speak.

Historical Perspective on Middle Childhood

Until the beginning of the 20th century, children were viewed primarily in economic terms within most European countries and the United States. Emphasis was placed on the child's productivity and ability to contribute to the family's financial well-being. Middle childhood represented a period during which children became increasingly able to play a role in maintaining or improving family status.

Beginning in the early 20th century, however, a radical shift occurred in the Western world's perceptions of children. Children passing through middle childhood became categorized as "school age" and their education became a societal priority. Child labor and compulsory education laws supported and reinforced this shift in societal values. There is incredible diversity among children falling within the developmental phase classified as middle childhood. Generally speaking, middle childhood has come to be viewed as a time when education, play, leisure, and social activities dominate daily life (Fass & Mason, 2000b).

The evolution of our perceptions of middle childhood continues. Traditionally perceived, in this century, as a relatively uneventful phase of development, it is increasingly recognized as an exciting and challenging time in every child's life. The age range classified as middle childhood is subject to debate—encompassing ages 5 to 11 for some (Sroufe, Cooper, & DeHart, 1996), 6 to 12 for others (Green, 1994)—and it is increasingly encroached on by adolescence. In educational circles, the ages of 10 to 14 are commonly labeled as early adolescence.

Images of middle childhood usually include children who are healthy and curious, making new friends and learning new things. But as Malik, Rhoda, and Juan demonstrate, middle childhood is filled with both opportunities and challenges. For some children, it is a period of particular vulnerability.

Middle Childhood in the Multigenerational Family

During middle childhood, the child's social world expands dramatically. Family is still the most significant influence on development, although the nuclear family is not the only relevant force in a child's life. In addition, families are in a constant state of change, and so the child's relationships with family members and the environment that the family inhabits are likely to be different from the child's first experiences of family. Consider the changes in Malik's family over time and the way that he has needed to continually renegotiate his family relationships.

How are Malik, Rhoda, and Juan affected by their multigenerational families?

Despite current geographical distances that often exist between family members today, nuclear families are still emotional subsystems of larger, multigenerational family systems. The nuclear family is significantly shaped by past, present, and anticipated future relationships within multigenerational family systems (Carter & McGoldrick, 1999b). Other important influences on individuals and families exist, such as culture and history. But these influences act on individuals through family systems. For example, the emotional wounds of slavery, segregation, and racism are often conveyed through generational ties. Children become directly connected to these events and phenomena even in the absence of similar experiences in the present generation. Cultural and historical influences also shape individual attitudes and development. Thus, the developing child is shaped not only by events and individuals explicitly evident in present time and physical space but also by events and individuals that have more directly influenced the lives of parents, grandparents, great-grandparents, and beyond.

Cognitive, Moral, and Spiritual Development in Middle Childhood

When Malik, Rhoda, and Juan first entered school, their readiness to confront the challenges and opportunities that school presents was shaped by prior experiences. Malik, for example, entered school generally prepared for and excited about the various experiences associated with kindergarten. For most children, the acquisition of cognitive abilities that occurs early in middle childhood allows the communication of thoughts with increasing complexity. As cognitive skills develop, the ability to understand people and situations in the surrounding environment matures (Green, 1994). The task for primary caregivers and others within the child's environment is to recognize and respond to this ability sensitively, nurturing and supporting the child's expanding cognitive abilities.

Several developmental theorists, including those listed in Exhibit 5.1, have described the developments and tasks associated with middle childhood. According to these traditional theorists, reasoning in middle childhood becomes more logical, the child's sense of morality expands and develops into a more internally based system, and the ability to understand the perspectives of others emerges. However, shortcomings in the methods and findings of many traditional developmental theorists are today widely recognized (see Gibbs & Huang, 1989; Gilligan, 1982, 1992; Langford, 1995; Mowrer & Klein, 2001). In particular, much developmental research historically lacked rigor and was biased against females and children belonging to nondominant groups. Although the need for additional developmental research is clear, many of the key developmental tasks during middle childhood, as identified by developmental theorists like Jean Piaget, Erik Erikson, and Lawrence Kohlberg, are widely agreed on.

Competence

How does a growing sense of competence promote the capacity for human agency in making choices?

Perhaps the most central developmental task of this period is the acquisition of feelings of **self-competence**. The child strives to recognize and value personal accomplishments and achievements. This is what Erik Erikson (1963) was referring to when he described the developmental task of middle childhood as industry versus inferiority (refer back to Exhibit 3.6 for a description of all eight of Erikson's psychosocial stages). *Industry* refers to a drive to acquire new skills and do meaningful work. The experiences of middle childhood foster or thwart the child's attempts to acquire an enhanced sense of **mastery** and self-efficacy. Family and community support may enhance the child's growing sense of competence; lack of such support undermines this sense. The child's definitions of self and accomplishment vary greatly according to interpretations in the surrounding environment. But superficial, external bolstering of self-esteem is not all

EXHIBIT 5.1
Phases and Tasks of Middle Childhood

Theorist	Phase or Task	Description
Freud (1938/1973)	Latency	Sexual instincts become less dominant; superego develops further.
Erikson (1950)	Industry versus inferiority	Capacity to cooperate develops; result is sense of either mastery or incompetence.
Piaget (1936/1952)	Concrete operational	Reasoning becomes more logical but remains at concrete level; principle of conservation is learned.
Piaget (1932/1965)	Moral realism and autonomous morality	Conception of morality changes from absolute and external to relative and internal.
Kohlberg (1969)	Preconventional and conventional morality	Reasoning based on punishment and reward is replaced by reasoning based on formal law and external opinion.
Selman (1976)	Self-reflective perspective taking	Ability develops to view own actions, thoughts, and emotions from another's perspective.

that children of this age group require. External appraisal must be supportive and encouraging but also accurate in order for children to value such feedback.

Children of this age must also learn the value of perseverance and develop an internal drive to succeed (Seligman, Reivich, Jaycox, & Gillham, 1995). Thus, opportunities to fail and succeed must be provided, along with sincere feedback and support. Ideally, the developing school-age child acquires the sense of personal competence and tenacity that will serve as a protective factor during adolescence and young adulthood.

Families play a critical role in supporting development of this sense. For example, as the child learns to ride a bike or to play a new musical instrument, parents can provide specific feedback and praise. They can counter their child's frustration by identifying and complimenting specific improvements and emphasizing the role of practice and perseverance in producing such improvements. Failures and setbacks can be labeled as temporary and surmountable rather than attributed to personal flaws or deficits. The presence of such feedback loops is a key feature of high-quality adult/child relationships, both in the family and in school.

Middle childhood is a critical time for children to acquire this sense of competence. In the process they gain an increasing awareness of their personal fit into the network of relationships in the surrounding environment. Each child experiences events and daily interactions that enhance or diminish feelings of self-competence. At this age, children's growing awareness of their surrounding environments and their changing emotional needs surface in the questions they consider about themselves and those affecting their lives (Green, 1994). A systems perspective is critical to understanding the multiple influences on children's development during this period.

Children are not equally positioned as they enter this developmental phase, as Malik's, Rhoda's, and Juan's stories suggest. Developmental pathways preceding entry into middle childhood are extremely diverse. Children experience this phase of life differently based not only on differences in the surrounding environment—such as family structure, socioeconomic status, and culture—but also on their personality differences. A particular personality and learning style may be valued or devalued, problematic or nonproblematic, in each of the child's expanding social settings (Green, 1994). Thus, although Malik, Rhoda, and Juan are moving through the same developmental period and facing many common tasks, they experience these tasks differently and will emerge into adolescence as unique individuals.

Social Sensitivity

Middle childhood is a critical time in moral development, a time when most children become intensely interested in moral issues. Advancing language capability serves not only as a communication tool but also as a vehicle for more sophisticated introspection. Language is also a tool for positive assertion of self and personal opinions as the child's social world expands (Coles, 1987, 1997). In recent years, many elementary schools have added character education to the curriculum. Some controversy has ensued about whether character education is best handled through a traditional approach of teaching children to conform to good habits or by helping them to engage in moral reasoning (White, 1997).

As children increasingly view their lives as part of the network of lives within their environment, communities gain greater potential to provide important support and structure. Today, however, many communities provide as many challenges as opportunities for development. Communities in which challenges outweigh opportunities have been labeled as "socially toxic," meaning that they threaten positive development (Garbarino, 1995). In contrast, within a socially supportive environment, children have access to peers and adults who can lead them toward more advanced moral and social thinking. This development occurs in part through the modeling of **prosocial behavior**, which injects moral reasoning and social sensitivity into the child's accustomed manner of reasoning and behaving. Thus, cognitive and moral development is a social issue. The failure of adults to take on moral and spiritual mentoring roles contributes significantly to the development of socially toxic environments.

This type of moral mentoring takes place in the **zone of proximal development**—the theoretical space between the child's current developmental level and the child's potential level if given access to appropriate models and developmental experiences in the social environment (Vygotsky, 1986). Thus, the child's competence alone interacts dynamically with the child's competence in the company of others. The result is developmental progress. This continuous process of social interaction and shaping is consistent with systems theory or with a biological model of equilibration, where organisms develop as they respond to environmental stimuli in a constant process of equilibrium, disruption, and reequilibration.

Several developmental theorists have refined our thinking about how such processes occur in children. The best-known theory of moral development is Lawrence Kohlberg's stage theory (for an overview of this theory, refer back to Exhibit 4.1). Kohlberg's research on moral reasoning found that children do not enter the second level of **conventional moral reasoning**, or morality based on approval of authorities or upon upholding societal standards, until about age 9 or 10, sometime after they have the cognitive skills for such reasoning. Moreover, Robert Coles (1987, 1997) has emphasized the distinction between moral imagination—the gradually developed capacity to reflect on what is right and wrong—and moral conduct, pointing out that a "well-developed conscience does not translate, necessarily, into a morally courageous life" (p. 3). To Coles, **moral behavior** is shaped by daily experiences, developing in response to the way the child is treated in his or her various environments such as home and school. The school-age child often pays close attention to the discrepancies between the "moral voices" and actions of the adults in his or her world, including parents, friends' parents, relatives, teachers, and coaches. Each new and significant adult sets an example for the child, sometimes complementing and sometimes contradicting the values emphasized in the child's home environment.

Emotional Intelligence

What are our societal expectations for emotional intelligence during middle childhood?

Only the emotionally intelligent are capable of both moral reasoning and moral conduct, according to Daniel Goleman (1995). As defined by Goleman, **emotional intelligence** refers to the ability to "motivate oneself and persist in the face of frustrations, to control impulse and delay gratification, to regulate one's moods and keep distress from swamping the ability to think, to empathize and to hope" (p. 34).

Although moral and emotional development occurs naturally, in order for the developmental process to result in a well-developed conscience and optimum emotional intelligence, positive social conditions and interactions must exist in a child's life. Thus, a child like Malik, with seemingly great academic promise, may not realize his potential without timely intervention targeting the development of critical emotional competencies. These competencies include, for example, self-awareness, impulse control, and the ability to identify, express, and manage feelings, including stress and anxiety. Fortunately, interventions targeting the development of emotional intelligence have been developed and appear to be promising, particularly when they are preventive in nature and provided during early and middle childhood.

Rhoda, like many girls her age, is at risk of developing depression and could benefit from intervention focusing on the development of emotional competence. Goleman (1995) argues that many cases of depression arise from deficits in two key areas of emotional competence: relationship skills and cognitive, or interpretive, style. In short, many children suffering from—or at risk of developing—depression likely possess a depression-promoting way of interpreting setbacks. Children with this pessimistic outlook attribute setbacks in their lives to internal, personal flaws. Appropriate preventive intervention, based on a cognitive behavioral approach, teaches these children that their emotions are linked to the way they think and facilitates productive, healthy ways of interpreting events and viewing themselves.

Certainly many children also experience depression as a result of trauma or significant loss. Children with close ties to extended family are particularly likely to experience loss of a close relative at a young age and therefore are more prone to this sort of depression. Loss, trauma, or violence may present monumental obstacles to the development of emotional intelligence. Research demonstrates, however, that many children are remarkably resilient (see Garmezy, 1994). Goleman (1995) argues that certain emotional skills may be essential to resilience. Appropriate, well-timed external intervention, however, seems crucial for children like Rhoda and Juan. Their present inability to establish mastery in any setting threatens each child's developing sense of self. It is particularly critical to attend to Juan's experiences and emotions to help him productively function and focus, particularly in the school environment.

Formal Schooling

During middle childhood, school becomes the primary context for complex developmental challenges and opportunities. The current importance of formal schooling in middle childhood cannot be overstated. Children entering school must learn to navigate a new environment quite different from the family. In school, they are evaluated on the basis of how well they perform tasks; people outside the family—teachers and peers—begin shaping the child's personality, dreams, and aspirations (Zastrow & Kirst-Ashman, 1997). At the same time, the school environment may serve as an important resource for the cognitive, emotional, and physical tasks of middle childhood. Schools offer a great deal of academic and social knowledge, through both teachers and peers (Kail & Cavanaugh, 1996).

Success in the school environment, then, is very important to the development of self-esteem. Malik, for instance, finds his school activities generally rewarding. Rhoda, however, finds school painful. Her inability to fit in with her peers compounds her academic difficulty. Rhoda's school experience is so threatening and unpleasant that she has begun to withdraw from the process, but her withdrawal represents a serious threat to her continued cognitive, emotional, and social development. Attention to Rhoda's social concerns and particular strengths may help prevent her complete withdrawal from school while providing her with the supports needed to gain crucial skills.

Students like Juan, however, face considerable challenges in the school setting. Juan's ability to focus in the school environment is compromised. Most schools are ill equipped to respond to the issues confronting children like Juan. If Juan is not supported and assisted by his school system, his educational experience in the United States may serve as another assault on his healthy development. But if Juan's support system can be expanded and mobilized, it may help him overcome his developmental challenges.

Today in the United States, Juan's situation is not rare. In 1999, about one in five elementary and high school students had at least one foreign-born parent (U.S. Census Bureau, 2001a). In general, elementary and high school students are more diverse than ever before. In 1999, 16% of such children were Hispanic, 15% were black (non-Hispanic), 4% were Asian or Pacific Islander, and 1% were American Indian or Alaska Native (Forum on Child & Family Statistics, 2000). The challenges facing children who have recently arrived in the United States, particularly those fleeing war-torn countries, are many. Language difficulties and their consequences are increasingly recognized. Research has established that children are best served when they are able to speak both their native language and the language of their host country (Vuorenkoski, Kuure, Moilanen, Penninkilampi, & Myhrman, 2000). But the consequences of growing up in an impoverished, war-torn environment are not as widely understood. Indeed, research regarding immigrant children in general is in its infancy (see Research Forum on Children, Families, and the New Federalism, 2002). Existing research suggests only that immigrant children are at heightened risk of school failure (Fuligni, 1997).

They are also at heightened risk of mental health problems (Escobar, Hoyos-Nervi, & Gara, 2000; Guarnaccia & Lopez, 1998; Pernice & Brook, 1996). Mental health status among immigrant populations, however, appears to be dependent on a wide number of factors. In general, **acculturation**, or a process by which two or more cultures remain distinct but exchange cultural features (such as foods, music, clothing), is easier on children than **assimilation**, or a process by which the minority culture must adapt and become incorporated into the majority culture, particularly in the school environment. Communication and interaction between parents and schools is important (Bhattacharya, 2000; U.S. Department of Health & Human Services, 2000).

Indeed, for all children, parental involvement in school is associated with better school performance. Schools serving diverse populations are becoming increasingly creative in their approaches to encouraging parent involvement, including the development of sophisticated interpretation and translation infrastructures (Pardington, 2002). Unfortunately, many schools lag behind, suffering from either inadequate resources or the consequences of exclusive and racist attitudes within the school and community environments (see Jones, 2002).

Trends in Schooling

Today, school has indisputable influence in the lives of children like Malik, Rhoda, and Juan. Although all parents now expect the school to play a fundamental role in the development of their children, they have not always felt this way. Our current conception of formal schooling—that is, public education—is only about 150 years old. It was conceived of by a new country eager to educate its citizens to participate fully in a democratic society (Constable, 1996).

A significant shift in the purpose of education occurred in the late 1800s. In order to meet the needs of the industrial era, the educational system shifted from the broad, liberal arts-oriented education necessary for civic participation. Subject matter was reorganized and segmented to prepare a workforce willing to accept clear delineation of job roles and repetition of work tasks (Spring, 1997, 2000).

Mirroring political ideals, public education in this country was intended to be an equalizer, enabling individuals from a variety of economic backgrounds to become righteous and economically successful citizens. Public schools were to be free and open to all. Instead, however, they reflected traditional public ambiguity toward poverty and diversity, and they embodied particular value systems and excluded certain groups. For instance, the first schools were "primarily agrarian . . . Protestant-Republican, and thus virtually guaranteed the exclusion of certain ethnic and religious groups" (Allen-Meares, Washington, & Walsh, 1996, p. 57). The first public schools were, in effect, open to European American males only, and throughout their history, public schools have often either excluded or marginalized members of nondominant groups.

What impact have these historical trends in public education had on middle childhood development?

Over time, however, the public schools gradually reflected changes occurring in other public institutions. They began to accept females, immigrants, African Americans, and other historically excluded groups. In most parts of the country, however, members of these groups did not receive equal treatment, and they were forced to attend segregated and inferior schools throughout most of the 20th century. However, various court rulings, most prominently the 1954 ***Brown v. Board of Education*** decision (347 U.S. 483), made equal, integrated education the right of all American citizens. Throughout the past few decades, the courts have continued to assert democratic ideology and have opposed school segregation (Constable, 1996).

Despite these court rulings and democratic ideals, public schooling continues to mirror the social systems with which it interacts, and thus often falls short. Informal segregation often persists in schools, for a variety of reasons (see Tatum, 1999). And racial and ethnic minorities and poor children still suffer in schools that frequently do not provide enough books, supplies, teachers, or curricula challenging enough to facilitate success in American society (Kozol, 1991, 2000). The juxtaposition of inner-city and suburban schools continues to point to substantial divisions between economically rich and impoverished communities.

Schools in economically impoverished areas simultaneously suffer from a lack of funding and an increasing number of educational challenges as the needs of their students grow more complex. Challenges such as poverty, changing family structures (dual-income and single-parent families) that decrease parents' involvement, lack of access to health and social services, and lack of high-quality, appropriate day care have forced schools to broaden their array of health and social services. Today, schools struggle to give increasing attention to the diverse needs that their students present (Dryfoos, 1994).

Physical and Symbolic Organization of the School

The structure of American schools plays an important role in shaping the experience of the children who attend them. Physical layout and functional systems create and maintain a symbolic structure for administrators, teachers, students, and families. The schools' combined symbolic and physical structures both reflect and help maintain the hierarchical nature of public education as well as the status quo within the larger society.

Physical Structure. Traditionally, most American school buildings have had the same general physical layout. Administrators have a suite of private offices with a common reception area and a secretary. These offices are walled off and often located in a wing separate from classrooms. Classrooms in schools are designed for one teacher and approximately 25 to 30 students. They traditionally contain desks that face the front of the room, thereby facilitating a lecture model of teaching (Swap, 1993). The front of the classroom has a chalkboard on which assignments are written and rules posted. The school day is structured into 40- to 50-minute periods, announced by the ringing of bells. With the exception of schools with extended day programs, the school day begins between 7:00 and 9:00 in the morning and rarely ends later than 3:00 in the afternoon.

The traditionally rigid physical structure of American schools is thought to contribute to the learning of essential academic course material (Oakes & Lipton, 1990). Yet, research suggests that the academic progress of many students is not well served by a rigid school structure. For example, sitting at desks and learning through the lecture format is not an appropriate way for most children to learn (Roueche & Baker, 1986).

Controversy over the structure most conducive to learning has prompted the development of a variety of alternative, model, and demonstration schools. These schools offer a variety of classroom settings, feature open floor plans, and provide a flexible approach to teaching and learning (Barr & Parrett, 1995). Although the traditional school structure prevails, interest is growing in the development of innovative structures and systems that are as attentive to developmental needs and as supportive of learning as possible. Indeed, educational reform movements have a long history, from the progressive educational movement encouraged by the writings of John Dewey in the early part of the 20th century to the informal classroom movement of the 1960s and 1970s. However, only in the last decade has clear and consistent educational research in the fields of literacy education and educational theory begun to detail effective instructional strategies and methodological approaches. Implementation of such research findings has disrupted the "stand and deliver," or lecture format, as the dominant approach to teaching and knowledge acquisition.

How do school settings promote and inhibit human agency in making choices?

Symbolic Structure. On entering a school, children—and their parents—may find the physical layout confusing and intimidating. Authoritarian communication systems and closed classrooms may act as a hindrance to open communication. The physical setting may act as a subtle barrier that prohibits meaningful dialogue between students and teachers, teachers and administrators, and parents and school personnel. Moreover, the school's structure typically delineates its members' roles. The most striking physical illustration of such delineation is the position of teacher at the head of the classroom and students in small desks facing the teacher. This physical organization of the classroom reinforces the passive learner role (Swap, 1993).

When parents, teachers, or students attempt to create new roles within traditional school systems, they often do not receive an encouraging response. Parents who come into school and request atypical services for their children are often quickly labeled "a problem" by school personnel. Personnel may then ignore the parents' requests or refuse to see them. From the school system's perspective, these parents have failed to adhere to their traditional role as supporter of the school's decisions for their child. Parents who wish to participate in their child's education are encouraged to do so in prescribed ways, such as helping with homework and attending parent-teacher meetings.

Thus, the traditional school system has often failed to accommodate students like Rhoda, who have special needs. At this point in her childhood, for example, Rhoda might benefit from an alternative to the traditional gym class. Rhoda's current gym class, rather than facilitating her social and physical development, instead highlights her weight and social insecurities. Adults and a physical education system that address Rhoda's insecurities while empowering her to work toward a healthy weight would support, rather than thwart, healthy development.

Another problematic aspect of the traditional American public educational structure is the practice of **tracking**, or grouping students by ability or attainment

(Oakes, 1985). It has been used to divide students into college-bound and noncollege-bound classes, accelerated and nonaccelerated classes, and regular and special education classes. This division of students into groups based on perceived or demonstrated ability often benefits accelerated students and eases teaching challenges, but it has traditionally disadvantaged students with special needs and has reduced educational opportunities for children from nondominant groups (Fuligni, Eccles, & Barber, 1995; Rodriquez, 1983). For a balanced assessment of the advantages and disadvantages of tracking, and recent attempts to detrack, see Tom Loveless's *The Tracking Wars: State Reform Meets School Policy.*

In addition, such division of students has often been based on standardized tests, which research suggests may be culturally and class biased. Students have also been divided based on school personnel reports. Such reports are often subjective and may inadvertently be based on assessments of students' dress, language, and behavior (Oakes, 1985; Oakes & Lipton, 1992). Throughout the history of public schooling, most counselors and teachers have belonged to dominant groups, and consciously or unconsciously, they may have awarded privilege and preference to learning styles, language, and dress that they find familiar.

In short, tracking has traditionally served as a two-tiered system of inequality. Special education, noncollege-bound, and nonaccelerated classes have been disproportionately populated by minority and poor students. These classes too often prepared students to work only in low-skilled, low-paying jobs. Conversely, regular education, college-bound, and accelerated classes have been disproportionately white and middle class. These classes typically prepared their members for college and leadership roles. Thus, the traditional structure of public education often both reflected and supported ethnic and class divisions within American society (Oakes, 1985; Oakes & Lipton, 1992; Winters, 1993).

For an example of the dangers of tracking, consider Malik. His behavior puts him at risk for eventual placement in specialized classes for emotionally disturbed children, even though his behavior may be a normal part of his developmental process. Currently, his fairly infrequent aggressive behavior seems to be dealt with by school personnel appropriately, which may prevent an escalation of the problem. Intervention with Traci and Jean may also facilitate a consistent, positive family response to Malik's behavior. However, the professionals making decisions at Malik's school and in his community could begin to interpret his behavior as serious and threatening. Thus, Malik faces an increased risk of placement outside the "regular" track. However, his generally prosocial personality and his parents' attentiveness may provide the buffers necessary to avoid such placement.

Formal Schooling and Cognitive Development

Public education plays a major role in the cognitive development of children in the United States, if only because children attend school throughout the formative years of such development. In Jean Piaget's (1936/1952) terms, children start school during the second stage (preoperational thought) and finish school when they are completing the fourth and final stage of cognitive development (formal operations). In the third stage (concrete operations), children are able to solve concrete problems using logical problem-solving strategies. By the end of middle childhood, they enter the formal operations stage and become able to solve hypothetical problems using abstract concepts (refer back to Exhibit 3.4 for an overview of Piaget's stages of cognitive development). School children rapidly develop conceptual thought, the ability to categorize complicated systems of objects, and the ability to solve problems (Allen-Meares, 1995).

Given these developmental tasks, traditional schooling in the United States has had four major shortcomings:

1. It did not typically put enough time into schooling students to increase their cognitive functioning.
2. It did not ask the students to think enough.
3. It provided too few substantive courses.
4. It often encouraged ineffective teaching methods.

Many schools are working toward changes in these four areas. Teachers are encouraged to use a variety of teaching methods, and recent federal and state initiatives seek to add substance to classes. And many teachers increase their effectiveness by encouraging active student involvement, giving a great deal of feedback to their students, contacting students outside of class, and adopting a flexible teaching approach and student-centered style (Roueche and Baker, 1986).

Today, schools typically try to ensure that students achieve their potential and acquire the cognitive skills that play an important role in economic and social success within the larger society. In fact, schools have become increasingly linked to the workplace. This shift represents a return to educational emphases of earlier historical eras (Fass & Mason, 2000a). Federal initiatives have been particularly influential in this area, emphasizing the need for schools to prepare a career-focused population. Schools have been encouraged through funding opportunities and legislative mandates to stay abreast of workforce trends and needs, including shifts in the demand for key skills (such as collaboration and critical thinking), and to ensure attention to the development of these skills.

In attempting to meet their diverse and multiple objectives, schools must recognize that children have individual cognitive styles. As a result, they benefit from diverse educational materials and varied activities that appeal to visual, auditory, and experiential learning styles. Such activities can include group work, student presentations, field trips, audiovisual presentations, written and oral skill activities, discussion, and lectures (Roueche & Baker, 1986).

Many school-age children have also benefited from new research and theory focusing on the concept of intelligence. Traditional views of intelligence and approaches to intelligence testing benefited European American children born in the United States. Howard Gardner's work, in particular, represents a paradigm shift in the field of education. He proposes that intelligence is neither unitary nor fixed, and argues that intelligence is not adequately or fully measured by IQ tests. More broadly, in his theory of **multiple intelligences,** intelligence is "the ability to solve problems or fashion products that are of consequence in a particular cultural setting or community" (Gardner, 1993, p. 15). Challenging the idea that individuals can be described, or categorized, by a single, quantifiable measure of intelligence, Gardner proposes that at least eight critical intelligences exist: verbal/linguistic, logical/mathematical, visual/spatial, musical/rhythmic, bodily/kinesthetic, naturalist, interpersonal, and intrapersonal. The paradigm shift in the education field prompted by Gardner's work encourages a culturally sensitive approach to students (Campbell, Campbell, & Dickinson, 1999) and a diminished role for standardized testing.

How might this increased emphasis on cognitive diversity alter the life course of students like Malik, Rhoda, and Juan?

In its practical application, multiple intelligence theory calls for use of a wide range of instructional strategies that engage the range of strengths and intelligences of each student (Kagan & Kagan, 1998). Gardner specifically calls for matching instructional strategies to the needs and strengths of students, stretching the intelligences—or maximizing development of each of the intelligences—by transforming education curriculum, and celebrating or (at a minimum) understanding the unique pattern of intelligences of each student. This last point is critical. Such understanding can facilitate self-knowledge and self-acceptance. Understanding and celebration of cognitive diversity, Gardner believes, will come from a transformation not of curricula or instructional methods but instead of the way in which adults view students and students view themselves and one another.

In addition to calling for changes in instructional strategies, multiple intelligence theory calls for movement away from norm-referenced testing and toward comprehensive assessments of student performance. Such assessment includes naturalistic, across-time observation and development of self-appraisal materials such as student portfolios (Lazear, 1994).

This shift, however, has occurred in tandem with the standards movement within the United States. Most schools have moved away from norm-referenced testing and toward criterion-referenced testing, which requires all graduating students to meet certain absolute scores and requirements. At present, all 50 states have established some form of learning standards that all students must achieve in order to graduate from high school. In New York, for example, the movement has spawned 29 new learning standards. The core learning standard areas (English language arts, mathematics, social studies, and science) have assessments attached to them at three checkpoints in the schooling process. The stated aim of this standards-based educational movement is to disrupt the tracking norm in schools in favor of an equity-based system that requires all students to meet common outcomes. It is still too early to determine the success of these changes. However, the standards reform movement does represent a major effort to disrupt the two-tiered tracking system prevalent in American schools throughout the 20th century.

In recent years, many schools have adopted innovative practices designed to advance cognitive development while benefiting all students. Studies of **heterogeneous grouping**—the educational practice of grouping students with a variety of different skill levels in the same classroom—show that such peer interaction often fosters cognitive development (Oakes, 1985; Oakes & Lipton, 1990, 1992). Structured peer group activities take advantage of the natural tendency of children to learn from and be influenced by their peers. Grouping peers in small heterogeneous groups to complete a variety of activities has resulted in positive gains for both high- and low-achieving students (Oakes, 1985; Viggiani, 1996). Students like Malik, with more academic skill, may model effective methods of mastering academic material for less advanced students while Malik simultaneously learns more appropriate school behavior from his socially adept peers. Furthermore, this teaching method may help Malik strengthen peer friendships, an important source of support as he confronts family transitions and conflict.

In recent years, **flexible grouping** has also been employed. It draws on both heterogeneous and homogenous grouping and recognizes that each method is useful to achieve distinct objectives. Grouping strategies include pairing students, forming cooperative and collaborative groups, modeling lessons for students, conducting guided practice, and setting up subject-based learning laboratories. A teacher may draw on any appropriate technique during a class period, day, or week. These approaches represent an attempt to adapt instruction to meet diverse student needs.

Formal Schooling and Physical Development

Middle childhood marks the beginning of many physical changes, a stage that leads from **prepubescence** (the period prior to commencement of the physiological processes and changes associated with puberty) to **pubescence** (the period during which the child begins to experience diverse and gradual physical processes associated with puberty). Because puberty is a process rather than an event, pubescence can be thought of as the initial stages of the process. In middle childhood, especially the latter part, boys and girls vary greatly in stature, weight, and sexual development. Although estimates of the age at which puberty commences diverge widely, some girls may begin puberty as early as 8 years of age, with research suggesting that African American girls develop sooner than European American girls by 1 to 2 years

(Peck, 1997). On average, puberty begins about 2 years earlier for girls than for boys (Sroufe, Cooper, & DeHart, 1996).

What impact do these differences in biological age have on psychological and social development during middle childhood?

Because physical development is outwardly visible, it affects the way a child is both viewed and treated by peers and teachers. Girls and boys who develop early are often treated as if they are older than their peers. Adults often give these children more responsibility, perhaps more than is ideal for their cognitive and emotional developmental stage. Early puberty may also result in higher expectations for mature behavior and understanding of academic material. Some students may thrive on these heightened expectations, but others may feel unable to meet the expectations and thus feel defeated. Adults who place more responsibility on physically mature students may also neglect or expect less from students who are physically immature. Because physical development is not necessarily consistent with cognitive development, however, adults should focus on children's actual ability level as represented by the successful completion of tasks.

During puberty, girls in general are often faced with unwanted sexual attention from both peers and adults (American Association of University Women, 1995). Breast and hip development often bring unwanted harassment and advances. Young girls may not understand their own bodies yet, so unwanted sexual attention is often a cause of great confusion and concern. Counseling on self-protection and individual rights may be beneficial for these girls, and schools committed to the safety of their students must diligently educate staff and students about sexual harassment and sexual abuse.

Physical development can also affect children's peer relationships. School-age children constantly compare themselves to others, and physical differences are often the topic of discussion. Whereas late developers may feel inferior about their size or lack of sexual development, early developers may feel awkward and out of place among their peers. Most children worry about being "normal." They want to be sure that they are "on track" in their development. Reassurance by adults that physical development varies among people and that all development is "normal" is therefore crucial.

Physical differences of other sorts are also often noticed by children. Thus, students who are overweight, underweight, very tall, or very short are often excluded from peer groups and exposed to harassment and name-calling. Students who have physical or developmental disabilities are at particular risk for being singled out by their peers. Teacher leadership aimed at educating children about disability and encouraging the support and acceptance of peers with disabilities may help to minimize negative attitudes and incidents (Ware, 1995).

Students with disabilities and others who feel misunderstood by their peers are particularly likely to feel alone, afraid, and isolated in the school setting. Students who are socially excluded by their peers often do not like school and dread going to class. Some students who are teased on a regular basis may simply skip school in order to avoid unpleasant experiences. Teachers, parents, and other school personnel who pay special attention to, and intervene with, students in this situation may prevent the escalation of such problems. Adults must be aware, however, that students react to peer harassment and bullying in diverse fashions, influenced to some extent by gender and ethnicity (Rigby, 1998; Robinson, 1998).

Rhoda is a good example. The fact that Rhoda is obese is apparent to her classmates and may be one reason they tease her. Rhoda's reaction is avoidance and withdrawal. But Rhoda's teacher and grandmother can help both Rhoda and her peers come to terms with physical difference. Identification of Rhoda's strengths and provision of opportunities for demonstration of these strengths would also be beneficial. Furthermore, considering Rhoda's concerns about her appearance, she may benefit from counseling regarding her weight. Good nutrition and a healthy level of self-selected, esteem-enhancing exercise may help improve Rhoda's appearance and, with it, her self-confidence.

At a broader level, federal and state legislative initiatives have encouraged school personnel to confront bullying and harassment in the school setting. Schools have been particularly responsive to these initiatives in the wake of well-publicized incidents of school violence. Today, many schools have policies in place designed to facilitate efficient and effective responses to aberrant behavior, sometimes due to legislative encouragement. In New York State, for example, legislation was enacted in 2000 that requires all school districts to develop and adopt as policy "Codes of Conduct." These Codes establish protocols and methods focused on preventing violence in school settings.

Formal Schooling and Self-Evaluation

As children move through the middle years, they become increasingly aware that they are evaluated on the basis of what they are able to do. In turn, they begin to evaluate themselves based on treatment by teachers and peers and on self-assessments of what they can and cannot do (Harter, 1988). Rhoda is beginning to develop a negative evaluation of herself because of her peers' reactions to her weight and hygiene. Her negative self-evaluation is further fueled by lack of academic success. Although Juan has many challenges in his life, it is important to help him get on track at school.

Formal schooling is significant in middle childhood in large part because children typically move from the safety and support of home and day care environments to the pressures of a system that closely monitors accomplishments. Sensitive to peer and teacher evaluation, children self-evaluate their abilities and competency based on how those in their new environment view them (Barr & Parrett, 1995). Specifically, children evaluate themselves based on their performance in school tasks and on their ability to interact successfully with their peers (Zastrow & Kirst-Ashman, 1997).

Children develop their sense of self-worth through the amount of positive regard they feel from people around them. School-age children consistently rate parents, classmates, friends, and teachers as the most important influences in their lives (Harter, 1988). Thus, children are likely to evaluate themselves in a positive manner if they receive encouraging feedback in both their academic and social environments.

Schools can help children develop a positive self-evaluation by providing a variety of activities that allow children with different strengths to succeed. For example, schools that assess children in many areas, including those described by Gardner, may help children who have a deficit in one area experience success in another realm. Children can also be encouraged to evaluate themselves positively through the creation of individual student portfolios and through school initiatives that promote new skill development. Classroom and extracurricular activities can build on children's abilities and help them develop or maintain self-confidence (Barr & Parrett, 1995). Conversely, schools can contribute to the development of a negative self-evaluation by emphasizing norm-referenced testing, judging students based on limited ability or skill areas, and providing little opportunity for skill development.

The Effects of Race, Ethnicity, Gender, and Class

How do racism, classism, and sexism affect middle childhood development?

Schools are microcosms of the larger American society and mirror its institutional structures. Thus, schools often uphold racism, classism, and sexism (Bowles & Gintis, 1976; Keating, 1994; Ogbu, 1994). Unequal treatment of members of nondominant groups reflects and maintains the status quo both in schools and in the larger society and has an impact on individual development (Bowles & Gintis, 1976; Kozol, 1991, 2000). Students belonging to nondominant groups are often viewed as inherently less capable and thus fail to receive the cognitive stimulation needed for optimal growth and development. During all phases of childhood, children benefit from equal treatment and attention.

Institutional discrimination—the systemic denial of access to assets, economic opportunities, associations, and organizations based on minority status—has traditionally occurred in a variety of ways within schools. For example, girls have a history of disadvantage in the school environment (American Association of University Women [AAUW], 1995; Gilligan, 1982). Textbooks and literature used in schools were rarely authored by women and generally minimized women's perspectives, including little mention of women's contributions to history. Girls have been less likely to receive positive teacher attention and feedback; moreover, girls have traditionally been either excluded or discouraged from pursuing courses or career tracks in mathematics, the sciences, or athletics. Finally, female students, particularly adolescents, have traditionally suffered from unwanted sexual advances by both peers and teachers (Sadker, Sadker, Fox, & Salata, 1994). We should perhaps not be surprised that girls appear to suffer a severe decline in academic achievement, body image acceptance, and general self-confidence during middle childhood (AAUW, 1995; Orenstein, 1994).

Many school systems have now recognized their historically unequal treatment of students and taken steps to reduce discrimination. One approach is **mainstreaming,** or **inclusion**, the practice of placing all children who could be assigned to special education classrooms into regular education classrooms (Slee, 1995). A particularly innovative approach in the disability arena is the **collaborative classroom**. Children with and without disabilities are team-taught by both a "regular" and a "special" education teacher. Heterogeneous grouping, discussed earlier, helps prevent students of different races, socioeconomic classes, and genders from being separated and treated unequally. Different approaches to teaching academic content are used in hopes of accommodating a variety of learning styles and social backgrounds. Teachers, students, and other school personnel receive training on diversity. And sexual harassment policies have slowly been implemented and enforced in public schools. The policies are enforced by the requirement that all schools receiving federal funds designate a Title IX hearing officer to inquire about and, if warranted, respond to all allegations of harassment in its many forms.

Schools have also begun to include, in their curricula, content that reflects the diversity of their students. As the topic of diversity has become prominent in academic and popular discourse, educational materials are increasingly likely to include the perspectives of traditionally nondominant groups. As a result, more literature and history lessons represent females and minorities who have contributed to American life.

Schools located in areas with high rates of poverty have also been targeted for extra attention. **Full-service schools** attempt to provide school-based or school-linked health and social services for school children and their families (Dryfoos, 1994). Similarly, school-based family resource centers attempt to provide children, families, and communities with needed supports. School-based services have several characteristics in common (Adler, 1993):

- Commitment to providing access to all necessary services for school-age children and their families at the school or some other neighborhood facility
- Provision of physical and mental health, job development, and child care services, among others
- Extensive collaboration among service providers
- Preventative services focused on community development and family support
- Commitment to new, flexible, empowering ways for schools and communities to work together

The move toward providing more holistic services illustrates public education's expanding community role and continuing effort to meet the ideal of equal and comprehensive education, allowing all Americans the opportunity to achieve economic and social success.

Home and School

The link between school and home is important, in poor, working-class, and affluent neighborhoods alike, because school and home are the two major spheres in which children exist. The more similar these two environments are, the more successful the child will be at school and at home. Students who experience vastly different cultures at home and at school are likely to have difficulty accommodating the two worlds (Ryan & Adams, 1995). A great deal of learning goes on before a child enters school. By the time Malik, Rhoda, and Juan began school, they had acquired routines and habits at home and had developed cognitive, social, emotional, and physical styles and skills (Kellaghan, Sloane, Alvarez, & Bloom, 1993). School is merely the next step in the educational process.

The transition is relatively easy for middle-class students, because schools typically present a mainstream, or middle-class, model for behavior and learning. As middle-class parents interact with their children, they model and promote the behavior acceptable in school. Children are taught the necessities of social interaction, such as saying "thank you" and "please" (Comer, 1994). Middle-class parents also teach their children the rules of the classroom, such as "sit in your chair" and "wait to speak until you are acknowledged." Children from such backgrounds are often well prepared for the school environment because, quite simply, they understand the rules; as a result, the school is accepting of them. Furthermore, the school environment helps reinforce rules and skills taught in the home environment, just as the home environment helps reinforce rules and skills taught in the school environment. Research indicates that this type of home-school continuity often predicts school success (Ameta & Sherrard, 1995; Comer, 1994; Epstein & Lee, 1995; Kellaghan et al., 1993; Ryan & Adams, 1995).

In contrast, children with a minority or impoverished background may not know mainstream speech patterns and may not have been exposed to school materials such as scissors and crayons. These children, although possessing skills and curiosity, are often viewed as "dumb" or "bad" by the school (Comer, 1994). Children viewed in this manner may feel inferior and either act out or disengage from the school process (Finn, 1989). Because the school environment does not support the home environment and the home environment does not support the school environment, these children face an increased risk of poor school outcomes.

Schools and professionals sensitive to this issue can take many steps to prevent such outcomes. Ruby Payne (2001) describes the many complex ways in which poverty in particular affects relationships between schools and children. She notes, for example, that virtually all children from nondominant groups, including lower-income Caucasian children, possess an "informal language register" that contains the communication rules needed to survive in the familial and cultural group to which the child belongs. Schools often ignore the potency of these informal registers as they work toward their mission of teaching the "formal register" of the dominant middle class, deemed necessary to survive in the world of work and school. The need for specific strategies to acknowledge and honor the "informal register" while teaching the formal has been identified by several literacy researchers (see Gee, 1996; Knapp, 1995). These researchers emphasize the importance of teaching children to recognize their internal, or natural, "register" and the "register" they use in the school environment. Identifying and mediating these processes is best accomplished in the context of a caring relationship (Noddings, 1984). By sensitively promoting an awareness of such differences in the home and school, social workers can help children experience less confusion and alienation.

Schools that recognize the contribution of home to school success also actively seek parental involvement. Parents can help establish the motivation for learning and provide learning opportunities within the home environment (Constable & Walberg, 1996). Children whose parents are involved in their education typically succeed academically (Kurtz, 1988; Kurtz & Barth, 1989). Unfortunately, poor communication between parents, children, and schools may short-circuit parental involvement. Traditionally, schools asked parents only to participate in Parent Teacher Association meetings, to attend parent-teacher meetings, to act as helpers in the classroom, and to review notes and written communications sent home with the schoolchild. This sort of parental participation does not always facilitate open communication. Schools can establish meaningful two-way communication with parents by reaching out to them, involving them as partners in decision making and school governance, treating parents (and their children) with respect, providing support and coordination to implement and sustain parental involvement, and connecting parents with resources (Comer, 1980; Dupper & Poertner, 1997; Kellaghan et al., 1993; Swap, 1993).

One successful method for facilitating open and constructive communication is the use of collaborative, goal-oriented teams in problem solving. Involving parents, teachers, students, and other school personnel has been successful in resolving school problems and promoting school success among children at risk for school failure (Bailey-Dempsey, 1993). In Malik's case, cooperation between a social worker, teacher, and parents may be the most effective way to determine the cause of his difficulties and forge effective remedies.

Malik's case points to another way that home and school can cooperate. His parents would undoubtedly appreciate quality, affordable before- and after-school care—as would many of today's working and job-seeking parents. It has long been recognized that quality child care is closely linked with children's social, cognitive, and language development (Helburn & Howes, 1996). But such child care facilities are few and far between. Some school districts have been able to implement before- and after-school programs through a mixture of parental fees and local, state, federal, and private dollars (Zigler & Finn-Stevenson, 1995). Many schools, however, have not been able to secure the necessary funding and have also had difficulty altering their schedules and structures to accommodate such changes.

Social Development in the Peer Group

Schools play a large role in children's lives and development. Nearly as influential during middle childhood are **peer groups**—collections of children with unique values and goals (Hartup, 1983). As children progress through middle childhood, peers have an increasingly important impact on such everyday matters as social behavior, activities, and dress. By this phase of development, a desire for group belongingness is especially strong. Within peer groups, children first learn about the functioning of social organizations and develop their skills in communication and social interaction. Whereas individual friendships facilitate the development of critical capacities such as trust and intimacy, peer groups foster learning about cooperation and leadership.

What role do peer groups play in developing the capacity for meaningful relationships in middle childhood?

Throughout middle childhood, the importance of **group norms** is highly evident. Children are sensitive, sometimes exceedingly so, to their peers' standards for behavior, appearance, and attitudes. Rhoda, for instance, is devaluing herself because she recognizes the discrepancy between her appearance and group norms. Not until early adolescence do group norms become more flexible and allow for more individuality, matching the increasing flexibility of cognition.

In most middle childhood peer groups, **dominance hierarchies** establish a social order among group participants. Those hierarchies may predict outcomes when conflict arises (Pettit, Bakshi, Dodge, & Coie, 1990; Savin-Williams, 1979); typically, the more dominant children prevail. Furthermore, through reinforcement, modeling, and direct pressure to conform to expectations, children's dominance hierarchies contribute to socialization.

Throughout middle childhood, gains in cognitive abilities promote more complex communication skills and a greater awareness of social norms. These developments, in turn, facilitate more complex peer interaction, which is a vital resource for the development of **social competence**—the ability to engage in sustained, positive, and mutually satisfactory peer interactions.

Cultural values, however, may influence the type and quantity of peer interaction observed among school-age children. Sociability, cooperativeness, and the value placed on play activities are all culturally shaped phenomena. The specific relationships between various cultures and peer interactions and preferences remain unclear, however, because the state of research in this area is significantly underdeveloped (Robinson, 1998).

Peer acceptance is a powerful predictor of psychological adjustment. One well-known study asked children to fit other children into particular categories. From the results, the researchers developed five general categories of social acceptance: popular, rejected, controversial, neglected, and average (Coie, Dodge, & Coppotelli, 1982). Common predictors of popular status include physical appearance (Adams & Crane, 1980) and prosocial behaviors in the social setting (Newcomb, Bukowski, & Pattee, 1993). Rejected children like Rhoda are those who are actively disliked by their peers. They are particularly likely to be unhappy and to experience achievement and self-esteem issues. Rejected status is strongly associated with poor school performance, antisocial behavior, and delinquency in adolescence (DeRosier, Kupersmidt, & Patterson, 1994; Ollendick, Weist, Borden, & Greene, 1992).

Support for rejected children may include interventions to improve peer relations and psychological adjustment. Most of these interventions are based on social learning theory and involve modeling and reinforcing positive social behavior—for example, initiating interaction and responding to others positively. Several of these programs have indeed helped children develop social competence and gain peer approval (Lochman, Coie, Underwood, & Terry, 1993; Mize & Ladd, 1990).

Gender Roles

During middle childhood, boys and girls seem to follow different paths in gender role development. Often, boys' identification with "masculine" role attributes increases while girls' identification with "feminine" role attributes decreases. As adults, females are the more androgynous of the two genders, and this movement toward androgyny appears to begin in middle childhood (Serbin, Powlishta, & Gulko, 1993).

These distinct paths have multiple causes, including both social and cognitive forces. Cross-gender behavior in girls is more socially acceptable than such behavior among boys. Most research to date suggests that, for both genders, a traditionally "masculine" identity is associated with a higher sense of overall competence and better academic performance (Boldizar, 1991; Newcomb & Dubas, 1992).

Our understanding of the structure of gender roles is derived from various theoretical perspectives. A behavioral perspective proposes that gender-related behaviors precede self-perception in the development of gender role identity; in other words, girls start imitating feminine behavior before they begin thinking of themselves as distinctly female, and boys go through the same sequence in developing a masculine identity. Cognitive developmental theory, however, assumes that self-perceptions emerge first and then guide children's behavior. Gender schema theory (see Bem, 1993), an information-processing approach to gender, combines behavioral and cognitive developmental theories, suggesting that social pressures and children's cognition work together to perpetuate gender-linked perceptions and behaviors.

In general, as children progress through middle childhood, gender stereotypes gradually become more flexible and children begin to accept that males and females can engage in the same activities and occupations (Carter & Patterson, 1982). In addition, children increasingly rely on unique characteristics, rather than a gender label, in attempting to predict the nature and behavior of a specific individual (Biernat, 1991).

Differences in gender stereotyping also exist. Boys appear to hold more gender stereotypical views throughout childhood than girls (Archer, 1992; Levy, Taylor, & Gelman, 1995). For instance, boys are more likely than girls to label a chore as a "girl's job" or a "boy's job." African American children may also hold less stereotyped views of females than do European American children (Bardwell, Cochran, & Walker, 1986). In addition, children from middle-income backgrounds appear to hold more flexible views of gender than children from lower-income backgrounds (Serbin et al., 1993).

The implications of gender stereotyping for individual gender role adoption are not clear cut. Even children well aware of gender role expectations may not conform to gender role stereotypes in their actual behavior (Downs & Langlois, 1988; Serbin et al., 1993). For example, girls who enjoy sports may readily refer to themselves as "tomboys." Perhaps children acquire gender role preferences before acquiring knowledge of gender role stereotypes, or perhaps they learn and interpret gender role stereotypes in diverse ways.

Friendship and Intimacy

Throughout middle childhood, children develop their ability to look at things from others' perspectives. In turn, their capacity to develop more complex friendships—based on awareness of others' thoughts, feelings, and needs—emerges (Selman, 1976). Thus, complex and fairly stable friendship networks begin to form for the first time in middle childhood (Hartup, 1983). Although skills such as cooperation and problem solving are learned in the peer group, close friendships facilitate understanding and promote trust and reciprocity. Most socially competent children maintain and nurture both close friendships and effective peer group interaction.

As children move through middle childhood, friendship begins to entail mutual trust and assistance and thus becomes more psychologically rather than behaviorally based (Damon, 1977). For example, Jane and Rhoda's friendship is based on the emotional support they provide for one another as much as, if not more than, their common interests and activities. The concept of friend is transformed from the playmate of early childhood to the confidant of middle childhood. Violations of trust during this period are perceived as serious violations of the friendship bond. As children move out of middle childhood and into adolescence, the role of intimacy and loyalty in friendship becomes even more pronounced. Moreover, children increasingly value mutual understanding and loyalty in the face of conflict among peers (Berndt, 1988).

Team Play

The overall incidence of aggression during peer activities decreases during middle childhood, and friendly rule-based play increases. This transition is due in part to the continuing development of a perspective-taking ability. In addition, school-age children are exposed to peers who differ in a variety of ways, including personality, ethnicity, and interests.

Peer communication also benefits from cognitive developments. School-age children are able to take their new understanding of others' needs and desires into account in peer interaction. Thus, their interaction reflects an enhanced ability to understand the role of multiple participants in activities. These developments facilitate the transition to rule-based activities, such as team sports (Rubin et al., 1983). Many young school-age children demonstrate this transition. Despite occasional arguments or fights with peers, involvement with team sports may provide great enjoyment and satisfaction.

Special Challenges in Middle Childhood

Society in the United States is changing. In the last several decades, family structures have become more diverse than ever. The percentage of children living with one parent increased from 20% in 1980 to 27% in 1999. Although most children living with a single parent live with their mothers, the proportion of children living with single fathers doubled over this same period (from 2 to 4%). Many single parents have a cohabiting partner. In 1999, 16% of children living with single fathers and 9% of children living with single mothers also resided with their parents' partners (Forum on Child and Family Statistics, 2000).

Dual-income families are also now commonplace. Economic trends are forcing more and more parents into the workforce in order to make ends meet. New legislation requires single parents who receive public assistance to enter the workforce. Because the school day often does not coincide with parents' work schedules, most children no longer come from school to a home supervised by a stay-at-home parent. Low- and middle-income parents have been forced to find affordable child care, which is rarely available, or leave their children home alone (McWhirter et al., 1993).

Unfortunately, available data suggest that the quality of child care experienced by the average child in the United States is less than ideal (Helburn & Howes, 1996; Vandell & Wolfe, 2000). This fact is particularly troubling because child care quality has been linked to children's health status as well as language, social, and cognitive development (Burchinal, 1999; Hayes, Palmer, & Zaslow, 1990; Vandell & Wolfe, 2000).

Children who receive high-quality child care are more likely to perform better on standardized cognitive tests (Vandell & Wolfe, 2000) and in school in general (see Gomby & Larner, 1995). On the other hand, children who receive poor-quality care are more likely to suffer from poor developmental outcomes, including behavior problems and poor school performance.

The association between high-quality child care and cognitive gains is particularly strong among low-income children. Compared to high-income children, low-income children appear more likely to experience positive outcomes from high-quality care *and* more likely to experience negative outcomes from low-quality care (Burchinal, Peisner-Feinberg, Bryant, & Clifford, 2000). And there is evidence that high-quality early childhood education interventions targeted at low-income children can improve children's educational achievements into early adulthood (Ramey, Campbell, & Blair, 1998). Moreover, high-quality child care settings are more likely to have better health and safety practices and as a result fewer infections and injuries among children (Vandell & Wolfe, 2000).

Providing quality child care is just one of the challenges facing young children—along with their parents and schools—in the 21st century. Others include poverty, family disruption, mixed ethnicity and biculturalism, attention deficits, physical disabilities, and family and community violence.

Poverty

How does poverty serve as a risk factor in middle childhood?

Foremost among threats to development is poverty, which creates challenges at multiple levels. Indeed, the detrimental impact of poverty on children has been well established (see Brooks-Gunn & Duncan, 1997; McLoyd, 1998; National Research Council, 1993; Vandivere, Moore, & Brown, 2000). That children should be protected from poverty is not disputed; in fact, this societal value dates back to the colonial period (Trattner, 1994). In practice, this belief has resulted in policies and programs targeted at ensuring that the minimal daily needs of children are met. The nature of these policies and programs, however, has shifted over time, as has our success in meeting this goal (Chase-Lansdale & Vinovskis, 1995).

The late 20th century brought a dramatic rise in the child poverty rate, which peaked at 22% in 1993 (Children's Defense Fund, 2001b). Recent evidence suggests that this trend may be reversing itself, with the child poverty rate dropping to 16% in 2000. However, it is important to note that between 1999 and 2000, child poverty rose among full-time working families. The proportion of children living in families where someone worked throughout the year but the family income remained below the poverty line increased from 18% in 1991 to 37% in 2000. With a shrinking social welfare safety net and a potentially worsening economy, the future outlook for children in working and nonworking poor families is unclear. In addition, the poverty rate for children in the

United States has historically exceeded that of all other Western industrialized nations with the exception of Australia (Smeeding & Rainwater, 1995).

Although in absolute numbers European American children compose the majority of poor children, children from Hispanic and African American families are consistently overrepresented among all children in poverty. Typically, the percentage of African American or Hispanic children living in poverty is at least twice as high as the percentage of European American children (Children's Defense Fund, 1996; U.S. Census Bureau, 1995).

Contrary to stereotypes, most poor children live in working families (National Center for Children in Poverty, 1996/1997). In any case, research demonstrates small or nonexistent differences in the developmental problems of the children and the quality of their home environments, between welfare children and poor children whose families do not receive welfare (Zill, Moore, Smith, Stief, & Coiro, 1995). Thus, moving parents off welfare and onto payrolls does not necessarily improve the overall well-being of their school-age children, perhaps because the challenges to development associated with poverty remain constant.

Welfare to Work. Several studies have focused on the impact of recent welfare-to-work initiatives on children. Such research suggests that the parents' employment stability and income growth, whether in the form of earnings or other financial or in-kind supports, is critical to facilitating positive child outcomes. But this research is in its infancy, and many factors—parent and child characteristics, family functioning, earnings supplements, employment stability, and the potential earnings growth associated with it—are critical determinants of the impact of welfare-to-work efforts on child outcomes. Child care circumstances are particularly critical; among low-income women, higher-quality care may increase the likelihood and stability of employment and improve mothers' later educational achievement (Hofferth, 1996; Vandell & Wolfe, 2000).

Existing research specifically suggests that initiatives that increase *both* parental employment and income may improve their children's academic achievement and reduce behavior problems (Moore, McGroder, & Zaslow, 2001; Morris, Duncan & Chase-Lansdale, 2001; Morris, Huston, Duncan, Crosby, & Bos, 2001). Initiatives that increase family income, whether through work or earnings supplements or other means, may improve children's academic achievement and reduce behavior problems, and potentially lead to other positive impacts on children.

Welfare-to-work initiatives can, however, be damaging. Unstable employment may threaten children's well-being. Transitions between employment and unemployment appear to increase anxious and depressed behavior among young school-age children (Kalil, Dunifon, & Danziger, 2001). Child well-being is detrimentally impacted by repeated changes in child care arrangements. Unstable employment and income contribute to such changes and other sources of turbulence in children's lives, and turbulence has been shown to lead to declines in school performance (Moore, Vandivere, & Ehrle, 2000). Also it should be noted that additional research focusing on the impact of welfare-to-work initiatives on infants and toddlers is needed, and research focusing on impacts on adolescents indicates quite distinct, and sometimes negative, findings.

It is also important to recognize that even children who benefit from welfare-to-work programs continue to face serious challenges. In recent research, one third of the children most positively affected still scored in the bottom 25th percentile on a nationally standardized test of language skills (Morris & Duncan, 2001). In general, the risk factors associated with child poverty are numerous, especially when poverty is sustained. Children who grow up in poverty are more likely (as Chapter 4 explains) to be born with low birth weight, to experience serious and chronic health problems, and to receive poorer health care and nutrition than children who grow up in better financial circumstances (Sroufe et al., 1996).

In addition, poor families often experience much higher levels of stress than families with adequate incomes, potentially leading to a wide variety of negative outcomes for children. They include heightened risk of exposure to **child maltreatment** (abuse and neglect) and exposure to domestic violence between adults in the home (Halpern, 1990; McLoyd, 1998). Children who have spent any part of their infancy or early childhood in poverty have often already encountered several developmental challenges by the time middle childhood begins. Children who enter, progress through, and leave middle childhood in poverty are at much greater risk of negative developmental outcomes than those who briefly enter and then exit poverty while still in middle childhood.

Moreover, in the United States, low income predicts child development problems more often than in other industrialized countries. Social policies in the United States tend to exaggerate rather than minimize the impact of family income on access to human services such as health care and child care (Bronfenbrenner, 1986). For example, in the United States, child- and health-care quality are linked to family income.

But what does it actually mean to be poor? Being poor is a relative concept, the meaning of which is defined by perceptions of exclusion (Garbarino, 1992, 1995). In our society, one must be *not* poor in order to be included. Lack of income and certain goods makes poor people feel that they do not possess what is expected among those who belong; thus, poverty results in feelings of inability and inadequacy. This is the essence of **relative poverty**. Fundamentally, then, poverty is more a social than an economic phenomenon.

The meaning of poverty for the school-age child is particularly profound. As evidence, James Garbarino (1995) points to an innocent question once asked of him by a child: "When you were growing up, were you poor or regular?" (p. 137). As the child struggles with the normal developmental tasks of feeling included and socially competent, poverty is a persistent reminder of exclusion and social incompetence.

Family Disruption

The divorce rate in the United States is the highest in the world. More than 1 million children experience the divorce of their parents each year, and at any given time approximately one child in four lives in a single-parent household (Meyer & Garasky, 1993). Between two thirds and three fourths of divorced parents marry a second time, and thus for many school-age children, divorce leads to new family relationships, as is occurring for Malik. But the likelihood of divorce is even greater for second marriages, and approximately half of these children experience the end of a parent's second marriage. Divorce and other types of family disruption often lead to a parade of new people and situations, including new housing and income arrangements and new family roles and responsibilities (Hetherington & Jodl, 1994). It may also immerse the child in poverty.

Divorce, or the loss of one or both parents, is stressful for all children. Great variation exists, however, in how children respond to this type of stress. Critical factors in outcomes for children include social supports within the family and surrounding community, the child's characteristics, and the psychological well-being of the parents. In addition, because middle childhood spans a wide age range, school-age children exhibit a wide range of cognitive and emotional responses to divorce. They may blame themselves and suffer from separation anxiety or may demonstrate a mature understanding of the reasons behind the divorce.

Children experiencing family disruption without supports or those who have experienced difficulties preceding the disruption are most likely to experience long-term emotional and behavioral problems. Children placed in foster care or exposed to domestic violence fall into this group. These children are likely to face additional trauma associated with the loss of familiar space, belongings, and social networks (Groves, 1997). Reaction to such trauma should be expected. However, with appropriate support and intervention, many children experiencing family disruption adjust over time (Hetherington & Clingempeel, 1992).

Mixed Ethnicity and Biculturalism

Juan, who speaks little English, represents many school-age children. An estimated 6 million American school-age children speak a language other than English at home, a figure that is expected to increase steadily over time (U.S. Census Bureau, 1995).

Bilingual, or **English as a second language (ESL),** children have traditionally been thought to be at risk of cognitive and language deficits. However, significant research evidence demonstrates that bilingualism may have a positive impact on development. Bilingual children often perform better than monolingual children on tests of analytical reasoning, concept formation, and cognitive flexibility (Hakuta, Ferdman, & Diaz, 1987).

Moreover, bilingual children may be more likely to acquire capacities and skills that enhance their reading achievement (Campbell & Sais, 1995). Despite such findings, however, bilingual children may receive little support for their native language and culture in the classroom.

Ethnicity—marked by skin color, language, and culture—is another potential challenge for school-age children. For European American children, ethnicity does not typically lead to comparison with others or exploration of identity (Rotheram-Borus, 1993). But for most children who are members of nondominant groups, ethnicity may be a central part of the quest for identity that begins in middle childhood and continues well into adolescence and young adulthood. School-age children of mixed ethnicity may also begin to struggle with issues of identity. Around age 7, cognitive advances allow children to view themselves and others as capable of belonging to more than one "category" at once, as capable of possessing two or more heritages simultaneously (Morrison & Bordere, 2001). As children like Malik mature, they may become more aware not only of their dual or multiple identity but also of the discrimination and inequality to which they are subjected. Issues related to ethnicity may in fact present overwhelming challenges for the school-age child belonging to a nondominant group. At a time when development of a sense of belonging is critical, these issues set some children apart from members of dominant groups and may increase the prejudice to which they are subjected.

Segregation based on ethnicity and social class is common in friendships at all ages, including middle childhood. Like adults, children are more likely to hold negative attitudes toward groups to which they do not belong. However, children, like adults, vary in the extent to which they hold ethnic and social class biases. Specific learning experiences appear to be influential in the development of childhood prejudice (Powlishta, Serbin, Doyle, & White, 1994). Verbalized prejudice declines during middle childhood as children learn to obey social norms against overt prejudice. However, children belonging to nondominant groups continue to face institutional discrimination and other significant challenges throughout this period of the life course (Bigler & Liben, 1993).

A particular challenge for children like Malik and Juan may be blending contradictory values, standards, and traditions. For Malik, his mother and father may give him different messages about who he is. Juan and Malik may respond to cultural contradictions by identifying with the mainstream American culture in which they are immersed or by developing negative attitudes about their subcultural group memberships. Research evidence indicates that rejection of ethnic identity is particularly likely among members of nondominant groups lacking a supportive social movement that stresses ethnic pride (Phinney, 1989). On the other hand, children whose experience in the mainstream culture challenges self-esteem and raises barriers to academic success may reject the dominant culture and define themselves in reaction against majority values (Matute-Bianchi, 1986). Other children begin to develop their own unique blend of the two cultures. Individual reactions, like those of Juan and Malik, will be shaped by the child's unique experiences and social influences.

Because blending the values of both dominant and nondominant groups in a manner that promotes self-esteem may be difficult and confusing (Bautista de Domanico, Crawford, & DeWolfe, 1994), children may avoid confronting their ethnic identity (Markstrom-Adams & Adams, 1995; Roebers & Schneider, 1999). It is a major developmental task to integrate dual or multiple racial and cultural identities into a consistent personal identity as well as a positive ethnic or racial identity (Gibbs & Huang, 1989).

Many models of identity development have been developed for children of mixed ethnicity, with new ideas and theories constantly emerging. It is clear that identity development for such children is diverse, extremely complex, and not well understood. As always, however, parents and professionals must start where the child is, with a focus on facilitating understanding and appreciation of heritage in order to promote development of an integrated identity and positive self-regard (Kopola, Esquivel, & Baptiste, 1994). Children should be provided with opportunities to explore their dual or multiple heritages and to select their own terms for identifying and describing themselves (Morrison & Bordere, 2001). Although studies have produced diverse findings, positive outcomes seem to be associated with supportive family systems and involvement in social and recreational activities that expose these children to their heritage and lead to self-affirmation (Fuligni, 1997; Gibbs & Huang, 1989; Guarnaccia & Lopez, 1998; Herring, 1995).

Key tasks for adults, then, include educating children about family histories and supporting the creation of an integrated sense of self. Individuals and organizations within the child's social system can provide support by being sensitive to issues related to ethnic origin and ethnic distinctions; they can also help by celebrating cultural diversity and trying to increase the cultural competence of European American children (Berk, 1997). Such interventions appear to encourage less negative stereotypes of peers belonging to nondominant groups (Rotheram-Borus, 1993).

In general, it is critical to the positive identity development of all children, but particularly those from nondominant groups, that schools value diversity and offer a variety of experiences that focus on ethnicity and identity development (Morrison & Bordere, 2001). Ensuring that schools respect nondominant cultures and learning styles is an important step. In order for schools to do this, educators must develop self-awareness. A variety of materials have been designed to facilitate this process among educators (see Lee, Menkart & Okazawa-Rae, 1998; Matsumoto-Grah, 1992; Seefeldt, 1993).

Attention Deficits

In recent years, children who have trouble concentrating on tasks have been among those most frequently referred to outside sources for help (Hinshaw, 1994). These children, who are often first recognized as "problems" in their middle years, may be stigmatized by teachers and peers alike because they are unable to control their behavior in large group settings. They often display high activity levels, inattention, aggression, defiance, poor academic performance, and antisocial behaviors (Hinshaw, 1994). Teachers often refer children displaying these behaviors to physicians, psychologists, and social workers.

Children referred to professionals because of suspected **attention deficit disorder (ADD)** or **attention deficit hyperactivity disorder (ADHD)** represent a population as heterogeneous and complex as the disorder itself (Hinshaw, 1994). Exhibit 5.2 provides the *DSM-IV* diagnostic criteria for ADHD. A comprehensive assessment by a professional who specializes in ADDs is a critical component of accurate diagnosis. Part of that assessment is a complete history of the disorder from a variety of sources. The specialist will also observe the child over time to detect variations in the child's behavior (Hinshaw, 1994).

It is important for parents to recognize that diagnosis is a complex issue and assessment methods and procedures vary widely from one professional to the next. Different professionals may reach conflicting diagnostic conclusions and recommend different treatments. Regardless of the assessor's background, a multimethod, multi-informant assessment process is critical. In this process, the assessor should pay attention to other conditions affecting behavior, relevant cultural and family issues, and treatment considerations such as cost, availability, and other feasibility issues (Anastopoulos & Shelton, 2001).

Children who are accurately diagnosed as ADD or ADHD may benefit from drug therapy, behavioral therapy, and cognitive behavioral therapy. The drug treatment must be well administered and monitored to avoid complications. Furthermore, it must be coupled with behavioral, or cognitive behavioral, interventions that teach the child with ADD or ADHD the skills needed for school success. The key point here is that drug therapy typically leads to desired outcomes only when combined with additional interventions (Dedmon, 1997).

Children who do not receive a comprehensive assessment by a qualified specialist are often misdiagnosed. Drug therapy may be prescribed hastily, with only a half-hearted recommendation for additional therapies. ADD and ADHD have become very popular labels for children who do not conform to school settings. Teachers often suggest to parents that their children have the disorder, the parents in turn suggest to their family physician or pediatrician that their child has the disorder, and thus a misdiagnosis is made. One result of this scenario is that children from nondominant groups are

EXHIBIT 5.2
Diagnostic Criteria for Attention-Deficit/Hyperactivity Disorder

Either (1) or (2):

(1) **Inattention**: Six (or more) of the following symptoms of inattention have persisted for at least 6 months to a degree that is maladaptive and inconsistent with developmental level:

- Often fails to give close attention to details or makes careless mistakes in schoolwork, work, or other activities
- Often has difficulty sustaining attention in tasks or play activities
- Often does not seem to listen when spoken to directly
- Often does not follow through on instructions and fails to finish schoolwork, chores, or duties in the workplace (not due to oppositional behavior or failure to understand instruction)
- Often has difficulty organizing tasks and activities
- Often avoids, dislikes, or is reluctant to engage in tasks that require sustained mental effort (such as schoolwork or homework)
- Often loses things necessary for tasks or activities (toys, school assignments, pencils, books, or tools)
- Is often easily distracted by extraneous stimuli
- Is often forgetful in daily activities

(2) **Hyperactivity-Impulsivity**: Six (or more) of the following symptoms of hyperactivity-impulsivity have persisted for at least 6 months to a degree that it is maladaptive and inconsistent with developmental level:

Hyperactivity

- Often fidgets with hands or feet or squirms in seat
- Often leaves seat in classroom or in other situations in which remaining seated is expected
- Often runs about or climbs excessively in situations in which it is inappropriate (in adolescents or adults, may be limited to subjective feelings of restlessness)
- Often has difficulty playing or engaging in leisure activities quietly
- Is often "on the go" or often acts as if "driven by a motor"
- Often talks excessively

Impulsivity

- Often blurts out answers to questions before they have been completed
- Often has difficulty awaiting turn
- Often interrupts or intrudes on others (e.g., butts into conversations or games)
- Some hyperactive-impulsive or inattentive symptoms that caused impairment were present before age 7
- Some impairment from the symptoms is present in two or more settings (e.g., at school [or work] and at home)
- There must be clear evidence of clinically significant impairment in social, academic, or occupational functioning
- The symptoms do not occur exclusively during the course of a pervasive developmental disorder, schizophrenia, or other psychotic disorder and are not better accounted for by another mental disorder (e.g., mood disorder, anxiety disorder, dissociated disorder, or a personality disorder)

Source: American Psychiatric Association, 1994.

disproportionately misdiagnosed with ADD and ADHD because their behavior often does not conform to classroom standards. Thus, those with social or emotional difficulties may be moved inappropriately to a special education class, where they face an increased risk of academic failure and premature departure from school (Oakes, 1985).

The popularity of the ADD and ADHD diagnoses most likely results from a combination of factors. These factors include limits on parents' time and resources, teachers' inability to control the classroom environment, too few resources for teachers to draw on in dealing with active children in the classroom, overcrowded classrooms, and discrimination. When resources are scarce and a teacher's time is limited, the easiest solution to the problem child may be either drug therapy or transfer to a different class. Neither route may be absolutely necessary to change or control a child's behavior, however. In some cases, individual attention or skill training may achieve the same end without unnecessary trauma to the child.

How might such educational initiatives minimize the risks associated with ADD and ADHD?

In the educational environment, "quality-first teaching" is an example of a step in this direction. Recognizing that educators need support in the classroom environment in order to fully implement the intent of the **Individuals with Disabilities Education Act** (IDEA, Part H of P.L.101-476) of 1990, this approach represents an attempt by schools to help teachers make adjustments in their instructional methods first rather than referring problematic children for assessment and diagnosis or removing children from the classroom for services. One tool used is pairing teachers who are well respected by their peers with less-experienced teachers in order to provide support. These "instructional support teachers" or "mentor teachers" discuss appropriate strategies and methods. In addition, they model suggested approaches and educate less-experienced teachers about appropriate support and delivery systems for children experiencing difficulties. The aim is to create an educational support system that uses ADD/ADHD classification as a last resort, promoting positive development and avoiding use of exclusion or tracking.

Physical Disabilities

Children's adjustment to their physical disabilities is highly dependent on the adjustment of those around them. Families may respond in a number of ways to a diagnosis of a disability or serious illness. Usually, however, they move through the following stages when they discover that a child is disabled: withdrawal or rejection, denial, fear and frustration, and ideally, adjustment and acceptance in the end (Ziolko, 1993). Awareness of and sensitivity to these stages is critical for those assessing the need for intervention. Typically, the parents of disabled children are helped by advocacy and support groups and access to information and resources.

Middle childhood is a critical time for children with either physical disabilities or chronic illness. For such children to acquire a clear sense of self and an ability to care for themselves and their own health needs, they need positive self-regard. The positive development of children with disabilities is facilitated by support at the micro, meso, and macro levels that promotes independence (Green, 1994).

Families of children with disabilities also typically desire independence and self-determination for their children. Family empowerment was an explicit focus of the Education for All Handicapped Children Act (P.L. 94-142) of 1975 (J. Gallagher, 1993), which stresses parental participation in the development of an **individual education plan (IEP)** for each child. The IEP charts a course for ensuring that each disabled child achieves as much as possible in the academic realm.

The need to include the family in decision making and planning is also embodied in the IDEA of 1990, which replaced the Education for All Handicapped Children Act. The 1990 act assures all children the right to a free and appropriate public education and supports the placement of children with disabilities into integrated settings. Prior to this act, the education of children with disabilities was left to individual states. As a result, the population labeled "disabled" and the services provided to them varied greatly. Today, however, through various pieces of legislation and several court decisions, society has stated its clear preference to educate children with disabilities in integrated settings to the maximum extent possible (Gent & Mulhauser, 1993).

Only full inclusion in family, school, and community life can allow children with special challenges to feel valued and to integrate their disabilities with other aspects of their lives (Green, 1994). The critical task for the school-age child with a disability is to confront successfully the reactions of other children, adults, and institutions. The critical task for individuals and institutional structures is to respond appropriately and supportively (W. Gallagher, 1993). Interventions that promote acceptance and support among children and adults without disabilities are thus necessary.

Family and Community Violence

Children are increasingly witness or subject to violence in their homes, schools, and neighborhoods (Guterman & Cameron, 1997). Although child maltreatment and domestic violence have always existed, they have been recognized as social problems only recently. Community violence is slowly becoming recognized as a social problem of equal magnitude, affecting a tremendous number of children and families. Exposure to violence is a particular problem in areas where a lack of economic and social resources already produces significant challenges for children (Groves, 1997). Among immigrant children from war-torn countries, like Juan, the atrocities witnessed or experienced are often unimaginable to children and adults who have resided in the United States all of their lives (see Gowen, 2001; Zea, Diehl, & Porterfield, 1997).

Witnessing violence deeply affects children, particularly when the perpetrator or victim of violence is a family member. In the United States, experts estimate that each

EXHIBIT 5.3
An Ecological Model of Child Maltreatment

Risk Category	Examples
Parental	Psychological disturbance Substance abuse
Child	Developmental disability Difficult temperament
Family	Low income Limited social support network
Community	Social isolation Limited family support services
Cultural	Condones use of physical force Has history of valuing children as property

Source: Based on Belsky, 1993.

year between 3.3 million and 10 million children witness domestic violence between adults in the home (Children's Defense Fund, 2000). But being a victim of violence is even more devastating, or even fatal. Child and teen firearm deaths increased dramatically in the United States between the early 1980s and early 1990s, and in 1999 nine children died each day from gunfire (Children's Defense Fund, 2000). Between 1994 and 2000, however, child and teen deaths by gunfire dropped 42% (Children's Defense Fund, 1998, 2000). Despite this decline, the rate of firearm deaths among children in the United States is much higher than that of almost all other industrialized countries (Children's Defense Fund, 2000).

Furthermore, 2.8 million victims of child maltreatment—including physical abuse, sexual abuse, neglect, and emotional abuse—were reported to authorities in 1998, and over 900,000 were confirmed as victims of abuse or neglect (Children's Defense Fund, 2000). African American and Native American children are consistently overrepresented among confirmed maltreatment victims. Until recently, research indicated a high, and increasing, incidence of maltreatment among school-age children, specifically among children ages 6 to 11. In 1999, however, the victimization rate was highest among the 0 to 3 age group. And in general, between 1998 and 1999, the rate of child victimization declined. This decline was small, however, and it is too soon to tell whether this will be a continuing trend (U.S. Department of Health and Human Services, 2001b).

A variety of factors contribute to child maltreatment and family violence. Exhibit 5.3 outlines Jay Belsky's (1993) ecological model of maltreatment, which specifies the multiple factors involved in children's victimization. These factors include parental, child, family, community, and cultural characteristics. Typically, the dynamic interplay of such characteristics leads to maltreatment.

Not surprisingly, children who experience abuse have been found to report more unhappiness and troubled behavior than children who only witness abuse (Sternberg et al., 1993). Witnesses, in turn, report more adjustment difficulties than children who have neither been abused nor witnessed domestic violence. Because of the strong association between domestic violence and child maltreatment, however, many children are likely to experience these challenges to healthy development simultaneously (McCloskey, Figueredo, & Koss, 1995).

Child maltreatment broadly affects the development of secure attachments, peer relationships, and cognitive and language skills (Groves, 1997). Emotionally abused or neglected children often experience lowered self-esteem and elevated anxiety (Sternberg et al., 1993). Also, over time, maltreated children show a variety of learning and adjustment problems, including difficulties with peers, academic failure, depression, substance abuse, and delinquency (Hotaling, Finkelhor, Kirkpatrick, & Strauss, 1988). Severe and chronic maltreatment may lead to more severe consequences, including a variety of psychopathologies (Terr, 1991).

Children who experience trauma, induced by either indirect or direct exposure to violence, may experience **post-traumatic stress disorder** (PTSD)—a set of symptoms that include feelings of fear and helplessness, reliving of the traumatic experience, and attempts to avoid reminders of the traumatic experience (Groves, 1997; Jenkins & Bell, 1997; Kaplan & Sadock, 1998). You will want to explore the possibility that the behaviors that Juan is exhibiting at school are related to traumatic experiences he experienced in El Salvador—first the political unrest and then the earthquake, as well as the traumatic resettlement to the United States. Researchers have also found changes in the brain chemistry of children exposed to chronic violence (Perry, 1997). Clearly, witnessing or experiencing violence adversely affects children in a number of areas, including the ability to function in school and the ability to establish stable peer relationships (Dyson, 1989). Evidence suggests that perhaps as many as one half of all children exposed to violence before the age of 10 develop psychiatric problems in adulthood (Davidson & Smith, 1990). Children who directly experience violence are at high risk of negative outcomes, but secondary exposure to violence and trauma—such as when a child's parents are suffering from PTSD—also may lead to negative outcomes for children (Hamblen, 2002; Monahon, 1997).

Prolonged exposure to violence has multiple implications for child development. Such children are forced to learn lessons about loss and death, perhaps before they have acquired the cognitive ability to understand. They may therefore come to believe that the world is unpredictable and violent, a belief that threatens children's natural curiosity and desire to explore the social environment. Multiple experiences in which adults are unable to protect them often lead children to conclude that they must take on such responsibility for themselves, a prospect that can easily overwhelm the resources of a school-age child.

Experiencing such helplessness may also lead to feelings of incompetence and hopelessness, to which children who experience chronic violence react in diverse ways. Responses may be passive, including withdrawal symptoms and signs of depression; or they may be active, including the use of aggression as a means of coping with and transforming the overwhelming feelings of vulnerability (Groves, 1997; Guterman & Cameron, 1997).

What protective factors can buffer the effects of neighborhood violence on school-age children?

The emotional availability of a parent or other caretaker who can support the child's need to process traumatic events is critical. However, in situations of crisis stimulated by child maltreatment, domestic violence, and national or international violence, families are often unable to support their children psychologically. Even with the best of parental resources, moreover, children developing in violent and chronically dangerous communities continue to experience numerous challenges to development. The child's need for autonomy and independence is directly confronted by the parent's need to protect the child's physical safety. Hours spent indoors to avoid danger do not promote the much-needed peer relationships and sense of accomplishment, purpose, and self-efficacy so critical during this phase of development (Groves, 1997).

Risk Factors and Protective Factors in Middle Childhood

School-age children face a variety of risks that undermine their struggles to develop a sense of purpose and self-worth. These risks include poverty, prejudice, and violence (Garbarino, 1995). More generally, risk factors are anything that increases the probability of a problem condition, its progression into a more severe state, or its maintenance (Fraser & Galinsky, 1997). Risk factors are moderated, however, by protective factors, either internal or external, which help children resist risk (Garmezy, 1993, 1994; Werner & Smith, 2001).

Resilience—or "survival against the odds"—arises from an interplay of risk and protective factors and manifests as adaptive behavior producing positive outcomes (Fraser & Galinsky, 1997). As Exhibit 5.4 illustrates, a variety of factors influence resilience during middle childhood. Whether a factor manifests as a risk or a protection often depends on its interaction with other factors influencing the individual child.

EXHIBIT 5.4
Factors Influencing Resilience During Middle Childhood

Dimension	Factors
Individual (child)	Earlier developmental history Personality Appearance Social competence Learning style Group membership (dominant/nondominant)
Family	Approach to child Continuity with school Social, emotional, and financial resources Group membership (dominant/nondominant)
Peer group	Approach to child Values, norms, and rules
School	Continuity with family Values, norms, and rules General child/parent/family orientation Flexibility and responsiveness Financial and social resources
Community	Approach to child and family Social, emotional, and financial resources General child/parent/family orientation
Socioeconomic system	Values, norms, and rules Societal orientation (preventive/reactive) Acceptance of cultural diversity

A multidimensional, or systems, perspective on resilience provides a tool for promoting positive development during middle childhood. This perspective also facilitates intervention efforts (discussed in greater detail in Chapter 4). As social workers, we must recognize that resilience is rarely an innate characteristic. Rather, it is a process (Egeland, Carlson, & Sroufe, 1993) that may be facilitated by influences within the child's surrounding environment. Indeed, research suggests that high-risk behavior among children increases as their perception of family involvement and community support declines (Benson, 1990; Blyth & Roehlkepartian, 1993). A primary goal of the social work profession must be to facilitate positive external supports for children and enhance the person/environment fit so as to maximize protective factors and minimize risk factors.

IMPLICATIONS FOR SOCIAL WORK PRACTICE

This discussion of middle childhood suggests several practice principles for social workers:

- Support family and community attempts to stabilize the environment for children.
- Support parents as the most important emotional resources for their children.
- Recognize and support resilience in children and families. Support the efforts of children and families to cope with adversity.
- Recognize the critical influence of the school environment on growth and development, and encourage attempts by school personnel to be responsive to all children and families.
- Understand the important role of peer groups in psychosocial growth and development; facilitate the development and maintenance of positive peer relationships.
- Understand the ways in which the organization of schools supports the status quo present in the larger society. Support schools in their efforts to alter discrepancies based on race, ethnicity, gender, and class.
- Facilitate teacher-parent-child communication about, and school responsiveness to, children with special needs.
- Understand the effects of violence on children, and establish a nurturing and nonviolent environment when possible.
- Become familiar with methods of teaching nonviolent conflict resolution skills to children and adults.
- Provide opportunities for moral and spiritual mentoring in the school environment.
- Help children recognize and accept diversity in physical development and ability levels during middle childhood.

Key Terms

acculturation
assimilation (culture)
attention deficit disorder (ADD)
attention deficit hyperactivity disorder (ADHD)
Brown v. Board of Education
child maltreatment
collaborative classroom
conventional level of moral reasoning
dominance hierarchy
emotional intelligence
English as a second language (ESL)
flexible grouping
full-service school
group norm
heterogeneous grouping
inclusion
individual education plan (IEP)
Individuals with Disabilities Education Act
institutional discrimination
mainstreaming
mastery
moral behavior
multiple intelligences
peer group
post-traumatic stress disorder
prepubescence
prosocial behavior
pubescence
relative poverty
self-competence
social competence
tracking
zone of proximal development

Active Learning

1. Form an even number of debate teams of three to four students. Half of the teams will argue the case for school tracking and the other half of the teams will argue the case against school tracking. Each team will have 2 minutes to present its case, starting first with the pro side of the question and then moving to the con side. Each team will also have 1 minute for rebuttal.

2. As a class, discuss the pros and cons of English-only school environments for children.

3. In small groups, compare and contrast the risk and protective factors present for Malik, Rhoda, and Juan. Brainstorm interventions you would consider if you were working with each child.

Web Resources

Forum on Child and Family Statistics

childstats.gov

Official web site of the Federal Interagency Forum on Child and Family Statistics offers easy access to federal and state statistics and reports on children and families, including international comparisons.

National Clearinghouse on Child Abuse and Neglect Information

www.calib.com/nccanch

Site presented by the Administration for Children and Families contains information for professionals and child abuse and neglect, including statistics, prevention information, state statutes, funding sources, and publications.

Search Institute

www.search-institute.org

Site presented by Search Institute, an independent, nonprofit, nonsectarian organization with the goal of advancing the well-being of adolescents and children, contains information on 40 developmental assets and methods for building assets for child and youth development.

Child Trauma Academy

www.childtraumaacademy.com

A site presented by the Child Trauma Academy contains information on the impact of child maltreatment on the brain, and the physiological and psychological effects of trauma on children.

American Association of University Women

www.aauw.org/home.html

Site maintained by the American Association of University Women contains information on education and equity for women and girls, including a report card on Title IX, a law that banned sex discrimination in education.

CHAPTER 6

Adolescence

Susan Ainsley McCarter

CHAPTER 6

Adolescence

Susan Ainsley McCarter
Charlotte, North Carolina

How do biological, psychological, social, and spiritual dimensions affect the adolescent phase of the life course?

Why do social workers need to understand theories of identity formation when working with adolescents?

What unique challenges do adolescents face when confronted with issues of sexuality and substance use and abuse?

Key Ideas

As you read this chapter, take note of these central ideas:

1. Adolescence is characterized by significant physical change, increased hormone production, sexual maturation, increased cognitive functioning, formative identity development, increased independence, and possible experimentation with sex and substances.
2. During adolescence, increased hormone production results in a period called puberty, during which persons become capable of reproduction. Other physical changes during this period include skeletal, musculature, and fat distribution changes as well as development of primary and secondary sex characteristics.
3. Psychological changes during this period include reactions to physical, social, and cultural changes confronting the adolescent, as well as cognitive development, in which most individuals develop the abilities to contemplate the future, to comprehend the nature of human relationships, to consolidate specific knowledge into a coherent system, and to envision possible consequences from a hypothetical list of actions.
4. The greatest task of adolescence is identity formation—determining who one is and where one is going.

5. Adolescents spend nearly a third of their waking hours at school, where they should receive skills and knowledge for their next step in life, but a school that follows a Eurocentric educational model without regard for other cultures may damage the self-esteem of students from minority ethnic groups.

6. Among the physical and mental health risks to today's adolescents are violence, poor nutrition, obesity, eating disorders, depression, and suicide.

Case Study 6.1

David's Coming-Out Process

As a social worker at Jefferson High School, you see many facets of adolescent life. Nothing much surprises you—especially not the way some of the kids hem and haw when they're trying to tell you what's really on their mind. Take David Cunha, for instance. When he shows up for his first appointment, you simply ask him to tell you about himself.

"Let's see, I'm 17," he began. "I'm a forward on the varsity soccer team. What else do you want to know? My parents are from Bolivia and are as traditional as you can imagine. My dad, David Sr., teaches history and is the varsity baseball coach here at Jefferson. My mom is a geriatric nurse. I have a younger sister, Patti. Patti Perfect. She goes to the magnet school and is in the ninth grade."

"How are things at home?" you ask him. "Whatever. Patti is perfect, and I'm 'a freak.' They think I'm 'different, arrogant, stubborn.' I don't know what they want me to be. But I don't think that's what I am. That may be because . . . because I'm gay. I haven't come out to my parents. That's all I need!"

This was obviously a difficult confession for David to make to an adult, but with a little encouragement he continues: "There are two other soccer players who are gay, and then we have some friends outside of soccer. Thank God! But basically when the whole team is together or when I'm with other friends, I just act straight. I talk about girls' bodies just like the other guys. I think that is the hardest. Not being able to be yourself. I'm at least glad that I've met other gay guys. It was really hard when I was about 13. I was so confused. I knew that men were supposed to be with women, not other men. What I was feeling was not 'normal,' and I thought I was the only one. I wanted to kill myself. That was a bad time."

David's tone changes. "Let's talk about something good. Let me tell you about Theo. I find Theo very attractive. I hope he likes my soccer build.

CASE STUDY 6.1

I wonder if he would like to hang out together—get to know one another. He's a junior, and if we got together, the other guys would razz me about seeing a younger guy. But I keep thinking about him. And looking at him during practice. I just need to say something to him. Some guys off the team are going out Thursday night after practice. He hasn't been invited in the past. Maybe if I invite him, he'll come."

CASE STUDY 6.2

CARL'S STRUGGLE FOR IDENTITY

Whereas David sought you out, Carl Fleischer, another 17-year-old, was sent to see you in your office at the high school. He matter-of-factly tells you that he is "an underachiever." He used to get an occasional B in his classes, but now it's mostly Cs with an occasional D.

When you ask Carl what he likes to do in his spare time, he replies, "I like to get high and surf the Net." Further probing elicits one-word answers until you ask Carl about girlfriends. His face contorts as he slaps his ample belly: "I'm not exactly a sex symbol. According to my doctor, I'm a fatso. He says normal boys my age and height weigh at least 50 pounds less than I do. He also tells me to quit smoking and get some exercise. Whatever. My mom says I'm big-boned. She says my dad was the same way. I wouldn't know. I never met the scumbag. He left when my mom was pregnant. But you probably don't want to hear about that."

Carl won't say more on that topic, but you finally get him to talk about his job, delivering pizzas two nights a week and on the weekends. "So if you need pizzas, call me at Antonio's. I always bring pies home for my mom on Tuesday and Friday nights. She works late those nights, and so we usually eat pizza and catch the Tuesday and Friday night lineups on TV. She lets me smoke in the house—cigarettes, not weed. Although I have gotten high in the house a couple times. Anyway, I am not what you would call popular. I am just a fat, slow geek and a pizza guy. But there are some heads who come into Antonio's. I exchange pies for dope. Works out pretty well: they get the munchies, and the pies keep me in with the heads."

Case Study 6.3

Monica's Quest for Mastery

Monica Golden, one of the peer counselors at Jefferson High, hangs around to chat after a meeting of the peer counselors. Monica is the youngest and tallest daughter in a family of five kids, with one younger brother. Monica's mother is the assistant principal at Grover Middle School, and her father works for the Internal Revenue Service. This year Monica is the vice president of the senior class, the treasurer for the Young Republicans, a starter on the track team, a teacher at Sunday School, and a Jefferson peer counselor.

When you comment on the scope of these activities, Monica replies: "I really do stay busy. I worked at the mall last year, but it was hard to keep my grades up. I'm trying to get into college, so my family and I decided I shouldn't work this year. So I just baby-sit sometimes. A lot of my aunts and uncles have me watch their kids, but they don't pay me. They consider it a family favor. Anyway, I am waiting to hear back from colleges. They should be sending out the letters this week. You know, the fatter the envelope the better. It doesn't take many words to say 'No. We reject you.' And I need to either get into a state school or get a scholarship so that I can use my savings for tuition."

You talk a little about Monica's options, and she tells you that her first choice is Howard University. "I want to surround myself with black scholars and role models and my dream is to be a pediatrician, you know. I love kids," Monica says. "I tried tons of jobs—that's where I got the savings. And, well, those with kids I enjoyed the most. Like I said, I've worked retail at the mall. I've worked at the supermarket as a cashier. I've worked at the snack bar at the pool. And I've been baby-sitting since I was 12. That's what I like the most."

"I'd love to have kids someday. But I don't even have a boyfriend. I wear glasses. My parents say I don't need contacts; they think I'm being vain. Not that I don't have a boyfriend because I wear glasses. Guys think I'm an overachiever. They think I'm driven and demanding and incapable of having fun. That's what I've been told. I think I'm just ambitious and extroverted. But really, I just haven't had much time to date in high school. I've been so busy. Well, gotta run."

The Social Construction of Adolescence Across Time

If you were asked to describe David, Carl, and Monica, you would probably draw attention to their status as adolescents. The importance of that status has changed across time and cultures, however. Adolescence was invented as a psychosocial concept in the late 19th and early 20th centuries as the United States made the transition from an agrarian to an urban-industrial society (Fass & Mason, 2000a). Prior to this time, and in many agrarian nations today, adolescents worked beside adults, doing what adults did for the most part. As the United States became urbanized and industrialized, child-labor legislation and compulsory education policies were passed, and adolescents were moved from the workplace to the school and became economically dependent on parents. The juvenile justice system was developed because juvenile offenders were seen as different from adult offenders, with less culpability for their crime because of their immaturity.

How have our views on adolescence changed over time?

In 1904, G. Stanley Hall, an American psychologist, published *Adolescence: Its Psychology and Its Relations to Physiology, Anthropology, Sociology, Sex, Crime, Religion, and Education.* Hall proposed that adolescence is a period of "storm and stress," a period when hormones cause many difficulties. That seems to be the image of adolescence that permeates the popular culture in the United States. In the past 25 years, however, behavioral scientists have made intensive study of the adolescent period and have found that, although adolescence presents special challenges, most adolescents do not experience a long stormy period (Lerner & Galambos, 1998). At the same time, there is growing agreement that the societal context in which adolescence is lived out in the United States is becoming increasingly less supportive for adolescent development (Fass & Mason, 2000a).

Sociologists caution against thinking of a monolithic adolescence. They suggest that, unfortunately, many adults dichotomize children and adolescents as *our own* children and *other people's* children (Graff, 1995). *Our own* children are expected to have "an innocent and secure childhood and dependent, prolonged adolescence" (Graff, 1995, p. 332). *Other people's* children are expected to be resilient in their childhood and accountable for their own behavior at increasingly younger ages, as we see in the declining ages for being treated as an adult in the criminal justice system. Sociologists conclude that there are multiple adolescences, with gender, race, and class as major influences on the ways they are constructed and their realities.

The Transition From Childhood to Adulthood

Adolescence is described as the transitional period between childhood and adulthood. It is more than that, of course. It is a very rich period of the life course in its own right. The word *adolescence* originates from the Latin verb *adolescere,* which means "to grow into maturity." It is a period of life filled with transitional themes in every dimension of the configuration of person and environment: biological, psychological, social, spiritual. These themes do not occur independently or without affecting one another.

For example, David's experience may be complicated because he is gay and because his family relationships are strained, but it is also strengthened by his supportive friendships and his participation in athletics. Carl's transition is marked by several challenges—his weight, his substance use, his lack of a relationship with his father, his academic performance—but also by the promise of his developing computer expertise and entrepreneurial skills. Monica's movement through adolescence may be eased by her academic, athletic, and social success, but it also could be taxed by her busy schedule and high expectations for herself. These themes interact as well with risk and protective factors.

Many cultures have specific **rites of passage**—ceremonies that demarcate the transition from childhood to adulthood. Often these rites include sexual themes, marriage themes, themes of becoming a man or a woman, themes of added responsibility, or themes of increased insight or understanding. For example, many American Jews celebrate the bar mitzvah for boys and bas mitzvah for girls at the age of 13 to observe their transition to adulthood and to mark their assumption of religious responsibility. Many Latino families, especially of Mexican heritage, celebrate Quinceanera, during which families attend Mass with their 15-year-old daughter, who is dressed in white and then presented to the community as a young woman. Traditionally, she is accompanied by a set of Padrinos, or godparents, who agree to support her parents in guiding her during this time. The ceremony is followed by a reception at which her father dances with her and presents her to the family's community of friends (Zuniga, 1992).

Mainstream culture in the United States, however, has few such rites. In the United States, many young adolescents go through confirmation ceremonies in Protestant and Catholic churches. Otherwise, the closest thing to a rite of passage may be getting a driver's license, graduating from high school, registering to vote, graduating from college, or getting married. But these events all occur at different times and thus do not provide a discrete point of transition. Moreover, not all youth participate in these rites of passage.

Even without a cultural rite of passage, all adolescents experience profound biological, psychological, psychosocial, social, and spiritual changes. In advanced industrial societies, these changes have been divided into three phases: early adolescence (ages 11 to 14), middle adolescence (ages 15 to 17), and late adolescence (ages 18 to 20). Exhibit 6.1 summarizes the typical biological, psychological, and social developments in these three phases. Of course, adolescent development varies from person to person and with time, culture, and other aspects of the environment. Yet, deviations from the normative patterns of adolescent change may have psychological ramifications, because adolescents are so quick to compare their own development to that of their peers.

EXHIBIT 6.1
Typical Adolescent Development

Stage of Adolescence	Biological Changes	Psychological Changes	Social Changes
Early (11 to 14)	Hormonal changes Beginning of puberty Physical appearance changes Possible experimentation with sex and substances	Reactions to physical changes, including early maturation Concrete/present-oriented thought Body modesty Moodiness	Changes in relationships with parents and peers Less school structure Distancing from culture/tradition Seeking sameness
Middle (15 to 17)	Completion of puberty and physical appearance changes Possible experimentation with sex and substances	Reactions to physical changes, including late maturation Increased autonomy Increased abstract thought Beginning of identity development Preparation for college or career	Heightened social situation decision making Consideration of physical attractiveness
Late (18 to 20)	Slowing of physical changes Possible experimentation with sex and substances	Formal operational thought Continuation of identity development Moral reasoning	Very little school/ life structure Beginning of intimate relationships Renewed interest in culture/tradition

Biological Aspects of Adolescence

What is the impact of biological age on psychological age, social age, and spiritual age during adolescence?

Those "raging hormones of adolescence" that we hear about are truly influential at this time of life. The hypothalamus, pituitary gland, adrenal glands, and **gonads** (ovaries and testes) begin to interact to stimulate increased hormone production. Although androgens are typically referred to as male hormones and estrogens as female hormones, males and females in fact produce all three major **sex hormones**: androgens, progestins, and estrogens. Sex hormones affect the development of the gonads, functioning of the gonads (including sperm production and ova maturation), and mating and child-caring behavior.

However, during **puberty** (the years during which adolescents become capable of reproduction), increased levels of androgens in males stimulate the development and functioning of the male reproductive system; increased levels of progestins and estrogens in females stimulate the development and functioning of the female reproductive system. Specifically, testosterone, which is produced in males by the testes, affects the maturation and functioning of the penis, prostate gland, and other male genitals; the secondary sex characteristics; and the sex drive. Estrogen, which is produced in females by the ovaries, affects the maturation and functioning of the ovaries, uterus, and other female genitals; the secondary sex characteristics; and child-caring behaviors.

Primary sex characteristics are those directly related to the reproductive organs and external genitalia. For boys, these include growth of the penis and scrotum. During adolescence, the penis typically doubles or triples in length. Girls' primary sex characteristics are not so visible but include growth of the ovaries, uterus, vagina, clitoris, and labia.

Secondary sex characteristics are those not directly related to the reproductive organs and external genitalia. Secondary sex characteristics are enlarged breasts and hips for girls, facial hair and deeper voices for boys, and hair and sweat gland changes for both sexes. Female breast development is distinguished by growth of the mammary glands, nipples, and areola. The tone of the male voice lowers as the larynx enlarges and the vocal cords lengthen. Both boys and girls begin to grow hair around their genitals and then under their arms. This hair begins with a finer texture and lighter color and then becomes curlier, coarser, and darker. During this period, the sweat glands also begin to produce noticeable odors.

Puberty is thought to begin with the onset of menstruation in girls and production of sperm in boys. Menstruation is the periodic sloughing off of the lining of the uterus. This lining provides nutrients for the fertilized egg. If the egg is not fertilized, the lining sloughs off and is discharged through the vagina. However, for a female to become capable of reproduction, she must not only menstruate but also ovulate. Ovulation, the release of an egg from an ovary, usually does not begin until several months after **menarche**, the onset of menstruation. For males to reproduce, **spermarche**—the onset of the ability to ejaculate mobile sperm—must occur. Spermarche does not occur until after several ejaculations.

Females typically first notice breast growth, then growth of pubic hair, then body growth, especially hips; they then experience menarche, then growth of underarm hair, and finally an increase in production of glandular oil and sweat, possibly with body odor and acne. Males typically follow a similar pattern, first noticing growth of the testes, then growth of pubic hair, body growth, growth of penis, change in voice, growth of facial and underarm hair, and finally an increase in the production of glandular oil and sweat, possibly with body odor and acne.

Generally, females begin puberty 2 years earlier than males. Normal pubertal rates (meaning they are experienced by 95% of the population) are for girls to begin menstruating between the ages of 9 and 16 and for boys to produce sperm between the ages of 10 and 19 (Tanner, 1990). The age at which puberty begins has been declining in this century, although it seems to be plateauing in industrialized countries (Friedman, 1992, p. 346).

In addition to changes instigated by raging sex hormones, adolescents experience growth spurts. Bones are augmented by cartilage during adolescence, and the cartilage calcifies later, during the transition to adulthood. Typically, boys develop broader shoulders, straighter hips, and longer forearms and legs; girls typically develop narrower shoulders and broader hips. These skeletal differences are then enhanced by the development of additional upper body musculature for boys and the development of additional fat deposits on thighs, hips, and buttocks for girls. These changes account for differences in male and female weight and strength.

Another important biological aspect of adolescence relates to sleep. Researchers are discovering that adolescents in the United States are the most sleep-deprived segment of a very sleep-deprived society (National Institutes of Health, 2001). Current research indicates that adolescent task performance drops substantially with less than 9½ hours of sleep. Even more important, sleep researchers are finding that the circadian clock varies with developmental stage. Adults with sufficient sleep are alert in the morning, sleepy in the afternoon, and alert again in the evening. Children with sufficient sleep are at maximum alertness in the morning and crash early in the evening. Adolescents with sufficient sleep are sleepy in the morning, dip even lower in the afternoon, and get a burst of alertness in the evening and going into the night. You may have seen media presentations of these research findings that suggest public schools are scheduling the school day for adolescents at the worst possible times, early morning to early afternoon. Some school districts are beginning to take note of these findings and explore a change in the school schedule for middle school and high school students.

Psychological Aspects of Adolescence

Psychological development in adolescence is multifaceted. Adolescents have psychological reactions, sometimes dramatic, to the biological, social, and cultural dimensions of their lives. They become capable of and interested in discovering and forming their psychological selves. They may show heightened creativity, as well as interest in humanitarian issues, ethics, religion, and reflection and record keeping, as in a diary (Kaplan & Sadock, 1998). Three areas of psychological development are particularly noteworthy: reactions to biological changes, changes in cognition, and the development of a self and an identity.

Psychological Reactions to Biological Changes

Imagine—or remember—being a sweaty, acne-ridden, gangly teenager whose body is changing every day and who is concerned with fitting in and being normal. The penis comparisons in the boys' locker room and the discussions of breasts, bras, and periods in the girls' locker room are examples of how adolescents try to cope with biological change.

Because the onset and experience of puberty vary greatly, adolescents need reassurance regarding their own growth patterns. Some adolescents will be considered early maturers, and some will be considered late maturers. Early maturing boys seem to get more attention than the other boys because they look more like adults (Brooks-Gunn, 1988). Perhaps as a result, early maturing boys seem to be more self-confident, but adult appearance can carry additional adult responsibilities as well. Conversely, late maturing boys tend to get less favorable attention. Because they still look like children, that is how they are often treated; for the most part, they are not given the additional responsibilities that are expected of early maturers. This difference in treatment may negatively affect their self-confidence.

For girls, unlike boys, early maturation often brings awkwardness (Alsaker, 1992; Brooks-Gunn, Petersen, & Eichorn, 1985) and even psychological distress (Ge, Conger, & Elder, 1996; Hayward et al., 1997). Early maturing girls may be taller and heavier than other girls and may find themselves having to wear a bra before their friends who want to wear a bra even pick one out. In addition to the psychological impact, early maturing girls may also feel early sexual pressure. Late maturing girls seem to be the least affected of all boys and girls. They seem to be given more psychological space to develop at their own pace.

Adolescents trying to make psychological accommodations to the dramatic biological changes they are experiencing benefit greatly from the compassion and support of caring adults. Judy Blume's *Are You There, God? It's Me, Margaret* (1970) captures the mixed feelings that some girls experience with their first menstrual period and models useful adult support. The book ends with the following scene:

> Then I looked down at my underpants and I couldn't believe it. There was blood on them. Not a lot—but enough. I really hollered, "Mom—hey Mom—come quick!"
>
> When my mother got to the bathroom she said, "What is it? What's the matter?"
>
> "I got it," I told her.
>
> "Got what?"
>
> I started to laugh and cry at the same time. "My period. I've got my period!" My nose started running and I reached for a tissue.
>
> "Are you sure, Margaret?" my mother asked.

> "Look—look at this," I said, showing her my underpants.
>
> "My God! You've really got it. My little girl!" Then her eyes filled up and she started sniffling too. "Wait a minute—I've got the equipment in the other room. I was going to put it in your camp trunk, just in case."
>
> "You were?"
>
> Then I got dressed and looked at myself in the mirror. Would anyone know my secret? Would it show? Would Moose, for instance, know if I went back outside to talk to him? Would my father know right away when he came home for dinner? I had to call Nancy and Gretchen and Janie right away. Poor Janie! She'd be the last of the [group] to get it. And I'd been so sure it would be me! How about that! Now I am growing for sure. Now I am almost a woman! (pp. 147-148)

This fictional representation mirrors what Karin Martin (1996) calls a "normative cultural scenario." A girl is "supposed to begin her period at home, with a supportive, informative mother, with knowledge of what is happening to her, with pads (or occasionally tampons) available" (p. 24). Margaret was indeed prepared, but not everyone has this experience. In any case, the reactions of significant others influence how the adolescent female begins to think and feel about her changing body.

From the male perspective, masturbation is a similarly sensitive topic. A young man interviewed by Martin (1996) had this to say:

> I pretty much knew everything. I was only worried about getting AIDS through like masturbating or something [laughs], but umm, I actually talked to my dad about that, so I wasn't really worried about anything after sixth grade. [Researcher asks what his dad said when he talked to him.] He said, he sort of laughed. He told me stories about how he used to do it too, and he said, "No, you can't get AIDS from doing that." And so I was happy, and he was happy, and that sort of opened the door for whatever conversations. (p. 50)

How the topic of masturbation is handled by adolescents and their families and peers may have lasting effects. Like Margaret's experience with menarche, this young man's situation was managed by a compassionate parent. A range of responses are possible, however, and some of them create enduring problems with attitudes toward the body and sex.

Changes in Cognition

During adolescence, most individuals develop cognitive abilities beyond those of childhood (Damon & Hart, 1988; Friedman, 1992), including these:

- Contemplation of the future
- Comprehension of the nature of human relationships
- Consolidation of specific knowledge into a coherent system
- Ability to envision possible consequences from a hypothetical list of actions (foresight)
- Abstract thought
- Empathy
- Internal control

Many of these abilities are components of Jean Piaget's fourth stage of cognitive development called formal operational thought (see Exhibit 3.4 for an overview of Piaget's stages of moral development). *Formal operational thought* suggests the capacity to apply hypothetical reasoning to various situations and the ability to use symbols to solve problems. David Cunha, for example, demonstrated formal operational thought when he considered the possibility of getting to know Theo. He considered the reactions from his other friends if he were to get together with Theo; he examined his thoughts, and he formulated a strategy based on the possibilities and on his thoughts.

Whereas younger children focus on the here-and-now world in front of them, the adolescent brain is capable of retaining larger amounts of information. Thus, adolescents are capable of hypothesizing beyond the present objects. This ability also allows adolescents to engage in decision making based on a cost/benefit analysis. In one study, 7th through 12th graders were asked to use a cost/benefit analysis to make decisions regarding sexual activity (Small, Silverberg, & Kerns, 1993). The data suggest that perceived costs are more important to sexual decision making than perceived benefits.

Adolescent cognition, however, mirrors adolescence in the sense that it is multifaceted. In addition to the increased capacity for thought, adolescents also bring with them experience, culture, personality, intelligence, family values, identity, and so on. If we conceptualize adolescent cognitive development along a linear continuum from simple intuitive reasoning to advanced, computational, rational, and objective reasoning (Case, 1998; Moshman, 1998), we miss many other facets of individuals and the influences on their cognition. For example, research suggests that older adolescents may not be more objective than younger adolescents, perhaps because irrational cognitive tendencies and biases increase with age (Baron, Granato, Spranca, & Teubal, 1993; Klaczynski, 2000; Klaczynski & Fauth, 1997). Older adolescents have more stereotypes, intuitions, memories, and self-evident truths that they may employ in processing information.

Development of an Identity

How do factors such as gender, race, ethnicity, and social class affect identity development?

Adolescents are fundamentally concerned with the question, "Who am I?" **Identity** is a combination of what you're born with and into; who you associate with; how others see you; what you've done; your attitudes, traits, abilities, habits, tendencies, and preferences; and what you look like. You might consider this issue of defining a self or an identity to be a psychosocial concept because it is a psychological task of adolescence developed in social transactions. What does the identity we so laboriously construct during adolescence do for us? Identity has five common functions (Adams & Marshall, 1996, p. 433):

1. To provide a structure for understanding who one is
2. To provide meaning and direction through commitments, values, and goals
3. To provide a sense of personal control and free will
4. To enable one to strive for consistency, coherence, and harmony between values, beliefs, and commitments
5. To enable one to recognize one's potential through a sense of future possibilities and alternative choices

Mature adults often incorporate all five functions of identity.

Theories of Self and Identity. A number of prominent psychologists have put forward theories that address self or identity development in adolescence. Exhibit 6.2 provides an overview of five theorists: Freud, Erikson, Marcia, Piaget, and Kohlberg. All five help to explain how a concept of self or an identity develops, and all five suggest that it cannot develop fully before adolescence. Piaget and Kohlberg suggest that some individuals may not reach these higher levels of identity development at all.

Sigmund Freud (1905/1953) thought of human development as a series of five psychosexual stages in the expression of libido (sensual pleasure). The fifth stage, the genital stage, occurs in adolescence, when reproduction and sexual intimacy become possible.

Building on Freud's work, Erik Erikson (1950, 1959b, 1963, 1968) proposed eight stages of psychosocial development (refer back to Exhibit 3.6). He viewed psychosocial crisis as an opportunity and challenge. Each Eriksonian stage requires the mastery of a particular developmental task related to identity. His fifth stage, identity versus role diffusion, is relevant to adolescence. The developmental task is to establish a coherent sense of identity; failure to complete this task successfully leaves the adolescent without a solid sense of identity.

EXHIBIT 6.2
Theories of Self or Identity in Adolescence

Theorist	Developmental Stage	Major Task or Processes
Freud	Genital stage	To develop libido capable of reproduction and sexual intimacy
Erikson	Identity versus role diffusion	To find one's place in the world through self-certainty versus apathy, role experimentation versus negative identity, and anticipation of achievement versus work paralysis
Marcia	Ego identity statuses	To develop one of these identity statuses: identity diffusion, foreclosure, moratorium, or identity achievement
Piaget	Formal operational thought	To develop the capacity for abstract problem formulation, hypothesis development, and solution testing
Kohlberg	Postconventional morality	To develop moral principles that transcend one's own society: individual ethics, societal rights, and universal principles of right and wrong

James Marcia (1966, 1980) expounded upon Erikson's notion that adolescents struggle with the issue of identity versus role diffusion. Marcia proposed that adolescents vary in how easily they go about developing personal identity, and described four categories of identity development in adolescents:

1. *Identity diffusion.* No exploration of or commitment to roles and values
2. *Foreclosure.* Commitment made to roles and values without exploration
3. *Moratorium.* Exploration of roles and values without commitment
4. *Identity achievement.* Exploration of roles and values followed by commitment

Jean Piaget proposed four major stages leading to adult thought (refer back to Exhibit 3.4 for an overview of Piaget's stages). He expected the last stage, the stage of formal operations, to occur in adolescence, enabling the adolescent to engage in more abstract thinking about "who I am." Piaget (1972) also thought that adolescents begin to use formal operational skills to think in terms of what is best for society.

EXHIBIT 6.3
Rosenberg's Model of Identity

Social Identity	Dispositions	Physical Characteristics
Social statuses: Basic classifications or demographic characteristics, such as sex, age, and socioeconomic status Membership groups: Groups with which the individual shares an interest, belief, origin, or physical or regional continuity (e.g., groups based on religion, political party, or race) Labels: Identifiers that result from social labeling (as when the boy who skips school becomes a delinquent) Derived statuses: Identities based on the individual's role history (e.g., veteran, high school athlete, or Harvard alumnus) Social types: Interests, attitudes, habits, or general characteristics (e.g., jock, geek, head, playboy, or go-getter) Personal identities: Unique labels attached to individuals (e.g., first name, first and last names, social security number, fingerprints, or DNA)	Attitudes (e.g., conservatism, liberalism) Traits (e.g., generosity, bravery) Abilities (e.g., musical talent, athletic skill) Values (e.g., efficiency, equality) Personality traits (e.g., introversion, extroversion) Habits (e.g., making lists, getting up early) Tendencies (e.g., to arrive late, to exaggerate) Likes or preferences (e.g., romance novels, pizzas)	Height Weight Body build Facial features

Source: Rosenberg, 1986.

Lawrence Kohlberg (1976, 1984) expanded on Piaget's ideas about moral thinking to describe three major levels of moral development (refer back to Exhibit 4.1 for an overview of Kohlberg's stage theory). Kohlberg thought that adolescents become capable of **postconventional moral reasoning**, or morality based on moral principles that transcend social rules but that many never go beyond conventional morality, or morality based on social rules.

These theories have been influential in conceptualizations of identity development. On perhaps a more practical level, however, Morris Rosenberg, in his book *Conceiving the Self* (1986), provides a very useful model of identity to keep in mind while working with adolescents—or perhaps to share with adolescents who are in the process of identity formation. Rosenberg suggests that identity comprises three major parts, outlined in Exhibit 6.3:

Exhibit 6.4
Examples of Adolescent Identity

Element of Identity	David	Carl	Monica
Social Identity			
Social statuses	Male, 17, middle class	Male, 17, working class	Female, 17, upper middle class
Membership groups	Bolivian American, gay	European American, heads	African American, Christian, Young Republicans
Labels	Freak	Fatso, underachiever, smoker	Overachiever
Derived statuses	Soccer player	Pizza deliverer	Senior class vice president, baby-sitter, supermarket cashier, track athlete
Social types	Jock	Greek, head (affiliate)	Brain, go-getter
Personal Identity	David Cunha	Carl Fleischer	Monica Golden
Disposition	Athletic	Underachiever, not popular, fat, slow, likes to get high, likes to surf the Internet	Athletic, ambitious, extroverted, likes children
Physical Characteristics	Soccer build	Overweight	Tall

- **Social identity** is made up of several elements derived from interaction with other people and social systems.
- **Dispositions** are self-ascribed aspects of identity.
- **Physical characteristics** are simply one's physical traits, which all contribute a great deal to sense of self.

Exhibit 6.4 uses Rosenberg's model to analyze the social identities of David, Carl, and Monica. Notice that disposition is an element of identity based on self-definition. In contrast, a label is determined by others, and physical characteristics are genetically influenced. David Cunha has an athletic body and thinks of himself as athletic, but his parents—and perhaps others—label him as a freak. He is working to incorporate the fact that he's different into his identity. Carl Fleischer has been labeled as a fatso, an underachiever, and a smoker. He seems to have incorporated these negative labels into his identity. Monica Golden has been labeled as an overachiever, but she does not absorb the negative label, reframing it instead as ambitious.

Identity Formation. How do adolescents construct an identity? We can think of adolescent identity formation as a trip to the salad bar of life. As adolescents move through the salad bar, they first have to decide on a base of iceberg lettuce or maybe romaine or perhaps spinach. Then they exercise more free will: broccoli, carrots, or tomatoes? cheese? croutons? sunflower seeds?

Scholars suggest that identity formation is structured by the sociocultural context (Adams & Marshall, 1996; Baumeister & Muraven, 1996). Thus, the options offered by any given salad bar will vary depending on the restaurant. Think about David, Carl, and Monica. What is the sociocultural context of their trip to the salad bar? What salad ingredients can they choose, given the restaurant they find themselves in?

For those salad options that individuals are able to choose—for those aspects of identity that we shape ourselves—individuals have four ways of trying on and developing a preference for certain identities:

1. *Future orientation.* By adolescence, youth have developed two important cognitive skills: they are able to consider the future and they are able to construct abstract thoughts. These skills allow them to choose from a list of hypothetical behaviors based on the potential outcomes resulting from those behaviors. David demonstrates future orientation in his contemplation regarding Theo. Adolescents also contemplate potential future selves.

2. *Role experimentation.* According to Erikson (1963), adolescence provides a psychosocial moratorium—a period during which youth have the latitude to experiment with social roles. Thus, adolescents typically sample membership in different cliques, build relationships with various mentors, take various academic electives, and join assorted groups and organizations—all in an attempt to further define themselves. Monica, for example, sampled various potential career paths before deciding on becoming a pediatrician.

3. *Exploration.* Whereas role experimentation is specific to trying new roles, exploration refers to the comfort an adolescent has with trying new things. The more comfortable the individual is with exploration, the easier identity formation will be.

4. *Self-evaluation.* During the quest for identity, adolescents are constantly sizing themselves up against their peers. Erikson (1968) suggested that the development

> of identity is a process of personal reflection and observation of oneself in relation to others. George Herbert Mead (1934) suggested that individuals create a **generalized other** to represent how others are likely to view and respond to them. The role of the generalized other in adolescents' identity formation is evident when adolescents act on the assumed reactions of their families or peers. For example, what Monica wears to school may be based not on what she thinks would be most comfortable or look the best but rather on what she thinks her peers expect her to wear. Thus, she does not wear miniskirts to school because "everyone" (generalized other) will think she is loose.

There are certainly added complexities during the identity formation of minority youth. Arthur Jones (1992) suggests that "the usual rifts between young adolescents (ages 13 to 15) and their parents are sometimes more intense in middle-class African American families, especially those in which middle-class economic status is new for the parents. This is because the generation gap is more exaggerated" (p. 29). Consider Monica Golden, who is an upper middle-class, African American teenager in a predominantly white high school. What are some of the potential added challenges of Monica's adolescent identity formation? Is it any wonder that she is hoping to attend Howard University, a traditionally black college, where she could surround herself with African American role models and professional support networks?

Gender Differences. Much has been written lately regarding the experiences of adolescent boys and girls (Garbarino, 1999; Kindlon & Thompson, 1999; Pipher, 1994; Rimm, 1999). Gender differences are getting a lot of attention for their particular role in the development of a strong identity and self.

Mary Pipher (1994), in her book *Reviving Ophelia: Saving the Selves of Adolescent Girls,* claims that "girls today are much more oppressed. They are coming of age in a more dangerous, sexualized and media-saturated culture. They face incredible pressures to be beautiful and sophisticated, which in junior high means using chemicals and being sexual. As they navigate a more dangerous world, girls are less protected" (p. 12).

Similar sentiments are presented regarding the forces that threaten adolescent boys in *Raising Cain: Protecting the Emotional Life of Boys* by Dan Kindlon and Michael Thompson (1999). They see boys in the United States who are hurting, sad, afraid, angry, and silent. Amid statistics that suggest increasing numbers of adolescent boys at risk for suicide, alcohol and drug abuse, violence, and loneliness, Kindlon and Thompson feel that "boys, beginning at a young age, are systematically steered away from their emotional lives toward silence, solitude, and distrust" (p. xv). They advocate giving boys the space and permission to be active and the emotional vocabulary and tools to develop in their social world.

As we work with adolescents and strive to be responsive to their particulars, we need to begin to consider what role being female or being male may play in who they are and what may be happening in their lives. How would David's situation be different if he were a lesbian versus a gay male? What if Carl was Carol? How are weight issues different for women and men? Are they different? And do successful black men have different experiences or expectations from successful black women? What if Monica were male?

Social Aspects of Adolescence

The social environment—family, peers, certain institutions, culture, and so on—is a significant element of adolescent life. For one thing, as already noted, identity develops through social transactions. For another, as adolescents become more independent and move into the world, they develop their own relationships with more elements of the social environment.

Relationships With Family

Answering the question, "Who am I?" includes a consideration of the question, "How am I different from my brothers and sisters, my parents, and other family members?" For many adolescents, this question begins the process of **individuation**—the development of a self or identity that is unique and separate. David seems to have started the process of individuation; he recognizes that he may not want to be what his parents want him to be. He does not yet seem comfortable with this idea, however. Carl is not sure how he is like and different from his absent father. Monica has begun to recognize some ways that she is different from her siblings, and she is involved in her own personal exploration of career options that fit her dispositions. It would appear that she is the furthest along in the individuation process.

Separation from parents has four components (Moore, 1987):

1. *Functional independence.* Literally being able to function with little assistance or independently from one's parents. An example would be getting ready for school: selecting an appropriate outfit, getting dressed, compiling school supplies, and feeding oneself.
2. *Attitudinal independence.* Not merely having a different attitude from parents, but developing one's own set of values and beliefs. An example might be choosing a presidential candidate based not on your parents' choice but on your values and beliefs.

3. *Emotional independence.* Not being dependent on parents for approval, intimacy, and emotional support. Emotional independence might mean discovering your own way to overcome emotional turmoil—for example, listening to your favorite CD after a fight with your girlfriend or boyfriend rather than relying on support from your parents.

4. *Conflictual independence.* Being able to recognize one's separateness from parents without guilt, resentment, anger, or other negative emotions. Conflictual independence is being comfortable with being different. Thus, instead of ridiculing your dad for wearing those shorts to the picnic, you are able to go to the picnic realizing that you would not wear those shorts but that your father's taste in shorts is not a reflection on you.

The concept of independence is largely influenced by culture. And mainstream culture in the United States places a high value on independence. However, as social workers, we need to recognize that the notion of pushing the adolescent to develop an identity separate from family is not acceptable to all cultural groups in the United States, including Italians, Jews, and Latinos (McGill & Pearce, 1996). Many Asian Indian families may view adolescent struggles for independence as a disloyal cutting off of family and culture (Hines et al., 1999). Our assessments of adolescent individuation should be culturally sensitive. Likewise, we must be realistic in our assessments of the functional independence of adolescents with disabilities.

Even when it is consistent with their cultural values, not all adolescents are able to achieve functional independence, attitudinal independence, emotional independence, and conflictual independence. Instead, many maintain a high level of conflict. Conflict is particularly evident in families experiencing additional stressors, such as divorce and economic difficulties (Flanagan, 1990; Smetana, Killen, & Turiel, 1991). Conflict also plays out differently in different arenas. Research suggests that, compared with childhood, adolescent conflict regarding chores, appearance, and politeness decreases overall; conflict regarding substance use stays the same; and conflict regarding finances increases (Galambos & Almeida, 1992).

How can families stay connected to their adolescents while also honoring their struggle for independence and increased agency in making choices?

Adolescent struggles for independence can be especially potent in multigenerational contexts (Preto, 1999). These struggles typically come at a time when parents are in midlife and grandparents are entering late adulthood and both are facing stressors of their own. Adolescent demands for independence may reignite unresolved conflicts between the parents and the grandparents and stir the pot of family discord. The challenge for the family is to stay connected while also allowing the adolescent to widen contact with the world. Most families make this adjustment well, but often after an initial period of confusion and disruption.

Relationships With Peers

Most adolescents would rather be anywhere with their peers than anywhere with their parents. In the quest for autonomy and identity, adolescents begin to differentiate themselves from their parents and associate with their peers. And whereas children seek same-sex peer groups, adolescents begin socializing more with opposite-sex peers. Peer relationships contribute to adolescents' identities, behaviors, and personal and social competence.

Peer relationships are a fertile testing ground for youth and their emerging identities (Connolly, White, Stevens, & Burstein, 1987). Many adolescents seek out a peer group with compatible members, and inclusion or exclusion from certain groups can affect their identity and overall development. David Cunha's peer groups include the soccer team and a group of gay males from school. Carl Fleischer seems to be gravitating toward the "heads" for his peer group—although this choice appears to be related to a perception of rejection by other groups. Monica Golden enjoys easy acceptance by several peer groups: the peer counselors at high school, the senior class officers, the Young Republicans, and the track team.

For some adolescents, participation in certain peer groups influences their behavior negatively. Peer influence may not be strong enough to undo protective factors, but if the youth is already at risk, the influence of peers becomes that much stronger. Sexual behaviors and pregnancy status are often the same for same-sexed best friends (Goldfarb et al., 1977; Holden, Nelson, Velasquez, & Ritchie, 1993; Smith, Udry, & Morris, 1985). Substance use is also a behavior that most often occurs in groups of adolescents (Jessor, 1987; Segal & Stewart, 1996). The same is true for violent and delinquent behaviors (Garbarino, 1999; Klein, 1995).

Finally, interaction with peers contributes significantly to the development of personal and social competence. A study of 266 ninth grade students (approximately 14 years old) suggested that adolescents have six goals in relationships with their peers: intimacy, nurturance, dominance, leadership, popularity, and avoidance of undesirable situations (Jarvinen & Nicholls, 1996). In addition, the researchers discovered six behaviors or circumstances that their adolescent participants believe contribute to success in peer relationships: being sincere, having status, being responsible, pretending to care, entertaining others, and being tough. When social workers interact with adolescents who are having trouble with peer relations, it is helpful to explore with them their goals in peer relationships and their perceptions about what behaviors are valued by their peers.

Relationships With Institutions

As adolescents loosen their ties to parents, they develop more direct relationships with such institutions as school, employment, and leisure activities. To study adolescent relationships with such institutions, Mihaly Csikszentmihalyi and Reed Larson (1984) gave pagers to 75 diverse 9th through 12th grade boys and girls. Throughout the day, the researchers periodically beeped their participants. When beeped, the adolescents were to complete a log identifying where they were, what they were doing, and who else was with them. Exhibit 6.5 provides an overview of the findings of this research.

The researchers found that these adolescents spent 41% of their time at home, 32% of their time at school, and 27% of their time in public. They spent 40% of their time in leisure activities such as socializing, playing sports, watching television, and listening to music. They spent 29% of their time on school or work activities: 13% in class, 12% on homework, and 4% on jobs. The other 31% was spent on maintenance activities such as eating, personal hygiene, transportation, rest, and errands. More than half of these adolescents' time was spent with peers: 29% with friends and 23% with classmates. Another 27% was spent alone, and 19% was spent with family. The remaining 2% was spent with others, including bosses, coworkers, and coaches (Csikszentmihalyi & Larson, 1984). As you can see, adolescents spend a substantial portion of their time interacting with, and in the context of, social institutions.

School. From the 32% of their time that is spent at school, adolescents are gaining skills and knowledge for their next step in life, either moving into the workforce or continuing their education. In school, they also have the opportunity to evolve socially and emotionally; school is a fertile ground for practicing future orientation, role experimentation, exploration, and self-evaluation.

Middle schools have a very structured format and a very structured environment; high schools are less structured in both format and environment, allowing a gradual transition to greater autonomy. The school experience changes radically, however, at the college level. Many college students are away from home for the first time and are in very unstructured environments. David, Carl, and Monica have had different experiences with structure in their environments to date. David's environment has required him to move flexibly between two cultures. That experience may help to prepare him for the unstructured college environment. Carl has had the least structured home life. It remains to be seen whether that has helped him to develop skills in structuring his own environment, or left him with insufficient models for doing so. Monica is accustomed to juggling multiple commitments and should have little trouble with the competing attractions and demands of college.

School is also an institutional context where cultures intersect, which may create difficulties for students who are not familiar or comfortable with mainstream culture. You may not realize how Eurocentric the educational model in the United States is until you view it through a different cultural lens. We can use a Native American lens as an example. Native Americans have the highest school dropout rate (35.5%) of any ethnic group in the United States (Hodgkinson, 1990). Michael Walkingstick Garrett (1995)

EXHIBIT 6.5
Adolescent Use of Time

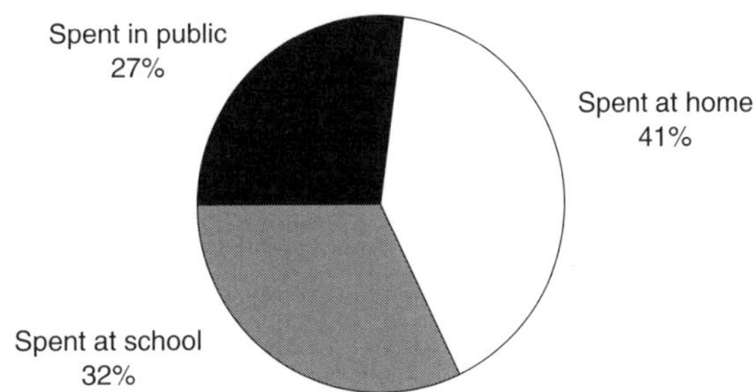

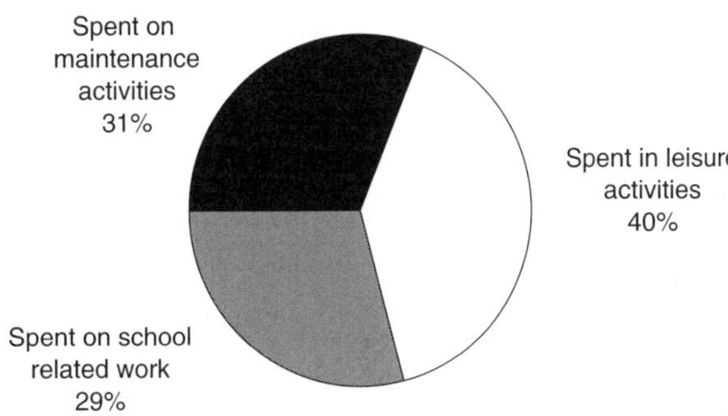

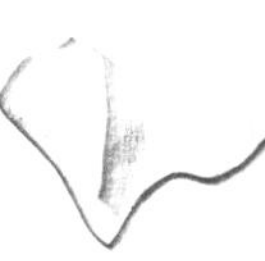

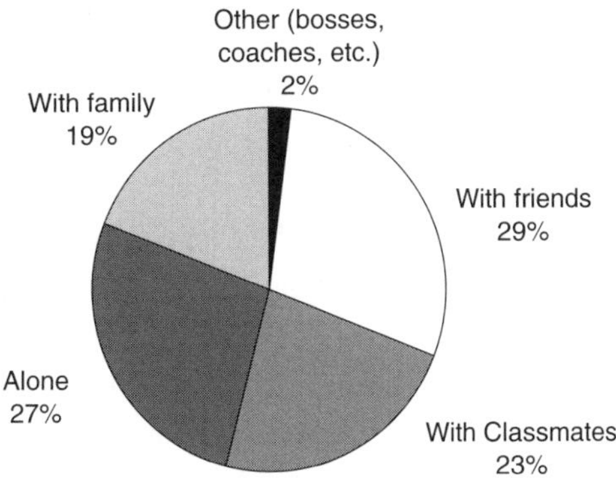

Source: Based on Csikszentmihalyi & Larson, 1984.

uses the experiences of the boy Wind-Wolf as an example of the incongruence between Native American culture and the typical education model:

> Wind-Wolf is required by law to attend public school. . . . He speaks softly, does not maintain eye contact with the teacher as a sign of respect, and rarely responds immediately to questions, knowing that it is good to reflect on what has been said. He may be looking out the window during class, as if daydreaming, because he has been taught to always be aware of changes in the natural world. These are interpreted by his teacher as either lack of interest or dumbness. (p. 204)

What are some ways that different cultural expectations regarding education affect adolescent development?

Children in the United States spend less time in school-related activities than do Chinese or Japanese children and have been noted to put less emphasis on scholastic achievement. Some researchers attribute oft-noted cross-cultural differences in mathematics achievement to these national differences in emphasis on scholastics (Fuligni & Stevenson, 1995). For adolescents, scholastic interest, expectations, and achievements may also vary, based not only on nationality but also on gender, race, ethnicity, economic status, and expectations for the future. Girls have been found to be more invested in school activities than boys (Shanahan & Flaherty, 2001). In a study of students in 33 middle and high schools, African American and Hispanic students were found to be more disengaged from school than Asian and white students, and economically disadvantaged teenagers were found to be more disengaged than more economically advantaged students (Csikszentmihalyi & Schneider, 2000). Recent longitudinal research found that adolescents with a future orientation and expectations of further schooling, marriage, and good citizenship devote a greater percentage of their time to school-related activities (Shanahan & Flaherty, 2001).

A 1988 report, *The Forgotten Half,* by the William T. Grant Foundation, cited 1980 census data that half of U.S. adults 25 and over had no formal education beyond high school and were vulnerable to a lifetime of poverty. Through the early 1990s, vocational education in the United States was stigmatized as the high school track for students with poor academic capabilities, special needs, or behavioral problems (Gamoran & Himmelfarb, 1994). Congress and most educators, however, believe that broadening the segment of the student population that participates in vocational education and adding academic achievement and postsecondary enrollment to the traditional objectives of technical competency, labor market outcomes, and general employability skills will improve the quality of these programs (Lynch, 2000). Recently, the National Women's Law Center has reported that there is pervasive sex segregation in high school vocational programs in the United States, with girls clustered in programs that train them for lower-paying jobs ("Sex Bias," 2002).

Work. Like many adolescents, Carl and Monica also play the role of worker in the labor market. Work can provide an opportunity for social interaction and greater financial independence. It may also lead to personal growth by promoting notions of contribution, responsibility, egalitarianism, and self-efficacy and by helping the adolescent to develop values and preferences for future jobs—answers to questions like "What kind of job would I like to have in the future?" and "What am I good at?" (Mortimer & Finch, 1996, p. 4). For example, Monica tried many jobs before deciding that she loves working with children and wants to become a pediatrician. In addition, employment may also offer the opportunity to develop job skills, time management skills, customer relation skills, money management skills, market knowledge, and other skills of value to future employers. The U.S. Department of Labor has launched a new initiative called YouthRules! which seeks to promote positive and safe work experiences for young workers. The YouthRules! Web site lists the hours teens can work and the types of jobs they can work. For example, did you know that if you are 14 or 15, you can work no more than 3 hours on a school day, 18 hours in a school week, 8 hours on a nonschool day, and 40 hours in a nonschool week? Learn more at www.youthrules.dol.gov.

Some of these Department of Labor guidelines may be the social policy result of research that suggests that for youth, work may also detract from development by cutting into time needed for sleep, exercise, maintenance of overall health, school, family relations, and peer relations. Adolescents who work more than 10 hours per week have been found to be at increased risk for poor academic performance, psychological problems such as depression, anxiety, fatigue, and sleep difficulties, and physical problems such as headaches, stomachaches, and colds. They are also more likely to use cigarettes, alcohol, or other drugs, regardless of ethnicity, socioeconomic status (SES), or age (Mortimer & Finch, 1996). Although we cannot draw causal conclusions, Carl is a good example of this linkage: he works more than 10 hours a week and also has declining grades and uses tobacco and marijuana. Employed adolescents also demonstrate higher rates of school tardiness and spend less time completing homework (Greenberger & Steinberg, 1986).

Leisure. A sizable portion of an adolescent's life is spent in leisure pursuits. These activities often have great influence on various aspects of the individual's development, such as identity formation. However, a study examining the relationship between leisure and identity formation for adolescents found that the patterns of influence are different for girls and boys (Shaw, Kleiber, & Caldwell, 1995). Participation in sports and physical activities has a positive effect on identity development for female adolescents but shows no effect for males. Watching television has a negative effect on identity development for male adolescents but shows no effect for females. And involvement in social activities and other leisure activities was not significantly correlated with identity development for either gender.

Research suggests that girls and boys spend their leisure time differently (Eder & Parker, 1987; Garton & Pratt, 1987). Favoring one particular type of activity is not necessarily a good thing, however. Some have recommended that adolescent girls be encouraged to undertake activities that stimulate independence and autonomy, because many of the activities they are involved in during their free time feature connectedness and social relationships (Shaw et al., 1995). Conversely, perhaps males need activities that support connectedness and social relationships.

Access to leisure activities varies. Leisure activities for rural adolescents are different from leisure activities for urban youth, for example. Adolescents living in urban areas have greater access to transportation and to public recreational activities and programs (Garton & Pratt, 1991). Rural youth lack this access and thus rely more heavily on school-related leisure activities (Garton & Pratt, 1991). Access to leisure activities also increases with SES.

Whatever an adolescent's gender, region, or SES, however, research suggests that those who consider their leisure time to be boring are more likely to use substances (Iso-Ahola & Crowley, 1991). They are also more likely to drop out of school (Widmer, Ellis, & Trunnell, 1996).

Relationships With Culture

Adolescents in the United States who are not of European American background face additional challenges as they encounter the many changes of adolescence. The greatest challenges may be faced by immigrants. Following a 5-year longitudinal study of immigrants, Patricia Arrendondo (1984) proposed the following three factors as necessary for satisfactory adjustment to a new culture:

1. Willingness and ability to confront the issue of belonging versus estrangement
2. Ability to rely on the values of the native culture
3. Supportive family relationships

Among the challenges facing immigrant youth is deciding what their relationship will be with their native culture and the mainstream culture. They generally have these options (Garrett, 1995):

- *Traditional.* Speaking in their native language and practicing traditional beliefs and practices
- *Transitional.* Speaking both their native language and English and not participating fully in either traditional practices or mainstream culture
- *Bicultural.* Participating in both native culture and mainstream culture
- *Assimilated.* Practicing only mainstream culture and values

For some youth, this decision is not theirs to make; it is imposed on them by family and community.

Many youth seek to distance themselves from their minority culture in early adolescence in order to emphasize their similarities with peers. These youth may then readopt their native culture in late adolescence if their self-concept and identity are adequately formed and allow the reconnection. For some youth, their heritage is a source of great pride; for others, it carries shame. These responses certainly affect the sense of self or identity of minority adolescents.

Some youth may be more likely to withdraw from the challenges of accessing mainstream culture rather than confronting those challenges and seeking workable options. Multiethnic (Markstrom-Adams & Adams, 1995), Mexican American (Abraham, 1986), and Native American (Markstrom & Mullis, 1986) youth are especially likely to have this response. Their perception that their options in mainstream culture are limited may pose psychological risk, depending on factors such as perceptions of their ethnic group's social status, available support systems, structures and patterns of family interactions, psychological characteristics of the individual, and explicit and implicit societal policies (Miller, 1992).

How can social workers use research like this to understand risk and protection in minority youth?

Researchers have recently taken an interest in how adolescents of different racial and ethnic backgrounds cope with stress. Paula Chapman and Ronald Mullis (2000) investigated racial differences in coping styles among a sample of lower middle-class white and African American adolescents who resided in rural communities in a southern state. Their findings indicate important racial differences in coping with stress, but caution must be used in interpreting their findings. African Americans were the majority racial group in the communities from which the sample was drawn, and the researchers were probably tapping minority-majority differences in coping styles, as well as racial differences. Keeping that in mind, Chapman and Mullis found that African American adolescents reported using several coping strategies more frequently than white adolescents: diversions, self-reliance, spiritual support, close friends, demanding activities, solution of family problems, and relaxation. White adolescents used two coping strategies more frequently than African American adolescents: ventilating feelings and avoidance. White females, as well as African American adolescents of both genders, reported more use of social support than white males. No racial differences were found in self-esteem. This research, and earlier work on which it was based, should alert white social workers to recognize the strengths in the coping styles of racial minority youth.

Social workers pursuing psychotherapeutic interventions with multiethnic youth should often aim at integrating the cultural features with which they have grown up instead of further dichotomizing their cultural differences (Nguyen, 1992). Each culture is likely to have imparted a distinctive set of psychological strengths and weaknesses.

Moreover, while recognizing the difficulties that may exist for minority youth, social workers must also be alert to the ethnocentrism that may be inherent in typical intervention strategies.

Spiritual Aspects of Adolescence

Another potential facet of adolescent development is spirituality or religiosity. As adolescents become capable of advanced thinking and begin to contemplate their existence, identity, and future, many also undertake spiritual exploration. One study found that 76% of adolescents between the ages of 13 and 17 believe in a personal God, 29% believe they have experienced the presence of God, 42% pray frequently, and 50% report attendance at religious services in the previous 7 days (Gallup & Lindsay, 1999). Yet, spirituality during adolescence has been largely unstudied.

In one of the few studies on the topic, using a review of the literature, Michael Donahue and Peter Benson (1995) examined the effects of religion on the well-being of adolescents (controlling for sociodemographic variables). They found a link between religiousness and "prosocial values and behavior." Religious adolescents are less likely to think of or attempt suicide, to abuse substances, to become prematurely involved in sexual activity, and to become "delinquent" (p. 145). In a similar vein, psychologist James Garbarino (1999) found a spiritual emptiness in violent adolescent males, whom he calls "lost boys." Garbarino advocates using spiritual values to build a positive attachment between boys and their communities, and working to make the boys' social environment (family, school, community) more competent to meet their needs. Garbarino believes this practice will anchor boys in empathy and socially engaged, moral thinking (p. 238).

Donahue and Benson (1995) suggest that cross-sectional research on religiousness by age reveals a persistent overall decline in religiousness during adolescence. Some attribute this decline to the period of questioning associated with the cognitive changes in adolescence; others suggest that during this period religiousness is merely evidenced in ways other than those typically studied, such as attendance at worship service (Donahue & Benson, 1995). This suggestion is supported by national survey data from the 1990s indicating that 65% of the youth in the United States are "very" or "somewhat" confident that they will be more religious than their parents and that 85% believe they will spend more time helping other people than their parents do (Gallup & Lindsay, 1999).

How important is it for social workers to assess the spirituality of adolescents with whom they work?

Research rather consistently finds that religiosity also breaks down along other demographic lines. Females demonstrate greater religiosity than males across all ages (Batson, Schoenrade, & Ventis, 1993; Donahue & Benson, 1995; Gallup & Lindsay, 1999). Both African American and Hispanic youth ascribe more importance to religion than do their European American counterparts (Benson, Yeager, Wood, Guerra, & Manno, 1986).

Thus, for many youth spirituality may be closely connected to culture. Jose Cervantes and Oscar Ramirez (1992) suggest that interventions with adolescents and their families should be consistent with their spirituality. For example, family therapy based on an understanding of mestizo spirituality and of the philosophy of ***curanderismo*** might profitably be used to guide clinical practice with Mexican American families.

The **mestizo perspective** "allows for an introspective attitude fostering culturally sanctioned inclination toward wholeness, harmony, and balance in one's relationship with self, family, community, and the physical and social environment. This attitude is embedded within a consciousness that understands learning from one's life history, diversity, and multicultural struggle" (Cervantes & Ramirez, 1992, p. 106). It is based on the following five tenets:

1. Every person has a valuable life story to tell and lesson to learn. There is a Mexican proverb, "Cada cabeza un mundo," which suggests that each person's life and experience is unique and important.
2. Harmony with the physical and social environment is crucial to psychological adjustment and reflects a recognition of balance and respect for all living things.
3. Openness to diversity fosters a multicultural attitude of mutual respect and acceptance of all peoples.
4. A willingness to learn from diversity advances the humanistic agenda of the people.
5. A theistic cosmology protects, influences, and engages all of life.

Curanderismo is a holistic folk medicine philosophy (Carrasco, 1990; Cervantes & Ramirez, 1992; De La Cancela & Martinez, 1983; Perrone, Stockel, & Krueger, 1989). It is based on the following beliefs (Cervantes & Ramirez, 1992, pp. 114-115):

- Divine will is central and the individual's responsibility is to have good intentions and do good deeds. If the individual deviates from this responsibility, misfortune and illness may result
- Social, emotional, and physiological successes or difficulties are also the result of the individual's interpersonal relationships within the family and community
- Supernatural forces can positively or negatively influence the individual, and the individual can take steps to restore balance with these forces
- There is no separation between mind and body, and this union is inextricably linked to the divine.

Although adolescents may not seem to be guided by their spirituality or religiosity, they may have underlying spiritual factors at work. As with any biological, psychological, or social aspect of the individual, the spiritual aspect of youth must be considered to gain the best understanding of the whole person.

Issues, Challenges, and Problems During Adolescence

The adolescent period is quite complex all on its own, and sexuality, substance use, juvenile delinquency, and other threats to physical and mental health further complicate the picture. Again, not all adolescents face all of these issues, and those who do face some of them follow no strict time line. We do know, however, that adolescents who are considered at risk may be more susceptible than others to these challenges or problems of adolescence. In the introduction to her book *Adolescents at Risk,* Joy Dryfoos (1990) states:

> Many children are growing up in the United States today without a hope of enjoying the benefits that come with adulthood. They are not learning the skills necessary to participate in the educational system or to make the transition into the labor force. They cannot become responsible parents because they have limited experience in family life and lack the resources to raise their own children. The gap between achievers and nonachievers is expanding. A new class of "untouchables" is emerging in our inner cities, on the social fringes of suburbia, and in some rural areas: young people who are functionally illiterate, disconnected from school, depressed, prone to drug abuse and early criminal activity, and eventually, parents of unplanned and unwanted babies. (p. 3)

Sexuality

Sexual identity is a significant component in the transition to adulthood. For the adolescent, sexual identity encompasses becoming familiar with the physical changes of puberty, recognizing one's sexual orientation, and making decisions about sexual activity; it may also include dealing with pregnancy and childbearing, sexually transmitted disease, and acquaintance rape.

Masturbation. As the pubertal hormones cause changes throughout the body, adolescents spend time becoming familiar with those changes. For many, exploration includes **masturbation**, the self-stimulation of the genitals for sexual pleasure. Almost 50% of boys and 30% of girls report masturbating by age 13; boys masturbate earlier and more often than girls (Leitenberg, Detzer, & Srebnik, 1993).

However, masturbation has negative associations for some boys and girls. Most girls do not like to touch or look at their genitals, so it makes sense that few masturbate.

For boys, any negative or anxious associations with sex at adolescence are usually in regard to masturbation (Martin, 1996). Thus, masturbation may have psychological implications for adolescents, depending on the way they feel about masturbation and on how they think significant others feel about it.

How does sexual orientation affect development during adolescence?

Sexual Orientation. During adolescence, many individuals, both homosexual and heterosexual, have homosexual experiences. But not all form a sexual identity based on those experiences. In a study of 38,000 7th through 12th graders, 88% classified themselves as heterosexual, 1% classified themselves as homosexual or bisexual, and 10% classified themselves as uncertain about their sexual orientation (Remafedi, Resnick, Blum, & Harris, 1992).

Still, adolescence is the time when most people develop some awareness of their sexual orientation. In their comprehensive investigation of gay and lesbian sexuality, Marcel Saghir and Eli Robins (1973) found that most adult gay men and lesbians reported the onset of homosexual arousal, homosexual erotic imagery, and homosexual romantic attachment during early adolescence before age 15. More recent research has produced similar findings (Herdt & Boxer, 1996). Recent studies indicate, however, that gay and lesbian youth may be "coming out" and accepting the homosexual identity at earlier ages than in prior eras (Taylor, 2000). One study found that the average age for both gay males and lesbians to accept the homosexual identity is 16 (Herdt & Boxer, 1996).

Gay and lesbian youth typically suffer from the awareness that they are different from most of their peers in an aspect of identity that receives a great deal of attention in our culture (Ryan & Futterman, 1998). Consider David's conflict over his homosexuality. Dennis Anderson (1994) suggests that a "crisis of self-concept occurs because the gay adolescent senses a sudden involuntary joining to a stigmatized group" (p. 15). He goes on to elaborate:

> To some gay and lesbian adolescents the experience of watching boys and girls in school walk hand-in-hand down the hallway, while their own desires must be kept secret, produces feelings of rage and sadness that are difficult to resolve. In addition to having no opportunity to experience social interactions with gay or lesbian peers, there is little likelihood that they will see gay or lesbian adult role models in their day-to-day lives. Low self-esteem, academic inhibition, truancy, substance abuse, social withdrawal, depressed mood, and suicidal ideation are not unusual and may be difficult to differentiate from depressive disorders. (p. 18)

Recall David's feelings of abnormality, isolation, depression, and suicidal thoughts in regard to his sexual orientation. As an adolescent, he is struggling to develop a sense of identity, including sexual identity, but society discourages him from expressing what he finds.

EXHIBIT 6.6
Questions to Ponder Prior to Coming Out

1. Are you sure about your sexual orientation?
2. Are you comfortable with your gay sexuality?
3. Do you have support?
4. Are you knowledgeable about homosexuality?
5. What's the emotional climate at home?
6. Can you be patient?
7. What's your motive for coming out now?
8. Do you have available resources?
9. Are you financially dependent on your parents?
10. What is your general relationship with your parents?
11. What is their moral societal view?
12. Is this your decision?

Source: Parents, Families and Friends of Lesbians and Gays, 2001.

Parents are often not very helpful to their gay and lesbian children:

> Unlike teenagers from other oppressed minority groups, gay teenagers find little or no support or understanding at home for their societal difference. Most often, family members are the most difficult people to reveal sexual orientation to, and are often the last to know. Considering the consequences, this is often a wise choice. Many teenagers who reveal their sexual orientation (or "come out") to their parents face extreme hostility, violence or sudden homelessness. (O'Conor, 1994, p. 10)

To forestall such damaging responses, the Parents, Families and Friends of Lesbians and Gays (PFLAG) (2001), a social movement with the goal of promoting a more supportive environment for gay males and lesbians, produced a brochure titled *Read This Before Coming Out to Your Parents.* This brochure lists 12 questions to ponder prior to coming out, reproduced in Exhibit 6.6. These are heavy questions for any adolescent, and few nonfamilial supports are available to assist adolescents in resolving their questions related to sexual orientation or easing the process of coming out. Researchers have found, as we might expect, that adolescents who feel close to their parents and supported and accepted by them are more likely to come out to their parents (Waldner & Magruder, 1999).

Sexual minority youth report more depression, hopelessness, and suicidal thinking and behavior than heterosexual adolescents (Safren & Heimberg, 1999). Perhaps we should not be surprised at the elevated risk of suicide among gay and lesbian youth. A task force on youth suicide commissioned by the U. S. Department of Health and Human Services (1993) found that

- Gay male and lesbian youth account for approximately 30% of all teen suicides.
- One in three gay male and lesbian youth reports committing at least one self-destructive act.
- Of the gay and lesbian youth who make one suicide attempt, nearly half attempt suicide repeatedly.
- Gay male and lesbian youth compose approximately one fourth of all homeless youth in the United States.

A study that examined suicidal behavior among gay and bisexual youth found that 30% reported at least one suicide attempt (Remafedi, Farrow, & Deisher, 1991). Following these attempts, only 21% received medical or psychiatric intervention; 74% went without any professional intervention. Many of the youth cited strife regarding their sexual orientation as impetus for the suicide attempt.

Sexual Decision Making. The decision to engage or not to engage in sexual activity is yet another decision that most adolescents make. Biological, psychological, social, cultural, spiritual, and moral factors all play a part in the decision. Biologically, changes in hormone production and the reaction to the changes in appearance based on hormones have been cited as possible catalysts for sexual activity (Udry, Billy, Morris, Groff, & Raj, 1985). Psychologically, adolescents are involved in making a wide range of decisions and developing their own identities, and sexuality is just one more decision. Socially, youth are influenced by the attitudes toward sexual activity that they encounter in the environment, at school, among peers, siblings, and family, in their clubs/organizations, in the media, and so on. When and how they begin to engage in sexual activity is closely linked to what they perceive to be the activities of their peers (Furstenberg, Moore, and Peterson, 1986). Research also suggests that youth who are not performing well in school are more likely to engage in sexual activity than are those who are doing well (Hofferth & Hayes, 1987). Finally, beliefs and behaviors regarding sexuality are also shaped by one's culture, religion/spirituality, and value system.

Data suggest that, on average, adolescents in the United States experience first sexual intercourse slightly earlier than adolescents in other industrialized countries. In 1998, one research team found that the average age of first intercourse in the United States was 15.8 years, compared to 16.2 in Germany, 16.8 in France, and 17.7 in the Netherlands (Berne & Huberman, 1999). Data from the United States indicate that most very young teens have not had intercourse, but the likelihood of having intercourse increases steadily with age, with most teens beginning to have intercourse in the mid to late teens. Seventy percent of females who have sex before age 13 did so nonvoluntarily (Alan Guttmacher Institute, 1999). One study found that the majority of teens in the

United States who are sexually active wish they had waited until they were older to begin to have sexual intercourse (National Campaign to Prevent Teen Pregnancy, 2002). In recent years, there has been a slight decline in teen sexual experience in the United States (Child Trends, n.d.).

Within the United States, there are some racial and ethnic differences in sexual activity among adolescents, but these differences have been declining in recent years. In 1995, 60% of African American teens reported having participated in sexual intercourse, compared with 55% of Hispanic American teens and 50% of European American teens (Child Trends, n.d.).

Early engagement in sexual intercourse has some negative consequences. The earlier a youth begins engaging in sexual intercourse, the more likely she or he is to become involved in delinquent behavior, problem drinking, and marijuana use (Costa, Jessor, Donovan, & Fortenberry, 1995). Young age, as well as use of substances, is associated with an increased number of sexual partners and nonuse of condoms (Shrier, Emans, Woods, & DuRant, 1996). Findings like these suggest that adolescents who report first sexual intercourse before age 13 are more likely to have nine or more sexual partners by the age of 20 (Shrier et al., 1996). Age aside, studies of AIDS transmission by the Centers for Disease Control, conducted every 2 years, indicate that among the approximately 75% of high school students who have had sexual intercourse by the 12th grade, less than 50% report using latex condoms, and about 20% have had more than four sexual partners (Healthtouch, 1997).

Rates of sexual activity among teens in the United States are fairly comparable to those in Western Europe, yet the incidence of adolescent pregnancy, childbearing, and STDs in the United States far exceeds the level of most other industrialized nations (Feijoo, 2001). For instance, the Netherlands, France, and Germany have far better sexual outcomes for teens than the United States. Teens in those countries begin sexual activity at slightly later ages and have fewer sexual partners than teens in the United States. The teen pregnancy rate in the United States is 9 times greater than the pregnancy rate in the Netherlands, nearly 4 times greater than the rate in France, and nearly 5 times greater than the rate in Germany. The teenage abortion rate in the United States is nearly 7 times the rate in the Netherlands, nearly 3 times the rate in France, and nearly 8 times the rate in Germany. There are similar differences in rates of sexually transmitted diseases among teens when comparing the United States to European countries (Advocates for Youth, 2002a). This discrepancy is probably related to three factors: teenagers in the United States make less use of contraception than teens in European countries, reproductive health services are more available in European countries, and sexuality education is more comprehensively integrated into all levels of education in most of Europe than in the United States (Feijoo, 2001; Huberman, 2001).

There is evidence that fewer teens in the United States than in the past are engaging in unprotected sex, however. During the 1980s, teenage women's use of contraception at first intercourse rose from 48% to 65%, and by 1995, 78% reported using contraception at first intercourse. Teenagers are less likely than adults, however, to be consistent in their use of contraception (Alan Guttmacher Institute, 1999). Only 40% of sexually active adolescent women have been found to visit a health care provider for contraceptives within 12 months of becoming sexually active. Most of the increased use of contraceptives among U.S. adolescents is related to increased use of condoms (Advocates for Youth, 2002b).

Why are adolescents in the United States engaging in so much unprotected sex? Many teens blame a double standard: they are taught about the benefits of condom use and are expected to practice safer sex, but they find condoms difficult to obtain. They report that they are harassed at local drug stores for buying condoms, and they find the price of condoms prohibitive (McCarter, 1998). Also, whereas few teens mention difficulty in communicating with sexual partners, they often cite reasons such as "He just won't wear one [a condom]," "He told me to trust him," "She was trying to trick me" (McCarter, 1998). Finally, substance use may cloud an adolescent's decision to engage in protected or safer sex (Shrier et al., 1996). (For a discussion of contraceptive methods, refer to Chapter 2.)

What factors might be producing this recent decline in the teen birthrate?

Pregnancy and Childbearing. Approximately 1 million adolescent girls become pregnant each year in the United States (Alan Guttmacher Institute, 1999). Of teen pregnancies, 56% end in birth (every day, 1,354 babies are born to teen mothers), 30% end in abortion, and 14% end in miscarriage (Alan Guttmacher Institute, 1999; Children's Defense Fund, 2001a). The Centers for Disease Control report that adolescents in the United States were less likely to become pregnant in 1997 than at any time since 1976 (National Center for Health Statistics, 1997a), and the adolescent birthrate fell for the 10th straight year to reach a new low in 2001 (National Center for Health Statistics, 2001a). The largest decline in teen pregnancy and the teen birthrate has been for black teens, and the smallest decline has been for Hispanic teens.

As discussed in Chapter 2, adolescent pregnancies carry increased physical risks to mother and infant, including less prenatal care and higher rates of miscarriage, anemia, toxemia, prolonged labor, premature delivery, and low birth weight. In many Asian, eastern Mediterranean, African, and Latin American countries, the physical risks of adolescent pregnancy are mitigated by social and economic support (Friedman, 1992, p. 346). In the United States, however, adolescent mothers are more likely than their counterparts elsewhere to drop out of school, to be unemployed or underemployed, to receive public assistance, and to have subsequent pregnancies and lower educational and financial attainment. Teenage fathers may also experience lower educational and financial attainment (Pirog-Good, 1995).

Even pregnant teens who choose to abort are at greater risk than older pregnant women:

> While an overall decline in fertility rates in adults in [Western] societies is largely attributable to contraceptive methods, the unmarried adolescent is more likely to choose induced abortion. Although safe abortion is generally more readily available than in traditional societies, the adolescent with less knowledge, resources, and experience, and often fearing the reaction of service providers, will go late or to the inappropriate sources, thus greatly increasing the danger of septic abortions, illness, future infertility, and death. (Friedman, 1992, p. 346)

The developmental tasks of adolescence are typically accomplished in this culture by going to school, socializing with peers, and exploring various roles. For the teenage mother, these avenues to development may be radically curtailed. The result may be long-lasting disadvantage. Consider Monica's path. She obviously loves children and would like to have her own someday, but she would also like to become a pediatrician. If Monica were to become pregnant unexpectedly, an abortion would challenge her religious values and a baby would challenge her future goals.

Sexually Transmitted Diseases. Youth have always faced pregnancy as a consequence of their sexual activity, but other consequences now include infertility and death as a result of **sexually transmitted diseases (STDs)**. As noted earlier, many adolescents are engaging in sexual intercourse without protection (Healthtouch, 1997). Adolescents are especially vulnerable (Shrier et al., 1996). They are likely to experiment with sex and be persuaded by potential partners about whom they know little. Health and sex education at home and in the schools often does not prepare adolescents for the difficult sexual decisions they must make, and they may be particularly ill informed about STDs (Berne & Huberman, 2000).

Thus, the prevalence of STDs and their consequences have been increasing among adolescents (Shrier et al., 1996). More than two thirds of the reported STD cases in the United States are in persons under the age of 25 ("Sexually transmitted diseases," 1996). Three million teenagers—one in every six individuals aged 13 to 19—contract an STD every year in the United States, and one fifth of U.S. AIDS cases occur in young people between the ages of 13 and 29 (State Legislatures, 1996).

Social workers providing services to adolescents need to be knowledgeable regarding these sexually transmitted diseases:

- *Chlamydia*. Each year, more people in the United States become infected with the bacterium *Chlamydia trachomatis*, or *T-strain Mycoplasma*, than any other sexually transmitted disease. Approximately 4 million new infections occur each year (National Institutes of Health–National Institute of Allergy and Infectious Diseases [NIH-NIAID], 1996). The annual reported rate of chlamydia cases increased 262% (from 48 to 182 cases per 100,000 people) in the United States from 1987 to 1995 (NIH-NIAID, 1996). The American Social Health Association (1995) estimates that 29 to 30% of sexually active teenage girls have chlamydia. The disease is typically transmitted through sexual contact, but can also be spread nonsexually, through contact with the mucus or feces of an infected person. The symptoms of chlamydia include vaginal itching and discharge in women (most women remain asymptomatic) or a thin, whitish discharge in men (approximately 40% remain asymptomatic). These symptoms appear 1 to 3 weeks after contact. Chlamydia is most often treated with tetracycline, but if left untreated can result in pelvic inflammatory disease (PID), a leading cause of infertility in women.

- *Genital warts.* Approximately 1 million people in the United States each year become infected with the human papilloma virus (HPV), which causes genital warts (NIH-NIAID, 1996). Estimating adolescent rates of HPV infection is difficult, but the American Social Health Association (1995) suggests that approximately 30% of sexually active adolescents are infected with the human papilloma virus. Genital warts may be contracted during vaginal or anal intercourse or during childbirth. The warts begin as hard, painless bumps that may appear 6 weeks to 8 months after transmission and may then become soft and resemble tiny cauliflower florets. They can appear in the vaginal area, on the penis, or around the anus, and they may itch. Genital warts may be hard to see without a colposcope, which magnifies them. Pap tests may reveal precancerous circumstances caused by HPV; more than 80% of invasive cervical cancer is associated with HPV. HPV can be treated with acid or podophyllin or with surgical, laser, or freezing treatments. Early treatment may prevent cancer of the cervix, vulva, or penis.

- *Gonorrhea.* An estimated 800,000 people a year are infected with gonorrhea in the United States (NIH-NIAID, 1996). For 1993, the rate of infection among adolescents aged 15 to 19 was 742.1 per 100,000 population (Centers for Disease Control [CDC], 1994). Gonorrhea is caused by the gonococcus bacteria *Neisseria gonorrhoeae,* which lives in mucous membranes such as those found in the mouth, vagina, urethra, and anus. Transmission can occur through oral, anal, or vaginal sexual activity with an infected person. Because gonorrhea can also be transmitted during childbirth, drops of silver nitrate are routinely placed in newborns' eyes immediately following delivery to prevent serious eye infections. After having intercourse once with an infected person, women have a 50% chance and men a 25% chance of contracting gonorrhea (Platt, Rice, & McCormack, 1983). Symptoms, which usually appear within 2 to 30 days after contact (average is 3 to 7 days), may include a change in vaginal discharge, painful urination, pelvic discomfort, or abnormal menstruation in women (approximately 80% experience mild or no symptoms), and painful urination with foul-smelling, thick, yellow urethral discharge in men (approximately 10% experience no symptoms). Gonorrhea is detected by microscopic examination of cultures taken from urethral or vaginal discharges and is treated orally by amoxicillin or ampicillin or intravenously by procaine penicillin. If left untreated, gonorrhea can cause arthritis, heart problems, central nervous system disorders, and pelvic inflammatory disease in women and prostate, testes, epididymis infections, and sterility in men.

- *Syphilis.* Rates of syphilis infection are rising in this country, with more than 130,000 cases reported annually (NIH-NIAID, 1996). This reported rate is almost 60 times greater for African Americans than for European Americans, a disparity not seen in the other STDs. Syphilis is caused by a spirochete bacterium, *Treponema pallidum,* acquired through sexual contact. It can be a four-stage disease. First, infection results in the formation of a chancre or sore on the mouth, cervix, vagina, urethra, rectum, anus, external genitals, or nipples, which appears 2 weeks to 1 month after exposure. This first symptom is relatively mild and goes away, often unnoticed. During the 2nd stage, 2 weeks to 2 months after the chancre disappears, infected persons may experience body rash, headache, fever, indigestion, sore throat, and painful joints. Syphilis is highly contagious during the first and second stages. During the third stage, syphilis becomes latent, with no external symptoms, but the spirochetes are actively invading the skeletal, cardiovascular, and nervous systems. For individuals who progress to the fourth stage of syphilis, treatment can kill the bacteria, but damage to internal organs may be irreparable at this point. Thus, syphilis should be detected as early as possible and treated with benzathine penicillin G.

- *Genital herpes.* Approximately 500,000 new cases of genital herpes occur each year, with an estimated 31 million people in the United States already infected (NIH-NIAID, 1996). The disease is caused by the herpes simplex II virus and is contracted by physical contact with the open herpes sores of an infected person (the disease is less contagious in the dormant phase). Genital herpes is characterized by small blisters, which appear in women on the labia, the clitoral hood, and the cervix and in men on the glans or foreskin of the penis 3 to 7 days after infection. The initial outbreak of blisters is typically the most painful and prompts many individuals to seek medical attention. There is no cure for genital herpes, but the medication acyclovir may reduce the pain in herpes outbreaks. Approximately 6% of women with genital herpes develop cervical cancer, and more than 80% of women with cervical cancer have herpes simplex II antibodies (Trimble, Gay, & Docherty, 1986).

- *Acquired immunodeficiency syndrome* (AIDS). AIDS is caused by the human immunodeficiency virus (HIV), which attacks the immune system and reduces the body's ability to combat other diseases. Transmission of the virus can occur through sexual contact, intravenous drug use, blood transfusion, and birth. Half of all new HIV infections in the United States are among those under the age of 25, and most of those are transmitted sexually (CDC, 2001). In 1999, HIV/AIDS was the ninth largest cause of death among black youth aged 15 to 19 years (Anderson, 2001). African Americans and Latinos are overrepresented among persons with AIDS

EXHIBIT 6.7
Facts About STDs

- STDs affect men and women of all backgrounds and economic levels but are most prevalent among teenagers and young adults. Nearly two thirds of all STDs occur in people younger than 25 years of age.
- The incidence of STDs is rising.
- Many STDs initially cause no symptoms, particularly in women. When symptoms develop, they may be confused with those of other diseases not transmitted through sexual contact. However, even when an STD causes no symptoms, a person who is infected may be able to pass on the disease to a sex partner. For this reason, many doctors recommend periodic testing for people who have more than one sex partner.
- Health problems caused by STDs tend to be more severe and more frequent for women than for men, in part because the frequency of asymptomatic infection means that many women do not seek care until serious problems have developed.
- When diagnosed and treated early, almost all STDs can be treated effectively.

Source: NIH-NIAID, 1992b.

(NIH-NIAID, 2002). NIAID reports that 36.1 million people worldwide were living with HIV/AIDS at the end of 2000, and the CDC estimates that 40,000 people in the United States become infected annually (CDC, 2001). Most people infected with HIV carry the virus for years before it destroys enough CD4+ T cells for AIDS to develop. Symptoms of HIV infection may include swollen lymph nodes, unexplained weight loss, loss of appetite, persistent fevers, night sweats, chronic fatigue, unexplained diarrhea, bloody stools, skin rashes, easy bruising, persistent and severe headaches, and unexplained chronic dry cough, all of which can result from opportunistic infections. As of 2002, there is no cure for AIDS. There are several anti-HIV drugs that can slow the immune system destruction, but these have not been tested extensively with children or adolescents.

Exhibit 6.7 lists some facts that social workers can use as a starting point for discussing STDs with adolescents. Some social workers who work with adolescents may face issues of infection, but all social workers should discuss prevention. Teaching communication skills to youth will probably benefit them the most, but in addition, they should be educated to

- Recognize the signs and symptoms of STDs
- Refrain from sexual contact if they suspect themselves or a partner of having any of these signs or symptoms and instead get medical attention as soon as possible

- Use a condom correctly during sexual activity
- Have regular checkups that include STD testing

For AIDS information, the U.S. Public Health Service has a confidential toll-free hot line in English (1-800-342-2437) and in Spanish (1-800-344-7432). The American Social Health Association provides an STD hot line at 1-800-227-8922, where callers can obtain STD information without leaving their names.

Acquaintance Rape. **Acquaintance rape** can be defined as forced, manipulated, or coerced sexual contact by someone you know. Women between 16 and 24 are the primary victims of acquaintance rape, but junior high school girls are also at great risk (U.S. Department of Justice Bureau of Justice Statistics, 2000).

Clear and up-to-date data on the incidence of date rape during adolescence are not available. In the late 1980s, a nationwide study of rape on college campuses found that 25% of female students had been victims of rape or attempted rape (Koss, Gidycz, & Wisniewski, 1987). Another researcher found that 52% of college women at one college had, at some point in their lives, experienced some form of sexual victimization on a date (Himelein, 1995).

One 4-year study of adolescent date rape and sexual assault, although not a national study, found that 23% of the sample experienced unwanted sexual activity by dates or boyfriends, and 15% were victims of date rape (Vicary, Klingaman, & Harkness, 1995). The researchers suggest that predictors of unwanted sexual activity may include reaching menarche at an early age, being sexually active, having sexually active same-sex friends, having poor peer relationships, and being emotionally fragile or distressed. The researchers conclude that parents, teachers, counselors, the legal system, and communities should be informed of the seriousness of this problem and should adequately address it (Vicary et al., 1995). A more recent study in South Dakota found that 14.9% of a statewide, random sample of female high school students reported being a victim of date rape (Schubot, 2001).

Although much research supports the notion that the majority of female victims know their assailants (Mynatt & Algeier, 1990; Russell, 1984), stranger rape is overrepresented in FBI statistics because acquaintance rape is much less likely to be reported. Stranger rape is also more likely to involve the use of a weapon and to result in physical injury to the victim (Mynatt & Algeier, 1990; Russell, 1984).

In recent years, there has been much attention in the news media on the use of so-called date rape drugs to assist in date rape. The date rape drugs are odorless and flavorless, but when mixed into a drink can cause the recipient to lose consciousness. If a blood test is done within a few hours after the drug is administered, it may not be detected (Soto, 2001). Three drugs are known to have been used to assist in date rape in recent years:

EXHIBIT 6.8

Percentage of Students Who Have Ever Used Alcohol, Tobacco, or Other Drugs (2001)

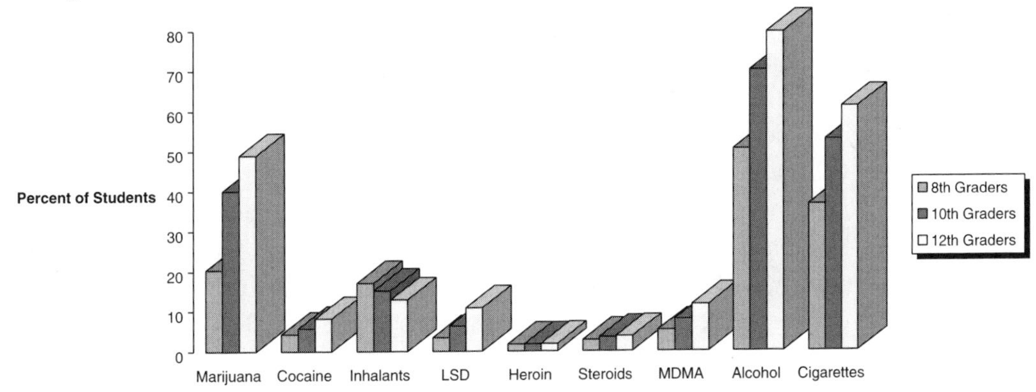

Source: NIH-NIDA, Monitoring the Future Study 2001.

1. Rohypnol (also known as Roofies, Rope, Ruffies, R2, Ruffles, Roche, Foget-pill)
2. Gamma Hydroxy Butyrate (also known as GHB, Liquid Extacy, Liquid X, Scoop, Easy Lay)
3. Ketamine Hydrochloride (also known as K, Special K, Vitamin K, Ket)

Substance Use and Abuse

Throughout this book, you have encountered a multiplicity of factors that contribute to the way individuals behave. Substance use is yet another variable in that mix. For example, Carl's use of tobacco and marijuana has several likely effects on his general behavior. Tobacco may make him feel tense, excitable, or anxious, and these feelings may amplify his concern about his weight, his grades, and his family relationships. On the other hand, the marijuana may make Carl feel relaxed, and he may use it to counteract or escape from his concerns.

According to the 2001 Monitoring the Future Study (National Institutes of Health-National Institute on Drug Abuse [NIH-NIDA], 2001), use of cigarettes by teenagers in the United States decreased from 2000 to 2001. The study also suggests that the rise in use of MDMA (ecstasy) in teenagers slowed during 2000-2001 among students in grades 8, 10, and 12. Rates of heroin use also decreased notably among 10th and 12th graders, and a gradual decline in the use of inhalants continued in 2001, with a significant decrease occurring among 12th graders. These are encouraging trends, but others are less positive. Alcohol prevalence rates remained relatively stable while steroid use by teenagers increased. Exhibit 6.8 summarizes some of the survey's findings regarding drug use in 2001.

Adolescents typically follow a pattern of substance use (Kandel & Logan, 1984, 1991; O'Malley, Johnston, & Bachman, 1991), beginning with tobacco, coffee, and alcohol. Thus, tobacco is considered a gateway drug to further substance use and abuse. According to a Youth Tobacco Survey conducted by the Office on Smoking and Health (2000), 80% of tobacco users began use before the age of 18 years.

Adolescence is the primary risk period for initiating the use of other substances as well; those who have not experimented with licit or illicit drugs by age 21 are unlikely to do so thereafter (Kandel & Logan, 1984). Each year approximately 3.3 million youth between the ages of 12 and 17 begin drinking alcohol, and alcohol use increases with age (CASA, 2002). Among high school seniors who had ever tried alcohol, 91.3% are still drinking in the 12th grade; of those students who had ever been drunk, 83.3% are still getting drunk in the 12th grade. Current alcohol use is nearly identical for male (40.2%) and female (41%) ninth graders, as is binge drinking for male (21.7%) and female (20.2%) ninth graders. Caucasian (52.5%) and Latino (52.8%) youth have comparable alcohol use rates, with lower rates for African American youth (39.9%). Eighth graders in rural areas are 29% more likely than their urban counterparts to have used alcohol and are 70% more likely to have been drunk (CASA, 2002).

Despite industry claims that alcohol is not marketed to children, animation, adolescent humor, and rock music are prevalent in alcoholic beverage advertising. Moreover, in the first 6 months of 2001, 217 varieties of "malternatives" (such as Rick's Spiked Lemonade, Tequiza, Hooper's Hooch, Smirnoff Ice, Skyy Blue) were approved by the Bureau of Alcohol, Tobacco, and Firearms (CASA, 2002). Forty-one percent of youth aged 14 to 18 have tried these sweet-tasting and colorfully packaged alcoholic beverages (CASA, 2002).

What are the risk factors for substance abuse in adolescence?

Decision Making About Substance Use. When asked why youth choose to use alcohol, adolescents cite the following reasons: to have a good time with friends, to relieve tension and anxiety, to deal with the opposite sex, to get high, to cheer up, and to alleviate boredom. When asked why youth use cocaine, the additional responses were to get more energy and to get away from problems. Overall drug use at a party is also cited quite often as a reason (O'Malley et al., 1991; Segal & Stewart, 1996). The following factors appear to be involved in adolescents' choice of drugs: the individual characteristics of the drug, the individual characteristics of the user, the availability of the drug, the current popularity of the drug, and the sociocultural traditions and sanctions regarding the drug (Segal & Stewart, 1996).

Adolescents who choose to abuse substances seem to differ from those who do not. In a 12-year longitudinal study, Richard Jessor (1987) found that adolescent problem drinkers differ from other adolescents in their personal qualities, their social environment, and their other patterns of behavior. Problem drinkers are less likely to hold traditional values about education, religion, or conformity. They perceive large differences between their family's values and their peers' values, are more influenced by their peers, and have peers who are also engaged in problem drinking. Finally, problem drinkers are also more likely to participate in other risk-taking behaviors, such as sexual activity and delinquency (Jessor, 1987). More recently, Jessor and colleagues have tested the stability of these findings using six adolescent samples that range the years from 1974 to 1992, two national samples and four local community samples. Even though there were significant changes in the sociohistorical context over the years of the six samples, the researchers found that the personal and environmental correlates of problem drinking remained the same across all samples, and were the same correlates as summarized above from Jessor's longitudinal study (Donovan, Jessor, & Costa, 1999).

Moreover, some adolescents are clearly more at risk for substance abuse than others. American Indian youth and Alaska Native youth begin using alcohol and other drugs at a younger age than other youth, use them more frequently, use a greater amount, and use more different substances in combination with each other (Cameron, 1999; Novins, Beals, Shore, & Manson, 1996). The death rate due to substance abuse among American Indian youth is twice that of other youth (Pothoff et al., 1998). In response to this social need, drug treatment to Native American teens is undergoing a rapid change, with direct service provided by Indian tribes, employing mainly American Indian staff, and using traditional Indian healing approaches in combination with standard addiction treatment approaches (Novins et al., 1996; Novins, Fleming, Beals, & Manson, 2000). It is too early to know how successful these new approaches will be.

Consequences of Substance Use and Abuse. Chemical substances pose a profound threat to the health of adolescents, because substance abuse affects metabolism, internal organs, the central nervous system, emotional functioning, and cognitive functioning (Segal & Stewart, 1996). Alcohol and opiates can cause severe intoxication, coma, and withdrawal symptoms. Sedative drugs can depress the nervous and respiratory systems; withdrawal may lead to disturbances in breathing, heart function, and other basic body functions. Intravenous use of cocaine has been linked to adolescent cases of hepatitis, HIV, heart inflammation, loss of brain tissue, and abnormally high fever. Extended use of inhalants can cause irreparable neuropsychological damage. And finally, substances can weaken the immune system and increase a youth's likelihood of disease or general poor health.

Substance abuse has significant psychosocial implications for adolescents as well:

> [It] compromises their adjustment and school performance, contributes to low achievements, poor academic performance and high school dropout. It disrupts normal psychosocial functioning, decreases social support, limits participation in age-appropriate activities, reduces psychological resources and produces anxiety, tension, and low self-esteem. Substance induced psychological reactions interfere with eating and sleeping, modify health related behavior and may be a cause of serious psychiatric disorders. (Segal & Stewart, 1996, p. 202)

As mentioned earlier, substance use can also affect the decision to engage in sexual activity. After substance use, youth are more likely to engage in sexual activity and are less likely to use protection; thus, they are more likely to become pregnant or impregnate and to contract a sexually transmitted disease (Brooks-Gunn & Furstenberg, 1989; Segal & Stewart, 1996; Shrier et al., 1996). In general, adolescents who use tobacco products, alcohol, marijuana, and other substances are more likely to be sexually active and to have more sexual partners (CASA, 2002; Lowry et al., 1994).

Juvenile Delinquency

Almost every adolescent violates rules at some time, disobeying parents or teachers, lying, cheating, and perhaps even stealing or vandalizing. Many adolescents smoke cigarettes, drink alcohol, skip school, or stay out past curfew. For some adolescents, this behavior is a phase, passing as quickly as it appeared. Yet for others, it becomes a pattern. These are the adolescents who are likely to come into contact with the juvenile justice system.

In the United States, persons older than 7 but younger than 18 can be arrested for anything for which an adult can be arrested. (Children under 7 are said not to possess mens rea, which means "guilty mind," and thus are not considered capable of criminal intent.) In addition, they can be arrested for what are called **status offenses**, such as running away from home, skipping school, violating curfew, and possessing tobacco or alcohol—behaviors not considered crimes when engaged in by adults. When adolescents are found guilty of committing either a crime (by adult standards) or a status offense, we refer to their behavior as **juvenile delinquency**. Recently, the philosophy of the courts has shifted from reform and rehabilitation of delinquent adolescents to punishment and restitution.

The Office of Juvenile Justice and Delinquency Prevention reports that in 1999, U.S. law enforcement agencies made an estimated 2.5 million arrests of persons under the age of 18 (Snyder, 2000). According to the FBI, juveniles accounted for 17% of all arrests and 16% of all violent crime arrests in 1999. Juveniles were involved in 9% of murder arrests, 14% of aggravated assault arrests, 33% of burglary arrests, 25% of robbery arrests, and 24% of weapons arrests. For the 5th consecutive year, the rate of juvenile arrests for violent crimes declined, and from 1993 to 1999, the juvenile arrest rate for murder decreased 68% to its lowest level since the 1960s. In 1999, the number of juvenile arrests declined in every violent crime category despite an 8% growth in the juvenile population since 1993.

The racial composition of the juvenile population in 1999 was 79% Caucasian, 15% African American, and 5% "other" (with most Hispanics classified as Caucasian). That same year, however, 57% of juvenile arrests for violent crimes involved Caucasian youth and 41% involved African American youth (Snyder, 2000). Research suggests that this disparity is based on a complex blend of psychological, racial, socioeconomic, familial, educational, structural, and political factors (McCarter, 1997).

Another area of concern is disproportionate delinquency among the adolescent children of welfare-to-work participants. Declines in educational outcomes among these adolescents have been noted (Brooks, Hair, & Zaslow, 2001; Gennetian et al., 2002), as well as increases in behavior problems as their parents transition to employment. Specifically, adolescents with parents enrolled in welfare-to-work programs have exhibited increased smoking, drinking, drug use, delinquent activity, and school disciplinary problems (Brooks et al., 2001; Morris et al., 2001). Some suggest that these impacts on adolescents may be related to decreased parental supervision and increased harsh or negative parenting (Brooks et al., 2001). Suggested strategies include limiting required hours of parental employment, developing more before- and after-school care programs targeted at adolescents, expanding child care (in order to limit family reliance on adolescents for care of younger siblings), providing guidance to parents about appropriate responsibility and autonomy for adolescents, and increasing financial supports to families (so that adolescent employment is less critical). Indeed, because recent research indicates that the adolescent children of welfare leavers are working more than other adolescents (Brown, 2001), the causes and consequences of employment among this population deserve further attention.

Threats to Physical and Mental Health

The U.S. Department of Health and Human Services (1991, 1995) reported the following statistics:

- Unintentional injury is the leading cause of death of adolescents.
- Homicide is the second leading cause of death for adolescents aged 15 to 19 (at a rate 8 times higher for African Americans than for European Americans) and the third leading cause of death for those aged 10 to 14.
- Suicide is the third leading cause of death for adolescents aged 15 to 19 and the fourth leading cause for those aged 10 to 14.
- Approximately 3 million adolescents contract an STD annually, and more than 1 million adolescent girls become pregnant each year (the highest rate of the world's developed countries).
- Among adolescents aged 12 to 17, 15% report having used illegal drugs, 41% report alcohol use, and 20% of teenagers will be smoking by the time they finish high school.
- Of youth aged 10 to 18, 20% have no health insurance.

- Between 15 and 30% of adolescents in the United States are obese, and the rate has increased over the past 20 years.
- More than half of underweight adolescents report being terrified of becoming overweight.

Thus, threats to adolescent health and well-being include not only pregnancy, STDs, and substance abuse, which have already been discussed, but also violence, problems with nutrition, and suicide.

Violence. Although researchers have studied the effects of family violence on youth, they are only beginning to address the effects of community violence. One study of 935 urban and suburban youth found that over 45% had witnessed a shooting or stabbing or other serious act of violence during the previous year (O'Keefe, 1997). This violence may be a significant predictor of aggressive acting-out behavior for both male and female adolescents (O'Keefe, 1997). Also, urban African American youth exposed to high levels of community violence have been found to experience more distress, such as anxiety and depression, than those with less or no exposure to community violence (Fitzpatrick & Boldizar, 1993).

One aspect of community violence that is especially pertinent to teens is the violence perpetrated by gangs. In 2000, the National Youth Gang Survey estimated that more than 24,500 gangs were active in the United States (Egley, 2002). In 1999, 47% of gang members in the United States were Hispanic, 31% were African American, 13% were Caucasian, 7% were Asian, and 2% were "other." It is important to note, however, that in 1999 only 37% of gang members were juveniles (under 18), and 63% were adults (18 and over) (Egley, 2002). Indeed, each wave of immigration in the United States has had its own incarnation of gangs, and most early gang members have been young adults (Huff, 1996). Historically, gang membership has been one way to become established and defend the ethnic neighborhood. Gangs have been a mixed blessing for ethnic communities, however. They provide some necessary services for their neighborhoods, but they also bring the threat of intergang violence.

Although most crime committed by gangs is nonviolent, it is the violent gang behavior that is best known to the public (U.S. Department of Health and Human Services, 2001c). Among cities with populations over 250,000 with persistent gang problems, 47% reported an increase in gang-related homicides from 1999 to 2000 (Egley, 2002). Armando Morales (1992) contends that "violent urban gangs are contributing to psychological pain and trauma, social disorganization, and dysfunction among many young clients referred for mental health services. Youth gangs and their violent behavior are a symptom; the members of a community are indicating that their needs are not being met by the family, neighborhood, social institutions, and health professions" (p. 129).

Nutrition, Obesity, and Eating Disorders. The dietary practices of some adolescents put them at risk for overall health problems. These practices include skipping meals, usually breakfast or lunch; snacking, especially on high-calorie, high-fat, low-nutrition snacks; eating fast foods; and dieting. Poor nutrition can affect a youth's growth and development, sleep, weight, cognition, mental health, and overall physical health.

An increasing minority of adolescents in the United States are obese. According to the third National Health and Nutrition Examination Survey, 1988-1994 (NHANES III), approximately 12% of adolescents aged 12 to 17 were overweight (CDC, 1997)—a significant increase over NHANES II in 1980. Teenagers in the United States are overweight as a result of biological tendency, diet, family attitudes and behaviors toward food, and lack of exercise (Maloney & Klykylo, 1983).

This chapter has emphasized how tenuous self-esteem can be during adolescence, but the challenges are even greater for profoundly overweight or underweight youth. Overweight adolescents may suffer exclusion from peer groups and discrimination in education, employment, marriage, housing, and health care (DeJong, 1993). Carl Fleischer has already begun to face some of these challenges. He thinks of himself as a "fat, slow geek" and assumes females would not be interested in him because of his weight.

Research is exposing the breadth of the problem. For instance, one study examined problematic eating attitudes or behaviors in preadolescent and early adolescent (fifth and sixth grade) girls and boys (Keel, Fulkerson, and Leon, 1997). The girls in the study reported more body dissatisfaction, more depression, and lower self-esteem than the boys, and endorsed more of the items on the survey that indicate disordered eating habits or attitudes (p. 213). In a national survey conducted in 1999, 42.7% of adolescents were trying to lose weight, the highest percentage since 1991 (Youth Risk Behavior Surveillance System [YRBSS], 1999).

Girls' body dissatisfaction reflects the incongruence between the societal ideal of thinness and the beginning of normal fat deposits in pubescent girls. Joan Brumberg (1997) used unpublished diaries to do a historical analysis of femaleness in adolescence. Her analysis suggests a strong trend for girls in the United States to define themselves more and more through their appearance. She suggests that we now have a situation in which girls are reaching sexual maturity at a younger age in a highly sexualized culture that exploits girls' normal sensitivity to their changing bodies, often using the prepubescent female body as a sexual symbol. Furthermore, girls are encountering this cultural tendency in micro bikinis, rather than in the corsets of their great-grandmothers. Micro bikinis are not very forgiving.

Blumbergh sees eating disorders, such as **anorexia nervosa** and **bulimia nervosa**, as one result of this situation:

- Anorexia nervosa means literally "loss of appetite due to nerves," but the disorder is actually characterized by a dysfunctional body image and voluntary starvation in the pursuit of weight loss. According to the *DSM-IV* (American Psychiatric Association [APA], 1994), the essential features of anorexia nervosa are that "the individual refuses to maintain a minimally normal body weight, is intensely afraid of gaining weight, and exhibits a significant disturbance in the perception of the shape or size of his or her body" (p. 539).

- Bulimia nervosa is characterized by a cycle of binge eating; feelings of guilt, depression, or self-disgust; and purging (producing vomiting or evacuation of the bowels). The *DSM-IV* (APA, 1994) suggests that individuals with bulimia nervosa are also excessively influenced by body shape and weight and exhibit binge eating followed by purging at least twice a week for at least 3 months.

Fad diets and unsafe nutrition may be precursors for anorexia nervosa and bulimia nervosa.

Depression and Suicide. Epidemiological studies suggest that as many as 8.3% of adolescents in the United States may have a major depressive disorder. Parents are less likely to recognize depression in their adolescents than the adolescents themselves. During adolescence, girls are about twice as likely as boys to have a major depressive disorder (National Institute of Mental Health [NIMH], 2000). The diagnoses may not accurately reflect the prevalence of male depression, however, because many "tough" male adolescents may find it hard to verbalize, admit, or identify feelings related to depression (Morales, 1992, p. 147). Research suggests that African American and Mexican American youth may be at increased risk for depression (Roberts, Roberts, & Chen, 1997).

Adolescent depression may also be underdiagnosed, among males and females alike, because it is difficult to detect. Many parents and professionals expect adolescence to be a time of ups and downs, moodiness, melodrama, anger, rebellion, and increased sensitivity. Researchers have found that parents are even less likely to recognize depression in their adolescents than the adolescents themselves (NIMH, 2000). There are, however, some reliable outward signs of depression in adolescents: poor academic performance, truancy, social withdrawal, antisocial behavior, changes in eating or sleeping patterns, changes in physical appearance, excessive boredom or activity, low self-esteem, sexual promiscuity, substance use, propensity to run away from home, and excessive family conflict. Additional symptoms of depression not unique to adolescence include pervasive inability to experience pleasure, severe psychomotor retardation, delusions, and a sense of hopelessness (Kaplan & Sadock, 1998).

The many challenges of adolescence sometimes prove overwhelming. I have already discussed the risk of suicide among gay male and lesbian adolescents. Overall, suicide is the third leading cause of death for adolescents in the United States (NIMH, 2000); it is number two (behind accidents) for European American males aged 15 to 24.

EXHIBIT 6.9
Suicide Signs in Adolescents

1. Change in eating and sleeping habits
2. Withdrawal from friends and family and from regular activities
3. Violent actions, rebellious behavior, or running away
4. Drug and alcohol use
5. Unusual neglect of personal appearance
6. Marked personality change
7. Persistent boredom, difficulty concentrating, or a decline in the quality of schoolwork
8. Frequent complaints about physical symptoms, often related to emotions, such as stomachaches, headaches, and fatigue
9. Loss of interest in pleasurable activities
10. Intolerance of praise or rewards

Source: American Academy of Child and Adolescent Psychiatry, 1995.

The American Academy of Child and Adolescent Psychiatry (1995) provides a list of warning signs for adolescent suicide, shown in Exhibit 6.9, and recommends that if one or more of these signs occur, professional help be sought.

Risk Factors and Protective Factors in Adolescence

What are the implications of research on risk and protection for social work program development?

There are many pathways through adolescence; both individual and group-based differences result in much variability. Some of the variability is related to the types of risk factors and protective factors that have accumulated prior to adolescence. Emmy Werner and associates (see Werner & Smith, 2001) have found, in their longitudinal research on risk and protection, that females have a better balance of risk and protection in childhood, but the advantage goes to males during adolescence. Their research indicates that the earlier risk factors that most predict poor adolescent adjustment are a childhood spent in chronic poverty, alcoholic and psychotic parents, moderate to severe physical disability, developmentally disabled siblings, school problems in middle childhood, conflicted relationships with peers, and family disruptions. The most important earlier protective factors are easy temperament, positive social orientation in early childhood, positive peer relationships in middle childhood, nonsex-typed extracurricular interests and hobbies in middle childhood, and nurturing from non-parental figures.

Much attention has also been paid to the increase in risk behaviors during adolescence (Lerner & Galambos, 1998). In the United States, attention has been called to a set of factors that are risky to adolescent well-being and serve as risk factors for adjustment in adulthood as well. These factors include use and abuse of alcohol and other drugs; unsafe sex, teen pregnancy, and teen parenting; school underachievement, failure, and dropout; delinquency, crime, and violence; and youth poverty. The risk and resilience research indicates, however, that many youth with several of these risk factors overcome the odds. Protective factors that have been found to contribute to resilience in adolescence include family creativity in coping with adversity, good family relationships, faith and attachment to religious institutions, social support in the school setting, and school-based health services.

In 1995, the Carnegie Corporation disseminated a report titled *Great Transitions: Preparing Adolescents for a New Century*. This report set out five core recommendations for ensuring the healthy development of adolescents in the current social environment in the United States:

1. *Reengage families with their adolescent children.* Schools and communities should help parents cope with the adolescent transition, through parent support groups and the like. Employers should develop family-friendly policies that allow parents to spend time with their young adolescents.

2. *Create developmentally appropriate schools for adolescents.* Middle schools and junior high schools should be transformed into small-scale, safe environments that promote stable relationships between students, teachers, and parents. Curricula that stimulate curiosity and the desire to explore should be developed.

3. *Develop health-promotion strategies for young adolescents.* Young adolescents should be helped to develop the knowledge, values, and skills that contribute to physical and mental health. A cadre of health providers should be trained to understand the developmental needs of adolescents. Both school-based and community-based health facilities for adolescents should be developed to address the issues of health care accessibility.

4. *Strengthen communities with young adolescents.* Communities should provide safe and attractive settings for young adolescents to socialize during out-of-school time.

5. *Promote the constructive potential of the media.* Families, schools, and religious institutions should help young adolescents become more critical consumers of media messages and work with media organizations to develop positive images of adolescence and for adolescents.

In recent years, concern has been voiced about the vulnerability of adolescents in societies that construct adolescence as a problem, and two social movements have attempted to reverse this trend by tying adolescents more securely to their communities. One, the **community youth development** movement, promotes youth as a community asset (Checkoway, 1998). For example, one nonprofit community development organization called on local youth to help to revitalize the main street of a small town after a mill closing (Twiss & Cooper, 2000). Another social movement revolves around the **Challenge Day** program (Challenge Day, n.d.), which was developed in 1987 as a day-long program for students, teachers, and administrators in middle schools and high schools. The purpose is to expose cultures of teasing and ostracizing in school settings and to create more supportive, accepting school cultures. The Challenge Day program developed a higher profile when it was invited to Colorado after the Columbine High School violence as a part of the healing process.

IMPLICATIONS FOR SOCIAL WORK PRACTICE

Adolescence is a vulnerable period. Adolescents' bodies and psyches are changing rapidly in transition from childhood to adulthood. Youth are making some very profound decisions during this life course period. Thus, the implications for social work practice are wide ranging.

- When working with adolescents, meet clients where they are "at," because that place may change frequently.
- Be familiar with typical adolescent development and with the possible consequences of deviations from developmental time lines.
- Be aware of and respond to the adolescent's level of cognition and comprehension. Assess the individual adolescent's ability to contemplate the future, to comprehend the nature of human relationships, to consolidate specific knowledge into a coherent system, and to envision possible consequences from a hypothetical list of actions.
- Recognize that the adolescent may see you as an authority figure who is not an ally. Develop skills in building rapport with adolescents.
- Assess the positive and negative effects of the school environment on the adolescent in relation to such issues as early or late maturation, popularity/sociability, culture, and sexual orientation.
- Where appropriate, advocate for change in maladaptive school settings, such as those with Eurocentric models or homophobic environments.

- Provide information, support, or other interventions to assist adolescents in resolving questions of sexual identity and sexual decision making.
- Where appropriate, link youth to existing resources, such as extracurricular activities, education on STDs, prenatal care, and gay and lesbian support groups.
- Provide information, support, or other interventions to assist adolescents in making decisions regarding use of tobacco, alcohol, or other drugs.
- Develop skills to assist adolescents with physical and mental health issues, such as nutritional problems, obesity, eating disorders, depression, and suicide.
- Participate in research, policy, and advocacy on behalf of adolescents.
- Work at the community level to develop and sustain recreational and social programs and places for young people.

Key Terms

acquaintance rape
acquired immunodeficiency syndrome (AIDS)
anorexia nervosa
bulimia nervosa
Challenge Day
community youth development
curanderismo
dispositions
generalized other
gonads
identity
individuation
juvenile delinquency
masturbation
menarche
mestizo perspective
physical characteristics
postconventional moral reasoning
primary sex characteristic
puberty
rites of passage
secondary sex characteristic
sex hormones
sexually transmitted diseases (STDs)
social identity
spermarche
status offenses

ACTIVE LEARNING

1. Recalling your own high school experiences, which case study individual would you most identify with—David, Carl, or Monica? For what reasons? How could a social worker have affected your experiences?
2. Visit a public library and check out some preteen and teen popular fiction or magazines. Which topics from this chapter are discussed and how are they dealt with?
3. Have lunch at a local high school cafeteria. Be sure to go through the line, eat the food, and enjoy conversation with some students. What are their concerns? What are their notions about social work?

WEB RESOURCES

Adolescence Directory On-Line

education.indiana.edu/cas/adol/adol/html

Site presented by the Center for Adolescent Studies at Indiana University contains an electronic guide to information on adolescent issues, including breaking news, conflict and violence, mental health issues, health issues, and resources for counselors and teens.

Puberty Information for Boys and Girls

www.aap.org/family/puberty.htm

Site presented by the American Academy of Pediatrics contains general information on the process of puberty for both boys and girls as well as advocacy issues and current research.

CDC Health Topic: Adolescents and Teens

www.cdc.gov/health/adolescent.htm

Site maintained by the Centers for Disease Control and Prevention contains links to a variety of health topics related to adolescents, including reproductive health, teen pregnancy, working teens, physical activity in adolescence, and youth smoking.

Adolescent Health and Mental Health

www.fenichel.com/adolhealth.shtml

Site presented by Dr. Michael Fenichel of the University of Nebraska-Lincoln contains links to information on adolescence and peer pressure, eating disorders, anxiety and panic, trauma, and depression.

Youth Risk Behavior Surveillance System (YRBSS)

www.cdc.gov/nccdphp/dash/yrbs/index.htm

Site presented by the National Center for Chronic Disease Prevention and Health Promotion contains latest research on adolescent risk behavior.

ABA Juvenile Justice Center

www.abanet.org/crimjust/juvjus/home.html

Site presented by the American Bar Association Juvenile Justice Center contains current events related to juvenile justice, and information on topics such as girls in the juvenile justice system, juvenile death penalty, and zero tolerance.

CHAPTER 7

Young Adulthood

Holly C. Matto

CHAPTER 7

Young Adulthood

Holly C. Matto
Virginia Commonwealth University

Why is it important for social workers to understand transitional markers associated with young adulthood from a *multidimensional* perspective, recognizing systemic-structural impacts on development as well as the psychosocial factors that are traditionally studied?

How do social class, culture, and gender affect the transition to adulthood?

Key Ideas

As you read this chapter, take note of these central ideas:

1. A new phase called "emerging adulthood" (ages 18-25) has been proposed as a time when individuals explore and experiment with different life roles, occupational interests, educational pursuits, religious beliefs, and relationships, with more focus than in adolescence but without the full commitment of young adulthood.
2. Traditional transitional markers associated with young adulthood have included obtaining independent housing, establishing a career, developing significant partnerships that lead to marriage, and becoming a parent; current research suggests that financial independence and authority in decision making are the markers considered important by emerging adults.
3. In young adulthood, cognitive capacities become more flexible; "moral conscience" expands in social awareness, responsibility, and obligation; and religious beliefs are often reexamined.
4. Identity development continues into adulthood and is not static, but is dynamic and ever evolving through significant interpersonal relationships.

5. Young adults struggle with the Eriksonian psychosocial crisis of intimacy versus isolation—the challenge of finding meaningful connections to others without losing oneself in the process.
6. Labor force experience and connection in young adulthood is associated with psychological and social well-being; advanced education is becoming increasingly important in attaining quality jobs.
7. Discrimination and multilevel racism-related stressors can directly and indirectly affect entry into young adulthood.

Case Study 7.1

Jerome's Break from School

Jerome is a 20-year-old white male living in a moderate-sized midwestern town. He went to college for a couple of years, but found it just wasn't for him and left to take a management position in his uncle's construction business. Jerome knows he will probably have to go back to school someday, but was excited at the prospect of doing something "more meaningful" in the real work world. He doesn't believe this job will be his lifelong career, but he says he feels good about having a steady paycheck, being able to have his own place, and being financially independent from his parents. Jerome has a strong work ethic (he usually gets to the construction site at 7:00 A.M. and works well into the evening), but lives by the mantra "work hard and play hard."

Jerome spends a lot of his free time with his friends, and says that having a family of his own right now is the furthest thing from his mind. Some of Jerome's friends from high school have children, and the emotional and financial stresses that he sees them endure lead him to say that he enjoys his freedom too much to be tied down right now. Jerome was dating a woman his age for about a year, but their relationship ended because he was not willing to get married. He is now in and out of dating relationships, each usually lasting a few months.

Jerome's parents have been divorced since he was 7 years old. He says he is not close to his father, who was physically abusive to him during his childhood, and says he "has never gotten along" with his stepmother. However, Jerome has a very close relationship with his mother, who is living with and caring for his ill grandmother. Jerome makes a point to see his mother and grandmother every Sunday.

CASE STUDY 7.1

Jerome is not very involved in his community and does not belong to a church, but he and a few work friends play basketball several nights a week at the local YMCA. Jerome says that, for the most part, he is comfortable with his life right now, but he has come to the family and youth services bureau where you work to participate in your outpatient substance awareness group because the courts have determined that his use of alcohol and marijuana has "gotten out of control." Jerome is currently fulfilling his 10-week court-mandated participation in your group as a result of a recent drug possession charge, and he is one of the few group members who presents as engaged in the treatment, despite openly stating that he does not have a substance abuse problem.

CASE STUDY 7.2

BEN'S NEW ENVIRONMENT

Ben is a 23-year-old second-generation Korean American. He comes from a very large family, all of whom live in a small rural community. They own the local grocery market, and Ben's two older brothers help in managing the store.

When Ben graduated from high school, he vowed to move out of the town and away from the "small-minded people who inhabit it." Ben says that he never really felt like he fit in during his high school years, partly because of his "immigrant" status and partly because he is gay. Ben had only a few close friends in high school, did not date, and dreamed of moving to New York City upon graduation. He did fairly well in his schoolwork and was admitted to a large state school close to New York City. Ben's family was proud that he graduated from high school and that he planned to go to college, but they were upset that he chose to move so far away from his family.

During college, Ben became much more comfortable socially, became active in student politics, and found a niche in the college running club. On the running team Ben met Michael, who became a close friend, and over time, they became romantically involved. Ben and Michael did everything together—they shared a lot of the same academic and political interests and

CASE STUDY 7.2

enjoyed intense political debates. Throughout his college years, Ben saw his family only infrequently, mostly at holiday breaks, and never brought Michael with him.

Ben continued to do well academically and, after finishing college, decided to go to graduate school in New York City for a master's degree in urban planning. His partner moved into the city with him, and they currently share an apartment near Ben's university. Ben and Michael are actively involved in gay social clubs, a city running club, and a community civic association. Ben wants to establish stronger ties with his parents and siblings back home but also feels as though he has "grown out of" that environment. He is afraid they will not understand all the changes he has been through in college and graduate school and that they will not accept his sexual identity or partnership. In addition, Ben knows that his parents still hold onto the expectation that he will come home when he finishes his graduate program.

Case Study 7.3

Carla's Transition to Parenthood

Carla is a 30-year-old Latina living in a large West Coast city. She graduated from the local college with a degree in business and is currently employed as an accountant. She has been married for 4 years to a man she met through her church and is 4 months pregnant with her first child.

In the midst of her excitement about the new baby, Carla is anxious about how she will juggle the new caretaking responsibilities with her career aspirations. She knows she wants both to have a meaningful career and to be a good mother but is very concerned about managing multiple demanding roles. Her husband, a consultant, works long hours and travels frequently for his job. Carla has discussed with you the disruption, strain, and lack of continuity she feels in their marriage as a result of her husband's intense work schedule, but she also knows that he makes good money and she respects the fact that he enjoys his work.

Carla and her husband are actively involved in their church group, where they meet monthly with other young adults for spirituality discussions.

CASE STUDY 7.3

They also participate in the church's various outreach projects, and Carla volunteers 2 hours each week with Streetwise Partners. However, they live in a very transient part of the city, and she is struggling to develop more meaningful connections with neighbors.

One of Carla's close friends, Marissa, was just diagnosed with breast cancer, which came as a shock to family and friends, because Marissa is only in her late 20s and does not have a family history of cancer. Carla has had a lot of difficulty dealing with her friend's diagnosis, and worries about her own risks for breast cancer, as she remembers her aunt had a malignant tumor removed 2 years ago.

Carla's mother died of liver failure the year before Carla graduated from high school, but Carla's father is still alive and is a significant support in her life. Most of Carla's extended family live nearby or in towns outside the central city, although some relatives still live in the Dominican Republic. Carla's mother-in-law, Jan, lives close by and just recently got divorced after 27 years of marriage. Jan relies heavily on her son and daughter-in-law for emotional (and some financial) support during this life transition.

Carla and her husband both say that they are having trouble dealing with the myriad roles they are faced with (such as young professionals, marriage partners, supportive family members), and are considering how the new role of first-time parents will affect their current lives and future life choices.

A Definition of Young Adulthood

Is it biological age, psychological age, social age, or spiritual age that best defines young adulthood?

Defining young adulthood and the transitional markers that distinguish this period from adolescence and middle adulthood has been the challenge and life's work of a number of developmental scholars. A broad challenge has been to determine a framework for identifying the developmental characteristics of young adulthood. For example, is a young adult one who has reached a certain biological or legal age? One who has achieved specific physiological and psychological milestones? Or perhaps one who performs certain social roles? Research, theory, and scholarly thinking about young adulthood presents a variety of perspectives related to each of these dimensions.

Typical chronological ages associated with young adulthood are 22 to 34 (Ashford, LeCroy, Lortie, 2001); some scholars define young adulthood even more broadly, from the age of 17 to about 40 (Levinson, 1978). Other scholars assert that such broad ranges encompass too much variety of experience:

> If ages 18-25 are young adulthood, what would that make the thirties? Young adulthood is a term better applied to the thirties, which are still young but are definitely adult in a way that the years 18-25 are not. It makes little sense to lump late teens, twenties, and thirties together and call the entire period young adulthood. The period from ages 18 to 25 could hardly be more distinct from the thirties. (Arnett, 2000, p. 479)

Although a wide age range can be useful in providing some chronological boundaries around this developmental period, from a life course perspective it is more useful to examine the social role transitions, important life events, and significant turning points associated with young adulthood. The major challenges facing young adults are attaining independent financial stability and establishing autonomy in decision making. Young adults ages 18 to 25 agree when asked about what they see as markers of entry into young adulthood (Arnett, 1998). Young persons who do not attend college are as likely as college students to say that making independent decisions based on their own values and belief systems is important for defining adult status (Arnett, 2000). Other social role changes young people face during the transition from adolescence to adulthood include

- Leaving home and becoming responsible for housing
- Taking on work and/or education tasks
- Marrying or committing to a significant partnership
- Raising children and caring for others
- Starting a career
- Making time commitments to their families of origin and to their newly created families

Some scholars also define young adulthood as the point at which young persons become functioning members of the community, demonstrated by obtaining gainful employment, developing their own social networks, and establishing independent housing (Halpern, 1996). From a psychosocial perspective, this period is seen as a time of progressive movement out of an individualized and egocentric sense of self and into greater connection with significant others. Social role transitions in young adulthood are summarized in Exhibit 7.1.

Timing of these transitions and psychological readiness for adopting adult roles are important factors in the individual's life course trajectory. However, research indicates that individual variation in the timing and sequence of transitions—when

EXHIBIT 7.1 Social Role Transitions in Young Adulthood

- Leaving home
- Gaining financial independence
- Gaining independence in decision making
- Pursuing an education or vocational skills
- Making a partnership commitment
- Becoming a parent
- Renegotiating relationships with parents
- Engaging with the community and the wider social world

and in what order the individual leaves home, starts a career, and forms a family, for example—does not have large-scale effects on the individual's eventual socioeconomic status (Marini, 1989). These findings contradict the popular notion that people who don't "grow up" on schedule will never "amount to much."

Nevertheless, young adulthood is a challenging and exciting time in life. Young people are confronted with new opportunities and the accompanying stressors associated with finances, occupational planning, educational pursuits, development of significant relationship, and new family roles (Havighurst, 1972). Kenneth Keniston, an eminent developmental scholar writing in the late 1960s, during an era of student activism and bold social expression, described young adulthood as a time of struggle and alienation between an individual and society (Keniston, 1966). Young adulthood remains a period of intrapersonal and interpersonal questing as well as a period of critiquing and questioning of social norms. Young persons grapple with decisions across several polarities: independence versus relatedness, family versus work, care for self versus care for others, individual pursuits versus social obligations.

Theoretical Approaches to Young Adulthood

There are no specific theories of young adulthood. However, two prominent developmental theories, promulgated by Erik Erikson and Daniel Levinson, specifically address this life course phase.

Erikson's Psychosocial Theory

Erik Erikson's psychosocial theoretical framework is probably one of the most universally known approaches to understanding life course development. Young adulthood is one of Erikson's original eight stages of psychosocial development (refer back to Exhibit 3.6). Erikson described it as the time when individuals move from the identity fragmentation, confusion, and exploration of adolescence into more intimate engagement with significant others (Erikson, 1968, 1978).

How is the capacity for intimacy affected by earlier social relationships?

Individuals who successfully resolve the crisis of intimacy versus isolation are able to achieve the virtue of love. An unsuccessful effort at this stage may lead the young adult to feel alienated, disconnected, and alone. A fear that exists at the core of this crisis is that giving of oneself through a significant, committed relationship will result in a loss of self and diminution of one's constructed identity. To successfully pass through this stage, young adults must try out new relationships and attempt to find a way to connect with others in new ways while preserving their individuality (Erikson, 1978; Fowler, 1981).

In Jerome's case, he seems to be struggling with this problem-solving process. He is tentatively trying out new relationships yet unwilling to fully commit to any one. It appears that Jerome is still exploring and expanding his own individual pursuits, and enjoys both his alone time and social time with friends. Jerome is also very connected to his work, and the psychological attachment and time commitment to his job may prevent him from developing more intimate personal relationships.

Levinson's Theory of Life Structure

Daniel Levinson (1978) describes adulthood as a period of undulating stability and stress, signified by transitions that occur at specific chronological times during the life course. He initially developed his theory based on interviews with men about their adult experiences; later he included women in the research (1996). From his research he developed the concept of **life structure,** which he described as the outcome resulting from specific decisions and choices made along the life course in such areas as relationships, occupation, and childbearing. He considered the ages of 17 to 33 to be the "novice phase" of adulthood. The transition into young adulthood, which occurs during the ages of 17 to 22, includes the tasks of leaving adolescence and making preliminary decisions about relationships, career, and belief systems; the transition out of this phase, which occurs about the age of 30, marks significant changes in life structure and life course trajectory.

During the novice phase, young persons' personality continues to develop, and they prepare to differentiate (emotionally, geographically, financially) from their families of origin (Levinson, 1978). The transition to adulthood takes hold primarily in two domains: work and relationships. Levinson suggested that it may take up to 15 years for some individuals to resolve the transition to adulthood and to construct a stable adult life structure.

Building on Levinson's concepts, others have noted that cultural and societal factors affect life structure choices during young adulthood by constraining or facilitating opportunities (Newman & Newman, 1995). For example, socioeconomic status, parental expectations, availability of and interactions with adult role models, neighborhood conditions, and community and peer group pressures may all contribute to a young person's decisions about whether to marry early, get a job before pursuing a college education or advanced training, or delay childbearing. Social factors may directly or indirectly limit a young person's access to alternative choices, thereby rigidifying a young person's life structure.

All three of the case studies at the beginning of the chapter reveal decision making that will affect life structure. Ben is currently struggling with what he perceives his parents' expectations to be (for him to move home to be with his family after completing his education) and his own desires to maintain the independent lifestyle he has constructed for himself. Jerome sees his friends who have children as struggling with pressures to make ends meet, and decides to put his own family plans on hold. And Carla may find herself curtailing some of her career aspirations in order to fulfill her familial obligations and responsibilities as a new parent. Especially in young adulthood, life structures are in constant motion, changing with time and evolving as new life circumstances unfold.

Decisions made during the young adulthood transition, such as forgoing postsecondary education or delaying childbearing, may not accurately or completely represent a young person's desired life structure or goals. Social workers need to explore goal priorities and the resources and obstacles that will help or hinder the individual in achieving these goals. Social workers are also often called on to help young adults negotiate conflicting, incompatible, or competing life roles throughout this novice phase, such as renegotiating family and work responsibilities as parenthood approaches.

Arnett's "Emerging" Adulthood

What historical trends are producing "emerging adulthood"?

A number of prominent developmental scholars who have written about the stages of adolescence and young adulthood have described phenomena called "prolonged adolescence" and "psychosocial moratorium," which represent an experimentation phase of young adulthood (Arnett, 2000; Erikson, 1968; Sheehy, 1995). Jeffrey Jensen Arnett has gone one step further, defining a phase he terms **emerging adulthood** in some detail. He describes emerging adulthood as a developmental phase distinct from both adolescence and young adulthood, occurring between the ages of 18 and 25 in industrialized societies (Arnett, 2000, p. 470). There is considerable variation in personal journeys from emerging adulthood into young adulthood, but most individuals make the transition by age 30 (Arnett, 2000). Arnett conceptualized this new phase of life based on research showing that a majority of young persons aged 18 to 25 believe they have not yet reached adulthood and that a majority of people in their 30s do agree they have reached adulthood.

According to Arnett, emerging adulthood is a period of prolonged exploration of social and economic roles. Emerging adults try out new experiences related to love, work, financial responsibilities, and educational interests without committing to any specific lasting plan. The social role experimentation of adolescence becomes further refined, more focused, and more intense, although commitment to adult roles is not yet solidified. Arnett explains this adulthood transition using an organizing framework that includes cognitive, emotional, behavioral, and role transition elements (Arnett & Taber, 1994).

Most young persons in emerging adulthood are in education, training, or apprenticeship programs working toward an occupation; most individuals in their 30s have established a more solid career path and are moving through occupational transitions (e.g., promotion to leadership positions and recognition for significant accomplishments). Studies do show more occupational instability during the ages 18 to 25 as compared to age 30 (Rindfuss, Cooksey, & Sutterlin, 1999).

Although marriage has traditionally been cited as a salient marker in the adulthood transition, current research shows that marriage has not retained its high status as the critical benchmark of adulthood. Today, independent responsibility for decision making and finances seems to be more significant in marking this transition than marriage is (Arnett, 1998). Overall, the emphasis in emerging adulthood is on trying out new roles without the pressure of making any particular commitment. The transition, then, from *emerging* adulthood into *young* adulthood is marked by solidifying role commitments.

Residential stability and mobility is another theme of this transition. Emerging adults in their early 20s may find themselves at various times living with family, living on their own in independent housing arrangements yet relying on parents for instrumental support, and living with a significant partner or friends. Indeed, residential instability and mobility is typically at its height in the mid-20s (Rindfuss et al., 1999). Thus, a traditional definition of the separation-individuation process may not be appropriately applied to emerging adulthood. True "separation" from the family of origin may appear only toward the end of young adulthood or, perhaps for some, during the transition to middle adulthood.

Ben's college experience exemplifies these transitions. It allowed him to test his interests through campus activities and engagements, which helped direct him into more focused relationships and educational pursuits. He has tried out a new geographical environment. However, Ben has still not emerged in the occupational world as a solid employee, as he is still in the process of obtaining his graduate degree. He demonstrates more refined focus and commitment, yet not strong or stable roots.

Demographic changes over the past several decades, such as delayed marriage and childbearing, have made young adulthood a significant developmental period filled with complex changes and possibilities (Arnett, 2000; Sheehy, 1995). Arnett's new theoretical perspective accounts for the prolongation of role experimentation and exploration during young adulthood within work, educational, relationship, family, and community domains. It also provides a framework for understanding the ebb and flow of a young person's journey toward increased stability. Endorsing the inevitability and normalcy of an experimental phase is important. Traditional models of human development that rely heavily on such criteria as enduring independent residence, stable employment, and new family formation may need to be revisited and updated in coming decades to expand on Arnett's insights.

How do culture and socioeconomic status affect the transition to adulthood?

Cultural Variations. Another advantage of the new theory of emerging adulthood is that it recognizes diversity. Individual routes of development (the timing and sequence of transitions) are contingent on socialization processes experienced within family, peer groups, school, and community. Specifically, environmental opportunities, expressed community attitudes, and family expectations may all influence the timing and sequencing of transitions during emerging adulthood. Socially constructed gauges of adulthood—such as stable and independent residence, completion of education, entry into a career path, and marriage or significant partnership—hold varying importance across families and culture.

For some young persons, decisions may be heavily weighted toward maintaining family equilibrium. For example, some may choose not to move out of the family home and establish their own residence in order to honor the family's expectation that children will continue to live with their parents, perhaps even into their 30s. This is a reality that Ben faces. For others, successful adult development may be defined through the lens of pragmatism; a young person may be expected to make decisions based on immediate, short-term, utilitarian outcomes. For example, they may be expected to enter the labor force and establish a career in order to care for a new family and release the family of origin from burden.

Culture and gender are significant influences on roles and expectations (Arnett & Taber, 1994). There may be different family expectations about what it means to be a "good daughter" or "good son," and these expectations may be consistent or inconsistent with socially prescribed gender roles, potentially creating competing role demands. For example, a young woman may internalize her family's expectations of going to college and having a career while at the same time being aware of her family's expectations that her brothers will go directly into a job to help support the family and her college expenses. In addition, this woman may internalize society's message that women can "do it all"—have a family and career and yet see her friends putting priority on having a family and raising children. As a result, she may feel compelled to succeed in college and a career to make good on the privilege that her brothers did not have while at the same time feeling anxious about putting a career over creating a new family of her own. Social norms may sanction the postponement of traditional adult roles (such as marriage) or may promote marriage and childbearing in adolescence. In addition, some environments may offer limited education and occupational opportunities. Carla seems to be struggling to uphold several Latina social norms, as seen through her emotional and financial commitments to her immediate and extended family, efforts to maintain a meaningful connection to her church, and creation of a family of her own. However, the multiple role demands experienced are considerable, as her own personal goals of maintaining a professional identity, being a good wife, and giving back to the community compete for Carla's time and emotional energy.

Economic structures also contribute to variations in transitions during emerging adulthood. An individual who grew up in a family with limited financial resources or who is making important transitions during an economic downturn has less time for lengthy exploration than others do and is encouraged to make an occupational commitment as soon as possible. Indeed, research shows that childhood socioeconomic status is an important mediating factor in young adult transitions (Smyer, Gatz, Simi, & Pedersen, 1998). Individuals with greater financial stability often have more paths to choose from and may have more resources to negotiate the stressors associated with this developmental period. In counseling Jerome, this may be a factor to investigate.

Multigenerational Concerns. In today's society, young persons are increasingly becoming primary caretakers for elderly family members. Such responsibilities can dramatically affect a young adult's developing life structure. Family life, relationships, and career may all be affected (Dellmann-Jenkins, Blankemeyer, & Pinkard, 2001, p. 1). The demographic trend of delaying childbearing, with an increase of first births for women in their 30s and 40s and a decrease of first births to women in their 20s (Ashford, LeCroy, & Lortie, 2001), suggests that young adults are also likely to face new and significant role challenges as primary caretakers for their own aging parents.

The concern is that young adults will face a substantial caregiving burden, trying to help their aging parents with later-in-life struggles while nurturing their own first children. We might see a shorter period of "emerging adulthood" for many people, which would mean that they have less opportunity to explore, to gain a sense of independence, and to form new families themselves. There may be less support for the notion of giving young people time to get on their feet and establish a satisfactory independent adulthood. In addition, young adults may increasingly experience the emotional responsibilities of supporting late-in-life divorcing parents or parents deciding to go back to school. Carla and her husband are clearly facing these multigenerational role demands as they become the main social support for Jan at the same time that they are trying to get ahead in their careers and prepare for their new baby. Luckily, Carla and her husband have the financial resources and an adequate support network themselves (Carla's father, some extended family, and their church) to help with logistical problem solving, such as finding day care, and to help them deal effectively with the emotional stressors of these role demands.

Physical Functioning in Young Adulthood

Physical functioning is typically at its height during early adulthood. But as young adults enter their 30s, an increased awareness of physical changes—changes in vision, endurance, metabolism, and muscle strength—is common (e.g., Ashford et al., 2001). With new role responsibilities in family and career, young adults may also spend less time in exercise and sports activities than during adolescence and pay less attention to their physical health. However, many young adults make an effort to maintain or improve their physical health, committing to new exercise regimens (such as kickboxing or spinning) and participating in wellness classes (such as yoga or meditation). They may choose to get more actively involved in community recreational leagues in such sports as hockey, soccer, racquetball, and ultimate Frisbee. Sometimes physical activities are combined with participation in social causes, such as Race for the Cure runs, AIDS walks, or organized bike rides.

Behavioral risks to health in emerging and young adulthood may include unprotected sex. The potential for STDs or HIV is related to frequent sexual experimentation, substance use (particularly binge drinking), and smoking or use of other tobacco products—although the age group with the highest number of cigarette smokers is adolescents ages 12 to 17, according to the National Cancer Institute (2002).

Data from the U.S. Department of Health and Human Services National Household Survey on Drug Abuse showed a 13% increase in hospital emergency intakes related to drugs or alcohol for young adults ages 18 to 25 compared to the adolescent group (data collected from years 1999-2000). Older age cohorts did not show any appreciable increase in drug-related emergency room visits during the same time period. Interestingly, substance abuse treatment facilities survey data (1991-1998) from the Uniform Facility Data Set showed an increase in clients under age 18 who were admitted for substance abuse treatment and an increase in clients over age 35, but a decrease in clients ages 25 to 34 (Substance Abuse and Mental Health Services Administration [SAMHSA], 2000). Combined, the data seem to indicate that young adults are at high risk for accidents and related health injuries associated with drug use but are less represented in substance abuse treatment facilities than other age groups.

Other health concerns include Type I diabetes ("juvenile diabetes"), typically diagnosed in children and young adults. Although this type of diabetes is less prevalent than Type II (diagnosed in older adults), young adults do have a risk of getting Type I diabetes in their 20s. Adults who are diagnosed with diabetes will have to adjust to lifestyle changes, such as more consistent exercise, modified diets, and monitoring of blood sugar levels.

Data from the American Cancer Society show that breast cancer rates for women ages 20 to 39 have not changed significantly over the past decade. Although women under age 40 are not usually at high risk for breast cancer, young women should have an understanding of the signs, symptoms, and risk factors associated with breast cancer and be vigilant of their own health as they age into middle adulthood.

In working with young adults who do have a health-related illness, social workers will want to assess the client's relationship to the illness and evaluate how the treatments are affecting the psychosocial developmental tasks of young adulthood (Dunbar, Mueller, Medina, & Wolf, 1998). For example, an illness may increase a young person's dependence on others at a time when independence from parents is valued, individuals may have concerns about finding a mate, societal stigma associated with the illness may be intense at a time when the individual is seeking more meaningful community engagements, and adjustment to the possibilities of career or parenthood delays may be difficult.

How does infertility alter the young adult phase of the life course?

In addition, young adult partners who struggle with infertility problems may have to confront disappointment from family members and adjust to feelings of unfulfilled social and family expectations. Costs of treatment may be prohibitive, and couples may experience a sense of alienation from peers who are moving rapidly into parenthood and child rearing.

The Psychological Self

Young adulthood is a time when an individual continues to explore personal identity and his or her relationship to the world. Cognition, spirituality, and identity are intertwined aspects of this process.

Cognitive Development

Psychosocial development will depend on cognitive and moral development, which are parallel processes (Fowler, 1981). Young adulthood is a time when individuals expand, refine, and challenge existing belief systems, and the college environment is especially fertile ground for such broadening experiences (Perry, 1994). Late adolescents and young adults are also entering Piaget's formal operations stage, during which they begin to develop the cognitive ability to apply abstract principles to enhance problem solving and to reflect on thought processes (refer back to Exhibit 3.4 for an overview of Piaget's stages of cognitive development). These more complex cognitive capabilities, combined with a greater awareness of personal feelings, characterize cognitive development in young adulthood (Labouvie-Vief, 1986).

The abstract reasoning capabilities of adulthood and the awareness of subjective feelings can be applied to life experiences in ways that help individuals negotiate life transitions, new roles, stressors, and challenges (Labouvie-Vief, 1986; Schaie, 1982). You might think of the development in cognitive processing from adolescence to young adulthood as a gradual switch from obtaining information to using that information in more applied ways (Arnett & Taber, 1994). Young adults are better able to see things from multiple viewpoints and from various perspectives than adolescents are.

With increasing cognitive flexibility, young adults begin to solidify their own values and beliefs. They may opt to retain certain traditions and values from their family of origin while letting go of others in order to make room for new ones. Ben is going through some of this tension as he prepares to confront his parents' traditional expectations. In the past, Ben dealt with his feeling that he did not fit in by removing himself geographically from the source of the problem. Through his college years, he has had more freedom psychologically, emotionally, and socially to find his niche, and is now at a point where he is trying to make sense of it all. His challenge is to reconcile the knowledge he has gained about himself (his sexual identity, political beliefs, career aspirations, geographic preferences) with the realities of his family ties. He is ready to revisit what he had let go of in its entirety at an earlier time, armed with new ideologies and values of his own.

During this sorting out process, young adults are also defining what community means to them and what their place in the larger societal context might be like. Individuals begin establishing memberships in and attachments to select social, service, recreational, and faith communities. Research indicates that religious beliefs, in particular, are reevaluated and critically examined in young adulthood, with individuals sorting out beliefs and values they desire to hold onto and those they choose to discard (Hoge, Johnson, & Luidens, 1993). However, there is a danger that discarded family beliefs may not be replaced with new meaningful beliefs (Arnett, 2000). Many emerging adults view the world as cold and disheartening and are somewhat cynical about the future. With this common pitfall in mind, we can take comfort from Arnett's finding that nearly all the 18- to 24-year-olds who participated in his study believed that they would ultimately achieve their goals at some point in the future (Arnett, 2000).

In terms of moral development, Lawrence Kohlberg (cited in Fowler, 1981) categorized individuals aged 16 and older as fitting into the postconventional stage, which has these characteristics (refer back to Exhibit 4.1 for an overview of Kohlberg's stages of moral reasoning):

- Greater independence in moral decision making
- More complex contemplation of ethical principles
- Development of a "moral conscience"
- Move from seeking social approval through conformity to redefining and revising values and selecting behaviors that match those values

- Recognition of larger systems and appreciation for community
- Understanding that social rules are relativistic, rather than rigid and prescribed

How does continued moral development affect the capacity for human agency in making choices?

Young adults begin to combine the principle of utility and production with the principle of equality, coming to the realization that individual or group gain should not be at the detriment of other individuals or social groups.

Kohlberg's research indicates that people do not progress in a straight line through the stages of moral development. Late adolescents and young adults may regress to conventional moral reasoning as they begin the process of critical reflection. In any case, successful resolution of the adolescent identity crisis, separation from home, and the willingness and ability to take responsibility for others are necessary, but not sufficient, conditions for postconventional moral development (Fowler, 1981).

Spiritual Development

As mentioned earlier, young adulthood is a time when individuals explore and refine their belief systems. Part of that process is development of **spirituality,** a focus on that which gives meaning, purpose, and direction to one's life. Spirituality manifests itself through one's ethical obligations and behavioral commitment to values and ideologies. It is a way of integrating values relating to self, other people, the community, and a "higher being" or "ultimate reality" (Hodge, 2001). Spirituality has been found to be associated with successful marriage (Kaslow & Robison, 1996), considerate and responsible interpersonal relations (Ellison, 1992), and positive self-esteem (Ellison, 1993).

Spirituality develops in three dimensions (Hodge, 2001):

1. *Cognition.* Beliefs, values, perceptions, meaning related to work, love, life
2. *Affect.* Sense of connection and support; attachment and bonding experiences; psychological attachment to work, love, life
3. *Behavior.* Practices, rituals, behavioral experiences

Generally, consistency across all three dimensions is necessary for a vigorous spiritual life. For Carla, for example, it is not enough just to attend church (behavior) or just to subscribe to a defined belief set (cognition); she also needs to feel that she is "making a difference" through her church service projects (affect).

Research has shown that religious behavioral practices are correlated with life course stages. One study found that religiosity scores (reflecting beliefs, practices, and personal meaning) were higher for a group of young adults (ages 18-25) than for a group of adolescents (ages 14-17) (Glover, 1996), suggesting a growing spiritual belief system with age. Individuals making the transition from adolescence into young adulthood seem to place a particularly high value on spirituality. In addition, religious participation has been found to increase with age, even within the young adulthood stage (Gallup & Lindsay, 1999; Stolzenberg, Blair-Loy, & Waite, 1995).

In an attempt to understand the development of spirituality, James W. Fowler (1981) articulated a theory of six stages of faith development. Fowler's research suggested that two of these stages of faith development occur primarily in childhood and two others occur primarily during late adolescence and young adulthood. Fowler's stages are very closely linked with the cognitive and moral development paradigms of Piaget and Kohlberg. Adolescents are typically in a stage characterized by **synthetic-conventional faith,** during which faith is rooted in external authority. Individuals aged 17 to 22 usually begin the transition to **individuative-reflective faith,** a stage when the person begins to let go of the idea of external authority and looks for authority within the self (Fowler, 1981). During this time, young adults establish their own belief system and evaluate personal values, exploring how those values fit with the various social institutions, groups, and individuals with whom they interact.

The transition from synthetic-conventional faith to individuative-reflective faith usually occurs in the early to mid-20s, although it may occur in the 30s and 40s, or may never occur at all (Fowler, 1981). An individual's faith development depends on his or her early attachments to other people, which serve as templates for understanding one's connection to more abstract relationships and help shape them. Faith growth, therefore, is heavily related to cognitive, interpersonal, and identity development.

The process also depends on crises confronted in the 20s and 30s; challenges and conflict are critical for change and growth in faith. In one study, young adult women who were HIV-positive were interviewed in order to explore coping strategies, women's experiences of living with the diagnosis, and life transformations or changes (Dunbar et al., 1998). The majority of women discussed the spiritual dimensions activated by their illness, such as renewing relationships, developing a new understanding of the self, experiencing heightened connections with nature and higher powers, and finding new meaning in the mundane. The interviews revealed several themes related to spiritual growth, including "reckoning with death," which led to the will to continue living and renewed "life affirmation"; finding new meaning in life; developing a positive sense of self; and achieving a "redefinition of relationships." These young women found new meaning and purpose in their lives, which gave them renewed opportunities for social connection (Dunbar et al., 1998).

Identity Development

Identity development is generally associated with adolescence and is often seen as a discrete developmental marker, rather than as a process spanning all stages of the life course. However, identity development—how one thinks about and relates to oneself in the realms of love, work, and ideologies—continues well into adulthood. Ongoing identity development is necessary to make adult commitments possible, to allow individuals to abandon the insular self, and to embrace connection with important others. In addition, continuing identity development is an important part of young adults' efforts to define their life's direction (Glover, 1996).

The classic work of James Marcia (1966) defined categories of identity formation in terms of level of exploration and commitment to life values, beliefs, and goals (as discussed in Chapter 6) as follows:

- Diffused (no exploration; no commitment)
- Foreclosed (no exploration; commitment)
- Moratorium (exploration; no commitment)
- Achievement (exploration; commitment)

Marcia (1993) has stated that people revisit and redefine their commitments as they age. As a result, identity is not static, but dynamic, open, and flexible.

Research exploring this notion that identity formation is a process that continues deep into adulthood shows several interesting outcomes. In one study the researchers interviewed women and men between the ages of 27 and 36 to explore the process of commitment in five domains of identity: religious beliefs, political ideology, occupational career, intimate relationships, and lifestyle (Pulkkinen & Kokko, 2000). Results showed that men and women differed in their overall commitment to an identity at age 27. Women were more likely to be classified in Marcia's "foreclosed" identity status, and men were more likely to be classified in the "diffused" identity status. However, these gender differences diminished with age, and by age 36, foreclosed and achieved identity statuses were more prevalent than diffused or moratorium statuses for both men and women. This trend of increasing commitment with age held constant across all domains except political ideology, which showed increased diffusion with age. Also, across ages, women were more likely than men to be classified in the achieved identity status for intimate relationships; for men, the diffused identity status for intimate relationships was more prevalent at age 27 as compared to age 36.

The young adult who is exploring and expanding identity experiences tension between independence and self-sufficiency on one hand and a need for connection with others and reliance on a greater whole on the other. Young adults are often challenged to find comfort in connections that require a loosening of self-reliant tendencies. Some suggest that the transition into adulthood is signified by increased self-control while simultaneously submitting to the social conventions, structure, and order of the larger community.

Another study of the development of identity well into adulthood used a sample of women in their 20s (Elliott, 1996). The researchers found that the transition into young adulthood excites new definitions of identity and one's place in society, leading to potential changes in self-esteem and psychological self-evaluations. Although self-esteem tends to remain stable in young adulthood, several factors appeared to influence self-esteem in a positive or negative direction:

- Marriage may have a positive effect on self-esteem if it strengthens a young adult's economic stability and social connectedness.
- Parenthood is likely to have a negative effect if the role change associated with this life event significantly increases stresses and compromises financial stability.
- Receiving welfare is likely to decrease a young woman's self-esteem over time.
- Employment may mitigate the negative effects brought about by the transition into parenthood.

Employment tends to expand one's self-construct and identity and can offer a new parent additional social support as well as a supplemental source of validation. However, the extent to which employment will operate as a stress buffer is contingent on the occupational context and conditions. Certainly, good-quality jobs with benefits may enhance, and certainly are unlikely to harm, a woman's psychological well-being (Elliott, 1996). However, dead-end, low-paying jobs do not help with the stresses of parenthood and have the potential to undermine a young woman's self-esteem.

Social workers need to be aware of how peoples' work life impinges on their development of identity. In our case example, Carla is beginning the process of exploring family benefits provided by her place of employment as she prepares for the new baby. She knows that some of her friends work in environments that have on-site day care, but she does not think her company has that service. She is aware that her work is central to her identity, but she also recognizes that she and her husband must find a way to balance their commitments to work and family.

Social Development and Social Functioning

What factors put individuals at risk when making the transition to adulthood?

There are, of course, many paths to early adulthood, and not all arrive at this phase of the life course with equal resources for further social role development. This section looks at some of the special challenges faced by young adults as they negotiate new social roles, and the impact on social functioning in young adulthood—particularly in regard to interpersonal relationships and work attachment.

Research has shown that problem behavior in young adults is linked to challenges experienced in negotiating new social roles (Hammer & Vaglum, 1990; Kandel, Davies, Karus, & Yamaguchi, 1986; Sampson & Laub, 1990). For example, although Jerome seems to be maintaining a sense of well-being currently through his connection to the work world, family members, and friends, the shift he is experiencing in becoming a responsible caregiver for his family and taking on financial independence, while still wanting to preserve the freedom of adolescent exploration without commitment, puts Jerome in a vulnerable period of transition. One behavioral expression of this transitional stress is his increased frequency of drinking and smoking marijuana with his friends. However, it is difficult to definitively capture the direction of influence. For example, does prior "deviant" behavior create difficulties in committing to work, or does a failure in finding a good job lead to problematic behaviors? Poor social functioning in young adulthood appears to be linked to a variety of difficulties in making the transition to new roles (Ronka & Pulkkinen, 1995):

- Problems in school and family in adolescence lead to social functioning problems in young adulthood.
- Unstable employment for males is associated with strained relationships, criminality, and substance abuse.
- Men who have many behavioral problems in young adulthood can be differentiated from young adult males who do not exhibit behavioral problems by several childhood factors, such as aggressive history, problems in school and family, and lack of formal educational attainment.

The transition to young adulthood from the secondary school environment can be challenging, particularly for students with learning disabilities. They drop out of high school at a higher rate than students without these challenges. Results from a qualitative study suggest some reasons why (Lichtenstein, 1993): many students with learning disabilities worked while in high school, often because employment provided an environment where they could gain control over decision making, exercise authority, garner support, and increase self-esteem—outcomes that such students were not able to experience in the traditional educational system.

In this study, working during the high school years was related to later employment but was also related to the risk of dropping out of high school altogether before graduation. These findings suggest a need for a well-tailored individual education plan (IEP) for each learning-disabled youth that outlines how that person can best make the transition out of high school and which postschool opportunities might be appropriate, as well as better transitioning services and active follow-up. In addition, the parents of students with learning disabilities need to be educated on their rights, and parent advocacy efforts within the school need to be strengthened (Lichtenstein, 1993).

Another special population that is likely to face challenges in making the transition into young adulthood is young persons with more severe emotional difficulties. They often have trouble forming meaningful interpersonal relationships, maintaining employment, managing physical health needs, and gaining financial independence. Many have tenuous experience with the labor market, much less strong connections to work. Often their families do not have sufficient resources to help them make the transition from high school, potentially delaying the youth's opportunity to live independently. Many of these young persons do not have a stable support network, and as a result, they are at higher than usual risk for homelessness (Davis & Vander Stoep, 1997).

Another group of youth at risk in the transition from late adolescence to early adulthood are those with poor relationships with their parents. Emotional intimacy in the parent-child relationship has been found to be important in the development of self-esteem, with the benefits lasting into adulthood. However, engaging and satisfying employment seems to mediate a poor parent-child relationship, increasing the youth's well-being (Roberts & Bengston, 1993).

This group of youth is often overlooked, but they have a great need for developmentally appropriate and culturally sensitive supportive services as they make the transition into young adulthood. Social workers should examine the ways in which formal services facilitate the transition to adulthood for youths who have no informal supports. Certainly, terminating services to these youths at the age of majority, without making arrangements for them to receive adult services, will undermine the efforts made during the youth's adolescence and put these individuals at a disadvantage as young adults (Davis & Vander Stoep, 1997).

Relationship Development in Young Adulthood

Erikson's concept of intimacy, which relies on connection with a significant partner, is at the core of relationship development during early adulthood. Typically, young adults develop sustained commitments to others and come to recognize a responsibility for others' well-being. This developmental process may manifest as thoughtful awareness in the early years, changing to more active behavioral commitment in later years—for example, caring for children or aging parents, getting involved in the community, and taking on social obligations.

Intimacy, which can be defined as a sense of warmth or closeness, has three components: interdependence with another person, self-disclosure, and affection (Perlman & Fehr, 1987). It may take the form of cognitive/intellectual intimacy, emotional intimacy, sexual intimacy, physical intimacy apart from a sexual relationship, and spiritual intimacy. When reflecting on intimate relations, some people talk about finding a "soul

EXHIBIT 7.2
Tasks in Fostering Intimacy

- Effectively negotiating expectations for the relationship
- Negotiating roles and responsibilities
- Making compromises
- Prioritizing and upholding values
- Deciding how much to share of oneself
- Identifying and meeting individual needs
- Identifying and meeting partnership needs
- Renegotiating identity
- Developing trust and security
- Allowing for reciprocal communication
- Making time commitments to partner
- Effectively resolving conflict and solving problems
- Demonstrating respect, support, and care

mate"; feeling intensely connected; sharing values, beliefs, and philosophical inquiries; and feeling as though the relationship has strong direction and purpose.

Establishing intimacy is a multifaceted process. Exhibit 7.2 lists some of the tasks involved in fostering an intimate relationship with someone. The ability to perform these tasks depends not only on personal abilities but also on external factors, such as the individual's family background. Research has found several family factors in adolescence to be important in the ability to develop intimate relationships during young adulthood: (a) a positive relationship with the mother (e.g., effective, clear communication with her, as well as mutual respect and empathy), and (b) adaptability of the family unit (e.g., good habits of conflict resolution and appropriate discipline) (Robinson, 2000). The young adult's ability to develop intimate relationships also depends on favorable environmental conditions, such as having adequate resources to accommodate stressors, handle life responsibilities, and deal effectively with the multiple life transitions of this developmental stage.

An individual's family relationships and attachment to the family unit as a whole are transformed during young adulthood. The family's life cycle stage and the psychosocial development of individual members will influence the nature of family relationships in young adulthood. Generally, though, young adults may see parents, siblings, and relatives less frequently as work, romantic attachments, and new family responsibilities take precedence. With greater independence, geographic distance may also preclude more visits. Thus, time spent together may center around holiday celebrations. As traditional family roles evolve, young adults may take more active responsibility for holiday preparations. They may find themselves wanting to spend less time with old friends and more time with family. As young adults have children, holiday activities and family interactions may increasingly focus on the new generation.

Romantic Relationships. Romantic relationships are a key element in the development of intimacy during early adulthood. **Romantic love** has been described as a relationship that is sexually oriented, is "spontaneous and voluntary," and occurs between equal partners (Solomon, 1988). Satisfaction in romantic partnerships depends on finding a delicate balance between positive and negative interactions across time (Gottman, 1994).

In the United States, heterosexual romantic love has traditionally been considered a precursor to marriage. A recent trend in romantic relationships is to have sex earlier but marry later. By the mid-1990s, more than half of all marriages occurred after a period of cohabitation (Steinhauer, 1995). It is important to remember, however, that in many recent immigrant groups, marriage is arranged and not based on romantic courtship. There are many other variations in relationship development as well, represented by single-parent families, childless couples, gay/lesbian partnerships, couples who marry and choose to live apart to establish individual career tracks, and couples where partners are in different life stages (e.g., early adulthood and middle adulthood).

In the past, increasing education decreased women's likelihood of marrying, but recent data suggest a reversal of that trend. The cohort of women who recently graduated from college, both black and white, are likely to marry later than women of their cohort without a college education, but their rate of eventual marriage will be higher (Goldstein & Kenney, 2001). The researchers interpret this trend to indicate that marriage is increasingly becoming a choice only for the most educated members of society. Given the advantages of a two-earner family, this trend may contribute toward the widening economic gap in our society.

How does sexual orientation affect young adult development?

An increasing awareness of variation in relationships has prompted research into all sorts of romantic attachments. One focus is homosexual relationships. One study that identified three "scripts" in lesbian relationships helps to differentiate romantic attachment from other kinds of intimacy (Rose & Zand, 2000): (1) the "romance" script combines emotional intimacy and sexual attraction. It is characterized by an attenuated dating period and quick commitment to a relationship; (2) "friendship" is a script in which individuals fall in love and are emotionally committed, though sexual behaviors are not necessarily a part of the relationship. Research shows that this is the most common script among lesbians, emphasizing emotional intimacy over sexuality. Women have suggested that the ambiguity implicit in this script often makes defining the relationship difficult; (3) "sexually explicit" focuses on sexual attraction and leaves emotional intimacy at the periphery. This script is void of any direct expression of future commitment. These scripts are summarized in Exhibit 7.3.

Lesbian and gay partnering becomes more complex if the coming out process begins in early adulthood. The individuals involved have to negotiate through their parents' own emotional reactions and responses at the same time as the new

EXHIBIT 7.3
Lesbian Relationship Development

Script	Descriptor
Romance	Emotional and sexual attraction; quick commitment
Friendship	Emotional commitment; sexual behavior may or may not be part of relationship
Sexually Explicit	Sexual attraction is focal point; emotional intimacy secondary

Source: Adapted from Rose & Zand, 2000.

relationship is developing. One study found that lesbian and gay partners are less likely to identify family as a significant social support as compared to heterosexual couples (Kurdek & Schmitt, 1987). One possible reason is that siblings and other relatives may be forced to confront their own comfort, biases, and values associated with the young adult's relationship. If gay/lesbian couples decide to have children, their own parents will inevitably be forced to confront the homosexual identity in order to develop their grandparent role with the new child.

Even in families where "acceptance" has taken root, people in the family's social network may have limited understanding that is difficult to work through. Family members who thought they had come to terms with the young adult's homosexual identity may find themselves harboring anger, hurt, disappointment, or confusion about how the young person's life trajectory is affecting their own life trajectories.

Other complicating factors related to gay/lesbian relationship development can be connections with the larger community and with the gay/lesbian community itself. Current legal inequities—such as the lack of legal sanction for marriage-like partnerships, the associated lack of benefits (e.g., survivorship and inheritance rights and housing loans), and the lack of authority in decision making for gay/lesbian partners (in such matters as child custody and health care/medical procedures)—can cause additional external strain on new couples.

Regardless of the sexuality of young adult clients, social workers need to consider the client's partner when exploring intimacy issues (LaSala, 2001). These partners may be a valuable resource in matters relating to the partnership itself as well as relations with the family of origin. Social workers also need to assess the adequacy of a young adult's support system across multiple dimensions and to identify and respond to any perceived gaps. Although marriages and partnerships typically expand a young adult's social support network, this might not be the case for all individuals, and social workers should be cautious about making such assumptions.

Parenthood. Parenting is an interactive process, with reciprocal parent-child and child-parent influences (Maccoby, 2002). The multiple role transitions that mark entry into parenthood during young adulthood can be both exciting and challenging, as new familial interdependencies evolve. New social obligations and responsibilities associated with caretaking affect the relationship between the young adult partners and between the young adults and their parents.

Often, the nature of the partners' relationship before parenthood will determine how partners will manage the demands of these changing roles (Durkin, 1995). Adjustment to parenthood, and successful role reorganization, depends on five dimensions (Cowan, 1991):

1. Individual factors, such as how role changes affect one's sense of self
2. Quality of the partners' relationship (e.g., how the couple negotiates responsibilities, their decision-making capabilities)
3. Quality of the relationship between the young adults and their children
4. Quality of each partner's relationships with his/her family of origin
5. Quality of external relationships (e.g., school, work, community)

How partners negotiate the division of labor along gender lines also influences parenting and marital satisfaction. Much of the parenting literature has focused on the role strain mothers face in maintaining work commitments alongside new parenting responsibilities. Some new literature has focused on the more positive aspects of mothers' participation in the workforce (Zaslow & Emig, 1997). However, fatherhood and the positive impact of paternal parenting on both child well-being and on the father's own successful male adult development need further exploration.

Some evidence of paternal parenting styles was provided in a longitudinal study of father-child relationships based on interviews with 240 working-class families (Snarey, 1993). Results showed that 35% of fathers in the study were "not very active," 41% reported being "substantially involved," and 24% were "highly involved" in fatherhood activities. Data showed that fathers were more involved during childhood as compared to adolescence or infancy. Socioemotional support was the most common support that fathers provided during activities shared with their children, followed by physical/athletic support and intellectual/academic support.

As for mothers, the evidence suggests that maternal employment may have a positive influence on her sense of self, leading to better outcomes for her children. With these findings in mind, it becomes necessary to identify groups for whom employment opportunities may be limited. Parents of children with disabilities fall into this category. Research shows that 12% of children in the United States have at least one developmentally related functional limitation that requires special attention and care (Hogan & Msall, 2002). Parenting a child with a functional disability demands extra care, which may decrease a parent's opportunity to enter or continue participation in the labor market. One study suggested that two thirds of families with a child who has a functional limitation will experience significant changes in labor force participation (Hogan & Msall, 2002).

Low-income mothers are another group for whom maternal employment is significantly related to child well-being (Zaslow & Emig, 1997). Employment often creates child care difficulties. However, characteristics associated with positive parenting (e.g., the mother's ability to express warmth to the child, her lack of depressive symptoms, and the quality of her verbal interaction with the child) have been found to mediate the ill effects on child well-being that may arise in welfare-to-work programs, which sometimes leave low-income mothers with poor child care options (McGroder, Zaslow, Moore, Hair, & Ahluwalia, 2002). Other studies have found that parents who have more social support are better at parenting (Marshall, Noonan, McCartney, Marx, & Keefe, 2001).

Helping young adults to develop parenting efficacy may help them overcome environmental conditions and improve their children's well-being. One study compared the effects of increasing the mother's parenting efficacy in white families and black families characterized by a weak marriage and living in economically disadvantaged neighborhoods (Ardelt & Eccles, 2001). The black families showed greater benefits in the form of increased academic success for their children. Parenting efficacy also contributed more to positive child outcomes in black families with a compromised marriage than in black families where the marriage was strong and secure.

Mentoring. Although young adults seek out older adult mentors in work as they begin establishing themselves in new careers, young persons also often serve as mentors themselves. Serving as a mentor can help young adults move through the adulthood transition by facilitating new experiences and helping them to develop new roles that require "taking care of others" as opposed to "being taken care of" themselves. As young adults refine their ideologies, beliefs, and values, they form group affiliations consistent with their emerging identity, career, relationships, community, and religious and political views.

Some examples of current groups and mentoring programs young adults might get involved in include 20 Something, a gay/lesbian young adult social group; Young Democrats/Young Republicans political groups; YMCA/YWCA; and Big Brothers/Big Sisters youth mentoring programs. Service-related groups young adults may choose to become involved with include Junior Achievement, a not-for-profit organization that brings young adults together with elementary school students to teach children economic principles, and Streetwise Partners, where young adults help low-income and unemployed persons with job skills training. College students may also get actively involved in Habitat for Humanity projects or student associations such as the College Hispanic American Society, Campus Crusaders for Christ, and Association of Black Students, which spearhead philanthropic and community-integration activities.

Work and the Labor Market

The transition into the world of work is an important element of social development during early adulthood. As important as individual factors are in that transition, the changing labor market and structural shifts in the economy may have an even greater influence by shaping a young person's opportunities for finding and maintaining productive work. Work in industry and manufacturing has been diminishing for 4 decades now, and the number of jobs in the service sector has increased (Portes & Rumbaut, 2001). Manufacturing jobs once offered unskilled youth with relatively little education an opportunity for good wages, employment benefits, and job security. However, the service sector is divided between low-wage, temporary or part-time service jobs, and work opportunities that call for advanced, technical skills. Today there is a high labor market demand for low-wage, low-skill jobs as well as a high demand among employers for workers with more specialized and technical skills (Portes & Rumbaut, 2001).

How do factors such as gender, race, ethnicity, and disability affect transitions into the labor market?

The dilemma facing disadvantaged youth entering adulthood is vexing. Labor market attachment is not only the surest route to material well-being but also has been found to be significantly related to mental health and psychosocial well-being. One study looked at factors associated with well-being and adjustment between ages 16 and 21. The study found that experiences of unemployment were significantly associated with thoughts of suicide, substance abuse, and crime (Fergusson, Horwood, & Woodward, 2001). Benefits of work include increased self-esteem, increased social interaction, and external validation through social recognition.

Increasingly, therefore, youths' life trajectories will be determined by access to advanced education and then good jobs. Jerome, at age 20, realizes that society demands education. But right now he is not worried about having dropped out of college, and he enjoys his work. He feels as though he has plenty of time to go back. In addition, his uncle needs Jerome's help and is not encouraging Jerome to go back to school. Although Jerome's mother would like to see him complete his education someday, she believes that what he really needs right now is a steady job.

Immigration and Work. Alejandro Portes and Ruben G. Rumbaut (2001), in their timely book *Legacies: The Story of the Immigrant Second Generation,* based on results from the Children of Immigrants Longitudinal Study (CILS), note that the structural labor market change of the past few decades disproportionately affects immigrants, particularly youth in late adolescence who will be emerging into this new occupational landscape. "Increasing labor market inequality implies that to succeed socially and economically, children of immigrants today must cross, in the span of a few years, the educational gap that took descendents of Europeans several generations to bridge" (p. 58). An important finding from the CILS is the contrast in job selection between older and younger generations of immigrants. Today's young people are more likely to turn down "traditional immigrant jobs" that are seen as unfulfilling, in contrast to older immigrants who often felt compelled to take any job available in their youth without such questioning (Portes & Rumbaut, 2001).

Another study investigated how migration affects the earnings prospects of Latino men making the transition into young adulthood (Padilla & Jordan, 1997). Specifically, seeking work opportunities in more favorable socioeconomic environments during early adulthood was found to be associated with decreased likelihood of poverty in adulthood. Increased education and cognitive ability were also associated with a decreased likelihood of being in poverty during the transition into adulthood.

It is important for social workers to understand the social and economic conditions that immigrant youth face. This large and growing group, born from the surge in immigration of recent decades, faces special challenges as young adults under recent economic conditions.

Role Changes and Work. A number of other factors are related to the type of work young adults secure, and thus their occupational prestige and income earned later in life. Across race and gender, educational attainment has a strong effect. Marriage itself is not a significant predictor of occupational prestige or earnings for males or females. Women who marry between ages 24 and 26 usually have higher earnings than women who marry earlier; but for males, entry into marriage before age 24 was associated with higher earnings than marriage at later ages (Marini, 1989). Parenthood showed no association with occupational prestige for either sex but negatively affected the income of women. Family role changes (marriage, parenthood) occurring before work transitions appear to have no relationship with individual socioeconomic status (SES). However, experience in the work force positively affects occupation and earnings (Marini, 1989).

For the social worker, it would be important to examine to what extent culture affects educational and work-related opportunities and timing sequences. Social workers also need to explore with individuals the extent of role overload that may exist. For example, an additional effect of employment on low-income earners may be the added expense that occurs when work and family pressures collide. Exploring the unique costs and benefits of employment decisions for each individual, recognizing the larger family context, can be helpful. Social workers should also assess clients' coping strategies and ask clients for their perceptions about how identified stressors are affecting the individual and family.

Race and Work. The association of race with work attachment has already received some attention. Labor force connection tends to be weakest for black males who have little formal education and who lack work experience (Laseter, 1997). Of course, the economic restructuring of past decades has made good-quality jobs for young adults without specialized skills hard to come by. Other barriers for young black men include discrimination in hiring, absence of adult mentors in the community who might help socialize youth toward work roles, a disconnect from a good-paying job with benefits, diminished self-efficacy related to perceptions of constricted economic opportunities, hopelessness about finding quality jobs, and the presence of alternative informal and more prosperous economic options (e.g., drug dealing, gambling). All may decrease the youth's ability or motivation to pursue formal work opportunities. But that is not to say that young black men do not want to succeed in the world of work:

> Young black men want jobs and wages comparable to white young men, and their reluctance to take inferior jobs, despite less experience, lengthens their period of unemployment. They share middle-class values and aspirations. The problem is how to achieve those aspirations. (Laseter, 1997, p. 74)

Racism may be a factor in job prospects for young black males as well. Racism can directly tax individuals and families and can indirectly deplete their buffering resources and weaken solutions to managing direct stressors (Harrell, 2000). Stressors and resources change over the life course, however, and social workers need to be able to assess the ways in which individuals and families are able to adapt to such changes.

Although social workers need to understand the effects of oppressive living conditions and environmental stressors on all groups, they should be aware of the disproportionate number of African Americans living in such conditions. Regardless of SES, African American males have the lowest well-being scores of any group studied (white women and men, African American women and men) (Woody & Green, 2001). Their low scores are potentially explained by social conditions such as stigma, constrained economic opportunities, health-related discrepancies, and a perception of lack of control over their lives. It is dually important, however, for social workers to understand the range of diversity within the African American community along many social dimensions, including SES, in order to avoid perpetuating the stereotypes that further stigmatize this diverse group.

Risk Factors and Protective Factors in Young Adulthood

How can social workers help to provide protective factors for the adult transition?

A longitudinal study that followed a cohort of individuals born in 1955 from infancy to age 40 identified clusters of protective factors at significant points across the lifespan (see Exhibit 7.4) that are associated with successfully making the transition to adulthood (Werner & Smith, 2001). The researchers identified high-risk individuals and then determined the specific factors that influenced their positive

EXHIBIT 7.4
Common Core Protective Factors Predicting Adult Adaptation

	Individual Characteristics	Caregiving Context
Infancy	Autonomy; social competence Health status	Maternal competence Emotional support # of stressful events
Middle childhood	Academic proficiency Health status	Emotional support to child (extended family; mentor) # of stressful events
Adolescence	Self-efficacy Health status	Emotional support to child (peer relations; feelings about family) # of stressful events
Young adulthood	Temperament Health status	Emotional support (quality of partner, work, & community relationships) # of stressful events

Source: Adapted from Werner & Smith, 2001, pp. 161-163.

adaptation to adulthood at age 32. The protective factors included successful early social, language, and physical development; good problem-solving skills in middle childhood; educational and work expectations and plans by age 18; and social maturity and a sense of mastery and control in late adolescence. Family factors included stable maternal employment when the child was 2 to 10 years old, access to a variety of social support sources, and the child's sense of belonging within the family unit at age 18. Community factors included having access to nurturing, caring adults in one's community, including the presence of adult mentors, and having access to "enabling," as opposed to "entrapping," community niches (see Saleebey, 1996).

Risk factors that the researchers found to be associated with the transition to adulthood included low family income during infancy, poor reading achievement by age 10, problematic school behavior during adolescence, and adolescent health problems (Werner & Smith, 2001). For men, an excessive number of stressful events, living with an alcoholic or mentally ill father, and substance abuse contributed to problematic coping in early adulthood. For women, a sibling death in early childhood, living with an alcoholic or mentally ill father, and a conflicted relationship with the mother were significant risk factors to successful coping at age 32.

Knowledge of risk and protective factors related to the adulthood transition can help social workers assess young adult clients' current challenges, vulnerabilities, strengths, and potentials. Gaining an accurate understanding of the client's developmental history provides guidance to the social worker in formulating appropriate goals and intervention strategies. It is important to remember to check out your own assumptions of "risk" with clients in order to clarify the unique impact such experiences have on individual clients.

IMPLICATIONS FOR SOCIAL WORK PRACTICE

This discussion of young adulthood suggests several practice principles for social workers:

- Recognize that social roles during emerging adulthood may be different from those later in young adulthood.
- Explore cultural values, family expectations, attitudes toward gender roles, and environmental constraints/resources that may influence life structure decisions and opportunities when working with young adult clients.
- Assess specific work and family conditions as they pertain to young adult clients' psychological and social well-being; be aware of any caregiving roles young adults may be playing.
- Where appropriate, help young adults to master the tasks involved in developing intimate relationships.
- Where appropriate, assist young adults with concerns about differentiating from family of origin and do so in a culturally sensitive manner.
- Work with other professionals to advocate for policies that promote transitional planning and connect youth to the labor market, particularly for youth aging out of foster care placements, correction facilities, group home environments, or other formal residential mental health settings.
- Take the initiative to develop mentoring programs that build relations between young adults and younger or older generations.
- Take the initiative to develop parenting classes for first-time parents.

Key Terms

emerging adulthood
individuative-reflective faith
intimacy
life structure
romantic love
spirituality
synthetic-conventional faith

Active Learning

1. Identify one current social issue as portrayed in the media (e.g., housing, immigration policies, health care access or coverage or affordability, living wage) and explore how this social issue uniquely affects young adults.

2. Create your own theory of young adulthood. What are some of the important characteristics? What makes someone a young adult? What differentiates this stage from adolescence and middle adulthood? Start the process by answering the following question: "Do you consider yourself to be an adult?"

3. Choose one of the case studies at the beginning of the chapter (Jerome, Ben, Carla). Change the gender for that case without changing any other major demographic variable. Explore how your assumptions change about the individual's problems, challenges, and potential. Now choose a different case. Change the race or ethnicity for that case and again explore your assumptions. Finally, using the remaining case, change the SES and again explore how your assumptions change.

Web Resources

Network on Transitions to Adulthood

www.macfound.org/research/hcd/hcd_21.htm

Site presented by the John D. and Catherine T. MacArthur Foundation contains information on a network of researchers focusing on the early years of adulthood and brief summaries of major findings from recent research.

American Diabetes Association

www.diabetes.org/main/application/commercewf

Site presented by American Diabetes Association contains basic diabetes information, community resources, healthy living guides, news updates, and even a recipe of the day.

National Alliance of Breast Cancer Organizations

www.nabco.org

Site presented by the National Alliance of Breast Cancer Organizations contains resources list, support groups by zip code, and news updates.

National Gay and Lesbian Task Force

www.ngltf.org

Site presented by the National Gay and Lesbian Task Force contains information about the task force, news and views, special issues, state and local organizations, and special events.

Sloan Work and Family Research Network

www.bc.edu/bc_ort/avp/wfnetwork

Site presented by the Sloan Work and Family Research Network of Boston College contains a literature database, research newsletter, resources for teaching, research profiles, and work and family links.

Chapter 8

Middle Adulthood

Elizabeth D. Hutchison

CHAPTER 8

Middle Adulthood

Elizabeth D. Hutchison
Virginia Commonwealth University

How are increased longevity, coupled with a declining birthrate, altering the life course phase of middle adulthood?

What do social workers need to know about biological, psychological, social, and spiritual changes in middle adulthood?

What are the antecedent risk factors and protective factors that affect resilience in middle adulthood as well as the effects of midlife behavior on subsequent health and well-being?

Key Ideas

As you read this chapter, take note of these central ideas:

1. Increased life expectancy and a declining birthrate in the United States and other industrial countries are leading to a trend of "mass longevity" and a large cohort of adults in midlife; very recently, this trend has led to an intense research interest in middle adulthood.
2. Theories about middle adulthood propose that midlife adults are deeply involved in care and concern for the generations to come and that midlife is a time when individuals attempt to find balance in opposing aspects of their lives.
3. Most biological systems reach their peak in the mid-20s, and gradual declines begin after that; by age 50, biological change becomes physically noticeable in most people, particularly changes in physical appearance, mobility, the reproductive system, and in vulnerability to chronic disease.
4. Middle adulthood is the period of peak performance of four mental abilities: inductive reasoning, spatial orientation, vocabulary, and verbal memory. Perceptual speed and numerical ability decline in middle adulthood.

5. There is good evidence of both stability and change in personality in middle adulthood; perhaps the greatest change in personality in middle adulthood is a gender crossover in personality.
6. Theory and research suggest that humans have the potential for continuous spiritual growth across the life course, with midlife adults having the capacity to recognize many truths and become more oriented to service to others.
7. The most central roles in middle adulthood are related to family and paid work.

Case Study 8.1

William George, on the Streets of San Diego at 42

William George spent the first 12 years of his life in a small town in Indiana, the next 20 years in Chicago, and moved to San Diego 10 years ago to "start over." Many of William's childhood memories involve moving. William was the second of three children born to Harold and Wilma George, a Caucasian couple of uncertain Anglo heritage. He remembers his first 4 years as being "pretty good." His dad made a fairly good living working as a security guard, and his parents were making plans to buy a small house and move out of the trailer park. Those plans were put to rest when Harold was shot and killed during a break-in at work. Wilma found it very hard to manage without Harold. The family was on and off welfare several times, and they finally moved into the public housing project. Wilma was admitted to the state hospital on two occasions to be treated for depression. Sometimes William and his siblings lived at home with their mother, sometimes with their maternal grandmother, and sometimes with their mother's younger sister, Ruby, and her family. William remembers these times with Aunt Ruby as the happiest times of his childhood.

When William was 10, his mother remarried, and the family moved to Chicago in search of better jobs. This marriage was turbulent from the beginning, and William remembers a small apartment that seemed to close in on a family that often had no working adult, a family where screaming and hitting were regular forms of communication. After living in a small town all his life, William found the streets of Chicago overwhelming. School was no refuge. With all the moving around, turbulence at home, violence in the neighborhood, going to school hungry, and perhaps an undiagnosed learning disability, William fell hopelessly behind. It seemed to him that his teachers gave up on him long before he gave up on himself. When he

CASE STUDY 8.1

dropped out of school at age 16, he felt a great sense of relief to be free of the failure and humiliation that he had come to associate with school.

After he left school, William worked a variety of odd jobs until he was hired as a semiskilled laborer in a manufacturing plant. He was a good worker and held the same job until the company where he worked went out of business. He was 23 by this time, married, and the father of two young children. The job market was not good for a young man who had dropped out of high school, and William worked sporadically over the next few years. He became depressed about his inability to support his family, because he had promised himself that his children would never have to suffer the kind of financial setback that had so altered the course of his childhood. He began to join neighborhood friends in trips to the bar, later in experimentation with marijuana, and finally in a love affair with crack cocaine.

William's preoccupation with getting and using drugs led to conflicts with his wife, and she finally asked him to leave. William went to live with his sister, but she also asked him to leave after a few months. He began to live in abandoned buildings with a group of men he met on the streets. Sometimes they found day labor work, and other times they begged and stole to stay alive. Whenever they had money, they bought crack. From time to time, William's sister or brother would let him move in with them, but it never worked for very long.

When William was 32, his Aunt Ruby convinced him to go into a detoxification program and to move to San Diego to live with her when he completed the program. Things went well for a while, but after a few months, William found his crack use getting out of control again. Before long he had lost his job and moved out of Aunt Ruby's apartment to avoid causing her more pain.

For the past few years, William has made his home in a series of abandoned buildings or "abandominiums," as he and his friends call them. He often works day labor jobs with one of the labor pools, arriving early in the morning, getting an assignment for the day, and being paid at the end of the day. Although the pay is low, the work unstable, and the supervisors harsh, he likes to work this way, because he can get some control of his drug use by controlling how much money he has in his pocket at any time. He has developed several chronic health problems, but receives no medical assistance. He talks occasionally with you at the homeless shelter and with the local parish priest, particularly when he is worried about the health and safety of other "street people." He has begun to let both of you know about the hold crack has on him and about the despair behind his bantering. He is too ashamed to get in touch with members of his family.

Case Study 8.2

Robert Johnson, A First-Time Father at 44

Robert Johnson was born into a stable black working-class family. His father was a longtime laborer in the steel industry, with an income that allowed the family to maintain a middle-class lifestyle. Robert's mother was a full-time housewife. Robert currently lives about 2 miles from his parents and keeps in close touch with them and with his two younger sisters and their families. He is proud of and grateful for the type of upbringing he was provided by his hardworking parents.

Robert's father had the good fortune, as many other black male workers did, of getting into the relatively high-paying, unionized steel industry before it began to crumble in the mid-1950s. Drawing on the equity accumulated in the family's modest home, he was able to provide financial assistance for Robert to attend college. Robert was the first member of his family to attend college, and now he has undergraduate and law degrees from a prestigious university.

With a good education, strong earning potential, and a positive self-image, Robert worked steadily toward building the kind of independence that is characteristic of the American middle class. He set his career goals high: to become a partner in his respected law firm. Soon after beginning work at the law firm, Robert set about repaying his school loans. At the same time, he began building his own investment program for the future.

After living together for 3 years, Robert and Cindy Marsh, an interior decorator, felt financially secure enough to get married. Soon after they were married, they bought a house. Once the house was furnished and Robert became a partner in the law firm, Robert and Cindy began to plan to have children. They were excited about this prospect and confident that they would make excellent parents. As the months went by and Cindy did not get pregnant, they became increasingly distressed. They attended a fertility clinic for about a year but found that their relationship was suffering from the constant pressure to become pregnant.

Finally, Robert and Cindy decided to go away for an extended vacation and take time to think about their plan to have children. They talked about their sadness over their inability to get pregnant, their love for each other, and their desire to share their many resources with children. They decided to work with children at their church, and they also began working toward adoption at your agency, Family Services Inc. Their adoption of 3- and 5-year-old brothers was recently finalized.

CASE STUDY 8.3

VERONICA PALMORE, NOT READY TO RETIRE AT 57

Veronica Palmore, a second-generation American of Polish heritage, married her high school boyfriend, Simon, when she graduated from college at age 22. Simon was 24 at the time and had been working as a laborer since he graduated from high school. Veronica had dreams of a career in teaching, but she did not know how she could combine that dream with her desire to have a family, because both she and Simon had very traditional expectations about gender roles. Veronica became pregnant during her first year of teaching and quit at age 23 to have a family, planning to return when the children were older.

Simon and Veronica's parents were thrilled about the baby, but Veronica did not feel ready to be a mother. She felt overwhelmed and was weepy for much of the first year, saying in retrospect that she was struggling with a stubborn postpartum depression. To make matters worse, Simon was laid off from work for a few months, and it became financially necessary to move in with Veronica's parents.

By the time Veronica was 25, Simon had a better job and they had an apartment of their own. Veronica decided it was time to have another baby, and to her surprise, she really enjoyed the second baby. Both she and Simon developed close relationships with the children.

When the younger child was 2, Veronica decided to try substitute teaching, and she found that she enjoyed being in the classroom more than she had during her earlier teaching experience. A year later, she took a full-time teaching position and hired a sitter for the children. Soon she began to take evening courses toward a master's degree. Simon seemed happy to help with household chores, and family was the center of his life. Work was important to him only because it allowed him to provide for his family. With Veronica and Simon both working, they could afford to buy their own house in a more middle-class neighborhood.

Veronica's starting salary was half that received by men in starting positions, and she felt that she had to prove to her male colleagues that she was dedicated to her work. She was careful never to say that she couldn't stay for a meeting because she had to get home to her children. After a few years as a full-time teacher, Veronica felt more confident and made a commitment to take a particular interest in children who were struggling in school.

CASE STUDY 8.3

When Veronica was 34, her father died suddenly of a heart attack, and her bereft mother lived with Veronica and Simon for 2 years until she remarried and moved out of town. Veronica was sad to lose the safety net of having a dependable mom and dad close by.

When Veronica was 39, Simon was seriously injured in an accident at work. He was hospitalized for several weeks, followed by a lengthy period in a rehabilitation center. This was a very hard time for the family. Veronica and the children missed Simon very much, and Veronica became concerned about whether she was giving too much responsibility to her adolescent daughters. She was happy for an opportunity to talk to the social worker at the rehabilitation center about the impact Simon's accident was having on the family. During these conversations, Veronica acknowledged that she and Simon were very different, but she also began to have a deep appreciation for the support Simon had offered to her over the years and for his close relationship with the children.

Simon made an excellent recovery from his accident and was able to return to work. A few years later, he was promoted into a better-paying position, the children were doing well in college, and Veronica was earning a reputation as a humane and dedicated teacher. She was assertively challenging school policies and enjoyed mentoring younger teachers. In her late 40s, she turned down an offer to be department head. As she approached 50, she looked forward to another 15 years of teaching, but as she approached menopause, she began to have occasional worries that she would either burn out or be pushed out. The question of "what next" became troublesome to Veronica. She was asked to join a coalition of county teachers who were developing guidelines for managing diversity in the public schools, and this activity brought new energy to her. Two years ago she left the classroom and now works full time as a trainer for the school system. Retirement looms on the horizon, but for now, Veronica enjoys her work.

The last few years have brought both challenge and reward. Simon's parents began to have major health problems, eventually moved in with Simon and Veronica, and both died in the past year. Simon and Veronica are actively involved in the lives of their children and grandchildren, who live nearby. Religion became less important to Veronica and Simon after the children left home, but has, once again, become an important part of their lives.

The Changing Social Construction of Middle Adulthood

Although there is a 15-year range in their ages, and their life paths have been very different, William George, Robert Johnson, and Veronica Palmore are all in the life course phase of middle adulthood. Not so long ago, middle adulthood was nearly an unstudied terrain. Recently, however, due to a confluence of demographic trends and research accomplishments, there has been intense interest in the middle adult years. Although we still have only a hazy picture of middle adulthood, that picture is coming into better focus.

Changing Age Demographics

How might these changing demographics affect the midlife phase of the life course?

In 1900, the median age of the U.S. population was 23 and the average life expectancy was 47.3 years (U.S. Census Bureau, 1999). By 1950, the median age was 30.2 and average life expectancy was 68.2. The 2000 census reports the median age as 35.3 and average life expectancy as 76.9 (National Center for Health Statistics, 2001b). These changing demographics are presented visually in Exhibit 8.1. These data do not mean that no one lived past what we now consider middle age in 1900. The average life expectancy in 1900 was deflated by high rates of infant mortality. Indeed, in 1900, 18% of the population of the United States was 45 years old or older. This compares to 28% in 1950 and 34% in 2000. Living past age 45 is not new, but more people are doing it. David Plath (1980) describes the current demographic trend in the United States, which exists as well in northern and Western Europe and in Japan, as a trend toward "mass longevity." This trend has an enormous impact on our understanding of the adult life course. Veronica Palmore is not surprised to be enjoying career renewal at age 57, and Robert Johnson assumes he will live to see his children into adulthood. On the other hand, William George already describes himself as "an old man."

This trend of increased life expectancy is juxtaposed with another important demographic trend, declining birthrate (Moen & Wethington, 1999). These two trends together have produced the large baby-boom generation currently moving through midlife in record numbers. The 50- to 54-year age group was the fastest growing age group from 1990 to 2000, with an increase of 55%, and the 45- to 49-year age group was the second fastest growing group, with a 45% increase. In 2000, there were over 96 million adults between the ages of 35 and 59, representing 34% of the U.S. population (U.S. Census Bureau, 2001b).

This trend varies across international populations. Certainly it holds true in advanced industrial societies; in poor and less-developed societies, however, the trends are radically different. International data show a high life expectancy of 83.5 years in Andorra and a low of 37.2 years in Zambia in 2000 (U.S. Census Bureau, 2001b). In

EXHIBIT 8.1
Changing Life Expectancy and Median Age

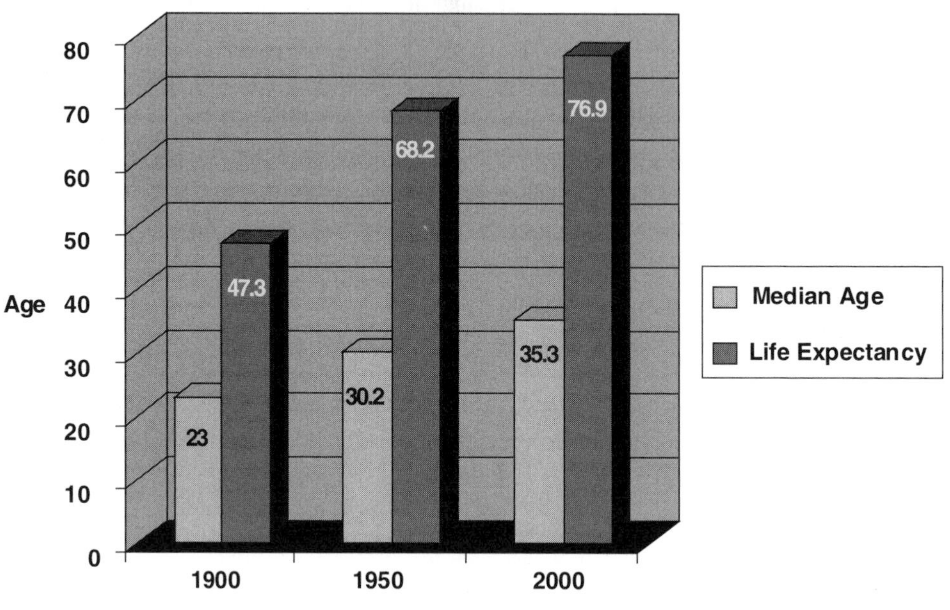

Source: Based on U.S. Census Bureau, 1999, and National Center for Health Statistics, 2001b.

that same year, the average life expectancy was less than 50 years in no fewer than 23 countries. Social workers who work in the international arena or with immigrant families will need to develop appropriate understanding of how the life course varies across world populations.

Given the trend in mass longevity and the current large cohort of adults in midlife, it is not surprising that researchers have begun to take a serious interest in the "lengthy central period" (Lachman, 2001, p. xiii) of the human life course. Beginning in the 1990s, an interdisciplinary group of researchers launched several large research projects to move our understanding of middle adulthood from mythology to science. These researchers span the fields of anthropology, economics, genetics, neurology, psychology, and sociology. One of the largest research projects is being conducted by the John D. and Catherine T. MacArthur Foundation Research Network on Successful Midlife Development (MIDMAC). Reports on the first 10 years of this project have begun to appear in disciplinary journals and form the basis of the first *Handbook of Midlife Development*. Because this project has produced some of the best research to date on middle adulthood, discussion in this chapter will draw heavily on it.

A Definition of Middle Adulthood

Is biological age, psychological age, social age, or spiritual age the best marker for middle adulthood?

Before we go further, we need to pause and consider *who* is included in middle adulthood. In the most general sense, we are talking about people who are in midlife, or the central part of the life course. Beyond that, we do not have generally agreed upon ages to include in middle adulthood. The most frequently used definition of middle adulthood includes those persons who are between the ages of 40 and 60, but some scholars use a lower limit as young as age 30 and an upper limit as late as age 65. The National Council on Aging (2000) found that one third of their sample in their 70s think of themselves as middle-aged, and other researchers have found that the older one is, the later the reported age of middle adulthood (Lachman & Bertrand, 2001).

Some authors argue that middle adulthood should not be thought of in terms of chronological age, but instead in terms of achieving certain developmental tasks. Generally, midlife adults have established a family, settled into and peaked in a career, and taken responsibility for their children, their parents, and their community (Staudinger & Bluck, 2001). Any definition of middle adulthood must also include biological aging processes, subjective perceptions, and social roles, as well as historical and generational contexts (Moen & Wethington, 1999). This suggestion is consistent with the major themes of a life course perspective discussed in Chapter 1 of this book.

Some authors have been critical of any approach to defining middle adulthood that includes such a wide age range as 40 to 60 (e.g., Staudinger & Bluck, 2001). They suggest that the beginning of midlife is very different from the latter part of midlife, and that lumping these parts of the life course together may lead to contradictory findings. You may recall a similar concern about the boundaries of young adulthood noted in Chapter 7. Late adulthood, which is divided into late adulthood and very late adulthood in this book, encompasses an even larger age span, potentially from 65 to 100+. As longevity increases, the adult portion of life is likely to be divided into finer and finer phases.

Culture and the Construction of Middle Adulthood

With the identification of a middlehood, societies must construct roles for and make meaning of middle adulthood. In his book *Welcome to Middle Age! (And Other Cultural Fictions),* Richard Shweder (1998) suggests that middle age is a "cultural fiction" and the fiction does not play out the same way in all cultures. He does not use *fiction* to mean false, but to mean, instead, that ideas about middle age are "fabricated, manufactured, invented, or designed" (p. x). Shweder suggests that the European American cultural construction of middle adulthood casts it primarily in terms of chronology (middle age), biology, and medicine. He argues that this cultural construction is a story of mental and physical decline. Other cultures, he suggests, organize the life course, including middle adulthood, in terms of "a social history of role transitions" (p. xi), focusing particularly on family roles.

Consider how middle adulthood is defined and understood in three cultures: upper-caste Hindu in rural India, middle-class Japanese, and middle-class Anglo American (Menon, 2001):

- Asian Indian Hindu beliefs and practices differ greatly according to region and caste, but middle adulthood is not defined as a separate, clearly distinguished life phase as it is in the United States. To the extent that it is recognized, it is thought of as "maturity" and seen in relation to transitions in family roles. Women become senior wives, and men replace their fathers as head of the family, responsible for family decision making and for the family's interaction with the community. Maturity is considered to be the best time in the life course.

- In Japan, aging is associated with power and creativity. This view of aging is tied to two central beliefs. First, life is about *becoming*, not *being*, and all phases of the life course offer "endless opportunities for continual personal improvement," to reach for human perfection (Menon, 2001, p. 52). A second central belief is that aging is a natural process. Although the Japanese recognize some loss and decline with the passing of years, the general view of middle adulthood is that it is the "prime of life," a time of fullness, activity, and spiritual growth.

- Empirical research about the meaning of midlife in the United States suggests two divergent cultural beliefs: one view sees middle adulthood as a positive time of having accumulated resources for coping; the other view sees middle adulthood as a negative time of decline and loss. This latter view of decline and loss (of being "over the hill") often seems to permeate popular culture (Gullette, 1998). However, much of the recent research on middle adulthood reveals an attempt to recast middlehood as the "prime of life." What images come to mind when you think of middle adulthood? Do you think first of sagging chins, wrinkles, reading glasses, thinning or graying hair, hot flashes, loss of sex drive, and so on, or do you think first of emotional and spiritual maturity that gives power and creativity? What images do you think William George, Robert Johnson, and Veronica Palmore hold of middle adulthood?

Comparing views of middlehood in these three cultures helps us recognize that our taken-for-granted views of this life course phase are, indeed, highly influenced by culture. It also alerts us to the possibility that our clients from different cultural groups may have different expectations for midlife roles.

Theories of Middle Adulthood

Few theories focus directly on middle adulthood, but a number of theories address middle adulthood as a part of a larger developmental framework. Themes from three of those theories are presented here.

Erikson's Theory of Generativity

How does generativity affect the capacity for interdependence?

According to Erik Erikson's (1950) life span theory, the psychosocial struggle of middle adulthood is **generativity** versus stagnation (refer back to Exhibit 3.6 for an overview of Erikson's psychosocial stage theory). Generativity is the ability to transcend personal interests to provide care and concern for generations to come; it encompasses procreation, productivity, and creativity (Erikson, 1982, p. 67). Generative adults provide "care, guidance, inspiration, instruction, and leadership" (McAdams, 2001, p. 395) for future generations. Failure to find a way to contribute to future generations, or to make a contribution to the general well-being, results in self-absorption and a sense of stagnation. Erikson saw generativity as an instinct that works to perpetuate society. Robert Johnson and Veronica Palmore are both finding a variety of ways to experience generativity, and it seems that William George may also be finding his own path to generativity, with his care and concern for younger homeless men he meets on the street. As a social worker, however, you will most likely encounter people who struggle with a sense of stagnation in middle adulthood.

More recently, Dan McAdams and Ed de St. Aubin (1992, 1998) have presented a model of generativity that includes the seven components found in Exhibit 8.2. McAdams and de St. Aubin (1992, 1998) see generativity coming from both the person (personal desire) and the social and cultural environment (cultural demand).

Even though Erikson outlined middlehood generativity in 1950, generativity was not a subject of empirical investigation until the 1980s. There is limited longitudinal research to answer the question, Are midlife adults more generative than people in other life course phases? Most of the cross-sectional research on generativity reports greater generativity during middle adulthood than in young adulthood or late adulthood (see review in McAdams, 2001). One notable exception is a cross-sectional study in which the researchers found that although midlife adults scored significantly higher than young adults and older adults on an overall measure of generativity, young adults scored just as high as midlife adults on some measures of generativity related to having concerns about making a contribution to the world (McAdams, de St. Aubin, & Logan, 1993). One longitudinal study (Stewart & Vandewater, 1998) found that *generativity motivation* decreased over time in two cohorts of college-educated women, but generative actions increase. The researchers suggest that young adults may have a generative spirit but lack the material, social, or emotional resources to accomplish generative

EXHIBIT 8.2
McAdams and de St. Aubins's Seven Components of Generativity

1. Inner desire for immortality and to be needed
2. Cultural demand for productivity
3. Concern for the next generation
4. Belief in the species
5. Commitment
6. Action: creating, maintaining, or offering
7. Development of a generative life story

Source: Adapted from McAdams, Hart, & Maruna, 1998.

goals until they reach middle adulthood. Although it is possible that the generative spirit wanes over time, resources for generative action increase. At any rate, research consistently finds that the cultural expectation in the United States is that adults become more generative in midlife (McAdams & de St. Aubin, 1998).

Research also finds that generativity is associated with gender, class, and race. Several researchers (McAdams & de St. Aubin, 1992; McKeering & Pakenham, 2000) have found that men who had never been fathers scored particularly low on measures of generativity, but not being a mother did not have the same effect for women. Generativity has been found to increase with educational level (Keyes & Ryff, 1998). Black adults have been found to score higher on some measures of generativity than white adults (Cole & Stewart, 1996; Hart, McAdams, Hirsch, & Bauer, 2001).

Jung's and Levinson's Theories of Finding a Balance

Both Carl Jung and Daniel Levinson suggest that middle adulthood is a time when individuals attempt to find balance in their lives in several ways. Jung (1971) sees middle adulthood as a time when we discover and reclaim parts of the self that were repressed in the search for conformity in the first half of life. He emphasizes the importance of gender identity in middle adulthood. In middlehood, adults begin to move from the stereotyped gender-role behavior of young adulthood to a more androgynous behavioral repertoire at this age. Jung also suggested that **extroversion**, or orientation to the external world, and **introversion,** or orientation to the internal world, come into greater balance in middle adulthood. He suggested that the challenges of establishing family and work roles demands extroversion in young adulthood, but in middle adulthood individuals tend to turn inward and explore their own subjective experience.

Daniel Levinson (Levinson, 1986, 1990; Levinson & Levinson, 1996; Levinson, Darrow, Klein, Levinson, & McKee, 1978) conceptualizes the life course as a sequence of eras, each with its own biopsychosocial character (Levinson & Levinson, 1996) with

EXHIBIT 8.3
Central Propositions of Life-Span Theory as They Relate to Middle Adulthood

- Human development is lifelong and no age period is supreme in the developmental trajectory. Midlife cannot be studied in isolation; it must be studied in terms of both its antecedents and its consequences.
- Development involves both gains and losses. In midlife, there is a tie in the relationship between gains and losses.
- Biological influences on development become more negative, and cultural support becomes more important, with increasing age in adulthood. A distinction can be made between early and late midlife.
- With increasing age in adulthood, there is an overall reduction in resources. At midlife, adults must put a major effort into managing resources.
- Even though challenges increase and biological resources decrease in midlife, there is still possibility for change.
- The experience of midlife adults may depend on cultural and historical contexts.

Source: Adapted from Staudinger & Bluck, 2001, pp. 17-18.

major changes from one era to the next. Changes do occur within eras, but these changes are small and do not involve major revision of the life structure. Adult life is composed of alternating periods of relative stability and periods of transition. As mentioned in Chapter 7, a key concept of Levinson's theory is life structure, by which he means "the underlying pattern or design of a person's life at a given time" (Levinson & Levinson, 1996, p. 22). In most cases, family and occupation are the central components in the life structure, but people vary widely in how much weight they assign to each. During the transition to middle adulthood, individuals often try to give greater attention to previously neglected components. That seems to be what Robert Johnson and Cindy Marsh were doing when they decided to become parents. Levinson sees this transition in terms of balancing four opposing aspects of identity: young versus old, creation versus destruction, feminine versus masculine, and attachment versus separating (Levinson, 1977).

Life-Span Theory and the Gain-Loss Balance

Life-span theory has much in common with the life course perspective introduced in Chapter 1 of this book. It is more firmly rooted in psychology, however, whereas the life course perspective has more multidisciplinary roots. Life-span theory is based in ongoing transactions between persons and environments and begins with the premise that development is lifelong. Six central propositions of the life-span theory as they relate to middle adulthood are summarized in Exhibit 8.3.

We focus here particularly on the proposition that in midlife there is a tie in the balance of gains and losses (Staudinger & Bluck, 2001). Life-span researchers have raised the question, What is the balance of gains and losses in midlife? (Baltes, Lindenberg, & Staudinger, 1998). For example, there is good evidence of gains in self-esteem and emotional maturity and of losses in biological functioning. There is beginning agreement that across adulthood, the balance shifts from a dominance of developmental gains in early midlife to a dominance of developmental losses in late midlife (e.g., Heckhausen, 2001; Staudinger & Bluck, 2001). This has led some researchers to suggest that middle adulthood should be divided into early midlife, which is a time of developmental gains, and late midlife, which is a time of developmental losses. It is important to note, however, that gains or losses are defined and given meaning in cultural contexts and are influenced by both group-based and individual-based differences. One might wonder if Robert Johnson and Veronica Palmore see the gain/loss balance in middle adulthood in a different light than William George.

William George seems to be making some gains in spiritual development, but already in early midlife he faces the challenges of a host of chronic health conditions that stem in large part from earlier environmental constraints and behavioral choice. Also in early midlife, Robert Johnson has many biological, social, emotional, and spiritual resources for coping with challenges. In early midlife, Veronica and Simon Palmore were doing better financially than ever, and Veronica was beginning to blossom in her career. She faced some challenges of declining biological functioning around age 50, but now in late midlife, losses in biological functioning seem more than compensated for by her growing capacity to make a meaningful contribution and spiritual development.

Biological Changes and Physical Health in Middle Adulthood

What factors have led to changes in biological age in middle adulthood?

There have been dramatic changes in the last few decades in the numbers of adults who enjoy healthy and active lives in the years between 45 and 65 and beyond. However, some physical and mental decline does begin to occur. Most biological systems reach their peak performance in the mid-20s. Age-related changes over the next 20 to 30 years are usually gradual, accumulating at different rates in different body systems. The changes are the result of interactions of biology with psychological, spiritual, and sociocultural factors, and individuals play a very active role in the aging process throughout adulthood, as we can see in the life trajectories of William George, Robert Johnson, and Veronica Palmore. However, by the age of 50, the accumulation of biological change becomes physically noticeable in most people.

The biggest stories in biological functioning and physical health in middle adulthood are changes in physical appearance; changes in mobility; changes in the reproductive system; and changes in health, more specifically the beginnings of chronic disease. There are enormous individual differences in the timing and intensity of these changes, but some changes affect almost everyone, such as presbyopia for both men and women and menopause for women.

Changes in Physical Appearance

Probably the most visible signs of physiological changes in middle adulthood are changes in physical appearance (see, e.g., Merrill & Verbrugge, 1999; Whitbourne, 2001). The skin begins to sag and wrinkle as it loses its firmness and elasticity. Small, localized areas of brown pigmentation, often called aging spots, may appear in parts of the body exposed to sunlight. As the sebaceous glands that secrete oils become less active, the skin becomes drier. Hair on the head often becomes thinner and grayer, and hair may appear in places where it is not wanted, such as ears, thicker clumps around the eyebrows, and the chin on women. Many midlife adults wear glasses for the first time because of the decreased ability to focus on near objects (presbyopia) that occurs in most adults between the ages of 45 and 55.

There are significant changes in body build as midlife adults begin to lose height and gain weight. Beginning in their 40s, people lose about one half inch in height per decade, due to loss of bone material in the vertebrae. Starting about age 20, there is a tendency to gain weight until about the mid-50s. Body fat begins to accumulate in the torso and accounts for a greater percentage of weight in middle adulthood than in adolescence and early adulthood. In the late 50s, people tend to begin to lose weight, but this weight loss comes from loss of lean body mass (bone and muscle) rather than from loss of fat.

Changes in skin can be minimized by using sunscreen, skin emollients, applications of vitamin E, facial massages, and by smoking cessation. Changes in body build can be minimized by involvement in aerobic exercise and resistance training to improve muscle tone, reduce fat, and offset bone loss. The current recommendation is 30 to 60 minutes of exercise 3 to 4 days per week.

Changes in Mobility

Beginning in the 40s, losses in muscles, bones, and joints start to have an impact on mobility. A progressive loss of muscle mass leads to loss of strength beginning at about age 45, and muscle strength continues to decline at the rate of 12% to 15% per decade thereafter (Whitbourne, 2001). The most apparent loss of muscle strength occurs in the legs and back (Merrill & Vertrugge, 1999). By engaging in strength training, midlife adults can minimize the loss of muscle mass. An effective strength training program involves three to four workouts per week for 8 to 12 weeks.

Maximum bone density is reached in early adulthood, and there is a progressive loss of bone mineral after that. The rate of bone loss accelerates in the 50s. Microcracks begin to develop in the bones in response to stress, and bones also begin to lose their elasticity. By the end of middle adulthood, bones are less strong and more brittle. The rate of bone loss is about 2 times greater in women than in men, linked to the loss of estrogens after menopause. Bone loss tends to be greater in people with fair skin, and black women have higher bone mineral than white women or Hispanic women. Bone loss is accelerated by smoking, alcohol use, and poor diet. It is slowed by aerobic activity, resistance training, increased calcium intake in young adulthood, and use of vitamin D (Whitbourne, 2001).

Changes in the joints begin to occur before skeletal maturity, but without injury, no obvious symptoms appear until the 40s. The cartilage that protects joints begins to degenerate, and an outgrowth of cartilage starts to develop and interfere with ease of movement. Unlike muscles, joints do not benefit from constant use. To prevent unnecessary wear and tear on joints, it is important to wear the proper footwear when engaging in exercise activities and to avoid repetitive movements of the wrists. Flexibility exercises help to expand the range of motion for stiff joints. Exercises to strengthen the muscles that support joints also help to minimize the mobility problems associated with changes in joints.

Changes in the Reproductive System and Sexuality

What effect do these sex differences in changes in the reproductive system have on middle adulthood?

Perhaps the most often noted biological change in middle adulthood is the lost or diminished reproductive capacity (see, e.g., Finch, 2001). Although both men and women experience reproductive changes during adulthood, the changes are more gradual for men than for women.

The pattern reported for men is a gradual decline in testosterone beginning in early adulthood and continuing throughout life (Finch, 2001; Merrill & Verbrugge, 1999). The quantity of viable sperm begins to decrease in the late 40s or 50s, and most births are fathered by men younger than 60 years (Finch, 2001; Merrill & Verbrugge, 1999).

The picture is somewhat different for women. In middle adulthood, women's capacity to conceive and bear children gradually declines until menopause, when the capacity for conceiving children ends (although reproductive technology to extend a woman's reproductive life may eventually become more generally available). **Menopause** is the permanent cessation of menstruation, and for research purposes is usually defined as 12 consecutive months with absence of menstruation (Avis, 1999). The median age of menopause is about 50; it occurs between the ages of 45 and 55 in 90% of women in the United States.

Although less gradual than the decline in reproductive capacity in men, menopause is a more gradual process than often recognized (Avis, 1999). The menopause process begins when the woman is in her 30s. At this time, called **premenopause,** the woman begins to have occasional menstrual cycles without ovulation, or the production of eggs. This change usually goes without notice.

By the mid- to late 40s, the supply of egg cells is depleted, ovarian production of hormone slows, and more and more menstrual cycles occur without ovulation. The menstrual cycle becomes irregular, some menstrual periods are skipped, and the production of estrogen drops. In this period, known as perimenopause, changes in the reproductive system begin to be noticed. The World Health Organization (1996) defines **perimenopause** as the period of time that begins immediately prior to menopause, when there are biological and clinical indicators that reproductive capacity is reaching exhaustion, and continues through the first year after the last menstrual period. One study using longitudinal data reported the median age for the beginning of perimenopause as 47.5 years (McKinlay, Brambilla, & Posner, 1992).

In popular culture, menopause is seen as a major milestone, a prominent biological marker, for women; it is popularly called the change of life. Cross-cultural studies suggest widely differing experiences with menopause, with many non-Western cultures viewing it as a positive change, ushering in a time of greater freedom for women, a time when they are allowed greater participation in the world beyond the family. In contrast, the Euro American perspective over time has focused on menopause as loss, decay, and more recently deficiency (estrogen deficiency) (Avis, 1999). In this tradition, menopause is assumed to be universally associated with hot flashes, night sweats, vaginal dryness, insomnia, fatigue, anxiety, depression, irritability, memory loss, difficulty concentrating, and weight gain.

Although perimenopause, and purported associated symptoms and discomforts, has received much attention in the popular media in recent years, it has not been the subject of intensive scientific study. Menopause did not receive much attention either until the 1980s. This increased interest seems to come from a confluence of factors. Chief among those factors is that the current baby boom generation of women, who are now in middlehood, have, as a cohort, asserted their control over their reproductive lives and challenged taboos about sexuality. Two other influential factors include epidemiological studies that identified estrogen decline in menopause as a risk factor for osteoporosis and cardiovascular disease, and the development of medications for the "treatment" of menopause. To date, however, research on the connection between menopause and most of the symptoms believed to be a consequence is far from conclusive.

Existing research suggests considerable variation in signs and symptoms of menopause across cultures. One recent large national research project compared menopausal symptoms across racial and ethnic groups in the United States, including Caucasian, African American, Chinese, Japanese, and Hispanic women (Avis et al., 2001; Bromberger et al., 2001). The researchers found that the Caucasian women reported significantly more psychosomatic symptoms than women from the other racial and ethnic groups. African American women were significantly more likely to report hot flashes or night sweats. These findings are consistent with earlier cross-cultural and cross-national research (Flint, 1975; Payer, 1991; Vatuk, 1992). It is hard to tease out the relative contribution of cultural beliefs about menopause from different patterns of diet and exercise. For example, Japanese diets are lower in fat and higher in phytoestrogens than diets in Canada and the United States (Adlercreutz, Hamalaiven, Gorbach, & Grodin, 1992).

Existing research also reports considerable individual variations in the signs and symptoms of menopause in the United States. Data from one longitudinal study in the United States report that only 19% of postmenopausal women report never experiencing a hot flash, but only 19% of those who experienced hot flashes report that the hot flashes were a problem (McKinlay et al., 1992). Data from this study indicate that the rate of hot flash reporting increases as the menstrual cycle becomes more irregular during perimenopause, peaking at about 50% just before menopause. The data also indicate that the longer the duration of perimenopause, the higher the rate of hot flashes.

Longitudinal research on depression and menopause indicates that there is a moderate increase in depression during perimenopause, but most women who become depressed during perimenopause had prior episodes of depression (Avis, Brambilla, McKinlay, & Vass, 1994). The researchers did find, however, that women who experienced a long perimenopausal period, lasting at least 27 months, were at greater risk of depression than women who experienced a shorter perimenopausal period. Existing research indicates that sleep disturbance is associated with menopause, but the exact mechanism for that association is not clear. Some research suggests that the sleep disturbance is directly related to hot flashes, finding that menopausal women who do not report hot flashes also do not report sleep disturbance (Shaver, Giblin, Lentz, & Lee, 1988).

Research does indicate that vaginal lubrication decreases as women age (Laumann, Paik, & Rosen, 1999). With lower estrogen levels, the blood supply to the vagina and surrounding nerves and glands is reduced. The tissues become thinner and drier and cannot produce sufficient lubrication for comfortable intercourse. There is also increased risk of infection unless estrogen replacement or an artificial lubricant is used. Longer periods of foreplay can also help with this situation.

Some social critics suggest that our latest construction of menopause as deficiency is a medical construction: menopause as disease (see, e.g., Bell, 1990). The treatment for the "disease of menopause" is hormone replacement therapy. There are two primary types of hormone therapy for menopause: estrogen alone (ERT) or estrogen combined with progestin (HRT, or hormone replacement therapy). ERT was introduced first, in the 1940s, and was promoted widely by pharmaceutical companies and by popular books such as *Feminine Forever* (Wilson, 1966) in the 1960s. In the 1970s, several research studies reported that ERT increased women's risk for endometrial cancer

(Mack et al., 1976; Smith, Prentice, Thompson, & Hermann, 1975; Ziel & Finkle, 1975). In response to these studies, pharmaceutical companies discovered that combining estrogen with progestin could prevent the excessive buildup of estrogen that increased the risk for endometrial cancer. HRT became the recommended treatment for menopausal women who still have an intact uterus.

Existing research on HRT presents midlife women with a difficult decision (Avis, 1999; Rexrode & Manson, 2002; Whitbourne, 2001). Like many baby boomers, Veronica Palmore and her friends have been confused about whether to use HRT. There is strong evidence that HRT retards bone loss, but only during the time the hormone is taken. Researchers consistently find that HRT decreases the incidence of hot flashing. Although earlier research had found HRT to be a protective factor against heart disease, recent research challenges that finding. There is some evidence that HRT helps prevent colon cancer, and some researchers are exploring the possible preventive effects of HRT on Alzheimer's disease.

Although manufacturers of hormone products have advertised the benefits to physical and mental health from HRT, research does not support this rosy picture (Rexrode & Manson, 2002). Little is known about the long-term effects of taking HRT, over a 20- to 30-year period, but the primary potential risk of long-term use is breast cancer. The Women's Health Initiative (WHI) was involved in a large, ongoing study, scheduled to end in 2005, comparing hormone therapy with a placebo. But in a surprising move, they called a halt to their study in the summer of 2002 because their preliminary findings indicated an increased risk of invasive breast cancer for women taking HRT compared to women taking the placebo. The preliminary findings also indicated higher rates of heart disease, strokes, and blood clots for the hormone therapy group compared to the placebo group (National Institutes of Health, 2002; Okie, 2002). This recent research suggests a small increase in risk of "cardiovascular events" during the first 2 years of HRT and the possibility of harm of HRT to women with established heart disease (Hlatky, Boothrody, Vittinghoff, Sharp, & Whooley, 2002; Rexrode & Manson, 2002). HRT has also been found to increase the risk of asthma and gallstones and to cause changes in blood sugar levels. In some women, it also causes such side effects as breast tenderness, headaches, and bloating.

Recently, some researchers have begun to explore another alternative to HRT, selective estrogen replacement modulaters (SERMs), such as raloxifene and tamoxifen. These newer alternatives are thought to have a more targeted effect on bone loss. It is important to note that lifestyle changes have also been shown to reduce the risks related to hormonal changes during menopause: quitting smoking, exercising, reducing cholesterol intake, taking calcium supplements, and losing weight.

The physical changes in middle adulthood require some adjustments in the sexual lives of midlife men and women. Beginning in their late 50s, men begin to experience a gradual slowdown in sexual responses. This includes decreased frequency and intensity

EXHIBIT 8.4 Death Rate (per 100,000 persons) in Selected Age Groups in 1999

		Male			Female		
Age Group	Overall	Overall	Black	White	Overall	Black	White
25 to 34 Years	108.3	150.2	268.4	134.5	66.9	122.0	58.4
35 to 44 Years	199.2	256.7	473.6	231.5	142.5	282.6	123.3
45 to 54 Years	427.3	546.7	1081.9	494.2	313.1	581.0	281.8
55 to 64 Years	1021.8	1280.0	2244.0	1200.2	786.5	1255.7	739.1
65 to 74 Years	2484.3	3109.3	4182.8	3043.2	1972.9	2732.1	1916.2

Source: Taken from Anderson, 2001.

of orgasms, increased difficulty in achieving erection, and longer time needed before achieving subsequent erection. For women, the vaginal dryness that often occurs during menopause may cause painful intercourse. Many couples adjust well to these changes, however, and with children out of the home, may find that their sexual lives become less inhibited and more passionate. The sex lives of midlife adults may benefit from improved self-esteem that typifies middle adulthood and, in relationships of some longevity, from better understanding of the desires and responses of the sexual partner. Currently, there are a number of treatments available to assist with deficient sexual responses in men, including Viagra and testosterone supplements, as well as a number of products being developed (Zonagen Sexual Dysfunction Program, 2002).

Changes in Health Status

What might be some reasons for these race and gender differences in health in middle adulthood?

As we can see in the stories of William George and Robert Johnson, who are about the same age, health during middle adulthood is highly variable. There are some positive changes: the frequency of accidents declines, as does susceptibility to colds and allergies. On the other hand, although many people live through middle adulthood with little disease or disability, the frequency of chronic illness, persistent symptoms, and functional disability begins to rise in middlehood. And the death rate increases continuously over the adult years, as demonstrated in Exhibit 8.4. You will also note that there are significant gender and race differences in the death rates in middle adulthood, with men having higher death rates than women in both white and black populations, and blacks of both genders having alarmingly higher death rates than their white counterparts. Data for other racial and ethnic groups are not reported because of inconsistencies in reporting race on death certificates.

In the past century, there has been a change in the types of diseases that are likely to affect health across the life course. In the early 1900s, when life expectancy was in the mid-40s, most deaths were caused by infectious diseases, such as pneumonia, tuberculosis, and influenza (CDC, 1999b). With the increase in life expectancy, chronic disease plays a more important role in the great stretch of middle adulthood and beyond. People are now living long enough to experience a chronic illness: "We are now living well enough and long enough to slowly fall apart. . . . [T]he diseases that plague us now are ones of slow accumulation of damage—heart disease, cancer, cerebrovascular disorders" (Sapolsky, 1998, p. 2).

The prevalence of chronic conditions increases with each decade from middle adulthood on. (Note: *Prevalence* measures the proportion of a population that has a disease at a point in time. *Incidence* measures the number of new cases of a disease or condition over a period of time, such as 1 year.) There is an increase in potentially fatal chronic conditions, as well as nonfatal chronic conditions. The important role of chronic illness as cause of death is demonstrated in Exhibit 8.5, which reports the five leading causes of death for selected age groups. Along with the middle adult age groups of 35 to 44, 45 to 54, and 55 to 64, the age groups on each side of middle adulthood are included for comparison purposes. Except for accident, suicide, and homicide, all the leading causes of death are chronic diseases: heart disease, cancer, HIV/AIDS, chronic liver disease, cerebrovascular disease (stroke), diabetes, chronic lower respiratory disease (COPD). Death due to accidents and suicide is relatively stable across age groups. Death due to homicide continues to decline throughout adulthood.

Exhibit 8.5 also demonstrates important gender and race differences in causes of death throughout adulthood. Cancer is a more common cause of death for women than for men, beginning in early adulthood and continuing into middle adulthood. Death due to accidents is more common among men than women beginning in early adulthood and continuing into middle adulthood. Homicide and HIV/AIDS play a more prominent role in the deaths of blacks than of whites in young and middle adulthood. Suicide plays a more prominent role in the deaths of whites than of blacks. It is important to note that these racial differences may be partly due to differences in socioeconomic status between whites and blacks.

Review of the data in Exhibit 8.6 indicates that most of the common chronic conditions in middle adulthood are not fatal, however. Men have been reported to have a higher prevalence of fatal chronic conditions in middle adulthood than women, and women have been reported to have a higher prevalence of nonfatal chronic conditions (Merrill & Verbrugge, 1999). Women in middle adulthood have higher rates of arthritis, sinusitis, and allergies than men but lower rates of heart disease and hearing impairments (Adams & Marano, 1995). Although most midlife adults do not experience limitations from chronic conditions, limits on activity generally increase from early midlife to later midlife. Data from household interviews of a sample of civilian noninstitutionalized children and adults taken in 1999 found that 13.1% of adults 45 to 54 years old and 21.1% of adults 55 to 64 years old reported some limitation of activity caused by chronic conditions (National Center for Health Statistics, 2001a). As

Exhibit 8.5

Five Leading Causes of Death and Percentage of Total Deaths in Selected Age Groups, Overall, for Men and Women, and for Black and White

	Overall	Men	Women	Black	White
25 to 34 Years	Accidents (29.0%) Suicide (12.4%) Homicide (10.3%) Cancer (9.8%) Heart Disease (7.5%)	Accidents (32.2%) Suicide (14.8%) Homicide (11.8%) Heart Disease (7.0%) Cancer (6.9%)	Accidents (21.8%) Cancer (16.0%) Heart Disease (8.4%) Suicide (7.1%) Homicide (6.9%)	Homicide (21.3%) Accidents (17.4%) HIV/AIDS (14.8%) Heart Disease (9.0%) Cancer (6.6%)	Accidents (32.9%) Suicide (14.8%) Cancer (10.7%) Heart Disease (7.0%) Homicide (6.6%)
35 to 44 Years	Cancer (18.7%) Accidents (17.1%) Heart Disease (15.2%) Suicide (7.2%) HIV/AIDS (7.0%)	Accidents (19.7%) Heart Disease (16.9%) Cancer (13.1%) Suicide (8.8%) HIV/AIDS (8.2%)	Cancer (28.8%) Accidents (12.4%) Heart Disease (12.3%) HIV/AIDS (4.7%) Suicide (4.5%)	Heart Disease (16.9%) HIV/AIDS (15.2%) Cancer (14.6%) Accidents (10.9%) Homicide (6.3%)	Cancer (19.9%) Accidents (19.1%) Heart Disease (14.8%) Suicide (8.9%) HIV/AIDS (4.5%)
45 to 54 Years	Cancer (30.5%) Heart Disease (22.9%) Accidents (7.6%) Liver Disease (4.2%) Stroke (3.6%)	Heart Disease (26.6%) Cancer (24.7%) Accidents (9.0%) Liver Disease (5.0%) Suicide (4.0%)	Cancer (40.2%) Heart Disease (16.6%) Accidents (5.3%) Stroke (4.5%) Diabetes (3.4%)	Cancer (24.7%) Heart Disease (23.7%) HIV/AIDS (6.6%) Accidents (6.1%) Stroke (5.3%)	Cancer (32.0%) Heart Disease (22.8%) Accidents (8.0%) Liver Disease (4.5%) Suicide (4.0%)
55 to 64 Years	Cancer (37.3%) Heart Disease (26.9%) COPD (4.7%) Stroke (4.0%) Diabetes (3.8%)	Cancer (34.2%) Heart Disease (30.6%) COPD (4.2%) Stroke (3.7%) Accidents (3.5%)	Cancer (41.8%) Heart Disease (21.3%) COPD (5.5%) Stroke (4.5%) Diabetes (4.4%)	Cancer (31.5%) Heart Disease (29.1%) Stroke (5.8%) Diabetes (5.4%) COPD (2.8%)	Cancer (38.5%) Heart Disease (26.5%) COPD (5.2%) Stroke (3.6%) Diabetes (3.4%)
65 to 74 Years	Cancer (33.7%) Heart Disease (28.6%) COPD (7.2%) Stroke (5.3%) Diabetes (3.7%)	Cancer (33.2%) Heart Disease (30.9%) COPD (6.9%) Stroke (4.8%) Diabetes (3.2%)	Cancer (34.3%) Heart Disease (25.5%) COPD (7.7%) Stroke (6.0%) Diabetes (4.4%)	Heart Disease (30.7%) Cancer (29.9%) Stroke (6.8%) Diabetes (5.6%) COPD (5.6%)	Cancer (34.3%) Heart Disease (28.3%) COPD (7.8%) Stroke (5.1%) Diabetes (3.4%)

Source: Adapted from Anderson, 2001.

EXHIBIT 8.6
Five Most Common Chronic Conditions in Men and Women Aged 45 to 64

Men	# Per 1,000 Persons	Women	# Per 1,000 Persons
Hypertension	220.0	Arthritis	297.0
Hearing Impairment	191.9	Hypertension	224.5
Arthritis	176.8	Sinusitis	210.2
Orthopedic Impairment	166.7	Orthopedic Impairment	173.2
Heart Disease	162.0	Hay Fever	133.4

Source: Based on Adams & Marano, 1995.

socioeconomic status decreases, limitations of activity due to chronic conditions become more common.

Intellectual Changes in Middle Adulthood

Perhaps no domain of human behavior in middle adulthood arouses more concern about the balance of gains and losses than intellectual functioning. A trip to your local pharmacy will confront you with the variety of supplements and herbal remedies that are marketed to midlife adults with promises of maintaining mental alertness and mental acuity. And yet, middle-aged adults are often at the peak of their careers and filling leadership roles. The most recent presidents of the United States were men older than 50.

Sherry Willis and K. Warner Schaie (1999) have tried to illuminate this dichotomy by summarizing findings from a large body of longitudinal research, drawing most heavily on the Seattle Longitudinal Study (SLS). The SLS is studying intellectual changes from the early 20s to very old age by following the same individuals over time as well as drawing new samples at each test cycle. Willis and Schaie summarize the findings about changes for selected mental abilities across the life course, paying attention to gender differences. By incorporating data on new participants as the survey progresses, they are also able to study generational (cohort) differences, addressing the question, Is the current baby boom midlife cohort functioning at a higher intellectual level than their parent's generation?

Willis and Schaie summarize the findings for six mental abilities:

1. *Vocabulary.* Ability to understand ideas expressed in words
2. *Verbal Memory.* Ability to encode and recall language units, such as word lists

3. *Number.* Ability to perform simple mathematical computations quickly and accurately
4. *Spatial Orientation.* Ability to visualize stimuli in two- and three-dimensional space
5. *Inductive Reasoning.* Ability to recognize and understand patterns in and relationships among variables to analyze and solve logical problems
6. *Perceptual Speed.* Ability to quickly make discriminations in visual stimuli

Willis and Schaie's analysis shows that middle adulthood is the period of peak performance of four of the six mental abilities: inductive reasoning, spatial orientation, vocabulary, and verbal memory. Two of the six mental abilities, perceptual speed and numerical ability, show decline in middle adulthood, but the decline in perceptual speed is much more dramatic than the decline in numerical ability. The authors note that the mental abilities that improve in middle adulthood—inductive reasoning, spatial orientation, vocabulary, and verbal memory—are among the more complex, higher-order mental abilities.

Willis and Schaie found gender differences in the changes in mental abilities during middle adulthood. They found that, on average, men reach peak performance somewhat earlier than women. Men reach peak performance on spatial orientation, vocabulary, and verbal memory in their 50s, and women reach peak performance on these same mental abilities in their early 60s. On the other hand, on average, women begin to decline in perceptual speed somewhat earlier than men, in their 20s compared to the 30s for men. The improvement in mental abilities in middle adulthood is more dramatic for women than for men. Across the adult life course, women score higher than men on vocabulary, verbal memory, perceptual speed, and inductive reasoning. Men, on the other hand, score higher than women across the adult life course on spatial orientation. Although findings are contradictory across research projects, the manufacturers of HRT suggest that menopause leads to declines in memory, which should be treated by HRT (see LeBlane, Janowsky, Benjamin, & Nelson, 2001). The findings cited by Willis and Schaie challenge this suggestion. Indeed, Willis and Schaie suggest that declines in verbal memory early in middle adulthood should be noted as a possible sign of early dementia.

What factors might be producing this historical trend toward declines in numerical ability?

Willis and Schaie also report on cohort differences in the selected mental abilities. They found that the baby boom cohort scored higher on two of the abilities, verbal memory and inductive reasoning, than their parents' generation did at the same chronological age. The baby boomers also scored higher than their parents on spatial orientation, but these differences were smaller than those for verbal memory and inductive reasoning. There were virtually no cohort differences on vocabulary and perceptual speed. The boomers did not score as well as their parents' generation on numerical ability, and the authors note that this is a continuation of a negative trend in numerical ability since the early 1900s found in other studies.

In spite of these optimistic findings about changes in intellectual functioning in middle adulthood, researchers have found that midlife adults often see themselves as deteriorating in mental abilities (Schaie, Willis, & O'Hanlon, 1994). Veronica Palmore has been heard to complain about her "senior moments." Willis and Schaie (1999) provide a databased rationale for why that might be. The data show that between 53 and 60, adults begin to show a modest decline in most mental abilities. At this point, they are still performing, on average, better than they did in early adulthood, but not as well as they did a few years earlier. The perception of decline is accurate, and it is easier to make comparisons over a short period than over a long period of time.

Personality Changes in Middle Adulthood

Does it appear to you that William George, Robert Johnson, and Veronica Palmore have grown "more like themselves" over their life course trajectories, or do you see changes in their personalities as they travel the life course? Little attention has been paid to the issue of personality in middle adulthood until quite recently. The literature that does exist on the topic consists largely of an argument about whether personality is stable or dynamic during middle adulthood. One theoretician has focused in recent years on identity processes in middle adulthood.

The Argument for Personality Stability

The idea that personality is stable in middle adulthood is an old one, rooted in Freud's psychoanalytic theory that saw personality as determined sometime in middle childhood. In this view, personality change past the age of 50 was practically impossible. The idea that personality is stable throughout adulthood comes from another very different approach to personality, commonly known as **trait theory**. According to this view, personality traits are enduring characteristics that are rooted in early temperament and are influenced by genetic and organic factors, but that remain relatively consistent across the life course. Recent empirical studies have focused on the degree to which individuals exhibit five broad personality traits, often referred to as the Big Five personality traits (Judge, Higgins, Thoresen, & Barrick, 1999):

1. *Neuroticism*: moody, anxious, hostile, self-conscious, and vulnerable
2. *Extroversion*: outgoing, friendly, lively, talkative, and active
3. *Conscientiousness*: organized, responsible, hardworking, persistent, and careful

4. *Agreeableness*: cooperative, cheerful, warm, caring, and gentle
5. *Openness to experience*: creative, imaginative, intelligent, adventurous, and nonconforming

Avshalom Caspi's **contextual model** also proposes personality stability across the life course, but it presents a different explanation for that stability (Caspi, 1987; Caspi & Roberts, 1999). Caspi and colleagues assert that personality influences both the environments we select for ourselves and how we respond to those environments. Personality leads us to choose similar environments over time, and these similar environments reinforce our personal styles. From this perspective we would ask what is it in William George's personality that led him to the streets of San Diego and how does his street existence reinforce that personality trait? We could ask the same question for the very different environments in which Robert Johnson and Veronica Palmore live out their lives.

The Argument for Personality Change

Some psychoanalysts have broken with Freud and proposed that personality continues to change across adulthood. More specifically, they propose that middle adulthood is a time when the personality ripens and matures. Most notable of these are Carl Jung, Erik Erikson, and George Vaillant. All three are consistent with humanistic models of personality that see middle adulthood as an opportunity for continued growth. Jung conceptualizes middle adulthood as a time of balance in the personality. Although Erikson sees early life as important, he suggests that societal and cultural influences call for different personal adaptations over the life course. Vaillant (1977, 2002) suggests that with age and experience, **coping mechanisms**, or the strategies we use to master the demands of life, mature. He divides coping mechanisms into immature mechanisms (denial, projection, passive aggression, dissociation, acting out, and fantasy) and mature mechanisms (sublimation, humor, altruism, and suppression). He proposes that as we age across adulthood, we make more use of mature coping mechanisms such as altruism, sublimation, and humor and less use of immature coping mechanisms such as denial and projection. Definitions for both the immature and mature coping mechanisms are found in Exhibit 8.7.

As you might imagine, life course theorists see possibilities for personality change in middle adulthood, as individuals experience life events and culturally influenced role changes. In fact, Daniel Levinson (Levinson, 1977, 1986; Levinson & Levinson, 1996), influenced by both Erikson and Jung, proposed that many adults experience a life event he called a "midlife crisis" in the transition to middle adulthood.

EXHIBIT 8.7
Coping Mechanisms

Immature Coping Mechanisms
Acting out. Ideas and feelings are acted on impulsively rather than reflectively.
Denial. Awareness of painful aspects of reality are avoided by negating sensory information about them.
Dissociation. Painful emotions are handled by compartmentalizing perceptions and memories, and detaching from the full impact.
Fantasy. Real human relationships are replaced with imaginary friends.
Passive-aggression. Anger toward others is turned inward against the self through passivity, failure, procrastination, or masochism.
Projection. Unacknowledged feelings are attributed to others.
Mature Coping Mechanisms
Altruism. Pleasure is attained by giving pleasure to others.
Mature humor. An emotion or thought is expressed through comedy, allowing a painful situation to be faced without individual pain or social discomfort.
Sublimation. An unacceptable impulse or unattainable aim is transformed into a more acceptable or attainable aim.
Suppression. Attention to a desire or impulse is postponed.

Source: Vaillant, 1977, 2002.

Evidence for Stability and Change in Midlife Personality

What can we conclude about personality in middle adulthood? Is it marked by stability or change? The available research suggests that we should think of the midlife personality in terms of both stability and change.

Research on the Big Five personality traits suggests that there is long-term stability in terms of the ranking of traits. For example, a person who is high in agreeableness at one point in adulthood will continue to be high in agreeableness across the life course (Costa & McCrae, 1994). Researchers have studied the genetic basis of the Big Five traits and found a small genetic contribution, particularly for neuroticism and agreeableness (Jang et al., 2001). In addition, a 40-year longitudinal study drawn from the Berkeley Guidance Study—which collected data during late childhood and again during young adulthood and middle adulthood—found a great deal of personality consistency over time (Caspi, 1987).

Nevertheless, a number of both cross-sectional and longitudinal studies report age-related changes in individual personality traits in middle and late adulthood

(Costa & McCrae, 1994; McCrae et al., 1999). Extroversion (activity and thrill seeking), neuroticism (anxiety and self-consciousness), and openness to experience have been found to decline with age. On the other hand, agreeableness has been found to increase with age, and conscientiousness has been found to peak in middle adulthood (Lachman & Bertrand, 2001). What's more, these patterns of age-related changes in personality have been found in cross-cultural research that included samples from Germany, Italy, Portugal, Croatia, and South Korea (McCrae et al., 1999).

Some researchers have found gender differences in personality traits to be greater than age-related differences (Lachman & Bertrand, 2001). Women score higher than men in agreeableness, conscientiousness, extroversion, and neuroticism. Men, on the other hand, score higher than women on openness to experience. These gender differences in personality have been found in 26 cultures, but the magnitude of differences varied across cultures. The researchers were surprised to find that the biggest gender differences occurred in European and American cultures, where traditional gender roles are less pronounced (Costa, Terracciano, & McCrae, 2001).

In spite of these gender differences, a number of researchers have found evidence for a gender-role shift during middle adulthood, as hypothesized by Jung, who suggested that in midlife both men and women become more androgynous. In fact, one research team found that scales measuring femininity/masculinity were among the scales that revealed the most change between the ages of 43 and 52 (Helson & Wink, 1992). Women were found by these and other researchers to increase in decisiveness, action orientation, and assertiveness during midlife. Men were found to increase in nurturance and affiliation (Havighurst et al., 1968; Neugarten & Gutmann, 1968). Writing from a different perspective, Joan Borysenko (1996), a cellular biologist, provides evidence for a gender crossover in personality in midlife that she attributes to changes in levels of sex hormones.

Although there is evidence that midlife adults often engage in review and reappraisal, there is much disagreement about whether that review and reappraisal is serious enough to constitute the midlife crisis proposed by Levinson and others. Most researchers who have studied this issue take a middle ground on this issue, suggesting that some midlife adults do reach crisis level in midlife, but in general, the idea of midlife crisis has been greatly overstated (see, e.g., Sterns & Huyck, 2001).

Whitbourne's Identity Process Model

Susan Whitbourne and colleagues (Whitbourne, 1986; Whitbourne & Connolly, 1999) propose that identity plays a central role in adult personality stability and change. Drawing on Piaget's theory of cognitive development, they suggest that identity continues to develop throughout adulthood through the processes of assimilation and accommodation. **Assimilation** is the process through which individuals incorporate new experiences into their existing identity. **Accommodation**, on the other hand, is the process through which an individual changes some aspect of identity in response to new experiences. Three identity styles are identified, based on the way that the midlife individual responds to new experiences (Whitbourne & Connolly, 1999):

1. *Assimilative identity style*. Midlife individuals see themselves as unchanging and may either deny the physical and other changes they are experiencing or rationalize them as something else.
2. *Accommodative identity style*. Midlife individuals overreact to physical and other changes, which undermines their identity and leaves it weak and incoherent.
3. *Balanced identity style*. Midlife individuals, combining goals and inner purpose with the flexibility to adapt to new experiences, recognize the physical and other changes of aging, engage in good health maintenance to minimize risk and enhance protection, and accept what cannot be changed.

How does a balanced identity style relate to human agency in making choices?

We might wonder if William George has an assimilative identity style, seeing little possibility for change in his life. On the other hand, Robert Johnson and Veronica Palmore appear to have a balanced identity style. Robert Johnson has moved with both purpose and flexibility to meet his goal of becoming a parent. Veronica Palmore was open to a new twist in her career path in midlife.

Spiritual Development in Middle Adulthood

Religion and a search for connectedness play a major role in the lives of Robert Johnson and Veronica Palmore and perhaps a growing role in William George's life. The same is true of many midlife adults. The major world religions also associate spiritual growth with advancing age (see, e.g., Biggs, 1999; Isenberg, 1992; Post, 1992; Thursby, 1992). And yet, burgeoning interest in middle adulthood among life course and human development scholars has almost entirely overlooked the issue of spiritual development. The primary effort has been models of spiritual development based on the idea that humans have the potential for continuous spiritual growth across the life course.

For example, James Fowler's Theory of Faith Development (1981) proposes six stages of faith. The first two stages occur primarily in childhood. These are the four stages that can occur in adulthood:

1. *Synthetic-conventional faith*. The basic worldview of this faith stage is that spiritual authority is found outside the individual. In this faith stage, the individual relies on a pastor or rabbi or other spiritual leader to define morality. Many people remain in this faith stage throughout their lives and never progress to the other stages.

2. *Individuative-reflective faith.* The adult no longer relies on outside authority and begins to look for authority within the self, based on moral reasoning. The individual also takes responsibility for examining the assumptions of his or her faith.

3. *Conjunctive faith.* Fowler proposes that many people never reach the stage of **conjunctive faith**, and if they do, they almost never reach it before middle adulthood. In this stage, the individual looks for balance in such polarities as independence and connection, recognizes that there are many truths, and opens out beyond the self in service to others.

4. *Universalizing faith.* In Fowler's final stage, **universalizing faith**, individuals lead selfless lives based on principles of absolute love and justice. Fowler notes that only the rare individual reaches this stage.

Fowler's theory has received support in cross-sectional research but has not yet been put to test in longitudinal research. Therefore, it should be applied with caution, recognizing that it may reflect the influences of historical time on faith development.

Interestingly, Fowler's description of conjunctive faith overlaps with theories of middle adulthood previously discussed in this chapter. For example, the reference to balance calls to mind the theories of Jung and Levinson, who saw middle adulthood as a time of bringing balance to personality and life structure. In addition, the idea of opening oneself in service to others is consistent with Erikson's idea of generativity as the psychosocial struggle of middle adulthood (Biggs, 1999; Dollahite, Slife, & Hawkins, 1998). Drawing on Jung, one theorist proposes that late midlife is "a time when our energy naturally moves beyond the concerns of our nuclear family into a concern with the world family" (Borysenko, 1996, p. 185). The emphasis is on spirituality as a state of "being connected."

One of the few studies of spiritual development in middle adulthood was described in Wade Clark Roof's *A Generation of Seekers* (1993), which reported on the "spiritual journeys of the baby boom generation." Drawing on survey data and interview responses, Roof suggested that the baby boom generation was "changing America's spiritual landscape" (Roof, 1993, p. 50). He reported that most baby boomers grew up in religious households, but 58% of his sample dropped their relationships with religious institutions for at least 2 years during their adolescence or young adulthood. Roof acknowledges that earlier generations have also dropped out of religion during early adulthood, but not in the numbers found in his sample of baby boomers. He suggests that the turmoil of the 1960s and 1970s, with a youth culture that questioned authority, is probably largely responsible for the high rate of dropout among baby boomers. Roof found that about one fourth of his sample that had dropped out had returned to religious activities by the end of the 1980s. For many of them, their return seemed to be related to having children at home.

Roof found that religious affiliation and activity did not tell the whole story about the spiritual lives of baby boomers, however. Regardless of religious affiliation, baby boomers were involved in an intense search for personal meaning (Roof, 1993). But for many of his sample, the current spiritual quest was a very personal, introspective quest, one that embraced a wide range of nontraditional as well as traditional beliefs.

In a follow-up study with the same sample from 1995 to 1997, Roof (1999) found that many boomers had shifted in their religious affiliation again. More than half of the earlier dropouts who had returned to religious activities by the late 1980s had dropped out again. But, on the other hand, one half of those who had dropped out in the 1980s had returned to religious activities by the mid-1990s. Presence of children in the home again seemed to be the factor that motivated a return to religion.

What does Roof's research suggest about spiritual age in middle adulthood?

Roof suggests that the baby boomers are leading a shift in American religious life away from an unquestioning belief to a questioning approach, and toward a belief that no single religious institution has a monopoly on truth. That shift is certainly not total at this point, however. Roof identifies five types of contemporary believers from his sample: 33% are born-again or Evangelical Christians, 25% are old-line mainstream believers, 15% are dogmatists who see one truth in the doctrine and form of their religious tradition, 15% are metaphysical seekers, and 12% are nonreligious secularists. Thus, almost three quarters of his sample could be classified as more or less unquestioning adherents of a particular system of beliefs but with an increasing trend toward recognition of the legitimacy of multiple spiritual paths.

Unfortunately, Roof does not analyze racial and ethnic differences in religious and spiritual expression for his baby boom sample. Others have found evidence, however, of strong racial and ethnic differences (Gallup & Lindsay, 1999). Black baby boomers have been much more constant in their religious beliefs and participation than white baby boomers and are far more likely to consider religion very important in their lives. Although not as steadfast as their black cohorts, Hispanic baby boomers have also been less fluid in their religious activity than their non-Hispanic white cohorts. Veronica Palmore, who dropped out of religious life while she was in college and again after her children left home, is typical of white baby boomers. On the other hand, Robert Johnson, who has been steadfast in his religious belief and activity throughout his life, is typical of black baby boomers.

Relationships in Middle Adulthood

In contemporary American life, both women and men fulfill multiple social roles in midlife (Antonucci, Akiyama, & Merline, 2001). The most central roles are related to family and paid work. Relationships with family, friends, and coworkers are an important part of life in middle adulthood.

In an analysis of longitudinal data, Elizabeth Paul (1997) found seven categories of relationships to be important to the well-being of midlife adults: relationships with mother, father, siblings, extended family, spouse or partner, children, and friends. Most midlife adults were involved in five or more of these types of relationships at one time or another, but the nature of the mix of relationships and their importance for personal well-being changed over time in complex ways. Paul concludes that people may need a variety of relationships for their psychological well-being.

Toni Antonucci and colleagues (Antonucci & Akiyama, 1987, 1997; Kahn & Antonucci, 1980) suggest that we each travel through life with a **convoy**, or a network of social relationships that protect, defend, aid, and socialize us. In one study, these researchers asked respondents in a representative sample of people aged 8 to 93 to map their convoys of support, using three concentric circles surrounding the individual respondent (Antonucci & Akiyama, 1997). In the inner circle, the respondents were asked to identify people who were so close and important to them that they could not imagine living without them. In the middle circle, respondents were asked to name people who were not quite that close but still very close and important to them. In the outer circle, respondents were asked to name people who were not as close as those in the two inner circles but who were still important enough that they came to mind as members of the support network. Exhibit 8.8 demonstrates how Veronica Palmore might respond to the request to map her current convoy. You can probably appreciate that she would map her convoy differently at different points in her life.

The size and structure of a person's convoy appear to vary with age and other demographic characteristics. For example, compared with other age groups, midlife adults (in a group aged 35-49 and a group aged 50-64) reported, on average, the largest convoys (Antonucci & Akiyama, 1997). The older midlife age group reported slightly fewer people in their convoys (average of almost 10) than the younger midlife age group (average of over 11). In both age groups, women reported more people in their convoys than men. The difference between men and women was larger in the 35 to 49 age group than in any other adult age group. What may be more important is that the gender differences show up in the closest inner circle, with midlife women reporting, on average, one more person in the inner circle than midlife men. There are also racial and ethnic differences. Whites have been found to have larger convoys than African Americans, and the convoys of African American adults have a higher proportion of kin in them than the convoys of white adults (Antonucci et al., 2001). One cross-national research project on convoys also indicates the important role of culture. In Japan, young adults in their 20s were the age group reporting the largest convoy of support (Antonucci & Akiyama, 1994).

Most of the other research that has been done on midlife adult relationships is based on the premise that the marital relationship is the focal relationship in middle adulthood. Consequently, too little is known about other familial and nonfamilial relationships. Recently, however, gerontologists have suggested that a variety of

EXHIBIT 8.8
Hypothetical Convoy for Veronica Palmore at Age 57

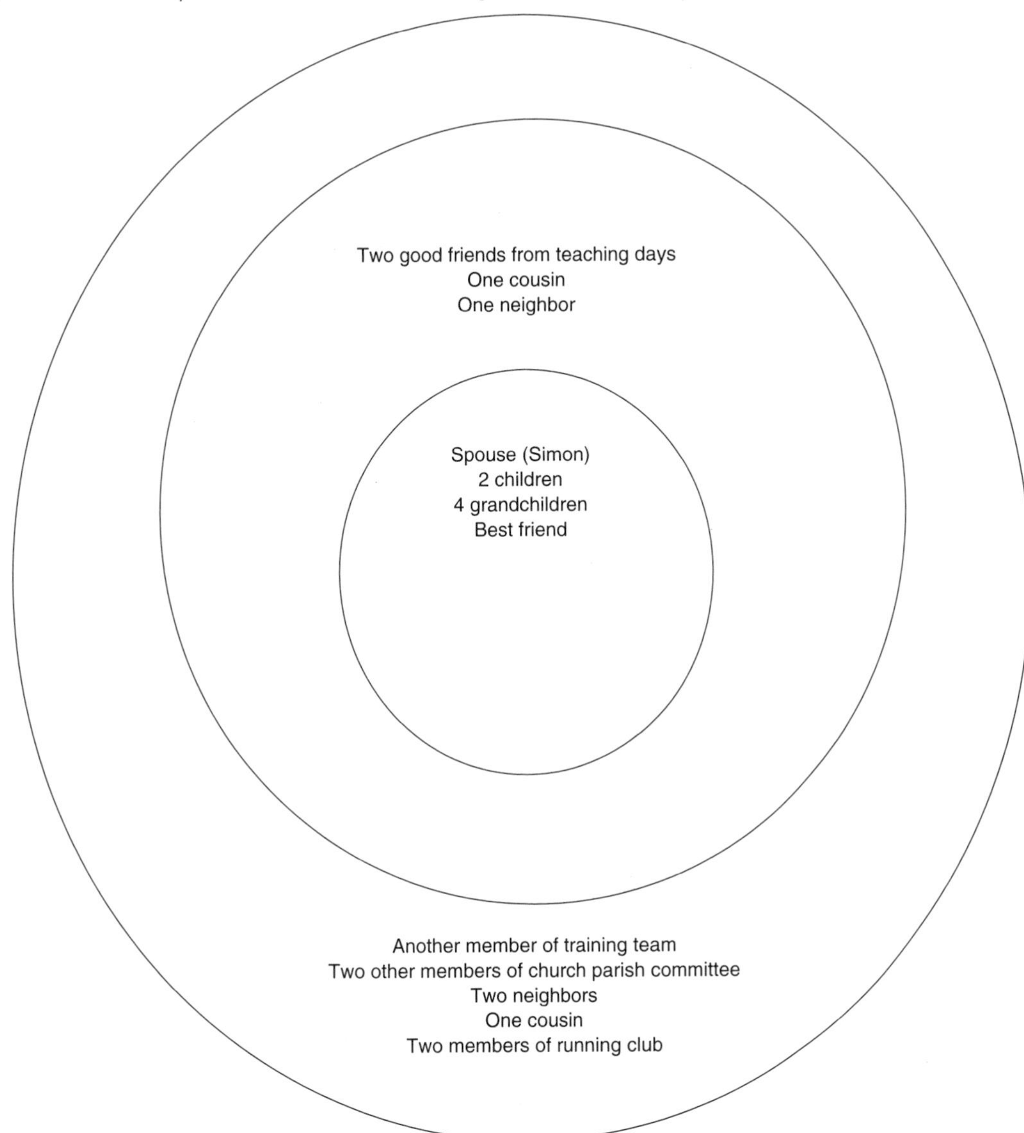

relationships are important to adults in late adulthood, and this hypothesis has led to preliminary investigations of a variety of relationships in middle adulthood (Paul, 1997). In the following sections, we look first at multigenerational family relationships and then review the limited research on friendship and community and organizational relationships.

Middle Adulthood in the Context of the Multigenerational Family

Because of increasing longevity, multigenerational families are becoming more common. By the early 1990s, three quarters of adults age 50 to 54 in the United States had a family with at least three generations; about 40% had families with four generations (Sweet & Bumpass, 1996). With a declining birthrate, the multigenerational family becomes increasingly vertical, with more generations but fewer people in each generation. This is the picture in all industrialized countries; the historical pyramid shape of the family has been replaced by a beanpole shape (tall and thin). There is also increasing complexity in the multigenerational family, with divorces and remarriages adding a variety of step-relationships to the mix.

There has been much popular speculation that family ties are weakening as geographic mobility increases. Research by Vern Bengtson and colleagues suggests, however, that there is more intergenerational solidarity than we may think (Bengtson, 2001; Putney & Bengtson, 2001). Using a national representative sample, these researchers have identified five types of extended family relationships. About one quarter (25.5%) of the families were classified as tightly knit, and another quarter (25.5%) was classified as sociable, meaning that family members are engaged with each other but do not provide to and receive concrete assistance from each other. The remaining families were about evenly split among the intimate-but-distant (16%), obligatory (16%), or those who have contact but no emotional closeness or shared belief system, and detached (17%) classifications. It is important to note that no one type of extended family relationships was found to be dominant, suggesting much diversity in intergenerational relationships in the United States. Ethnicity is one source of that variation. For example, black and Hispanic families report stronger maternal attachments than were reported in white families.

Another way of categorizing extended families is as collectivist oriented or individualistic (Pyke & Bengtson, 1996). In families with a strong collectivist orientation, kinship ties and family responsibilities take precedence over nonfamily roles. In families with a strong individualistic orientation, personal achievement and independence take precedence over family ties. The researchers found that most families were some mix of collectivist and individualistic—as appears to be the case with the families of Robert Johnson and Veronica Palmore.

Despite the evidence that intergenerational family relationships are alive and well, there is also evidence that many family relationships include some degree of conflict. One longitudinal study concluded that about one in eight adult intergenerational relationships can be described as "long-term lousy relationships" (Bengtson, 1996).

After studying multigenerational family relationships for several decades, Bengtson (2001) suggests that, with increased marital instability and a declining birthrate, multigenerational family relationships are once again becoming more important in the United States and may replace some nuclear family functions. We should perhaps think of the multigenerational family as a "latent kin network" (Bengtson, 2001, p. 12) that may be activated only at times of crisis. Of course, strong multigenerational families are still the norm in many parts of the world, and many immigrant groups bring that approach to family life with them to the United States.

The trend toward multiple generations in extended families has particular relevance for midlife adults, who make up the generation in the middle. Several researchers (see, e.g., Fry, 1995; Rosenthal, 1985) have found that midlife adults are the kinkeepers in multigenerational families and that this holds true across cultures. **Kinkeepers** are family members who work at keeping family members across the generations in touch with one another and who make sure that both emotional and practical needs of family members are met. Historically, when nuclear families were larger, kinkeepers played an important role in working to maintain ties among large sibling groups. With increased longevity and multiple generations of families, kinkeepers play an important role in the multigenerational family, working to maintain ties across the generations, ties among grandparents, parents, children, grandchildren, siblings, aunts, uncles, nieces, nephews, and cousins.

Researchers have found that most kinkeepers are middle-aged women (Aronson, 1992; Gerstel & Gallagher, 1993; Ross & Rossi, 1990). Women help larger numbers of kin than men and spend three times as many hours helping kin (Gerstel & Gallagher, 1993). Because of this kinkeeping role, midlife women have been described as the "sandwich generation" (Brody, 1985). This term was originally used to suggest that midlife women are simultaneously caring for their own children as well as their parents. Recent research suggests that with demographic changes, few women still have children at home when they begin to care for parents, but midlife women continue to be "sandwiched" with competing demands of paid work roles and intergenerational kinkeeping (Putney & Bengston, 2001).

Relationships With Spouse or Partner. In recent decades, there has been an increased diversity of marital statuses at midlife. Some men and women have been married for some time, some are getting married for the first time, some are not yet married, some will never marry, some were once married but now are divorced, some are in a second or third marriage, and some are not married but are living in a long-term committed relationship with someone of the same or opposite sex (Antonucci et al., 2001). About 75% of midlife adults are in married or partnered relationships (W. Gallagher, 1993).

For heterosexual marriages, midlife appears to be a time of both good news and bad news. On the one hand, midlife has been found to be the time of peak marital happiness (White & Edwards, 1993). Marital happiness has a first peak in the first few years, drops off during the child-rearing years, and peaks again after the last child is launched. Midlife marriages seem to combine friendship, companionship, shared interests, tolerance, and equality (Dowling, 1996). Midlife gay and lesbian partnerships have been described in a similar way, as "more companionable and less passionate" (Blacker, 1999, p. 304) than young adult gay and lesbian partnerships.

On the other hand, the divorce rate is high during midlife. There is a dramatic increase in divorce 15 to 18 years after marriage and again 25 to 28 years after marriage (Shapiro, 1996). The first increase occurs at a time when there are usually adolescent children in the family. The second increase occurs at a time when the couple has typically launched young adult children. Although many marriages flourish once the children have been launched, some marriages cannot survive without the presence of children to buffer conflicts in the marriage. Men at midlife report more marital satisfaction than women at midlife (Antonucci & Akiyama, 1997), and most divorces are initiated by women (Carter & McGoldrick, 1999a).

Although there is a period of adjustment to divorce, midlife adults cope better with divorce than young adults (Marks & Lambert, 1998). Some individuals actually report improved well-being after divorce (Antonucci et al., 2001). It is true, however, that the financial consequences of divorce for women are negative (Scott, 1997). After divorce, men are more likely to remarry than women, and whites are more likely to remarry than African Americans.

Relationships With Children. Although a growing number of midlife adults, like Robert Johnson, are parenting young children, most midlife adults are parents of adolescents or young adults. Parenting adolescents can be a challenge, and launching young adult offspring from the nest is a happy experience for most families. It is a family transition that has been undergoing changes in the past 20 years, however, coming at a later age for the parents and becoming more fluid in its timing and progress (Antonucci & Akiyama, 1997).

What factors are producing these trends in family life?

In the United States and the industrialized European countries, it became common for young adults to live outside the family prior to marriage in the 1960s, as was the case with Robert Johnson. Then, in the 1980s, two trends became evident: increased age at first leaving home and increased incidence of returning home. Popular culture has used phrases such as "prolonged parenting," "cluttered nest," and "boomerang generation" to describe these trends (Putney & Bengtson, 2001). Recent data indicate that 30 to 40% of parents between the ages of 40 and 60 live with their adult children. Approximately half of these young adult children have never left home, and the other half have left home but returned one or more times. About 40% of recent cohorts of young adults have returned home at least once after leaving home (Putney & Bengtson, 2001).

These shifts in the timing of young adult launching from the family home have created uncertainty in the expectations of both parents and young adults about realistic age norms for this family transition. In general, parents are more positive than their young adult children about living together. Fathers, in particular, seem to derive satisfaction from living with their young adult children (Spitze, Logan, Joseph, & Lee, 1994).

Young adults who live with their parents report slightly less affection toward their parents than do nonresident young adults (White & Rogers, 1997).

Attitudes toward co-residence of young adults with their parents are influenced by ethnicity and religion. Every group in the United States is more supportive of the arrangement than white, nonfundamentalist Protestants (Goldscheider & Lawton, 1998). Hispanics and non-Hispanic Catholics are the groups with the most positive attitudes toward young adults living with parents. Blacks have ambiguous attitudes: although black families tend to be more collectivist oriented than white families, among low-income blacks preference for co-residence is confounded with inadequate resources in the family. Although attitudes in Germany, France, the Netherlands, and Great Britain are similar to the attitudes of white, nonfundamentalist Protestants in the United States, young adults in Italy and Spain are expected to remain in the parental home until they form their own family, as are young adults from Asian cultures (Goldscheider, 1997). Conflicts with adolescent and young adult children often develop when midlife immigrant parents wish to maintain these cultural traditions (Antonucci et al., 2001).

Although marital happiness has been found to increase after adult children leave the house, staying closely connected to their children is important for the well-being of midlife adults (White & Edwards, 1993). In general, mothers have closer relationships with their young adult children than fathers, and divorced fathers have been found to have weaker emotional attachments with their adult children than either married fathers or divorced mothers (Silverstein & Bengtson, 1997). Young adults are more likely to continue living with parents if the family is "intact" than if the parents are divorced; the presence of a stepparent further decreases the likelihood of co-residence (Aquilino, 1990). Although the dominant culture in the United States emphasizes the importance of the marital relationship, some suggest that the parent/child relationship is the "single most important kinship tie in Western industrial societies," particularly because marital relationships are becoming less stable (Bahr, Dechaux, & Stiehr, 1994, p. 116).

Relationships With Parents. Most research shows that middle-aged adults are deeply involved with their aging parents (Antonucci & Akiyama, 1997; Cicirelli, 1983). This is the case for Robert Johnson and was the case for Veronica Palmore while her parents and Simon's parents were alive and close by.

The nature of the relationship with aging parents changes over time, however. Aging parents provide comfort, aid, and support for their midlife children, particularly while the parents are in their 60s and 70s (see, e.g., Akiyama, Antonucci, & Campbell, 1990; Bengtson & Harootyan, 1994). Robert Johnson receives much comfort and aid from his parents in his transition to parenthood. But as the parents' health begins to deteriorate, they turn more to their midlife children for help, as was the case with Simon's parents. In one study (Marks, 1998), about one in eight employed midlife adults reported giving personal care for 1 month or more to a disabled or frail relative. By age 54, one in three reported providing this type of care at some point in the past.

Traditionally, and typically still, caregivers to aging parents are daughters or daughters-in-law (Blacker, 1999). This is the case even though, by 1997, over 75% of women between the ages of 45 and 54 were employed (U.S. Bureau of Labor Statistics, 1997). At least one researcher found that unmarried women are more likely to be called upon to be the primary caregiver than other daughters (Allen, 1989). In spite of competing demands from spouses and children, providing limited care to aging parents seems to cause little psychological distress (Marks, 1998). Extended caregiving, on the other hand, has been found to have a negative effect on the emotional well-being of married women (Putney & Bengtson, 2001).

Culture plays a role in whether providing care to aging parents is experienced as a burden. Both collectivist-oriented and individualistic families meet the caregiving needs of their elders, but their motivations and processes differ (Pyke & Bengtson, 1996). Collectivist families engage in caregiving out of affection, often share the caregiving among family members, and experience little caregiver burden. This seems to have been the situation for Veronica and Simon Palmore. Individualistic families, on the other hand, engage in caregiving out of a sense of obligation, often use formal care, and are more likely to report caregiver burden. Collectivist-oriented families, such as Latino, Asian American, African American, and Native American families, normalize family caregiving. Individualistic families, such as those of Irish and Czech background, value individual independence and find elder care particularly troublesome to both caregiver and care recipient (McGoldrick, Giordano, & Pearce, 1996). Even in collectivist-oriented families, however, midlife caregivers are at high risk for stress-related illnesses. Greene (1991) has identified the issues presented in Exhibit 8.9 as points of stress for midlife caregivers.

Other Family Relationships. Midlife is typically a time of launching children and a time when parents die. It is also a time when new family members get added by marriage and the birth of grandchildren. Until recently, however, family relationships other than marital relationships and parent/child relationships have received little research attention. One notable exception is the line of research that studies extended kinship systems (Hatchett & Jackson, 1993; Paz, 1993). The grandparent/grandchild relationship has received the next greatest amount of research attention, followed by a growing body of research on sibling relationships.

For those adults who become grandparents, the onset of the grandparent role typically occurs in their 40s or 50s. This role is often gratifying to midlife adults, especially women. One study found that relationships with grandchildren are particularly important for the well-being of midlife women (Paul, 1997). Another study found that grandmothers have more affection for their grandchildren than do grandfathers (Silverstein & Long, 1998). Other researchers have noted two potential problems for

EXHIBIT 8.9
Points of Stress for Midlife Caregivers

- Shift in generational intimacy, as caregivers learn personal details and provide intimate physical care
- Shift in power and responsibility
- *Financial burden*. If midlife caregivers provide financial assistance to their parents, they may do so at the time that they are paying college tuitions and saving for retirement
- *Competing roles*. Caregivers may also be employees, students, volunteers, mothers, partners, and homemakers
- *Emotional ambivalence*. Providing intimate physical care can stimulate a variety of emotions, including embarrassment, anger, and guilt
- Confrontation of one's own aging

Source: Based on Greene, 1991.

grandparents. First, if adult children divorce, custody agreements may fail to attend to the rights of grandparents for visitation (Bergquist, Greenberg, & Klaum, 1993). Second, if adult children become incapacitated by substance abuse, illness, disability, or incarceration, grandparents may be recruited to step in to raise the grandchildren. The number of children cared for by grandparents has risen dramatically in the past 30 years. In one national representative sample, 30% of black grandmothers, 19% of Hispanic grandmothers, and 12% of white grandmothers reported that they had been surrogate parents for a grandchild at some point in their lives (Szinovacz, 1998).

Most midlife adults have at least one sibling. Sibling relationships have been found to be important for the well-being of both men and women in midlife (Paul, 1997). Siblings often drift apart in young adulthood, but contact between siblings increases in late midlife (Carstensen, 1998; Circirelli, 1995). They are often brought together around the care and death of aging parents. Their collaboration at such times may bring them closer together or may stir new as well as unresolved resentments. Although step- and half-siblings tend to stay connected to each other, their contact is less frequent than the contact between full siblings.

Relationships With Friends

Midlife adults have more family members in their social convoys than do younger and older adults, but they also continue to report at least a few important friendships (Adams & Allan, 1998). In an attempt to account for this phenomenon, one theorist suggests that midlife adults become more selective about their relationships (Carstensen, 1992). The emphasis shifts from having a large number of friends to having a smaller number of more intimate friends. This idea has some support from research (Carney & Cohler, 1993), but midlife friendships are studied less than friendships in other life phases (Sherman, de Vries, & Lansford, 2000). It is important to remember that midlife adults report larger social convoys than any other adult age group, but the bulk of those convoys are intergenerational family members. This gives credence to the suggestion that midlife adults have less time than other adult age groups for friendships (Antonucci et al., 2001).

Friendships appear to have an impact on midlife well-being for both men and women, although they do not seem to be as important as close familial relationships (Julian, 1992). For instance, the adequacy of social support, particularly from friends, at age 50 predicts physical health for men at age 70 (Vaillant, 1998). Likewise, midlife women who have a confidant or a close group of female friends report greater well-being than midlife women without such interpersonal resources (McQuaide, 1998). Women who report positive feelings toward their women friends also have fewer depressive symptoms and higher morale than women who report less positive feelings toward female friends (Paul, 1997). Whether good feelings toward friends protect against depression or depression impairs the quality of friendships remains to be determined, however.

Why is it important for social workers to recognize the role of fictive kin in the lives of their clients?

It appears that the importance of friends in the social convoy varies by sexual orientation, race, and marital status. Friends are important sources of support in the social convoys of gay and lesbian midlife adults, often serving as an accepting "chosen family" for those who have traveled the life course in a homophobic society (Johnson & Colucci, 1999; Kimmel & Slang, 1995; Weston, 1991). These chosen families provide much care and support to each other, as evidenced by the primary caregiving they have provided in times of serious illness such as AIDS and breast cancer (McGoldrick, 1999). Friends also become family in many African American families. In one study, two thirds of the black participants reported having **fictive kin**, or friends who are neither biologically nor romantically related to the family but who are adopted as family and given the same rights and responsibilities as family members (Chatters & Jayakody, 1995). Friendships also serve an important role in the social convoys of single midlife adults, serving as a chosen family rather than a "poor substitute" for family (Berliner, Jacob, & Schwartzberg, 1999; Marks & Lambert, 1998).

Community/Organizational Relationships

Little information is available about midlife relationships in the community and within organizations, but it is increasingly recognized that these relationships are important in the lives of midlife adults (Antonucci et al., 2001). The two most frequently cited places for forming friendships are workplace and neighborhood (Fischer & Phillips, 1982). Mentoring younger employees at work has been found to provide a good forum for the expression of generativity (McDermid, Heilbrun, & DeHaan, 1997). Contacts with neighbors and with volunteer associations are positively correlated with health and well-being in middle adulthood, as in other periods of the adult life course.

Black midlife women have been found to score higher on political participation than white middle-aged women in one cross-sectional study. The relationship between this participation and well-being deserves further study (Cole & Steward, 1996). Participation in a religious community is consistently found to be associated with health and well-being (Antonucci et al., 2001). Participation in voluntary associations becomes a more important part of the social convoy after retirement (Moen, 1997).

Work in Middle Adulthood

Like Robert Johnson, Veronica Palmore, and William Goerge, the majority of midlife adults engage in paid labor. Between the ages of 40 and 59, only 20% of people are unemployed, and 24% of the people between the ages of 51 and 59 are unemployed. Of those who are unemployed, 54% are retired but have been employed some in the past 5 years and 46% are dependents who have not been employed in the past 20 years. Nonemployed midlife men are more likely to be retired (85%) than nonemployed midlife women (44%). That ratio may change in future midlife cohorts, however, given the trend toward convergence of the work patterns for women and men (Elman & O'Rand, 1998).

Work and retirement have different meanings for different people. Among the meanings work can have are the following (Friedmann & Havighurst, 1954):

- A source of income
- A life routine and way of structuring time
- A source of status and identity
- A context for social interaction
- A meaningful experience that provides a sense of accomplishment

Given these meanings, employment is an important role for midlife adults in the United States, for men and women alike (Kim & Moen, 2001). However, the last few decades have seen a continuing decline in the average age of retirement, particularly for men (Kim & Moen, 2001). This trend is a little surprising in view of the lengthening of years of both midlife and late adulthood and the fact that adults are entering midlife healthier and better educated than in previous eras. Improved pension plans may be at least partially responsible for this trend.

Overall, the work patterns of middle-aged workers have changed considerably in the past 3 decades. Four trends stand out (Elman & O'Rand, 1998):

1. *Greater job mobility among middle-aged workers.* Changes in the economic institution have produced job instability for middle-aged workers. Midlife white-collar

workers who had attained midlevel management positions in organizations have been vulnerable to downsizing and reorganization efforts aimed at flattening organizational hierarchies. Midlife blue-collar workers have been vulnerable to changes in job skill requirements as the U.S. economy shifts from an industrial base to a service base. Within these broad trends, gender, class, and race have all made a difference in the work patterns of midlife adults (Elman & O'Rand, 1998). Women are more likely than men to have job disruption throughout the adult life course, although those with higher education and higher income are less vulnerable to job disruption. Race is a factor in the midlife employment disruption for men but not for women. Although black men were found to have more job disruptions than white men, there were no race differences for women when other variables were controlled.

2. *Greater variability in the timing of retirement.* Like many others in their age group, Robert Johnson has given some thought to the idea that he could retire in his late 50s, and Veronica Palmore plans to retire in her mid-60s. Today, many other midlife adults anticipate working into their late 60s or early 70s. The decision to retire is driven by both health and financial status (more particularly, the availability of pension benefits) (Han & Moen, 1999). The National Academy on an Aging Society (in Sterns & Huyck, 2001) found that 55% of persons who retired between the ages of 51 and 59 reported a health condition as a major reason for retirement. Although availability of a pension serves as inducement for retirement, men and women who work in physically demanding jobs often seek early retirement whether or not they have access to a pension. Some leave the workforce as a result of disability and become eligible for Social Security disability benefits.

3. *Blurring of the lines between working and retirement.* Many people now phase into retirement. Some middle-aged retirees return to work in different occupational fields than those from which they retired. Others leave a career at some point in middle adulthood for a part-time or temporary job. Increasing numbers of middle-aged workers leave a career position because of downsizing and reorganization and find reemployment in a job with less financial reward, a "bridge job" that carries them into retirement (Sterns & Huyck, 2001). As many as half of all the people who permanently retire have left these lower-quality jobs (Elman & O'Rand, 1998).

4. *Increasing educational reentry of midlife workers.* This trend has received little research attention. However, workers with high levels of educational attainment prior to middle adulthood are more likely than their less-educated peers to retrain in middle adulthood (Elman & O'Rand, 1998). This difference is consistent with the theory of cumulative advantage; those who have accumulated resources over the life course are more likely to have the resources for retraining in middle adulthood. But in this era of high job obsolescence, relatively few middle-aged adults will have the luxury of

choosing to do one thing at a time; to remain marketable, many middle-aged adults will have to combine work and school.

These trends aside, there is both good news and bad news for the middle-aged worker in the beginning of the 21st century. Research indicates that middle-aged workers have greater work satisfaction, organizational commitment, and self-esteem than younger workers (Matheson, 1991). Veronica Palmore is a good example of this constellation of attitudes. However, with the current changes in the labor market, employers are ambivalent about middle-aged employees. Employers may see middle-aged workers as "hard-working, reliable, and motivated" (Sterns & Huyck, 2001, p. 476). But they also often cut higher-wage older workers from the payroll as a short-range solution for reducing operating costs and staying competitive.

For some midlife adults, like William George, the issue is not how they will cope with loss of a good job but rather how they will find gainful employment at all. Some people arrive in middle adulthood still trying to establish themselves in the labor market. In the previous industrial phase, poverty was due to unemployment. In the current era, the major issue is the growing proportion of low-wage, no-benefit jobs. Black men with a high school education or less have been particularly disadvantaged in the current phase of industrialization, largely because of the declining numbers of routine production jobs. Adults with disabilities have an even harder time finding work that can support them (West, 1991). Even with legislation of the past 2 decades, much remains to be done to open educational and work opportunities to persons with disabilities.

Thus, middle-aged workers, like younger workers, are deeply affected by a changing labor market. Like younger workers, they must understand the patterns in those changes and be proactive in maintaining and updating their skills. As researchers are finding, however, that task is easier for middle-aged workers who arrive in middle adulthood with accumulated resources (e.g., Elman & O'Rand, 1998). Marginalization in the labor market in adulthood is the result of "cumulative disadvantage" over the life course. Adults, like William George, who have employment disruptions early in the adult life course have more job disruption in middle adulthood.

Risk Factors and Protective Factors in Middle Adulthood

Why is it important for social workers to understand both antecedents and consequences of midlife behavior?

From a life course perspective, midlife behavior has both antecedents and consequences. Earlier life experiences can serve either as risk factors or as protective factors for health and well-being during middle adulthood. And midlife behaviors can serve either as risk factors or as protective factors for future health and well-being. The rapidly growing body of literature on risk, protection, and resilience based on longitudinal research has recently begun to add to our understanding of the antecedents of midlife behavior.

One of the best known programs of research is a study begun by Emmy Werner and associates with a cohort born in 1955 on the island of Kauai, Hawaii. The research participants turned 40 in 1995, and Werner and Ruth Smith (2001) capture their risk factors, protective factors, and resilience in *Journeys from Childhood to Midlife.* They summarize their findings by suggesting that they "taught us a great deal of respect for the self-righting tendencies in human nature and for the capacity of *most* individuals who grew up in adverse circumstances to make a successful adaptation in adulthood" (p. 166). At age 40, compared to previous decades, the overwhelming majority of the participants reported "significant improvements" in work accomplishments, interpersonal relationships, contributions to community, and life satisfaction. Most adults who had a troubled adolescence had recovered by midlife. Many of these adults who had been troubled as youth reported that the "opening of opportunities" (p. 168) in their 20s and 30s had led to major *turning points.* Such turning points included continuing education at community college, military service, marriage to a stable partner, religious conversion, and survival despite a life-threatening illness or accident. At midlife, participants were still benefiting from the presence of a competent, nurturant caregiver in infancy, as well as from the emotional support along the way of extended family, peers, and caring adults outside the family.

Although this research is hopeful, Werner and Smith (2001) also found that one of six of the study cohort was doing poorly at work and in relationships. The earlier risk factors associated with poor midlife adjustment include severe perinatal trauma, small for gestational age birth weight, early childhood poverty, serious health problems in early childhood, problems in early schooling, parental alcoholism and/or serious mental illness, health problems in adolescence, and health problems in the 30s. William George's early life produced several of these risk factors: early childhood poverty, problems in early schooling, and parental mental illness. For men, the most powerful risk factor was parental alcoholism from birth to age 18. Women were especially negatively affected by paternal alcoholism during their adolescence. It is interesting to note that the long-term negative effects of serious health problems in early childhood and adolescence were just beginning to show up at age 40.

Several studies have also examined the effects of midlife behavior, specifically the effects on subsequent health (Stamler et al., 1999; Vita, Terry, Hubert, & Fries, 1998). They have found a number of health behaviors that are risk factors for more severe and prolonged health and disability problems in late adulthood. These include smoking, heavy alcohol use, diet high in fats, overeating, and sedentary lifestyle. Economic deprivation and high levels of stress have also been found to be risk factors throughout the life course (Auerback & Krimgold, 2001; Spiro, 2001). A health behavior that is receiving much research attention as a protective factor for health and well-being in late adulthood is a physical fitness program that includes stretching exercises, weight training, and aerobic exercise (Whitbourne, 2001).

IMPLICATIONS FOR SOCIAL WORK PRACTICE

This discussion has several implications for social work practice with midlife adults:

- Be familiar with the unique pathways your clients have traveled to reach middle adulthood.
- Recognize the role that culture plays in constructing beliefs about appropriate midlife roles and assist clients to explore their beliefs.
- Help clients to think about their own involvement in generative activity and the meaning that this involvement has for their lives.
- Become familiar with biological changes and special health issues in middle adulthood. Engage midlife clients in assessing their own health behaviors.
- Be aware of your own beliefs about intellectual changes in middle adulthood and evaluate those against the available research evidence.
- Be aware of both stability and the capacity for change in personality in middle adulthood.
- Help clients assess the role that spirituality plays in their adjustments in middle adulthood and, where appropriate, to make use of their spiritual resources to solve current problems.
- Engage midlife clients in a mutual assessment of their involvement in a variety of relationships, including romantic relationships, relationships with parents, relationships with children, other family relationships, relationships with friends, and community/organizational relationships.
- Collaborate with social workers and other disciplines to advocate for governmental and corporate solutions to work and family life conflicts.

KEY TERMS

accommodation
assimilation (identity)
conjunctive faith
contextual model
convoy
coping mechanism

extroversion
fictive kin
generativity
introversion
kinkeepers
life-span theory
menopause
premenopause
perimenopause
trait theory
universalizing faith

Active Learning

1. Think about how you understand the balance of gains and losses in middle adulthood. Interview three midlife adults ranging in ages from 40 to 60 and ask them whether they see the current phase of their lives as having more gains or more losses over the previous phase.

2. Draw your social convoy as it currently exists with three concentric circles:

   - Inner circle of people who are so close and important to you that you could not do without them
   - Middle circle of people who are not quite that close but are still very close and important to you
   - Outer circle of people who are not as close and important as those in the two inner circles but still close enough to be considered part of your support system

   What did you learn from engaging in this exercise? Do you see any changes you would like to make in your social convoy?

3. What evidence do you see of antecedent risk factors and protective factors that are affecting the midlife experiences of William George, Robert Johnson, and Veronica Palmore? What evidence do you see of current behaviors that might have consequences, either positive or negative, for their experiences with late adulthood.

Web Resources

Max Planck Institute for Human Development

www.mpib-berlin.mpg.de

Site presented by the Max Planck Institute for Human Development, Berlin, Germany, contains news and research about life course development.

Network on Successful Midlife Development

www.macfound.org/research/hcd/hcd_20.htm

Site presented by the John D. and Catherine T. MacArthur Foundation Research Network on Successful Midlife Development (MIDMAC) contains an overview of recent research on midlife development and links to other human development research projects.

Boomers International

boomersint.org

Site presented by Boomers International: World Wide Community for the Baby Boomer Generation contains information from the trivial to the serious on the popular culture of the baby boomer generation.

MEDLINEplus: Hormone Replacement Therapy

www.nlm.nih.gov/medlineplus/hormonereplacementtherapy.html

Site presented by the National Institute on Aging contains the latest news on research on hormone replacement therapy to treat menopause in midlife women.

Families and Work Institute

www.familiesandwork.org

Site presented by the Families and Work Institute contains information on work-life research, community mobilization forums, information on the Fatherhood Project, and frequently asked questions.

National Center for Health Statistics Fast Stats

www.cdc.gov/nchs/fastats/lifexpec.htm

Site presented by National Center for Health Statistics contains statistics on life expectancy for different groups and links to other relevant sites.

CHAPTER 9

Late Adulthood

Peter Maramaldi

Matthias J. Naleppa

CHAPTER 9

Late Adulthood

Peter Maramaldi
University of Utah

Matthias J. Naleppa
Virginia Commonwealth University

How will the trend toward increased longevity affect family life and social work practice?

What do social workers need to understand about coping mechanisms in late adulthood?

What formal and informal resources are available for meeting the needs of elderly persons?

Key Ideas

As you read this chapter, take note of these central ideas:

1. Unlike in earlier historical eras, many people in the United States today reach the life phase of late adulthood, and the older population is a very heterogeneous group, including the young-old (65-74 years), the middle-old (75-84 years), and the oldest-old (85 and above). In this chapter, we consider the young-old and the middle-old.
2. The most commonly discussed theories of social gerontology are disengagement theory, activity theory, continuity theory, social construction of aging, feminist theories of aging, social exchange theory, life course theory, and the age stratification perspective; the most common theories of biological aging are the programmed aging theories and random error theories.
3. All systems of the body appear to be affected during the aging process.

4. It has been difficult to understand psychological changes in late adulthood without long-term longitudinal research, but recent longitudinal research suggests that with age and experience, individuals tend to use more adaptive coping mechanisms.

5. Families play an important role in late adulthood, and as a result of increased longevity, multigenerational families are more common than ever.

6. Although most persons enter retirement in late adulthood, some individuals continue to work even after they are eligible to retire, either out of financial necessity or by choice.

7. Older adults rely on a number of both informal and formal resources to meet their changing needs.

Case Study 9.1

The Smiths in Early Retirement

The Smiths are a European American couple in their early retirement years who have come to you for couples counseling. Lois Smith is 66 and Gene Smith is 68 years of age. They have lived in the same quiet suburban neighborhood since they married 20 years ago. When they met, Gene was a widower and Lois had been divorced for 3 years. They have no children from this marriage but three children from Lois's first marriage. The Smiths are grandparents to the three children of their married daughter, who lives 4 hours away. Their two sons are both single and also live in a different city. The Smiths visit their children frequently, but family and holiday gatherings usually take place at the Smiths' house.

The Smiths live in a comfortable home, but their neighborhood has changed over the years. When they bought the house, many other families were in the same life stage, raising adolescent children and seeing them move out as young adults. Many of the neighbors from that time have since moved, and the neighborhood has undergone a change to young families with children. Although the Smiths feel connected to the community, they do not have much interaction with the people in their immediate neighborhood. Only one other neighbor, a woman in her mid-80s, is an older adult. This neighbor has difficulty walking and no longer drives a car. The Smiths help her with chores around the house and often take her shopping.

Until her divorce, Lois had focused primarily on raising her children. After the divorce at age 43, she needed to enter the job market. Without

CASE STUDY 9.1

formal education beyond high school, she had difficulty finding employment. She worked in a number of low-paying short-term jobs before finding a permanent position as a secretary at a small local company. She has only a small retirement benefit from her 12 years on that job. Gene had worked as bookkeeper and later assistant manager with a local hardware store for more than 30 years. Although their combined retirement benefits enable them to lead a comfortable retirement, Gene continues to work at the hardware store on a part-time basis.

The transition into retirement has not been easy for the Smiths. Both Gene and Lois retired last year, which required them to adjust all at once to a decrease in income. Much more difficult, however, has been the loss of status and feeling of void that they are experiencing. Both were accustomed to the structure that was provided by work. Gene gladly assists in his former company on a part-time basis, but he worries that his employer will think he's getting too old. Lois has no plans to reenter the workforce. She would like her daughter to live closer so she could spend more time with the grandchildren. Although the infrequency of the visits with the grandchildren has placed some strain on Lois's relationship with her daughter, especially in the period following her retirement, Lois has now begun to enjoy the trips to visit with her daughter as a welcome change in her daily routine. But those visits are relatively infrequent, and Lois often wishes she had more to do.

CASE STUDY 9.2

MS. RUBY JOHNSON, CARETAKER FOR THREE GENERATIONS

Ms. Ruby Johnson is a handsome woman who describes herself as a "hard-boiled, 71-year-old African American" who spent the first 30 years of her life in Harlem, until she settled in the Bronx, New York. She married at 19 and lived with her husband until her 30th birthday. During your initial assessment for case management services, she explained her divorce with what appeared to be great pride. On her 29th birthday, Ruby told her husband that he had one more year to choose between "me and the bottle." She tolerated his daily drinking for another year, but when he came home

CASE STUDY 9.2

drunk on her 30th birthday, she took their 6-year-old daughter and left him and, she explained, "never looked back."

Ruby immediately got a relatively high-paying—albeit tedious—job working for the postal service. At the same time, she found the Bronx apartment, in which she has resided for the past 41 years. Ruby lived there with her daughter, Darlene, for 18 years until she "put that girl out" on what she describes as the saddest day of her life.

Darlene was 21 when she made Ruby the grandmother of Tiffany, a vivacious little girl in good health. A year later, Darlene began using drugs when Tiffany's father abandoned them. By the time Darlene was 24, she had a series of warnings and arrests for drug possession and prostitution. Ruby explained that it "broke my heart that my little girl was out there sellin' herself for drug money." Continuing the story in an unusually angry tone, she explained that "I wasn't gonna have no 'hoe' live in my house."

During your initial interview, Ruby's anger was betrayed by a flicker of pride when she explained that Darlene, now 46, has been drug free for more than 20 years. Tiffany is 25 and lives with her husband and two children. They have taken Darlene into their home to help Ruby. Ruby flashed a big smile when she told you that "Tiffany and Carl [her husband] made me a great-grandma twice, and they are taking care of Darlene for me now." Darlene also has a younger daughter—Rebecca—from what Ruby describes as another "bad" relationship with a "no good man." Rebecca, age 16, has been living with Ruby for the past 2 years since she started having difficulty in school and needed more supervision than Darlene was able to provide.

In addition, about a year ago, Ruby became the care provider for her father, George. He is 89 and moved into Ruby's apartment because he was no longer able to live independently after his brother's death. On most weeknights, Ruby cooks for both her father, her granddaughter, and everyone at Tiffany's house as well. Ruby says she loves having her family around, but she just doesn't have half the energy she used to have.

Ruby retired 5 years ago from the postal service, where she worked for 36 years. In addition to her pension and Social Security, she now earns a small amount for working part time providing child care for a former coworker's daughter. Ruby explains that she has to take the extra work in order to cover her father's prescription expenses not covered by his Medicare benefits, and help pay medical/prescription bills for Tiffany's household. Tiffany and Carl receive no medical benefits from their employers and are considering lowering their income in order to qualify for Medicaid

CASE STUDY 9.2

benefits. Ruby wants them to keep working, so she has been trying to use her connections to get them jobs with the postal service. Ruby reports this to be her greatest frustration, because her best postal service contacts are "either retired or dead."

Although Ruby's health is currently stable, she is particularly concerned that her own health may worsen. She is diabetic and insulin dependent and worries about all the family members for whom she feels responsible. During your initial interview, Ruby confided that she thinks that her physical demise has begun. Her greatest fear is death; not for herself, she tells you, but for the effect it would have on her family. She asked you to help her find a way to ensure their well-being after her death.

Case Study 9.3

The Moros' Increasing Needs for Care

Frank Moro is an 82-year-old married man who lives with his 80-year-old wife, Camille, in their own home. Both Frank and Camille are second-generation Italian Americans. Frank had a stroke 1 year ago that resulted in a right-side paralysis. He has several other limiting medical conditions, including arthritis, hypertension, and a partial loss of vision. He perceives his health to be fair, even though his level of functioning in activities of daily living is very low. He needs assistance in using the toilet, rising from a chair, getting in and out of bed, moving around, and personal care. Frank has a wheelchair that he rarely uses. He shows a slight cognitive decline on a standardized measurement tool. Camille is the primary caregiver, assisting her husband in his personal care, helping him in and out of bed, and assisting him with toileting. The two sons who live in the area also provide assistance, especially with home repairs and financial arrangements.

Frank was referred by his physical therapist to the case management program for which you work as a case manager. Since his stroke, he is not able to ambulate independently. His wife and sons have reported being overwhelmed by round-the-clock caregiving.

During your first home visit, you identified several needs: Frank needed assistance with his personal care and mobility, and he did not use his wheelchair. Furthermore, Camille needed some respite. After exploring Frank's

CASE STUDY 9.3

personal care needs, you told the Moros about the services available to them. Then the three of you agreed to undertake a couple of tasks: you would contact a home health aide to set up a meeting, and the Moros would discuss their needs and make arrangements with the home health aide. These tasks were completed quickly, and the aide began providing services within a week.

Two other target problems can be met by the same solution. After some discussion, it was decided that Frank would benefit from medical adult day care, which could assist in maintaining his mobility. Day care would also provide respite for Camille. Implementing this plan took a little longer, however, because the Moros had to visit an adult day care center, apply, and arrange for transportation before Frank could begin to attend.

Another area of need, identified by Camille, related to Frank's unwillingness to use the wheelchair. In his culture, he said, men do not advertise physical limitations and dependence on others. His self-esteem as well as cultural factors seemed to be hindering efforts to increase his mobility. With a great deal of persuasion, you helped Frank see the benefits of using a wheelchair, and he finally agreed to try it out for a few days. Although he began very reluctantly, after several weeks Frank got used to the wheelchair. He uses it on a daily basis now and concedes that it has significantly enhanced his independence.

Demographics of the Older Population

Every client in these stories could be considered old, and yet, they are functioning in different ways and at different levels. The term *old* can have many meanings. In discussing life course trajectories, we commonly use the terms *older population* or *elderly persons* to refer to those over 65 years of age. But an Olympic gymnast is "old" at age 25, a president of the United States is "young" at age 50, and a 70-year-old may not consider herself "old" at all.

Late adulthood is perhaps a more precise term than *old*, but it can still be confusing because of the 50-year range of ages it may include. *Late adulthood* starts at 65, continues through the 85-and-older range (which is the fastest growing segment of the older population), and includes increasing numbers of people 100 years and older. With a life expectancy in the United States of 79 years for women and 74 years for men, many people today reach the life stage of late adulthood (Federal Interagency Forum on Aging-Related Statistics, 2000a).

EXHIBIT 9.1 Dependency Ratio: Percentage of Children and Elderly in the U.S. Population, 1900, 1980, 2030

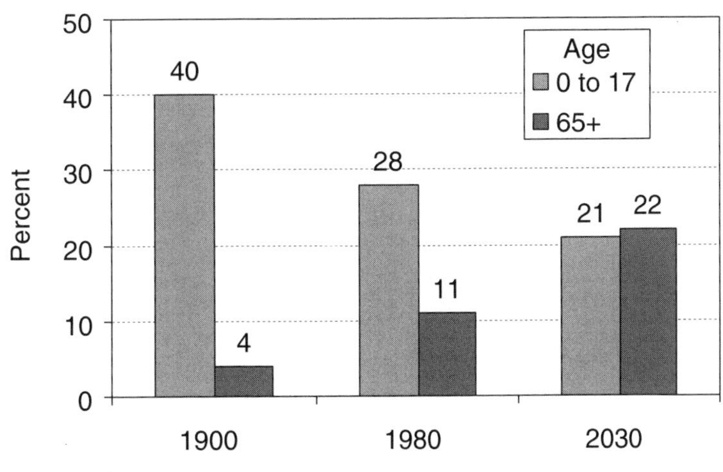

Source: Moody, 1998, p. 220.

What factors are leading to this trend toward increased longevity?

Just a century ago, it was uncommon to reach 65. The first population census of the United States, conducted in 1870, estimated about 3% of the population to be over 65 years of age. Today, more than three fourths of all persons in the United States live to be 65 (Walker, Manoogian-O'Dell, McGraw, & White, 2001). More than 12% of the U.S. population is 65 or older, and a person reaching 65 can expect to live another 17 years (Hobbs & Damon, 1997). The U.S. Census Bureau estimates that in the next 50 years, the elderly population will double to 80 million, representing approximately 20% of the estimated total population.

An interesting side effect of the growing elderly population is a shifting **dependency ratio**—a demographic indicator that expresses the degree of demand placed on society by the young and the aged combined (Morgan & Kunkel, 1996). Currently, the dependency ratio is stable, because the increase in elderly dependents is being offset by a decrease in dependents under 18 (Soldo & Agree, 1988). However, the nature of the U.S. dependency ratio has changed gradually over the past century, as the percentage of children in the population has decreased and the percentage of dependent older adults has increased. This demographic shift toward aged dependents suggests, as Exhibit 9.1 shows, that by the year 2030, there will be more people over 65 than under 18 in the United States (Moody, 1998).

Because today it encompasses such a broad age range, the older population is often categorized into subgroups: the young-old (age 65 to 74), the middle-old (age 75 to 84), and the oldest-old (over 85). The Smiths and Ruby Johnson exemplify the young-old, the Moros the middle-old. In this chapter, we discuss those persons in the young-old and middle-old categories, ages approximately 65 to 84. Very late adulthood is discussed in Chapter 10, covering ages 85 and over.

Census 2000 revealed that among the older population, women continue to outnumber men across all racial and ethnic groups. In addition, the proportion of men steadily drops with age—with 82 men for every 100 women in the 65 to 74 age group, 65 men for every 100 women in the 75 to 84 age group, and 41 men for every 100 women in the 85 years and older age group (U.S. Census Bureau, 2001b).

One of the biggest differences in life circumstances for elderly women and men is the difference in their marital status. In 1998, 55% of women and 79% of men between 65 to 74 years who were not living in an institutional setting were married (Federal Interagency Forum on Aging-Related Statistics, 2000b). This is an important consideration, because marital status influences a person's emotional and economic status, living arrangement, and caregiving needs. In 1998, about 48% of the elderly women were widowed, compared to 14% of the elderly men. Moreover, the current cohort entering the older population is seeing an increase in divorced or separated elderly.

Not surprisingly, elderly women are more likely than elderly men to live alone, and living arrangements for older women vary by race and ethnicity. In 1998, the proportion of white and black women living alone was similar (about 41%). Fewer older Hispanic women lived alone (27%) and even fewer Asian and Pacific Island women lived alone (21%) (Federal Interagency Forum on Aging-Related Statistics, 2000c). Although one can draw inferences about cultural differences and familial support from these comparisons, take caution to consider the complex relationship between culture, socioeconomic status, and individual personality.

Fewer elderly persons are institutionalized than we generally assume, but the risk for entering a nursing home increases significantly with age. During the past decade, the percentages of older people living in nursing homes actually declined from 5.1% in 1990 to 4.5% in 2000. However, the risk of entering a nursing home continues to increase with age. Only 1.1% of older adults between the age of 65 and 74 are in nursing homes, but 18.2% of those 85 years and older are (U.S. Census Bureau, 2001b). It remains to be seen whether Gene Smith, Lois Smith, Ms. Johnson, Frank Moro, or Camille Moro will spend some time before death in a nursing home.

As Exhibit 9.2 demonstrates, the elderly population is becoming increasingly diverse in race and ethnic background. Census 2000 data indicate that 16% of adults over age 65 are nonwhite, with 8% non-Hispanic black, 6% Hispanic, 2% Asian and Pacific Islander. The U.S. Census Bureau estimates that between 2000 and 2050, the non-Hispanic white population will decline from 84% to 64% of the total late adult population. Hispanic people are expected to account for 16% of the older population, with 12% projected to be non-Hispanic black people and 7% identified as non-Hispanic Asian and Pacific Island people (Administration on Aging, 2002).

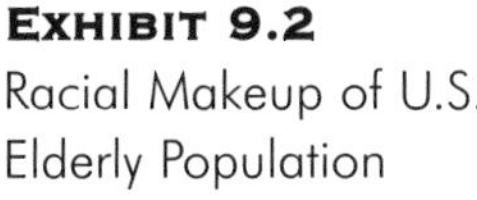

EXHIBIT 9.2
Racial Makeup of U.S. Elderly Population

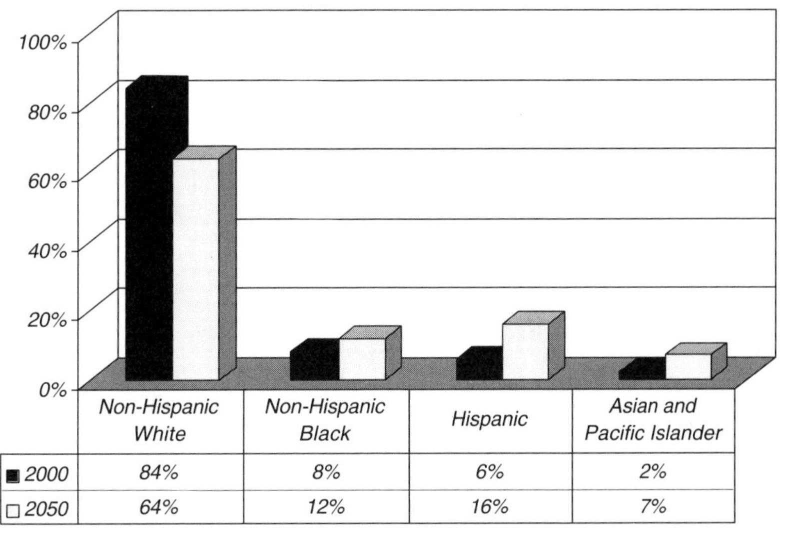

	Non-Hispanic White	Non-Hispanic Black	Hispanic	Asian and Pacific Islander
■ 2000	84%	8%	6%	2%
□ 2050	64%	12%	16%	7%

Source: Based on Administration on Aging, 2002.

How are gender, race, and social class related in late adulthood?

Gender, race, and ethnicity have a significant effect on the economic status of elderly individuals. In general, poverty rates increase with age across the late adult years. According to U.S. Census data, 10.5% of the population over age 65 fell below the federal poverty threshold in 1998. The poverty rate for persons 65 to 74 was 9%, 12% for the population between the ages of 65 to 74, and 14% for those age 85 and older. However, elderly men have a significantly lower poverty rate than elderly women (7% vs. 17%). The poverty rates also differ for racial groups, with black elderly persons having the highest poverty rate (26.4%), followed by Hispanics (21%), non-Hispanic Asian and Pacific Islanders (16%), and whites (8.2%) (Administration on Aging, 2002). Trends indicate that the poverty rate is currently declining for all racial and ethnic groups of older adults.

The geographic distribution of the elderly population across the United States is also varied. Between 1990 and 2000, every state experienced population increases in the proportion of age 65 and older, ranging from a 1% increase in Rhode Island to a 79% increase in Nevada. Only the District of Columbia showed a decrease in the proportion of people age 65 and older. The greatest regional increases in percentages of older people occurred in the West (20%) and the South (16%). Increases occurred at significantly lower rates in the Midwest (7%) and the Northeast (5%) (U.S. Census Bureau, 2001b).

Residential mobility has a significant impact on the distribution of the elderly population. The migration of older persons to Florida after retirement contributes to its high percentage of elderly residents. On the other hand, high percentages of elderly residents in some other regions are the result of outward migration by younger people (Hobbs & Damon, 1997).

Residential mobility can also lead to changing age structures within neighborhoods and thus affect the elderly person's life. For example, the Smiths used to be a "typical" family in their neighborhood. Now, as one of only two households with elderly occupants, they are the exception.

Cultural Construction of Late Adulthood

How important is social age in defining late adulthood?

The ethnic/racial diversity of the older population in the United States underscores the importance of taking cultural differences in perceptions of aging into account. A salient example of cultural differences in approaches to aging are the contrasts between traditional Chinese and U.S. beliefs and values. China has been described in the anthropological literature as a "gerontocracy," wherein older people are venerated, given deference, and valued in nearly every task. Benefiting from the Confucian values of filial piety, older people hold a revered position in the family and society.

By contrast, consider the traditional cultural influences in the United States, where fierce independence and self-reliance are core values that inherently conflict with the aging process. In the United States, older people have traditionally been collectively regarded as dependent, and cultural values dictate that older people living independently are given higher regard than those requiring assistance. As people age, they strive to maintain the independence and avoid—at all costs—becoming a burden to their family. Older people in the United States typically resort to intervention from private or social programs to maintain their independence rather than turning to family. By contrast, Chinese elders traditionally looked forward to the day when they would become part of their children's household, to live out their days being venerated by their families (Kao & Lam, 1997). No discussion of comparisons between cultures would be complete without mention of differences that occur within groups. An individual Chinese person might value independence. And an individual in the United States might be closer to the Confucian value of filial piety than traditional U.S. values. In fact, U.S. values of aging appear to be shifting, influenced in part by political and market forces. In the United States, we are now bombarded with contradictory information about aging—media presentations of long-lived, vibrant older adults are juxtaposed with media presentations of nursing home horror stories (Vaillant, 2002).

In his recent book, *Aging Well,* George Vaillant (2002) raises the question, "Will the longevity granted to us by modern medicine be a curse or a blessing?" (p. 3). The answer, he suggests, is influenced by individual, societal, and cultural values, but his research makes him optimistic. Vaillant reports on the most long-term longitudinal research available, the Study of Adult Development. The study includes three separate cohorts of 824 persons, all of whom have been studied since adolescence:

1. 268 socially advantaged graduates of Harvard University born about 1920. These research participants were selected for their physical and psychological health as they began college.
2. 456 socially disadvantaged inner-city men born in 1930. These research participants were selected because they were nondelinquent at age 14. Half of their families were known to five or more social agencies, and more than two thirds of their families had been recent public welfare recipients.
3. 90 middle-class intellectually gifted women born about 1910. These participants were selected for their high IQs when they were in California elementary schools.

A major limitation of the study is the lack of racial and ethnic diversity among the participants, who are almost exclusively white. The great strength of the study is its ability to control cohort effects by following the same participants over such a long period of time.

How much choice do we have over the six traits for "growing old with grace"?

Much of the news from the Study of Adult Development is good news. Vaillant reminds us that Immanuel Kant wrote his first book of philosophy at 57, Titian created many art works after 76, Ben Franklin invented bifocals at 78, and Will Durant won a Pulitzer Prize for history at 83. Unless they develop a brain disease, the majority of older adults maintain a "modest sense of well-being" (p. 5) until a few months before they die. Older adults are less depressed than the general population. Many older adults acknowledge hardships of aging but also see a reason to continue to live. Vaillant concludes that "positive aging means to love, to work, to learn something we did not know yesterday, and to enjoy the remaining precious moments with loved ones" (p. 16). Although he found many paths to successful aging, Vaillant identifies six traits for "growing old with grace," found in Exhibit 9.3.

Vaillant reports that he had originally planned to study only the rate of physical deterioration as individuals age. He had absorbed the cultural bias that aging was only about decay. He recounts a letter he received from one study participant, who wrote, "You ask us what we can no longer do . . . but I detect little curiosity about our adaptability, our zest for life, how our old age is, or isn't, predictable from what went before" (p. 36). This feedback influenced Vaillant to pursue the possibilities in late adulthood, without denying the special hardships of this life phase. Note that this study participant and other members of the current generation of older adults are exercising human agency and, in the process, producing changes in some of the culture of aging in the United States.

EXHIBIT 9.3
Six Traits for Growing Old With Grace

1. Caring about others and remaining open to new ideas
2. Showing cheerful tolerance of the indignities of old age
3. Maintaining hope
4. Maintaining a sense of humor and capacity for play
5. Taking sustenance from past accomplishments while remaining curious and continuing to learn from the next generation
6. Maintaining contact and intimacy with old friends

Source: Vaillant, 2002, pp. 310-311.

EXHIBIT 9.4
Theoretical Perspectives on Social Gerontology

Theory	Primary Concept
Disengagement theory	Elderly persons gradually disengage from society.
Activity theory	Level of life satisfaction is related to level of activity.
Continuity theory	Elderly persons continue to adapt and continue their interaction patterns.
Social construction theory	Self-concepts arise through interaction with the environment.
Feminist theory	Gender is an important organizing factor in the aging experience.
Social exchange theory	Resource exchanges in interpersonal interactions change with age.
Life course perspective	Aging is a dynamic, lifelong process characterized by many transitions.
Age stratification perspective	Society is stratified by age, which determines people's roles and rights.

Theoretical Perspectives on Social Gerontology

How we as social workers see and interpret aging will inspire our interventions with an older adult. **Social gerontology**—the social science that studies human aging—offers several theoretical perspectives that can explain the process of growing old. Eight predominant theories of social gerontology are introduced here. An overview of the primary concepts of each theory is presented in Exhibit 9.4.

1. *Disengagement theory.* Disengagement theory suggests that as elderly individuals grow older, they gradually decrease their social interactions and ties and become increasingly self-preoccupied (Cumming & Henry, 1961). Considering Frank Moro, for example, you might interpret his initial lack of initiative to increase his mobility by using the wheelchair as a sign of his disengagement from others. In addition, society disengages itself from older adults. Although disengagement is seen as a normative and functional process of transferring power within society, the theory does not explain, for example, the fact that a growing number of older persons like Gene and Lois Smith continue to assume active roles in society. Disengagement theory has received much criticism and little research support (Neugarten, Havighurst, & Tobin, 1968).

2. *Activity theory.* **Activity theory** states that higher levels of activity and involvement are directly related to higher levels of life satisfaction in elderly people (Havighurst, 1968). If they can, individuals stay active and involved, and carry on as many activities of middle adulthood as possible. Activity theory has received some criticism for not addressing relatively high levels of satisfaction for individuals like Ms. Johnson, whose level of activity is declining. It also does not address the choice made by many older individuals to adopt a more relaxed lifestyle.

3. *Continuity theory.* **Continuity theory** was developed in response to critiques of the disengagement and activity theories. According to continuity theory, individuals adapt to changes by using the same coping styles they have used throughout the life course, and they adopt new roles that substitute for roles lost because of age (Neugarten et al., 1968). Individual personality differences are seen as a major influence in adaptation to old age. Those individuals who were active earlier in life stay active in later life, whereas those who adopted a more passive lifestyle continue to do so in old age. Older adults also typically retain the same stance concerning religion and sex as they always did. Continuity theory might help you counsel someone like Lois Smith. Just as she adapted actively to her divorce by reentering the job market later in life, she might actively seek new roles in retirement. She might find great satisfaction in volunteering in her church and in being a grandmother.

4. *Social construction theory.* **Social construction theory** aims to understand and explain the influence of social definitions, social interactions, and social structures on the individual elderly person. The individual's self-conceptions about aging arise through interaction with the social environment (Dannefer & Perlmutter, 1990). For instance, George Vaillant's conceptions of aging changed as he followed research participants into late adulthood.

5. *Feminist theory.* Proponents of **feminist theories** of aging suggest that gender is a key factor in understanding a person's aging experience. They contend that because

gender is an organizing principle in our society, we can only understand aging by taking gender into account (Arber & Ginn, 1995). Think, for example, about Camille Moro's experience as a caregiver to her husband and about Ms. Johnson's experience as a single older woman. How might their personal situations differ if they were men?

6. *Social exchange theory.* **Social exchange theory** is built on the notion that an exchange of resources takes place in all interpersonal interactions (Blau, 1964; Homans, 1961). Individuals will only engage in an exchange if they perceive a favorable cost/benefit ratio or if they see no better alternatives (Hendricks, 1987). As individuals become older, however, the resources they are able to bring to the exchange begin to shift. Exchange theory bases its explanation of the realignment of roles, values, and contributions of older adults on this assumption. For example, many older persons get involved in volunteer activities; this seemingly altruistic activity may also be seen as fulfilling an emotional need that provides a personal gain. Older individuals who withdraw from social activities may perceive their personal resources as diminished to the point where they have little left to bring to an exchange, thus leading to their increasing seclusion from social interactions. You might want to explore how Frank and Camille Moro are dealing with the shift in resources within their relationship.

7. *Life course perspective.* From the life course perspective, aging is a dynamic, lifelong process. Individuals go through many transitions in the course of their life span. The era they live in, the cohort they belong to, and personal and environmental factors influence these transitions.

8. *Age stratification perspective.* The framework of **age stratification** falls into the tradition of the life course perspective (Foner, 1995; Riley, 1971). The age stratification perspective suggests that, similar to the way society is structured by socioeconomic class, it is also stratified by age. Roles and rights of individuals are assigned based on their membership in an age group or cohort. Individuals proceed through their life course as part of that cohort. Their experience of aging differs because cohorts differ in size, composition, and experience with an ever-changing society.

Biological Changes in Late Adulthood

How important is the impact of biological age on the experience of the late adult phase of the life course?

Every day, our bodies are changing. In a sense, then, our bodies are constantly aging. As social workers, however, we need not be concerned with the body's aging until it begins to affect the person's ability to function in her or his world, which typically begins to occur in old age.

Several physiological theories of aging try to explain how and why our bodies age. Leonard Hayflick (1994) suggests that these theories can be divided into two categories: **programmed aging theories** and **random error theories**. Programmed aging theories start from the assumption that the aging process is genetically determined. One example, *cellular aging theory,* proposes that cells cannot replicate themselves indefinitely. A slowing down in the replication of cells occurs as we become older. Hayflick (1994) has proven that human cells can only divide a limited number of times, approximately 50 times. On this basis, the upper limit of the human life span would be 110 to 120 years.

Random error theories propose that physiological aging occurs because of damaging processes that become more frequent in late adulthood but are not a part of a genetic unfolding process. The five theories described here are all random error theories with some popularity, but none has received uniform support in the scientific community:

1. *Wear and tear theory*. As we age, our body simply wears out. This theory was once in great favor but in recent years has become less popular among scientists.

2. *Waste product accumulation theory*. As we age, waste products build up in the body's cells and interfere with bodily functioning (Whitbourne, 2001).

3. *Cross-linkage theory*. This theory, also termed collagen theory, is based on the fact that collagen, the connective tissue of the body, stiffens with age. The wrinkling of skin is a visible result of this process. Other effects are the slower healing of wounds, decreased elasticity of muscle tissue and blood vessels, and changes in the eyes and other organs (Hooyman & Kiyak, 1988).

4. *Autoimmune theory*. The aging body loses some of its ability to recognize foreign bacteria, viruses, and other invaders. The body also starts to attack some of its own healthy cells by producing antibodies against itself, thus possibly producing autoimmune diseases.

5. *Free radical theory*. Changes occur in cells because of the production of free radicals, which are highly reactive elements formed by some molecules. Free radicals cause damage when they attach to other molecules. There is some experimental support for the free radical theory.

However the complex process of physiological aging is described, it has an impact on the functional capacity of both the body and the mind.

Health and Longevity

Mortality rates—the frequency at which death occurs within a population—have declined significantly for all segments of the population in the United States during the last century. This decline in death rates includes people over age 65. Between 1980 and 1997, death rates for heart disease and stroke in the 65 and older segment of the population declined by one third. However, death rates for chronic obstructive pulmonary disease increased by 57%, and death rates for diabetes increased by 37%. In 1997, the leading causes of death for people 65 and older were, in descending order, heart disease, cancer, chronic obstructive pulmonary disease, influenza, and diabetes. Overall death rates in 1997 were higher for older men than for older women (Federal Interagency Forum on Aging-Related Statistics, 2000a).

As mortality has decreased, **morbidity**—the incidence of disease—has increased. In other words, the proportion of the population suffering from age-related chronic conditions has increased in tandem with the population of elderly persons. In 1995, for people 70 years or older, the most prevalent chronic conditions in descending order were arthritis, hypertension, heart disease, cancer, diabetes, and stroke.

However, the prevalence of chronic conditions varies significantly by gender, race, and ethnicity. For example, in comparison with older women, men were less likely to report having arthritis or hypertension but more likely to report heart disease and cancer. Arthritis was reported by 67% of non-Hispanic African American people, 58% of non-Hispanic white people, and 50% of Hispanic people. Non-Hispanic African Americans were also more likely to report diabetes, stroke, and hypertension than were non-Hispanic whites or Hispanics. Interestingly, cancer was reported by 21% of non-Hispanic white people, 11% of Hispanic people, and 9% of non-Hispanic African American people (Federal Interagency Forum on Aging-Related Statistics, 2000a). Physical decline is also related to socioeconomic status. Vaillant (2002) found the physical conditions of his inner-city men aged 68 to 70 to be similar to the physical conditions of the women and the Harvard men aged 78 to 80.

A chronic condition can have considerable impact on a family system. In Ms. Johnson's case, the seven people for whom she cares—including two toddlers, an adolescent, an adult daughter who is functionally impaired, a granddaughter and her husband who are at risk of leaving the workforce, and an aging father—are all affected by her chronic diabetes. This case illustrates the untold impact of chronic conditions in aging populations that are rarely described by national trend reports.

For many people, illness and death can be postponed through lifestyle changes. In recent years, the importance of preventing illness by promoting good health has received considerable attention. The goals of health promotion for older adults include preventing or delaying the onset of chronic disease and disability; reducing the severity of chronic diseases; and maintaining mental health, physical health, and physical functioning as long as possible (Hess, 1991). Ways to promote health in old age include improving dietary habits, increasing activity levels and physical exercise, stopping smoking, and getting regular health screenings (blood sampling, blood pressure measurement, cancer screening, glaucoma screening).

Age-Related Changes in Physiology

All systems of the body appear to be affected during the aging process. Consider the *nervous system.* In the brain, neurons and synapses are the transmitters of information throughout the nervous system. Because neurons are not replaced by the body after birth, the number of neurons decreases throughout the life span (Santrock, 1995). The result is a slow decrease of brain mass after age 30. Because we are born with many more neurons and synapses than we need to function, problems usually do not arise. Also, if the older adult develops brain deficits in one area of the brain, he or she may make up for these deficits by increasing activity in other brain regions (Whitbourne, 2001). However, a neurological injury or disease may result in more permanent and serious consequences for an older person. This is just one of the changes that may affect the brain, spinal cord, nerves, and mechanisms controlling other organs in the body.

Our *cardiovascular system* changes in several ways as we become older. The cardiac output—the amount of blood pumped per minute—decreases throughout adult life, and the pulse slows with age (Whitbourne, 2001). The arteries become less elastic and harden, which can result in arteriosclerosis. Fatty lipids accumulate in the walls of the blood vessels and make them narrower, which can cause atherosclerosis. As a result of these changes, less oxygen is available for muscular activities (Whitbourne, 2001).

The respiratory system too changes with age. Beginning at about 20 years of age, a person's lung capacity decreases throughout the lifespan (Whitbourne, 2001). The typical decrease from age 20 to age 80 is about 40% for a healthy person.

The most important age-related change in our *skeletal system* occurs after age 30, when the destruction of bones begins to outpace the reformation of bones. The gradual decrease in bone mass and bone density can cause osteoporosis (Whitbourne, 2001). It is estimated that bone mineral content decreases by 5 to 12% per decade from the 20s through the 90s. One result is that we get shorter as we age. As the cartilage between the joints wears thin, arthritis, a chronic inflammation of the joints, begins to develop. Although many individuals suffer from some form of arthritis in their 40s, the symptoms are often not painful until late adulthood. Some of these changes can be ameliorated by diet and exercise and by avoiding smoking and alcohol (Whitbourne, 2001).

With increasing age, the *muscular system* declines in strength and endurance. As a consequence, an elderly person may become fatigued more easily. In addition, muscle contractions begin to slow down, which contributes to deteriorating reflexes and incontinence, which becomes more prevalent with age. However, the muscular system of older individuals can be successfully strengthened through weight training and changes in diet and lifestyle (Whitbourne, 2001).

Changes in the neurological, muscular, and skeletal systems have an impact on the *sensory system* and the sense of balance, which contributes to the increase in accidental falls and bone fractures in late adulthood. Vision decreases with age, and older persons need more light to reach the retina in order to see. The eye's adaptation to the dark slows with age, as does visual acuity, the ability to detect details (Fozard, 1990). Age-related decreases in hearing are caused by degenerative changes in the spiral organ of the ear and the associated nerve cells. Many older adults have a reduced ability to hear high-pitched sounds (Fozard, 1990). Because taste receptors are constantly replaced, age-related changes in taste are minimal (Bornstein, 1992). Differences may reflect individual factors, such as exposure to environmental conditions like smoking, rather than general processes of aging. The smell receptors in the nose can decrease with age, however, and become less sensitive.

The *integumentary system* includes the skin, hair, and nails. The skin comprises an outer layer (epidermis) and an inner layer (dermis). With age, the epidermis becomes thinner and pigment cells grow and cluster, creating age spots on the skin (Thomas, 1992). The sweat and oil-secreting glands decrease, leaving the skin drier and more vulnerable to injury (Whitbourne, 2001). Much of the fat stored in the hypodermis, the tissue beneath the skin, is lost in age, causing wrinkles. The skin of an older person often feels cool because the blood flow to the skin is reduced (Spence, 1989).

Sexual potency begins to decline at age 20, but without disease, sexual desire and capacity continue in late adulthood. According to a 1998 survey, half of all persons in the United States age 60 or older are sexually active. Among those who are sexually active, 74% of the men and 70% of the women report that they are as satisfied or more satisfied with their sex lives now than they were in their 40s (National Council on the Aging, n.d.). Vaillant (2002) reports that *frequency* of sexual activity decreases, however. He found that partners in good health at 75 to 80 often continue to have sexual relations, but that the average frequency is approximately once in every 10 weeks. Interestingly, he found that among the women in his study, mastering the life task of generativity, rather than mastering the task of intimacy, was the predictor of regular attainment of orgasm.

Contemporary views on the physiology of aging focus on longevity. Antiaging medicine focuses on developing interventions that will delay age-related pathology or other changes that are not officially listed as disease or decreases in bone and muscle mass. Science and technology are achieving gains that show great promise for the future. However, to date, there is no evidence that these gains have increased the maximum life span of humans (International Longevity Center-USA, 2001). Some of the more promising gains in this area include the following (Dychtwald, 1999):

- Supernutrition is the only technique that has extended life in humans with consistency. Supernutrition involves properly dosed dietary supplements of multivitamins and multiminerals, along with restricted fats and fresh, whole, unprocessed foods. The convergence of nutritional sciences and the emphasis on preventive medicine is likely to yield a new generation of supernutritional foods in the not-so-distant future.

- Hormone therapy is already used in some medical conditions today. Further breakthroughs with the use of estrogen, testosterone, Melatonin, dehydroepiandrosterone (DHEA), and human growth hormone (HGH) hold promise but are wrought with potentially dangerous side effects to date.

- Gene manipulation will potentially have the greatest impact of all interventions on human aging. But despite recent advances in gene mapping, the technology is not yet developed enough for large-scale human applications.

- Bionics would have seemed like science fiction a generation ago, but the convergence of biological science and engineering may produce limbs and organs to replace those worn out or deteriorated with age.

- Organ or tissue cloning is an approach similar to bionics. Tissue cloning has particular appeal for brain diseases such as Parkinson's or Alzheimer's because it could provide patients with healthy neural tissue identical to their own.

In each of these areas, significant research efforts are being conducted the world over (Dychtwald, 1999). Whether any of these technologies will come into widespread use is uncertain. It is certain that economic and ethical considerations and debates will be as unprecedented as the technologies themselves.

Psychological Changes in Late Adulthood

Without good longitudinal research, it has been difficult to understand psychological changes in late adulthood. Because cross-sectional research cannot control for cohort effects, we need to exercise great caution in interpreting findings of age differences in human psychology. Three areas that have received a lot of attention are changes in personality, changes in intellectual functioning, and mental health and mental disorders in late adulthood.

Personality Changes

A couple of theorists have addressed the issue of how personality changes as individuals age. As noted in Chapter 8, Erik Erikson's (1950) life-span theory proposes that the struggle of middle adulthood is generativity versus stagnation (refer back to Exhibit 3.6 for an overview of Erikson's stages of psychosocial development). You may recall that generativity is the ability to transcend personal interests to guide the next generation. The struggle of late adulthood, according to Erikson, is **ego integrity versus ego despair**. *Integrity* involves the ability to make peace with one's "one and only life cycle" and to find unity with the world. Erikson (1950) also noted that from middle adulthood on, adults participate in a "wider social radius," with an increasing sense of social responsibility and interconnectedness. Some support was found for this notion in a 50-year follow-up of adult personality development (Haan, Millsap, & Hartka, 1986). The researchers found that in late adulthood, three aspects of personality increased significantly: outgoingness, self-confidence, and warmth.

Do you have any "keepers of the meaning" in your multigenerational family?

Vaillant (2002) has also considered the personality changes of late adulthood. He found that for all three of the cohorts in the Study of Adult Development, mastery of generativity tripled the likelihood that men and women would find their 70s to be a time of joy instead of despair. He also proposes that another life task, Keeper of the Meaning, comes between generativity and integrity. The **Keeper of the Meaning** takes on the task of passing on the traditions of the past to the next generation. In addition, Vaillant suggests that humans have "elegant unconscious coping mechanisms that make lemonade out of lemons" (2002, p. 91). As discussed in Chapter 8, Vaillant reports that with age and experience, individuals tend to use more adaptive coping mechanisms.

The proposition that coping mechanisms mature with age requires longitudinal research. And indeed, Vaillant finds support for this idea in his Study of Adult Development. He found that over a 25-year period, the Harvard men made significant increases in their use of altruism and humor and significant decreases in their use of projection and passive aggression. Overall, he found that 19 of 67 Harvard men made significant gains in use of mature coping mechanisms between the ages of 50 and 75, 28 men were already making strong use of mature mechanisms at age 50, use of mature mechanisms stayed the same for 17 men, and only 4 out of the 67 men used less mature coping mechanisms with advancing age. These findings are consistent with findings from another longitudinal study of aging that found that in late adulthood, participants became more forgiving, more able to meet adversity cheerfully, less prone to take offense, and less prone to venting frustrations on others (McCrae & Costa, 1990).

In Chapter 8, we read that there are controversies about whether personality changes or remains stable in middle adulthood. There are similar controversies in the literature on late adulthood. Using longitudinal research, Vaillant (2002) found evidence for both change and continuity of personality. He suggests that personality has two components: temperament and character (p. 284). Temperament, he concludes, doesn't change, and adaptation in adolescence is one of the best predictors of adaptation in late adulthood. On the other hand, character, or adaptive style, does change, influenced both by experiences with the environment and the maturation process. Vaillant attributes this change in adaptive style over time to the fact that many genes are "programmed to promote plasticity," or the capacity to be shaped by experience (p. 285). One personality change that was noted in Chapter 8 to occur in middle age is gender crossover, with women becoming more dominant and men becoming more passive. This pattern continues into late adulthood.

Intellectual Changes, Learning, and Memory

Answering the question about how our intellectual capabilities change in late adulthood is a complex and difficult task. One often-cited study on age-related intellectual changes found that fluid intelligence declines with age, but crystallized intelligence increases (Horn, 1982). **Fluid intelligence** is the capacity for abstract reasoning and involves such things as the ability to "respond quickly, to memorize quickly, to compute quickly with no error, and to draw rapid inferences from visual relationships" (Vaillant, 2002, p. 238). **Crystallized intelligence** is based on accumulated learning and includes the ability to reflect and recognize (e.g., similarities and differences, vocabulary) rather than to recall and remember. This theory has received much criticism, however, because it was based on a comparison of two different age groups. Researchers who followed a single cohort over time found no general decline of intellectual abilities in late adulthood (Schaie, 1984). Rather, they found considerable individual variation. Other longitudinal research has found that fluid intelligence declines earlier than crystallized intelligence, which has been found to remain the same at 80 as at 30 in most healthy older adults (Vaillant, 2002).

Learning and memory are closely related; we must first learn before we can retain and recall. When we process information, it moves through several stages of memory (Kaplan & Sadock, 1998; Thomas, 1992):

- *Sensory memory*. New information is initially recorded in sensory memory. Unless the person deliberately pays attention to the information, it is lost within less than a second. There seems to be little age-related change in this type of memory.
- *Primary memory.* If the information is retained in sensory memory, it is passed on to the primary memory, also called recent or short-term memory. Primary memory has only limited capacity; it is used to organize and temporarily hold information. Working memory refers to the process of actively reorganizing and manipulating information that is still in primary memory. Although there are some age-related declines in working memory, there seems to be little age-related decline in primary memory.
- *Secondary memory.* Information is permanently stored in secondary memory. This is the memory we use daily when we remember an event or memorize facts for an exam. The ability to recall seems to decline with age, but recognition capabilities stay consistent.

- *Tertiary memory*. Information is stored for extended periods, several weeks or months, in tertiary memory, also called remote memory. This type of memory experiences little age-related changes.

Another way to distinguish memory is between intentional and incidental memory. **Intentional memory** relates to events that you plan to remember. **Incidental memory** relates to facts you have learned without the intention to retain and recall. Research suggests that incidental memory declines with old age, but intentional memory does not (Sinnott, 1986).

Another element of intellectual functioning studied in relation to aging is *brain plasticity*, the ability of the brain to change in response to stimuli. Research indicates that even older people's brains can rewire themselves to compensate for lost functioning in particular regions, and in some instances, may even be able to generate new cells. As a result, people are capable of lifelong learning, despite myths to the contrary. In fact, adult education and intellectual stimulation in later life may actually help maintain cognitive health. Not only are humans capable of lifelong learning, but the stimulation associated with learning new things may reduce the risk of impairments (Institute for the Study of Aging, 2001).

For reasons that are unknown, the rate at which the human brain can receive and process information slows with age. However, contemporary thinking about cognitive vitality is based on the assumption that having a clear mind is more important than processing speed to quality of life—especially for older women and men. Hence the concern about **dementia**, a brain disease in which memory and cognitive abilities deteriorate over time. Dementia is greatly feared because it is disruptive and has the effect of robbing people of their personality. Dementia affects 3 to 10% of people over age 65. Researchers do not currently know why some people develop dementia and others do not.

The initial stage of cognitive dysfunction is called age-associated memory impairment (AAMI). It is followed by even greater memory loss and diagnosed as mild cognitive impairment (MCI), which may progress to dementia. AAMI and MCI are limited to memory loss alone, whereas dementia results in disruption of daily living and an inability to function normally. The most common cause of dementia is Alzheimer's disease. However, not all people with dementia have Alzheimer's, nor do all people with MCI develop dementia. Risk factors for cognitive decline and dementia include genetic factors; female gender; medical conditions, including, but not limited to, hypertension, heart disease, and diabetes; lifestyle choices such as smoking or substance abuse; psychological and psychosocial factors such as low educational achievement, lack of physical activity, lack of social interaction and leisure activities, and excessive response to stress (Institute for the Study of Aging, 2001).

Mental Health and Mental Disorders

A number of longitudinal studies indicate that, without brain disease, mental health improves with age (Vaillant, 2002). Although older adults are more predisposed to certain brain diseases such as dementia, these disorders are not a part of the normal aging process. However, the prevalence of mental disorders in residents of long-term care facilities is over 80% (Conn, 2001). Although few institutionalized individuals with mental disorders receive care from mental health professionals, many of the more common mental disorders associated with older age can be diagnosed and treated in elderly persons much as they would be in earlier adulthood (Hooyman & Kiyak, 1988). Given the aging of the population, the need for gero-psychiatric research and clinical practice is sure to increase.

Some of the more commonly diagnosed mental disorders in late adulthood include the following:

- *Anxiety*. Anxiety in older adults is similar to that in the younger population. Diagnosis and treatment, however, are often more complex and difficult, because anxiety in older adults often does not follow any direct stimulus. Rather, anxiety is frequently an indication of an underlying mental or physical disorder (Tueth, 1993). Situational stressors that may trigger anxiety in older adults include financial concerns, physical stressors, and loss and loneliness. Symptoms of anxiety include tension, worry, apprehension, and physiological symptoms such as dizziness, gastrointestinal distress, palpitations, urinary disturbance, sweating, and tremors.

- *Depression*. The most common mental health problem in older adults is depression, and major depression is the leading cause of suicide in late adulthood (Blazer, 1995). Many depressive episodes in older adults are associated with problems in coping with difficult life events, such as death of a loved person or physical illness. Symptoms of depression include sadness and depressed mood, loss of interest, weight loss, insomnia, and fatigue. To be diagnosed, the depressive episode has to persist for at least 2 weeks.

- *Delirium*. One of the two most prevalent cognitive disorders in the elderly population (Kaplan & Sadock, 1998), **delirium** is characterized by an impairment of consciousness. The syndrome has a sudden onset (a few hours or days), follows a brief and fluctuating course that includes an impairment of consciousness, and has the potential for improvement when the causes are treated. Prevalent causative factors include not only central nervous system disturbances but also outside factors such as renal or hepatic failure (Kaplan & Sadock, 1998). The prevalence of delirium is high among hospitalized elderly persons, with approximately 30 to 40% of hospital patients over age 65 experiencing an episode (Kaplan & Sadock, 1998). Toxicity from prescribed medications is a very common cause of delirium.

- *Dementia*. The other most prevalent cognitive disorder among older adults is dementia, which was discussed earlier in the context of memory loss. Dementia has a slower onset than delirium and is not characterized by an impairment of consciousness. Rather, dementia is characterized by multiple impairments of the person's cognitive functioning. *Reversible dementia* is caused by factors such as drug and alcohol use, nutritional deficits, a brain tumor, or severe depression, and the cognitive decline is reversible if identified and treated early enough (Kaplan & Sadock, 1998). *Irreversible dementia* is not curable. The two most prevalent types of irreversible dementia are senile dementia of the Alzheimer's type (SDAT) and vascular dementia (multiinfarct dementia), which together account for approximately 75% of all cases. SDAT alone accounts for almost two thirds of all dementia cases (Moody, 1998). Other causes of dementia include Parkinson's disease, Huntington's disease, Pick's disease, Creutzfeldt-Jakob disease, and HIV. Having a family member with dementia is emotionally trying for all involved. In the advanced stages, the person may repeat the same words over and over again, may have problems using appropriate words, and may not recognize a spouse or other family members. At the same time, the person may still be able to recall and vividly describe events that happened many years ago.

- *Substance abuse*. Alcohol is the drug of choice among today's older adults. The prevalence of alcoholism in the older population is estimated to be between 10 and 18%. It is the second most frequent reason (after depression) for admitting older adults to an inpatient psychiatric facility (Moss, Mortens, & Brennan, 1993). The general consumption of alcohol is lower for older adults than for younger adults, but many heavy drinkers do not reach old age, and alcohol abuse is often more hidden among older adults. Although the consequences of alcoholism are the same for older adults as for younger persons, the attitudes held by family members and society are often very different. Notions such as "He's too old to change," "If I were old I would drink too," or "Don't take away her last pleasure" often prevent efforts to intervene. Contrary to these common attitudes, however, many older persons respond as well to treatment as younger adults do.

Social Role Transitions and Life Events of Late Adulthood

Transitions are at the center of the life course perspective, and people experience many transitions, some of them very abrupt, in late adulthood. Retirement, death of a spouse or partner, institutionalization, and one's own death are among the most stressful events in human existence, and they are clustered in late adulthood. Several other events are more benign but may still enter into the social worker's analysis of the changing configuration of person and environment represented by each case.

Families in Later Life

As you saw with the Smiths, the Moros, and Ms. Johnson, families continue to play an important role in the life of an older person. With increased longevity, however, the postempty nest and postretirement period lengthens (Walsh, 1999). Thus, the significance of the marital or partner relationship increases in late adulthood. As older individuals are released from their responsibilities as parents and members of the workforce, they are able to spend more time together. Some studies have suggested a U-shaped curve of marital satisfaction, with the highest levels during the first period of the marital relationship and in late adulthood, and lower levels during the childbearing years (Bengtson, Rosenthal, & Burton, 1990). Moreover, overall satisfaction with the quality of life seems to be higher for married elderly individuals than for the widowed or never married. For married couples, the spouse is the most important source of emotional, social, and personal support in times of illness and need of care.

The most common living arrangement for men over 65 is with their wife; in 1990, 75% of men over 65 lived with their spouse. The picture is different for older women, who are more likely than older men to be living alone. By age 75, over one half of women are living alone. Older black and Hispanic women are less likely than white women to live with a spouse, but they are also less likely to live alone, opting instead to live with relatives (Himes, 2001). Family relationships have been found to be closer and more central for older women than for older men. Mother-daughter relationships have been found to be particularly strong (Silverstein & Bengtson, 2001).

The never married constitute a very small group of the current elderly population. It will further decrease for some time as the cohort of baby boomers, with its unusually high rate of marriage, enters late adulthood (Bengtson et al., 1990). However, the proportion of elderly singles and never married will probably increase toward the middle of the next century, because the cohort that follows the baby boomers has had an increase in the number of individuals remaining single.

Singlehood due to divorce in late adulthood is increasing, however, as divorce is becoming more socially accepted in all population groups. As in all stages of life, divorce in later life may entail financial problems, especially for older women, and it may be especially difficult to recuperate financially in postretirement. Divorce also results in a change of kinship ties and social networks, which are important sources of support in later life. The incidence of remarriage after divorce or widowhood is significantly higher for older men than for older women. The fact that there are more elderly women than men contributes to this trend. Even if older adults are not themselves divorced, they may need to adjust to the enlarged and complicated family networks that come from the divorces and remarriages of their children and grandchildren.

One group of older adults that has often been neglected in the discussion of late adulthood are elderly gay men and lesbians. Estimates of the proportion of gay men and lesbians among elderly persons are similar to those for younger age groups (Teitelman, 1995). Being faced not only with ageist but also with homophobic attitudes, elderly gay men and lesbians may be confronted by a double jeopardy. Eligibility requirements for many services to elderly adults continue to be based on a norm of heterosexuality. Although growing in number, services catering directly to older gay or lesbian persons are still few and far between in many parts of the country. But the most problematic aspect of being an elderly homosexual may be the lack of societal sanction to grieve openly when the partner dies (Teitelman, 1995).

Sibling relationships play a special role in the life of older adults. Siblings share childhood experiences and are often the personal tie with the longest duration. Siblings are typically not the primary source of personal care, but they often play a role in providing emotional support. Sibling relationships often change over the life course, with closer ties in preadulthood and later life and less involvement in early and middle adulthood. Women's ties with siblings have been found to be more involved than those of men (Cicirelli, 1995).

Relationships with children and grandchildren are also significant in late adulthood. The "myth of the golden age" suggests that in the past, older people were more likely to live in a multigenerational family, be well taken care of, and have valued emotional and economic roles. This heartwarming picture is a myth, however, because people died earlier and multigenerational families were less prevalent than they are in our era of increased longevity (Hareven, 2000). Furthermore, even in the past, elderly individuals valued independent living, and they typically resided in separate households from their adult children, although they usually lived in close proximity.

In fact, multigenerational families have become more common in recent years, resulting in more interactions and exchanges across generations. Contrary to common belief, intergenerational exchanges between adult children and elderly parents are not one-directional. Children often take care of their elderly parents, but healthy elderly persons also provide significant assistance to their adult children, as is the case with Ms. Johnson. Research on elderly parents living with their adult children suggests that for the young-old, more assistance flows from the elderly parents to the adult children than the other way around (Speare & Avery, 1993). In another study (Ward, Logan, & Spitze, 1992), older parents living with their adult children reported doing more than three quarters of the housework. Patterns of co-residence between parents and adult children vary by race. Non-Hispanic white elderly are the least likely to co-reside with their children; Asian elderly are the most likely to live with their children (Speare & Avery, 1993).

Grandparenthood

In some cases, older people such as Ms. Johnson are assuming full responsibility for parenting their grandchildren, because their children have problems with drugs,

HIV infection, or crime. Beginning in the early 1990s, the U.S. Census Bureau began to note an increasing number of children under 18 living with grandparents, rising from 3% of children under age 18 in 1970 to 5.5% in 1997 (Bryson & Casper, 1999). This has been viewed as a negative trend, although there is no inherent reason why grandchildren co-residing with grandparents is problematic, and, indeed, across time and place, grandparents have sometimes been seen as appropriate caregivers. It does appear, however, that the current trend is based on the growth of drug use among parents, teen pregnancy, and the rapid rise of single-parent families (Bryson & Casper, 1999). As a result, new physical, emotional, and financial demands are placed on grandparents with already limited resources. Some speculate that custodial grandparents may also be caring for their own impaired adult child, because two thirds of grandparent-headed households have a member of the "skipped generation" in residence (Burnette, 1999).

How do culture, social class, and gender affect grandparenting styles?

Grandparenthood is a normative part of the family life cycle, but the majority of grandparents do not co-reside with their grandchildren. The timing of grandparenthood influences the way it is experienced and the roles and responsibilities that a grandparent will take on. Many first-time grandparents are middle-aged adults in their early 50s. Yet, others do not become grandparents until they are 70 or 80 years old. Because individuals are enjoying longer lives, more and more assume the role of grandparent, and they assume it for more years. Many spend the same number of years being a grandparent as being a parent of a child under the age of 18.

In general, being a grandparent is a welcome and gratifying role for most individuals, but it may increase in significance and meaning for an older person. The Smiths, for example, both enjoy being grandparents, and Lois Smith especially gains pleasure and satisfaction from her role as grandmother to her daughter's children.

Family researchers have begun to take a strong interest in the grandparenting role, but little is actually known about grandparent-grandchild relationships. A classic study of middle-class grandparents in the early 1960s identified several styles of grandparents: formal grandparents, fun seekers, distant figures, surrogate parents, and mentors (Neugarten and Weinstein, 1964).

A recent study by Margaret Mueller and her associates has focused particularly on the relationships between grandparents and adolescent grandchildren; the average age of grandparents in this study was 69 years old (Mueller, Wilhelm, & Elder, 2002). This study identified five dimensions of the grandparenting role in 451 families: face-to-face contact, activities done together, intimacy, assistance, and authority/discipline. Each of these grandparenting dimensions is defined in Exhibit 9.5. Using a statistical clustering method, the researchers identified five styles of grandparenting:

1. *Influential grandparents* are highly involved in all aspects of grandparenting, scoring high on all five dimensions. These grandparents constituted 17% of the sample. Ms. Johnson is grandparenting Rebecca in this manner.

EXHIBIT 9.5
Dimensions of Grandparenting Role

Dimension	Definition
Face-to-face contact	How often grandparents see their grandchildren.
Activities done together	Participation in shared activities, such as shopping, working on projects together, attending grandchildren's events, teaching the grandchild a skill.
Intimacy	Serving as confidant, companion, or friend; discussing grandparent's childhood.
Assistance	Providing instrumental assistance, such as financial aid and/or interpersonal support.
Discipline and authority	Disciplining the grandchild or otherwise serving as an authority figure.

Source: Based on Mueller, Wilhelm, & Elder, 2002.

2. *Supportive grandparents* are highly involved in the lives of their grandchildren but do not see themselves in a role of disciplinarian or authority figure. About a quarter of the sample fit this pattern.

3. *Passive grandparents* are moderately involved in their grandchildren's lives, but they do not provide instrumental assistance and do not see themselves as discipline/authority figures. About 19% of the sample fit this pattern. Lois and Gene Smith seem to be following this pattern of grandparenting.

4. *Authority-oriented grandparents* see their role as authority figures as the central component in their grandparenting, and they are relatively inactive in their grandchildren's lives compared with both influential and supportive grandparents. These grandparents constitute about 13% of the sample.

5. *Detached grandparents* are the least involved of the grandparents, scoring lowest on all the dimensions of grandparenting. This was the largest group, comprising about 28% of the sample.

This research is helpful because it demonstrates that the grandparent role may be played in many different ways. A number of factors may influence the style of grandparenting, including geographic proximity, ages of grandparents and grandchildren, number of grandchildren, and family rituals. There is a major drawback to the sample, however; it is entirely white and midwestern. It does not, therefore, address the possibility of cultural variations in grandparenting roles.

A smaller-scale study of grandparenting in 17 Native American families, including Sioux, Creek, Seminole, Choctaw, and Chickasaw, partially addresses the issue of cultural variation (Weibel-Orlando, 2001). Like the research of Mueller and her associates, this study identified five styles of grandparenting:

1. *The distanced grandparent* lives at considerable geographic distance from grandchildren but also has psychological and cultural distance. This type of grandparenting is not common among Native Americans. It is most likely to occur if the family has migrated to an urban area and the grandparents return to their ancestral homeland after retirement.
2. *The ceremonial grandparent* also lives at considerable geographic distance from grandchildren but visits regularly. Intergenerational visits are times for ethnic ceremonial gatherings, and grandparents model appropriate ceremonial behavior.
3. *The fictive grandparent* assumes the elder role with children who are not biologically related. These grandparents may have no grandchildren of their own or may live at a great distance from their biological grandchildren.
4. *The custodial grandparent* lives with the grandchildren and is responsible for their care. This style of grandparenting is usually the result of parental death, incapacitation, or abandonment, and is based on necessity rather than choice.
5. *The cultural conservator grandparent* actively pursues the opportunity to have grandchildren live with her (all such grandparents were women in this study) so that she might teach them the Indian way of life.

Think about your relationships with your grandparents. How would you characterize their grandparenting styles? Did you have different types of relationships with different grandparents? Did your grandparents have different types of relationships with different grandchildren? What might explain any differences?

Work and Retirement

How do these social trends affect the late adult phase of the life course?

Until the 20th century, the average worker retired about 3 years before death. In 1890, 90% of men in the United States over age 70 were still in the workforce. Increased worker productivity, mass longevity, and Social Security legislation changed that situation, however, and by 1986, only 31% of 65-year-old men were in the workforce. In the past century, with the combined impact of increased longevity and earlier retirement, the average number of years spent in retirement before death is almost 15 years (Vaillant, 2002).

EXHIBIT 9.6
Amended Age to Receive Full Social Security Benefits (1983)

Year of Birth	Full Retirement Age
1937 and earlier	65
1938	65 and 2 months
1939	65 and 4 months
1940	65 and 6 months
1941	65 and 8 months
1942	65 and 10 months
1943-1954	66
1955	66 and 2 months
1956	66 and 4 months
1957	66 and 6 months
1958	66 and 8 months
1959	66 and 10 months
1960 and later	67

Source: Social Security Administration, n.d.

Retirement patterns vary with social class, however. Vaillant found that only 20% of his sample of surviving inner-city men were still in the workforce at age 65, but half of the sample of Harvard men were still working full time at 65. The inner-city men retired, on average, 5 years earlier than the Harvard men. Poor health often leads to earlier retirement among less advantaged adults (Sterns & Huyck, 2001). In addition, higher levels of education make workers eligible for more sedentary jobs, which are a better fit with the declining energy levels in late adulthood (Vaillant, 2002).

Data about retirement have been based on the work patterns of men, probably because women's labor force involvement has been less uniform. A trend was noted in the early 1990s, however, in which labor force participation rates for men over 50 were falling while labor force participation rates of women over 50 were increasing. Labor force participation for women 60 to 64 increased considerably between 1950 and 1970 and then began to level off (Gendell & Siegal, 1992).

The "appropriate" age for retirement in the United States is currently understood to be age 65. This cultural understanding has been shaped by Social Security legislation enacted in 1935. However, the 1983 Social Security Amendments included a provision for a gradual increase in the age at which a retired person could begin receiving social security retirement benefits. Exhibit 9.6 shows the schedule for increasing the age for receiving full benefits. In arguing for this legislative change, members of Congress noted increased longevity and improved health among older adults (Social Security Administration, n.d.).

Certainly, some older individuals continue to work for many years after they reach age 65 (Morgan & Kunkel, 1996). Individuals who continue to work fall into two groups: those who could afford to retire but choose to continue working and those who continue to work because of a financial need. Older adults of the first group usually receive great satisfaction in sharing their knowledge and expertise and gain a feeling of purpose from being productive. Members of the second group continue to work out of necessity. Because economic status in old age is influenced by past employment patterns and the resultant retirement benefits, this second group consists of individuals who had lower-paying employment throughout their life. This group also includes elderly divorced or widowed women who depended on their husband's retirement income and are now faced with poverty or near poverty. Gene Smith falls into the first category, because he continued working even though he and his wife had sufficient combined benefits to retire. However, Lois Smith's own benefits would not have enabled her to lead a financially comfortable retirement if she were not married, and she would probably face some financial hardship if she were to become a widow. Ruby Johnson continues to be employed on a part-time basis out of financial necessity.

When we think about retirement, we often picture individuals cleaning up their desks to stop working completely and sit in a rocking chair on the front porch. Yet, there are many ways of retiring from the workforce. Some individuals do cease work completely, but others continue with part-time or part-year employment. Others may retire for a period and then reenter the labor market, as Gene Smith did when his former employer offered him a part-time position. Retirement is a socially accepted way to end an active role in the workforce. Most persons retire because of advancing age, mandatory retirement policies, health problems, a desire to pursue other interests, or simply a wish to relax and lead the life of a retiree.

Retirement brings with it a shift in roles, social interactions, and financial resources. Robert Atchley (1976) has suggested that these changes occur in seven stages of adjustment, summarized in Exhibit 9.7:

1. *Remote stage.* Before actual retirement, most individuals spend little time thinking about it. They may do some financial planning, but the actual event of retiring still seems far away.

2. *Near stage.* As retirement comes closer, individuals begin thinking about what it will be like not to work. Many start looking into their retirement benefits and pensions.

3. *Honeymoon stage.* In the period immediately following the retirement event, individuals often experience a feeling of elation accompanied by a sense of loss.

4. *Disenchantment stage.* Many feel a continuing sense of loss that lasts from a few months to several years. Not everything works out as they had planned for

EXHIBIT 9.7
Seven Phases of Retirement Adjustment

Stage	Primary Tasks
Remote stage	Only few thoughts spent on upcoming retirement
Near stage	More thoughts about retirement; evaluation of benefits
Honeymoon stage	Period of elation; adjustment to recent retirement
Disenchantment stage	Sense of loss experienced in varying degrees
Reorientation stage	Reevaluation of lifestyle and routine
Stability stage	Feeling well adapted; few thoughts about retirement
Termination stage	Declining health; facing the end of retirement and of life

Source: Adapted from Atchley, 1976.

retirement. For some elderly persons, this disenchantment may cause depression. Those whose life centered around work often have a harder time adjusting than those who were more actively involved in activities outside of work.

5. *Reorientation stage.* Most people progress to the next stage, which involves reevaluation of the lifestyle and the routine adopted in retirement. Some, like Gene Smith, may decide at this point to return to work. Others may decide that the choices they made are satisfying.

6. *Stability stage.* During this phase, the individual feels well adapted and does not spend much time thinking about retirement. Adjustment to retirement seems to be easiest for those who are healthy and active, are better educated, have a higher retirement income, and participate in an active social network (Palmore, Burchett, Fillenbaum, George, & Wallman, 1985).

7. *Termination stage.* The end of retirement nears when a person becomes dependent on others for care and assistance because of frailty and declining health and begins to face death.

With the blurring of the lines between working and retirement (see Chapter 8), many people will be phasing into retirement over time. Such societal changes may seriously undermine the usefulness of this stage model of adjustment to retirement and others like it.

Individuals vary in whether they view retirement as something to dread or something to look forward to. Most often, however, retirement is a positive experience. Vaillant (2002) argues that "retirement is highly overrated as a life problem" (p. 220). He found no evidence in his longitudinal research that retirement is bad for physical health; in fact, for every person who indicated that retirement was bad for her or his health, four retirees indicated that retirement had improved their health. Vaillant did note, however, four conditions under which retirement is stressful (p. 221):

1. Retirement was involuntary or unplanned.
2. There are no other means of financial support besides salary.
3. Work provided an escape from an unhappy home life.
4. Retirement was precipitated by preexisting bad health.

As Vaillant notes, these conditions are present among only a fraction of retirees, but those are the retirees with whom social workers are likely to come into contact.

Vaillant found that retirement has generally been very rewarding for many of the participants of his study. Four basic activities appear to make retirement rewarding:

1. Replacing work mates with another social network.
2. Rediscovering how to play.
3. Engaging in creative endeavors.
4. Continuing lifelong learning.

Vaillant also suggests that retirement would be less stressful if the culture provided rituals for the transition, as it does for other life transitions. He found little evidence of such rituals in his research. Some people with a long tenure in a job are given retirement parties by their employers.

Caregiving and Care Receiving

As retirement unfolds, declining health may usher in a period of intensive need for care. Eighty percent of older adults who need long-term care receive that care in the community rather than in an institution. Women are the primary source of caregiving in old age (Walsh, 1999). Daughters are more likely than sons to take care of elderly parents. Moreover, elderly men tend to be married and thus are more likely to have a wife available as caregiver.

Caregiving can be a 24-hour, around-the-clock task and often leaves caregivers overwhelmed and exhausted. Camille Moro is a good example of the burden that can be experienced by an elderly spouse. Programs that can assist caregivers like Camille in reducing their exceptional levels of stress have received much attention. Many programs combine educational components—for example, information about and training in adaptive coping skills—with ongoing support through the opportunity to share personal feelings and experiences. Respite programs for caregivers are also available. In-home respite programs provide assistance through a home health aide or a visiting nurse. Community-based respite is often provided through adult day care and similar programs.

How can such programs buffer the stress of caregiving and care receiving?

When caregiving becomes too overwhelming, a nursing home placement may be pursued. Yet, caregiving often continues after a family member enters a nursing home. Although caregivers are relieved from direct care, they continue to be involved in the emotional and social aspects of care in the nursing home.

Stress and burden are not experienced only by the caregiver. The care recipient also often experiences significant strain. Requiring care is a double loss: the person has lost the capability to perform the tasks for which he or she needs assistance and has lost independence. Having to rely on others for activities that a person has carried out independently throughout adult life can be the source of tremendous emotional and psychological stress. Some individuals respond by emotional withdrawal; others become agitated and start blaming others for their situation. The levels of stress that an elderly care recipient may experience depend on "(1) personal and situational characteristics of the elderly recipient; (2) characteristics of the caregiver; (3) social support provided to caregiver and recipient; (4) aspects of the relationship between family caregiver and recipient; and (5) characteristics of caregiving" (Brubaker, Gorman, & Hiestand, 1990, p. 268).

Think of Frank Moro. His stress was amplified by culturally defined norms promoting independence, individuality, and pride. Helping Frank overcome his uneasiness about receiving assistance and support was a matter of asking him to verbalize his worries, listening to him express his feelings, and looking together at ways that he could overcome his uneasiness in small steps. Getting him to accept a wheelchair also reduced his stress by increasing his independence. Such assistive technology can often greatly reduce the care recipient's reliance on help and thus decrease her or his stress.

Widowhood

The death of a spouse has been found to be the most stressful event in a person's life. In most cases, it is the loss of someone with whom the individual has shared a major part of life. Moreover, the marital relationship is one of the most important relationships for a person in later life. Because they have a longer life expectancy, more women than men face this life event.

Losing a spouse signifies the end of one phase in a person's life course and the beginning of a new phase called widowhood. It requires the individual to readjust to a new social role and a new way of relating to others. Those who saw the world through the eyes of a spouse have to learn to see everything from a new perspective. Widowhood also confronts the person with his or her own mortality. There seems to be some evidence that the loss of a spouse is associated with subsequent illness and earlier mortality (Minkler, 1985). Loss, grief, and bereavement are discussed in greater detail in Chapter 10.

Adjustment to widowhood is facilitated by a person's own inner strength, family support, a strong network of friends and neighbors, and membership in a church or an active community. The family is the most important source of emotional, social, and financial support during this time.

Widowhood may be especially difficult if the surviving spouse provided intensive caregiving for a prolonged period. In this case, the partner's death may be a relief from the burdensome caregiving task, but it may also mean the loss of a role and sense of purpose. In addition, during the period of intensive caregiving, the survivor may have had to give up many social interactions and thus have a shrunken social support network.

Institutionalization

Another myth of aging is that older individuals are being abandoned and neglected by their families and being pushed into nursing homes to get them out of the way. Most children and spouses do not use nursing homes as a dumping ground for their elderly relatives. They turn to nursing homes only after they have exhausted all other alternatives. Nor is institutionalization a single, sudden event. It is a process that starts with the need to make a decision, continues through the placement itself, and ends in the adjustment to the placement (Naleppa, 1996).

Researchers have taken a close look at the factors that predict a person's entry into a nursing home. Among the most important are the condition and needs of the elderly individual. Functional and behavioral deficits, declining health, previous institutionalization, and advanced age all contribute to the decision to enter a nursing home. Family characteristics that are good predictors of institutionalization include the need for 24-hour caregiving, caregiver feelings of distress, caregiver health and mental status, and caregiving environment (Naleppa, 1996). Marital status is a strong predictor of institutionalization for elderly men. Unmarried and never married men have the highest risk of entering a nursing home (Dolinsky & Rosenwaike, 1988; Hanley, Alecxih, Wiener, & Kennell, 1990). Individuals without a spouse who live alone in the community are at a higher risk of entering a nursing home than those living with spouses, family members, or friends (Montgomery & Kosloski, 1994).

How can social workers help to protect human agency for making choices in institutional settings?

The placement decision itself is emotionally stressful for all involved and can be viewed as a family crisis. Yet, it can be considered a normative part of the family life cycle. The process of making a placement decision itself unfolds in four stages: "the recognition of the potential for institutionalization; discussion of the institutionalization option; implementation of action steps toward institutionalization; and placement of the relative in the institutional setting" (Gonyea, 1987, p. 63).

Because many nursing home placements are arranged from the hospital for an elderly individual who entered the hospital expecting to return home, many people may not have time to progress well through these stages. For those who unexpectedly enter a nursing home from the hospital, it may be advisable to arrange a brief visit home to say farewell to their familiar environment. While society has developed rituals for many occasions, unfortunately no rituals exist for this difficult life transition.

Entering a nursing home means losing control and adjusting to a new environment. How well a person adjusts depends on many factors. If the elderly individual sees entering the nursing home in a favorable light and feels in control, adjustment may proceed well. Frequent visits by relatives and friends also help in the adaptation to the new living arrangement. Despite the commonly held belief that families do not visit their relatives, continued family involvement seems to be the norm. About two thirds of nursing home residents receive one or more visitors a week, and only a very small group is never visited (Bitzan & Kruzich, 1990).

The Search for Personal Meaning

As adults become older, they spend more time reviewing their life achievements and searching for personal meaning. In gerontology, the concept of **life review** as a developmental task of late adulthood was introduced by Robert Butler (1963). He theorized that this self-reflective review of one's life is not a sign of losing short-term memory, as had been assumed. Rather, life review is a process of evaluating and making sense of one's life. It includes a reinterpretation of past experiences and unresolved conflicts.

The life review can lead to diverse outcomes, including depression, acceptance, or satisfaction (Butler, 1987). If the life review is successful, it leads the individual to personal wisdom and inner peace. But the reassessment of one's life may also lead to despair and depression. This idea that the process of life review may lead to either acceptance or depression is similar to the eighth stage of Erikson's theory of adult development: through the life review, the individual tries to work through the conflict between ego integrity (accepting oneself and seeing one's life as meaningful) and despair (rejecting oneself and one's life).

The ways in which individuals review their lives differ considerably. Some undertake a very conscious effort of assessing and reevaluating their achievements; for others, the effort may be subtle and not very conscious. Regardless of how they pursue it, life review is believed to be a common activity for older adults that occurs across cultures and time.

The concept of **reminiscence** is closely related to life review. Most older persons have a remarkable ability to recall past events. They reminisce about the past and tell their stories to anyone who is willing to listen, but they also reminisce when they are on their own. This reminiscing can serve several functions (Sherman, 1991):

- Reminiscing may be an enjoyable activity that can lift the spirits of the listener and of the person telling the story.
- Some forms of reminiscing are directed at enhancing a person's image of self, as when individuals focus on their accomplishments.
- Reminiscing may help the person cope with current or future problems, letting her or him retreat to the safe place of a comfortable memory or recall ways of coping with past stressors.
- Reminiscing can assist in the life review, as a way to achieve ego integrity.

Reminiscing combines past, present, and future orientations (Sherman, 1991). It includes the past, which is when the reviewed events occurred. However, the construction of personal meaning is an activity that is also oriented to the present and the future, providing purpose and meaning to life.

Another factor in the search for personal meaning is religious or spiritual activity. Cross-sectional research has consistently found that humans become more religious or spiritual in late adulthood (Gallup & Lindsay, 1999). Vaillant's (2002) longitudinal research did not find support for this idea, however. He found that the importance of religion and spirituality, on average, did not change in the lives of his study participants over time. He suggests that the cross-sectional finding may be picking up a cohort effect, and that subsequent cohorts may be less religious or spiritual in adolescence and young adulthood than the current cohort of older adults was. What Vaillant fails to address is whether his cohort reaches a higher faith stage in late adulthood, as developmental theorists would suggest.

Resources for Meeting the Needs of Elderly Persons

The persons in the case studies at the beginning of this chapter needed several kinds of assistance. Lois and Gene Smith, for example, needed some counseling to help them settle comfortably into retirement together. Gene went back to work to fill some of his leisure hours, but Lois needed some suggestions about the volunteer opportunities that could give meaning to her life. The Moros' needs were quite different. Frank is confronted with several chronic conditions for which he needs assistance. Much of this assistance has been provided by his wife. Camille, in turn, needs some respite services to prevent her from being overwhelmed by the demands of giving care. Ms. Johnson requires a level of assistance most practically provided by effective and comprehensive case management.

The types of support and assistance that elderly persons receive can be categorized as either formal or informal resources. Formal resources are those provided by formal service providers. They typically have eligibility requirements that a person has to meet in order to qualify. Some formal resources are free, but others are provided on a fee-for-service basis, meaning that anyone who is able to pay can request the service. Informal resources are those provided through families, friends, neighbors, and churches. Elderly persons receive a considerable amount of support through these informal support networks.

Informal Resources

What types of social service programs can enhance informal supports for older adults?

The family is the most important provider of informal resources for many older individuals. It is estimated that 80 to 90% of the care provided to elderly persons living in the community is provided by family members (Manton & Liu, 1984). Usually family members can provide better emotional and social support than other providers of services. Family members know the person better and are more available for around-the-clock support. Different family members tend to provide different types of assistance. Daughters tend to provide most of the caregiving and are more involved in housekeeping and household chores. Sons are more likely to provide assistance with household repairs and financial matters.

However, the family should not be considered a uniformly available resource or support. Not all family networks are functional and able to provide needed support. As Ms. Johnson's story illustrates, even when family members are involved in the elderly person's life, they may place additional demands on the older person instead of relieving the burden. The increased presence of women in the labor market places them in a particularly difficult position—trying to balance the demands of raising children, taking care of their parents, and being part of the workforce. Furthermore, the size of the family network available to support elderly persons is decreasing as a consequence of the decreasing average number of children in a family (T. Brubaker, 1990).

A second source of informal resources is friends and neighbors, who often provide a significant amount of care and assistance. Although they may be less inclined than family members would be to provide personal care, friends and neighbors like Gene and Lois Smith in our first case study often offer other forms of assistance, such as running errands or performing household chores. Sometimes a system of informal exchanges evolves—for example, an elderly woman invites her elderly neighbor over for meals while he mows her lawn and drives her to medical appointments.

Finally, informal resources are also provided by church and community groups. Church-related resources include social and emotional support through group activities and community events. It is this form of support that an active retired person like Lois Smith finds most helpful. In addition, some churches are involved in providing more formal resources, such as transportation or meal services.

Formal Resources

The second type of support for older adults is the formal service delivery system, which offers a wide range of services. Four different Social Security trust funds are the backbone of formal resources to older people in the United States:

1. *Old-Age and Survivors Insurance (OASI).* The retirement and survivors' component of the U.S. Social Security system is a federally administered program that covers almost all workers. To qualify, a person must have worked at least 10 years in employment covered by the program. The benefit is based on the individual's earnings and is subject to a maximum benefit amount. Through cost-of-living adjustments, the amount is adjusted annually for inflation. Many older individuals are able to supplement this benefit with private pension benefits.
2. *Hospital Insurance Trust Fund (Medicare Part A).* This fund covers a major part of the cost of hospitalization, as well as a significant part of the costs of skilled nursing facility care, approved home health care, and under certain conditions, hospice care. Depending on the type of service needed, beneficiaries pay a one-time copayment or a percentage of the actual costs. Most beneficiaries do not need to pay a monthly premium (Kingson & Berkowitz, 1993).
3. *Supplementary Medical Insurance (Medicare Part B).* This fund covers medical costs such as physicians' services, inpatient and outpatient surgery, and ambulance services, as well as laboratory services, medically necessary home health care, and outpatient hospital treatment. Beneficiaries pay a small monthly premium (Kingson & Berkowitz, 1993). Some services require a copayment or a deductible.
4. *Disability insurance.* This component provides benefits for workers younger than 62 with a severe long-term disability. There is a 5-month waiting period, but the benefits continue as long as the disability exists.

How do these federal programs serve as protective factors in late adulthood?

In addition, Supplementary Social Security Income (SSI) is a financial need-based program that provides cash benefits to low-income, aged, blind, and disabled persons. It is not part of the Social Security trust funds but is a federal welfare program.

Other formal services are available regionally. Here is an overview of some of the most important ones:

- *Adult day care.* Some elderly individuals have conditions that prevent them from staying at home while their caregiver is at work, or the caregiver may benefit from respite. Two forms of adult day care exist for such situations. The social adult day care model provides meals, medication, and socialization, but no personal care. The medical adult day care model is for individuals who need medical care, nursing services, physical or occupational therapy, and more intensive personal care.
- *Senior centers.* Community forums for social activities, educational programs, and resource information are available even in small communities.
- *Home health care services.* Several types of home health care are available, varying greatly in level of assistance and cost. They range from homemakers who assist with household chores, cleaning, and errands to registered nurses who provide skilled nursing service, use medical equipment, and provide IV therapy.
- *Hospice programs.* The purpose of a hospice program is to provide care to the terminally ill. Through inpatient or outpatient hospice, patients typically receive treatment by a team of doctors, nurses, social workers, and care staff.
- *Senior housing.* An elderly person may require a change in his or her living arrangement for a number of reasons, and several alternative living arrangements are available. Senior apartments and retirement communities are for persons who can live independently. They typically offer meals and housekeeping services, but no direct care. Many offer transportation, community rooms, and senior programs.
- *Adult homes* are for seniors in need of more assistance. They usually have rooms, rather than apartments, and provide meals, medication management, and supervision.
- *Health-related senior facilities* are for those in need of nursing care and intensive assistance with activities of daily living. Rooms are private or semiprivate, and residents share living and dining rooms. Medications, meals, personal care, and some therapeutic services are provided. The skilled nursing facility provides the highest level of care, including nursing and personal care and an array of therapeutic services. Several noninstitutional alternatives to the nursing home exist, including *adult foster care* programs that operate in a similar way to foster care programs for children and adolescents.
- *Nutrition programs.* Deficits in nutrition can affect a person's health and the aging process. Nutritional services are provided through a number of programs, the best known being Meals on Wheels (Wacker, Roberto, & Piper, 1997).
- *Transportation services.* Public and private providers offer transportation for elderly persons with mobility problems.

- *Power of attorney.* Some elderly persons have difficulty managing their legal and financial affairs. A **power of attorney (POA)** is a legal arrangement by which a person appoints another individual to manage his or her financial and legal affairs. The person given the POA should be a person the client knows and trusts. Standard POA forms are available at stationery stores, but the POA can be tailored to the individual's situation. It then needs to be notarized, a service provided by attorneys and some banks. A POA can be limited (for a limited time period), general (no restrictions), or durable (begins after the client reaches a specified level of disability) (Wacker et al., 1997).

With so many types of services available, the social worker's most daunting task is often assessing the elderly person's needs. It may also be a challenge, however, to find quality services that are affordable. Thus, advocacy on behalf of older adults remains a concern of the social work profession.

Risk Factors and Protective Factors in Late Adulthood

Chapter 8 suggests that midlife behavior has both antecedents and consequences. The same can be said for late adulthood. Early life experiences can serve either as risk factors or as protective factors for health and well-being during late adulthood. And late adult behaviors can serve either as risk factors or as protective factors for future health and well-being.

As the longest-term longitudinal research available on late adult behavior, Vaillant's Study of Adult Development (2002) provides the clearest understanding of the antecedents of late adult well-being. Like Emmy Werner, who has studied a cohort until midlife (see Chapter 8), Vaillant is impressed with the self-righting tendencies in human nature. He summarizes the antecedent risk factors and protective factors for late adulthood in this way: "What goes right in childhood predicts the future far better than what goes wrong" (p. 95). He also suggests that unhappy childhoods become less important over the stages of adulthood. Consequently, Vaillant suggests that it is more important to count up the protective factors than to count up the risk factors. Although he found childhood experiences to diminish in importance over time, Vaillant also found that much of the resilience, or lack thereof, in late adulthood is predicted by factors that were established by age 50. He suggests that risk factors and protective factors change over the life course.

Exhibit 9.8 lists six variables that Vaillant was surprised to find did not predict healthy aging and seven factors that he did find to predict healthy aging. Some of the factors that did not predict healthy aging did predict good adjustment at earlier adult stages. In terms of stress, Vaillant found that if we wait a few decades, many people recover

EXHIBIT 9.8 Variables That Affect Healthy Aging

Variables That Do Not Predict Healthy Aging	Variables That Do Predict Healthy Aging
Ancestral longevity	Not smoking, or stopping young
Cholesterol	Using mature coping mechanisms
Stress	Not abusing alcohol
Parental characteristics	Healthy weight
Childhood temperament	Stable marriage
General ease in social relationships	Some exercise
	Years of education

Source: Vaillant, 2002.

from psychosomatic illness. In terms of parental characteristics, he found that they are still important for predicting adaptation at age 40 but not by age 70. In terms of both childhood temperament and general ease in social relationships, he found that they are strong predictors of adjustment in young adulthood but no longer important at age 70.

On the other hand, Vaillant found that the seven factors on the right side of Exhibit 9.8, collectively, are strong predictors of health 30 years in the future. He also found that each variable, individually, predicted healthy aging, even when the other six variables were statistically controlled. Vaillant has chosen to frame each of these predictive factors in terms of protection; he sees risk as the flip side of protection. He notes the danger of such a list of protective factors: that it be used to "blame the victim" rather than provide guidance for aging well. He sees the list of predictors as "good news," however, because they all represent something that can be controlled to some extent.

By following cohorts across the period of young-old and middle-old, Vaillant (2002) also has some suggestions about the consequences of late adult behavior. We have already taken a look at his prescription for growing old gracefully. In addition, he notes the following personal qualities in late adulthood to bode well for continued well-being:

- Good self-care
- Future orientation, ability to anticipate, plan, and hope
- Capacity for gratitude and forgiveness
- Capacity for empathy, to imagine the world as the other sees it
- Desire to do things *with* people rather than *to* them

IMPLICATIONS FOR SOCIAL WORK PRACTICE

Several practice principles for social work with older adults can be recommended:

- When working with an older adult, take into account the person's life history.
- Develop self-awareness of your views on aging and how different theoretical perspectives may influence your practice.
- Be conscious that age-related social roles change over time and that they vary for different cohorts.
- Identify areas in which you can assist an elderly client in preventing future problems, such as health-related difficulties.
- Develop an understanding of and skills to assess the difference between the physical, biological, psychological, and socioemotional changes that are part of normal aging and those that are indicative of a problematic process. Develop an understanding of how such factors may affect the intervention process.
- Develop an understanding of the different types of families in later life. Because older adults continue to be part of their families, it may be beneficial to work with the entire family system.
- Develop an understanding of the retirement process and how individuals adjust differently to this new life stage.
- Carefully assess an elderly person's caregiving network. Be conscious of the difficulties that the caregiving situation poses for both the caregiver and the care recipient. Be conscious of the potential for caregiver burnout, and familiarize yourself with local caregiver support options.
- Develop an understanding of the process of institutionalizing an older adult. Be careful not to label it as an act of abandonment. Rather, be aware that institutionalization is stressful for all involved and is typically done only as a last resort. Develop an understanding of the process of adaptation to nursing home placement and skills to assist an older adult and his or her family with that adaptation.
- When assessing the need for service, be conscious of the availability of formal and informal support systems. Develop an understanding and knowledge of the formal service delivery system.

- Avoid treating older persons as if they were incapable of making decisions simply because they may not be able to carry out the decision. Rather, involve them to the maximum extent possible in any decisions relating to their personal life and care, even if they are not able to carry out the related actions.

Key Terms

activity theory
age stratification perspective
continuity theory
crystallized intelligence
delirium
dementia
dependency ratio
ego integrity versus ego despair
feminist theory (of aging)
fluid intelligence
incidental memory
intentional memory
keeper of the meaning
life review
morbidity
mortality rate
power of attorney (POA)
programmed aging theories
random error theories
reminiscence
social construction theory (of aging)
social exchange theory (of aging)
social gerontology

Active Learning

1. Think about the three case studies presented at the outset of this chapter (Smith, Johnson, and Moro). Which theory/theories of social gerontology seems to be the best fit with each of these individuals?

2. Think of examples of how older adults are presented in the media (TV, movies, advertisements). How are they typically characterized? What does this say about our society's views on aging? Think of examples of how older adults could be presented in an age-appropriate way in the media. Develop a short script for an advertisement that features older adults.

3. Think about your own extended family. What roles do the members of the oldest generation play in the family? How do the different generations interact, exchange resources, and influence each other? How do the different generations deal with their role changes and life transitions as they age? In what ways do the different generations support and hinder each other in life transitions?

WEB RESOURCES

National Institute on Aging

www.nia.nih.gov

Site presented by the National Institute on Aging (NIA) contains information about the NIA, news and events, health information, research programs, funding and training, and National Advisory Council on Aging.

Duke University Center for the Study of Aging and Human Development

www.geri.duke.edu.resource/resource.html

Site presented by the Duke University Center for the Study of Aging and Human Development contains links to a number of aging resources.

Indiana University Center for Aging Research

iucar.iu.edu/links/link.php3

Site presented by the Indiana University Center for Aging Research contains a large number of links to other aging centers and institutes, aging directories, and information resources.

National Council on the Aging

www.ncoa.org/visitor/index.html

Site presented by the National Council on the Aging (NCOA) contains information on advocacy, programs, publications, and a number of good links to other aging resources.

Social Security Online

www.ssa.gov

Site maintained by the U.S. Social Security Administration contains benefits information and online direct services.

AgingStats.Gov

www.agingstats.gov

Site presented by the Federal Interagency Forum on Aging-Related Statistics covers 31 key indicators of the lives of older people in the United States and their families.

CHAPTER 10

Very Late Adulthood

Pamela J. Kovacs

Key Terms

Active Learning

Web Resources

CHAPTER 10

Very Late Adulthood

Pamela J. Kovacs
Virginia Commonwealth University

What are some of the reasons for the fast growth and increased diversity among very late-life adults, and what are some of the main challenges associated with increased longevity?

What do social workers need to know about how people respond to crises such as severe illness, acquired disability, and loss when working with clients in very late adulthood?

What are some of the implications for intimacy among very late-life adults as their families and peers die and they become less mobile and independent?

Key Ideas

As you read this chapter, take note of these central ideas:

1. People 85 and older are the fastest growing segment of the older adult population. Never have so many people lived so long.
2. Among very late-life adults, women outnumber men five to two, and four out of five centenarians are women.
3. Because the more frail individuals die sooner, those surviving to very late adulthood tend to be a relatively robust group, but they face an increased incidence of chronic disease and disability.
4. In very late adulthood, individuals continue to desire and need connections to other people.
5. In very late adulthood, spirituality is often associated with making meaning of loss and finding a way to stay connected to others.

6. Very late adulthood is the one life course phase when dying is considered on time, and very late-life adults seem to have less denial about the reality of death than those in other age groups.
7. Theoreticians and researchers continue to try to understand the multidimensional process of grief.

Case Study 10.1

Carmen Ruiz Is Institutionalized

Carmen Ruiz has lived in the same ground floor apartment, next to the city bus station, since she immigrated to the United States in the mid-1950s. When she reflects on her 89 years, she reminisces about growing up on a farm in Puerto Rico, raising her family, and then moving to the United States with her husband when she was 41 years old. Carmen has lived on her own since her husband died 20 years ago, and her two sons returned to Puerto Rico upon their retirement a few years ago. She is the last family member of her generation who is still alive. Carmen's granddaughter, Gloria, who is 45 years old, lives in a nearby suburb and visits regularly. Although Carmen does not understand or speak English, she manages by only interacting with Spanish-speaking individuals and uses services provided in her language. When she requires assistance with English, she calls Gloria.

Carmen was recently hospitalized for 6 days because of complications related to a recurring heart condition. The original plan was to discharge Carmen to a nursing home for a short-term stay for rehabilitation. But at Gloria's request, that plan was changed, and Carmen was discharged to her apartment with home health aides, visiting nurse services, and in-home physical therapy and occupational rehabilitation services. Now, 4 weeks later, Carmen is feeling better, and she is back in her routine, shopping in the community, sitting on the steps talking with neighbors, and tending to her own health needs.

As the social worker assigned to Carmen's case, you were involved in the discharge planning and are still following her through long-term care services. Gloria has asked to speak with you now. After Carmen's discharge, Gloria has grown increasingly concerned about her grandmother's safety in the apartment. She explains that Carmen has her own unique form of logic, which is "inviolate and untouchable." Gloria thinks that Carmen "invents her own world and you either buy into it or get frozen out." Absolutely everything has to be at Carmen's convenience. The minute she steps into her primary care doctor's office, having made an appointment or not, the doctor must see her right away or she leaves. While Carmen was in the hospital,

CASE STUDY 10.1

she became more and more confused, at times not remembering where she was. Since being discharged, Carmen's memory has continued to fail. Several times she has left the stove burning unattended. In-home health care services are an option right now, but soon Carmen will need constant supervision and assistance. Thus, Gloria has made the very difficult decision to pursue a nursing home placement.

When you spoke to Carmen about these issues, she expressed anger and resentment. No one in her family had lived in a nursing home before, and it was not the way she had planned to spend her last years. She insisted that she will stay in her apartment until "God" takes her. Finally, after three incidents where the police had to help Carmen find her way back to the apartment, and a smoky oven fire, Carmen said that God appeared to her and told her that she could leave the apartment.

Fortunately, you found a nursing home with a Spanish-speaking staff and an immediate opening. Carmen moved from her apartment of almost 50 years to the nursing home. Carmen's first days there were painfully difficult. She had to share a room with a woman experiencing dementia, who repeated the same phrases over and over again. During the day, Carmen did not want to spend any time in her new room. So, in addition to being upset about losing her independence and the hope of returning home, she felt trapped in an unfamiliar environment without a place to retreat. During these first days, Carmen felt very lonely and had a hard time finding companionship among the nursing home residents. You encouraged her to establish some new routines to take the place of her old ones. Gloria continues to visit Carmen daily, and they spend time together on the weekends. They continue to be close and are planning to spend a weekend together when Gloria's father visits from Puerto Rico.

Case Study 10.2

Bina Patel Outlives Her Son

Bina Patel is a 90-year-old immigrant who moved to the United States 25 years ago from India with her son and his family. Like other South Asian older adults, Bina prefers to reside with her adult children and values the mutual interdependency among generations common in their culture. Upon arriving in this country at age 65, Bina, a widow, played a critical

CASE STUDY 10.2

role in the family, providing child care, assisting with meals and various household tasks, and offering companionship and support for her adult children. True to her cultural tradition, Bina expects adult children, especially sons, to provide for parents in their old age, and believes that the role of the elder is to provide crucial functions such as passing on wisdom and guidance to children and grandchildren, being constantly available to them.

Bina had been in remarkably good health until she had a mild stroke last year. She was managing well at home with weekly physical therapy and her family's assistance with bathing. She and her family have been unprepared for her longevity; and in fact it appears that she will outlive her son, who at age 69 was recently diagnosed with pancreatic cancer with a prognosis of 6 to 12 months. Her daughter-in-law is home full time with Bina, but does not drive, and currently is emotionally distraught over her husband's rapid decline. Bina's two grandchildren, who are in their 30s, have relocated with their own families due to employment. They are in frequent telephone contact, but they live a 2-hour plane ride away and are busy with work and children's school and activities. Although this family has traditionally handled their family needs on their own or with the help of a small South Asian network, the son's decline in health has caused tremendous concern regarding Bina's future well-being.

As the hospital social worker, you have been asked to meet with the son and daughter-in-law during his hospitalization to explore possible sources of assistance during the son's pending decline as well as to help strategize for Bina's anticipated increased need of physical care, given her recent decline in cognitive and physical capacity.

Case Study 10.3

Pete Mullin Loses His Sister's Support

Pete Mullin and Lucy Rauso, brother and sister, ages 96 and 92, have lived together since the death of Lucy's husband, Tony, 25 years ago. Pete and Lucy are second-generation Irish Catholic Americans and Tony Rauso was Italian American. Pete was married in his 30s, but had lived alone since his divorce at age 55. Pete and Lucy were both in their early 70s when they decided to pool

CASE STUDY 10.3

their limited savings and retirement income to buy a condominium in south Florida. The promise of lower cost of living and milder winters and the fact that many of their friends had moved or died helped Lucy and Pete leave the community in Massachusetts where they had spent their entire lives.

Pete has been estranged from his one daughter since his divorce but is in touch with a granddaughter who "found" him when she moved to Florida a few years ago. Lucy has one surviving son in New Jersey and several grandchildren who provide limited financial support and some social support via phone calls and an occasional visit. Pete has enjoyed his life and, despite some difficulty with his vision and hearing, manages to get around well in his familiar surroundings and is especially fond of tending his orchids in the back porch.

Lucy has just been hospitalized with chronic heart failure and is not expected to make it through the night. A neighbor has brought Pete to the ICU to be with Lucy. Pete states that together he and Lucy managed to provide for each other and served as each other's durable power of attorney, health care surrogate, and in general made it possible for each of them to remain in their home. He wonders what will happen to him after Lucy's death. He knows that many people his age live in nursing homes, but he prefers to stay in his own home. He wonders if the Meals on Wheels will still come to the home, because their eligibility was based on Lucy's diagnosis of chronic heart failure. He hopes he will die soon and quickly like Lucy.

As the social worker employed for the Meals on Wheels program, you have been asked to make a home visit within the week following Lucy's death to reassess Pete's eligibility for services. You had not realized how much your work would involve working with people who have experienced a major loss, whether death of a loved one as in Pete's case or the accompanying losses that come with illness, disability, and aging.

Very Late Adulthood: Charting New Territory

How does the fact that the current cohort of very late-life adults are charting new territory affect their experience with this life course phase?

At 89, 90, 92, and 96, Carmen Ruiz, Bina Patel, Lucy Rauso, and Pete Mullin are charting new territory. They are a part of the rapidly growing population over age 85. Bina Patel—and perhaps Carmen Ruiz, Pete Mullin, and Lucy Rauso as well—has surprised herself, as well as her family, by living so long. Never have so many people lived to be so old.

In the first edition of this book, written 4 years ago, the chapter on late adulthood covered all persons 65 and older. The fact that this edition presents this content in two chapters ("Late Adulthood" and "Very Late Adulthood") indicates the scope and rapidity of the demographic changes taking place in the United States and other late industrial societies. Only within the past 5 to 10 years have researchers begun to methodically consider age distinctions after age 65 or 75; much research on aging still does not make such distinctions.

This chapter summarizes some of the emerging literature on very late adulthood. (Much of what appears in the previous chapter on late adulthood applies as well.) However, current knowledge about very late adulthood is limited. After all, until recently there were not enough adults over 85 to warrant special study. And at the current time, we do not have any longitudinal studies that have followed a cohort from early adulthood deep into very late adulthood. Consequently, it is impossible to tease out the cohort effects in the available cross-sectional research.

One issue that comes up at all adult stages is, What ages are you including? As you have seen throughout this book, chronological markers of age are arbitrary at best, and influenced by biological age, psychological age, social age, and spiritual age. But it is fairly standard to think of 85 and older as old old, oldest old, or very late adulthood. In this chapter, we use "very late adulthood" to describe the life course phase. For the most part, we use "very late-life adults" to describe people in this life course phase, but we also use "old old" and "oldest old" when citing work where those terms are used. Keep in mind that chronological age may not be the appropriate marker for categorizing very late-life adults, however (Pipher, 1999). Loss of health might be a better criterion for very late adulthood categorization as old old. Nevertheless, in keeping with the other chapters in the book, this chapter uses a chronological distinction.

The drawback to using a chronological marker for entry into very late adulthood is that the path through very late adulthood is quite diverse, and for many people over 85, ill health is not a central theme of their lives. In his book *Aging Well*, George Vaillant (2002) reminds us that

- Frank Lloyd Wright designed the Guggenheim Museum at age 90.
- Dr. Michael DeBakey obtained a patent for a surgical innovation at age 90.
- Pablo Casals was still practicing cello daily at 91.
- Leopold Stokowski signed a 6-year recording contract at 94.
- Grandma Moses was still painting at 100.

In addition, we would add that

- Sarah and Elizabeth Delany published their book *Having Our Say: Our First 100 Years* when Sarah (Sadie) was 103 and Elizabeth (Bessie) was 101.

- Sadie Delany published *On My Own at 107: Reflections on Life Without Bessie* at the age of 107.

So there is much variation in the age at which health issues take on great importance. Carmen Ruiz and Bina Patel reached this stage in their late 80s, Lucy Rauso reached it in her early 90s, and it does not yet seem to have overtaken Pete Mullin in his mid-90s. But sooner or later in very late adulthood, health issues and impending death become paramount.

With our current ways of living, with pressed work schedules and families geographically scattered, late industrial societies are not organized to make aging easy. That portion of the physical environment attributable solely to human efforts was designed, in the main, by and for those in young and middle adulthood, not for children, persons with disabilities, or older adults. Not only is the current cohort of very late-life adults charting new territory, but as a society we are also charting new territory that will become more and more familiar when the large baby boom generation reaches very late adulthood. What can we learn from people who reach 85 and beyond, and what do social work practitioners need to know to provide meaningful interventions?

As Erik Erikson suggested, we have one and only one life cycle (at least in this incarnation). Sooner or later, each of us will complete that life cycle and die. For some of us, that death will come quickly, but for others of us, death will come after a protracted period of disease and disability. One of the life tasks of late adulthood is to come to terms with that one and only life cycle, and the evidence suggests that most very late-life adults do that remarkably well. We began this book with a discussion of conception and birth, the starting line of the life course, and in this chapter we end the book with a discussion of death and dying, the finish line of the life course.

Very Late Adulthood in Historical and Cultural Perspective

There have always been those who outlive their cohort group, but greater numbers of people are surpassing the average life expectancy and more are becoming centenarians. Although very few persons aged 100 years were known to exist in 1900, by 2000 there were an estimated 61,000, and by 2050 the number is expected to reach 600,000 (Dunkle, Roberts, & Haug, 2001). Between 1990 and 2000, the 90- to 94-year-old group tied for second place in terms of the fastest growing segments of the U.S. population. The largest percentage growth occurred in the baby boom 50- to 54-year age group, which grew 55%. The 90- to 94-year age group grew 45%, as did another baby boom group, the 45- to 49-year-old age group (U.S. Census Bureau, 2001b).

Growth in the midlife age groups is the result of the high birthrates in the baby boom generation. But what accounts for the fact that persons 85 and older are the fastest growing segment of the older adult population? Several factors contribute to the growth among old-old adults, including better health care in early and middle years, earlier diagnosis and improved technology for treatment and overall health care, and improved health habits, including less smoking, less consumption of alcohol and saturated fats, and increased exercise in some groups. Fewer people die of infectious diseases. Although more are living with chronic illnesses, fewer of these are debilitating illnesses (Hooyman & Kiyak, 1996).

The U.S. Census data refers to persons 65 and older as "elderly" and those 85 and older as the "oldest old" (Administration on Aging, 2002b). Between 1900 and 1994, the elderly population increased elevenfold compared to threefold for those under age 65. Of interest to this chapter, however, is that from 1960 to 1994, persons aged 85 and older (the oldest old) increased by 274% compared to 100% for those 65 and older and 45% for the total population. The oldest old population is projected to double from the 1994 census to 7 million in 2020.

Because both group-based and individual differences within this age group are great, one is cautioned against stereotyping very late-life adults in an attempt to describe them (Field & Gueldner, 2001). For instance, gender and racial/ethnic differences are embedded within these overall statistics. Life expectancy at birth in 1991 was about 80 years for white females, 74 years for black females, 73 years for white males, and 65 years for black males. Among very late-life adults, women outnumber men five to two, and four out of five centenarians are women. At this point, very late adulthood is largely a woman's territory. Pete Mullin is an exception to this trend. Culturally, the most significant fact is that very late-life adults, like other age groups, are becoming more diverse. As of 1999, 86% of the U.S. population 85 and older was non-Hispanic white, 7% was black, 4.5% was of Hispanic origin, 1.5% was Asian Pacific Islander, and less than 1% was Native American (U.S. Census Bureau, 2000).

Census data such as these are of interest to researchers studying *ethnogerontology,* the study of the causes, processes, and consequences of race, national origin, and culture on individual and population aging (Hooyman & Kiyak, 1996). Some gender and racial differences are thought to be associated more with socioeconomic status than with physiological factors. Usually low income and female gender create a double risk. Women are poorer than men throughout their lives, including this final phase. Income and poverty differences are also significant for racial subgroups. The poverty rates in 1992 were higher for elderly blacks (33%) and Hispanics (22%) than for whites (11%) (Hobbs & Damon, 1997).

Chapter 1 suggests that one of the themes of the life course perspective is that individual and family development must be understood in historical context. It is particularly important when we interact with very late-life adults to be aware of the historical worlds in which their life journeys have taken place. To help us to keep this in mind, Exhibit 10.1 captures some historical events faced by the current cohort of

EXHIBIT 10.1
Historical Events Witnessed by an 85-Year-Old Born in 1917 (as of 2002)

When he or she was . . .	Historical Event
An infant	The United States enters World War I.
3	Women win the right to vote in the United States.
6	The National Woman's Party launches a campaign for an equal rights amendment. First shopping center opens in Kansas City.
11	First color motion picture is demonstrated.
A teenager	Mount Rushmore is completed. "Star Spangled Banner" is adopted as national anthem. The Great Depression becomes a worldwide phenomenon. Social Security legislation is passed.
20-something	American Medical Association approves birth control. New York's La Guardia Airport opens. U.S. Supreme Court rules blacks are entitled to first class services on railroad trains. United States enters World War II after the attack at Pearl Harbor. GI Bill is signed, giving broad benefits to returned servicemen.
30-something	Minimum wage is raised from 40 to 75 cents. U.S. Supreme Court outlaws racial segregation in public schools. Rosa Parks refuses to relinquish her seat to a white man on a bus in Montgomery, Alabama. Jonas Salk develops polio vaccine.
40-something	Russia sends first satellite into space, and United States follows soon behind. The computer microchip is invented. BankAmericard and American Express issue credit cards. Alaska and Hawaii become the 49th and 50th states. President Kennedy becomes the first Catholic president of the United States. John Glenn becomes the first American to orbit Earth. Black Civil Rights Movement reaches its peak. National Organization for Women (NOW) is formed. United States involvement in Vietnam deepens. Lyndon Johnson begins a War on Poverty.
50-something	First human heart transplant takes place. Antiwar sentiment against U.S. involvement in Vietnam intensifies. Student protest movement against war and racism spreads. Neil Armstrong walks on the moon.

(continued)

EXHIBIT 10.1
Historical Events Witnessed by an 85-Year-Old Born in 1917 (as of 2002) *(continued)*

When he or she was . . .	Historical Event
	Thousands flock to music festival at Woodstock, New York. Computerized axial tomography (CAT) scan is developed. Watergate break-in ultimately causes Richard Nixon to resign. OPEC imposes a 6-month oil embargo on the United States. *Roe v. Wade* imposes constitutional protections on abortion. *Saturday Night Live* television show debuts.
60-something	First "test-tube baby" is born. The World Health Organization announces that smallpox has been eradicated worldwide. CNN, the first 24-hour TV news channel, is launched. IBM introduces the first generation of personal computers. MTV is created. Sandra Day O'Connor becomes the first woman on the U.S. Supreme Court. Astronaut Sally Ride is the first U.S. woman to travel in space. Crack cocaine addiction becomes a serious problem. Terrorism becomes a fact of life. The space shuttle *Challenger* explodes immediately after takeoff.
70-something	Communism loses its hold in Eastern Europe, and the Soviet Union disintegrates. The Americans with Disabilities Act recognizes the civil rights of persons with disabilities. The U.S. wages Operation Desert Storm to liberate Kuwait from Iraq. Basketball star "Magic" Johnson announces on TV that he had contracted AIDS. Islamic terrorists bomb New York's World Trade Center, killing five people. The computer-based worldwide network (Internet) revolutionizes communications. Former President Ronald Reagan reveals he is suffering from Alzheimer's disease. War veteran Timothy McVeigh bombs the Alfred P. Murrah Building in Oklahoma City. President Bill Clinton signs legislation that ends "welfare as we knew it." The Taliban gains control in Afghanistan.
80-something	Researchers in Great Britain clone a sheep. President Clinton is impeached after a sex scandal with a White House intern. The stock market hits unprecedented highs, before deflating. On September 11, 2001, terrorists fly hijacked airplanes into the World Trade Center in New York City and the Pentagon. Scandals at major big businesses in the United States reveal accounting fraud and greed.

Source: Based on National Geographic Society, 1998.

85-year-olds (as of June 2002). Of course, many of these events have also been shared by young adults, midlife adults, and late-life adults, but at different life phases.

Chapter 1 also discusses the concept of *cohort effects,* which suggests that a historical event affects one cohort differently than it affects subsequent cohorts because of the life phase in which it occurred. Let's look, for example, at the development of the computerized worldwide network (the Internet). It was experienced

- By the current cohort of 85-year-olds when they were in their 70s
- By the current cohort of 65-year-olds in their 50s
- By the current cohort of 45-year-olds in their 30s
- By the current cohort of 25-year-olds in their teens
- By the current cohort of 10-year-olds as a staple of life from infancy

What differences do you think this cohort effect makes for cognitive and social development?

Individuals' cultural backgrounds also play a role in their perceptions of very late adulthood. Remember that Carmen Ruiz's first 41 years were spent in Puerto Rico, and Bina Patel lived the first 65 years of her life in India—both places in which the very old are expected to live out their lives under the care of their extended families. In contrast, Pete Mullin and Lucy Rauso relocated from Massachusetts to Florida in their 70s, moving away from family and friends. Social workers need to try to understand clients' years in these prior settings and any important historical markers in those settings. They also need to know something about migration experiences as well.

What We Can Learn From Centenarians

"Forget about Generation X and Generation Y. Today, the nation's most intriguing demographic is Generation Roman numeral C—folks age 100 and over" ("Aging," 2002). Phrases such as "master survivors" and "successful agers" have been used to describe those who reach their 80s. Those who reach their 100s are "expert agers" (Poon et al., 1992, p. 7).

How will this longevity trend alter our views on appropriate roles for other adult phases?

The number of centenarians doubled in the 1980s and again in the 1990s, with a total of 70,000 reported in 2002. In the next 50 years, midrange projections anticipate that over 800,000 people in the United States could reach the century mark. Other industrialized countries report the same trends. Future editions of human behavior textbooks might in fact report on another group that demographers are now counting—supercentenarians, people age 110 and over ("Aging," 2002).

More than counting numbers, researchers want to know the answers to fundamental questions about human health and longevity such as:

- What does it take to live a long life?
- How much do diet, exercise, and other lifestyle factors matter compared with "good" genes and other genetic factors?
- What is the quality of life among very late-life adults?
- What role do individual characteristics such as gender, personality, and socio-economic status play in longevity?
- What is the role of social support, religiosity, and social environment in longevity?
- Basically, what is the secret?

Much of what is known about centenarians comes from the work of Leonard Poon and his colleagues in the Georgia Centenarian Study (1992) and from the New England Centenarian Study (Perls & Wood, 1996). These and other centenarian studies are trying to understand the interrelationship between multiple variables such as family longevity, gender, environmental support, adaptational skills, individual traits, life satisfaction, and health.

These studies reveal that because the more frail individuals die sooner, those remaining are a relatively robust group. While these "extra" years are for the most part healthy years, several studies report high levels of dementia (66% in one study and 51% in another) and cardiovascular disease (72%), urinary incontinence (60%), and osteoarthritis (54%). What is notable, however, is that the period of serious illness and disability for those who make it to 100 tends to be brief ("Aging," 2002). Some factors thought to contribute to centenarians' robustness are physical activity such as walking, biking, golfing, and swimming, as well as mental exercise such as reading, painting, and playing a musical instrument.

However, 100 is still old and life expectancy is short at 100, with most only living 1 to 2 more years. In the New England Study, 75% of the people were still living at home and taking care of themselves at 95. By age 102, this number had dropped to 30%—which is still quite remarkable.

How does the gender gap affect the experience of very late adulthood?

The gender gap in very late adulthood widens further past the age of 100, with female centenarians outnumbering males 9 to 1. However, men who reach their 100th birthday are, on the whole, more healthy than their female counterparts, reporting lower incidence of dementia and other serious medical problems. Estrogen may give women an edge in longevity. Another possibility is that there may be some protective genes in the X chromosome, of which women have two but men only one. Others theorize that menstruation and systems related to childbirth better equip women to eliminate toxins from the body. Another hypothesis is that genetics are relatively neutral, but women tend to be more social, and these connections are thought to be critical in weathering old age ("Aging," 2002). Cross-cultural studies in which differences in diet, physical activity, and other lifestyle factors can be compared will be important in helping researchers better understand the influence of these multiple contributing variables.

Functional Capacity in Very Late Adulthood

Although persons who reach 85 years of age and older demonstrate resilience in the simple fact of their longevity, they continue to face an increased incidence of chronic illness and debilitation with age. Chapter 9 provides a good overview of changes in physiology and mental functioning that begin to occur in late adulthood and only become more prevalent with advancing age. Unfortunately, much of the available information does not distinguish the 85 and older cohort group from the larger 65 and older group. We do know that of the 85 and older age group, 24% lived in a nursing home in 1990 and 50% of those who were noninstitutionalized reported the need for personal assistance with everyday activities (Administration on Aging, 2002b). We also know, however, that the functional level of older adults showed some improvement between 1990 and 2000.

We can extrapolate from existing data to get some better understanding of the functional capacity of persons 85 and over. We have data that show that in 1997, 50% of adults 75 and over reported some limitation of activity caused by chronic conditions. The good news is that by 1999, this percentage had dropped to about 45%. In 1999, about 10% of the population 75 and over reported some limitations in **activities of daily living** (**ADL**), or basic self-care activities. About 21% of this same population reported some limitations in **instrumental activities of daily living (IADL)**, which are more complex everyday tasks (National Center for Health Statistics, 2001a). Exhibit 10.2 lists common ADLs and IADLs. Looking at earlier data from 1994 to 1995, which did break out the 85+ age group, may help to interpret the 1999 data reported for the 75+ group. That data shows that 18% of the population 85 and over reported problems with two or more ADLs. In contrast, only about 8% of the 75- to 84-year-old age group reported problems with two or more ADLs (Adams & Marano, 1995). These findings suggest that the percentages reported above for the 75+ age group would probably double if we broke out the 85+ group.

In general, all persons experience **primary aging**, or changes that are a normal part of the aging process. There is a recognized slowing with age—slowing of motor responses, sensory responses, and intellectual functioning. "Older individuals can do

EXHIBIT 10.2
Common Activities of Daily Living (ADLs) and Instrumental Activities of Daily Living (IADLs)

Activities of Daily Living
Bathing
Dressing
Walking a short distance
Shifting from a bed to a chair
Using the toilet
Eating
Instrumental Activities of Daily Living
Doing light housework
Doing the laundry
Using transportation
Handling finances
Using the telephone
Taking medications

what younger ones can, but it takes more time. The causes of the slowing are not fully understood, although animals of all species become slower as they age" (Seifert, Hoffnung, & Hoffnung, 1997, p. 589). For example, the percentage of older adults in the United States with significant visual loss increases during late and very late adulthood: 9% among the 65- to 75-year-olds, 16% among the 75- to 84-year-olds, and 28% among those over 85. Similarly, in terms of hearing, 23% of 65- to 74-year-olds, 34% of 75- to 84-year-olds, and 51% of persons 85+ years old experience significant hearing loss.

How much control do we have over secondary aging?

In addition, many experience **secondary aging** caused by health-compromising behaviors such as smoking or environmental factors such as pollution (Seifert et al., 1997). Access to health care, ample and nutritious food, safe and affordable housing, safe working conditions, and other factors that influence the quality of life also affect longevity.

Although late adulthood is a time of loss of efficiency in body systems and functioning, the body is an organism that repairs and restores itself as damage occurs. Those persons who live to be 85 and older may be blessed with a favorable genetic makeup. But they may also have found ways to compensate, to prevent, to restore, and to maintain other health-promoting behaviors. One cross-sectional study of individuals age 85 and over found that most report well-being despite their physical and social losses (Johnson & Barer, 1997). Most very late-life adults come to think of themselves in ways that fit their circumstances. They narrow the scope of their activities to those that are most cherished, and they carefully schedule their activities to make the best use of their energy and talents.

Sooner or later, however, most very late-life adults come to need some assistance with ADLs and IADLs. As a society, we have to grapple with the question of who will provide that assistance. Currently, most of the assistance is provided by family members. But as families grow smaller, fewer adult children exist to provide such care. A number of family theorists have begun to suggest that multigenerational families will need to renegotiate their relationships. One sign of the strain is the current crisis of care, with too many very late-life adults having some of their personal needs neglected while "a thousand miles away their grandchildren are not getting the love and attention they desperately need" (Pipher, 1999, p. 11). These are some of the costs of the high value our culture places on rugged individualism.

Relationships in Very Late Adulthood

How do current social arrangements threaten and/or support the desire for social connections among very late-life adults?

Much of what is presented in Chapter 9 under the section called Families in Later Life applies also to very late adulthood. Research that looks specifically at relationship patterns among very late-life adults is limited, but two themes are clear (Carstensen, 2001):

1. Individuals continue to desire and need connections to other people throughout life.
2. In very late adulthood, people interact with others less frequently, but old-old adults make thoughtful selections about the persons with whom they will interact.

After intensive interviews with groups that she labeled as young-old and old-old, Mary Pipher (1999) concludes that "the situations that work for people in the young-old stage are not feasible for the old-old. Young-old people may love their mountain cabin or Manhattan townhouse, but old-old people need relatives nearby" (p. 32). That is one of the issues that will need to be explored as our society charts the new demographic territory.

Relationships With Family and Friends

Social isolation is considered to be a powerful risk factor not only for the development of cognitive and intellectual decline in very late adulthood but also for physical illness (McInnis-Dittrich, 2002). A sense of connectedness with family and friends can be achieved in person, on the phone, and more recently via chat rooms and e-mail. Pets, plants, and other connections with nature bring comfort, as with any age group.

Pertinent to very late-life adults is the increased likelihood that one will have lost spouses/partners, friends, and other family members to death, illness, debilitation, or relocation. Loss is more prevalent during this stage than at other times of life, but there is also greater opportunity for intergenerational family contact as four-, five-, and six-generation families become more common.

Siblings often provide companionship and caregiving for each other, as Pete and Lucy did in the case study. Siblings are comforting because they are part of one's cohort and also have experienced many of the same family events. In addition, siblings tend to be the most long-standing relationships in a person's life (Cicirelli, 1995). Obviously, sibling relationships may range from loving and close to ambivalent, distant, or even hostile. Sharing responsibility for aging parents may create greater closeness between siblings or increase tension. There is some evidence that sibling relationships are especially important sources of support among members of lower socioeconomic groups. Close relationships with sisters in very late adulthood have been found to be positively related to positive mental health, but close relationships with brothers do not have the same benefit (Cicirelli, 1995).

Relationships with adult children are another important part of the social networks of very late-life adults. However, one study of a predominantly white sample in San Francisco found that most older people prefer to be independent from their children when possible, with adult children serving more as managers of social supports than providing direct care (Johnson & Barer, 1997). Very late-life adults are in fact institutionalized more often for social reasons than for medical reasons (Hooyman & Kiyak, 1996). One reason is that approximately one in five women 80 and older has been childless throughout her life or has outlived her children. In addition, baby boomers and their children tended to have more divorces and fewer children, decreasing the caregiving options for their parents and grandparents (Hooyman & Kiyak, 1996). Racial and ethnic variations exist, however. As in Bina Patel's case, families with a collectivist heritage prefer to have elderly parents reside with their grown children. It is important to understand and honor historical and cultural expectations of each family when addressing the caregiving and health care needs of aging members.

Relationships with friends remain important in very late adulthood. In general, women have fewer economic resources, but more social resources, and richer, more intimate relationships than do older men (Hooyman & Kiyak, 1996). But over time, women tend to outlive partners, friends, and other key members of their social support system, often being left to deal with end-of-life decisions at an advanced age, without the social and perhaps financial support of earlier life.

Relationships with a domestic partner become much less likely in very late adulthood than in earlier phases of life. Very late-life adults have the potential to have shared 60 to 70 years with a spouse or partner, but one study found that was the case for no more than 20% of a white sample in San Francisco (Johnson & Barer, 1997). Such long-term relationships, where they do exist, present the risk of tremendous loss when one member of the relationship dies. (Widowhood is presented in more detail in Chapter 9.) Because women outnumber men five to two over the age of 85, heterosexual men stand a greater chance of starting a new relationship than heterosexual women. With the current gender demographics, lesbian domestic partnerships have the greatest opportunity for continued long-term relationships in very late adulthood.

Intimacy and Sexuality in Very Late Adulthood

Given the scarcity of men and the fact that many partners and friends have died, many persons 85 and older, especially women, are more alone than at other times in their lives. The implications for intimacy and sexuality are significant. Although minimal research has been conducted specifically about intimacy and sexuality with this age group, some tentative conclusions can be drawn from literature on aging. In particular, a summer 2002 issue of *Generations* focused on "Intimacy and Aging," including the expressions of intimacy in a variety of relationships, challenges related to physical and mental illness, gay and lesbian relationships, and separation of couples due to institutionalization.

Intimacy can be seen as much broader than sexuality, which has been identified as only one of five major components of intimacy (Moss & Schwebel, cited in Blieszner & deVries, 2001). These are the five major components of intimacy in this view:

1. *Commitment.* Feeling of cohesion and connection
2. *Affective intimacy.* A deep sense of caring, compassion, and positive regard and the opportunities to express the same
3. *Cognitive intimacy.* Thinking about and awareness of another, sharing values and goals
4. *Physical intimacy.* Sharing physical encounters ranging from proximity to sexuality
5. *Mutuality.* A process of exchange or interdependence

Closeness is inherent in cognitive, affective, and physical intimacy. Communication, or self-disclosure, facilitates intimacy.

Although sexuality is only one aspect of intimacy, it deserves additional attention; it should not be neglected, as it often is in our interaction with older adults: "Sexuality is a major quality-of-life issue, even into advanced age" (Bortz & Wallace, 1999, p. 167). It is important for social workers to assess the impact of physical and psychosocial conditions on the sexual interest level, satisfaction, and performance of older adults. Medical conditions such as arthritis, pain, and medications that restrict sexual positions, limit movement, and ultimately reduce sexual pleasure are primary factors in reducing sexual desire over age 50 (Ducharme, 2001). Because of these conditions, many very late-life adults are relieved to move into a less sexualized type of intimacy (Pipher, 1999).

Some of the more common psychosocial factors associated with reduced sexual desire or sexual dysfunction include restrictive beliefs about sexuality and aging, role changes due to illness or disability in one or both of the partners, anxiety about sexual function, and psychological disorders. Depression and substance abuse are especially prevalent in older adults with sexual dysfunction. Also, cultural ideals about body image and perceived sexual attractiveness make it more difficult for some older adults to embrace age-related changes (Zeiss & Kasl-Godley, 2001). Many older adults grew up in a time when older people were generally expected to be asexual or not interested in forming new romantic attachments. This cultural conditioning may make it difficult to accept today's greater openness about sexual and romantic relationships, sexual orientation, and varying partnership choices at all ages (Huyck, 2001).

Relationships With Organizations and Community

Relationships with the wider world peak in young and middle adulthood. They grow more constricted as access to social, occupational, recreational, and religious activities becomes more difficult due to decrease in mobility and independence, and as the physical and cognitive impairments associated with age increase. As mobility declines, community-based programs like Meals on Wheels can become important resources to people like Pete Mullin and Lucy Rauso, providing them not only with essential resources such as food but serving also as a connection to the community.

One organizational relationship becomes more likely with advancing age, however. As people live longer and need greater assistance, many move into some form of institutional care. When reading the following discussion about the continuum of housing options, consider the benefits and the challenges each presents as a source of relationships.

The Housing Continuum

As people live longer, the likelihood of illness and disability increases; spouses, partners, and friends die, and the chance of needing more support than is available to the very late-life adults in their own home increases (Maddox, 2001). Review the section on informal and formal resources in Chapter 9 for a description of the variety of options along the continuum as needs for assistance increase.

How do gender, race, ethnicity, and social class affect access to physical assistance in very late adulthood?

Other than skilled nursing care reimbursed by Medicare and other health insurance, the majority of assistance that people need must be paid for privately. Financing is a major problem for low-income and even many middle-income people. Women, especially women of color, are overrepresented in lower socioeconomic categories, and in very late adulthood, safe, affordable housing options are a serious concern for them, as in the case of Carmen Ruiz. But even Pete Mullin and Lucy Rauso found housing a problem until they moved in together and pooled their resources.

Current trends indicate that in the future, the following housing options will become more needed and hopefully more prevalent (Hogstel, 2001):

- Shared housing, shared expenses, and support by family members and friends
- Options for care and assistance in the home with education and support available to family and other informal caregivers
- Housing options such as assisted living facilities, which provide 24-hour assistance, and continuing care retirement communities, which offer a range of services and options for aging in place, without a large initial investment
- Inner-city high-rise retirement communities close to medical, cultural, and recreational activities
- Governmental benefits for home health skilled care services

At the same time, the number of skilled nursing facilities that provide custodial care is likely to decrease, their role taken over by assisted living facilities.

Access and receptivity to this continuum of options are influenced by several factors: geographic location, including urban and rural location; socioeconomic status; race; ethnicity; gender; family support; and health care status. In particular, African American and Latino women historically have been admitted to nursing homes at less than one half the rate of Caucasian women, due to access barriers such as location, cost, language, and acceptability (Johnson & Tripp-Reimer, 2001). A cultural bias against nursing homes may also be a factor for the low use of such facilities among these groups. As social workers we must recognize the unfortunate reality that, as Mary Pipher (1999) suggests, "being old-old costs a lot of money" (p. 50). Many of the current cohort of very late-life adults have arrived at that stage without any expectation that they would live so long, or any preparation for such a prolonged life. And some arrive there after a full life course of limited resources.

Spirituality in Very Late Adulthood

When I called my 85-year-old aunt to wish her a happy birthday, my uncle said, "She has been thinking a lot more about the hereafter." Curious about what sounded like a connection to aging and spirituality, I asked her to tell me more. She added with a chuckle, "Yes, I go into a room and I wonder 'What am I here after?'" On one hand, she was joking about her short-term memory loss. But I also know that she has been questioning the meaning of her life and wondering about her own death, especially since the recent death of her 58-year-old son to cancer.

The following discussion about spirituality refers to aging in general, not specifically to the very late-life adults, but is included in this chapter because of the connection between aging, loss, spirituality, and meaning making. It is when faced by crises, particularly those of severe illness and disability, that one tends to reexamine the meaning of life (Ai, 2000). And while illness, disability, and loss occur throughout life, they tend to accumulate and come at a faster pace during very late adulthood.

Many definitions of spirituality exist. Some social work educators suggest that spirituality refers to the way in which persons seek, find, create, use, and expand personal meaning in the context of their universe, with each person having a unique spiritual style (Ellor, Netting, & Thibault, 1999). More simply, spirituality represents the way in which people seek meaning and purpose in their lives (Bullis, 1996; Canda & Furman, 1999).

The search for meaning is a central element of Erik Erikson's (1963) eighth and final developmental task, referred to as maturity. It involves the challenge of *ego integrity versus ego despair* and centers on one's ability to process what has happened in life and accept these experiences as integral to the meaning of life. Other important spiritual challenges facing elders include transcendence beyond oneself and a sense of connectedness to others (McInnis-Dittrich, 2002). An elderly person's struggle to maintain independence and the ability to make choices in the face of multiple challenges, versus becoming dependent on others, is both psychosocial and spiritual, calling for a social work response addressing both. It is important to remember, however, the cultural, racial, and religious variations that influence each person's spiritual journey. (For more information on aging, diversity, and spirituality see Fried & Mehrotra, 1998; McInnis-Dittrich, 2002.)

Spirituality late in life is often associated with loss (Armatowski, 2001, p. 75). Over time, losses accumulate in the following areas:

- *Relationships*: to children, spouses and partners, friends, and others
- *Status and role*: in family, work, and society

- *Health*: stamina, mobility, hearing, vision, and other physical and cognitive functions
- *Control and independence*: finances, housing, health care, and other decision-making arenas

Whether incremental or sudden, these losses can be difficult for members of a society where personal autonomy, independence, and sense of control are highly valued. Ironically, this increased focus on spirituality often coincides with decreased mobility and independence and diminishing social contact, limiting access to church services and other opportunities for spiritual fulfillment and social support (Harrigan & Farmer, 2000; Watkins, 2001). Spirituality that develops over a lifetime is most responsive to the challenges and the immediacies of old age (Koenig, 1990). Consider, for example, the way that Carmen Ruiz depended on her relationship with God to make the difficult decisions she faced when she could no longer care for herself in her own home.

For older adults, the meaning of spirituality often takes the form of these five themes (Fischer, 1993):

1. Embrace the moment.
2. Find meaning in past memories as part of constructing meaning in one's life.
3. Confront your own limitations.
4. Seek reconciliation and forgiveness.
5. Reach out to others through prayer or service.

These themes suggest a process of slowing down, looking back, and reaching out, steps that make sense developmentally as one nears the end of life.

The subject of spirituality is separated in this chapter from the subject of dying to emphasize the point that spirituality is not just about preparing for death. Rather, it is about finding meaning in life, transcending oneself, and remaining connected to others (McInnis-Dittrich, 2002).

The Dying Process

The topic of death and dying is almost always in the last chapter of a human behavior textbook, reflecting the hope that death will come as late as possible in life. Obviously, people die in all stages of life, but very late adulthood is the time when dying is considered "on time."

Starting with Elisabeth Kübler-Ross's book *On Death and Dying* in 1969, there have been several efforts to talk about death, despite our strong cultural predisposition toward denial of the topic. In recent years, efforts like the Project on Death in America (PDIA) have set out to change mainstream attitudes. The mission of PDIA is to understand and transform the culture and experience of dying and bereavement. It promotes initiatives in research, scholarship, the humanities, and the arts, and fosters innovations in the provision of care, education, and policy. Television programs such as the Public Broadcasting Service's "On Our Own Terms: Moyers on Dying" have facilitated public education and community dialogue.

On a more individual level, many factors influence the ways in which a person adjusts to death and dying, including one's religion and philosophy of life, culture, personality, and other personal traits. Adjustment may also be affected by the conditions of dying. A person with a long terminal illness has more time to accept death than someone with a very short time to face death.

The following adjectives used to describe death were found in both the professional and popular literature: good, meaningful, appropriate, timely, peaceful, sudden, and natural. One can be said to die well, on time, before one's time, and in a variety of ways and places. This terminology reflects an attempt to embrace, acknowledge, tame, and integrate death into one's life.

As with life, the richness and complexity of death is best understood from a multidimensional framework involving the biological, psychological, social, and spiritual dimensions (Bern-Klug & Chapin, 1999; Bern-Klug, Gessert, & Forbes, 2001). The following conceptualizations of the dying process, starting with the well-known work of Kübler-Ross, help capture the notion that dying and other losses, and the accompanying bereavement, are processes that differ for each unique situation, yet share some common aspects.

In *On Death and Dying,* Kübler-Ross (1969) described the stages that persons go through in accepting their own inevitable death or that of others, summarized in Exhibit 10.3. While these stages were written with death in mind, they have application to other loss-related experiences, including the aging process. Given time, most individuals experience these five reactions, although not necessarily in this order. People often shift back and forth between the reactions rather than experience them in a linear way, and some people get stuck in some phases and skip over others. Kübler-Ross (1969) suggests that, on some level, hope of survival persists through all phases of dying.

Although these reactions may fit people in general, very late-life adults appear to experience far less denial about the reality of death than other age groups (McInnis-Dittrich, 2002). As they confront their limitations of physical health and become socialized to death with each passing friend and family member, most very late-life adults become less fearful of death. Unfortunately, professionals and family members are not

Exhibit 10.3
Stages of Accepting Impending Death

Denial: The person denies that death will occur: "This is not true. It can't be me." This denial is succeeded by temporary isolation from social interactions.
Anger: The individual asks, "Why me?" The person projects his or her resentment and envy onto others and often directs the anger toward a supreme being, medical caregivers, family members, and friends.
Bargaining: The individual starts bargaining in an attempt to postpone death, proposing a series of deals with God, self, or others: "Yes, me, but I will do . . . in exchange for a few more months."
Depression: A sense of loss follows. Individuals grieve about their own end of life and about the ones that will be left behind. A frequent reaction is withdrawal from close and loved persons: "I just want to be left alone."
Acceptance: The person accepts that the end is near and the struggle is over: "It's okay. My life has been . . ."

Source: Based on Kübler-Ross, 1969.

usually as comfortable talking about their feelings related to death and dying, leaving the elder feeling more isolated.

In addition to the need to talk about death, most very late-life adults have other needs related to dying. A fear of prolonged physical pain or discomfort, as well as fear of losing a sense of control and mastery trouble very late-life adults most. Some have suggested that older adults who are dying need a safe and accepting relationship in which to express the fear, sadness, anger, resentment, or other feelings related to the pending loss of life and opportunity, especially separation from loved ones (Bowlby, 1980).

Ira Byock (1997) suggested that dying persons with unfinished business might benefit from focusing on "five tasks of completion." Saying the following five phrases to family and loved ones, using these exact words or their own, has been found to help some patients greet their final days "with courage and determination" (p. 140): "I forgive you. Forgive me. Thank you. I love you. Goodbye." As with Kübler-Ross's stages, this technique may not work for everyone, but social workers may find it useful as a guide for working with individuals who are confronting death.

Advance Directives

How do advance directives promote a continued sense of human agency in making choices?

On a more concrete level, social workers can help patients and families discuss, prepare, and enact health care **advance directives**, or documents that give instructions about desired health care if, in the future, individuals cannot speak for themselves. Such discussions can provide an opportunity to clarify values and wishes regarding end-of-life treatment. Ideally, this conversation has started prior to very late adulthood (see Chapter 9 regarding a power of attorney and other health care decision-making processes). If not, helping people communicate their wishes regarding life-sustaining measures, who they want to act on their behalf when they are no longer competent to make these decisions, and other end-of-life concerns helps some people feel empowered.

Since the passage of the Patient Self-Determination Act in 1990, hospitals and other health care institutions receiving Medicare or Medical Assistance funds are required to inform patients that should their condition become life-threatening, they have a right to make decisions about what medical care they would wish to receive (McInnis-Dittrich, 2002). The two primary forms of advance directive are the living will and the durable power of attorney for health care.

A **living will** describes the medical procedures, drugs, and types of treatment that you would choose for yourself if you were able to do so in certain situations. It also describes the situations for which you would want treatment withheld. For example, you may instruct medical personnel not to use any artificial means or heroic measures to keep you alive if your condition is such that there is no hope for your recovery. Although a living will allows you to speak for yourself in advance, a durable power of attorney designates someone else to speak for you.

The promotion of patient rights as described above has helped many patients feel empowered and comforted some family members, but this topic is not without controversy. Because the laws vary from state to state, lay and professionals must inquire about the process if one relocates. Also, rather than feeling comforted by knowing a dying person's wishes, some family members experience the burden of difficult decision making that once was handled by the physician. Advance directives are not accepted or considered moral by some ethnic, racial, and religious groups. Because of historical distrust of the white medical establishment, some African American and Hispanic families have preferred life-sustaining treatment to the refusal of treatment inherent in advance directives. Among some religious groups, the personal control represented in advance directives is seen to interfere with a divine plan and is considered a form of passive suicide. As discussed below in Culture and Bereavement, do not assume you know the patient's and family's values and wishes.

Care of the Dying

Although some associate hospice and palliative care with "giving up" and there being "nothing left to do," in fact **palliative care** is active care of patients who have received a diagnosis of a serious, life-threatening illness. It is a form of care focusing on pain and symptom management as opposed to curing disease. Palliative care attends to the psychological, social and spiritual issues in addition to the physical needs. The goal

EXHIBIT 10.4
Key Ideas of Hospice Care

- The patient and the family (as defined by the patient) are the u.
- Care is provided by an interdisciplinary team composed of physician, ... nurse's aide, social worker, clergy, volunteer, and other support staff who attend to the spectrum of biopsychosocial and spiritual needs of the patient and family.
- The patient and family have chosen hospice services and are no longer pursuing aggressive, curative care, but selecting palliative care for symptom management.
- Bereavement follow-up is part of the continuum of care available to family members after the patient's death.

Source: Based on Lattanzi-Licht, Mahoney, & Miller, 1998; McInnis-Dittrich, 2002; Wilkinson & Lynn, 2001.

of palliative care is achievement of the best possible quality of life for patients and their families.

Hospice is one model of palliative care, borrowed from the British, that began to address the needs of dying persons and their loved ones in the United States in the mid-1970s. It is more a philosophy of care than a place, with the majority of persons receiving hospice services in their homes. It is typically available to persons who have received a prognosis of surviving 6 months or less and who are no longer receiving care directed toward a cure. As the hospital social worker, you may want to give Bina Patel and her daughter-in-law information about hospice care, as an additional support during her son's illness. Exhibit 10.4 summarizes the key ideas that distinguish hospice care from more traditional care of the dying.

The National Hospice and Palliative Care Organization (NHPCO) estimates that the United States has 3,100 operational hospice programs serving most communities: solely urban (13%), solely rural (49%), and both rural and urban areas (38%). In 2000, approximately one in four people who died in the United States received hospice services. Hospice continues to serve predominantly people with cancer (57%), but increasingly, noncancerous causes of death are included for conditions such as end-stage heart disease (10%), dementia (6%), lung disease (6%), end-stage kidney disease (3%), and end-stage liver disease (2%) (NHPCO, 2002).

Persons of color have been underserved by hospice, and NHPCO has a task force exploring minority access to hospice services. Recent initiatives through the Soros Foundation's Faculty Scholar program, as well as the Robert Wood Johnson Foundation's Promoting Excellence in End-of-Life Care, are focusing on program development specific to the needs of patients and families in African American, Hispanic, Native American, and other communities that have been underserved by more traditional hospice programs (Crawley et al., 2000).

Palliative care programs are emerging in hospital settings to address pain and symptom management in patients who might not fit the hospice criteria. Some hospitals have palliative care units specializing in management of short-term, acute symptoms; others have palliative care consultative services that bring their expertise to medical, oncology, pediatric, and other units throughout the hospital.

End-of-Life Signs and Symptoms

Family and others caring for a dying person often experience a great deal of anxiety when they do not have adequate information about the dying process. Most families appreciate knowing what to expect, and honest, factual information can help allay their fears of the unknown (Herbst, Lynn, Mermann, & Rhymes, 1995). Pete Mullin might benefit by knowing what to expect during his vigil with his sister. Many hospice services provide written information about symptoms of death for those families anticipating the death of a loved one at home. Exploring how much information people have and want is an important part of the social worker's assessment.

Obviously, each individual situation will differ, but the following general information about symptoms of impending death, summarized in Exhibit 10.5, helps people prepare (Bon Secours Hospice, 2002; Herbst et al., 1995; Kemp, 1999):

- *Temperature and circulation changes.* The patient's arms and legs may become cool to the touch, and the underside of the body may darken in color as peripheral circulation slows down. Warm blankets will help prevent the patient from becoming too cold.

- *Sleeping.* The dying patient will gradually spend more time sleeping and at times may be difficult to arouse as metabolism decreases. The patient will gradually retreat from the surroundings. It is best to spend more time with the patient during the most alert times.

- *Vision and hearing.* Clarity of vision and hearing may decrease. Patient may want the lights on as vision decreases. Hearing is the last of the five senses to be lost, so do not assume than an unresponsive patient cannot hear. Speak softly and clearly, but not louder than necessary. Many patients talk until minutes before death and are reassured by the exchange of words between loved ones.

- *Secretions in the mouth and congestion.* Oral secretions may become more profuse and collect in the back of the throat. Most people are familiar with the term *death rattle*, a result of a decrease in the body's intake of fluids and inability to cough up normal saliva. Tilting the head to the side and elevating the head of the bed will ease breathing. Swabbing the mouth and lips also provides comfort.

EXHIBIT 10.5
Signs and Symptoms of Impending Death

- Lowered temperature and slowed circulation
- Deeper and longer periods of sleep
- Decreased acuity of vision and hearing
- Increased secretions in the mouth and congestion
- Incontinence
- Restlessness and confusion
- Reduced need for eating and drinking and difficulty swallowing
- Irregular and interrupted breathing
- Increased signs of pain

Source: Bon Secours Hospice, 2002; Herbst et al., 1995; Kemp, 1999.

- *Incontinence.* Loss of bowel and bladder function may occur around the time of death or as death is imminent, as the muscles begin to relax. The urine will become very dark in color. If needed, pads should be used to keep skin clean and dry.
- *Restlessness and confusion.* The patient may become restless or have visions of people or things that do not exist. These symptoms may be a result of a decrease in the oxygen circulation to the brain and a change in the body's metabolism. Stay with the patient; reassure the person in a calm voice; tell the person it is okay to let go; use oxygen as instructed by the nurse. Soft music, back rubs, and gentle touch may help soothe the patient. Do not interfere with or try to restrain the patient, yet prevent falling.
- *Eating, drinking, and swallowing.* Patients will have decreased need for food and drink. It may be helpful to explain that feeding will not improve the condition, and in fact may exacerbate symptoms. Slight dehydration may be beneficial in reducing pulmonary secretions and easing breathing. Dehydration also generally results in mild renal insufficiency that is mildly sedating. To withhold food and water feels counterintuitive, however, because food and water are usually equated with comfort and sustaining life. Ice chips, small sips of water, and small amounts of food that have meaning to the patient and family are more helpful than forcing food or liquids.
- *Breathing changes.* Breathing may become irregular, with periods of 10 to 30 seconds of no breathing. This symptom is very common and indicates a decrease in circulation and buildup of body waste products. Elevating the head of the bed and turning the patient on his or her side often helps relieve irregular breathing patterns. Use oxygen as instructed.

- *Pain.* Frequent observation will help you determine if the patient is experiencing pain. Signs of discomfort include moaning, restlessness, and a furrowed brow. Give medication as instructed or contact the nurse or physician if pain persists.

Dying may take hours or days; no one can predict the time of death even when the person is exhibiting signs and symptoms of dying. The following are signs that death has occurred:

- Breathing stops.
- The heart stops beating.
- Bowel or bladder control is lost.
- There is no response to verbal commands or shaking.
- Eyelids may be slightly open with eyes fixed on a certain spot.
- Mouth may fall open slightly as the jaw relaxes.

Such explicit discussion of death with those attending a dying family member or close friend may seem upsetting, but this knowledge is also comforting and can help ease the anxiety related to the fear of the unknown. Dying persons are also comforted knowing that their family members have the informational, medical, and social support they need to help them in their caregiving role. It is also helpful to have funeral plans in place so that at the time of death one phone call to the mortuary facilitates the process.

Loss, Grief, and Bereavement

Loss is a common human experience. There is strong ethnographic evidence that people of all cultures have strong, painful reactions to the death of the people to whom they are emotionally attached (Counts & Counts, 1991). Sadness, loneliness, disbelief, and anxiety are only a few of the feelings a person may experience in times of bereavement.

The following terms are likely to be used in dealing with individuals who have suffered a loss (Stroebe, Stroebe, & Hansson, 1993):

- **Loss**. The severing of an attachment an individual has with a loved one, a loved object (such as a pet, home, or country), or an aspect of one's self or identity (such as a body part or function, physical or mental capacity, or role or position in family, society, or other context)
- **Bereavement**. The state of having suffered a loss

- **Grief**. The normal internal reaction of an individual experiencing a loss. Grief is a complex coping process and is highly individualized
- **Mourning**. The external expression of grief, also a process, influenced by the customs of one's culture

The rituals associated with death vary in historical and cross-cultural context (Counts & Counts, 1991). In some cultures, the dead are buried; in other cultures, the dead are burned and the ashes are spread. In some places and times, a surviving wife might have been burned together with her husband. In the United States, death rituals can be as different as a traditional New Orleans funeral, with street music and mourners dressed in white or a somber and serene funeral with hushed mourners dressed in black. Some cultures prescribe more emotional expression than others. Some cultures build ritual for expression of anger, and some do not. However, the death rituals in most cultures include the following (Counts & Counts, 1991):

- Social support provided to grievers
- Ritual and ceremony used to give meaning to death
- Visual confrontation of the dead body
- A procession

Did these earlier experiences with loss serve as either risk factors or protective factors for coping with current losses?

Throughout life, we are faced with many losses, some that occur by death but many that occur in other ways as well. For example, Bina Patel lost a homeland when she immigrated to be near her children, and she lost some physical functioning after her stroke. Carmen Ruiz lost her home, her privacy, and her routines when she moved into the nursing home. Pete Mullin lived through the losses related to divorce and retirement. Recently, the burgeoning literature on loss, grief, and bereavement has recognized that there may be similar processes for grieving all losses, including those that occur for reasons other than death. Loss is one of the most important themes in the work that social workers do. For example, we encounter loss due to foster care placement, divorce, disease and disability, migration and immigration, forced retirement, and so on.

Theories and Models of Loss

A variety of theorists have sought to make sense of the complex experience of loss. Much of the literature on grief and bereavement for the past century has been influenced by Sigmund Freud's (1917/1957) classic article "Mourning and Melancholia." Freud described the "work of mourning" as a process of severing a relationship with a lost person, object, or ideal. He suggested that this happens over time as the bereaved person is repeatedly faced with situations that remind him or her that the loved person (object or ideal) has, indeed, been lost. From this classic work came the idea of a necessary period of **grief work** to sever the attachment bond, an idea that has been the cornerstone of a number of stage models of the grief process.

In the United States, Erich Lindemann (1944) was a pioneer in grief research. Through his classic study of survivors of a fire at the Cocoanut Grove Lounge in Boston, he conceptualized grief work as both a biological and psychological necessity. The common reactions to loss that he identified included the following:

- *Somatic distress*, occurring in waves lasting from 20 minutes to an hour, including tightness in throat, choking and shortness of breath, need for sighing, empty feeling in abdomen, lack of muscular power, and intense subjective distress
- *Preoccupation with image of deceased*, yearning for the lost one to return, wanting to see pictures of the deceased or touch items that are associated with the deceased
- *Guilt*
- *Hostile reactions*, toward the deceased as well as toward others
- *Loss of patterns of conduct*, where the ability to carry out routine behaviors is lost

Lindemann proposed that grief work occurs in stages, an idea that has been popular with other theorists and researchers since the 1960s. A number of stage models of grief have been proposed, and four are presented in Exhibit 10.6. As you can see, although the number and names of stages vary somewhat among theorists and researchers, in general the stage models all agree that grief work progresses from disbelief and feelings of unreality, to painful and disorganizing reactions, to a kind of "getting over" the loss.

J. William Worden (1991) took a somewhat different approach, writing about the "tasks of mourning" rather than stages of mourning. Worden was interested in helping clinicians working with persons in the mourning process. He considered *task* to be "more consonant with Freud's concept of grief work and imply that the mourner needs to take action and can do something," whereas "phases imply a certain passivity, something that the mourner must pass through" (p. 35). Worden suggests that the following four tasks of mourning are important when a person is adapting to a loss:

> *Task I: To accept the reality of the loss.* Working through denial takes time, because this involves an intellectual and an emotional acceptance. Some people have traditional rituals that help with this process.

EXHIBIT 10.6
Four Stage Models of Grief

Typical Stages of Stage Models of Grief	Erich Lindemann (1944)	Elizabeth Kübler-Ross (1969)	John Bowlby (1980)	Therese Rando (1993)
Disbelief and feelings of unreality	Shock and disbelief	Denial and isolation	Numbness	Avoidance
Painful and disorganizing reactions	Acute mourning	Anger Bargaining Depression	Yearning Disorganization Despair	Confrontation
A kind of "getting over" the loss	Resolution	Acceptance	Reorganization	Accommodation

Task II: To work through to the pain of grief. Because people are often uncomfortable with the outward displays of grief, our society often interferes with this task. People often seek a geographic cure or quickly replace the lost person in a new relationship but often still have this task to complete.

Task III: To adjust to an environment in which the deceased is missing.

Task IV: To emotionally relocate the deceased and move on with life.

In the past decade or so, there has been a critique of the idea of grief work. A highly influential article, "The Myths of Coping With Loss" (Wortman & Silver, 1989), disputed two major themes of the traditional view of grief work: distress is an inevitable response to loss, and the failure to experience distress is a sign of improper grieving. In fact, a number of researchers have found that those who show the highest levels of distress immediately following a loss are more likely than those who show little distress to be depressed several years later.

Camille Wortman and Roxanne Silver (1990) proposed that at least four different patterns of grieving are possible:

1. *Normal grief.* Relatively high level of distress soon after the loss, followed by a relatively rapid recovery.

2. *Chronic grief.* High level of distress continues over a number of years.

3. *Delayed grief.* Little distress in the first few months after the loss, but high levels of distress at some later point.

4. *Absent grief.* No notable level of distress either soon after the loss or at some later time.

In their own research, Wortman and Silver (1990) found absent grief in 26% of their bereaved participants, and other researchers have had similar findings (Levy, Martinkowski, & Derby, 1994). These same researchers have found a high rate (over 30%) of chronic grief.

Given these critiques of the traditional model of grief, theorists and researchers have looked for other ways to understand the complex reactions to loss. Recently, the study of bereavement has been influenced by developments in the study of stress and trauma reactions. Research on loss and grief has produced the following findings (Bonanno & Kaltman, 1999):

- It is the evaluation of the nature of the loss by the bereaved survivor that determines how stressful the loss is.
- How well a coping strategy works for dealing with loss depends on the context, the nature of the person-environment encounter.
- Maintaining some type of continued bond with the deceased, a strong sense of the continued presence of the deceased, may be adaptive.
- The capacity to minimize negative emotions after a loss allows the bereaved to continue to function in areas of personal importance.
- Humor can aid in the grief process by allowing the bereaved to approach the enormity of the loss without maximizing psychic pain or alienating social support.
- In situations of traumatic loss, there is a need to talk about the loss, but not all interpersonal relationships can tolerate such talk.

In summary, grief is a multidimensional process that theorists and practitioners continue to try to understand. There seems to be general agreement that culture, past experience, gender, age, and other personal characteristics shape how one copes with loss.

Culture and Bereavement

It is important to be informed about the impact of each individual's culture and religious and spiritual practices on the bereavement process. Historically, because of sensitivity about racial issues, there has been some hesitancy to address issues of race and ethnicity in the health care arena. Unfortunately, when ethnic differences are not taken into consideration, too often it is assumed that the norm is white and middle class. But the United States is becoming increasingly multiethnic (Irish, Lundquist, & Nelsen, 1993, p. 2). You will need to continually inform yourself about cultural, ethnic, and religious traditions of individuals and families with whom you work so as not to become unintentionally ethnocentric. Remember, however, that given the tremendous diversity within groups as well as among them, the individual and the family are your best teachers. Ask them, "What do I need to know about you (your family, cultural, or religious and spiritual traditions) so that I can be of help to you?"

Why is it important for social workers to learn about cultural variations in grief and bereavement?

Grief is expressed differently across cultures. In the United States, we tend to psychologize grief, understanding it in terms of sadness, depression, anger, and other emotions. There may be a cohort divide in the United States on this issue, however, and the current generation of very late-life adults are often much more matter-of-fact about death than younger adults are (Pipher, 1999). In China and other Eastern societies, grief is somatized, or expressed in terms of physical pain, weakness, and other physical discomfort. We need to be aware of the possibility of somatization when working with many clients from different cultures, as well as with some older adults of Anglo heritage.

Cultural variation also exists regarding the acceptable degree of emotional expression of grief, from "muted" to "excessive" grief, with many variations between these two ends of the continuum. Gender differences exist in many cultures, including the dominant U.S. culture, where men have learned to be less demonstrative with emotions of grief and sadness than women are.

Mourning and funeral customs also differ a great deal. For example, among African Americans, customs vary depending on whether the family is Southern Baptist, black Catholic, northern Unitarian, Black Muslim, or Pentecostal. Yet, "in general one thinks of funerals in the white culture as more formal and less emotional than within black death rituals" (Perry, 1993, p. 33). Perhaps because of some vestiges of traditional African culture and slavery, and a strong desire to celebrate the person's life and build up a sense of community, funerals are important external expressions of mourning in many black communities.

The complex, and at times, impersonal health care system in the United States often is insensitive to cultural traditions. In some cultures, proper handling of the body, time to sit with the deceased, and other traditions are important. For example, the Hmong believe that proper burial and worship of ancestors directly influence the safety and health of the surviving family members. They believe that the spiritual world coexists with the physical world. Because they believe that each person has several souls, it is important that the souls be "sent back appropriately" (Bliatout, 1993, p. 83).

Tremendous diversity exists within the Hispanic cultures in the United States, depending upon country of origin, degree of acculturation, and religious background.

Historically, conquest and death have been an important part of the history of Mexican, Cuban, Guatemalan, and other cultures (Younoszai, 1993). Mexican culture, for example, celebrates the Day of the Dead with colorful traditions honoring those who have died. Additional saints' days provide ongoing bereavement opportunities.

Given approximately 350 distinct Native American tribes in the United States and more than 596 different bands among the First Nations in Canada, and because of the differing degrees of acculturation and religious practices from one group to another, it is difficult to provide useful generalizations about this cultural group (Brokenleg & Middleton, 1993). Although most Native Americans believe in an afterlife, the Navajo do not. Some tribes believe that talking directly about death helps the death occur. This belief makes discussing hospice and end-of-life plans challenging. Among the Zuni, it is important to address the eldest son, not the other parent, when a parent is ill.

These are only a few examples of the rich diversity among some of the peoples in our increasingly multiethnic society. You cannot possibly know all the specific traditions, but it is important to assume that you do not know, and therefore to inquire of the family how you can assist them.

The Life Course Completed

In this book, we have explored the seasons of the life course. These seasons have been and will be altered by changing demographics. Current demographic trends have led to the following predictions about the future of the life course (Hogstel, 2001):

- The size and inevitable aging of the baby boom generation will continue to drive public policy debate and improve services for very late-life adults.
- Women will continue to live longer than men.
- Educational attainment levels of the very late-life adult will increase, with more women having been in the labor force long enough to have their own retirement income.
- Six-generation families will be common, although the generations will live in geographically dispersed settings, making care of very late-life adults difficult.
- Fewer family caregivers will be available for very late-life adults because the baby boomers and their children tended to marry later and have fewer children. At the same time, the need for informal or family caregiving to supplement formal care will be increasing.

- Assessment and management of health care, as well as health care education, will increasingly be available via telephone, computer/Internet, and television, providing greater access in remote areas but running the risk of rendering the service more impersonal.

As a society, we have a challenge ahead of us, to see that newborns begin the life course on a positive foot and that everyone reaches the end of life with the opportunity to see his or her life course as a meaningful whole. As social workers, we have a responsibility to take a look at our social institutions and evaluate how well they guarantee the opportunity for each individual to meet basic needs during each season of life, as well as whether they guarantee the opportunity for interdependence and connectedness appropriate to the season of life.

IMPLICATIONS FOR SOCIAL WORK PRACTICE

All the implications for practice listed in chapter 9 on late adulthood apply in very late adulthood as well. In addition, the following practice principles focus on the topics of spirituality, relationships, the dying process, and loss, grief, and bereavement:

- Given the link between aging, disability, loss, and spirituality, consider doing a spiritual assessment to find ways to help very late-life adults address increasing spiritual concerns.
- Assess the impact of loss in the lives of your very late-life clients—loss of partners, friends, children, and other relationships, but also loss of roles and statuses, physical and mental capacities.
- Recognize and be delighted when very late-life adults are grateful for their "extra time."
- Assess the loneliness and isolation that may result from cumulative loss.
- Know available formal and informal resources to help minimize isolation.
- Be aware of your own feelings about death and dying so that you may become more comfortable being physically and emotionally present with clients and their loved ones.
- Identify literature, cultural experiences, key informants, and other vehicles for ongoing education about your clients' cultural, ethnic, and

religious practices that are different from your own. Remember, the client may be your best teacher.

- Assume that the very late-life adult continues to have needs for intimacy. Stretch your conceptualization of intimacy to include any relationship the person might have, wish for, or grieve, including spouse/partner, friends, children, self, and community.

KEY TERMS

activities of daily living (ADL)
advance directive
bereavement
grief
grief work
hospice
instrumental activities of daily living (IADL)
living will
loss
mourning
palliative care
primary aging
secondary aging

ACTIVE LEARNING

1. Take an inventory of your assumptions about what it is like to be 85 and older. What are your biggest fears? What do you think would be the best part of reaching that age? Think about how these assumptions might influence your feelings about working with clients in very late adulthood.

2. You have recently been hired as the activities director and social worker at an assisted living facility, and Carmen Ruiz, Bina Patel, and Pete Mullin have all recently moved in. All three are unhappy to be there, preferring their prior living arrangements. Bina's son and Pete's sister recently died. You want to help them share some of their recent experiences related to loss but want to be sensitive to the diversity in life experience that they bring with them. What barriers might you face in accomplishing your goal? What are some ways that you might begin to help them?

3. Think about the relationships between poverty, gender, and race as one ages in the United States today. Identify ways that social workers can influence policies that affect housing, health care, and other essential services directly related to quality of life in very late-life adulthood.

Web Resources

AARP

www.aarp.org

Site maintained by American Association of Retired Persons contains health and wellness information, information on legislative issues, and links to online resources regarding aging.

APA ONLINE Aging Issues Office

www.apa.org/pi/aging

Site presented by the Office of Aging of the American Psychological Association contains news briefs, publications, and links to aging organizations.

APA ONLINE Public Topics

www.apa.org/psychnet/aging.html

Site presented by the American Psychological Association contains news briefs, APA publications, and links to a number of aging organizations.

Hospice Foundation of America

www.hospicefoundation.org

Site maintained by the Hospice Foundation of America contains information on locating hospice programs, a newsletter, and links to a variety of hospice-related resources.

The National Hospice and Palliative Care Organization

www.nhpco.org/body.cfm

Site maintained by the National Hospice and Palliative Care Organization contains information on the history and current development of hospice and palliative care programs and four downloadable grief and bereavement guides.

Project on Death in America

www.Capcmsssm.org/content/1/topic=14

Site presented by the Center to Advance Palliative Care contains information on the Project on Death in America, as well as descriptions of physician, nursing, social work, and pastoral care roles on interdisciplinary teams.

Partnership for Caring

www.partnershipforcaring.org

Site presented by Partnership for Caring, an organization devoted to public education about the use of living wills and durable powers of attorney for health care, provides links to other legal and social organizations promoting responsible use of advance directives as well as the capacity to download appropriate forms from each of the 50 states.

Solutions for Better Aging

www.caregivers.com

Site maintained by AgeNet Inc., a good place for both family and professional caregivers to start when seeking information about financing caregiving services, purchasing products helpful in providing care, contains linkage to online caregiver support groups and other topics.

Hospice Net

hospicenet.org

Site maintained by Hospice Net provides information for dying persons, their families, and professionals about the hospice movement, advance directives, pain and symptom management, and the grieving process.

Hacer es Poder

A Community Prevention Project With a Life Course Framework

Elizabeth D. Hutchison
Virginia Commonwealth University

Marian A. Aguilar
Texas A & M International University

Ernesto Arce is a prevention specialist for the state department of mental health. For the past 2 years, he has directed Hacer es Poder (Action Is Power), a prevention project in a community where he lived as a child—a community that is predominantly Mexican American but has a growing population of other Latino groups. Located in the central city of a major urban center in the Southwest, this community has been identified as an area of concentrated poverty. The housing stock is deteriorating, and rates of unemployment and early school leaving are high. Some residents are new immigrants, some are the children of immigrants, some have ancestors whose presence in the region predated the Anglo American settlers, and some have moved back and forth across the border with changing labor conditions in both the United States and Mexico. Some are U.S. citizens, and some are undocumented. Some speak English, some speak Spanish, and many are bilingual. Most are Catholic, but some are Protestant; some weave Christian beliefs with healing rituals.

Having grown up in the community, Ernesto is well aware of its problems. Since he was a child, he has heard a lot about problems in the community. In his work at the state department of mental health, he is familiar with data that indicate a variety of community troubles: high rates of unemployment, teen pregnancy, early school leaving, substance abuse, depression and anxiety, serious health problems, and family and community violence. Ernesto is also familiar with many strengths in the community: the natural support systems made up of extended family, *compradzo* (church sponsors or godparents), and the barrios (tightly knit neighborhoods); the religious institutions; the merchants who run the cultural *hierberia* shops (that sell herbs) and grocery shops; and the social and recreational clubs. He knows that the community has been able to absorb and support new immigrants and to survive prejudice and discrimination from the outside world.

In the early days of Hacer es Poder, Ernesto and project staff wanted to identify community assets and community problems—from the perspective of community members. They talked to a lot of community people, including community leaders (from teens to older adults), religious leaders, traditional healers, merchants, members of the social and recreational clubs, self-help groups, advocacy groups, parent groups in the schools, youth groups, and so on. They also talked to staff in the schools, social service agencies, the medical clinic, the legal clinic, and to leaders in civic organizations that have provided resources to the community.

These conversations identified an assortment of community assets—many of them already familiar to Ernesto, but some new ones as well—including

- Strong family and neighborhood support systems, including mutual support between older adults and grandchildren
- Deep religious faith of many community members and their involvement in church activities, such as religious education, fund-raisers, social activities, and social services
- Committed merchants who provide many kinds of aid to community members
- An active Catholic Services agency, St. Vincent de Paul, that provides a soup kitchen, a clothing closet, a legal clinic, and adult education programs
- Interested and committed organizations from outside the community, such as the Junior League, a suburban church, and the university medical school
- Community festivals that help to develop cultural pride
- Community activists who have formed safety patrol groups

The conversations also identified the community problems most troublesome to community members:

- Financial hardship
- Child and maternal health problems

- Parenting difficulties
- Early school leaving
- Family conflict about acculturation issues
- Caregiver burden
- Substance abuse
- Youth gangs creating unsafe schools, playgrounds, and neighborhoods
- Physical and mental health problems among community elders

An advisory council was formed to help the Hacer es Poder staff develop programs that use community assets to address community problems. The council is made up of people who represent the community, rather than those who come from the outside to offer services—community leaders from teens to older adults. They recommended a life course perspective as the best framework for improving community life and strengthening families (see Mrazek & Haggerty, 1994). This framework was used to analyze the risk factors and protective factors for each age group in the community, and the following targets were identified for intervention specific to each age-graded period:

- *Conception, pregnancy, and birth.* Provide better information for community women of childbearing age about the hazards of tobacco, alcohol, and other drugs, diabetes, and HIV during pregnancy. Secure early, regular, and comprehensive prenatal care for pregnant women.
- *Infancy and early childhood.* Provide more widespread immunization. Strengthen parenting skills. Develop more child care options. Develop programs to improve nutrition.
- *Middle childhood.* Strengthen relationships between home and school. Provide earlier intervention for children with behavioral problems or at risk for school failure. Prevent the use of alcohol and other drugs.
- *Adolescence.* Improve school retention rates. Reduce the use of alcohol and other drugs. Prevent HIV, teen pregnancy, and gang involvement. Strengthen cultural pride.

- *Adulthood.* Reduce stress related to unemployment, work conditions, immigrant status, caregiver burden, and chronic illness.
- *Late adulthood.* Reduce depressive symptoms and social isolation among elder widows. Enhance mutual aid with younger generations.

Still in an early stage, Hacer es Poder counts the following activities among its accomplishments:

1. The department of mental health and the public health department have provided brochures—written in both Spanish and English—on the hazards of tobacco, alcohol, and other drugs, diabetes, and HIV during pregnancy. These brochures are now prominently displayed in the *hierberia* shops, grocery shops, music stores, and beauty shops. Local merchants—who received some training about these hazards—often engage customers in conversations about the content of the brochures.
2. Catholic Services is collaborating with the public health department and the medical school to ensure that more pregnant women in the community—regardless of citizenship status—receive prenatal care. They are working to ensure that language interpretation will be available when needed. In addition, the public health department has provided brochures on physiological and emotional changes during pregnancy and on fetal development—in both Spanish and English—to community merchants. These brochures are prominently displayed, and merchants draw them to the attention of pregnant customers, asking if they have received prenatal care.
3. The medical clinic—located in the community and run by the medical school—has stepped up its efforts to vaccinate infants and young children. They are collaborating with community merchants, religious leaders, and social clubs to get the word out about the immunization program.
4. Catholic Services, Head Start, and the Junior League are working together to seek funding to expand parent education in the community. They hope to provide weekend workshops for mothers and fathers. They also hope to begin a mother-to-mother program that pairs experienced mothers (trained in parenting skills) with new mothers and provides home visitation and telephone reassurance.
5. A subcommittee of the Hacer es Poder Advisory Council is exploring several options for addressing the shortage of child care providers in the community.

With project staff, they are investigating funding possibilities for a child development center.

6. The advisory council has worked with primary and secondary schools in the community—public and private—to develop collaborative teams of administrators, teachers, other school personnel, parents, and students to resolve school problems and to promote academic success. This process has not always been smooth, but there have been important breakthroughs in relationships between parents and school personnel, particularly with regard to the hot topic of honoring the bicultural and bilingual nature of the students' lives. Parents have begun to feel a greater sense of ownership of the schools. Teachers have learned how much the parents value education. An elementary school collaborative team has sought help from the department of mental health to develop special programs for aggressive and peer-rejected children and children at risk of school failure. The collaborative team at the high school has focused on the inability of many parents to help their children with schoolwork. They have begun to think about ways to support parents in their efforts to support their children's educational achievement. They have also used community heroes as role models of school achievement.

7. With consultation from the department of mental health and the advisory council, school social workers and the Girls and Boys Clubs are developing a peer education program to prevent substance abuse. They are also exploring alternatives for jobs for adolescents, neighborhood safety, and recreation sites.

8. The Hacer es Poder Advisory Council has worked with the legal clinic, churches, and merchants to publicize materials developed by national immigrants' rights groups and to assist in legalizing status whenever possible. Hacer es Poder staff have made efforts to educate teachers, social workers, and medical providers about the special stresses of undocumented immigrants—to help them understand the fear behind the evasive and resistant behaviors they sometimes encounter.

9. Catholic Services and Hacer es Poder staff, with consultation from the advisory council, have developed separate curricula for teens and for parents to help them understand the family conflict and emotional problems that develop when teens and parents have different approaches to handling their bicultural existence. Cultural pride is emphasized in the teen curriculum.

These curricula are being used by school social workers, the Girls and Boys Clubs, and the churches.

10. The medical clinic is developing a support group for family caregivers of chronically ill and disabled community members and another support group for community members with disabilities. They are seeking funds for assistive technology for community members with disabilities.

11. Catholic Services has developed two widow support groups in the community. One of these groups has begun to plan a program to pair older adults and youth for mentoring and mutual aid. They are also providing Meals on Wheels and transportation to health facilities.

Something to Think About

Ernesto Arce knew that this community had many troubles. His social work education has helped him to think about the relationships between these troubles. Ernesto also knew that this community had many assets. His social work education has taught him how to assess and enhance those assets. The following questions will help you think about how you might use what you have been learning to minimize risks and strengthen protective factors for people of every age:

- How did Ernesto and his staff go about assessing the assets and problems of this community? What information did they use? Whom did they involve in the assessment process? How did they make sure their assessment was grounded in the culture and tradition of the community?

- Hacer es Poder is targeting interventions at all age periods of the life course. Why do you think this approach is important to them? If prevention is their goal, why not confine the focus to prenatal and early childhood issues? How important do you think it is for the advisory council to include people of different ages?

- The assessment indicated that financial hardship is a major community problem. Given the pervasive risks of poverty for all age groups, how does action bring power to this community? Do you see any risk factors being reduced? Protective factors strengthened?

- What have you learned about the life course that could help you be a competent member of the Hacer es Poder staff? How might you use what you have learned about conception, pregnancy, and childbirth? What you have learned about early childhood? Middle childhood? Adolescence? Adulthood? Late adulthood?

- In what ways does this project build on family and neighborhood support systems? What other ways could it use?

Works Cited

Abel, E. L., & Sokol, R. J. (1987). Incidence of fetal alcohol syndrome and economic impact of FAS-related anomalies. *Drug and Alcohol Dependence, 19,* 51-70.

Aberman, S., & Kirchoff, K. T. (1985). Infant-feeding practices: Mother's decision-making. *Journal of Obstetric, Gynecologic, and Neonatal Nursing, 14,* 394-398.

Abraham, K. (1986). Ego differences among Anglo-American and Mexican-American adolescents. *Journal of Adolescence, 9*(2), 151-166.

Achata, C. (1993). Immunization of Mexican migrant farm workers' children, on site at a day care center in a rural Tennessee County: Three successful summers. *Journal of Health and Social Policy, 4*(4), 89-101.

Achievements in Public Health: 1900-1999. (1999). Healthier mothers and babies. *Morbidity and Mortality Weekly, 49*(38), 849-858.

Adams, G. R., & Crane, P. (1980). An assessment of parents' and teachers' expectations of preschool children's social preference for attractive or unattractive children and adults. *Child Development, 51,* 224-231.

Adams, G. R., & Marshall, S. K. (1996). A developmental social psychology of identity: Understanding the person-in-context. *Journal of Adolescence, 19,* 429-442.

Adams, P., & Marano, M. (1995). Current estimates from the National Health Interview Survey, 1994. *Vital Health Statistics, 10*(193), 83-84. Hyattsville, MD: National Center for Health Statistics.

Adams, R., & Allan, G. (1998). *Placing friendship in context.* New York: Cambridge University Press.

Adler, L. (1993). Introduction and overview. *Journal of Education Policy, 8*(5-6), 1-16.

Adlercreutz, H., Hamalaiven, O., Gorback, S., & Grodin, B. (1992). Dietary phytoestrogens and the menopause in Japan. *Lancet, 339,* 12333.

Administration on Aging. (2002a). *Facts and figures: Statistics on minority aging in the U.S. (Population and projected population by race and Hispanic origin).* Retrieved September 3, 2002, from www.aoa.dhhs.gov/minorityaccess/stats.html.

Administration on Aging. (2002b). *The many faces of aging: Resources to effectively serve minority older persons.* Retrieved June 10, 2002, from www.aoa.gov.

Advocates for Youth (2002a). *Adolescent sexual health in Europe and the U.S.: Why the difference?* Retrieved June 6, 2002, from www.advocatesforyouth.org.

Advocates for Youth (2002b). *Adolescent contraceptive use.* Retrieved June 6, 2002, from www.advocatesforyouth.org.

Africa News Services (2001, May 26). *Breastfeeding ups death risk in HIV mothers: New study.* Electronic Collection A75056717.

Aging—Living to 100: What's the secret? (2002). *Harvard Health Letter, 27*(3). Cambridge, MA: President and Fellows of Harvard.

Ahrons, C. (1999). Divorce: An unscheduled family transition. In B. Carter & M. McGoldrick (Eds.), *The expanded life cycle: Individual, family, and social perspectives* (3rd ed., pp. 381-398). Boston: Allyn & Bacon.

Ai, A. L. (2000). Spiritual well-being, spiritual growth, and spiritual care for the aged: A cross-faith and interdisciplinary effort. *Journal of Religious Gerontology, 11*(2), 3-28.

Ainsworth, M., Blehar, M., Waters, E., & Wall, S. (1978). *Patterns of attachment: A psychological study of the strange situation.* Hillsdale, NJ: Lawrence Erlbaum.

Akiyama, H., Antonucci, T., & Campbell, R. (1990). Exchange and reciprocity among two generations of Japanese and American women. In J. Sokolovski (Ed.), *Cultural context of aging: Worldwide perspectives* (pp. 127-138). Westport, CT: Greenwood Press.

Alan Guttmacher Institute. (1999). *Teen sex and pregnancy.* Retrieved June 6, 2002, from www.agi-usa.org/pubs/fb_teen_ sex.html.

Allen, K. (1989). *Single women; family* ties. Newbury Park, CA: Sage.

Allen-Meares, P. (1995). School failure and special populations. In P. Allen-Meares (Ed.), *Social work with children and adolescents* (pp. 143-164). White Plains, NY: Longman.

Allen-Meares, P., Washington, R. O., & Walsh, B. (1996). *Social work services in schools* (2nd ed.). Englewood Cliffs, NJ: Prentice Hall.

Alsaker, F. D. (1992). Pubertal timing, overweight, and psychological adjustment. *Journal of Early Adolescence, 12*, 396-419.

American Academy of Child & Adolescent Psychiatry. (1995). *Facts for families: Fact no. 10. Teen suicide.* Author.

American Academy of Pediatrics (2001a). Condom use by adolescents. *Pediatrics, 107*(6), 1463.

American Academy of Pediatrics. (2001b). WIC Program. *Pediatrics, 108*(5), 1216-1218.

American Association of University Women (1995). *How schools shortchange girls*. New York: Marlowe.

American Dietetic Association (2001). Position of the Journal of the American Dietetic Association: Breaking the barriers to breastfeeding. *Journal of the American Dietetic Association, 101*(11), 1213.

American Medical Association. (2002). *Emergency contraception*. Retrieved September 9, 2002, from www.ama-assn.org/special/contrmergenca/support/ppfa/emergenc.htm.

American Psychiatric Association. (1994). *Diagnostic and statistical manual of mental disorders (DSM-IV)* (4th ed.). Washington, DC: Author.

American Social Health Association. (1995). *STD fact sheet.* Research Triangle Park, NC: Author.

American Society for Reproductive Medicine. (2002, October 12-17). *Highlights from the ASRM 58th Annual Meeting,* Seattle, Washington. Retrieved November 6, 2002, from www.asrm.org/Media?Press/1700000babies.html.

Ameta, E. S., & Sherrard, P. A. (1995). Inquiring into children's social worlds: A choice of lenses. In B. A. Ryan, G. R. Adams, T. P. Gullotta, R. P. Weissberg, & R. L. Hampton (Eds.), *The family-school connection: Theory, research, and practice* (pp. 29-74). Thousand Oaks, CA: Sage.

Anastopoulos, A. D., & Shelton, T. L. (2001). *Assessing attention deficit/hyperactivity disorder*. New York: Kluwer Academic/Plenum.

Anderson, C. (1999). Single-parent families: Strengths, vulnerabilities, and interventions. In B. Carter & M. McGoldrick, *The expanded family life cycle: Individual, family, and social perspectives* (3rd ed., pp. 399-416). Boston: Allyn & Bacon.

Anderson, D. A. (1994). Lesbian and gay adolescents: Social and developmental considerations. *High School Journal, 77*(1-2), 13-19.

Anderson, R. (2001, October 12). Deaths: Leading causes for 1999. *National Vital Statistics Report, 49*(11). Hyattsville, MD: National Center for Disease Control.

Anderson, R. E., & Anderson, D. A. (1999). The cost-effectiveness of home birth. *Journal of Nurse Midwifery, 44*(1), 30-35.

Andrews, L. B. (1994). *Assessing genetic risks: Implications for health and social policy.* Washington, DC: National Academy Press.

Ankum, W. M. (2000). Diagnosing suspected ectopic pregnancy. *British Medical Journal, 321*(7271), 1235-1237.

Antonucci, T., & Akiyama, H. (1987). Social networks in adult life and a preliminary examination of the convoy model. *Journal of Gerontology: Social Sciences, 42*, S519-S527.

Antonucci, T., & Akiyama, H. (1994). *Social relations and mental health over the life course.* Final report to the National Institute of Mental Health.

Antonucci, T., & Akiyama, H. (1997). Concern with others at midlife: Care, comfort, or compromise? In M. Lachman & J. James (Eds.), *Multiple paths of midlife development* (pp. 145-169). Chicago: University of Chicago Press.

Antonucci, T., Akiyama, H., & Merline, A. (2001). Dynamics of social relationships in midlife. In M. Lachman (Ed.), *Handbook of midlife development* (pp. 571-598). New York: Wiley.

Aquilino, W. (1990). The likelihood of parent-adult child coresidence: Effects of family structure and parental characteristics. *Journal of Marriage and the Family, 52*, 405-419.

Arber, S., & Ginn, J. (1995). *Connecting gender and aging: A sociological approach.* Philadelphia: Open University Press.

Archer, J. (1992). Childhood gender roles: Social content and organization. In H. McGurk (Ed.), *Childhood social development* (pp. 31-62). Hillsdale, NJ: Erlbuam.

Ardelt, M., & Eccles, J. S. (2001). Effects of mothers' parental efficacy beliefs and promotive parenting strategies on inner-city youth. *Journal of Family Issues, 22*(8), 944.

Argetsinger, A. (2001, August 27). An oversupply of undergrads. *Washington Post*, pp. A1, A5.

Armatowski, J. (2001). Attitudes toward death and dying among persons in the fourth quarter of life. In D. O. Moberg

(Ed.), *Aging and spirituality: Spiritual dimensions of aging theory, research, practice, and policy* (pp. 71-83). New York: Haworth Pastoral Press.

Armstrong, E. M. (2000). Lessons in control: Prenatal education in the hospital. *Social Problems, 47*(4), 583-611.

Arnett, J. J. (1998). Learning to stand alone: The contemporary American transition to adulthood in cultural and historical context. *Human Development, 41*(5), 295-297.

Arnett, J. J. (2000). Emerging adulthood: A theory of development from the late teens through the twenties. *American Psychologist, 55*(5), 469-480.

Arnett, J. J., & Taber, S. (1994). Adolescence terminable and interminable: When does adolescence end? *Journal of Youth & Adolescence, 23*(5), 517-538.

Aronson, J. (1992). Women's sense of responsibility for the care of old people: But who else is going to do it? *Gender and Society, 6*, 8-29.

Arrendondo, P. M. (1984). Identity themes for immigrant young adults. *Adolescence, 19*, 977-993.

Ascribe Higher Education News Service (2002, February 27). *UCLA study reports on role father's attitudes play in mother's successfully_breastfeeding their babies.* Electronic collection: A98328192.

Ashford, J. B., LeCroy, C. W., & Lortie, K. L. (2001). *Human behavior in the social environment* (2d ed.). Belmont, CA: Wadsworth.

Atchley, R. C. (1976). *The sociology of retirement.* Cambridge, MA: Schenkman.

Auerbach, J., & Krimgold, B. (Eds.). (2001). *Income, socioeconomic status, and health.* Washington, DC: National Policy Association.

Avis, N. (1999). Women's health at midlife. In S. Willis & J. Reid (Eds.), *Life in the middle: Psychological and social development in middle age* (pp. 105-146). San Diego: Academic Press.

Avis, N., Brambilla, D., McKinlay, S., & Vass, K. (1994). A longitudinal analysis of the association between menopause and depression: Results from the Massachusetts Women's Health Study. *Annals of Epidemiology, 4*, 214-220.

Avis, N., Stellato, R., Crawford, S., Bromberger, Ganz, P., Cain, V., & Kagawa-Singer, M. (2001). Is there a menopausal syndrome? Menopausal status and symptoms across racial/ethnic groups. *Social Science & Medicine, 52*(3), 345.

Bahr, H., Dechaux, J., & Stiehr, K. (1994). The changing bonds of kinship: Parents and adult children. In S. Langlois (Ed.), *Convergence or divergence? Comparing recent social trends in industrial societies* (pp. 115-171). Buffalo, NY: McGill-Queen's University Press.

Bailey, J., & Zucker, K. (1995). Childhood sex-typed behavior and sexual orientation: A conceptual analysis and quantitative review. *Developmental Psychology, 31*, 43-55.

Bailey-Dempsey, C. A. (1993). *A test of a task-centered case management approach to resolve school failure.* Unpublished doctoral dissertation, State University of New York at Albany.

Baillargeon, R. (1987). Object permanence in 3½ and 4½ month old infants. *Developmental Psychology, 23*, 655-664.

Bain, M. D., Gau, D., & Reed, G. B. (1995). An introduction to antenatal and neonatal medicine, the fetal period and perinatal ethics. In G. B. Reed, A. E. Claireaux, & F. Cockburn (Eds.), *Diseases of the fetus and newborn* (2nd ed., pp. 3-23). London: Chapman & Hall.

Bakan, R., Birmingham, C. L., & Goldner, E. M. (1991). Chronicity in anorexia nervosa: Pregnancy and birth complications as risk factors. *International Journal of Eating Disorders, 10*, 631-645.

Baker, A. (1990). The psychological impact of the Intifada on Palestinian children in the occupied West Bank and Gaza: An exploratory study. *American Journal of Orthopsychiatry, 60*, 496-505.

Baltes, P., Lindenberger, U., & Staudinger, U. (1998). Life-span theory in developmental psychology. In R. Lerner (Ed.) *Handbook of child psychology* (5th ed., pp. 1029-1143). New York: Wiley.

Bandura, A. (1977). Self-efficacy: Toward a unifying theory of behavioral change. *Psychological Review, 84*, 191-215.

Bandura, A. (1977). *Social learning theory*. Englewood Cliffs, NJ: Prentice-Hall.

Bandura, A. (1986). *Social foundations of thought and action: A social cognitive theory.* Englewood Cliffs, NJ: Prentice-Hall.

Barak, B., & Stern, B. (1986). Subjective age correlates: A research note. *The Gerontologist, 26*(5), 571-578.

Baranowski, T. (1983). Social support, social influence, ethnicity, and the breastfeeding decision. *Social Science Medicine, 17*, 1599-1611.

Bardwell, J. R., Cochran, S. W., & Walker, S. (1986). Relationship of parental education, race, and gender to sex role stereotyping in five year old kindergartners. *Sex Roles, 15*, 275-281.

Barker, K. K. (1998). "A ship upon a stormy sea": The medicalization of pregnancy. *Social Science and Medicine, 47*(8), 1067-1076.

Baron, J., Granato, L., Spranca, M., & Teubal, E. (1993). Decision-making biases in children and early adolescents: Exploratory studies. *Merrill-Palmer Quarterly, 39*, 22-46.

Barr, R. D., & Parrett, W. H. (1995). *Hope at last for at-risk youth*. Boston: Allyn & Bacon.

Barth, R. (1994). Long-term in home services. In D. J. Besharov (Ed.). *When drug addicts have children* (pp. 175-194). Washington, DC: Child Welfare League of America.

Bartley, M., Blane, D., & Montgomery, S. (1997). Health and the life course: Why safety nets matter. *British Medical Journal, 314*(7088), 1194-1196.

Bartz, K., & Levine, E. (1978). Childrearing by black parents: A description and comparison to Anglo and Chicano parents. *Journal of Marriage and the Family, 40*, 709-719.

Bassali, R., & Benjamin, J. (2002, July 12). Failure to thrive. *EMedicine Journal, 3*(7). Retrieved August 21, 2002 from www.emedicine.com/PED/topic738.htm.

Batson, C. D., Schoenrade, P., & Ventis, W. L. (1993). *Religion and the individual: A social-psychological perspective.* New York: Oxford University Press.

Baumeister, R. F., & Muraven, M. (1996). Identity as adaptation to social, cultural, and historical context. *Journal of Adolescence, 19*, 405-416.

Baumrind, D. (1971). Current patterns of parental authority. *Developmental Psychology Monographs, 41*(1, Pt. 2).

Bautista de Domanico, Y., Crawford, I. & DeWolfe, A. (1994). Ethnic identity and self-concept in Mexican-American adolescents: Is bicultural identity related to stress or better adjustment? *Child & Youth Care Forum, 23*(3), 197-206.

Beckman, D., & Brent, R. (1994). Effects of prescribed and self-administered drugs during the second and third trimesters. In G. Avery, M. Fletcher, & M. MacDonald (Eds.), *Neonatology: Athophysiology and management of the newborn* (4th ed., pp. 197-206). Philadelphia: Lippincott.

Beckwith, L. (1984). Parent interaction with their preterm infants and later mental development. *Early Child Development and Care, 16*(1-2), 27-40.

Beeman, S. K., Kim, H., & Bullerdick, S. K. (2000). Factors affecting placement of children in kinship and nonkinship foster care. *Children and Youth Services Review, 22*(1), 37-54.

Bell, S. (1990). Sociological perspectives on the medicalization of menopause. *Annals of New York Academy of Sciences, 592*, 173-178.

Belsky, J. (1987). Infant day care and socioemotional development: The United States. *Journal of Child Psychology and Psychiatry, 29*, 397-406.

Belsky, J. (1993). Etiology of child maltreatment: A developmental ecological analysis. *Psychological Bulletin, 114*, 414-434.

Belsky, J., & Braungart, J. M. (1991). Are insecure-avoidant infants with extensive day care experience less stressed by and more independent in the strange situation? *Child Development, 62*, 567-571.

Bem, S. (1989). Gender schema theory: A cognitive account of sex-typing. *Psychological Review, 88*, 354-364.

Bem, S. L. (1993). *The lenses of gender: Transforming the debate on sexual inequality.* New Haven, CT: Yale University Press.

Benenson, J. (1993). Greater preference among females than males for dyadic interaction in early childhood. *Child Development, 64*, 544-555.

Bengtson, V. (1996). Continuities and discontinuities in intergenerational relationships over time. In V. Bengtson & K. Schaie (Eds.), *Adulthood and aging* (pp. 246-268). New York: Springer.

Bengtson, V., & Harootyan, R. (1994). *Intergenerational linkages: Hidden connections in American society.* New York: Springer.

Bengtson, V., Rosenthal, C., & Burton, L. (1990). Families and aging: Diversity and heterogeneity. In R. H. Binstock & L. K. George (Eds.), *Handbook of aging and the social sciences* (3rd ed., pp. 405-426). San Diego: Academic Press.

Benson, P. L., Yeager, R. J., Wood, P. K., Guerra, M. J., & Manno, B. V. (1986). *Catholic high schools: Their impact on low-income students.* Washington, DC: National Catholic Educational Association.

Benson, P. L. (1990). *The troubled journey: A portrait of 6th-12th grade youth.* Minneapolis, MN: Search Institute.

Bentgson, V. (2001). Beyond the nuclear family: The increasing importance of multigenerational bonds. *Journal of Marriage and Family, 63*(1), 1-16.

Bengtson, V., Rosenthal, C., & Burton, L. (1990). Families and aging: Diversity and heterogeneity. In

R. Binstock & L. Geroge (Eds.), *Handbook of aging and the social sciences* (3rd ed. pp. 263-287). New York: Academic Press.

Bergquist, W., Greenberg, E., & Klaum, G. (1993). *In our fifties: Voices of men and women reinventing their lives.* San Francisco: Jossey-Bass.

Berk, L. (1997). *Child development* (4th ed.). Boston: Allyn & Bacon.

Berk, L. (2002). *Infants, children & adolescents.* Boston: Allyn & Bacon.

Berkeley Planning Associates (1996). *Priorities for future research: Results of BAs' Delphi Survey of Disabled women.* Retrieved November 6, 2002, from www.ncddr.org/rr/women/priorities.html.

Berliner, K., Jacob, D., & Schwartzberg, N. (1999). The single adult and the family life cycle. In B. Carter & M. McGoldrick (Eds.), *The expanded family life cycle: Individual, family, and social perspectives* (3rd ed., pp. 362-372). Boston: Allyn & Bacon.

Berndt, T. J. (1988). Friendships in childhood and adolescence. In W. Damon (Ed.), *Child development today and tomorrow* (pp. 332-348). San Francisco: Jossey-Bass.

Berne, L., & Huberman, B. (1999). *European approaches to adolescent sexual behavior & responsibility.* Washington, DC: Advocates for Youth.

Bern-Klug, M., & Chapin, R. (1999). The changing demography of death in the United States: Implications for human service workers. In B. deVries (Ed.), *End of life issues: Interdisciplinary and multidimensional perspectives* (pp. 265-280). New York: Springer.

Bern-Klug, M., Gessert, C., & Forbes, S. (2001). The need to revise assumptions about the end of life: Implications for social work practice. *Health and Social Work, 26*(1), 38-48.

Berryman, J. C., & Wendridge, K. (1991). Having a baby after 40: A preliminary investigation of women's experience of pregnancy. *Journal of Reproduction and Infant Psychology, 9,* 3-18.

Berryman, J. C., & Wendridge, K. (1996). Pregnancy after 35 and attachment to the fetus. *Journal of Reproduction and Infant Psychology, 14,* 133-143.

Best, K. (2002). Medical barriers often unnecessary: Barriers with no scientific basis can limit choice and endanger health (facilitating contraception choice). *Network: 21*(3), 4-14.

Betts, S. (2002). *Childhood immunizations.* Unpublished manuscript.

Bhattacharya, G. (2000). The school adjustment of South Asian immigrant children in the United States. *Adolescence, 35,* 77-85.

Biernat, M. (1991). Gender stereotypes and the relationship between masculinity and feminity: A developmental analysis. *Journal of Personality and Social Psychology, 61,* 351-365.

Biggs, S. (1999). *The mature imagination: Dynamics of identity in midlife and beyond.* Philadelphia, PA: Open University Press.

Bigler, R. S., & Liben, L. S. (1993). A cognitive-developmental approach to racial stereotyping and reconstructive memory in Euro-American children. *Child Development, 64,* 1507-1518.

Billingsley, A. (1999). *Mighty like a river: The black church and social reform.* New York: Oxford University Press.

Bishop, K. (1993). Psychosocial aspects of genetic disorders: Implications for practice. *Families in Society, 74,* 207-212.

Bitzan, J. E., & Kruzich, J. M. (1990). Interpersonal relationships of nursing home residents. *The Gerontologist, 30,* 385-390.

Blacker, L. (1999). The launching phase of the life cycle. In B. Carter & M. McGoldrick (Eds.), *The expanded family life cycle: Individual, family, and social perspectives* (3rd ed., pp. 287-306). Boston: Allyn & Bacon.

Blass, E., & Ciaramitaro, V. (1994). A new look at some old mechanisms in human newborns: Taste and tactile determinants of state, affect, and action. *Monographs of the Society for Research in Child Development, 59*(1).

Blau, P. M. (1964). *Exchange and power in social life.* New York: Wiley.

Blazer, D. G. (1995). Depression. In G. L. Maddox (Ed.), *The encyclopedia of aging: A comprehensive resource in gerontology and geriatrics* (2nd ed., pp. 265-266). New York: Springer.

Bliatot, B. (1993). Hmong death customs: Traditional and acculturated. In D. Irish, K. Lundquist, & V. Nelsen (Eds.), *Ethnic variations in dying, death, and grief: Diversity in universality* (pp. 77-99). Washington, DC: Taylor & Francis.

Blieszner, R., & deVries, B. (2001). Perspectives on intimacy. *Generations, 25*(2), 7-8.

Blinn, C. (1997). *Maternal ties: A selection of programs for female offenders.* Lanham, MD: American Correctional Association.

Bloch, J., & Seitz, M. (1989). Parents as assessors of children: a collaborative approach to helping. *Social Work in Education, 11*(4), 226-244.

Bloom, B., & Steinhart, D. (1993). *Why punish the children? A reappraisal of the children of incarcerated mothers in America.* San Francisco: National Council on Crime and Delinquency.

Blume, J. (1970). *Are you there, God? It's me, Margaret.* New York: Dell.

Blyth, D. A., & Roehlkepartian, E. C. (1993). *Healthy communities, healthy youth.* Minneapolis, MN: Search Institute.

Boldizar, J. P. (1991). Assessing sex typing and androgyny in children: The children's sex role inventory. *Developmental Psychology, 27,* 505-515.

Bon Secours Hospice (2002). *Signs and symptoms of approaching death.* Richmond, VA: Author.

Bonanno, G., & Kaltman, S. (1999). Toward an integrative perspective on bereavement. *Psychological Bulletin, 125*(6), 760-776.

Bonne, O. B., Rubinoff, B., & Berry, E. M. (1996). Delayed detection of pregnancy in patients with anorexia nervosa: Two case reports. *International Journal of Eating Disorders, 20,* 423-425.

Borke, H. (1973). The development of empathy in Chinese and American children between 3 and 6 years of age: A cross-cultural study. *Developmental Psychology, 9,* 102-108.

Bornstein, M. H. (1992). Perception across the life span. In M. H. Bornstein & M. E. Lamb (Eds.), *Developmental psychology: An advanced textbook* (3rd ed., pp. 155-210). Hillsdale, NJ: Lawrence Erlbaum.

Bornstein, M. (1995). Parenting infants. In M. Bornstein (Ed.), *Handbook of parenting: Vol 1: . Children and parenting* (pp. 3-41). Mahway, NJ: Lawrence Erlbaum.

Bortz, W. M., & Wallace, D. H. (1999). Physical fitness, aging, and sexuality. *Western Journal of Medicine, 170*(3), 167-169.

Borysenko, J. (1996). *A woman's book of life: The biology, psychology, and spirituality of the feminine life cycle.* New York: Riverhead Books.

Bowlby, J. (1969). *Attachment and loss.* New York: Basic Books.

Bowlby, J. (1980). *Attachment and loss: Loss, sadness, and depression* (Vol. 3). New York: Basic Books.

Bowlby, J. (1982). *Attachment and loss* (Vol. 1). New York: Basic Books.

Bowles, S., & Gintis, H. (1976). *Schooling in capitalist America: Educational reform and the contradictions of economic life.* New York: Basic Books.

Bradley, R., Whiteside, L., Mundfrom, D., Casey, P., Kelleher, K., & Pope, S. (1994). Early indications of resilience and their relation to experiences in the home environments of low birthweight, premature children living in poverty. *Child Development, 65,* 346-360.

Brantlinger, E. (1992). Professionals' attitudes toward the sterilization of people with disabilities. *Journal of the Association for Severe Handicaps, 17*(1), 4-18.

Braungart, J., Plomin, R., DeFries, J. C., & Fulker, D. (1992). Genetic influences on tester-rated infant temperament as assessed by Bayley's Infant Behavior Record: Non-adoptive and adoptive siblings and twins. *Developmental Psychology, 28,* 40-47.

Brayden, R., Altemeier, W., Tucker, D., Dietrich, M., & Veitze, P. (1992). Antecedents of child neglect in the first two years of life. *Journal of Pediatrics, 120*(3), 426-429.

Brazelton, T. B. (1983). *Infants and mothers: Differences in development.* New York: Delta/Seymour Lawrence.

Breastfeeding protects against childhood cancers (2001). *Contemporary OB/GYN, 46*(5), 130.

Bredekamp, S. (Ed.). (1992). *Developmentally appropriate practice in early childhood programs serving children from birth through age 8.* Washington, DC: National Association for the Education of Young Children.

Brinch, M., Isager, T., & Tolstrup, K. (1988). Anorexia nervosa and motherhood: Reproduction pattern and mothering behavior of 50 women. *Acta Psychiatrica Scandinavica, 77,* 611-617.

Brody, E. (1985). Parent care as normative family stress. *The Gerontologist, 25*(1), *19-29.*

Brokenleg, M., & Middleton, D. (1993). Native Americans: Adapting, yet retaining. In D. Irsih, K. Lundquist, & V. Nelsen (Eds.), *Ethnic variations in dying, death, and grief: Diversity in universality* (pp. 101-112). Washington, DC: Taylor & Francis.

Bromberger, J., Meyer, P., Kravitz, H., Sommer, B., Cordal, A., Powell, L., Ganz, P., & Sutton-Tyrrell, K. (2001). Psychological distress and natural menopause: A multi-ethnic community study. *American Journal of Public Health, 91*(9), 1435.

Bronfenbrenner, U. (1986). Ecology of the family as a context for human development research perspectives. *Developmental Psychology, 22,* 723-742.

Brooks, J. L., Hair, E. C., & Zaslow, M. J. (2001, July). *Welfare reform's impact on adolescents: Early warning signs.* (Child Trends Research Brief). Washington, DC: Child Trends.

Brooks-Gunn, J. (1988). Antecedents and consequences of variations in girls' maturational timing. *Journal of Adolescent Health, 9,* 365-373.

Brooks-Gunn, J., & Duncan, G. (1997). The effects of poverty on children. *Future of Children, 7*(2), 55-71.

Brooks-Gunn, J., & Furstenberg, F. (1989). Adolescent sexual behavior. *American Psychologist, 44,* 249-257.

Brooks-Gunn, J., Petersen, A. C., & Eichorn, D. (1985). The study of maturational timing effects in adolescence. *Journal of Youth and Adolescence, 14,* 149-161.

Brosco, J. (1999). The early history of the infant mortality rate in America. *Pediatrics, 103*(2), 78.

Brown, B. (2001, August). *Teens, jobs, and welfare: Implications for social policy.* (Child Trends Research Brief). Washington, DC: Child Trends.

Brown, J., Eichenberger, S., Portes, P., & Christensen, D. (1991). Family functioning and children's divorce adjustment. *Journal of Divorce and Remarriage, 17*(1/2), 81-97.

Brubaker, E., Gorman, M. A., & Hiestand, M. (1990). Stress perceived by elderly recipients of family care. In T. H. Brubaker (Ed.), *Family relationships in later life* (2nd ed., pp. 267-281). Newbury Park, CA: Sage.

Brubaker, T. H. (1990). An overview of family relationships in later life. In T. H. Brubaker (Ed.), *Family relationships in later life* (2nd ed., pp. 13-26). Newbury Park, CA: Sage.

Bruer, J. (1999). *The myth of the first three years of life.* New York: Free Press.

Brumberg, J. (1997). *The body project: An intimate history of American girls.* New York: Random House.

Brunner, E. (1997). Stress and the biology of inequality. *British Medical Journal, 314*(7092), 1472-1476.

Bryson, K., & Casper, L. (1999). *Coresident grandparents and grandchildren.* Washington, DC: U.S. Census Bureau.

Buchmann, M. (1989). *The script of life in modern society: Entry into adulthood in a changing world.* Chicago: University of Chicago Press.

Bullis, R. K. (1996). *Spiritality in social work practice.* Washington, DC: Taylor and Frances.

Bullis, R. K., & Harrigan, M. (1992). Religious denominational policies on sexuality. *Families in Society, 73,* 304-312.

Burchinal, M. R., Peisner-Feinberg, E. S., Bryant, D. M., & Clifford, R. M. (2000). Children's social and cognitive development and child care quality: Testing for differential associations related to poverty, gender, or ethnicity. *Applied Developmental Science, 4,* 149-165.

Burchinal, M.R. (1999). Childcare experiences and developmental outcomes. *Annals of the American Academy of Political Science, 563,* 73-98.

Berne, L., & Huberman, B. (2000). Lessons learned: European approaches to adolescent sexual behavior and responsibility. *Journal of Sex Education & Therapy, 25*(2-3), 189-199.

Burnette, D. (1999). Custodial grandparents in Latino families: Patterns of service use and predictors of unmet needs. *Social Work, 44*(1), 22-34.

Bustan, N. M. (1994). Maternal attitudes toward pregnancy and the risk of neonatal death. *American Journal of Public Health, 84,* 411-414.

Butler, R. N. (1963). The life review: An interpretation of reminiscence in the aged. *Psychiatry, 26,* 65-70.

Butler, R. N. (1987). Life review. In G. L. Maddox (Ed.), *The encyclopedia of aging: A comprehensive resource in gerontology and geriatrics* (2nd ed., pp. 397-398). New York: Springer.

Byock, I. (1997). *Dying well: Peace and possibilities at the end of life.* New York: Riverhead Books.

Cahill, D., & Wardle, P. (2002). Management of infertility. *British Medical Journal, 325*(7354), 28-32.

Cahill, J., & Wagner, C. (2002). Challenges in breastfeeding: Maternal considerations. *Contemporary Pediatrics, 19*(5), 94-107.

Call, J. (1995). On becoming a good enough infant. *Infant Mental Health Journal, 16*(1), 52-57.

Cameron, L. (1999). Understanding alcohol abuse in American Indian/Alaskan native youth. *Pediatric Nursing, 25*(3), 297.

Campbell, L., Campbell, B., & Dickinson, D. (1999) (2nd ed). *Teaching and learning through multiple intelligences.* Needham Heights, MA: Allyn & Bacon.

Campbell, R., & MacFarlane, A. (1986). Place of delivery: A review. *British Journal of Obstetrics and Gynaecology, 93*(7), 675-683.

Campbell, R., & Sais, E. (1995). Accelaterated metalinguistic (phonological) awareness in bilingual children. *British Journal of Developmental Psychology, 13,* 61-68.

Canda, E. (1997). Spirituality. *Encyclopedia of social work: 1997 supplement* (19th ed.). Washington, DC: National Association of Social Workers Press.

Canda, E. R., & Furman, L. D. (1999). *Spiritual diversity in social work practice*. New York: Free Press.

Canino, I., & Spurlock, J. (1994). *Culturally diverse children and adolescents*. New York: Guilford Press.

Carey, T. A. (1994). "Spare the rod and spoil the child." Is this a sensible justification for the use of punishment in child rearing? *Child Abuse and Neglect, 18,* 1005-1010.

Carnegie Corporation of New York. (1995). *Great transitions: Preparing adolescents for a new century*. New York: Carnegie Corp.

Carney, J., & Cohler, B. (1993). Developmental continuities and adjustment in adulthood: Social relations, morale, and the transformation from middle to late life. *The course of life: Late adulthood* (Vol. 6, pp. 199-226). Madison, CT: International Universities Press.

Carrasco, D. (1990). *Religions of Mesoamerica*. New York: Harper Collins.

Carstensen, L. (1992). Social and emotional patterns in adulthood: Support for socioemotional selectivity theory. *Psychology and Aging, 7,* 331-338.

Carstensen, L. (1998). A life-span approach to social motivation. In J. Heckhausen & C. Dweck (Eds.), *Motivation and self-regulation across the life span* (pp. 341-364). New York: Cambridge University Press.

Carstensen, L. (2001). Selectivity theory: Social activity in life-span context. In A. Walker, M. Manoogian-O'Dell, L. McGraw, & D. White (Eds.), *Families in later life: Connections and transitions* (pp. 265-275). Thousand Oaks, CA: Pine Forge.

Carter, B., & McGoldrick, M. (Eds.). (1989). *The changing family life cycle: A framework for family therapy* (2nd ed.). New York: Allyn & Bacon.

Carter, B., & McGoldrick, M. (1999a). The divorce cycle: A major variation in the American family life cycle. In B. Carter & M. McGoldrick (Eds.), *The expanded family life cycle: Individual, family, and social perspectives* (3rd ed., pp. 373-380). Boston: Allyn & Bacon.

Carter, B., & McGoldrick, M. (1999b). *The expanded family life cycle: Individual, family and social perspectives* (3rd ed.). Boston: Allyn & Bacon.

Carter, D. B., & Patterson, C. J. (1982). Sex roles as social conventions: The development of children's conceptions of sex-role stereotypes. *Developmental Psychology, 18,* 812-824.

CASA. (2002). *CASA 2002 teen survey.* New York: National Center on Addiction and Substance Abuse at Columbia University (CASA).

Case, R. (1998). The development of conceptual structures. In D. Kuhn & R. Siegler (Eds.), *Handbook of child psychology: Vol. 2. Cognition, perception, and language* (5th ed., pp. 745-800). New York: Wiley.

Caspi, A. (1987). Personality in the life course. *Journal of Personality and Social Psychology, 53*(6), 1203-1213.

Caspi, A., & Roberts, B. (1999). Personality continuity and change across the life course (pp. 300-326). In L. A. Pervin & O. P. John (Eds.), *Handbook of personality: Theory and research* (2nd ed., pp. 300-326). New York: Guilford Press.

Cavanaugh, J. (1996). *Adult development and aging* (3rd ed.). Pacific Grove, CA: Brooks/Cole.

CDC: 30,000 babies born by ART in 1999. (2002, January 13). *Medical Letter on the CDC and FDA, 7.*

Centers for Disease Control and Prevention. (1994). *STD surveillance, 1993.* Atlanta, GA: Author.

Centers for Disease Control and Prevention. (1997, March 7). Analysis of the third National Health and Nutrition Examination Survey, 1988-1994 (NHAMES III). *Morbidity and Mortality Weekly Report, 46*(9), 11-32.

Centers for Disease Control and Prevention. (1999a). 1999 assisted reproductive technology success rates. Retrieved September 9, 2002, from www.cdc.gov/nccdphp/drh/art.htm.

Centers for Disease Control and Prevention. (1999b). *Chronic diseases and their risk factors: The nation's leading causes of death.* Atlanta, GA: Author.

Centers for Disease Control & Prevention. (2000). *Abortion surveillance: Preliminary analysis: United States, 1997.* Retrieved November 6, 2002, from www.infoplease.com/ipa/A0764203.html.

Centers for Disease Control and Prevention. (2001). *HIVAIDS surveillance report, 13*(1). Retrieved August 26, 2002, from www.cdc.gov/hiv/stats/has1301.pdf.

Cervantes, J., & Ramirez, O. (1992). Spirituality and family dynamics in psychotherapy with Latino children. In L. Vargas & J. Koss-Chioino (Eds.), *Working with culture: Psychotherapeutic interventions with ethnic minority children and adolescents.* San Francisco: Jossey-Bass.

Chadiha, L., & Danziger, S. (1995). The significance of fathers for inner-city African-American mothers. *Child and Adolescent Social Work Journal, 12*(2), 83-100.

Chadwick, R., Levitt, M., & Shickle, D. (1997). *The right to know and the right not to know.* Brookfield, VT: Avebury.

Challenge Day. (n.d.). Retrieved June 17, 2002 from www.challengeday.org/history.html.

Chang, L. (2001). The development of racial attitudes and self concepts of Taiwanese preschoolers (China). *Dissertation Abstracts International: Section A: Humanities & Social Sciences, 61*(8-A), 3045.

Chapman, P., & Mullis, R. (2000). Racial differences in adolescent coping and self-esteem. *Journal of Genetic Psychology, 161*(2), 152-160.

Chase-Lansdale, P. L., & Vinovskis, M. A. (1995). Whose responsibility? An historical analysis of the changing roles of mothers, fathers, and society. In P. L. Chase-Lansdale & J. Brooks-Gunn (Eds.), *Escape from poverty: What makes a difference for children?* (pp. 11-37). New York: Cambridge University Press.

Chasnoff, I. (1998). Silent violence: Is prevention a moral obligation? *Pediatrics, 102*, 145-148.

Chatfield, J. E. (2002). FDA approves weekly birth control patch. *American Family Physician, 65(*12), 329.

Chatters, L., & Jayakody, R. (1995). Commentary: Intergenerataional support within African-American families: Concepts and methods. In V. Bengtson, K. Schaie, & L. Burton (Eds.), *Adult intergenerational relations: Effects of social change* (pp. 97-118). New York: Springer.

Checkoway, B. (1998). Involving young people in neighborhood development. *Children and Youth Services Review, 20*(9/10), 765-795.

Chen, Y., Yu, S., & Li, W. (1988). Artificial feeding and hospitalization in the first 18 months of life. *Pediatrics, 81*, 58-62.

Child Trends. (n.d.). *Trends in sexual activity and contraceptive use among teens.* Washington, DC: Child Trends. Retrieved August 19, 2002, from www.childtrends.org.

Children's Defense Fund. (1996). *The state of America's children, 1996.* Washington, DC: Author.

Children's Defense Fund. (1997). *The state of America's children, 1997.* Washington, DC: Author.

Children's Defense Fund. (1998). *Annual report: The state of America's children.* Washington, DC: Author.

Children's Defense Fund. (2000). *Yearbook 2000: The state of America's children.* Washington, DC: Author.

Children's Defense Fund. (2001a). *The state of America's children, 2001.* Washington, DC: Author.

Children's Defense Fund (2001b). Overall child poverty rate dropped in 2000 but poverty rose for children in full-time working families. Retrieved February 15, 2002 from www.childrensdefense.org/release010925.html.

Chomsky, N. (1968). *Language and mind.* New York: Harcourt Brace Jovanovich.

Chudacoff, H. (1989). *How old are you?* Princeton, NJ: Princeton University Press.

Cicerelli, V. (1995). *Sibling relationships across the life span.* New York: Plenum Press.

Cicirelli, V. (1983). Adult children's attachment and helping behavior to elderly parents: A path model. *Journal of Marriage and the Family, 45*, 815-825.

Clark, H. (2001). Residential substance abuse treatment for pregnant and postpartum women and their children: Treatment and policy implications. *Child Welfare, 80*(2), 179-198.

Clark, K., & Clark, M. (1939). The development of consciousness of self and the emergence of racial identification in Negro preschool children. *Journal of Social Psychology, 10*, 591-599.

Clarke-Stewart, K. A. (1988). "The 'effects' of infant day care reconsidered" reconsidered: Risks for parents, children, and researchers. *Early Childhood Research Quarterly, 3*(3), 293-318.

Clarke-Stewart, K. A. (1989). Infant day care: Maligned or malignant? *American Psychologist, 17*, 454-462.

Clearinghouse on International Developments in Child, Youth and Family Policies at Columbia University. Retrieved June 7, 2002, from www.childpolicyintl.org.

Coates, M. M. (Ed.). (1993). Policy statements. In LaLeche League International, *The lactation consultant's topical review and bibliography of the literature on breastfeeding.* Franklin Park, IL: LaLeche League International.

Coie, J. D., Dodge, K. A., & Coppotelli, H. (1982). Dimensions and types of social status: A cross age perspective. *Developmental Psychology, 18*, 557-570.

Cole, E., & Stewart, A. (1996). Meanings of participation among black and white women: Political identity and social responsibility. *Journal of Personality and Social Psychology, 71*(1), 130-140.

Cole, S. S., & Cole, T. M. (1993). Sexuality, disability, and reproductive issues through the lifespan. In F. P. Haseltine, S. S. Cole, & D. B. Gray (Eds.), *Reproductive issues for persons with physical disabilities* (pp. 3-21). Baltimore: Brookes.

Coleman, M., & Ganong, L. (1983). Parent-child interaction: A prototype for parent education. *Home Economics Research Journal, 11*(3), 235-244.

Coles, R. (1987). *The moral life of children.* Boston: Houghton/Mifflin.

Coles, R. (1997). *The moral intelligence of children.* New York: Random House.

Collins, A., Freeman, E. W., Boxer, A. S., & Tureck, R. (1992). Perceptions of infertility in females as compared to males entering in vitro fertilization treatment. *Fertility and Sterilization, 57,* 350-356.

Comer, J. P. (1980). *School power: Implications of an intervention project.* New York: Free Press.

Comer, J. P. (1994). Home, school, and academic learning. In K. I. Goodland & P. Keating (Eds.), *Access to knowledge: The continuing agenda for our nation's schools.* New York: College Board.

Conger, R., Conger, K., Elder, G., Jr., Lorenz, F., Simons, R., & Whitbeck, B. (1993). Family economic stress and adjustment of early adolescent girls. *Developmental Psychology, 29*(2), 206-219.

Conger, R., Elder, G., Jr., Lorenz, F., Simons, R., & Whitbeck, L. (1992). A family process model of economic hardship and adjustment of early adolescent boys. *Child Development, 63,* 526-541.

Conn, D. K. (2001). Mental health issues in long-term care facilities. In D. Conn, N. Herrmann, A. Kaye, D. Rewilak, & B. Schogt (Eds.), *Practical psychiatry in the long-term care facility: A handbook for staff* (pp. 1-16). Seattle, WA: Hogrefe & Huber.

Connie, T. A. (1988). *Aids and adaptations for disabled parents: An illustrated manual for service providers and parents with physical or sensory disabilities* (2nd ed.). Vancouver: University of British Columbia, School of Rehabilitation Medicine.

Connolly, J., White, D., Stevens, R., & Burstein, S. (1987). Adolescent self-reports of social activity: Assessment of stability and relations to social adjustment. *Journal of Adolescence, 10,* 83-95.

Constable, R. (1996). General perspectives on theory and practice. In R. Constable, J. P. Flynn, & S. McDonald (Eds.), *School social work: Practice and research perspectives* (3rd ed., pp. 3-16). Chicago: Lyceum Books.

Constable, R., & Walberg, H. (1996). School social work: Facilitating home-school partnerships in the 1990s. In R. Constable, J. P. Flynn, & S. McDonald (Eds.), *School social work: Practice and research perspectives* (3rd ed., pp. 182-196). Chicago: Lyceum Books.

Coohey, C. (1996). Child maltreatment: Testing the isolation hypothesis. *Child Abuse and Neglect, 20*(3), 241-254.

Coohey, C. (1998). Home alone and other inadequately supervised children. *Child Welfare, 77*(3), 291-310.

Cook, E. A., Jelen, T. G., & Wilcox, C. (1992). *Between two absolutes: Public opinion and the politics of abortion.* Boulder, CO: Westview Press.

Cooksey, E., Menaghan, E., & Jekielek, S. (1997). Life-course effects of work and family circumstances on children. *Social Forces, 76*(2), 637-665.

Cooper, P. G. (2000). Ectopic pregnancy. *Clinical Reference Systems, Annual 2000,* 565.

Copeland, V. (1996). Immunization among African American children: Implications for social work. *Health and Social Work, 21*(2), 105-114.

Corbin, J. M. (1987). Women's perceptions and management of pregnancy complicated by chronic illness. *Health Care Women International, 8*(5-6), 317-337.

Cordero, L., Hines, S., Shibley, K. A., & Landon, M. B. (1992). Perinatal outcome for women in prison. *Journal of Perinatology, 12,* 205-209.

Corsaro, W. (1997). *The sociology of childhood.* Thousand Oaks, CA: Pine Forge.

Costa, F. M., Jessor, R., Donovan, J. E., & Fortenberry, J. D. (1995). Early initiation of sexual intercourse: The influence of psychosocial unconventionality. *Journal of Research on Adolescents, 5,* 93-121.

Costa, P., & McCrae, R. (1994). Set like plaster? Evidence for stability of adult personality. In T. F. Heatherton & S. L. Weinberger (Eds.), *Can personality change?* (pp. 21-40). Washington, DC: American Psychological Association.

Costa, P., Terracciano, A., & McCrae, R. (2001). Gender differences in personality traits across cultures: Robust and surprising findings. *Journal of Personality and Social Psychology, 81*(2), 322.

Counts, D. R., & Counts, D. A. (1991). *Coping with the final tragedy: Cultural variation in dying and grieving.* Amityville, NY: Baywood.

Cowan, P. A. (1991). Individual and family life transitions: A proposal for a new definition. In P. A. Cowan & M. Hetherington (Eds.), *Family transitions* (pp 3-30). Hillsdale, NJ: Lawrence Erlbaum.

Cowley, C., & Farley, T. (2001). Adolescent girls' attitudes toward pregnancy. *Journal of Family Practice, 50*(7), 603-617.

Crawley, L., Payne, R., Bolden, J., Payne, T., Washington, P., & Williams, S. (2000). Palliative and end-of-life care in the

African American community. *Journal of the American Medical Association, 284*(19), 2518-2521.

Cronenwett, L. R., & Reinhardt, R. (1987). Social support and breastfeeding: A review. *Birth, 14,* 199-203.

Csikszentmihalyi, M., & Larson, R. (1984). *Being adolescent: Conflict and growth in the teenage years.* New York: Basic Books.

Csikszentmihalyi, M., & Schneider, B. (2000). *Becoming adult: How teenagers prepare for the world of work.* New York: Basic Books.

Cumming, E., & Henry, W. (1961). *Growing old.* New York: Basic Books.

Cummings, E. M., Iannotti, R., & Zahn-Waxler, C. (1989). Aggression between peers in early childhood: Individual continuity and developmental change. *Child Development, 60,* 887-895.

Damon, W. (1977). *The social world of the child.* San Francisco: Jossey-Bass.

Damon, W., & Hart, D. (1988). *Self understanding in childhood and adolescence.* Cambridge, UK: Cambridge University Press.

Dannefer, D., & Perlmutter, M. (1990). Development as a multidimensional process: Individuals and social constituents. *Human Development, 33,* 108-137.

Danziger, S. K., & Danziger, S. (1993). Child poverty and public policy: Toward a comprehensive antipoverty agenda. *Daedalus, 122,* 57-84.

David, H. P. (1996). Induced abortion: Psychosocial aspects. In J. J. Sciarra (Ed.), *Gynecology and obstetrics* (Vol. 6, pp. 1-8). Philadelphia, PA: Lippincott-Raven.

Davidson, J., & Smith, R. (1990). Traumatic experiences in psychiatric outpatients. *Journal of Traumatic Stress Studies, 3,* 459-475.

Davies, D. (1999). *Child development: A practitioner's guide.* New York: Guilford.

Davis, M., & Vander Stoep, A. (1997). The transition to adulthood for youth who have serious emotional disturbance: Developmental transition and young adult outcomes. *Journal of Mental Health Administration, 24*(4), 400-427.

De Casper, A., & Fifer, W. (1980). Of human bonding: Newborns prefer their mothers' voices. *Science, 208,* 1174-1176.

Dedmon, S. R. (1997). Attention deficiency and hyperactivity. In M. Fraser (Ed.), *Risk and resilience in childhood: An ecological perspective* (pp. 73-94). Washington, DC: NASW Press.

DeHart, G. B., Sroufe, L. A., & Cooper, R. G. (2000). *Child development: Its nature and course.* (4th ed.). Boston: McGraw-Hill.

DeJong, W. (1993). Obesity as a characterological stigma: The issue of responsibility and judgments of task performance. *Psychological Reports, 73,* 963-970.

De La Cancela, V., & Martinez, I. (1983). An analysis of culturalism in Latino mental health: Folk medicine as a case in point. *Hispanic Journal of Behavioral Sciences, 5*(3), 251-274.

Delany, S., & Delany, E., with Hearth, A. (1993). *Having our say: The Delany sisters' first 100 years.* New York: Kodansha International.

Delany, S., with Hearth, A. (1997). *On my own at 107: Reflections on life without Bessie.* New York: Harper Collins.

Dellmann-Jenkins, M., Blankemeyer, M., & Pinkard, O. (2001). Incorporating the elder caregiving role into the developmental tasks of young adulthood. *International Journal of Aging and Human Development, 52*(1), 1.

Denham, S., Zoller, D., & Couchoud, E. (1994). Socialization of preschoolers' emotion understanding. *Developmental Psychology, 30,* 928-936.

DeRosier, M. E., Kupersmidt, J. B., & Patterson, C. J. (1994). Children's academic and behavioral adjustment as a function of the chronicity and proximity of peer rejection. *Child Development, 65,* 1799-1813.

Devitt, N. (1977). The transition from home to hospital births in the United States. *Birth and Family Journal, 4,* 47-58.

Devore, W., & Schlesinger, E. (1999). *Ethnic sensitive social work practice* (5th ed.) Boston: Allyn & Bacon.

de Vries, B. (Ed.) (1999). *End of life issues: Interdisciplinary and multidimensional perspectives.* New York: Springer Publishing Company.

de Vries, B., & Watt, D. (1996). A lifetime of events: Age and gender variations in the life story. *International Journal of Aging and Human Development, 42*(2), 81-102.

de Vries, M., & Sameroff, A. (1984). Culture and temperament: Influences on infant temperament in three East African societies. *American Journal of Orthopsychiatry, 54,* 83-96.

Dhooper, S., & Schneider, P. (1995). Evaluation of a school-based child abuse prevention program. *Research on Social Work Practice, 5*(1), 36-46.

Dickason, E. J., Schult, M., & Silverman, B. L. (1990). *Maternal-infant nursing care.* St. Louis, MO: Mosby.

Dickason, E. J., Silverman, B. L., & Kaplan, J. A. (1998). *Maternal-infant nursing care* (3rd ed.). St. Louis, MO: Mosby.

Dick-Read, G. (1944). *Childbirth without fear: Principles and practices of natural childbirth.* New York: Harper & Row.

Dodge, D. T. (1995). The importance of curriculum on achieving quality child care programs. *Child Welfare, 74,* 1171-1188.

Dolinsky, A. L., & Rosenwaike, I. (1988). The role of demographic factors in the institutionalization of the elderly. *Research on Aging, 10,* 235-257.

Dollahite, D., Slife, B., & Hawkins, A. (1998). Family generativity and generative counseling: Helping families keep faith with the next generation. In D. McAdams & E. de St. Aubin (Eds.), *Generativity and adult development: How and why we care for the next generation* (pp. 449-481). Washington, DC: American Psychological Association.

Donahue, M. J., & Benson, P. L. (1995). Religion and the well-being of adolescents. *Journal of Social Issues, 51*(2), 145-161.

Donovan, J., Jessor, R., & Costa, F. (1999). Adolescent problem drinking: Stability of psychosocial and behavioral correlates across a generation. *Journal of Studies on Alcohol, 60*(3), 352-361.

Dowling, C. (1996). *Red hot mamas: Coming into our own at fifty.* New York: Bantam.

Downs, A. C., & Langlois, J. H. (1988). Sex typing: Construct and measurement issues. *Sex Roles, 18*(1-2), 87-100.

Drisko, J. (1992). Intimidation and projective identification in group therapy of physically abused early adolescent boys. *Journal of Child and Adolescent Group Therapy, 2*(1), 17-30.

Dryfoos, J. G. (1990). *Adolescents at risk.* New York: Oxford University Press.

Dryfoos, J. G. (1994). *Full-service schools: A revolution in health and social services for children, youth, and families.* San Francisco: Jossey-Bass.

Dubrow, N., & Garbarino, J. (1989). Living in the war zone: Mothers and young children in a public housing development. *Child Welfare, 68,* 3-20.

Ducharme, S. (2001). Aging and sexuality (results of the Association for Advancement of Retired Persons survey). *Paraplegia News, 55*(2), 18-20.

Duggan, A. & Windham, A. (2000). Hawaii's healthy start program of home visiting for at-risk families: Evaluation of family identification, family engagement, and service delivery. *Pediatrics, 105*(1), 250-260.

Dunbar, H. T., Mueller, C. W., Medina, C., & Wolf, T. (1998). Psychological and spiritual growth in women living with HIV. *Social Work, 43,* 144-154.

Dundas, S., & Kaufman, M. (2000). The Toronto Lesbian Family Study. *Journal of Homosexuality, 34*(2), 65-79.

Dunkle, R., Roberts, B., & Haug, M. (2001). *The oldest old in everyday life: Self perception, coping with change, and stress.* New York: Springer.

DuPlessis, H. M., Bell, R., & Richards, T. (1997). Adolescent pregnancy: Understanding the impact of age and race on outcomes. *Journal of Adolescent Health, 20*(3), 187-197.

Dupper, D. R., & Poertner, J. (1997). Public schools and the revitalization of impoverished communities: School-linked, family resource centers. *Social Work, 42,* 415-422.

Durkin, K. (1995). *Developmental social psychology.* Malden, MA: Blackwell.

Dychtwald, K. (1999). *Age power: How the 21st century will be ruled by the new old.* New York: Jeremy P. Tarcher/Putnam.

Dyson, J. (1989). Family violence and its effects on academic underachievement and behavior problems in school. *Journal of the National Medical Association, 82,* 17-22.

East, P. L. (1996). The younger sisters of childbearing adolescents: Their attitudes, expectations, and behaviors. *Child Development, 67,* 267-282.

East, P. L., & Shi, C. R. (1997). Pregnant and parenting adolescents and their younger sisters: The influence of relationship qualities and younger sister outcomes. *Journal of Developmental and Behavioral Pediatrics, 18*(2), 84-90.

Easterlin, R., Schaeffer, C., & Macunovich, D. (1993). Will the baby boomers be less well off than their parents? Income, wealth, and family circumstances over the life cycle in the United States. *Population and Development Review, 19,* 497-522.

Eder, D., & Parker, S. (1987). The cultural production and reproduction of gender: The effect of extracurricular activities on peer-group culture. *Sociology of Education, 60,* 200-213.

Edwards, C. (1992). Normal development in the preschool years. In E. V. Nuttall, I. Romero, & J. Kalesnik (Eds.), *Assessing and screening preschoolers* (pp. 9-22). Boston: Allyn & Bacon.

Egeland, B., Carlson, E., & Sroufe, L. A. (1993). Resilience as process. *Development and Psychopathology, 5,* 517-528.

Egley, A., Jr. (2002). *National youth gang survey trends from 1996-2000*. Office of Juvenile Justice and Delinquency Prevention-Fact Sheet, February 2002, *3*.

Egley, C., Miller, D., Granados, J., & Ingram-Fogel, C. (1992). Outcome of pregnancy during imprisonment. *Journal of Reproductive Medicines, 37*, 131-134.

Ego, A. (2001). Survival analysis of fertility after ectopic pregnancy. *JAMA, The Journal of the American Medical Association, 285*(23), 2955.

Eisenberg, N., & Strayer, J. (1987). Critical issues in the study of empathy. In N. Eisenberg & J. Strayer (Eds.), *Empathy and its development* (pp. 3-13). Cambridge, UK: Cambridge University Press.

Elder, G., Jr. (1974). *Children of the Great Depression*. Chicago: University of Chicago Press.

Elder, G., Jr. (1986). Military times and turning points in men's lives. *Developmental Psychology, 22*, 233-245.

Elder, G., Jr. (1992). Life course. In E. Borgatta & M. Borgatta (Eds.), *Encyclopedia of sociology* (pp. 1120-1130). New York: Macmillan.

Elder, G., Jr. (1994). Time, human agency, and social change: Perspectives on the life course. *Social Psychology Quarterly, 57*(1), 4-15.

Elder, G., Jr. (1998). The life course as developmental theory. *Child Development, 69*(1), 1-12.

Elkind, D. (1981). *The hurried child: Growing up too fast too soon*. Reading, MA: Addison-Wesley.

Elley, N. (2001). Early birds, too early: Prematurity may mean poor performance. *Psychology Today, 34*(15), 28.

Elliott, M. (1996). Impact of work, family, and welfare receipt on women's self-esteem in young adulthood. *Social Psychology Quarterly, 59*(1), 80-95.

Ellison, C. G. (1992). Are religious people nice? Evidence from a national survey of Black Americans. *Social Forces, 71*(2), 411-430.

Ellison, C. G. (1993). Religious involvement and self-perception among Black Americans. *Social Forces, 71*(4), 1027-1055.

Ellman, B., & Taggart, M. (1993). Changing gender norms. In F. Walsh (Ed.), *Normal family processes* (2nd ed., pp. 377-404). New York: Guilford.

Ellor, J. W., Netting, F. E., & Thibault, J. M. (1999). *Understanding religious and spiritual aspects of human service practice*. Columbia, SC: University of South Carolina Press.

Elman, C., & O'Rand, C. (1998). Midlife work pathways and educational entry. *Research on Aging, 20*(4), 475-505.

Emde, R., Biringen, Z., Clyman, R., & Oppenheim, D. (1991). The moral self of infancy: Affective core and procedural knowledge. *Developmental Review, 11*, 51-270.

Epps, S., & Jackson, B. J. (2000). *Empowered families, successful children: Early intervention programs that work*. Washington, DC: American Psychological Association.

Epstein, J. L., & Lee, S. (1995). National patterns of school and family connections in the middle grades. In B. A. Ryan, G. R. Adams, T. P. Gullotta, R. P. Weissberg, & R. L. Hampton (Eds.), *The family-school connection: Theory, research, and practice* (pp. 108-154). Thousand Oaks, CA: Sage.

Epstein, N., Bishop, D., Ruan, C., Miller, I., & Keitner, G. (1993). The McMaster model: View of healthy functioning. In F. Walsh (Ed.), *Normal family processes* (pp. 138-160). New York: Guilford.

Epstein, S. (1973). The self-concept revisited: Or, a theory of a theory. *American Psychologist, 28*, 404-416.

Epstein, S. (1991). Cognitive-experiential self-theory: An integrative theory of personality. In R. Cutis (Ed.), *The self with others: Convergences in psychoanalytic, social, and personality psychology* (pp. 111-137). New York: Guilford.

Epstein, S., Lipson, A., Holstein, C., & Huh, E. (1993). Irrational reactions to negative outcomes: Evidence for two conceptual systems. *Journal of Personality and Social Psychology, 62*, 328-339.

Erikson, E. H. (1950). *Childhood and society*. New York: Norton.

Erikson, E. H. (1959b). The problem of ego identity. *Psychological Issues, 1*, 101-164.

Erikson, E. H. (1963). *Childhood and society* (2nd ed.). New York: Norton.

Erikson, E. H. (1968). *Identity: Youth and crisis*. New York: Norton.

Erikson, E. H. (Ed.). (1978). *Adulthood*. New York: Norton.

Erikson, E. H. (1982). *The life cycle completed*. New York: Norton.

Erikson, R. (1993). Abortion trauma: Application of a conflict model. *Pre- and Peri-natal Psychology Journal, 8*(1), 33-42.

Escobar, J., Hoyos-Nervi, C., & Gara, M. (2000). Immigration and mental health: Mexican Americans in the United States. *Harvard Review of Psychology, 8*(2), 64-72.

Fabelo-Alcover, H. (2001). *Black beans and chopsticks: A refugee Latino social worker collaborates with Vietnamese survivors of reeducation camps*. Unpublished manuscript, Virginia Commonwealth University.

Fabes, R., Eisenberg, N., Nyman, M., & Michealieu, Q. (1991). Young children's appraisals of others' spontaneous emotional reactions. *Developmental Psychology, 27*, 858-866.

Fahy, T. (1991). Fasting disorders in pregnancy. *Psychological Medicine, 21*, 577-580.

Falicov, C. (1999). The Latino family life cycle. In B. Carter & M. McGoldrick (Eds.), *The expanded family life cycle: Individual, family, and social perspectives* (3rd ed., pp. 141-152). Boston: Allyn & Bacon.

Fass, P., & Mason, M. (Eds.). (2000a). *Childhood in America*. New York: New York University Press.

Fass, P. S., & Mason, M. A. (2000b). Childhood in America: Past and present. In P. S. Fass & M. A. Mason (Eds.), *Childhood in America* (pp. 1-7). New York: New York University Press.

Federal Interagency Forum on Aging-Related Statistics. (2000a). *Older Americans 2000: Key indicators of well-being* (Health status indicator 12-life expectancy). Washington, DC: U.S. Government Printing Office.

Federal Interagency Forum on Aging-Related Statistics. (2000b). *Older Americans 2000: Key indicators of well-being* (Population indicator 3-marital status). Washington, DC: U.S. Government Printing Office.

Federal Interagency Forum on Aging-Related Statistics. (2000c). *Older Americans 2000: Key indicators of well-being* (Population indicator 5-living arrangements). Washington, DC: U.S. Government Printing Office.

Feijoo, A. (2001). Adolescent pregnancy, birth, and abortion rates in Western Europe far outshine U.S. rates. *Transitions, 14*(2), 4-5.

Fergusson, D. M., Horwood, L. J., & Woodward, L. J. (2001). Unemployment and psychosocial adjustment in young adults: Causation or selection? *Social Science & Medicine, 53*(3), 305.

Fertility Plus. (n.d.). *Frequently asked questions about intrauterine insemination (IUI)*. Retrieved November 6, 2002, from www.fertilityplus.org/faq/iui.html.

Field, D., & Gueldner, S. H. (2001). The oldest-old: How do they differ from the old-old? *Journal of Gerontological Nursing, 27*(8), 20-27.

Field, T., Woodson, R., Greenberg, R., & Cohen, C. (1982). Discrimination and imitation of facial expressions by neonates. *Science, 218*, 179-181.

Figueira-McDonough, J. (1990). Abortion: Ambiguous criteria and confusing policies. *Affilia, 5*(4), 27-54.

Finch, C. (2001). Toward a biology of middle age. In M. Lachman (Ed.), *Handbook of midlife development* (pp. 77-108). New York: Wiley.

Finn, J. D. (1989). Withdrawing from school. *Review of Educational Research, 59*, 117-142.

Fischer, C., & Phillips, S. (1982). Who is alone? Social characteristics of people with small networks. In L. A. Peplau & D. Perlman (Eds.), *Loneliness: A sourcebook of current theory, research and therapy* (pp. 21-39). New York: Wiley Interscience.

Fischer, K. (1993). Aging. In M. Downey (Ed.), *The new dictionary of Catholic spirituality* (pp. 31-33). Collegeville, MN: Liturgical Press.

Fitzpatrick, K. M., & Boldizar, J. P. (1993). The prevalence and consequences of exposure to violence among African American youth. *Journal of the American Academy of Child and Adolescent Psychiatry, 56*, 22-34.

Flanagan, C. A. (1990). Change in family work status: Effects on parent-adolescent decision making. *Child Development, 61*, 163-177.

Fleming, A. R. (2000). Welcoming the stork later in life. *Insight on the News, 16*(46), 32.

Fletcher, A. B. (1994). Nutrition. In G. B. Avery, M. A. Fletcher, & M. G. MacDonald (Eds.), *Neonatology: Pathophysiology and management of the newborn* (4th ed., pp. 330-350). Philadelphia, PA: Lippincott.

Flint, M. (1975). The menopause: Reward or punishment? *Psychosomatics, 15*, 161-163.

Flint, M. M., & Perez-Porter, M. (1997). Grandparent caregivers: Legal and economic issues. *Journal of Gerontological Social Work, 28*(1/2), 63-76.

Foner, A. (1995). Social stratification. In G. L. Maddox (Ed.), *The encyclopedia of aging: A comprehensive resource in gerontology and geriatrics* (2nd ed., pp. 887-890). New York: Springer.

Foner, A. (1996). Age norms and the structure of consciousness: Some final comments. *The Gerontologist, 36*(2), 221-223.

Forrest, G. (1993). Preterm labour and delivery: Psychological sequelae. *Bailliere's Clinical Obstetrics and Gynaecology, 7*, 653-669.

Forste, R., Weiss, J., & Lippincott, E. (2001). The decision to breastfeed in the United States: Does race matter? *Pediatrics, 108*(12), 291-296.

Forum on Child and Family Statistics (2000). *America's children 2000: Highlights*. Retrieved March 1, 2002, from www.childstats.gov/ac2000/highlight.asp.

Fost, N. (1981). Counseling families who have a child with severe congenital anomaly. *Pediatrics, 67,* 321-323.

Fowler, J. (1981). *Stages of faith: The psychology of human development and the quest for meaning*. San Francisco: Harper.

Fozard, J. L. (1990). Vision and hearing in aging. In J. E. Birren & K. W. Schaie (Eds.), *Handbook of the psychology of aging* (3rd ed., pp. 150-170). San Diego, CA: Academic Press.

Fracasso, M., Busch-Rossnagel, N., & Fisher, C. (1994). The relationship of maternal behavior and acculturation to the quality of attachment in Hispanic infants living in New York City. *Hispanic Journal of Behavioral Sciences, 16,* 143-154.

Frank, M., Bell, S., Nowik, R., & Faber, M. (1989). Caring for day care: A pilot project. *Child Welfare, 68*(1), 69-78.

Frank, R., Strobino, D., Salkever, D., & Jackson, C. (1992). Updated estimates of the impact of prenatal care on birth weight outcomes by race. *Journal of Human Resources, 27,* 629-642.

Frankel, A. (1991). Social work and day care: A role looking for a profession. *Child and Adolescent Social Work Journal, 8*(1), 53-67.

Franklin, C., & Corcoran, J. (2000). Preventing adolescent pregnancy: A review of programs and practices. *Social Work, 45*(1), 40-48.

Fraser, M. (Ed.). (1997). *Risk and resilience in childhood: An ecological perspective*. Washington, DC: NASW Press.

Fraser, M. W., & Galinsky, M. J. (1997). Toward a resilience-based model of practice. In M. W. Fraser (Ed.), *Risk and resilience in childhood: An ecological perspective* (pp. 265-275). Washington, DC: NASW Press.

Frederick, I. B., & Auerbach, K. G. (1985). Maternal-infant separation and breastfeeding: The return to work or school. *Journal of Reproductive Medicine, 30,* 523-526.

Freeman, E., & Dyer, L. (1993). High risk children and adolescents: Family and community environments. *Families in Society, 74,* 422-431.

Freeman, L., Shaffer, D., & Smith, H. (1996). Neglected victims of homicide: The needs of young siblings of murder victims. *American Journal of Orthopsychiatry, 66,* 337-345.

Freud, S. (1905/1953). Three essays on the theory of sexuality. In J. Strachey (Ed. and Trans.), *The standard edition of the complete works of Sigmund Freud* (Vol. 7, pp. 135-245). London: Hogarth.

Freud, S. (1917/1957). Mourning and melancholia. In J. Strachey (Ed. and Trans.). *The standard edition of the complete psychological works of Sigmund Freud* (Vol. 14, pp. 237-258). London: Hogarth.

Freud, S. (1927). Some psychological consequences of the anatomical distinction between the sexes. *International Journal of Psycho-Analysis, 8,* 133-142.

Freud, S. (1938/1973). *An outline of psychoanalysis.* London: Hogarth Press.

Frey, A. (1989). Treating children of violent families: A sibling group approach. *Social Work With Groups, 12*(1), 95-107.

Fried, S. B., & Mehrotra, C. M. (1998). *Aging and diversity: An active learning experience*. Washington, DC: Taylor and Francis.

Friedman, H. L. (1992). Changing patterns of adolescent sexual behavior: Consequences for health and development. *Journal of Adolescent Health, 13,* 345-350.

Friedmann, E., & Havighurst, R. (1954). *The meaning of work and retirement*. Chicago: University of Chicago Press.

Frodi, A. (1981). Contribution of infant characteristics to child abuse. *American Journal of Mental Deficiency, 85*(4), 341-349.

Fry, D. (1995). Kinship and individuation: Cross-cultural perspectives on intergenerational relations. In V. Bengtson, K. Schaie, & L. Burton (Eds.), *Adult intergenerational relations: Effects of social change* (pp. 126-156). New York: Springer.

Fu, H., Darroch, J., Haas, T., & Ranjit, N. (1999). Contraceptive failure rates: New estimates from the 1995 National Survey of Family Growth. *Family Planning Perspectives, 31*(2), 52-58.

Fuligni, A. (1997). The academic achievement of adolescents from immigrant families: The roles of family background, attitudes, and behavior. *Child Development, 68*(2), 351-363.

Fuligni, A., & Stevenson, H. (1995). Time use and mathematics achievement among American, Chinese and Japanese high school students. *Child Development, 66*(3), 830-842.

Fuligni, A., Eccles, J., & Barber, B. (1995). The long-term effects of seventh-grade ability grouping in mathematics. *Journal of Early Adolescence, 15*(1), 58-59.

Furstenberg, F. (1994). Good dads-bad dads: Two faces of fatherhood. In A. S. Skolnick & J. H. Skolnick (Eds.),

Family in transition (8th ed., pp. 348-368). New York: Harper Collins.

Furstenberg, F., Jr., Cook, T., Eccles, J., Elder, G., Jr., & Sameroff, A. (1999). *Managing to make it: Urban families and adolescent success.* Chicago: University of Chicago Press.

Furstenberg, F. F., Moore, K. A., & Peterson, J. L. (1986). Sex education and sexual experience among adolescents. *American Journal of Public Health, 75,* 1221-1222.

Gabel, K., & Johnston, D. (Eds.) (1995). *Children of incarcerated parents.* New York: Lexington Books.

Galambos, N. L., & Almeida, D. M. (1992). Does parent-adolescent conflict increase in early adolescence? *Journal of Marriage and the Family, 54,* 737-747.

Gallagher, J. J. (1993). The future of professional/family relations in families with children with disabilities. In J. L. Paul & R. J. Simeonsson (Eds.), *Children with special needs: Family, culture, and society* (2nd ed., pp. 295-310). Fort Worth, TX: Harcourt Brace Jovanovich.

Gallagher, W. (1993, May). Midlife myths. *Atlantic Monthly,* 551-568.

Gallup, G., Jr., & Lindsay, D. M. (1999). *Surveying the religious landscape: Trends in U.S. beliefs.* Harrisburg, PA: Morehouse.

Gamoran, A., & Himmelfarb, H. (1994). *The quality of vocational education.* Washington, DC: U.S. Department of Education.

Gandelman, R. (1992). *Psychobiology of behavioral development.* New York: Oxford University Press.

Garbarino, J. (1992). The meaning of poverty to children. *American Behavioral Scientist, 35,* 220-237.

Garbarino, J. (1995). *Raising children in a socially toxic environment.* San Francisco: Jossey-Bass.

Garbarino, J. (1999). *Lost boys: Why our sons turn violent and how we can save them.* New York: Free Press.

Gardner, H. E. (1993). *Multiple intelligences: The theory in practice.* New York: Basic Books.

Garmezy, N. (1993). Vulnerability and resilience. In D. C. Funder, R. D. Parke, C. Tomlinson-Keasey, & K. Widaman (Eds.), *Studying lives through time* (pp. 377-398). Washington, DC: American Psychological Association.

Garmezy, N. (1994). Reflections and commentary on risk, resilience, and development. In R. J. Haggerty, L. R. Sherrod, N. Garmezy, & M. Rutter (Eds), *Stress, risk, and resilience in children and adolescents: Processes, mechanisms, and interventions* (pp. 1-18). New York: Cambridge University Press.

Garrett, M. W. (1995). Between two worlds: Cultural discontinuity in the dropout of Native American youth. *The School Counselor, 10,* 199-208.

Garton, A. F., & Pratt, C. (1987). Participation and interest in leisure activities by adolescent schoolchildren. *Journal of Adolescence, 10,* 341-351.

Garton, A. F., & Pratt, C. (1991). Leisure activities of adolescent school students: Predictors of participation and interest. *Journal of Adolescence, 14,* 305-321.

Gartrell, N., Hamilton, J., Banks, A., Mosbacher, D., Reed, N., Sparks, C., & Bishop, H. (1996). The national lesbian family study: 1. Interviews with prospective mothers. *American Journal of Orthopsychiatry, 66,* 272-281.

Garver, K. L. (1995). Genetic counseling. In G. B. Reed, A. E. Claireaux, & F. Cockburn (Eds.), *Diseases of the fetus and newborn* (2nd ed., pp. 1007-1012). London: Chapman & Hall.

Garvey, C. (1984). *Children's talk.* Cambridge, MA: Harvard University Press.

Garvin, V., Kalter, N., & Hansell, J. (1993). Divorced women: Factors contributing to resiliency and vulnerability. *Journal of Divorce and Remarriage, 21*(1/2), 21-39.

Ge, X., Conger, R. D., & Elder, G. H., Jr. (1996). Coming of age too early: Pubertal influences on girls' vulnerability to psychological distress. *Child Development, 67,* 3386-3401.

Gee, J. P. (1996). *Social linguistics and literacies: Ideology in discourses* (2nd ed.). London: Falmer.

Gelles, R. (1989). Child abuse and violence in single-parent families: Parent absence and economic deprivation. *American Journal of Orthopsychiatry, 59,* 492-501.

Gelles, R., & Hargreaves, E. (1981). Maternal employment and violence toward children. *Journal of Family Issues, 2,* 509-530.

Gendell, M., & Siegal, J. (1992). Trends in retirement age by sex, 1950-2005. *Monthly Labor Review, 115*(7), 22-29.

Generations (2002, Summer) *25*(2).

Gennetian, L., Duncan, G., Knox, V., Vargas, W., Clark-Kauffman, E., & London, A. (2002). *How welfare and work policies for parents affect adolescents: A synthesis of research.* New York: Manpower Demonstration Research Corporation.

Gent, P. J., & Mulhauser, M. B. (1993). Public integration of students with handicaps: Where it's been, where it's going, and how it's getting there. In M. Nagler (Ed.),

Perspectives on disability (2nd ed., pp. 397-409). Palo Alto, CA: Health Markets Research.

George, L. (1993). Sociological perspectives on life transitions. *Annual Review of Sociology, 19,* 353-373.

George, L. (1996). Missing links: The case for a social psychology of the life course. *The Gerontologist, 36*(2), 248-255.

George, L., & Gold, D. (1991). Life course perspectives on intergenerational and generational connections. *Marriage & Family Review, 16*(1-2), 67-88.

Gerstel, N., & Gallagher, S. (1993). Kinkeeping and distress: Gender, recipients of care, and work-family conflict. *Journal of Marriage and the Family, 55,* 598-607.

Gibbs, J. T., & Huang, L. N. (1989). A conceptual framework for assessing and treating minority youth. In J. T. Gibbs & L. N. Huang (Eds.), *Children of color: Psychological interventions with minority youth* (pp 1-29). San Francisco: Jossey-Bass.

Gilligan, C. (1982). *In a different voice: Psychological theory and women's development.* Cambridge, MA: Harvard University Press.

Gilligan, C. (1992). *Meeting at the crossroads: Women's psychology and girls' development.* Cambridge, MA: Harvard University Press.

Glass, P. (1994). The vulnerable neonate and the neonatal intensive care environment. In G. B. Avery, M. A. Fletcher, & M. MacDonald (Eds.), *Neonatology: Pathophysiology and the management of the newborn* (4th ed., pp. 77-94). Philadelphia, PA: Lippincott.

Glover, R. (1996). Religiosity in adolescence and young adulthood: Implications for identity formation. *Psychological Reports, 78,* 427-431.

Goldenberg, R. L., & Jobe, A. H. (2001). Prospects for research in reproductive health and birth outcomes. *Journal of the American Medical Association, 285*(5), 633-642.

Goldenberg, R. L., Hauth, J. C., & Andrews, W. W. (2000). Intrauterine infection and premature delivery. *New England Journal of Medicine, 342*(20), 1500-1508.

Goldfarb, J., Mumford D., Schum, D., Smith, P., Flowers, C., & Schum, C. (1977). An attempt to detect "pregnancy susceptibility" in indigent adolescent girls. *Journal of Adolescence, 6,* 127-144.

Goldscheider, F. (1997). Recent changes in U.S. young adult living arrangements in comparative perspective. *Journal of Family Issues, 18,* 708-724.

Goldscheider, F., & Lawton, L. (1998). Family experiences and the erosion of support for intergenerational coresidence. *Journal of Marriage and the Family, 60,* 623-632.

Goldstein, J., & Kenney, C. (2001). Marriage delayed or marriage forgone? New cohort forecasts of first marriage for U.S. women. *American Sociological Review, 66*(4), 506-519.

Goleman, D. (1995). *Emotional intelligence.* New York: Bantam.

Golembiewski, R. (1994). Is organizational membership bad for your health? Phases of burnout as covariants of mental and physical well-being. In A. Farazmand (Ed.), *Modern organizations: Administrative theory in contemporary society* (pp. 211-227). Westport, CT: Praeger.

Gomby, D. S., & Larner, M. B. (1995). Long-term outcomes of early childhood programs. *The Future of Children, 5*(3).

Gomes, J. S., Cimo, S., & Cook, T. (2001). Baby-friendly hospital initiative improves breastfeeding initiation rates in a U.S. hospital setting. *Pediatrics, 108*(3), 677.

Gomez, N. (2001). EEG during different emotions in 10 month old infants of depressed mothers. *Journal of Reproductive and Infant Psychology, 19*(4), 295-313.

Gonyea, J. G. (1987). The family and dependency: Factors associated with institutional decision-making. *Journal of Gerontological Social Work, 10,* 61-77.

Good news for men. (2002). *Discover, 23*(1), 16.

Goodman, C. C. (2001). Advances through second changes: Grandparents raising grandchildren. *Reflections, 7*(2), 2-5.

Googins, B. (1991). *Work/family conflicts: Private lives public responses.* New York: Auburn House.

Gopaul-McNicol, S. (1988). Racial identification and racial preference of Black preschool children in New York and Trinidad. *Journal of Black Psychology, 14*(2), 65-68.

Gottlieb, S. (2000). In vitro fertilization [sic] is preferable to fertility drugs. *British Medical Journal, 321*(7254), 134.

Gottman, J. M. (1994, May/June). Why marriages fail. *Family Therapy Networker,* 41-48.

Gowen, A. (2001, December 6). School is new world for child immigrants. *Washington Post,* p. GZ14.

Graff, H. (1995). *Conflicting paths: Growing up in America.* Cambridge, MA: Harvard University Press.

Grant, R. (2000). The special needs of children in kinship care. *Journal of Gerontological Social Work, 33*(3), 17-33.

Green, M. (1994). *Bright futures: Guidelines for health supervision of infants, children, and adolescents.* Arlington, VA:

National Center for Education in Maternal and Child Health.

Greenberger, E., & Steinberg, L. D. (1986). *When teenagers work: The psychological and social costs of adolescent employment.* New York: Basic Books.

Greene, C. (1991). Clinical considerations: Midlife daughters and their aging parents. *Journal of Gerontological Nursing, 17,* 6-12.

Griffith, S. (1996). *Amending attachment theory: Ambiguities among maternal care, day care peer group experience, general security and altruistic prosocial proclivities in 3, 4 & 5 year old children.* Unpublished doctoral dissertation, Adelphi University, New York.

Grossman, L. K., Larsen-Alexander, J. B., Fitzsimmons, S. M., & Cordero, L. (1989). Breastfeeding among low-income, high risk women. *Clinical Pediatrics, 28,* 38-42.

Groves, B. M. (1997). Growing up in a violent world: The impact of family and community violence on young children and their families. *Topics in Early Childhood Special Education, 17*(1), 74-102.

Gruszinski, R., Brink, J., & Edleson, J. (1988). Support and education groups for children of battered women. *Child Welfare, 67,* 431-444.

Guarnaccia, P., & Lopez, S. (1998). The mental health and adjustment of immigrant and refugee children. *Child and Adolescent Psychiatric Clinic of North America, 7*(3), 537-553.

Guay, L. A., & Ruff, A. J. (2001). HIV and infant feeding: An ongoing challenge. *Journal of the American Medical Association, 286*(19), 2462-2465.

Guillemard, A., & van Gunsteren, H. (1991). Pathways and prospects: A comparative interpretation of the meaning of early exit. In M. Kohli, M. Rein, A. M. Guillemard, & H. van Gunsteren (Eds.), *Time for retirement.* Cambridge, UK: Cambridge University Press.

Gullete, M. (1998). Midlife discourses in the twentieth-century United States: An essay on the sexuality, ideology, and politics of middle-ageism. In R. Shweder (Ed.), *Welcome to middle age (and other cultural fictions)* (pp. 3-44). Chicago: University of Chicago Press.

Guterman, N. B., & Cameron, M. (1997). Assessing the impact of community violence on children and youths. *Social Work, 42,* 495-505.

Gutman, H. (1976). *The Black family in slavery and freedom, 1750-1925.* New York: Pantheon.

Guyer B., Hoyert, D. L., Martin, J. A., Ventura, S. J., MacDorman, M. R., Strobino, D. (1999). Annual summary of vital statistics—1998. *Pediatrics 104*(6), 1229-1246.

Haan, N., Millsap, R., & Hartka, E. (1986). As time goes by: Change and stability in personality over fifty years. *Psychology and Aging, 1,* 220-232.

Hack, M., Breslau, N., & Aram, D. (1992). The effects of very low birthweight and social risk on neurocognitive abilities at school age. *Journal of Developmental and Behavioral Pediatrics, 13,* 412-420.

Hack, M., Taylor, G., Klein, N., & Eiben, R. (1994). Outcome of <750 gram birthweight children at school age. *New England Journal of Medicine, 331,* 753-759.

Hagestad, G. (1991). Trends and dilemmas in life course research: An international perspective. In W. Heinz (Ed.), *Theoretical advances in life course research* (pp. 23-57). Weinheim, Germany: Deutscher Studien Verlag.

Hakuta, K., Ferdman, B. M., & Diaz, R. M. (1987). Bilingualism and cognitive development: Three perspectives. In S. Rosenberg (Ed.), *Advances in applied psycholinguistics: Vol. 2. Reading, writing, and language learning* (pp. 284-319). New York: Cambridge University Press.

Hall, G. (1904). *Adolescence: Its psychology and its relations to physiology, anthropology, sociology, sex, crime, religion, and education.* New York: Appleton.

Halpern, A. (1996). Transition: A look at foundations. *Exceptional Children, 51,* 479-486.

Halpern, R. (1990). Poverty and early childhood parenting: Toward a framework for intervention. *American Journal of Orthopsychiatry, 6,* 6-18.

Halpern, R. (1992). Challenges in evaluating community-based health and social intervention: The case of prenatal care outreach. *Journal of Social Service Research, 16*(3/4), 117-131.

Halpern, R. (1993). Neighborhood based initiative to address poverty: Lessons from experience. *Journal of Sociology and Social Welfare, 20*(4), 111-135.

Hamblen, J. (2002). Terrorism and children. National Center for Post-Traumatic Stress Disorder. Retrieved January 23, 2002, from www.ncptsd.org/facts/disasters/fs_children_disaster.html.

Hammer, T., & Vaglum, P. (1990). Use of alcohol and drugs in the transitional phase from adolescence to young adulthood. *Journal of Adolescence, 13,* 129-142.

Han, S., & Moen, P. (1999). Clocking out: Temporal patterning of retirement. *American Journal of Sociology, 105*, 191-236.

Hanley, R. J., Alecxih, L. M., Wiener, J. M., & Kennell, D. L. (1990). Predicting elderly nursing home admissions: Results from the 1982-1984 National Long-Term Care Survey. *Research on Aging, 12*, 199-227.

Hareven, T. (Ed.). (1978). *Transitions: The family and the life course in historical perspective*. New York: Academic Press.

Hareven, T. (1982a). American families in transition: Historical perspectives on change. In F. Walsh (Ed.), *Normal family processes* (pp. 446-466). New York: Guilford.

Hareven, T. (1982b). *Family time and industrial time: The relationship between the family and work in a New England industrial community*. New York: Cambridge University Press.

Hareven, T. (Ed.). (1996). *Aging and generation relations over the life course: A historical and cross-cultural perspective*. New York: Walter de Gruyter.

Hareven, T. (2000). *Families, history, and social change*. Boulder, CO: Westview.

Harkness, S. (1990). A cultural model for the acquisition of language: Implications for the innateness debate. *Developmental Psychobiology, 23*, 727-739.

Harrell, S. P. (2000). A multidimensional conceptualization of racism-related stress: Implications for the well-being of people of color. *American Journal of Orthopsychiatry*, 70(1), 42-57.

Harrigan, M. P., & Farmer, R. L. (2000). The myths and facts of aging. In R. L. Schneider, N. P. Kropf, & A. J. Kisor (Eds.), *Gerontological social work: Knowledge, service settings, and special populations* (2nd dd., pp. 26-64). Belmont, CA: Wadsworth.

Hart, D. A. (1992). *Becoming men: The development of aspirations, values, & adaptational styles*. New York: Plenum.

Hart, H., McAdams, D., Hirsch, B., & Bauer, J. (2001). Generativity and social involvements among African-American and among Euro-American adults. *Journal of Research in Personality, 3*(2), 208-230.

Harter, S. (1988). Developmental processes in the construction of self. In T. D. Yawkey & J. E. Johnson (Eds.), *Integrative processes and socialization: Early to middle childhood* (pp. 45-78). Hillsdale, NJ: Lawrence Erlbaum.

Hartup, W. W. (1983). Peer relations. In E. M. Hetherington (Ed.), *Handbook of child psychology: Vol. 4. Socialization, personality, and social development* (4th ed., pp. 103-196). New York: Wiley.

Harvey, S. M., Carr, C., & Bernheime, S. (1989). Lesbian mothers' health care experiences. *Journal of Nurse-Midwives, 34*(3), 115-119.

Harvey, S. M., Beckman, L. J., Sherman, C., & Petitti, D. (1999). Women's experience and satisfaction with emergency contraception. *Family Planning Perspectives, 31*, 237-240, 260.

Harwood, R. (1992). The influence of culturally derived values on Anglo and Puerto Rican mothers' perceptions of attachment behavior. *Child Development, 63*, 822-839.

Hatchett, S., & Jackson, J. (1993). African American extended kin systems: An assessment. In H. McAdoo (Ed.), *Family ethnicity: Strength in diversity* (pp. 90-108). Newbury Park, CA: Sage.

Hatecher, R. A., Trussel, J., Stewart, F., Stewart, G. K., Kowal, D., Guest, F., Cates, W., & Policar, M. S. (1994). *Contraception technology* (16th ed.). New York: Irvington.

Havighurst, R. J. (1968). Personality and patterns of aging. *The Gerontologist, 8*, 20-23.

Havighurst, R. J. (1972). *Developmental tasks and education* (3rd ed.). New York: David McKay.

Havighurst, R., Neugarten, B., & Tobin, S. (1968). Personality and patterns of aging. In B. L. Neugarten (Ed.), *Middle age and aging* (pp. 173-177). Chicago: University of Chicago Press.

Hayes, C., Palmer, J., & Zaslow, M. (Eds.). (1990). *Who cares for America's children? Child care policy for the 1990s*. Washington, DC: National Academy Press.

Hawley, D. R., & DeHaan, L. (1996). Toward a definition of family resilience: Integrating life-span and family perspectives. *Family Process, 35*, 283-298.

Hayflick, L. (1994). *How and why we age*. New York: Ballantine Books.

Hayward, C., Killen, J. D., Wilson, D. M., Hammer, L. D., Litt, I. F., Kraemer, H. C., Haydel, F., Varady, A., & Taylor, C. B. (1997). Psychiatric risk associated with early puberty in adolescent girls. *Journal of the American Academy of Child and Adolescent Psychiatry, 36*, 255-263.

Healthtouch. (1997). [On-line] Available at www.healthtouch.com.

Healthy People 2010 (2000). Retrieved April 6, 2002, from www.health.gov/healthypeople/default.htm.

Heck, K. E., Schoendorf, K. C., & Chavez, G. F. (2002). The influence of proximity of prenatal services on small-for-gestational age birth. *Journal of Community Health, 27*(1), 15-27.

Heckhausen, J. (2001). Adaptation and resilience in midlife. In M. Lachman (Ed.), *Handbook of midlife development* (pp. 345-394). New York: Wiley.

Helburn, S. W., & Howes, C. (1996). Child care cost and quality. *The Future of Children: Financing Child Care, 6*(2), 62-82.

Helson, R., & Wink, P. (1992). Personality change in women from the early 40s to the early 50s. *Psychology and Aging, 7*, 46-55.

Hemenway, D., Solnick, S., & Carter, J. (1994). Child-rearing violence. *Child Abuse and Neglect, 18*, 1011-1020.

Henderson, K., Goldsmith, R., & Flynn, L. (1995). Demographic characteristics of subjective age. *Journal of Social Psychology, 135*(4), 447-457.

Hendricks, J. (1987). Exchange theory in aging. In G. L. Maddox (Ed.), *The encyclopedia of aging* (pp. 238-239). New York: Springer.

Herbst, L. J., Lynn, J., Mermann, A. C., & Rhymes, J. (1995, February 28). What do dying patients want and need? *Patient Care*, 27-39.

Herdt, G., & Boxer, A. (1996). *Children of horizons: How gay and lesbian teens are leading a new way out of the closet.* Boston, MA: Beacon Press.

Hernandez, M., & McGoldrick, M. (1999). Migration and the family life cycle. In B. Carter & M. McGoldrick (Eds.), *The expanded family life cycle: Individual, family, and social perspectives* (3rd ed., pp. 169-184). Boston: Allyn & Bacon.

Herring, R. D. (1995). Developing biracial ethnic identity: A review of the increasing dilemma. *Journal of Multicultural Counseling and Development, 23*(1), 29-38.

Hess, J. P. (1991). Health promotion and risk reduction for later life. In R. F. Young & E. A. Olson (Eds.), *Health, illness, and disability in later life: Practice issues and interventions* (pp. 25-44). Newbury Park, CA: Sage.

Hetherington, E. M., & Clingempeel, W. G. (1992). Coping with marital transitions: A family systems perspective. *Monographs of the Society for Research in Child Development, 57* (2-3, Serial No. 227).

Hetherington, E. M., & Jodl, K. M. (1994). Stepfamilies as settings for child development. In A. Booth & J. Dunn (Eds), *Stepfamilies: Who benefits? Who does not?* (pp. 55-79). Hillsdale, NJ: Lawrence Erlbaum.

Higgins, S. (2002). Smoking in pregnancy. *Current Opinions in Obstetrics and Gynecology, 14*(2), 145-151.

Hill, R. B. (1972). *The strengths of black families.* New York: National Urban League.

Himelein, M. (1995). Risk factors for sexual victimization in dating: A longitudinal study of college women. *Psychology of Women Quarterly, 19*(1), 31-48.

Himes, C. (2001). Social demography of contemporary families and aging. In A. Walker, M. Manoogian-O'Dell, L. McGraw, & D. L. White (Eds.), *Families in later life: Connections and transitions* (pp. 47-50). Thousand Oaks, CA: Pine Forge Press.

Hines, P. M. (1999). The family life cycle of African American families living in poverty. In B. Carter & M. McGoldrick (Eds.). *The expanded family life cycle: Individual, family and social perspectives* (3rd ed., pp. 327-345).

Hines, P., Preto, N., McGoldrick, M., Almeida, R., & Weltman, S. (1999). Culture and the family life cycle. In B. Carter & M. McGoldrick (Eds.), *The expanded family life cycle: Individual, family, and social perspectives* (3rd ed., pp. 69-87). Boston: Allyn & Bacon.

Hinshaw, S. P. (1994). *Attention deficits and hyperactivity in children.* Thousand Oaks, CA: Sage.

Hirshman, C., & Butler, M. (1981). Trends and differentials in breast feeding: An update. *Demography, 18*, 39-54.

Hlatky, M., Boothrody, D., Vittinghoff, E., Sharp, P., & Whooley, M. (2002). Quality-of-life and depressive symptoms in postmenopausal women after receiving hormone therapy: Results from heart and estrogen/progestin replacement study (HERS) trial. *JAMA, The Journal of the American Medical Association, 287*(5), 591-597.

Hobbs, F., & Damon, B. (1997, April 25). *Sixty-five plus in the United States: Statistical brief.* U.S. Census Bureau. Retrieved from www.census.gov/socdemo/www/agebrief.

Hodge, D. R. (2001). Spiritual assessment: A review of major qualitative methods and a new framework for assessing spirituality. *Social Work, 46*(3), 203-214.

Hodges, W., Tierney, C., & Buchsbaum, H. (1984). The cumulative effect of stress on preschool children of divorced and intact families. *Journal of Marriage and the Family, 46*(3), 611-617.

Hodgkinson, H. L. (1990). *The demographics of American Indians: One percent of the people; fifty percent of the diversity.* Washington, DC: Institute for Educational Leadership.

Hofferth, S. (1996). Child care in the United States today. *The Future of Children: Financing Child Care, 6*(2), 41-61.

Hofferth, S. L., & Hayes, C. D. (Eds.). (1987). *Risking the future: Adolescent sexuality, pregnancy, and childbearing: 2. Working papers and statistical reports.* Washington, DC: National Academy Press.

Hogan, D. (1978). The variable order of events in the life course. *American Sociological Review, 43,* 573-586.

Hogan, D. (1981). *Transitions and social change: The early lives of American men.* New York: Academic Press.

Hogan, D. P., & Msall, M. E. (2002). Family structure and resources and the parenting of children with disabilities and functional limitations. In J. G. Borkowski, S. Landesman Ramey, & M. Bristol-Power (Eds.), *Parenting and the child's world.* (pp. 311-344). Mahwah, NJ: Lawrence Erlbaum.

Hoge, D., Johnson, B., & Luidens, D. (1993). Determinants of church involvement of young adults who grew up in Presbyterian churches. *Journal for the Scientific Study of Religion, 32*(3), 242-255.

Hogoel, L., Van-Raalte, R., Kalekin-Fishman, D., & Shlfroni, G. (1995). Psychosocial and medical factors in pregnancy outcome: A case study of Israeli women. *Social Science and Medicine, 40,* 567-571.

Hogstel, M. (2001). *Gerontology: Nursing care of the older adult.* Albany, NY: Delma-Thompson Learning.

Holden, G., Nelson, P., Velasquez, J., & Ritchie, K. (1993). Cognitive, psychosocial, and reported sexual behavior differences between pregnant and nonpregnant adolescents. *Adolescence, 28,* 557-572.

Hollander, D. (2001). Women exposed to DES in utero have elevated levels of fertility impairment and adverse pregnancy. *Family Planning Perspectives, 33*(1), 43.

Holmes, M. M., Resnick, H. S., Kilpatrick, D. G., & Best, C. L. (1996). Rape-related pregnancy: Estimates and descriptive characteristics from a national sample of women. *American Journal of Obstretics and Gynecology, 175,* 320-324.

Holmes, T. (1978). Life situations, emotions, and disease. *Psychosomatic Medicine, 19,* 747-754.

Holmes, T., & Rahe, R. (1967). The social readjustment rating scale. *Journal of Psychosomatic Research, 11,* 213-218.

Homans, G. C. (1961). *Social behavior: Its elementary forms.* New York: Harcourt Brace Jovanovich.

Homer, L. (2001). Home Birth: Alternative medicine in obstetrics. *Clinical Obstetrics and Gynecology, 44*(4), 671-680.

Hooyman, N. R., & Kiyak, H. A. (1988). *Social gerontology: A multidisciplinary perspective.* Boston: Allyn & Bacon.

Hooyman, N., & Kiyak, H. A. (1996). *Social gerontology: A multidisciplinary perspective* (4th ed.). Boston: Allyn & Bacon.

Hopper, R., & Naremore, R. (1978). *Children's speech: A practical introduction to communication development.* New York: Harper & Row.

Horn, J. L. (1982). The theory of fluid and crystallized intelligence in relation to concepts of cognitive psychology and aging in adulthood. In F. I. M. Craik & S. Trehub (Eds.), *Aging and cognitive processes* (237-278). New York: Plenum.

Hosmer, L. (2001). Home birth, alternative medicine, and obstetrics. *Clinical Obstetrics and Gynecology, 44*(4), 671-680.

Hotaling, G. T., Finkelhor, D., Kirkpatrick, J. T., & Strauss, M. A. (Eds). (1988). *Family abuse and its consequences: New directions in research.* Newbury Park, CA: Sage.

Household pesticides could affect fertility. (2000). *Organic Gardening, 47*(3), 16.

Howie, P. W., Forsyth, J. S., Ogston, S. A., Clark, A., & Florey, C. D. (1990). Protective effect of breastfeeding against infection. *British Medical Journal, 300,* 11-16.

Hoybert, D.L., Friedman, M.A., Strobino, D.M., & Guyer, B. (2001). Annual summary of vital statistics: 2000. *Pediatrics, 108*(16), 1241-1346.

Huberman, B. (2001). The lessons learned: A model to improve adolescent sexual health in the United States. *Transitions, 14*(2), 6.

Huff, C. (Ed.). (1996). *Gangs in America* (2nd ed.). Thousand Oaks, CA: Sage.

Hughes, H. (1988). Psychological and behavioral correlates of family violence in child witnesses and victims. *American Journal of Orthopsychiatry, 58,* 77-90.

Human Genome Project. (2002). Human genome project information. Retrieved September 9, 2002 from www.ornl.gov/ hgmis.

Humphreys, A.S., Thompson, N.J., & Miner, K.R. (1998). Intention to breastfeed in low-income pregnant women: The role of social support and previous experience. *Birth, 25,* 169-174.

Huttenlocher, P., & Kabholkar, A. (1997). Regional differences in synaptogenesis in human cerebral cortex. *Journal of Comparative Neurology, 387,* 167-178.

Huyck, M. H. (2001). Romantic relationships in later life. *Generations, 25*(2) 9-17.

Iannotti, R. (1985). Naturalistic and structured assessments of prosocial behavior in preschool children: The influence of empathy and perspective taking. *Developmental Psychology, 21*, 46-55.

Infant mortality and low birth weight among Black and White infants: United States 1980-2000. *Morbidity and Mortality Weekly Report, 51*(27), 589-592. Retrieved November 6, 2002, from www.cdc.gov/mmwr/preview/mmwrhtml/ mm5127al.htm.

Institute for the Study of Aging (2001). *Achieving and maintaining cognitive vitality with aging.* (International Longevity Center Workshop Report). New York: Author.

International Longevity Center-USA. (2002). *Is there an "anti-aging" medicine?* (Workshop Report D17692). New York: Author.

Irish, D., Lundquist, K., & Nelsen, V. (1993). *Ethnic variations in dying, death, and grief: Diversity in universality.* Washington, DC: Taylor & Francis.

Ironson, G. (1992). Work, job stress, and health. In S. Zedeck (Ed.), *Work, families, and organizations* (pp. 33-69). San Francisco: Jossey-Bass.

Is driving a risk factor for male infertility? (2000). *Contemporary Urology, 12*(11), 88. Electronic Collection A7107868.

Isenberg, S. (1992). Aging in Judaism. In T. Cole, D. van Tassel, & R. Kastenbaum (Eds.), *Handbook of the humanities and aging* (pp. 147-174). New York: Springer.

Iso-Ahola, S. E., & Crowley, E. D. (1991). Adolescent substance abuse and leisure boredom. *Journal of Leisure Research, 23*, 260-271.

Jackson, J. (1993). Multiple caregiving among African Americans and infant attachment: The need for an emic approach. *Human Development, 36*, 87-102.

Jang, K., Liveseley, J., Riemann, R., Vernon, P., Hu, S., Angleirner, A., Ando, J., Ono, Y., & Hamer, D. (2001). Covariance structure of neuroticism and agreeableness: A twin and molecular genetic analysis of the role of the serotonin transporter gene. *Journal of Personality and Social Psychology, 81*(2), 295.

Jans, L., & Stoddard, S. (1999). *Chartbook on woman and disability in the United States. AnIinfoUse Report.* Washington, DC: US Department of Education. National Institute on Disability and Rehabilitation Research.

Jarvinen, D. W., & Nicholls, J. G. (1996) Adolescents' social goals, beliefs about the causes of social success, and satisfaction in peer relations. *Developmental Psychology, 32*, 435-442.

Jendrek, M. (1993). Grandparents who parent their grandchildren: Effects on lifestyle. *Journal of Marriage & Family, 55*(3), 609-622.

Jenkins, E., & Bell, C. (1997). Exposure and response to community violence among children and adolescents. In J. Osofosky (Ed.), *Children in a violent society* (pp. 9-31). New York: Guilford.

Jessor, R. (1987). Problem-behavior theory, psychosocial development, and adolescent problem drinking. *British Journal of Addiction, 82*, 331-342.

Joffe, G.M., Symonds, R., Alverson, D., & Chilton, L. (1995). The effect of a comprehensive prematurity prevention program on the number of admissions to the neonatal intensive care. *Journal of Perinatalogy, 15*, 305-309.

Johanson, R., Newburn, M., & Macfarlane, A. (2002). Has the medicalisation of childbirth gone too far? *British Medical Journal, 324*(7342), 892-895.

Johnson, C. L., & Barer, B. M. (1997). *Life beyond 85 years: The aura of survivorship*. New York: Springer Publishing Company, Inc.

Johnson, C., Ironsmith, M., Snow C., & Poteat, M. (2000). Peer acceptance and social adjustment in preschool and kindergarten. *Early Childhood Education Journal, 27*(4) 207-212.

Johnson, M.P. (2002). An exploration of men's experience and role at childbirth. *The Journal of Men's Studies, 10*(12), 165-183.

Johnson, R. S., & Tripp-Reimer, T. (2001). Aging, ethnicity, and social support: A review. *Journal of Gerontological Nursing, 27*(6), 15-21.

Johnson, T., & Colucci, P. (1999). Lesbians, gay men, and the family life cycle. In B. Carter & M. McGoldrick (Eds.), *The expanded family life cycle: Individual, family, and social perspectives* (3rd ed., pp. 346-361). Boston: Allyn & Bacon.

Jones, A. (1992). Self-esteem and identity in psychotherapy with adolescents from upwardly mobile middle-class African American families. In L. Vargas & J. Koss-Chioino (Eds.), *Working with culture: Psychotherapeutic interventions with ethnic minority children and adolescents.* San Francisco: Jossey-Bass Publishers.

Jones, A. (2002, January 11). Immigrants' needs unmet, educators say. *The Atlanta Journal-Constitution.* Retrieved on January 16, 2002: http:// www.accessatlanta.com/ajc/epaper/editions/Friday.

Jones, H.P., Guildea, S.E.S., Stewart, J.H., & Cartlidge, P.H.H. (2002). The health status questionnaire: Achieving concordance of public health and disability criteria. *Archives of Disease in Childhood, 86*(11), 15-16.

Judge, T., Higgins, C., Thoresen, C., & Barrick, M. (1999). The big five personality trits, general mental ability, and career success across the life span. *Personnel Psychology, 52*(3), 621-652.

Julian, T. (1992). Components of men's well-being at mid-life. *Issues in Mental Health Nursing, 13,* 285-299.

Jung, C. (1971). *The portable Jung*. New York: Viking Press.

Kagan, S., & Kagan, M. (1998). *Multiple intelligences: The complete multiple intelligences book*. San Clemente, CA: Kagan Cooperative Learning.

Kahn, R., & Antonucci, T. (1980). Convoys over the life course: Attachment, roles, and social support. In P. Baltes & O. Brim (Eds.), *Life-span development and behavior* (Vol. 3, pp. 253-286). New York: Academic Press.

Kail, R. V., & Cavanaugh, J. C. (1996). *Human development.* Pacific Grove, CA: Brooks/Cole.

Kalil, A., Dunifon, R., & Danziger, S. (2001). When single mothers work—effects on child development. *Poverty Research News, 5*(4).

Kamerman, S. (1996). Child and family policies: An international overview. In E. Zigler, S. Kagan, & N. Hall (Eds.), *Children, families, & government: Preparing for the twenty-first century* (pp. 31-48). New York: Cambridge University Press.

Kamerman, S., & Kahn, A. (1995). Innovations in toddler day care and family support services: An international overview. *Child Welfare, 74*(6), 1281-1300.

Kandel, D. B., & Logan, J. A. (1984). Patterns of drug use from adolescence to young adulthood: Periods of risk for initiation, stabilization and decline in use. *American Journal of Public Health, 74,* 660-666.

Kandel, D. B., & Logan, J. A. (1991). Cocaine use in a national sample of U.S. youth: Ethnic patterns, progression and predictors. *NIDA Monographs, 110,* 151-188.

Kandel, D. B., Davies, M., Karus, D., & Yamaguchi, K. (1986). The consequences in young adulthood of adolescent drug involvement: An overview. *Archives of General Psychiatry*, 43, 746-754.

Kao, R. S., & Lam, M. L. (1997). Asian American elderly. In E. Lee (Ed.), *Working with Asian Americans: A guide for clinicians* (pp. 208-223). New York: Guilford.

Kaplan, D.W., Feinstein, R.A., Fisher, M.M., Klein, J., Olmedo, L.F., Rome, E.S., Yancy, W.S., Adams,-Hillard, P.J., Sacks, P., Pearson, G., Frankowski, B., Hurley, T.P., & American Academy of Pediatrics Committee on Adolescence (2001). Condom use by adolescents. *Pediatrics, 107*(6), 1463-1469.

Kaplan, H., & Sadock, B. (1998). *Synopsis of psychiatry* (8th ed.). Baltimore: Williams & Wilkins.

Kaplan, M.S. & Sasser, J.E. (1996). Women behind bars: Trends and policy issues. *Journal of Sociology and Social Welfare, 23*(4), 43-56.

Kaslow, F., & Robison, J. A. (1996). Long-term satisfying marriages: Perceptions contributing factors. *The American Journal of Family Therapy, 24*(2), 153-170.

Katz, L., Kling, J., & Liebman, J. (1999). *Moving to opportunity in Boston: Early impacts of a housing mobility program.* Working paper. Industrial Relations Section, Princeton University.

Katz, P. (1976). *Toward the elimination of racism.* New York: Pergamon Press.

Kaufman, K. J., & Hall, L. A. (1989). Influences of the social network on choice and duration of breast-feeding in mothers of preterm infants. *Research in Nursing and Health, 12,* 149-159.

Kayne, M., Greulich, M., & Albers, L. (2001). Doulas: An alternative yet complementary addition to care during childbirth. *Clinical Obstetrics and Gynecology, 44*(4), 692-703.

Keating, P. (1994). Striving for sex equity in schools. In K. I. Goodland & P. Keating (Eds.), *Access to knowledge: The continuing agenda for our nation's schools* (pp. 91-106). New York: The College Board.

Keel, P. K., Fulkerson, J. A., & Leon, G. R. (1997). Disordered eating precursors in pre- and early adolescent girls and boys. *Journal of Youth and Adolescence, 26,* 203-216.

Kellaghan, T., Sloane, K., Alvarez, B., & Bloom, B. S. (1993). *The home environment and school learning: Promoting parental involvement in the education of children.* San Francisco: Jossey-Bass.

Kellam, S., & Van Horn, Y. (1997). Life course development, community epidemiology, and preventive trials: A scientific structure for prevention research. *American Journal of Community Psychology, 25*(2), 177-188.

Kemp, C. (1999). *Terminal illness: A guide to nursing care.* New York: Lippincott.

Kempe, C., & Kempe, R. (1976). Assessing family pathology. In R.E. Helfer & C.H. Kempe (eds). *Child abuse and neglect. The family and the community*. Cambridge, MA: Ballinger.

Keniston, K. (1966). *The uncommitted: Alienated youth in American society*. New York: Harcourt, Brace, & World.

Kenney, J. W., Reinholtz, C., & Angelini, P. J. (1997). Ethnic differences in childhood and adolescent sexual abuse and teenage pregnancy. *Journal of Adolescent Health, 21*(1), 3-10.

Kent, G. (2002). Breastfeeding vs formula-feeding among HIV-infected women in resource-poor areas. *Journal of the American Medical Association, 287*(9), 1110-1114.

Kertzer, D. (1989). Age structuring in comparative and historical perspective. In D. Kertzer & K. W. Schaie (Eds.), *Age structuring in comparative perspective* (pp. 3-20). Hillsdale, NJ: Lawrence Erlbaum.

Keye, W. R. (1995). Psychological issues of infertility. In J. J. Sciarra (Ed.), *Gynecology and obstretics* (Vol. 5, pp. 1-14). Philadelphia: Lippincott-Raven.

Keyes, C., & Ryff, C. (1998). Generativity in adult lives: Social structural contours and quality of life consequences. In D. McAdams & E. de St. Aubin (Eds.), *Generativity and adult development: How and why we care for the next generation* (pp. 227-263). Washington, DC: American Psychological Association.

Kim, J., & Moen, P. (2001). Moving into retirement: Preparation and transitions in late midlife. In M. Lachman (Ed.), *Handbook of midlife development* (pp. 487-527). New York: Wiley.

Kimmel, D. (1990). *Adulthood and aging* (3rd ed.). New York: Wiley.

Kimmel, D., & Sang, B. (1995). Lesbians and gay men in midlife. In A.R. D'Augelli & C. Patterson (Eds.), *Lesbian, gay, and bisexual identities over the lifespan: Psychological perspectives* (pp. 190-214). New York: Oxford University Press.

Kindlon, D., & Thompson, M. (1999). *Raising Cain: Protecting the emotional life of boys*. NY: Random House.

King, B.R. (2001). Ranking of stigmatization toward lesbians and their children and the influence of perceptions of controllability of homosexuality. *Journal of Homosexuality, 41*(2), 77-97.

Kingson, E. R., & Berkowitz, E. D. (1993). *Social Security and Medicare: A policy primer.* Westport, CT: Auburn House.

Kirby, L., & Fraser, M. (1997). Risk and resilience in childhood. In M. Fraser (Ed.), *Risk and resilience in childhood* (pp. 10-33). Washington, DC: NASW Press.

Klaczynski, P. (2000). Motivated scientific reasoning biases, epistemological beliefs, and theory polarization: A two-process approach to adolescent cognition. *Child Development, 71*(5).

Klaczynski, P., & Fauth, J. (1997). Developmental differences in memory-based intrusions and self-serving statistical reasoning biases. *Merrill-Palmer Quarterly, 43*, 539-566.

Klaus, M.H., Kennel, J.H., & Klaus, P.H. (1993). *Mothering the mother.* New York: Addison-Wesley.

Klebanov, P., Brooks-Gunn, J., Gordon, R., & Chase-Lansdale, P. (1997). The intersection of the neighborhood and home environment and its influence on young children. In J. Brooks-Gunn, G. Duncanc, & J. Aber (Eds.), *Neighborhood poverty: Context and consequences for children* (pp. 79-118). New York: Russell Sage.

Klein, M. (1995). *The American street gang: Its nature, prevalence, and control.* NY: Oxford University Press.

Klerman, L. (1991). The health of poor children. In A. C. Huston (Ed.), *Children and poverty* (pp. 136-157). New York: Cambridge University Press.

Kliman, J., & Madsen, W. (1999). Social class and the family life cycle. In B. Carter & M. McGoldrick (Eds.), *The expanded family life cycle: Individual, family, and social perspectives* (3rd ed., pp. 88-105). Boston: Allyn & Bacon.

Klotter, J. (2002). Pregnancy and older women. *Townsend Letter for Doctors and Patients,* (Jan 2002), 17-19.

Knapp, M.S. (1995). *Teaching for meaning in high-poverty classrooms.* New York: Teachers College Press.

Koenig, H. G. (1990). Research on religion and mental health in later life: A review and commentary. *Journal of Geriatric Psychiatry, 23*(1), 23-53.

Koeske, G., & Koeske, R. (1990). The buffering effect of social support on parental stress. *American Journal of Orthopsychiatry, 60*(3), 440-451.

Koeske, G., & Koeske, R. (1992). Parenting locus of control: Measurement, construct validation, and a proposed conceptual model. *Social Work Research and Abstracts, 28*(3), 37-45.

Kohlberg, L. (1969). Stage and sequence: The cognitive developmental approach to socialization. In D. A. Goslin (Ed.), *Handbook of socialization theory and research* (pp. 347-480). Chicago: Rand McNally.

Kohlberg, L. (1976). Moral stages and moralization: The cognitive-developmental approach. In T. Lickona (Ed.), *Moral development and behavior: Theory, research, and social issues* (pp. 31-53). New York: Holt.

Kohlberg, L. (1984). *Essays on moral development: Vol. 2. The psychology of moral development.* San Francisco: Harper & Row.

Kohli, M. (1986). The world we forgot: A historical review of the life course. In V. Marshall (Ed.), *Later life* (pp. 271-303). Beverly Hills, CA: Sage.

Kohut, H. (1971). *The analysis of the self.* New York: International Universities Press.

Kopola, M., Esquivel, G., & Baptiste, L. (1994). Counseling approaches for immigrant children: Facilitating the acculturative process. *The School Counselor, 41*, 352-359.

Kopp, C. (1989). Regulation of distress and negative emotions: A developmental view. *Developmental Psychology, 25*, 343-354.

Korbin, J. (Ed.). (1981). *Child abuse and neglect: Cross-cultural perspective.* Berkeley and Los Angeles: University of California Press.

Koshar, J.H. (2001). Teen pregnancy 2001-Still no easy answers. *Pediatric Nursing, 25*(5), 505-512.

Koss, M. P., Gidycz, C. A., & Wisniewski, N. (1987). The scope of rape: Incidence and prevalence of sexual aggression and victimization in a national sample of higher education students. *Journal of Consulting and Clinical Psychology, 55*, 162-170.

Kotch, J., Browne, D., Ringwalt, C., Dufort, V., Ruina, E., Stewart, P., & Jung, J. (1997). Stress, social support, and substantiated maltreatment in the second and third years of life. *Child Abuse and Neglect, 21*(11), 1026-1037.

Kowalski, K. (1996). The emergence of ethnic/racial attitudes in preschool-age children. *Dissertation Abstracts International: Section B: The Sciences & Engineering, 56*(8-B), 4604.

Kozol, J. (1991). *Savage inequalities: Children in America's schools.* New York: HarperPerennial.

Kozol, J. (2000). *Ordinary resurrections: Children in the years of hope.* New York: Crown Publishers.

Kramer, M. (1991). Poverty, WIC & breast feeding. *Pediatrics, 87*(3), 399-400.

Kübler-Ross, E. (1969). *On death and dying.* New York: Macmillan.

Kuh, D., & Ben-Shlomo, Y. (Eds.) (1997). *A life course approach to chronic disease epidemiology.* New York: Oxford University Press.

Kuhl, P. (1987). Perception of speech and sound in early infancy. In P. Salapatek & L. Cohen (Eds.), *Handbook of infant perception* (Vol. 1). Orlando, FL.: Academic Press.

Kurdek, L. A., & Schmitt, J. P. (1987). Perceived emotional support from family and friends in members of homosexual, married, and heterosexual cohabitating couples. *Journal of Homosexuality, 14*(3/4), 57-68.

Kurtz, L. (1995). The relationship between parental coping strategies and children's adaptive processes in divorced and intact families. *Journal of Divorce and Remarriage, 24*(3/4), 89-110.

Kurtz, P. D. (1988). Social work services to parents: Essential to pupils at risk. *Urban Education, 22*, 444-457.

Kurtz, P. D., & Barth, R. P. (1989). Parent involvement: Cornerstone of school social work practice. *Social Work, 34*, 407-413.

Labouvie-Vief, G. (1986). Modes of knowing and the organization of development. In M. L. Commons, L. Kohlberg, F. Richards, & J. Sinnott (Eds.), *Beyond formal operations 3: Models and methods in the study of adult and adolescent thought.* New York: Praeger.

Lachman, M. (2001). Preface. In M. Lachman (Ed.), *Handbook of midlife development.* New York: Wiley.

Lachman, M., & Bertrand, R. (2001). Personality and the self in midlife. In M. Lachman (Ed.), *Handbook of midlife development* (pp. 279-309). New York: Wiley.

LaDue, R A. (2001). Fetal alcohol syndrome. In R. Carson (Ed.), *Encyclopedia of drugs, alcohol and addictive behavior* (Vol. 2. 2nd ed., pp. 533-537). New York: Macmillian.

Laird, J., & Green, R. ((Eds.) (1996). *Lesbian and gays in couples and families: A handbook for therapists.* San Francisco: Jossey-Bass.

Lamaze, F. (1958). *Painless childbirth: Psychoprophylactic method* (L. R. Celestin, Trans.). London: Burke.

Langford, P.E. (1995). *Approaches to the development of moral reasoning.* Hillsdale: Lawrence Erlbaum.

Larson, E. J. (1995). The effects of maternal substance abuse on the placenta and fetus. In G. B. Reed, A. E. Claireaux, & F. Cockburn (Eds.), *Diseases of the fetus and newborn* (2nd ed., pp. 353-361). London : Chapman & Hall.

LaSala, M. C. (2001). The importance of partners to lesbians' intergenerational relationships. *Social Work Research, 25*(1), 27-40.

Laseter, R. (1997). The labor force participation of young black men: A qualitative examination. *Social Service Review*, 71, 72-88.

Lattanzi-Licht, M., Mahoney, J.J., & Miller, G. W. (1998). *The hospice choice: In pursuit of a peaceful death.* New York: Fireside.

Laumann, E., Paik, A., & Rosen, R. (1999). Sexual dysfunction in the United States: Prevalence and predictors. *Journal of the American Medical Association, 279*, 537-544.

Lazear, D. (1994). *Multiple intelligence approach to assessment: Solving the assessment conundrum*. Tucson, AZ: Zephyr Press.

Leblane, E., Janowsky, K., Benjamin, K., & Nelson, H. (2001). Hormone replacement therapy and cognition: Systematic review and meta-analysis. *JAMA, The Journal of the American Medical Association, 285*(11), 1489.

Lee, B., & George, R. (1999). Poverty, early childbearing and child maltreatment: A multinomial analysis. *Children & Youth Services Review, 21*(9-10), 755-780.

Lee, E., Menkart, D., & Okazawa-Rae, M. (1998). *Beyond holidays and heroes: A practical guide to K-12 anti-racist multicultural education and staff development*. Washington, DC: Network of Educators in the Americas.

Leitenberg, H., Detzer, M. J., & Srebnik, D. (1993). Gender differences in masturbation and the relationship of masturbation experience in preadolescence and/or early adolescence and sexual behavior and sexual adjustment in young adulthood. *Archives of Sexual Behavior, 22*, 299-313.

Lerner, R., & Galambos, N. (1998). Adolescent development: Challenges and opportunities for research. *Annual Review of Psychology, 49*, 413-446.

Levine, E., & Sallee, A. (1999). *Child welfare: Clinical theory and practice*. Dubuque, IA: Eddie Bowers Publishing.

Levinson, D. (1977). The mid-life transition. *Psychiatry*, 40, *99-112*.

Levinson, D. (1978). *The seasons of a man's life*. New York: Knopf.

Levinson, D. (1980). Toward a conception of the adult life course. In N. J. Smelser & E. H. Erikson (Eds.), *Themes of work and love in adulthood* (pp. 265-290). Cambridge, MA: Harvard University Press.

Levinson, D. (1986). A conception of adult development. *American Psychologist, 41*(1), 3-13.

Levinson, D. (1990). A theory of life structure development in adulthood. In C. N. Alexander & E. J. Langer (Eds.), *Higher stages of human development* (pp. 35-54). New York: Oxford University Press.

Levinson, D., & Levinson, J. (1996). *The seasons of a woman's life*. New York: Ballantine Books.

Levinson, D., Darrow, C., Klein, E., Levinson, M., & McKee, B. (1978). *The seasons of a man's life*. New York: Knopf.

Levy, G. D., Taylor, M. G., & Gelman, S. A. (1995). Traditional and evaluative aspects of flexibility in gender roles, social conventions, moral rules and physical laws. *Child Development*, *66*, 515-531.

Levy, L., Martinkowski, K., & Derby, J. (1994). Differences in patterns of adaptation in conjugal bereavement: Their sources and potential significance. *Omega, 29*, 71-87.

Lewis, T. (1994). A comparative analysis of the effects of social skills training and teacher directed contingencies on social behavior of preschool children with disabilities. *Journal of Behavioral Education, 4*, 267-281.

Lichtenstein, S. (1993). Transition from school to adulthood: Case studies of adults with learning disabilities who dropped out of school. *Exceptional Children, 59*(4), 336-347.

Light, J., Irvine, K., & Kjerulf, L. (1996). Estimating genetic and environmental effects of alcohol use and dependence from a national survey: A "quasi adoption" study. *Journal of Studies on Alcohol, 57*, 507-520.

Lindemann, E. (1944). Symptomatology and management of acute grief. *American Journal of Psychiatry, 101*, 141-148.

Lipsky, D., & Abrams, A. (1994). *Late bloomers*. New York: Times Books.

Lochman, J. E., Coie, J.D., Underwood, M. K., & Terry, R. (1993). Effectiveness of a social relationship intervention program for aggressive and nonaggressive, rejected children. *Journal of Consulting and Clinical Psychology, 61*, 1053-1058.

Locke, A., Ginsborg, J., & Peers, I. (2002). Development and disadvantage: Implications for the early years and beyond. *International Journal of Language & Communication Disorders, 37*(1), 3-15.

Logan, S. L., Freeman, E. M., & McRoy, R. G. (Eds.). (1990). *Social work practice with black families: A culturally specific perspective*. New York: Longman.

Loveless, T. (1999). *The tracking wars: State reform meets school policy*. Washington, DC: Brookings Institution Press.

Lowery, G.H. (1986). *Growth and development of children* (8th edition). Chicago: Year Book.

Lowry, R., Holtzman, D., Truman, B. I., Kann, L., Collins, J. L., & Kolbe, L. J. (1994). Substance use and HIV-related sexual behaviors among U.S. high school students: Are they related? *American Journal of Public Health, 84,* 1116-1120.

Lydon-Rochelle, M., Holt, V.L., Martin, D.P., & Easterling, T.R. (2000). Association between method of delivery and the maternal rehospitalization. *Journal of the American Medical Association, 55*(10), 605-607.

Lynch, R. (2000). *New directions for high school career and technical education in the 21st century.* Washington, DC: U.S. Department of Education.

Lyons-Ruth, K., Connell, D., Grunebaum, H., & Botein, S. (1990). Infants at social risk: Maternal depression and family support services as mediators of infant development and security of attachment. *Child Development, 61,* 85-98.

Maccoby, E. (1980). *Social development: Psychological growth and the parent-child relationship.* San Diego: Harcourt Brace Jovanovich.

Maccoby, E. (1992). The role of parents in the socialization of children: An historical overview. *Developmental Psychology, 28,* 1006-1017.

Maccoby, E. E. (2002). Parenting effects: Issues and controversies. In J. G. Borkowski, S. Landesman Ramey, & M. Bristol-Power (Eds.), *Parenting and the child's world* (pp. 35-45). Mahwah, NJ: Lawrence Erlbaum.

Mack, R., Pike, M., Henderson, M. Pfeffer, R., Gerkins, V., Arthur, M., & Brown, S. (1976). Estrogens and endometrial cancer in a retirement community. *The New England Journal of Medicine, 294,* 1262-1267.

MacLennan, B. (1994). Groups for poorly socialized children in the elementary school. *Journal of Child and Adolescent Group Therapy, 4,* 243-250.

Maddox, G. L. (2001). Housing and living arrangements: A transactional perspective. In R. H. Binstock & L. K. Geroge (Eds.), *Handbook of aging and the social sciences* (pp. 426-443).New York: Academic Press.

Magwaza, A., Kilian, B., Peterson, I., & Pillay, Y. (1993). The effects of chronic violence on preschool children living in South African townships. *Child Abuse and Neglect, 17,* 795-803.

Main, M., & Hesse, E. (1990). Parents' unresolved traumatic experiences are related to infant disorganized attachment status: Is frightened and/or frightening parental behavior the linking mechanism? In M. Greenberg, D. Cicchetti, & E. M. Cumming (Eds.), *Attachment in the preschool years: Theory, research and intervention* (pp. 161-182). Chicago: University of Chicago Press.

Maloney, M. J., & Klykylo, W. M. (1983). An overview of anorexia nervosa, bulimia and obesity in children and adolescents. *Journal of the American Academy of Child Psychiatry, 22,* 99-107.

Manton, K. G., & Liu, K. (1984). *The future growth of the long-term care population: Projections based on the 1977 national nursing home survey and the 1981 long-term care survey.* Washington, DC: Health Care Financing Administration.

Marcia, J. E. (1966). Development and validation of ego-identity status. *Journal of Personality and Social Psychology, 3,* 551-558.

Marcia, J. E. (1980). Identity in adolescence. In J. Adelson (Ed.), *Handbook of adolescent psychology* (pp. 159-187). New York: Wiley.

Marcia, J. E. (1993). The ego identity status approach to ego identity. In J. E. Marcia, A. S. Waterman, D. R. Mattesson, S. L. Arcjer, & J. L. Orlofksy (Eds.), *Ego identity: A handbook for psychosocial research.* New York: Springer.

Marini, M. M. (1989). Socioeconomic consequences of the process of transition to adulthood. *Social Science Research,* 18, 89-135.

Marino, R., Weinman, M., & Soudelier, K. (2001). Social work intervention and failure to thrive in infants and children. *Health & Social Work, 26*(2), 90-98.

Markides, K., & Boldt, J. (1983). Change in subjective age among the elderly: A longitudinal analysis. *The Gerontologist, 23*(24), 422-427.

Marks, N. (1998). Does it hurt to care? Caregiving, work-family conflict, and midlife well-being. *Journal of Marriage and the Family, 60,* 951-966.

Marks, N., & Lambert, J. (1998). Marital status continuity and change among young and midlife adults. *Journal of Family Issues, 19,* 652-686.

Markstrom, C., & Mullis, R. (1986). Ethnic differences in the imaginary audience. *Journal of Adolescent Research, 1*(3), 289-301.

Markstrom-Adams, C., & Adams, G. R. (1995). Gender, ethnic group, and grade differences in psychosocial functioning during middle adolescence. *Journal of Youth and Adolescence, 24,* 397-417.

Marshall, N. L., Noonan, A. E., McCartney, K., Marx, F., & Keefe, N. (2001). It takes an urban village: Parenting networks of urban families. *Journal of Family Issues, 22*(2), 163.

Marsiglio, W. (1986). Teenage fatherhood: High school accreditation and educational attainment. In A. B. Elster & M. E. Lamb (Eds.), *Adolescent Fatherhood.* Hillside, NJ: Lawrence Erlbaum.

Martin, K. A. (1996). *Puberty, sexuality, and the self: Boys and girls at adolescence.* New York: Routledge.

Martin, J., Hamilton, B., Ventura, J., Menacker, F., & Park, M. (2002). Births: Final data for 2000. *National Vital Statistics Reports, 50*(5). Hyattsville, MD: National Center for Health Statistics.

Martin, S. L., Clark, K.A., Lynch, S.R., Kupper, L.L. & Cilenti, D. (1999). Violence in the lives of pregnant teenage women: Associations with multiple substance abuse. *American Journal of Drug and Alcohol Use, 25*(3), 425-431.

Martin, S. L., Kim, H., Kupper, L.L., Meyer, R.E., & Hays, M. (1997). Is incarceration during pregnancy associated with infant birthweight? *American Journal of Public Health, 87,* 1526-1531.

Matheson, N. (1991). *The influence of organization-based self-esteem on satisfaction and commitment: An analysis of age differences.* Unpublished doctoral dissertation, University of Akron, OH.

Matsumoto-Grah, K. (1992). Diversity in the classroom: A checklist. In D. Byrnes & G. Kiger (Eds.), *Common bonds: Anti-bias teaching in a diverse society* (pp. 105-108). Olney, MD: Association for Childhood Education International.

Matute-Bianchi, M. E. (1986). Ethnic identities and patterns of school success and failure among Mexican-descent and Japanese-American students in a California school: An ethnographic analysis. *American Journal of Education, 95,* 233-255.

McAdams, D. (2001). Generativity in midlife. In M. Lachman (Ed.), *Handbook of midlife development* (pp. 395-443). New York: Wiley.

McAdams, D., & de St. Aubin, E. (1992). A theory of generativity and its assessment through self-report, behavioral acts, and narrative themes in autobiography. *Journal of Personality and Social Psychology, 62,* 1003-1015.

McAdams, D., & de St. Aubin, E. (Eds.). (1998). *Generativity and adult development: How and why we care for the next generation.* Washington, DC: American Psychological Association.

McAdams, D., de St. Aubin, E., & Logan, R. (1993). Generativity among young, midlife, and older adults. *Psychology and Aging, 8,* 221-230.

McAdams, D., Hart, H., & Maruna, S. (1998). The anatomy of generativity. In D. McAdams & E. de St. Aubin (Eds.), *Generativity and adult development: How and why we care for the next generation* (pp. 7-43). Washington, DC: American Psychological Association.

McAdoo, H. (1986). Societal stress: The black family. In J. Cole (Ed.), *All American women: Lines that divide, ties that bind* (pp. 187-197). New York: Free Press.

McCarter, S. (1997). *Understanding the overrepresentation of minorities in Virginia's juvenile justice system.* Unpublished doctoral dissertation, Virginia Commonwealth University, Richmond.

McCarter, S. (1998). Interviews with adolescents regarding health topics. Work in progress, Virginia Commonwealth University, School of Social Work.

McCarton, C. (1986). The long term impact of a low birth weight infant on the family. *Zero to Three, 267*(16), 6-10.

McCloskey, L. A., Figueredo, A. J., & Koss, M. P. (1995). The effects of systemic family violence on children's mental health. *Child Development, 66,* 1239-1261.

McCluskey, U., & Duerden, S. (1993). Pre-verbal communication: The role of play in establishing rhythms of communication between self and others. *Journal of Social Work Practice, 7*(1), 17-27.

McCrae, R., & Costa, P., Jr. (1990). *Personality in adulthood.* New York: Guilford Press.

McCrae, R., Costa, P., Jr., Ostendorf, F., Angleitner, A., Caprara, G., Barbaranelli, C., de Lima, M., Simoes, A., Marusic, I., Bratko, D., Chaie, J., & Piedmont, R. (1999). Age differences in personality across the adult life span: Parallels in five cultures. *Developmental Psychology, 35*(2), 466.

McDermid, S., Heilbrun, G., & DeHaan, L. (1997). The generativity of employed mothers in multiple roles: 1979 and 1991. In M. Lachman & J. James (Eds.), *Multiple paths of midlife development* (pp. 207-240). Chicago: The University of Chicago Press.

McDermott, S., Cokert, A. L., & McKeown, R. E. (1993). Low birthweight and risk of mild mental retardation by ages 5 and 9 to 11. *Paediatric and Perinatal Epidemiology, 7*(2), 195-204.

McElhatton, P.R. (2000). Fetal effects of substances of abuse. *Journal of Toxicology: Clinical Toxicology, 38*(2), 194-195.

McFalls, J. Jr. (1998). Population composition. *Population Bulletin, 53*(3), 26-34.

McGill, D., & Pearce, J. (1996). American families with English ancestors from the colonial era: Anglo Americans. In M. McGoldrick, J. Giordanao, & J. Pearce (Eds.), *Ethnicity and family therapy* (pp. 451-466). New York: The Guilford Press.

McGoldrick, M. (1999). Becoming a couple. In B. Carter & M. McGoldrick (Eds.), *The expanded family life cycle: Individual, family, and social perspectives* (3rd ed., pp. 231-248). Boston: Allyn & Bacon.

McGoldrick, M., Broken Nose, M., & Potenza, M. (1999). Violence and the family life cycle. In B. Carter & M. McGoldrick (Eds.), *The expanded family life cycle: Individual, family, and social perspectives* (3rd ed., pp. 470-491). Boston: Allyn & Bacon.

McGoldrick, M., Giordano, J., & Pearce, J. (1996). *Ethnicity and family therapy* (2nd ed.). New York: Guilford.

McGroder, S. M., Zaslow, M. J., Moore, K. A., Hair, E. C., & Ahluwalia, S. K. (2002). The role of parenting in shaping the impacts of welfare-to-work programs on children. In J. G. Borkowski, S. Landesman Ramey, & M. Bristol-Power (Eds.), *Parenting and the child's world.* (pp. 383-410). Mahwah, NJ: Lawrence Erlbaum.

McInnis-Dittrich, K. (2002). *Social work with elders: A biopsychosocial approach to assessment and intervention.* Boston: Allyn & Bacon.

McIntosh, P. (1988). *White privilege: Unpacking the invisible knapsack.* (Available from Peggy McIntosh, Wellesley College Center for Research on Women, Wellesley, MA 02181.)

McIntyre, J., & Gray, G. (2002). What can we do to reduce mother to child transmission of HIV? (Education and debate). *British Medical Journal, 324*(7331), 218-222.

McKeering, H., & Pakenham, K. (2000). Gender and generativity issues in parenting. Do fathers benefit more than mothers from involvement in child care activities? *Sex Roles, 43*(7-8), 459-480.

McKinlay, S., Brambilla, D., & Posner, J. (1992). The normal menopause transition. *Journal of Human Biology, 4,* 37-46.

McLaren, L. (1988). Fostering mother-child relationships. *Child Welfare, 67*(4), 353-365.

McLoyd, V. (1990). The impact of economic hardship on black families and children: Psychological distress, parenting, and socioemotional development. *Child Development, 61,* 311-346.

McLoyd, V. C. (1998) Socioeconomic disadvantage and child development. *American Psychologist, 53*(2), 185-204.

McLoyd, V., & Wilson, L. (1991). The strain of living poor: Parenting, social support and child mental health. In A. C. Huston (Ed.), *Children and poverty* (pp. 105-136). New York: Cambridge University Press.

McQuaide, S. (1998). Women at midlife. *Social Work, 43*(1), 21-31.

McWhirter, J. J., McWhirter, B. T., McWhirter, A. M., & McWhirter, E. H. (1993). *At-risk youth: A comprehensive response.* Pacific Grove, CA: Brooks/Cole.

Mead, G. H. (1934). *Mind, self and society.* Chicago: University of Chicago Press.

Mechcatie, E. (2002). Patch, vaginal ring offer steady hormone levels. *OB GYN News, 37*(4), 18-20.

Meek, M. (2000). Foreword. In K. Roskos & J. Christie (Ed.), *Play and literacy in early childhood: Research from multiple perspectives* (pp. vii-xiii). Mahwah, NJ: Lawrence Erlbaum.

Menon, U. (2001). Middle adulthood in cultural perspective: The imagined and the experienced in three cultures. In M. Lachman (Ed.), *Handbook of midlife development* (pp. 40-74). New York: Wiley.

Merriam Webster, Inc. (1998). *Merriam-Webster's collegiate dictionary* (10th ed.). Springfield, MA: Author.

Merrill, S., & Verbrugge, L. (1999). Health and disease in midlife. In S. Willis & J. Reid (Eds.), *Life in the middle: Psychological and social development in middle age* (pp. 78-103). San Diego, CA: Academic Press.

Merton, R. (1968). The Matthew Effect in science: The reward and communications systems of science. *Science, 199,* 55-63.

Meyer, D. R., & Garasky, S. (1993). Custodial fathers: Myths, realities, and child support policy. *Journal of Marriage and the Family, 55,* 73-89.

Meyer, J. (1986). The institutionalization of the life course and its effects on the self. In A. Sorensen, F. Weinert, & L. Sherrod (Eds.), *Human development and the life course: Multidisciplinary perspectives* (pp. 199-216). Hillsdale, NJ: Lawrence Erlbaum.

Meyers, D. (2001). Promoting and supporting breastfeeding. *American Family Physician, 64*(6), 931-934.

Miller, B. (1992). Adolescent parenthood, economic issues, and social policies. *Journal of Family and Economic Issues, 13*(4), 467-475.

Minkler, M. (1985). Social support and health in the elderly. In S. Cohen & S. L. Syme (Eds.) *Social support and health* (pp. 199-216). Orlando: Academic Press.

Miyake, K., Campos, J., Kagan, J., & Bradshaw, D. (1986). Issues in socioemotional development in Japan. In H. Azuma, I. Hakuta, & H. Stevenson (Eds.), *Dodoma: Child development and education in Japan* (pp. 239-261). New York: W. H. Freeman.

Mize, J., & Ladd, G. W. (1990). A cognitive-social learning approach to social skill training with low status preschool children. *Developmental Psychology, 26,* 388-397.

Modell, J., Furstenberg, F., Jr., & Hershberg, T. (1976). Social change and transitions to adulthood in historical perspective. *Journal of Family History, 1,* 7-32.

Moen, P. (1997). Women's roles and resilience: Trajectories of advantage or turning points? In I. H. Gotlib & B. Wheaton (Eds.), *Stress and adversity over the life course: Trajectories and turning points* (pp. 133-156). New York: Cambridge University Press.

Moen, P., & Wethington, E. (1999). Midlife development in a life course context. In S. Willis & J. Reid (Eds.), *Life in the middle* (pp. 3-24). San Diego, CA: Academic Press.

Molfese, V., Holcomb, L., & Helwig, S. (1994). Biomedical and social-environmental influences on cognitive and verbal abilities in children 1 to 3 years of age. *International Journal of Behavioral Development, 17,* 271-287.

Monahon, C. (1997). *Children and trauma: A guide for parents and professionals.* San Francisco: Jossey-Bass.

Montgomery, R. J. V., & Kosloski, K. (1994). A longitudinal analysis of nursing home placement for dependent elders cared for by spouses vs. adult children. *Journal of Gerontology: Social Science, 49,* S62-S74.

Moody, H. R. (1998). *Aging: Concepts and controversies.* (2nd ed.). Thousand Oaks, CA: Pine Forge.

Moore, D. (1987). Parent-adolescent separation: The construction of adulthood by late adolescents. *Developmental Psychology, 23,* 298-307.

Moore, K. L., & Persaud, T. V. N. (1993). *Before we are born* (4th ed.). Philadelphia: Saunders.

Moore, K., McGroder, S., & Zaslow, M. (2001, May). Measuring child and family outcomes. Paper presented at Fourth Annual Welfare Reform Evaluation Conference, Arlington, VA.

Moore, K. A., Vandivere, S., & Ehrle, J. (2000, June). *Turbulence and child well-being. New Federalism National Survey of American Families, No. B-16.* Washington, DC: The Urban Institute.

Morales, A. (1992). Therapy with Latino gang members. In L. Vargas & J. Koss-Chioino (Eds.), *Working with culture: Psychotherapeutic interventions with ethnic minority children and adolescents.* San Francisco: Jossey-Bass.

Morgan, L., & Kunkel, S. (1996). *Aging: The social context.* Thousand Oaks, CA: Pine Forge.

Morris, P. A.,& Duncan, G. J. (2001). *Which welfare reforms are best for children? Welfare Reform & Beyond, Policy Brief No. 6.* Washington, DC: Brookings Institution.

Morris, P. A., Duncan, G. J., & Chase-Lansdale, L. (2001). Welfare reform's effects on children. *Poverty Research News, 5*(4), 5-8.

Morris, P. A., Huston, A. C., Duncan, G. J., Crosby, D. A. & Bos, J. M. (2001). *How welfare and work policies affect children: A synthesis of research.* New York: Manpower Demonstration Research Corporation.

Morrison, J. W., & Bordere, T. (2001). Supporting biracial children's identity development. *Childhood Education, 77*(3), 134-138.

Mortimer, J. T., & Finch, M. D. (1996). *Adolescents, work, and family: An intergenerational developmental analysis.* Thousand Oaks, CA: Sage.

Moshman, D. (1998). Cognitive development beyond childhood. In D. Kuhn & R. Siegler (Eds.), *Handbook of child psychology: Vol. 2. Cognition, perception, and language* (5th ed., pp. 947-978). New York: Wiley.

Moss, N. E. (1987). Effects of father-daughter contact on use of pregnancy services by Mexican, Mexican-American, and Anglo adolescents. *Journal of Adolescent Health Care, 8,* 419-425.

Moss, R. H., Mortens, M. A., & Brennan, P. L. (1993). Patterns of diagnosis and treatment among late-middle-aged and older substance abuse patients. *Journal of Studies in Alcohol, 54,* 479-487.

Mowrer, R., & Klein, S. (Eds.). (2001). *Handbook of contemporary learning theories.* Mahwah, NJ: Lawrence Erlbaum.

Moyer, K. (1974). Discipline. In K. Moyer, *You and your child: A primer for parents* (pp. 40-61). Chicago: Nelson Hall

Moyers, B. (1993). *Healing and the mind.* New York: Doubleday.

Mueller, M., Wilhelm, B., & Elder, G. (2002). Variations in grandparenting. *Research on Aging, 24*(3), 360-388.

Munakata, Y., McClelland, J., Johnson, M., & Siegler, R. (1997). Rethinking infant knowledge: Toward an adaptive process account of successes and failures in object permanence tasks. *Psychological Review, 104(4),* 618-713.

Murphy, J., Jellinek, M., Quinn, D., Smith, G., Poitrast, F., & Goshko, M. (1991). Substance abuse and serious child maltreatment: Prevalence, risk, and outcome in a court sample. *Child Abuse & Neglect, 15*(3), 197-211.

Mynatt, C. R., & Algeier, E. R. (1990). Risk factors, self-attributions and adjustment problems among victims of sexual coercion. *Journal of Applied Social Psychology, 20,* 130-153.

Naleppa, M. J. (1996). Families and the institutionalized elderly: A review. *Journal of Gerontological Social Work, 27,* 87-111.

National Campaign to End Teen Pregnancy. (2002). *General facts and stats.* Retrieved August 26, 2002, from www.teenpregnancy.org/resources/data/genlfact.asp.

National Cancer Institute (2002). *Statistics.* Retrieved September 7, 2002, from www.nci.nih.gov.

National Center for Child Abuse and Neglect. (1995). *Child maltreatment 1995: Reports of the states to the National Child Abuse Neglect Data Systems.* Retrieved from www/calib.com/nccanch/services/stats.htm#NIS-3.

National Center for Children in Poverty. (1996/97). One in four: America's youngest poor. *News and Issues, 6*(2), 1-2.

National Center for Children in Poverty. (2002, March). *Early childhood poverty: A statistical profile.* Retrieved August 23, 2002, from cpmcnet.columbia.edu/dept/nccp/ecp302.html.

National Center for Clinical Infant Programs. (1992). How community violence affects children, parents, and practitioners. *Public Welfare, 50*(4), 25-35.

National Center for Health Statistics. (1993). Advance report of final natality statistics, 1991. *Monthly Vital Statistics Report, 42*(3), Suppl. Hyattsville, MD: Public Health Service. Retrieved from www.cdc.gov/nchwww/products/pubs/pubd/mvsr/ supp/44-43/mvs44_3s.htm.

National Center for Health Statistics (1995). *1994-1995 national health interview survey on disability (Phase I).* Hyattsville, MD: Author.

National Center for Health Statistics. (1997a). *Teen pregnancy rate reaches a record low in 1997.* Retrieved August 26, 2002, from www.cdc.gov/nchs/releases/02news/birthlow.htm.

National Center for Health Statistics. (1997b). 1995 birth statistics released. In MVSR Vol. 45, No. 11(S). *Report of final natality statistics, 1995.* Public Health Service. Retrieved from www.cdc.gov/nchwww/releases/97facts/97sheets/95natrel.htm.

National Center for Health Statistics (2000). *NICHS-2000 fact-sheet.* Retrieved September 20, 2001, from www.ced.gov/nchs/ releases/00facts/trends.htm.

National Center for Health Statistics (2001a). *Health, United States, 2001.* Hyattsville, MD: Author.

National Center for Health Statistics (2001b). *Trends in deaths caused by infectious diseases in the United States, 1900-1994.* Retrieved September 4, 2001, from www.cdc.gov/ncidod/emergplan/box01.htm.

National Commission to Prevent Infant Mortality. (1992). One-stop shopping for infants and pregnant women. *Public Welfare, 50*(1), 26-34.

National Council on the Aging. (2000, March). *Myths and realities 2000 survey results.* Washington, DC: National Council on Aging.

National Council on the Aging. (n.d.). *Facts about older Americans.* Retrieved June 29, 2002, from www.ncoa.org/press/facts.html.

National Geographic Society. (1998). *Eyewitness to the 20th century.* Washington, DC: Author.

National Hospice and Palliative Care Organization. (2002). *NHPCO facts and figures.* Retrieved June 15, 2002. from www.nhpco.org.

National Institute of Mental Health. (2000). *Depression in children and adolescents.* Bethesda, MD: Author. Retrieved August 27, 2002, from www.nimh.nih.gov/publicat/depchildresfact.cfm.

National Institutes of Health. (2001). *Vital connections: Science of mind-body interactions. A report on the interdisciplinary conference held at NIH March 26-28, 2001.* Bethesda, MD: Author.

National Institutes of Health (2002). *NHLBI stops trial of estrogen plus progestin due to increased cancer risk, lack of overall benefit.* Retrieved September 3, 2002, from www.nhlbi.nih.gov/new/press/02-07-09.htm.

National Institutes of Health—National Institute of Allergy and Infectious Diseases (1996, August). An introduction to sexually transmitted diseases. Bethesda, MD: U.S. Department of Health and Human Services, Public Health Service.

National Institutes of Health-National Institute of Allergy and Infectious Diseases (2002). *Basic information about AIDS and HIV.* Retrieved July 2, 2002, from www.niaid.nih.gov/aidsvaccine/basicinfo.htm.

National Institutes of Health-National Institute on Drug Abuse. (2001). *Monitoring the future study.* Bethesda,

MD: U.S. Department of Health and Human Services, National Institutes of Health, National Institute on Drug Abuse.

National Research Council (1990). *Who cares for America's children?* Washington, DC: Author.

National Research Council (1993). *Understanding child abuse & neglect.* Washington, DC: National Academy Press.

National Vaccine Information Center. (n.d). *History of NVIC.* Retrieved June 7, 2002, from www.909shot.comnvichistory.htm.

National Vital Statistics Report. (2002, January 30). Volume *50*(4). Retrieved from www.cdc.gov/nchs/data/ibid/nvsr50_04-+2.pdf.

Nettles, S., Mucherah, W., & Jones, D. (2000). Understanding resilience: The role of social resources. *Journal of Education for Students Placed at Risk, 5*(1&2), 47-60.

Neugarten, B. L., & Weinstein, K. K. (1964). The changing American grandparent. *Journal of Marriage and the Family, 26,* 199-204.

Neugarten, B., & Gutmann, D. (1968). Age-sex roles and personality in middle age: A thematic apperception study. In B.L. Neugarten (Ed.), *Middle age and aging* (pp. 58-71). Chicago: University of Chicago Press.

Neugarten, B., & Hagestad, G. (1976). Age and the life course. In R. Binstock & E. Shanas (Eds.), *Handbook of aging and the social sciences* (pp. 35-55). New York: Van Nostrand Reinhold.

Neugarten, B. L., Havighurst, R. J., & Tobin, S. S. (1968). Personality and patterns of aging. In B. L. Neugarten (Ed.), *Middle age and aging.* Chicago: University of Chicago Press.

Newcomb, A. F., Bukowski, W. M., & Pattee, L. (1993). Children's peer relations: A meta-analytic review of popular, rejected, neglected, controversial, and average sociometric status. *Psychological Bulletin, 113,* 99-128.

Newcomb, N., & Dubas, J. S. (1992). A longitudinal study of predictors of spatial ability in adolescent females. *Child Development, 63,* 37-46.

New Gel tested against STDs as well as sperm. (2002, January 21). *Health and Medicine Week.* Electronic Collection A81887337.

Newman, B. M., & Newman, P. R. (1995). *Development through life: A psychosocial approach* (6th ed.). Pacific Grove, CA: Brooks/Cole.

Newman, P., & Newman, B. (1997). *Childhood and adolescence.* Pacific Grove, CA: Brooks/Cole.

Nguyen, N. A. (1992). Living between two-cultures: Treating first-generation Asian Americans. In L. Vargas & J. Koss-Chioino (Eds.), *Working with culture: Psychotherapeutic interventions with ethnic minority children and adolescents.* San Francisco: Jossey-Bass.

Noddings, N. (1984). *Caring: A feminine approach to ethics and moral education.* Berkeley, CA: University of California Press.

Nosek, M. (1995). Findings on reproductive health and access to health care. *National study of women with physical disabilities.* Houston, TX: Baylor College of Medicine, Department of Physical Medicine and Rehabilitation.

Nosek, M. A., Howland, C. A., Rintal, D. H., Young, M. E. & Chanpong, G. F. (1997). *National study of women with physical disabilities: Final report.* Houston, TX: Center for Research on Women with Disabilities.

Novak, J. C., & Broom, B. (1995). *Maternal and child health nursing.* St. Louis, MO: Mosby.

Novins, D., Beals, J., Shore, J., & Manson, S. (1996). Substance abuse treatment of American Indian adolescents: Comorbid symptomatology, gender differences, and treatment patterns. *Child & Adolescent Psychiatry, 35*(12), 1593-1601.

Novins, D., Fleming, C., Beals, J., & Manson, S. (2000). Commentary: Quality of alcohol, drug, and mental health services for American Indian children and adolescents. *American Journal of Medicine Quarterly, 15*(4), 148-156.

Oakes, J. (1985). *Keeping track of tracking: How schools structure inequality.* New Haven, CT: Yale University Press.

Oakes, J., & Lipton, M. (1990). *Making the best of schools: A handbook for parents, teachers, and policymakers.* New Haven, CT: Yale University Press.

Oakes, J., & Lipton, M. (1992). Detracking schools: Early lessons from the field. *Phi Delta Kappan, 73,* 448-454.

Oakley, A., Hickey, D., Rojan, L., & Rigby, A. S. (1996). Social support in pregnancy: Does it have long-term effects? *Journal of Reproductive and Infant Psychology, 14*(1), 7-22.

Oberklaid, F., Sanson, A., Pedlow, R., & Prior, M. (1993). Predicting preschool behavior problems from temperament and other variables in infancy. *Pediatrics, 91,* 113-120.

O'Brien, M. (1992). Gender identity and sex roles. In V. B. Van Hasselt & M. Hersen (Eds.), *Handbook of social development: A lifespan perspective* (pp. 325-345). New York: Plenum.

O'Conor, A. (1994). Who gets called queer in school? Lesbian, gay and bisexual teenagers, homophobia and high school. *High School Journal, 77*(1-2), 7-12.

Odent, M. (1998). *Men's role in the labour room.* Conference presentation at the Royal Society of Medicine, London.

Odent, M. (1999). *The scientification of love.* London: Free Association Books.

Office on Smoking and Health. (2000). *Youth tobacco surveillance-United States, 1998-1999.* Washington, DC: Author.

Ogbu, J. U. (1994). Overcoming racial barriers to equal access. In K. I. Goodland & P. Keating (Eds.), *Access to knowledge: The continuing agenda for our nation's schools* (pp. 59-90). New York: The College Board.

O'Keefe, M. (1994). Adjustment of children from maritally violent homes. *Families in Society, 75,* 403-415.

O'Keefe, M. (1997). Adolescents' exposure to community and school violence: Prevalence and behavioral correlates. *Journal of Adolescent Health, 20,* 368-376.

Okie, S. (2002, February 6). Hormone therapy no panacea; Study tracks menopause treatments' effect on well-being. *Washington Post,* p. A7.

Olds, D., Eckenrode, J., Henderson, C., Kitzman, H., Powers, J., Cole, R., Sidora, K., Morris, P., Pettitt, L., & Luckey, D. (1997). Long-term effects of home visitation on maternal life course and child abuse and neglect: Fifteen-year follow-up of a randomized trial. *JAMA, 278*(8), 637-643.

Ollendick, T. H., Weist, M. D., Borden, M. C., & Greene, R. W. (1992). Sociometric status and academic, behavioral, and psychological adjustment: A five year longitudinal study. *Journal of Consulting and Clinical Psychology, 60,* 80-87.

O'Malley, P. L., Johnston, L., & Bachman, J. (1991). Quantitative and qualitative changes in cocaine use among American high school seniors, college students, and young adults. *NIDA Monographs, 110,* 19-43.

Opitz, J. M. (1996). Origins of birth defects. In J. J. Sciarra (Ed.), *Gynecology and obstetrics* (rev. ed., pp. 23-30). Philadelphia, PA: Lippincott-Raven.

O'Rand, A. (1996). The precious and the precocious: Understanding cumulative disadvantage and cumulative advantage over the life course. *The Gerontologist, 36*(2), 230-238.

Orenstein, P. (1994). *Schoolgirls: Young women, self-esteem, and the confidence gap.* New York: Doubleday.

Osofsky, J. D., Hann, D., & Peebles, C. (1993). Adolescent parenthood: Risks and opportunities for mothers and infants. In C. Zeanah, Jr. (Ed.), *Handbook of infant mental health* (pp. 106-119). New York: Guilford.

Osofsky, J. D., Osofsky, H. J., & Diamond, M. O. (1988). The transition to parenthood: Special tasks and risk factors for adolescent mothers. In G. Y. Michaels & W. A. Goldberg (Eds.), *The transition to parenthood* (pp. 209-234). Cambridge, UK: Cambridge University Press.

Oyserman, D., Bybee, D., Mowbray, C. & MacFarlane, P. (2002). Positive parenting among African American mothers with a serious mental illness. *Journal of Marriage and Family, 65,* 65-77.

Padilla, Y. C., & Jordan, M. W. (1997). Determinants of Hispanic poverty in the course of the transition to adulthood. *Hispanic Journal of Behavioral Sciences, 19*(4), 416-433.

Palmore, E. B., Burchett, B. M., Fillenbaum, C. G., George, L. K., & Wallman, L. M. (1985). *Retirement: Causes and consequences.* New York: Springer.

Panksepp, J. (1986). The psychobiology of prosocial behaviors: Separation distress, play, and altruism. In C. Zahn-Waxler, E. M. Cummings, & R. Iannotti (Eds.), *Altruism and aggression: Biological and social origin* (pp. 465-492). Cambridge, UK: Cambridge University Press.

Pardington, S. (2002, January 13). Multilingual pupils pose a challenge to educators. *Contra Costa Times.* Retrieved January 17, 2002, from www.uniontrib.com/news/uniontrib/sun/news/news_0n13lingos.html.

Parents, Family and Friends of Lesbians and Gays [PFLAG]. (2001). *Read this before coming out to your parents.* Washington, DC: Sauerman.

Parette, H. (1995, November). *Culturally sensitive family-focused assistive technology assessment strategies.* Paper presented at the DEC Early Childhood Conference on Children with Special Needs, Orlando, FL.

Pascoe, J. M., Pletta, K., Beasley, J., & Schellpfeffer, M. (2002). Best start breastfeeding promotion campaign. *Pediatrics, 109*(1), 170.

Paul, E. (1997). A longitudinal analysis of midlife interpersonal relationships and well-being. In M. Lachman & J. James (Eds.), *Multiple paths of midlife development* (pp.171-206). Chicago: University of Chicago Press.

Payer, L. (1991). The menopause in various cultures. In H. Burger & M. Boulet (Eds.), *A portrait of the menopause.* Park Ridge, NJ: Parthenon.

Payne, R. K. (2001). *A framework for understanding poverty.* Highlands, TX: aha! Process Inc.

Paz, J. (1993). Support of Hispanic elderly. In H. McAdoo (Ed.), *Family ethnicity: Strength in diversity* (pp. 177-183). Newbury Park, CA: Sage.

Pearlin, L., & Skaff, M. (1996). Stress and the life course: A paradigmatic alliance. *The Gerontologist, 36*(2), 239-247.

Peck, P. (1997). Study shows puberty hits girls at a young age. *Family Practice News, 27*(16), 61.

Pelligrini, A., & Galda, L. (2000). Cognitive development, play, and literacy: Issues of definition and developmental function. In K. Roskos & J. Christie (Eds.), *Play and literacy in early childhood: Research from multiple perspectives* (pp. 63-76). Mahwah, NJ: Lawrence Erlbaum.

Pena, R., & Wall, S. (2000). Effects of poverty, social inequality and maternal education on infant mortality in Nicaragua, 1988-1993. *American Journal of Public Health, 90*(1), 64-69.

Pennekamp, M. (1995). Response to violence. *Social Work in Education, 17,* 199-200.

Perlman, D., & Fehr, B. (1987). The development of intimate relationships. In D. Perlman & S. Duck (Eds.), *Intimate relationships: Development, dynamics, & deterioration* (pp. 13-42). Newbury Park, CA: Sage.

Perlman, J. M. (2001). Neurobehavioral deficits in premature graduates of intensive care—potential medical and neonatal environmental risk factors. *Pediatrics, 108*(16), 1339-1449.

Perloff, J., & Buckner, J. (1996). Fathers of children on welfare: Their impact on child well being. *American Journal of Orthopsychiatry, 66,* 557-571.

Perls, T. T., & Wood, E. R. (1996). Acute care costs of the oldest old. *Archives of Internal Medicine, 156,* 754-760.

Pernice, R., & Brook, J. (1996). Refugees' and immigrants' mental health: Assocation of demographic and post-immigration factors. *Journal of Social Psychology, 136*(4), 511-519.

Perrone, B., Stockel, H., & Krueger, V. (1989). *Medicine women, curanderas, and women doctors.* Norman: University of Oklahoma.

Perry, B. (1997). Incubated in terror: Neurodevelopmental factors in the "cycle of violence." In J. Osofsky (Ed.), *Children in a violent society* (pp. 124-149). New York: Guilford.

Perry, H. (1993). Mourning and funeral customs of African Americans. In D. Irish, K. Lundquist, & V. Nelsen (Eds.), *Ethnic variations in dying, death, and grief: Diversity in universality* (pp. 51-65). Washington, DC: Taylor & Francis.

Perry, W. G. (1994). Forms of intellectual and ethical development in the college years: A scheme. In B. Puka (Ed.), *Defining perspectives in moral development. Moral development: A compendium* (pp. 231-248). New York: Garland.

Pesa, J. A., & Shelton, M. M. (1999). Health-enhancing behaviors correlated with breastfeeding among a national sample of mothers. *Public Health Nursing, 16,* 120-124.

Peterson, M. B., Greisen, G., & Kovacs, R. (1994). Outcome of < 750 gm birthweight children at school age. *New England Journal of Medicine, 331,* 753-759.

Pettit, G. S., Bakshi, A., Dodge, K. A., & Coie, J. D. (1990). The emergence of social dominance in young boy's play groups: Developmental differences and behavioral correlates. *Developmental Psychology, 26,* 1017-1025.

Philipp, B. L., Merewood, A., Miller, L. W., Chawla, N., Murphy-Smith, M. M., Gorners, J. S., Cimo, S., & Cook, J. T. (2001). Baby-friendly hospital initiatives improve breastfeeding: Initiation rates in a U.S. hospital setting. *Pediatrics, 108*(3), 677.

Philipp, B. L., Merewood, A., Miller, L. W., Chawla, N., Murphy-Smith, M. M., & Ryan, A. S. (1997). The resurgence of breastfeeding in the United States. *Pediatrics, 99*(4). Retrieved from www.pediatrics.org/cgi/content/full/99/4/e12.

Phinney, J. S. (1989). Stages of ethnic identity development in minority group adolescents. *Journal of Early Adolescence, 9,* 34-49.

Piaget, J. (1936/1952). *The origins of intelligence in children.* New York: International Universities Press.

Piaget, J. (1932/1965). *The moral judgment of the child.* New York: Free Press.

Piaget, J. (1972). Intellectual evolution from adolescence to adulthood. *Human Development, 15,* 1-12.

Pipher, M. (1994). *Reviving Ophelia: Saving the selves of adolescent girls.* New York: Ballantine Books.

Pipher, M. (1999). *Another country: Navigating the emotional terrain of our elders.* New York: Riverhead Books.

Pirke, K. M., Dogs, M., Fichter, M. M., & Tuschil, R. J. (1988). Gonadotrophin, oestradiol, and progesterone during the menstrual cycle in bulimia nervosa. *Clinical Endocrinology Metabolism, 60,* 1174-1179.

Pirog-Good, M. (1995). The family background and attitudes of teen fathers. *Youth and Society, 26*(3), 351-376.

Plante, M. (2000). Fertility preservation in the management of gynecological cancers. *Current Opinion in Oncology, 12*(5), 497-507.

Plath, D. (1980). *Long engagements.* Stanford, CA: Stanford University Press.

Platt, R., Rice, P., & McCormack, W. (1983). Risk of acquiring gonorrhea and prevalence of abnormal adnexal findings among women recently exposed to gonorrhea. *Journal of the American Medical Association, 250,* 3205-3209.

Poehlmann, J., & Fiese, B. (1994). The effects of divorce, maternal employment, and maternal social support on toddlers' home environments. *Journal of Divorce and Remarriage, 22*(1/2), 121-135.

Pomeroy, C., & Mitchell, J. E. (1989). Medical complications and management of eating disorders. *Psychiatric Annals, 19*(9), 488-493.

Poon, L. W., Clayton, G. M., Martin, P., Johnson, M. A., Courtenay, B. C., Sweaney, A. L., Merriam, S. B., Pless, B. S., & Thielman, S. B. (1992). The Georgia Centenarian Study. *International Journal of Aging and Human Development, 34*(1), 1-17.

Population Council Inc. (1999). CDC on infant and maternal mortality in the United States: 1900-1999. *Population and Development Review, 25*(25), 821-824.

Portes, A., & Rumbaut, R. G. (2001). *Legacies.* Berkeley: University of California Press.

Post, S. (1992). Aging and meaning: The Christian tradition. In T. Cole, D. van Tassel, & R. Kastenbaum (Eds.), *Handbook of the humanities and aging* (pp. 127-146). New York: Springer.

Pothoff, S., Bearinger, L., Skay, C., Cassuto, N., Blum, R., & Resnick, M. (1998). Dimensions of risk behaviors among American Indian youth. *Archives of Pediatric & Adolescent Medicine, 152,* 157-163.

Powlishta, K. K., Serbin, L. A., Doyle, A., & White, D. R. (1994). Gender, ethnic, and body type biases: The generality of prejudice in childhood. *Developmental Psychology, 30,* 526-536.

Preto, N. (1999). Transformation of the family system during adolescence. In B. Carter & M. McGoldrick (Eds.), *The expanded family life cycle: Individual, family, and social perspectives* (3rd ed., pp. 274-286). Boston: Allyn & Bacon.

Pridham, K., & Chang, A. (1992). Transition to being the mother of a new infant in the first 3 months: Maternal problem solving and self-appraisals. *Journal of Advanced Nursing, 17,* 204.

Providers examine teen contraceptive use. (2001, September). *Contraceptive Technology Update.* Electronic Collection A77711625.

Pulkkinen, L., & Kokko, K. (2000). Identity development in adulthood: A longitudinal study. *Journal of Research in Personality,* 34, 445-470.

Putney, N., & Bengtson, V. (2001). Families, intergenerational relationships, and kinkeeping in midlife. In M. Lachmann (Ed.), *Handbook of midlife development* (pp. 528-570). New York: Wiley.

Pyke, D., & Bengtson, V. (1996). Caring more or less: Individualistic and collectivist systems of family eldercare. *Journal of Marriage and the Family, 58,* 379-392.

Rabkin, J., Balassone, M., & Bell, M. (1995). The role of social workers in providing comprehensive health care to pregnant women. *Social Work in Health Care, 20*(3), 83-97.

Ramey, C. T., Campbell, F. A., & Blair, C. (1998). Enhancing the life-course for high-risk children: Results from the Abecedarian Project. In J. Crane (Ed.), *Social programs that work* (pp. 163-183). New York: Russell Sage.

Rando, T. (1993). *Treatment of complicated mourning.* Champaign, IL: Research Press.

Rauch, J. (1988). Social work and the genetics revolution: Genetic services. *Social Work, 9/10,* 389-395.

Reed, G. B. (1996). Introduction to genetic screening and prenatal diagnoses. In J. J. Sciarra (Ed.), *Gynecology and obstetrics* (rev. ed., pp. 999-1003). Philadelphia, PA: Lippincott-Raven.

Remafedi, G., Farrow, J. A., & Deisher, R. W. (1991). Risk factors for attempted suicide in gay and bisexual youth. *Pediatrics, 87,* 869-875.

Remafedi, G., Resnick, M., Blum, R., & Harris, L. (1992). Demography of sexual orientation in adolescents. *Pediatrics, 89,* 714-721.

Research Forum on Children, Families and the New Federalism (2002). Lack of appropriate research leads to gaps in knowledge about children in immigrant families. *Forum, 5*(1).

Rexrod, K., & Manson, J. (2002) Postmenopausal hormone therapy and quality of life: No cause for celebration. *JAMA, The Journal of the American Medical Association, 287*(5), 591-597.

Richmond, M. (1917). *Social diagnosis.* New York: Russell Sage.

Riedmann, G. (1996). Preparation for parenthood. In J. J. Sciarra (Ed.), *Gynecology and obstetrics* (Vol. 2, 2nd ed., pp. 1-8). Philadelphia, PA: Lippincott-Raven.

Rigby, K. (1998). Gender and bullying in schools. In P.T. Slee & K. Rigby (eds), *Children's Peer Relations* (pp. 47-59). New York, NY: Routledge.

Riley, M. (1996). Discussion: What does it all mean? *The Gerontologist, 36*(2), 256-258.

Riley, M. W. (1971). Social gerontology and the age stratification of society. *The Gerontologist, 11,* 79-87.

Rimm, S. (1999). *See Jane win.* New York: Three Rivers Press.

Rindfuss, R. R., Cooksey, E. C., & Sutterlin, R. L. (1999). Young adult occupational achievement: Early expectations versus behavioral reality. *Work & Occupations, 26*(2), 220-263.

Rindfuss, R., Swicegood, G., & Rosenfeld, R. (1987). Disorder in the life course: How common and does it matter? *American Sociological Review, 52,* 785-801.

Riordan, J. (1993a). The cultural context of breastfeeding. In J. Riordan & K. Auerbach (Eds.), *Breastfeeding and human lactation.* Boston, MA: Jones & Bartlett.

Riordan, J. (1993b). Viruses in human milk. In J. Riordan & K. Auerbach (Eds.), *Breastfeeding and human lactation.* Boston: Jones & Bartlett.

Roberts, E., Burchinal, M., & Bailey, D. (1994). Communication among preschoolers with and without disabilities in same-age and mixed-age classes. *American Journal on Mental Retardation, 99,* 231-249.

Roberts, M. (1979). Reciprocal nature of parent-infant interaction: Implications for child maltreatment. *Child Welfare, 58*(6), 383-392.

Roberts, R. E. L., & Bengston, V. L. (1993). Relationship with parents, self-esteem, & psychological well-being in young adulthood. *Social Psychology Quarterly, 56*(4), 263-278.

Roberts, R. E., Roberts, C. R., & Chen, Y. R. (1997). Ethnocultural differences in prevalence of adolescent depression. *American Journal of Community Psychology, 25*(1), 95-111.

Robinson, J. A. (1998). The impact of race and ethnicity on children's peer relations. In P. T. Slee & K. Rigby (Eds.), *Children's peer relations* (pp. 76-88). New York: Routledge.

Robinson, L. C. (2000). Interpersonal relationship quality in young adulthood: A gender analysis. *Adolescence, 35*(140), 775-785.

Rock, P. (1996). Eugenics and euthanasia: A cause for concern for disabled people, particularly disabled women. *Disability & Society, 11*(1), 121-127.

Rodriquez, A. (1983). Educational policy and cultural plurality. In G. Powell, J. Yamamoto, A. Romero, & A. Morales (Eds.), *The psychosocial development of minority group children* (pp. 499-512). New York: Brunner/Mazel.

Roe, K., & Minkler, M. (1998/99). Grandparents raising grandchildren: Challenges and responses. *Generations, 22*(4), 28-33.

Roebers, C., & Schneider, W. (1999). Self-concept and anxiety in immigrant children. *International Journal of Behavioral Development, 23*(1), 125-147.

Rogers, R. (1989). Ethnic and birth-weight differences in cause-specific infant mortality. *Demography, 26,* 335-341.

Ronka, A., & Pulkkinen, L. (1995). Accumulation of problems in social functioning in young adulthood: A developmental approach. *Journal of Personality and Social Psychology, 69*(2), 381-391.

Roof, W. (1993). *A generation of seekers: The spiritual journeys of the baby boom generation.* San Francisco: HarperCollins.

Roof, W. (1999). *Spiritual marketplace: Baby boomers and the remaking of American religion.* Princeton, NJ: Princeton University Press.

Roopnarine, J., Shin, M., Donovan, B., & Suppal, P. (2000). Sociocultural contexts of dramatic play: Implications for early education. In K. Roskos & J. Christie (Eds.), *Play and literacy in early childhood: Research from multiple perspectives* (pp. 205-220). Mahway, NJ: Lawrence Erlbaum.

Rose, S., & Zand, D. (2000). Lesbian dating and courtship from young adulthood to midlife. *Journal of Gay & Lesbian Social Services, 11*(2/3), 77-104.

Rosenbaum, J. (1991). Black pioneers: Do their moves to the suburbs increase economic opportunity for mothers and children? *Housing Policy Debate, 2*(4), 1179-1213.

Rosenberg, M. (1986). *Conceiving the self.* Malabar, FL: Robert E. Krieger.

Rosenfeld, J. A., & Everett, K. D. (1996). Factors related to planned and unplanned pregnancies. *Journal of Family Practice, 43*(2), 161-166.

Rosenthal, C. (1985). Kinkeeping in the familial division of labor. *Journal of Marriage and the Family, 47,* 965-974.

Roskos, K., & Christie, J. (2000). *Play and literacy in early childhood: Research from multiple perspectives.* Mahway, NJ: Lawrence Erlbaum.

Rosow, I. (1978). What is a cohort and why? *Human Development, 21*, 65-75.

Ross, L. J. (1992). African-American women and abortion: A neglected history. *Journal of Health Care for the Poor and Underserved, 3*, 274-284.

Ross, M., & Holmberg, D. (1992). Are wives' memories for events in relationships more vivid than their husband's memories? *Journal of Social and Personal Relationships, 9*, 585-604.

Ross, S. (1996). Risk of physical abuse to children of spouse abusing parents. *Child Abuse and Neglect, 20*, 589-598.

Rossi, A., & Rossi, P. (1990). *Of human bonding: Parent-child relations across the life course*. New York: Aldine de Gruyter.

Rotheram-Borus, M. J. (1993). Biculturalism among adolescents. In M. Bernal & G. Knight (Eds.), *Ethnic identity* (pp. 81-102). Albany: State University of New York Press.

Rothman, B. K. (1991). *In labor, women and power in the birthplace*. New York and London: Norton.

Roueche, J. E., & Baker, G. A., III. (1986). *Profiling excellence in America's schools*. Arlington, VA: American Association of School Administrators.

Rovee-Collier, C. (1999). The development of infant memory. *Current directions in psychological science, 8*(3), 80-85.

Rubin, K. (1986). Play, peer interaction, and social development. In A. Gottfried & C. Brown (Eds.), *Play interactions: The contribution of play materials and parental involvement to children's development* (pp. 163-174). Lexington, MA: Heath.

Rubin, K., Fein, G., & Vandenberg, B. (1983). Play. In E. M. Hetherington (Ed.). *Handbook of child psychology: Vol. 4. Socialization, personality, and social development* (4th ed., pp. 693-744). New York: Wiley.

Rubin, R. (1995). *Maternal identity and the maternal experience: Childbirth educator.* New York: Springer.

Russell, D. E. H. (1984). *Sexual exploitation: Rape, child sexual abuse, and workplace harassment.* Beverly Hills, CA: Sage.

Rutter, M. (1996). Transitions and turning points in developmental psychopathology: As applied to the age span between childhood and mid-adulthood. *International Journal of Behavioral Development, 19*(3), 603-636.

Ryan, A. S. (1997). The resurgence of breastfeeding in the United States. *Pediatrics, 99*(4), E12./

Ryan, B. A., & Adams, G. R. (1995). The family-school relationships model. In B. A. Ryan, G. R. Adams, T. P. Gullotta, R. P. Weissberg, & R. L. Hampton (Eds.), *The family-school connection: Theory, research, and practice* (pp. 3-28). Thousand Oaks, CA: Sage.

Ryan, C., & Futterman, D. (1998). *Lesbian and gay youth: Care and counseling.* New York: Columbia University Press.

Ryder, N. (1965). The cohort as a concept in the study of social change. *American Sociological Review, 30*, 843-861.

Sacchetti, A. D., Gerardi, M., Sawchuck, P., & Bihl, I. (1997). Boomerang babies: Emergency department utilization at early discharge neonates. *Pediatric Emergency Care, 13*, 365-368.

Sadker, M., Sadker, D., Fox, L., & Salata, M. (1994). Gender inequity in the classroom. In J. I. Goodlad & P. Keating (Eds.), *Access to knowledge: The continuing agenda for our nation's schools* (rev. ed., pp. 321-328). New York: College Entrance Examination Board.

Sadovsky, R. (2002). Evaluation and management of male infertility. *American Family Physician, 66*(77), 1299.

Safren, S., & Heimberg, R. (1999). Depression, hopelessness, suicidality, and related factors in sexual minority and heterosexual adolescents. *Journal of Consulting and Clinical Psychology, 67*(6), 859-866.

Saghir, M. T., & Robins, E. (1973). *Male and female homosexuality: A comprehensive examination.* Baltimore. MD: Williams & Wilkins.

Saleeby, D. (1996). The strengths perspective in social work practice: Extensions and cautions. *Social Work, 41*(3), 296-304.

Sampson, R. J., & Laub, J. H. (1990). Crime and deviance over the life course: The salience of adult social bonds. *American Sociological Review, 55*, 609-627.

San Francisco Fertility Centers. (2002). *Non-IVF treatments: Intrauterine insemination.* Retrieved September 9, 2002, from www.sffertility.com/nonivf/non_ivf_iui.htm.

Sands, R., & Goldberg, G. (2000). Factors associated with stress among grandparents raising their grandchildren. *Family Relations, 49*(1), 97-105.

Santrock, J. W. (1995). *Life-span development* (5th ed.). Madison, WI: Brown & Benchmark.

Sapolsky, R. (1998). *Why zebras don't get ulcers: An updated guide to stress, stress-related diseases, and coping.* New York: W.H. Freeman

Savin-Williams, R. C. (1979). Dominance hierarchies in groups of early adolescents. *Child Development, 50*, 923-935.

Sawin, K. S. (1998). Health care concerns for women with physical disability and chronic illness. In E. Q. Youngkin & M. S. Davis (Eds.), *Women's health: A primary care clinical guide* (2nd ed., pp. 905-941). Stamford, CT: Appleton & Lange.

Scannapieco, M., & Jackson, S. (1996). Kinship care: The African American response to family preservation. *Social Work, 41*(2), 190-196.

Schachere, K. (1990). Attachment between working mothers and their infants: The influence of family processes. *American Journal of Orthopsychiatry, 60*, 19-34.

Schaie, K. W. (1982). Toward a stage theory of adult cognitive development. In K. W. Schaie & J. Geiwitz (Eds.), *Readings in adult development and aging*. Boston, MA: Little, Brown.

Schaie, K. W. (1984). The Seattle Longitudinal Study: A 21-year exploration of psychometric intelligence in adulthood. In K. W. Schaie (Ed.), *Longitudinal studies of adult psychological development* (pp. 64-135). New York: Guilford.

Schaie, K., Willis, S., & O'Hanlon, A. (1994). Perceived intellectual performance change over seven years. *Journal of Gerontology: Psychological Sciences, 49*, 108-118.

Schild, S., & Black, R. (1984). *Social work and genetics: A guide for practice*. New York: Haworth.

Schmitt, B. (1988). Failure to thrive: The medical evaluation. In D. Bross, R. Krigman, M. Lenherr, D. Rosenberg, & B. Schmitt (Eds.), *The new child protection team handbook* (pp. 82-101). New York: Garland.

Schmitz, C., & Hilton, A. (1996). Combining mental health treatment with education for preschool children with severe emotional and behavioral problems. *Social Work in Education, 18*, 237-249.

Schubot, D. (2001). Date rape prevalence among female high school students in a rural Midwestern state during 1993, 1995, and 1997. *Journal of Interpersonal Violence, 16*(4), 291-296.

Schuetze, P., Lewis, A., & DiMartino, D. (1999). Relation between time spent in daycare and exploratory behavior. *Infant Behavior & Development Special Issue, 22*(2), 267-276.

Scott, J. (1997). Family relationships of midlife and older women. In J. Coyle (Ed.), *Handbook on women and aging* (pp. 367-384). Westport, CT: Greenwood Press.

Scott, K. D., Berkowitz, G., & Klaus, M. H. (1999). A comparison of intermittent and continuous support during labor: A meta-analysis. *American Journal of Obstetrics and Gynecology, 180*(5), 1054.

Seefeldt, C. (1993). Educating yourself about diverse cultural groups in our country by reading. *Young Children, 48*, 13-16.

Segal, B. M., & Stewart, J. C. (1996). Substance use and abuse in adolescence: An overview. *Child Psychiatry and Human Development, 26*(4), 193-210.

Seifer, R., & Dickstein, S. (2000) Paternal mental illness and infant development. In C. Zeanah (Ed.), *Handbook of infant mental health* (2nd ed., 145-160). New York: Guilford.

Seifert, K. L., Hoffnung, R. J., & Hoffnung, M. (1997). *Lifespan development*. New York: Houghton Mifflin.

Seligman, M. E. P., Reivich, K., Jaycox, L., & Gillham, J. (1995). *The optimistic child*. New York: Houghton Mifflin.

Selman, R. L. (1976). Social-cognitive understanding: A guide to educational and clinical practice. In T. Lickona (Ed.), *Moral development and behavior: Theory, research, and social issues* (pp. 219-316). New York: Holt, Rinehart, & Winston.

Serbin, L. A., Powlishta, K. K., & Gulko, J. (1993). The development of sex typing in middle childhood. *Monographs of the Society for Research in Child Development, 58*(2), Serial No. 232.

Settersten, R., Jr. (1998). A time to leave home and a time never to return? Age constraints on the living arrangements of young adults. *Social Forces, 76*(4), 1373-1400.

Settersten, R., Jr., & Lovegreen, L. (1998). Educational experiences throughout adult life: New hopes or no hope for life-course flexibility? *Research on Aging, 20*(4), 506-538.

Settersten, R. A., & Mayer, L. U. (1997). The measurement of age, age structuring, and the life course. *Annual Review of Sociology, 23*, 233-261.

Severy, L. J., & Spieler, J. (2000). New methods of family planning: Implications for intimate behavior. *Journal of Sex Research, 37*(3), 258-264.

Sex bias cited in vocational ed. (2002, June 6). *Washington Post*, pp. 18-19.

Sexually transmitted diseases and adolescents. (1996). *State Legislatures, 22*(4),7.

Shanahan, M. (2000). Pathways to adulthood in changing societies: Variability and mechanisms in life course perspective. *Annual Review of Sociology, 27*, 667-692.

Shanahan, M., & Flaherty, B. (2001). Dynamic patterns of time use in adolescence. *Child Development, 72*(2), 385-401.

Shanahan, M., Miech, R., & Elder, G., Jr. (1998). Changing pathways to attainment in men's lives: Historical patterns of school, work, and social class. *Social Forces, 77*(1), 231-266.

Shapiro, P. (1996). *My turn: Women's search for self after the children leave.* Princeton, NJ: Peterson's.

Shaver, J., Giblin, E., Lentz, M., & Lee, K. (1988). Sleep patterns and stability in perimenopausal women. *Sleep, 11,* 556-561.

Shaw, S., Kleiber, D., & Caldwell, L. (1995). Leisure and identity formation in male and female adolescents: A preliminary examination. *Journal of Leisure Research, 27,* 245-263.

Sheehy, G. (1995). *New passages.* New York: Random House.

Shepard, M. (1992). Child visiting and domestic abuse. *Child Welfare, 71,* 357-367.

Sherman, A., de Vries, B., & Lansford, J. (2000). Friendship in childhood and adulthood: Lessons across the life span. *International Journal of Aging and Human Development, 51*(1), 31-51.

Sherman, E. (1991). *Reminiscence and the self in old age.* New York: Springer.

Shonkoff, J., & Phillips, D. (Eds.) (2000). *From neurons to neighborhoods: The science of early childhood development.* Washington, DC: National Academy Press.

Shonkoff, J., Hauser-Cram, P., Krauss, M, & Upshur, C. (1992). Development of infants with disabilities and their families: Implications for theory and service delivery. *Monographs of the Society for Research in Child Development, 57*(6), 230-239.

Shrier, L. A., Emans, S. J., Woods, E. R., & DuRant, R. H. (1996). The association of sexual risk behaviors and problem drug behaviors in high school students. *Journal of Adolescent Health, 20,* 377-383.

Shweder, R. (Ed.). (1998). *Welcome to middle age (and other cultural fictions).* Chicago: University of Chicago Press.

Siefert, K., & Pimlott, S. (2001). Improving pregnancy outcome during imprisonment: A model residental care program. *Social Work, 46*(2), 125-134.

Silvern, L., & Kaersvang, L. (1989). The traumatized children of violent marriages. *Child Welfare, 68,* 421-436.

Silverstein, M., & Bengtson, V. (1997). Intergenerational solidarity and the structure of adult child-parent relationships in American families. *American Journal of Sociology, 103,* 429-460.

Silverstein, M., & Bengtson, V. (2001). Intergenerational solidarity and the structure of adult child-parent relationships in American families. In A. Walker, M. Manoogian-O'Dell, L. McGraw, & D. L. White (Eds.), *Families in later life: Connections and transitions* (pp. 53-61). Thousand Oaks, CA: Pine Forge.

Silverstein, M., & Long, J. (1998). Trajectories of grandparents' perceived solidarity with adult grandchildren: A growth curve analysis over 23 years. *Journal of Marriage and the Family, 60,* 912-923.

Sinnott, J. D. (1986). Prospective/intentional and incidental everyday memory: Effects of age and passage of time. *Psychology and Aging, 1,* 110-116.

Sitzer, A. R. (1998). Early discharge and the neonate. *Clinical Pediatrics, 37*(10), 617-620.

Skinner, B. F. (1957). *Verbal behavior.* Englewood Cliffs, NJ: Prentice-Hall.

Skolnick, A., & Skolnick, J. (1996). *The family in transition* (9th ed.). Reading, MA: Addison-Wesley.

Slee, R. (1995). Inclusive education: From policy to school implementation. In C. Clark, A. Dyson, & A. Millward (Eds.), *Towards inclusive schools?* New York: Teachers College Press.

Small, S., Silverberg, S., & Kerns, D. (1993). Adolescents' perceptions of the costs and benefits of engaging in health-compromising behaviors. *Journal of Youth and Adolescence, 22,* 73-87.

Smeeding, T., & Rainwater, L. (1995). Cross-national trends in income, poverty, and dependence: The evidence for young adults in the eighties. In K. McFate (Ed.), *Poverty, inequality, and the future of social policy.* New York: Russell Sage.

Smetana, J. G., Killen, M., & Turiel, E. (1991). Children's reasoning about interpersonal and moral conflicts. *Child Development, 62,* 629-644.

Smith, A., Dannison L., & Vach-Hasse, T. (1998). When grandma is mom. *Childhood Education, 75*(1), 12-16.

Smith, D., Prentice, R., Thompson, D., & Hermann, W. (1975). Association of extrogenous estrogen and endometrial carcinoma. *New England Journal of Medicine, 293*(23), 1164-1167.

Smith, D., Stormshak, E., Chamberlain, P., & Whaley, R. (2001). Placement disruption in foster care. *Journal of Emotional and Behavioral Disorders, 9,* 200-211.

Smith, E., Udry, J., & Morris, N. (1985). Pubertal development and friends: A biosocial explanation of adolescent sexual behavior. *Journal of Health and Social Behavior, 26*, 183-192.

Smith, J. D., & Polloway, E. A. (1993). Institutionalization, involuntary sterilization, and mental retardation: Profiles from the history of the practice. *Mental Retardation, 314*, 208-214.

Smith, J., O'Connor, I., & Berthelsen, D. (1996). The effects of witnessing domestic violence on young children's psycho-social adjustment. *Australian Social Work, 49*(4), 3-10.

Smith, M. A., Acheson, L. S., Byrd, J. E., Curtis, P., Day, T. W., Frank, S. H., Franks, P., Graham, A. V., LeFevre, M., Resnick, J., & Wall, E. M. (1991). A critical review of labor and birth care. *Journal of Family Practice, 33*(3), 281-293.

Smyer, M. A., Gatz, M., Simi, N. L., & Pedersen, N. L. (1998). Childhood adoption: Long-term effects in adulthood. *Psychiatry: Interpersonal and Biological Processes, 61*(3), 191.

Snarey, J. (1993). *How fathers care for the next generation: A four-decade study.* Cambridge, MA: Harvard University Press.

Snyder, H. (2000, December). *Juvenile arrests 1999.* Washington, DC: Office of Juvenile Justice and Delinquency Prevention-Juvenile Justice Bulletin.

Social Security Administration. (n.d.). Full retirement age goes from 65 to . . . 66 . . . 67. Retrieved June 25, 2002, from www.ssa.gov/pub/retirechart.htm.

Soldo, B. J., & Agree, E. M. (1988). America's elderly. *Population Bulletin, 43*, 1-51.

Solomon, R. C. (1988). *About love: Reinventing romance for modern times.* New York: Simon & Schuster.

Song, Y., & Lu, H. (2002). *Early childhood poverty: A statistical profile (March 2002).* New York: National Center for Children in Poverty. Retrieved August 21, 2002, from cpmcnet.columbia.edu/dept/nccp/ecp302.html.

Soto, O. (2001, June 3). Drug-assisted date rapes on rise, hard to prosecute. *San Diego Union Tribune*. Retrieved August 26, 2002, from www.vachss.com/help_text/archive/drug_assisted.html.

Speare, A., Jr., & Avery, R. (1993). Who helps whom in older parent-child families? *Journal of Gerontology, 48*, S64-S73.

Speckland, A. (1993). Complicated mourning: Dynamics of impacted post abortion grief. *Pre- and Peri-natal Psychology Journal, 8*(1), 5-32.

Spence, A. P. (1989). *Biology of aging.* Englewood Cliffs, NJ: Prentice-Hall.

Spencer, M. (1985). Black children's race awareness, racial attitudes and self concept: A reinterpretation. *Annual Progress in Child Psychiatry & Child Development*, 616-630.

Spencer, N., & Logan, S. (2002). Social influences on birth weight: Risk factors for low birth weight are strongly influenced by the social environment. *Archives of Disease in Childhood: Fetal and Neonatal Edition, 86*(1), 6-8.

Spiro, A. (2001). Health in midlife: Toward a life-span view. In M. Lachmann (Ed.), *Handbook of midlife development* (pp. 156-187). New York: Wiley.

Spitze, G., Logan, J., Joseph, G., & Lee, E. (1994). Middle generations and the well-being of men and women. *Journal of Gerontology: Social Sciences, 49*, S107-S116.

Splete, J. (2002). New tool assesses ectopic pregnancy (Microculdoscopy). *OB GYN News, 37*(3), 1-2.

Spring, J. H. (1997). *Conflict of interests: The politics of American education.* Boston: McGraw-Hill.

Spring, J. H. (2000). *The American school 1642-2000.* Boston: McGraw-Hill.

Sroufe, L. A., Cooper, R. G., & DeHart, G. B. (1996). *Child development: Its nature and course* (3rd ed.). New York: McGraw-Hill.

Stacey, J. (1996). *In the name of the family: Rethinking family values in the postmodern age.* Boston, MA: Beacon.

Stack, C. (1974). *All our kin.* New York: Harper & Row.

Stack, D., & Muir, D. (1992). Adult tactile stimulation during face-to-face interactions modulates five-month-olds' affect and attention. *Child Development, 63*, 1509-1525.

Stamler, J., Stamler, R., Neaton, J., Wentworth, D., Daviglus, M., Garside, D., Dyer, A., Lin, K., & Greenland, P. (1999). Low risk-factor profile and long-term cardiovascular and noncardiovascular mortality and life expectancy: Findings for 5 large cohorts of young adult and middle-aged men and women. *Journal of the American Medical Association, 282*, 2012-2018.

Starbird, E. H. (1991). Comparison of influences on breast-feeding initiation of firstborn children, 1960-69 vs. 1979. *Social Science and Medicine, 33*, 627-634.

Staudinger, U., & Bluck, S. (2001). A view on midlife development from life-span theory. In M. Lachman (Ed.), *Handbook of midlife development* (pp. 3-39). New York: Wiley.

Steinhauer, J. (1995, April 10). Big benefits in marriage, studies say. *New York Times*. p. A10.

Stepp, L. (2001, July 31). Welfare reform's unexpected difficulties: Study finds problems among adolescents. *Washington Post*, p. A3.

Sternberg, K. J., Lamb, M. E., Greenbaum, C., Cicchetti, D., Dawut, S., Cortes, R. M., Krispin, O., & Lorey, F. (1993). Effects of domestic violence on children's behavior problems and depression. *Developmental Psychology, 29,* 44-52.

Sterns, H., & Huyck, M. (2001). The role of work in midlife. In M. Lachman (Ed.), *Handbook of midlife development* (pp. 447-486). New York: Wiley.

Stevens, L. M. (2002). Low birth weight. *Journal of the American Medical Association, 287*(2), 270.

Stevens, S. J., & Patton, T. (1998). Residential treatment for drug addicted women and their children: Effective treatment strategies. *Drugs and Society, 13,* 235-249.

Stewart, A., & Vandewater, E. (1998). The course of generativity. In D. McAdams & E. de St. Aubin (Eds.), *Generativity and adult development: How and why we care for the next generation* (pp. 75-100). Washington, DC: American Psychological Association.

Stokes, J., & Greenstone, J. (1981). Helping black grandparents and older parents cope with child rearing: a group method. *Child Welfare, 60*(10), 691-701.

Stolzenberg, R. M., Blair-Loy, M., & Waite, L. J. (1995). Religious participation in early adulthood: Age and family life cycle effects on church membership. *American Sociological Review, 60*(1), 84-104.

Stovall, K., & Dozier, M. (1998). Infants in foster care: An attachment theory perspective. *Adoption Quarterly, 2*(1), 55-88.

Strathearn, L., Gary, P., & O'Callaghan, M., (2001). Childhood neglect and cognitive development in extremely low birth weight infants: A prospective study. *Pediatrics, 108*(1), 142-152.

Stroebe, M., Stroebe, W., & Hansson, R. (1993). *Handbook on bereavement: Theory, research and intervention.* New York: Cambridge University Press.

Substance Abuse and Mental Health Services Administration. (2000). *Uniform Facility Data Set (UFDS).* DHHS: Pub No (SMA) 00-3463. Rockville, MD.

Suh, E., & Abel, E. (1990). The impact of violence on the children of the abused. *Journal of Independent Social Work, 4*(4), 27-43.

Sun, A., Shillington, A., Hohman, M., & Jones, L. (2001). Caregiver AOD use, case substantiation, and AOD treatment: Studies based on two southwestern counties. *Child Welfare, 80*(2), 151-177.

Swap, S. M. (1993). *Developing home-school partnerships: From concepts to practice.* New York: Teachers College Press.

Sweet, J., & Bumpass, L. (1996). *The national survey of families and households-Waves 1 and 2.* Madison, WI: Center for Demography and Ecology, University of Wisconsin-Madison.

Szinovacz, M. (1998). Grandparents today. A demographic profile. *The Gerontologist, 38,* 37-52.

Taddio, A., Shah, V., Gilbert-Macleod, C., & Katz, J. (2002). Conditioning and hyperalgesia in newborns exposed to repeated heel lances. *Journal of American Medical Association, 288*(7), 857-861.

Takahashi, E. A., & Turnbull, J. E. (1994). New findings in psychiatric genetics: Implications for social work practice. *Social Work in Health Care, 20*(2), 1-21.

Takahashi, K. (1990). Are the key assumptions of the "strange situation" procedure universal? A view from Japanese research. *Human Development, 33,* 23-30.

Tanner, J. M. (1990). *Fetus into man: Physical growth from conception to maturity.* Cambridge, MA: Harvard University Press.

Tatum, B. D. (1999) *Why are all the Black kids sitting together in the cafeteria? And other conversations about race* (rev. ed). New York: Basic Books.

Tay, J. I., Moore, J., & Walker, J. J. (2000). Ectopic pregnancy. *British Medical Journal, 320*(7239), 916-922.

Taylor, H. (2000). Meeting the needs of lesbian and gay young adolescents. *Clearing House, 73*(4), 221-224.

Teicher, M. (2002). Scars that won't heal: The neurobiology of child abuse. *Scientific American, 286*(3), 68-75.

Teitelman, J. L. (1995). Homosexuality. In G. L. Maddox (Ed.), *The encyclopedia of aging: A comprehensive resource in gerontology and geriatrics* (2nd ed., p. 270). New York: Springer.

Teplin, S. W., Burchinal, M., Johnson-Martin, N., Humphrey, R. A., & Kraybill, E. N. (1991). Neurodevelopmental, health, and growth status at age 6 years of children with birth weights less than 1000 grams. *Journal of Pediatrics, 118,* 751-760.

Terr, L. C. (1991). Childhood traumas: An outline and overview. *American Journal of Psychiatry, 148,* 10-20.

Thapa, S., Short, R. V., & Potts, M. (1988). Breastfeeding, birthspacing, and their effects on child survival. *Nature, 335,* 679-682.

Thoits, P. (1985). Social support and psychological well-being: Theoretical possibilities. In I. Sarason & B. R. Sarason (Eds.), *Social support theory, research and applications* (pp. 51-72). Boston, MA: Martinus Nijhoff.

Thomas, A., & Chess, S. (1986). The New York longitudinal study: From infancy to early adult life. In R. Plomin & J. Dunn (Eds.), *The study of temperament: Changes, continuities, and challenges* (pp. 39-52). Hillside, NJ: Lawrence Erlbaum.

Thomas, A., Chess, S., & Birch, H. G. (1968). *Temperament and behavior disorders in children.* New York: New York University Press.

Thomas, A., Chess, S., & Birch, H.G. (1970). The origin of personality. *Scientific American, 223,* 102-109.

Thomas, J. L. (1992). *Adulthood and aging.* Needham Heights, MA: Allyn & Bacon.

Thompson, R., & Nelson, C. (2001). Developmental science and the media: Early brain development. *American Psychologist, 56*(1), 5-15.

Thursby, G. (1992). Islamic, Hindu and Buddhist conceptions of aging. In T. Cole, D. van Tassel, & R. Kastenbaum (Eds.), *Handbook of humanities and aging* (pp. 175-196). New York: Springer.

Tiedje, L. B. (2001). Fathers' coping style, antenatal preparation, and experiences of labor and postpartum. *MCN, The American Journal of Maternal and Child Nursing, 26*(2), 108.

Tiet, Q., Bird, H., Hoven, C., Wu, P., Moore, R., & Davies, M. (2001). Resilience in the face of maternal psychopathology and adverse life events. *Journal of Child and Family Studies, 10*(3), 347-365.

Tomal, A., (1999). Determinants of teenage birth rates as an unpooled sample: Age matters for socioeconomic predictors. *American Journal of Economics and Sociology, 58*(1), 57.

Trattner, W. I. (1994). *From poor law to welfare state: A history of social welfare in America* (5th ed.). New York: Free Press.

Trifiletti, R. (2001). Febrile seizures following childhood vaccinations: A risk worth taking. *Neurology Alert, 20*(2), 15.

Trimble, J., Gay, H., & Docherty, J. (1986). Characterization of the tumor-associated 38-kd protein of herpes simples virus Type II. *Journal of Reproductive Medicine, 31*(5), 399-409.

Tueth, M. J. (1993). Anxiety in the older patient: Differential diagnosis and treatment. *Geriatrics, 48,* 51-54.

Tutty, L., & Wagar, J. (1994). The evolution of a group for young children who have witnessed family violence. *Social Work With Groups, 17*(1/2), 89-104.

Twiss, P., & Cooper, P. (2000). Youth revitalizing Main Street: A case study. *Social Work in Education, 22*(3), 162-176.

Update: Interim recommendations for antimicrobial prophylaxis for children and breastfeeding mothers and treatment for children with anthrax. (2001, November 16). *Morbidity and Mortality Weekly Report.* Electronic collection: A80485416.

U.S. Bureau of Labor Statistics. (1997). Developments in women's labor force participation. *Monthly Labor Review, September 1977* (pp. 41-46). Washington, DC: U.S. Government Printing Office.

U.S. Bureau of the Census. (1995). *Statistical abstract of the United States* (115th ed.). Washington, DC: U.S. Government Printing Office.

U.S. Bureau of the Census. (1999). *Statistical abstract of the United States.* Washington, DC: U.S. Government Printing Office.

U.S. Bureau of the Census. (2000). *Statistical abstract of the United States: 2000.* Washington, DC: Author.

U.S. Bureau of the Census (2001a). Children of "baby boomers" and immigrants boost school enrollment to equal all-time high. Retrieved February 22, 2002, from www.census.gov/press-release/www/2001/cb01-52.html.

U.S. Bureau of the Census. (2001b). *Age: 2000.* Washington, DC: U.S. Government Printing Offfce.

U.S. Bureau of the Census. (2001c). *The 65 years and over population: 2000.* (C2KBR/01-10). Washington, DC: U.S. Department of Commerce.

U.S. Department of Energy Human Genome Program (October 2001*). Genomics and its impact on medicine and society: A 2001 primer.* Washington, DC: U.S. Department of Energy.

U.S. Department of Health and Human Services. (1993). Gay male and lesbian youth suicide. *Report of the Secretary's Task Force on Youth Suicide, 93,* 110-142. Washington, DC: U.S. Government Printing Office.

U.S. Department of Health and Human Services (1995). *A nation's shame: Fatal child abuse and neglect in the United States* (Report of the U.S. Advisory Board on Child Abuse and Neglect). Washington, DC: U.S. Government Printing Office.

U.S. Department of Health and Human Services (2000). *Trends in the well-being of America's children and youth.* Washington, DC: U.S. Government Printing Office.

U.S. Department of Health and Human Services (2001a). New CDC report shows teen birth rate hits record low. *HHS News*. Retrieved April 7, 2002, from www.cdc.gov/nchs/releases/01news/newbirth.html.

U.S. Department of Health and Human Services. (2001b). *Child maltreatment 1999: Reports from the states to the National Child Abuse and Neglect Data System.* Washington, DC: U.S. Government Printing Office.

U.S. Department of Health and Human Services. (2001c). *Youth violence: A report of the surgeon general.* Rockville, MD: U.S. Department of Health and Human Services, Substance Abuse and Mental Health Services Administration, Center for Mental Health Services.

U.S. Department of Health and Human Services, Health Resources and Services. Administration, Maternal and Child Health Bureau. (1995). *Adolescent health fact sheet.* Washington, DC: U.S. Government Printing Office.

U.S. Department of Health and Human Services, Public Health Service. (1991). *Healthy people 2000.* Washington, DC: U.S. Government Printing Office.

U.S. Department of Justice Bureau of Justice Statistics. (2000). *Women ages 16 to 24 experience the highest rates of violence by current or form partners.* Washington, DC: Author.

U.S. Federal Bureau of Prisons (1998). *A profile of female offenders.* Washington, DC: Author.

Udry, J. R. (1993). The politics of sex research. *Journal of Sex Research, 30*(2), 103-110.

Udry, J. R., Billy, J. O. G., Morris, N. M., Groff, T. R., & Raj, M. H. (1985). Serum androgenic hormones motivate sexual behavior in boys. *Fertility and Sterility, 43*(1), 90-94.

Uhlenberg, P. (1996). Mutual attraction: Demography and life-course analysis. *The Gerontologist, 36*(2), 226-229.

Ulizzi, L., & Zonta, L. (1994). Sex ratio and selection by early mortality in humans: Fifty year analysis in different ethnic groups. *Human Biology, 66*(6), 1037-1048.

Uotinen, V. (1998). Age identification: A comparison between Finnish and North-American cultures. *International Journal of Aging & Human Development, 46*(2), 109-125.

Use of assisted reproductive technology: United States 1996 and 1998. *Morbidity and Mortality Weekly Report, 51*(5). Retrieved November 6, 2002, from www.cdc.gov/mmwr/PDF/wk/mm5105.pdf.

Vaillant, G. (1977). *Adaptation to life.* Boston: Little, Brown.

Vaillant, G. (1998). Are social supports in late midlife a cause or a result of successful physical aging? *Psychological Medicine, 28*, 1159-1168.

Vaillant, G. (2002). *Aging well: Surprising guideposts to a happier life from the Landmark Harvard Study of Adult Development.* Boston: Little Brown.

Vallacher, R., & Nowak, A. (1998). *Dynamical social psychology.* New York: Guilford.

Valsiner, J. (1989a). *Human development and culture: The social nature of personality and its study.* Lexington, MA: Lexington Books.

Valsiner, J. (1989b). Social development in infancy and toddlerhood. In *Human development and culture: The social nature of personality and its study* (pp. 163-253). Lexington, MA: Lexington Books.

Van Riper, M. (2001). Family-provider relationships and well-being in families with preterm infants in the NICU. *Heart and Lung: The Journal of Acute and Critical Care, 30*(1), 74-84.

Vandell, D. L., & Wolfe, B. (2000). *Child care quality: Does it matter and does it need to be improved?* (Special Report #78). Madison, WI: Institute for Research on Poverty.

Vandivere, S., Moore, K. A., Brown, B. (2000). Child well-being at the outset of welfare reform: An overview of the nation and 13 states. *New Federalism, National Survey of American Families*, Series B, No. B-23. Washington, DC: The Urban Institute.

Vatuk, S. (1992). Sexuality and the middle-aged woman in South Asia. In V. Kerns & J. K. Brown (Eds.), *In her prime: New views of middle-aged women.* Urbana: University of Illinois Press.

Vekemans, M. (1996). Cytogenetics. In J. J. Sciarra (Ed.), *Gynecology and obstetrics* (rev. ed., pp. 57-66). Philadelphia, PA: Lippincott-Raven.

Vellery-Rodot, R. T. (1926). *The life of Pasteur.* Garden City, NY: Doubleday.

Veltkamp, L., & Miller, T., (1994). *Clinical handbook of child abuse and neglect.* Madison, CT: International Universities Press.

Veltman, M., & Browne, K. (2001). Three decades of child maltreatment research: Implications for the school years. *Trauma Violence & Abuse, 2*(3), 215-239.

Ventura, S. J., Martin, J.A., Curtin, S. C., & Mathews, T. J. (1998). Report of final natality statistics:1996. *Monthly Vital Statistics Report, 46*(225), 1-99.

Vicary, J. R., Klingaman, L. R., & Harkness, W. L. (1995). Risk factors associated with date rape and sexual assault of adolescents. *Journal of Adolescence, 18,* 289-307.

Viggiani, P. A. (1996). *Social worker-teacher collaboration.* Unpublished doctoral dissertation, State University of New York at Albany.

Vissing, Y., Straus, M., Gelles, R., & Harrop, J. (1991). Verbal aggression by parents and psychosocial problems of children. *Child Abuse & Neglect, 15*(3), 223-238.

Vita, A., Terry, R., Hubert, H., & Fries, J. (1998). Aging, health risks, and cumulative disability. *New England Journal of Medicine, 338,* 1035-1041.

Vohr, B. R., Wright, L. L., Dusick, A. S., Mele, L., Verter, J., Steicher, J. J., Simon, N. P., Wilson, D. C., Broyles, S., Bauer, C. R., Delaney-Black, V., Yolton, K. A., Fleisher, B. E., Papile, L. A., & Kaplan, M. D. (2000). Neurodevelopmental and functional outcomes of extremely low birth weight infants: National Institute of Child Health and Human Development Neonatal Research Network 1994. *Pediatrics, 105*(6), 1216-1227.

Vuorenkoski, L., Kuure, O., Moilanen, I., Penninkilampi, V., & Myhrman, A. (2000). Bilingualism, school achievement, and mental wellbeing: A follow-up study of return migrant children. *Journal of Child Psychology and Psychiatry and Allied Disciplines, 41*(2), 261-266.

Vygotsky, L. (1986). *Thought and language.* Cambridge, MA: MIT Press.

Wachs, T. D. (2000). *Necessary but not sufficient: The respective roles of single and multiple influences on individual development.* Washington, DC: American Psychological Association.

Wacker, R. R., Roberto, K. A., & Piper, L. E. (1997). *Community resources for older adults: Programs and services in an era of change.* Thousand Oaks, CA: Pine Forge.

Waldner, L., & Magruder, B. (1999). Coming out to parents: Perceptions of family relations, perceived resources, and identity expression as predictors of identity disclosure for gay and lesbian adolescents. *Journal of Homosexuality, 37*(2), 83-84.

Walker, A., Manoogian-O'Dell, M., McGraw, L., & White, D. (2001). *Families in later life: Connections and transitions.* Thousand Oaks, CA: Pine Forge.

Walker, L., & Taylor, J. (1991). Family interactions and the development of moral reasoning. *Child Development, 62,* 262-283.

Walker, L. (1989). A longitudinal study of moral reasoning. *Child Development, 5,* 33-78.

Walker, L. O. (1992). *Parent-infant nursing science: Paradigms, phenomena, methods.* Philadelphia, PA: Davis.

Walker, S., Berthelsen, D., & Irving, K. (2001). Temperament and peer acceptance in early childhood: Sex and social status differences. *Child Study Journal, 31*(3), 177-192.

Wallerstein, J. S. (1983). Children of divorce: The psychological task of the child. *American Journal of Orthopsychiatry, 53,* 230-243.

Wallerstein, J. S., & Blakeslee, S. (1989). *Second chances: Men, women and children a decade after divorce.* New York: Ticknor & Fields.

Wallerstein, J. S., & Corbin, S. (1991). The child and the vicissitudes of divorce. In M. Lewis (Ed.), *Child and adolescent psychiatry: A comprehensive textbook* (pp. 1108-1118). Baltimore, MD: Williams & Wilkins.

Wallerstein, J. S., Corbin, S., & Lewis, J. (1988). Children of divorce: A ten year study. In E. Hetherington & J. Arasteh (Eds.), *Impact of divorce, single-parenting and step-parenting on children* (pp. 198-214). Hillsdale, NJ: Lawrence Erlbaum.

Wallerstein, J. S., & Kelly, J. (1980). *Surviving the breakup.* New York: Basic Books.

Walling, A. D. (2001). What is optimal strategy in diagnosing ectopic pregnancy? *American Family Physician, 64*(18), 1420-1421.

Walsh, F. (1998). *Strengthening family resilience.* New York: Guilford.

Walsh, F. (1999). Families in later life. In B. Carter & M. McGoldrick (Eds.), *The expanded family life cycle: Individual, family, and social perspectives* (3rd ed., pp. 307-326). Boston: Allyn & Bacon.

Ward, R. R., Logan, J., & Spitze, G. (1992). The influence of parent and child needs on coresidence in middle and later life. *Journal of Marriage and the Family, 54,* 209-221.

Ware, L. (1995). The aftermath of the articulate debate: The invention of inclusive education. In C. Clark, A. Dyson, & A. Millward (Eds.), *Towards inclusive schools?* (pp. 127-146). New York: Teachers College Press.

Waterstone, M., Bewley, S., Wolfe, C., & Murphy, D. J. (2001). Incidence and predictors of severe obstetric morbidity: Case-control study. *British Medical Journal, 322*(7294), 1089-1092.

Watkins, D. R. (2001). Spirituality in social work practice with older persons. In D. O. Moberg (Ed.), *Aging and spirituality: Spiritual dimensions of aging theory, research, practice, and policy*, (pp. 133-146). New York: Haworth Pastoral.

Watson, J., & Crick, F. (1953). Molecular structure of nucleic acids. *Nature, 171,* 737-738.

Waxman, B. F. (1994). Up against eugenics: Disabled women's challenge to receive reproductive health services. *Sexuality and Disability, 12*(2), 155-171.

Weibel-Orlando, J. (2001). Grandparenting styles: Native American perspectives. In A. Walker, M. Manoogian-O'Dell, L. McGraw, & D. White (Eds.), *Families in later life: Connections and transitions* (pp. 139-145). Thousand Oaks, CA: Pine Forge.

Welsh, R. (1985). Spanking: A grand old American tradition? *Children Today, 14*(1), 25-29.

Werner, E. (2000). Protective factors and individual resilience. In J. Shonkoff & S. Meisels (Eds.), *Handbook of early childhood intervention* (2nd ed., pp. 115-132). New York: Cambridge University Press.

Werner, E. E., & Smith, R. S. (1992). *Overcoming the odds: High risk children from birth to adulthood.* Ithaca, NY: Cornell University Press.

Werner, E. E., & Smith, R. S. (2001). *Journeys from childhood to midlife.* Ithaca, NY: Cornell University Press.

West, J. (Ed.). (1991). *The Americans with Disabilities Act.* New York: Millbank Fund.

Weston, K. (1991). *Families we choose: Lesbians, gays, kinship*. New York: Columbia University Press.

What to expect in the next five years: Innovative contraceptive delivery. (2001, May). *Contraceptive Technology Update.* Electronic Collection A74405631.

Wheaton, B., & Gotlib, I. (1997). Trajectories and turning points over the life course: concepts and themes. In I. Gotlib & B. Wheaton (Eds.), *Stress and adversity over the life course: Trajectories and turning points* (pp. 1-25). Cambridge, UK: Cambridge University Press.

Whitbourne, S. (1986). *The me I know: A study of adult identity*. New York: Springer Verlag.

Whitbourne, S. (2001). The physical aging process in midlife: Interactions with psychological and sociocultural factors. In M. Lachman (Ed.), *Handbook of midlife development* (pp. 109-155). New York: Wiley.

Whitbourne, S., & Connolly, L. (1999). The developing self in midlife. In S.Willis & J. Reid (Eds.), *Life in the middle: Psychological and social development in middle age* (pp. 25-45). San Diego, CA: Academic Press.

White, C. (1997). The moral dimension of civic education in the elementary school: Habit or reason. *Journal of Education, 179*(2), 35-46.

White, L., & Edwards, J. (1993). Emptying the nest and parental well-being: An analysis of national panel data. *American Sociological Review, 55,* 235-242.

White, L., & Rogers, S. (1997). Strong support but uneasy relationships: Coresidence and adult children's relationships with their parents. *Journal of Marriage and the Family, 59,* 62-76.

Whiting, B. B., & Whiting, J. W. (1975). *Children of six cultures: A psycho-cultural analysis.* Cambridge, MA: Harvard University Press.

Widmayer, S., Peterson, L., & Larner, M. (1990). Predictors of Haitian-American infant development at twelve months. *Child Development, 61,* 410-415.

Widmer, M. A., Ellis, G. D., & Trunnell, E. P. (1996). Measurement of ethical behavior in leisure among high- and low-risk adolescents. *Adolescence, 31,* 397-408.

Wilber, K. (1977). *The spectrum of consciousness.* Wheaton, IL.: Quest.

Wilber, K. (1995). *Sex, ecology, spirituality: The spirit of evolution*. Boston: Shambhala.

Wilkinson, A., & Lynn, J. (2001). The end of life. In R. H. Binstock & L. K. Geroge (Eds.), *Handbook of aging and the social sciences* (pp. 444-461). New York: Academic Press.

William T. Grant Foundation, Commission on Work, Family, and Citizenship. (1988). *The forgotten half: Pathways to success for America's youth and young families*. New York: Author.

Willis, S., & Schaie, K. (1999). Intellectual functioning in midlife. In S. Willis & J. Reid (Eds.), *Life in the middle: Psychological and social development in middle age* (pp. 234-247). San Diego, CA: Academic Press.

Wilson, R. (1966). *Feminine forever.* New York: M. Evans.

Winnicott, D. (1971). *Playing and reality*. London: Routledge.

Winters, W. G. (1993). *African American mothers and urban schools: The power of participation.* New York: Lexington Books.

Wittenberg, J. (1990). Psychiatric considerations in premature births. *Canadian Journal of Psychiatry, 35,* 734-740.

Wolfner, G., & Gelles, R. (1993). A profile of violence toward children: A national study. *Child Abuse and Neglect, 17,* 197-212.

Woody, D. J., & Green, R. (2001). The influence of race/ethnicity and gender on psychological and social well-being. *Journal of Ethnic & Cultural Diversity in Social Work, 9*(3/4), 151-166.

Wooldredge, J. D. & Masters, K. (1993). Confronting problems faced by pregnant inmates in state prisons. *Crime and Delinquency, 39*(2), 195-203.

Woollett, A., Dosanjh-Matwala, N., Nicolson, P., Marshall, H., Djhanbakhch, O., & Hadlow, J. (1995). The ideas and experiences of pregnancy and childbirth of Asian and non-Asian women in East London. *British Journal of Medical Psychology, 68*, 65-84.

Worden, J. W. (1991). *Grief counseling and grief therapy: A handbook for the mental health practitioner* (2nd ed.). New York: Springer.

World Health Organization Scientific Group. (1996). *Research on the menopause in the 1990s.* World Health Organization Technical Services Report Series No. 886. Geneva: World Health Organization.

Wortman, C., & Silver, R. (1989). The myths of coping with loss. *Journal of Consulting and Clinical Psychology, 57*, 349-357.

Wortman, C., & Silver, R. (1990). Successful mastery of bereavement and widowhood. A life course perspective. In P. Baltes & M. Baltes (Eds.), *Successful aging: Perspectives from the behavioral sciences* (pp. 225-264). Cambridge, UK: Cambridge University Press.

Wright, A., Holberg, C., & Taussig, L .M., & The Group Health Medical Associates Pediatricians (1988). Infant-feeding practices among middle-class Anglos and Hispanics. *Pediatrics, 82*, 496-503. Retrieved from www.ornl.gov/hgmis/elsi.html.

Wrigley, E. (1966). Family limitation in pre-industrial England. *Economic History Review, 19*, 82-109.

Young, D. S. (1996). Contributing factors to poor health among incarcerated women: A conceptual model. *Affilia: Journal of Women and Social Work, 11*(4), 440-461.

Youniss, J. (1980). *Parents and peers in social development. A Piaget-Sullivan perspective.* Chicago: University of Chicago Press.

Younoszai, B. (1993). Mexican American perspectives related to death. In D. Irish, K. Lundquist, & V. Nelsen (Eds.), *Ethnic variations in dying, death, and grief: Diversity in universality* (pp. 67-78). Washington, DC: Taylor & Francis.

Youth Risk Behavior Surveillance System [YRBSS]. (1999). *Youth risk behavior surveillance system.* Atlanta, GA: National Center for Chronic Disease Prevention and Health Promotion. Centers for Disease Control and Prevention.

Yu, V. Y. H., Jamieson, J., & Asbury, J. (1981). Parents' reactions to unrestricted parental contact in the intensive care unit nursery. *Medical Journal of Australia, 1*, 294-296.

Zaslow, M. J., & Emig, C. A. (1997). When low-income mothers go to work: Implications for children. *Future of Children, 7*(1), 110-115.

Zastrow, C., & Kirst-Ashman, K. K. (1997). *Understanding human behavior and the social environment* (4th ed.). Chicago: Nelson-Hall.

Zea, M. C., Diehl, V. A., & Porterfield, K. S. (1997). Central American youth exposed to war violence. In J. Garcia & M. C. Zea (Eds), *Psychological interventions and research with Latino populations* (pp. 39-55). Needham Heights, MA: Allyn & Bacon.

Zeiss, A. M., & Kasl-Godley, J. (2001). Sexuality in older adults' relationships. *Generations, 25(2)*, 18-25.

Ziel, H., & Finkle, W. (1975). Increased risk of endometrial carcinoma among users of conjugated estrogens. *New England Journal of Medicine, 293*(23), 1167-1170.

Zigler, E. F., & Finn-Stevenson, M. (1995). The child care crisis: Implications for the growth and development of the nation's children. *Journal of Social Issues, 51*, 215-231.

Zill, N., Moore, K. A., Smith, E. W., Stief, T., & Coiro, M. J. (1995). The life circumstances and development of children in welfare families: A profile based on national survey data. In P. L. Chase-Lansdale & J. Brooks-Gunn (Eds.), *Escape from poverty: What makes a difference for children?* (pp. 38-59). New York: Cambridge University Press.

Ziolko, M. E. (1993). Counseling parents of children with disabilities: A review of the literature and implications for practice. In M. Nagler (Ed.), *Perspectives on disability* (2nd ed., pp. 185-193). Palo Alto, CA: Health Markets Research.

Zipper, I., & Simeonsson, R. (1997). Promoting the development of young children with disabilities. In M. Fraser (Ed.), *Risk and resilience in childhood* (pp. 10-33). Washington, DC: NASW Press.

Zonagen Sexual Dysfunction Program. (2002). *Background on sexual dysfunction.* Retrieved September 4, 2002, from www.zonagen.com/html/sexdys.htm.

Zucker, K. (1985). The infant's construction of his parents in the first six months of life. In T. Field & N. Fox (Eds.), *Social perception in infants*. Norwood, NJ: Ablex.

Zuckerman, B., & Kahn, R. (2000). Pathways to early child health and development. In S. Danziger & J. Waldfogel (Eds.), *Securing the future: Investing in children from birth to college* (pp. 87-121). New York: Russell Sage.

Zuniga, M. (1992). Families with Latino roots. In E. Lynch & M. Hanson (Eds.), *Developing cross-cultural competence: A guide for working with young children and their families* (pp. 151-179). Baltimore, MD: Paul H. Brookes.

Zuravin, S., & DiBlasio, F. (1996). The correlates of child physical abuse and neglect by adolescent mothers. *Journal of Family Violence, 11*(2), 149-166.

Life Course Glossary/Index

Education:
childbirth education, 65-66
child care and, 149
individual education plan, 238
risk prevention and, 151
social effects of, 40
standards-based/equity-based system, 217-218
tracking system, 214-215
See also Formal schooling experience
Education for All Handicapped Children Act, 238
Efficacy expectation, 37
Egocentrism, 166, 184
Ego integrity versus ego despair The psychosocial crisis of Erik Erikson's eighth and final stage of development, which centers on one's ability to process what has happened in life and accept these experiences as integral to the meaning of life, 410, 458
Egocentrism The assumption by children in the preoperational stage of cognitive development that others perceive, think, and feel just the way they do. Inability to recognize the possibility of other perspectives
Elder, G., Jr., 21, 29, 34, 37, 39
Elderly gravidas, 89-90
Embryo The stage of prenatal development beginning in the 2nd week and lasting through the 8th week, 82
Emerging adulthood A developmental phase distinct from both adolescence and young adulthood, occurring between the ages of 18 and 25 in industrialized societies, 313
characteristics of, 314-315
cultural variations in, 315-316
economic structures and, 316
multigenerational concerns and, 316
Emotional intelligence The ability to motivate oneself to persist in the face of frustration, to control impulses, to delay gratification, to regulate one's moods, and to empathize with others; theory proposed by Daniel Goleman, 209-210
Emotions. *See* Socioemotional development
Empathy Ability to understand another person's emotional condition, 169-170
Employment factors, 35, 36:
English as a second language (ESL) Term used to describe individuals or groups in the United States whose first, or native, language is a language other than English, 232-233
Environmental issues:
barriers, 8
language acquisition, 167
neighborhood effects, 36
Erikson, E., 129, 207, 261, 262, 265, 311, 351, 409, 410, 445, 458
Ethics issues:
delayed pregnancy, 89-90
genetic engineering, 73
Ethnic identity. *See* Race
Event history The sequence of significant events, experiences, and transitions in a person's life from birth to death
Extroversion Orientation to the external world, in contrast to introversion, which is orientation to the internal world, 352

Failure to thrive, 147
Faith development theory, 33, 369-370
Family:
adolescents and, 267-268
child-care sharing, 138, 141-142, 149-150
child maltreatment and, 238-241, 239 (exhibit)
divorce, 183-184, 232
grandparenthood, 416-419, 418 (exhibit)
interdependency within, 34-36
late adulthood and, 415-416
life course trajectories and, 38, 39
middle adulthood and, 374-379, 379 (exhibit)
multigenerational groups, 61-62, 144-145, 179-180, 205
parent-school link, 211-212, 223-225
pluralism and, 61
teen pregnancy, response to, 88
See also Conception-pregnancy-birth cycle; Parents
Family leave, 141-142, 143 (exhibit)
Family and Medical Leave Act (FMLA), 141
Family pluralism Recognition of many viable types of family structures, 61
Feminist theory (of aging) Theory of social gerontology suggesting that, because gender is a central organizing principle in our society, we can only understand aging by taking gender into account, 402 (exhibit), 403-404

Generativity The ability to transcend personal interests to provide care and concern for generations to come, 351-352, 352 (exhibit)

Gene replacement therapy Implantation of genetic material to alter the genotype, 100

Genes Basic units of heredity, made of DNA, and found on chromosomes, 70

Genetic counseling Providing appropriate knowledge about human genetics and advice to guide the decisions of persons concerned about hereditary abnormalities, 72-73

Genetic heterogeneity A genetic principle that a trait, such as mental retardation, can have a different etiology in different persons, 98

Genetic liability The state of being prone to hereditary disorders, 98

Genotype The totality of the hereditary information present in an organism, 70

Germ cells The ova and spermatozoa whose function is to reproduce the organism, 70

Gestation The length of maturation time from conception to birth. In humans it averages 280 days, with a range of 259 to 287 days, 81

Gestational age The number of completed weeks of pregnancy counting from the 1st day of the last normal menstrual cycle to the birth of the neonate, 81

Gonads Sex glands—ovaries in females and testes in males, 255

Grief The normal internal reaction of an individual experiencing a loss, a complex process that is highly individualized

Grief work A necessary period of working to sever the attachment bond to a lost person or object, 468-470

Group norms A group's collective standards for its members in areas such as behavior, appearance, and attitude, 225

Heterogeneous grouping The practice of placing children with varying academic abilities in the same classroom. This practice is distinct from homogeneous grouping, or *tracking,* in which students with similar abilities are placed in the same classroom, 218

Hospice Program that provides care to the terminally ill. Patients typically receive treatment by a team of doctors, nurses, social workers, and care staff through inpatient or outpatient hospice, 463

Hostile aggression Aggression that occurs while fighting over toys and space, etc., 171

Human agency The use of personal power to achieve one's goals, 36-37, 38

Identity A combination of what you're born with and into; who you associate with; how others see you; what you've done; your attitudes, traits, abilities, habits, tendencies, and preferences; and what you look like

Immunization A method of administering microorganisms, bacteria, or viruses that have been modified or killed to stimulate the body's immune system to build a defense against a specific disease; also known as vaccination or inoculation, 124-125

Incidental memory Memory that relates to facts a person has learned without the intention to retain and recall. Compare *intentional memory*, 412